VOLUME TWO

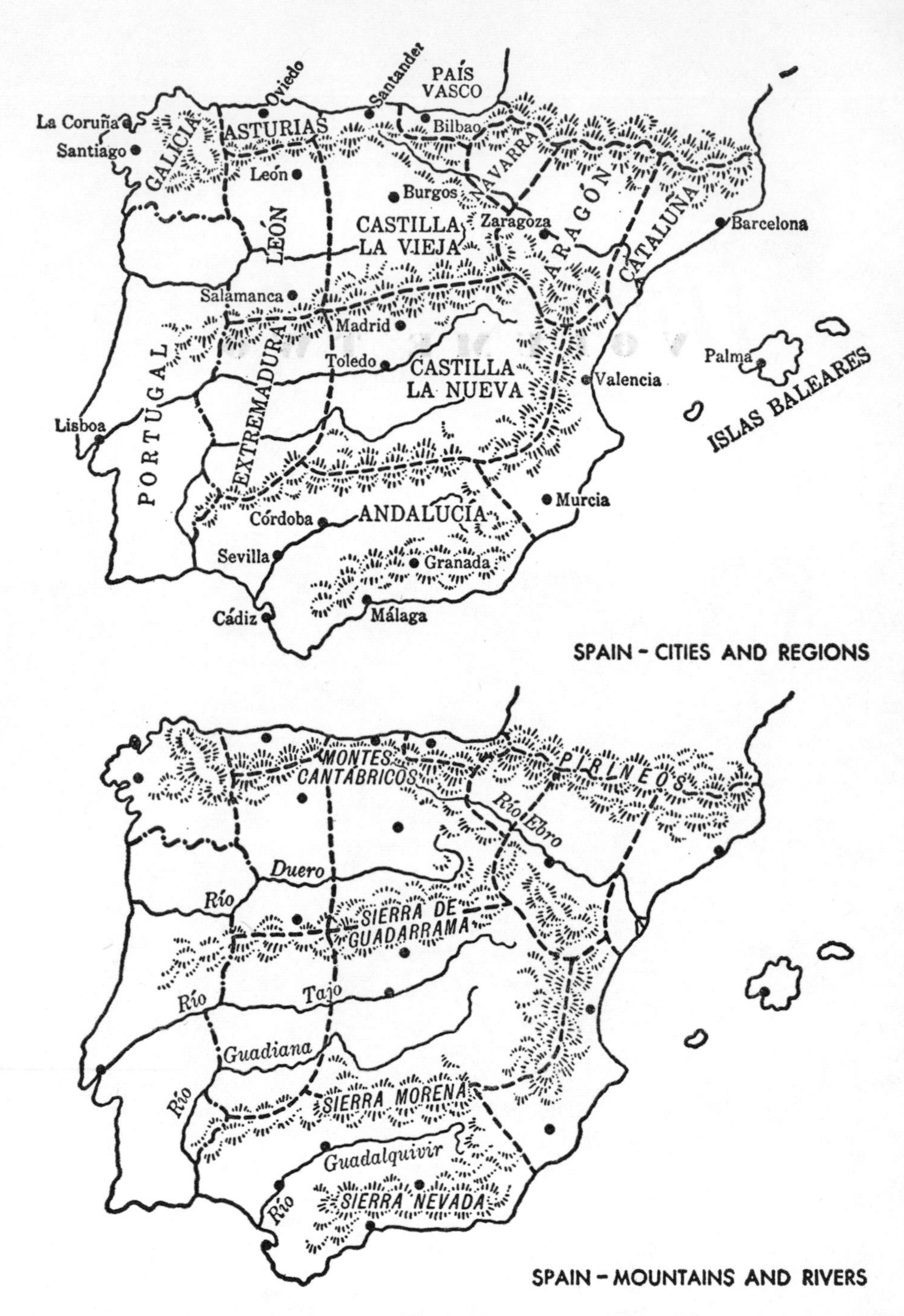

SPAIN - CITIES AND REGIONS

SPAIN - MOUNTAINS AND RIVERS

(Note to student: Cover the upper map; then name the cities and regions on the lower one. Next try naming the rivers and mountains on the upper map without looking at the lower one.)

REPRESENTATIVE
Spanish Authors

WALTER T. PATTISON
PROFESSOR OF ROMANCE LANGUAGES, UNIVERSITY OF MINNESOTA

IN TWO VOLUMES
VOLUME TWO
SECOND EDITION

NEW YORK
OXFORD UNIVERSITY PRESS
1963

Library of Congress Catalogue Card Number: 58-5378

First edition of *Representative Spanish Authors,* Vol. II, copyright 1942 by Oxford University Press, Inc.

PRINTED IN THE UNITED STATES OF AMERICA

Preface to the Second Edition

The task of selecting outstanding and representative works of the modern period of Spanish literature is a difficult one. There is no universally accepted canon of literary worth, as there is for the earlier periods; furthermore, the twentieth century, with its swarm of well-established authors, demands an ever larger share of our attention. There are numerous authors who deserve inclusion in an anthology, but, within the scope and purpose of this book, a few must represent all the rest.

Over the twenty years which have elapsed since the first publication of this volume a great many of my friends and colleagues have made suggestions for its enlargement or revision. It is impossible to thank all of them by name: suffice it to say that their ideas have been greatly appreciated and given thoughtful consideration—even when they were mutually exclusive! Of course, the responsibility for the final choices remains my own.

I also wish to thank the authors who gave me permission to publish selections from their works and the heirs or agents of deceased authors who granted similar courtesies. Finally, I am grateful for the helpfulness of the staff of the Oxford University Press and the constant co-operation of my wife.

W. T. P.

Minneapolis, Minnesota
February 1963

Acknowledgments

The editor gratefully acknowledges permission to print excerpts from the following authors granted by the individuals or the publishing houses listed.

Emilia Pardo Bazán, Editorial Renacimiento; Benito Pérez Galdós, Doña María Galdós de Verde; José María de Pereda, Librería Victoriano Suárez; Pío Baroja, Don Julio Caro Baroja; Ramón del Valle-Inclán, Don Carlos de Valle-Inclán; Miguel de Unamuno, Prof. Manuel García Blanco; José Ortega y Gasset, Revista de Occidente S. A.; Azorín, the author; Jacinto Benavente, Los Sucesores de Hernando; Rubén Darío, Don José Villazactin; Federico García Lorca, from *Selected Poems of Federico Garcia Lorca:* Copyright 1955 by New Directions. Reprinted by permission of New Directions, Publisher.

Permission granted by the Sociedad de Autores, Madrid, to reprint material by Juan Valera, Ramón de Campoamor, Antonio Machado, and Juan Ramón Jiménez is also gratefully acknowledged.

To

THE MEMORY OF MY FATHER

GEORGE HENRY PATTISON

AUGUST 28, 1868–MAY 2, 1939

Y aunque la vida murió,
Nos dejó harto consuelo
Su memoria.

Contents

VOLUME TWO

Representative Spanish Authors

The Eighteenth Century in Spain

History

IN general, the eighteenth century in Spain was an epoch of inactivity in all lines. The nation seemed to be exhausted after a period of violent expansion and constant wars during which Spain discovered and colonized America, fought the Turks in the Mediterranean, the French in both Italy and France, the Flemish and Dutch in the Low Countries, and the English on the sea. Spain needed a long and profound rest. Even the population had fallen from some ten millions to about six millions during the course of the seventeenth century. While pursuing its double ideal of one universal religion and a single universal monarchy, Spain had struggled against practically the whole world.

Spain's decadence was also of an economic nature, and the country needed to replenish its stores and build up its national wealth. The gold from America, which had flowed into Spain in great quantities, had passed through Spain and ended in the coffers of the Italian bankers. Very little manufacturing took place in Spain itself. The well-to-do preferred luxurious imported articles, and the poor, glorying in the great deeds of the Spanish military forces, had developed a distaste for manual work and had conceived the idea that the only honorable ways of earning one's bread were by following the career of soldier, writer, priest, or government official. Heavy taxes had to be imposed to carry on the disastrous military campaigns. The most nefarious of these was the *alcabala,* a 10 per cent sales tax which affected every article, either manufactured or raw material, each time it changed hands. Furthermore, the expulsion of the Jews in 1492 and of the *moriscos* early in the seventeenth century was an economic mistake, as these classes had more industrial initiative than the other Spaniards.

In the last place, the monarchs steadily declined in quality from generation to generation until the famous Hapsburg line ended with the impotent Carlos II, in 1700.

The eighteenth century opened, then, with a new line of kings ascending the Spanish throne, of whom the first, Felipe V, was the grandson of Louis XIV of France, consequently a Frenchman and a Bourbon. Although the Bourbon kings ruled Spain down to 1931, they were always looked on as outsiders or foreigners by the Spaniards. We may also say that they represented an idea of monarchy quite different from that of the earlier Spanish kings, who had felt themselves to be representatives of God and, as a result, responsible to His high authority. The Bourbon concept is best seen in the phrase said to be used by Louis XIV, the greatest monarch of that line: *'L'état, c'est moi'*;[1] or, on passing some decree, giving as his reason: *'car c'est notre bon plaisir.'*[2] It is obvious that the Bourbons always thought of their rule as absolute and personal, a policy which was continued by the Spanish branch of the line.

We must, however, give the eighteenth-century monarchs credit for representing an enlightened despotism. They brought many institutions into Spain which had already been established elsewhere, notably in France. Among these were the *Biblioteca Nacional* (1711), the *Academia Española*[3] (1714), and the *Academia de Medicina* (1734). Considerable advance was made in scholarship, manufacturing techniques, and the rudimentary science of the day. This policy of enlightenment reached its high point during the reign of Carlos III (1759–88); but immediately afterwards the decadence of the Bourbon line began with Carlos IV (1788–1808), who left the government of the nation to Godoy, a common soldier raised to the rank of prime minister, and a royal favorite through the attachment the queen had for him.

Intellectual and literary currents

As in most periods of Spanish intellectual history, there was a struggle between two conflicting ideas: one, the desire of a few cultured people of the upper classes to bring Spain, which they felt to be benighted and behind the times, abreast of contemporary thought; and the other, *casticismo,* or the clinging to good old Spanish ways of thinking and doing. The members of the first group were looked down upon as partisans of the always unpopular French cause; hence their name *afrancesados*. In reality, it was out of patriotism they tried to bring in new ideas from outside, in the hope of seeing Spain equal what they considered to be the brilliant civilization of the rest of Europe.

As French thought dominated all of Europe, naturally they turned to French theories of literature and attempted to propagate them in Spain. During the seventeenth century the French had developed a school of literature called *classicism,* which still dominated their literary produc-

[1] 'I am the state.'
[2] 'for it is our good pleasure'
[3] A group of 36 literary men, whose object was to decide on all disputed questions of language. Its dictionary, although not perfect, is the best in existence. Election to this group is a great honor, although the Spaniards have never revered their *Academia* to the same extent as the French their corresponding institution, *L'Académie française*.

tions in the eighteenth century. This was what the *afrancesados* attempted to introduce into Spain, with very little success, due to the fact that classicism was in no way compatible with Spanish temperament or with the literature the Spaniards has been used to in the past.

Classicism may be defined as a restrained, mature, authoritarian point of view towards life and literature. It starts from the premise that the ancient Greek and Latin authors were better writers than any modern man could be. Consequently, the modern must imitate the essence of their work. Fundamentally, classicism strove for universality in plots, ideas, and characters. Thus, it depicted things, people, and ideas which could be true not just at the present time, but in any age, and not just in one nation, but anywhere in the world. It tended to reject original ideas and new or unique characters. Originality was not considered to be a virtue among the classicists, for the very cornerstone of their literary theory was imitation. Often they were content merely to retell a story from ancient literature in their modern language. Because of their feeling that they must always subject themselves to the authority of the 'ancients' they inherited certain restraints, most notable of which are the rules for the different forms, or genres, of literature. Each genre was subject to a series of strict limitations, among which the outstanding example is the three unities (time, place, and action) which governed the drama.

We have already emphasized the individualism of the Spaniard. As the classicists, in their effort to attain universality, sacrified everything exceptional, picturesque, or individual, they were necessarily running contrary to the current of Spanish feeling. In reality, they achieved no successes at all in Spain until the eighteenth century was three-quarters over, and even in the last quarter of that century and the beginning of the nineteenth, such successes as they did attain were only minor ones. The first drama acted in Spain, written according to classic rules, appeared in 1770 (*Hormesinda,* of Nicolás Fernández de Moratín) and ran only six nights. Only one classical tragedy had any real success (*Raquel,* of Vicente García de la Huerta, 1778). The classical comedy achieved only two notable successes, both plays of Leandro Fernández de Moratín (*La comedia nueva,* 1792, and *El sí de las niñas,* 1806). The two important schools of lyric poetry of the century, namely those of Salamanca and Sevilla, did not come into being until the century was three-quarters spent. In fact, only one classical work of any significance comes earlier in the century, Luzán's *Arte Poética* (1737), in which he laid down the rules by which he hoped his compatriots would produce classic masterpieces. A later and far more readable codification of the rules and attitudes of classicism is Tomás de Iriarte's *Fábulas literarias* (1782).

The great masses of the people of Spain were always opposed to the innovations of the *afrancesados,* although they did little to produce a literature of their own. However, they maintained a constant preference for the dramas of the Golden Age, which continued to be acted in the theaters throughout this period. These dramas had nothing in common with classicism, as they respected none of the rules so sacred to that school. Furthermore, the immense success of the playwright Ramón de la Cruz is a reflection of the popular taste, for he made no attempt to abide by rules, but followed the deep-seated Spanish tendency towards pictorial realism. His little one-act plays, or *sainetes,* which continue the tradition of the *pasos* of Lope de Rueda and the *entremeses* of Cervantes, simply show some picturesque or characteristic detail of Madrid life. The same type of realism abounds in the works of Leandro Fernández de Moratín, which leads us to believe that his comedies owe their success not to their adherence to the forms of classicism, but to their ingrained *españolismo.* García de la Huerta's successful tragedy was also only externally classic, for its subject matter was a legend from the Spanish Middle Ages which had already been treated in a Spanish drama of the Golden Age. In fact, much of the success of the play lay in its hidden attack on French dominance in politics at the very time that the author was following the French lead in literature. The best works of the lyric poets also are generally those in which they adhere least strictly to classicism. Thus, we find that the school of Sevilla, whose members were doctrinaire classicists, is far less important than that of Salamanca, some of whose members, such as Meléndez Valdés, Cadalso, and Cienfuegos, showed many moments of independence and originality.

The influence of France and of classicism continued in Spain until the death of the most despotic of the Spanish monarchs, Fernando VII (1833), primarily because he exiled some 40,000 men who were liberal in politics and consequently liberal also in their literary point of view. Therefore, the new literary current, known as *romanticism,* which was developing in France and England in the early nineteenth century, was not free to appear in Spain until an amnesty, granted just before the monarch's death, made possible the return of these exiles. Logically, we should consider the first third of the nineteenth century as belonging to the eighteenth century in literature and intellectual history.

Tomás de Iriarte

Fábulas Literarias

El burro flautista

(Sin reglas del arte, el que en algo acierta, acierta por casualidad.)

Esta fabulilla,
salga bien o mal,
me ha ocurrido ahora
por casualidad.
Cerca de unos prados 5
que hay en mi lugar,
pasaba un Borrico
por casualidad.
Una flauta en ellos
halló, que un zagal 10
se dejó olvidada
por casualidad.
Acercóse a olerla
el dicho animal,
y dió un resoplido 15
por casualidad.
En la flauta el aire
se hubo de colar,[1]
y sonó la flauta
por casualidad. 20
«¡Oh!—dijo el Borrico—:
¡Qué bien sé tocar!
¡Y dirán que es mala
la música asnal!»
Sin reglas del arte, 25
borriquitos hay
que una vez aciertan
por casualidad.

La cabra y el caballo

(Hay malos escritores que se lisonjean fácilmente de lograr fama póstuma cuando no han podido merecerla en vida.)

Estábase una Cabra muy atenta
largo rato escuchando
de un acorde violín[2] el eco blando.
Los pies se le bailaban de contenta,[3]
y a cierto Jaco, que también suspenso 5
casi olvidaba el pienso,
dirigió de esta suerte la palabra:
«¿No oyes de aquellas cuerdas la armonía?
Pues sabe que son tripas de una Cabra
que fué en un tiempo compañera mía. 10
Confío (¡dicha grande!) que algún día
no menos dulces trinos
formarán mis sonoros intestinos.»
Volvióse el buen Rocín y respondióla:
«A fe que no resuenan esas cuerdas 15
sino porque las hieren con las cerdas
que sufrí me arrancasen de la cola.
Mi dolor me costó, pasé mi susto;

[1] *se hubo de colar,* went through, penetrated
[2] *acorde violín,* well-tuned violin
[3] *de contenta,* because she was so happy, for joy

pero, al fin, tengo el gusto
de ver qué lucimiento 20
debe a mi auxilio el músico[4] instrumento.
Tú, que satisfacción igual esperas,
¿cuándo la gozarás? Después que mueras.»
Así, ni más ni menos, porque en vida
no ha conseguido ver su obra aplaudida 25
algún mal escritor, al juicio apela
de la posteridad, y se consuela.

El pollo y los dos gallos

(No ha de considerarse en un autor la edad, sino el talento.)

Un Gallo, presumido
de luchador valiente,
y un Pollo[5] algo crecido,
no sé por qué accidente
tuvieron sus palabras, de manera 5
que armaron una brava pelotera.
Dióse el Pollo tal maña,
que sacudió a mi Gallo lindamente,[6]
quedando ya por suya la campaña,
y el vencido sultán de aquel serrallo[7] 10
dijo, cuando el contrario no le oía:
«¡Eh!, con el tiempo no será mal Gallo;
el pobrecillo es mozo todavía.»
Jamás volvió a meterse con el Pollo;
mas en otra ocasión, por cierto embrollo, 15
teniendo un choque con un Gallo anciano,
guerrero veterano,
apenas le quedó pluma ni cresta,
y dijo al retirarse de la fiesta:
«Si no mirara que es un pobre viejo . . . 20
Pero chochea y por piedad le dejo."
Quien se meta en contienda,
verbigracia, de asunto literario,
a los años no atienda,
sino a la habilidad de su adversario. 25

[4] *músico,* here, musical
[5] *Pollo,* cockerel, young rooster
[6] *sacudió . . . lindamente,* dusted off neatly, gave a good beating
[7] *sultán de aquel serrallo,* the sultan of that harem, i.e. the cock

Juan Meléndez Valdés

Oda VIII

A Lisi,[1] que siempre se ha de amar

La primavera derramando flores,
El céfiro bullendo licencioso,[2]
Y el trino de las aves sonoroso
Nos brindan[3] a dulcísimos amores
En lazo delicioso. 5
Viene el verano, y la insufrible llama
Agosta de su aliento congojado
Árboles, plantas, flores, yerba y prado:
Todo cede a su ardor, sólo quien ama
Lo arrostra sin cuidado. 10
El amarillo otoño asoma luego,
De frutas, yedra y pámpanos ceñido:
La luz febea,[4] su vigor perdido,
Se encoge, mientra[5] amor dobla su fuego
Blando y apetecido. 15
Y en el ceñudo invierno, cuando atruena
Más ronco el aquilón tempestuoso,
Entre lluvias y nieves en reposo
Canta su ardor, y ríe en su cadena[6]
El amador dichoso. 20
Que así plácido amor sabe del año
Las estaciones, si gozarlos quieres,
Colmar, Lisi, de encantos y placeres.
¡Ay! cógelos, simplilla; ve tu engaño,
Y a la vejez no esperes. 25

Epístola VI

El filósofo en el campo

Bajo una erguida populosa encina,
Cuya ancha copa en torno me defiende
De la ardiente canícula, que ahora
Con rayo abrasador angustia el mundo,
Tu oscuro amigo, Fabio,[1] te saluda. 5

[1] *Lisi.* Even when writing about his friends or his sweetheart, the classical author addresses them with assumed names, usually taken from Latin literature.
[2] *licencioso,* wantonly, haphazardly
[3] *brindan,* here, invite
[4] *luz febea,* light of the sun
[5] *mientra,* poetic for *mientras,* to preserve the rhythm of the line by permitting synalepha with the following word
[6] *cadena,* bonds (of love)

[1] *Fabio.* A name often used for a friend in classical poetry. Meléndez Valdés uses it in another poem to designate his friend Manuel María Cambronero, a prominent lawyer who was secretary of state under the French regime during the Napoleonic invasion.

Mientras tú en el guardado gabinete
A par del feble[2] ocioso cortesano
Sobre el muelle sofá tendido yaces,
Y hasta para alentar vigor os falta;
Yo en estos campos por el sol tostado 10
Lo afronto sin temor, sudo y anhelo;
Y el soplo mismo que me abrasa ardiente,
En plácido frescor mis miembros baña.
Miro y contemplo los trabajos duros
Del triste labrador, su suerte esquiva, 15
Su miseria, sus lástimas; y aprendo
Entre los infelices a ser hombre.
Ay Fabio ¡Fabio! en las doradas salas,
Entre el brocado y colgaduras ricas,
El pie hollando entallados pavimentos;[3] 20
¡Qué mal al pobre el cortesano juzga!

. . .

Insensibles nos hace la opulencia,
Insensibles nos hace. Ese bullicio,
Ese contino[4] discurrir[5] veloces
Mil doradas carrozas, paseando[6] 25
Los vicios todos por las anchas calles,
Esas empenachadas[7] cortesanas,
Brillantes en el oro y pedrería
Del cabello a los pies; esos teatros,
De lujo y de maldades docta escuela, 30
Do un ocioso indolente a llorar corre
Con Andrómaca o Zaira;[8] mientras sordo
Al anciano infeliz vuelve la espalda,
Que a sus umbrales su dureza implora;
Esos palacios y preciosos muebles, . . . 35
Ese incesante hablar de oro y grandezas;
Ese anhelo pueril por los más viles
Despreciables objetos, nuestros pechos
De diamante tornaron:[9] nos fascinan,
Nos embebecen, y olvidar nos hacen 40
Nuestro común origen y miserias. . . .
El potentado distinguirse debe
Del tostado arador; próvido el cielo
Así lo ha decretado, dando al uno
El arte de gozar, y un pecho al otro 45
Llevador del trabajo: su vil frente
Del alba matinal a las estrellas[10]

[2] *a par de,* like; *feble,* weak
[3] *entallados pavimentos,* parquet floors
[4] *contino,* poetic for *continuo*
[5] *discurrir,* to run on, roll by
[6] *paseando,* here, displaying
[7] *empenachadas,* bedecked
[8] *Andrómaca o Zaira,* heroines of the French classical plays *Andromaque* by Racine and *Zaïre* by Voltaire. These plays were also acted in Madrid in Spanish translations.
[9] *nuestros . . . tornaron,* made our hearts as hard as diamonds
[10] *a las estrellas,* until the stars come out

En amargo sudor los surcos bañe,
Y exhausto expire a su señor sirviendo;
Mientras él coge venturoso el fruto 50
De tan ímprobo afán, y uno devora
La sustancia de mil. ¡Oh cuánto! ¡cuánto
El pecho se hincha con tan vil lenguaje!
Por más que grite la razón severa,
Y la cuna y la tumba nos recuerde[11] 55
Con que justa natura[12] nos iguala.

. . .

¿Y estos miramos con desdén? ¿la clase
Primera del estado, la más útil,
La más honrada, el santuario augusto
De la virtud y la inocencia hollamos? 60
¿Y para qué? Para exponer tranquilos
De una carta al azar ¡oh noble empleo
Del tiempo y la riqueza! lo que haría
Próvido heredamiento a cien hogares;
Para premiar la audacia temeraria 65
Del rudo gladiador, que a sus pies deja
El útil animal que el corvo arado
Para sí nos demanda;[13] los mentidos
Halagos con que artera al duro lecho,
Desde sus brazos, del dolor nos lanza 70
Una impudente cortesana; el raro
Saber de un peluquero, que elevando
De gasas y plumaje una alta torre
Sobre nuestras cabezas, las rizadas
Hebras de oro en que ornó naturaleza 75
A la beldad, afea y desfigura
Con su indecente y asquerosa mano.

. . .

Huye, Fabio, esa peste. En tus oídos
De la indigencia mísera ¿no suena
El suspirar profundo, que hasta el trono 80
Sube del sumo Dios? ¿su justo azote
Amenazar no ves? ¿no ves la trampa,
El fraude, la bajeza, la insaciable
Disipación, el deshonor lanzarlos[14]
En el abismo del oprobio, donde 85
Mendigarán sus nietos infelices,
Con los mismos que hoy huellan confundidos?
Húyelos, Fabio: ven, y estudia dócil
Conmigo las virtudes de estos hombres

[11] *nos recuerde,* recalls to us, reminds us of (subject: *la razón*)

[12] *natura* for *naturaleza*

[13] *el útil animal . . . nos demanda,* freely, the bull which could prefer to be hitched to the plow.

[14] *lanzarlos. Los* refers to the inhabitants of the court, whose dissipation and sins will bring their descendants to poverty.

No conocidos en la corte. Admira, 90
Admira su bondad: ve cuál su boca
Llana y veraz como su honrado pecho,
Sin velo, sin disfraz, celebra, increpa
Lo que aplaudirse o condenarse debe.
Mira su humanidad apresurada 95
Al que sufre, acorrer: de boca en boca
Oirás volar, oh Fabio, por la corte
Esta voz celestial;[15] mas no imprudente
En las almas la busques, ni entre el rico
Brocado blando abrigo al infelice.[16] 100
Sólo los que lo son, sólo en los campos
Los miserables condolerse saben . . .
Admira su paciente sufrimiento;
O más bien llora, viéndolos desnudos,
Escuálidos, hambrientos, encorvados, 105
Lanzando ya el suspiro postrimero
Bajo la inmensa carga que en sus hombros
Puso la suerte. El infeliz navega,
Deja su hogar, y afronta las borrascas
Del inmenso océano, porque el lujo 110
Sirva a tu gula, y tu soberbio hastío
El café que da Moca perfumado,[17]
O la canela de Ceilán. La guerra
Sopla en las almas su infernal veneno,
Y en insano furor las cortes arden; 115
Desde su esteva[18] el labrador paciente,
Llorando en torno la infeliz familia,
Corre a la muerte; y en sus duros brazos
Se libra de la patria la defensa.
Su mano apoya el anhelante fisco:[19] 120
La aciaga mole de tributos carga
Sobre su cerviz ruda, y el tesoro
Del Estado hinche de oro la miseria.
Ese sudor amargo con que inunda
Los largos surcos que su arado forma, 125
Es la dorada espiga que alimenta,
Fabio, del cortesano el ocio muelle.
Sin ella el hambre pálida . . . ¿Y osamos
Desestimarlos? Al robusto seno
De la fresca aldeana confiamos 130
Nuestros débiles hijos, porque el dulce
Néctar y la salud felices hallen,[20]

[15] *esta voz celestial,* i.e. *humanidad,* three lines above. A strong current of sentimental humanitarianism developed in France during the 18th century. It influenced Meléndez Valdés and other Spanish writers not only in the eighteenth but also in the nineteenth century.

[16] *infelice,* poetic for *infeliz*

[17] Understand as follows: *y el café perfumado que da Moca o la canela de Ceilán sirva tu soberbio hastío. Moca,* Mokka in Arabia; *Ceilán,* Ceylon.

[18] *esteva,* plough handle

[19] *fisco,* treasury

[20] It was customary to hire wet nurses for the children of the middle and upper classes.

De que los privan nuestros feos vicios:
¿Y por vil la tenemos? ¿Al membrudo
Que nos defiende, injustos desdeñamos? 135
Sus útiles fatigas nos sustentan;
¿Y en digna gratitud con pie orgulloso
Hollamos su miseria, porque al pecho
La roja cinta o la brillante placa,
Y el ducal manto para el ciego vulgo 140
Con la clara Excelencia nos señalen?[21]
¿Qué valen tantas raras invenciones
De nuestro insano orgullo, comparadas
Con el montón de sazonadas mieses
Que crió el labrador? Débiles niños 145
Fináramos[22] bien presto en hambre y lloro
Sin el auxilio de sus fuertes brazos.

[21] *porque . . . nos señalen,* so a ribbon or a medal or a duke's mantle with their nobility may distinguish us from the common people. This passage is, of course, ironical.

[22] *Débiles niños,* supply *como* before this phrase; *Fináramos,* we would die

The Nineteenth Century in Spain

WHEN we try to find some unifying or connecting idea running through the history of nineteenth-century Spain, we are confronted with such political chaos and intellectual conflict that our task seems practically impossible. The history of the century is a kaleidoscopic succession of ministers; kings who abdicate, are deposed, or restored; civil wars, assassinations, and military dictators.

The century opens with Carlos IV reigning. Under his prime minister, Godoy, a policy of close alliance with France was followed, which brought disaster to Spain in the destruction of its fleet in the battle of Trafalgar in 1805. With the invasion of Napoleon in 1808, Carlos IV abdicated in favor of his son Fernando VII (1808–33). At first a prisoner of Napoleon, he was set free by the Spanish liberals who, during the king's absence, drew up the famous Constitution of 1812, declaring that the people were the true sovereigns, subjecting the king to the will of elected ministers, and making all citizens equal before the law.

The whole century was a battle to put these reforms into force. No sooner did the liberals win an apparent victory than the king and other traditional forces undid their triumph by swinging the nation back to despotic absolutism. Throughout the rule of Fernando VII, the nation moved like a restless pendulum between the two extremes of personal rule by the king and advanced liberalism.

At the time of Fernando's death in 1833, many liberals had just returned from exile outside of Spain, while in the country, the Carlist party, which believed in the strictest adherence to old traditions, was seeking power. Thus, the beginning of the reign of Isabel II (1833–68) is also the beginning of a civil war between the liberals, who supported Isabel, and the Carlists, who desired the absolute rule of her uncle, Don Carlos. Isabel showed a frivolity typical of Bourbon monarchs, for after having gained the throne through the support of the liberals, she rejected the constitution which they wished to impose and ruled by personal whim and decree. She was finally deposed in 1868, largely because of her immoral private life.

Spain now found itself in the curious situation of believing in monarchial government (the Cortes voted three to one in favor of a monarchy) and not being able to find a king. The crown was offered to three princes who turned it down. After two years had passed in these futile attempts, Amadeo de Saboya was persuaded to take over the ruling of the nation in 1871, but on the very day he landed in Spain, his chief supporter, General Prim, was assassinated. In spite of Amadeo's sincere efforts to bring some order to the country, he failed, and abdicated in 1873. The same Cortes which had voted for a monarchy only five years before now voted for the establishment of a republic. It was doomed to failure, because its leaders were idealistic and impractical theorists. Chief among them was Pi y Margall, a believer in federalism, by which each region of Spain would be practically independent, being only loosely bound to the central government. But when even single villages set themselves up as independent states, chaos could be the only result, and in desperation the country called back the Bourbon line, in the person of the son of Isabel II, Alfonso XII (1875–85).

Alfonso proved himself a conscientious monarch, and the country, which had gone through a second Carlist war during the unsettled years preceding his restoration, was now in need of a complete rest. Political strife was held down and the country made rapid industrial progress. Alfonso XII died while still young, during an epidemic of cholera. At the king's death, his son Alfonso XIII, the last king of Spain, had not yet been born. Therefore, during his minority, which covered the rest of the nineteenth century, the policies of his father were continued, and the country paid greater attention to economic development than to the conflicts of political factions. However, the progress of a quarter of a century was checked by the disastrous defeat of Spain by the United States in the Spanish-American War (1898).

Even from this brief account the unrest and turbulence which ran throughout nineteenth-century Spain will be apparent. We can never understand this century unless we realize that fundamentally it is a great struggle between the traditionalists and the liberals. The fight to establish the Constitution of 1812 is symbolic of the fight which ran through all aspects of life. On one hand there were entrenched and well-organized traditionalists, who may be subdivided into three classes: first of all, the king and the nobility dependent upon him, who wished to maintain all of their old privileges; in the second place, the clergy and church; and in the third place, especially in the second half of the century, the wealthy. The liberal side, which was always advanced or even radical in its thought, was largely unorganized. It consisted at the beginning of the century mainly of intellectuals whose ambition was to give the country a constitutional monarchy, but as time went on these intellectuals allied themselves with labor movements and demanded much more—namely, the abolition of the monarchy and the establishment of a democratic form of government. Spain never has had a numerous middle class, which in other countries did much to check the ambitions of the two extremes.

One other great force in Spanish life, the army, remains to be described. We must remember that the army in Spain, with its large number of officers and its political generals, has always wielded a powerful influence in the formation of internal policy. Generals often deposed the constitutional government and stepped into power, moved by a desire to cut red tape and believing that they were called on to serve the country through a temporary dictatorship. During the early part of the century, the army was definitely a force for liberalism, yet in later years it lined up on the opposite side. How can we explain this change? The ideal of the army seems to have been a constitutional monarchy, so while the king exercised absolute power, it was against him, hence somewhat liberal. But when the country moved towards a democracy, the army again was against that movement, hence somewhat conservative.

The conflict we have outlined manifests itself constantly in Spanish literature of the nineteenth century. Early in the century, the desire to get rid of the oppressive Bourbon monarch, Fernando VII, was identified in the minds of the liberals with their desire to get rid of French classicism, and the triumph of liberalism seemed to them akin to the liberalization of literature by romanticism. Later on, many of the novelists wrote tendentious works of propaganda. For example, we see Fernán Caballero defending the church and the good old way of living; Pereda, in *Peñas arriba,* upholds the old-fashioned virtues and simple life of the country; while on the other hand, Galdós, in *Doña Perfecta,* attacks savagely the benighted ways and backward religion of a small Spanish town; and Larra, in his *cuadros de costumbres,* is constantly criticizing outmoded Spanish ways.

We will not understand the literature of this century unless we realize that it, as every other manifestation of life, was a battlefield where the traditionalists and the liberals were each constantly attempting to wrest victory from the other camp.

Romanticism

WE have already seen that up to 1833 a general tendency in literature, called classicism, was being advocated in Spain by the small, cultured upper class. Classicism, with its conservative, mature, well-proportioned point of view towards life, was a submission to society's point of view. The author showed more deference to other people's feelings than to his own.

But a revolt developed throughout Europe against the classic point of view—a revolt which came to be called romanticism, at first derisively, because of the frequence of the adjective 'romantic' in the works of one of the early adherents of the movement. Romanticism deliberately opposed every rule of classicism. Thus, romanticism was primarily an exuberant, youthful point of view in which the individual stressed the value of his own feelings and thoughts as opposed to those usually accepted by the group. In its opposition to classicism at every point, romanticism found its inspiration in national legends, usually of the Middle Ages (as opposed to inspiration from the ancient Greek and Roman classics). It found its characters in unusual men, often outcasts from society and oppressed by fate (rather than in the typical, universal man of classicism). Where classicism showed restraint in form (i.e. rules), romanticism imposed no rules at all. While the classic author restrained his personal emotion and concealed his own personality, the romantic author gave free rein to both personality and emotions, which were usually melancholy, since the real world always fell far short of his dreams.

Romanticism swept over Europe about the beginning of the nineteenth century, but did not reach Spain in force until considerably later. As we have seen, all the liberals in politics, who were also liberals in literature, had been exiled by Fernando VII, and at his death swarmed back into Spain and immediately began producing in the new liberal literary vein. But in Spain romanticism was no particular surprise. The Spanish literature of the Golden Age had not adhered to any set of rules; furthermore, the classicism of the eighteenth century had gained no real hold here. Thus, the Spaniards felt that the movement was more of a return to their own national tradition and a patriotic release from the tyranny of an imposed foreign literature than an outright literary revolt.

The productions of romanticism in Spain are not very numerous, as it lasted only to about 1845. While attempts were made to write romantic novels after the pattern of Walter Scott or Dumas *père,* none was successful. Lyric poetry produced four great names: Espronceda, Rivas, Zorrilla, and the later, but still romantic, poet, Bécquer. In the drama, a series of plays appeared between 1834 and 1837, including as its chief successes: *La conjuración de Venecia,* by Martínez de la Rosa; *Macías,* by Larra; *Don Álvaro,* by the Duque de Rivas; *El trovador,* by García Gutiérrez; and *Los amantes de Teruel,* by Hartzenbusch. A few years later (1844) Zorrilla revived the romantic drama in his masterpiece, *Don Juan Tenorio.*

The force of romanticism in the drama was not exhausted, even though purely romantic plays were no longer written. The eclectic drama became popular: an attempt to compromise between classicism (by showing some respect for the unities of time and place) and romanticism (from which the romantic hero, romantic passion, and national historical setting were taken). Without the authors' realizing it, a considerable element of realism entered the new type of play, which was the dominant dramatic form for about half a century.

As is the case with almost every intellectual movement in Spain, romanticism split into a traditionalistic and a liberal faction. The conservative group wanted only to revive the glamorous past and to present its legendary lore with all its local color; while the radical wing wanted to make reforms in both the political and religious life of the country. The romantic revival is well exemplified by Zorrilla, the romantic revolt by Espronceda.

All in all, the production of romanticism in Spain was small, and here, as in the rest of the world, its emphasis on the exceptional, picturesque, and imaginative elements of life often led one into an unreal, fantastic world which could not possibly exist. Yet the elements of romanticism which lived on in later days, after the movement itself was spent, are sufficient to justify it in our eyes. Furthermore, its works, although often disturbingly unreal and melodramatic, contain many real beauties.

José de Espronceda

ESPRONCEDA (1808–42), one of the greatest lyric poets of the romantic period and of the whole century, lived a life very similar to that of the heroes of romantic works. From his childhood he was a rebellious liberal. As a student he was involved in a political society against the tyrannical Fernando VII, for which he was imprisoned. Still untamed despite this punishment, he had to flee into exile when only eighteen because of his plotting against the king. He first went to Lisbon, then to England, where he fell in love with a married woman, Teresa Mancha de Bayo. Espronceda joined her in Paris where he showed his contempt for social laws by persuading her to leave her husband for him. There he is said to have fought at the barricades in the Revolution of 1830, he enlisted in an army which was to set Poland free but which was soon dissolved, and finally he joined an army to liberate Spain from the rule of Fernando VII. At the latter's death in 1833, Espronceda returned to Madrid with Teresa, whom, however, he soon abandoned. She died in 1839, and the poet survived her by only three years. He published but three slim volumes of poetry during his life.

Espronceda has often been called the Byron of Spain, and there is undoubtedly a considerable amount of imitation of Byron in his work. Whether or not his Byronic attitude of rebellion against the world is real or merely a pose is a matter of debate. What is certain is that he hoped to get much more out of life than he actually found in it. In a passage recalling his youthful aspirations he exclaims:

Yo me arrojé, cual rápido cometa,
En alas de mi ardiente fantasía:
Doquier mi arrebatada mente inquieta
Dichas y triunfos encontrar creía.

As we shall see in the *Canto a Teresa,* this ardent yearning for glory, liberty, and happiness was never satisfied. Consequently, Espronceda feels that he has been cheated by life. His melancholy is that of one who believes that life has nothing but disappointments to offer him. Again, in the *Canción del pirata* he shows an outcast from society, but one who glories in his isolation. We cannot doubt that Espronceda identified himself with this hero, as with the heroes of *El mendigo, El verdugo, El reo de muerte,* and his other poems on social outcasts.

In two longer poems, *El estudiante de Salamanca,* a reworking of the Don Juan theme,* and *El diablo mundo,* a protest against the senselessness of a world which can offer the protagonist but one disillusionment after another, Espronceda aspired to be both a poet and a thinker. It must be confessed, however, that it is chiefly as a poet that he triumphed. The ever present music in his verse and his great variety of meters have done more to give him the high place which he deserves than any profundity of thought. Rather than original thought, the content of his work is conventional romanticism, just as his life was one of typical romantic rebellion.

José de Espronceda

Canción del pirata

Con diez cañones por banda,
Viento en popa a toda vela
No corta el mar, sino vuela
Un velero bergantín:
Bajel pirata[1] que llaman 5
Por su bravura el *Temido,*
En todo mar conocido
Del uno al otro confín.

La luna en el mar rïela,
En la lona gime el viento, 10
Y alza en blando movimiento
Olas de plata y azul;
Y ve el capitán pirata,[1]
Cantando alegre en la popa,
Asia[2] a lado, al otro Europa[2] 15
Y allá a su frente Stambul.[2]

«Navega, velero mío,
Sin temor,
Que ni enemigo[1] navío,
Ni tormenta, ni bonanza 20
Tu rumbo a torcer alcanza,
Ni a sujetar tu valor.

«Veinte presas[3]
Hemos hecho
A despecho 25
Del inglés,
Y han rendido
Sus pendones
Cien naciones[4]
A mis pies. 30

«Que es mi barco mi tesoro,
Que es mi Dios la libertad,
Mi ley la fuerza y el viento,
Mi única patria la mar.

«Allá muevan feroz guerra 35
Ciegos reyes
Por un palmo más de tierra:
Que[5] yo tengo aquí por mío
Cuanto abarca el mar bravío,
A quien nadie impuso leyes. 40

«Y no hay playa,
Sea cualquiera,
Ni bandera

* See Vol. I, p. 138.
[1] An adjective here
[2] Objects of *ve* (l. 13)
[3] prizes, captured ships
[4] Subject of *han rendido*
[5] Omit in translating

De esplendor,[6]
Que no sienta 45
Mi derecho,
Y dé pecho[7]
A mi valor.

«Que es mi barco mi tesoro,
Que es mi Dios la libertad, 50
Mi ley la fuerza y el viento,
Mi única patria la mar.

«A la voz de ‹¡barco viene!›[8]
Es de ver[9]
Como vira y se previene 55
A todo trapo[10] a escapar:
Que yo soy el rey del mar,
Y mi furia es de temer.

«En las presas
Yo divido 60
Lo cogido[11]
Por igual:
Sólo quiero
Por riqueza
La belleza 65
Sin rival.

«Que es mi barco mi tesoro,
Que es mi Dios la libertad,
Mi ley la fuerza y el viento,
Mi única patria la mar. 70

«¡Sentenciado estoy a muerte!
Yo me río:
No me abandone la suerte,
Y al mismo que me condena,
Colgaré de alguna entena, 75
Quizá en su propio navío.

«Y si caigo,
¿Qué es la vida?
Por perdida
Ya la di,[12] 80
Cuando el yugo[13]
Del esclavo,
Como un bravo,
Sacudí.

«Que es mi barco mi tesoro, 85
Que es mi Dios la libertad,
Mi ley la fuerza y el viento,
Mi única patria la mar.

«Son mi música mejor
Aquilones, 90
El estrépito y temblor
De los cables sacudidos,
Del negro mar los bramidos
Y el rugir de mis cañones.

«Y del trueno 95
Al son[14] violento,
Y del viento
Al rebramar,
Yo me duermo
Sosegado 100
Arrullado
Por el mar.

«Que es mi barco mi tesoro,
Que es mi Dios la libertad,
Mi ley la fuerza y el viento, 105
Mi única patria la mar.»

[6] *bandera de esplendor,* glorious flag
[7] *dar pecho,* to pay tribute
[8] Ship ahoy
[9] you should see
[10] Here, sail
[11] the booty (what is taken)
[12] considered
[13] Object of *sacudí*
[14] sound. Tranlate l. 96 before l. 95, and l. 98 before l. 97.

El diablo mundo

Canto II

A Teresa: Descansa en paz[1]

¿Por qué volvéis a la memoria mía,
Tristes recuerdos del placer perdido,
A aumentar la ansiedad y la agonía
De este desierto corazón herido?
¡Ay, que[2] de aquellas horas de alegría, 5
Le quedó al corazón sólo un gemido,
Y el llanto que al dolor los ojos niegan,
Lágrimas son de hiel que el alma anegan!

¿Dónde volaron ¡ay! aquellas horas
De juventud, de amor y de ventura, 10
Regaladas de músicas sonoras,
Adornadas de luz y de hermosura?
Imágenes[3] de oro bullidoras,[4]
Sus alas de carmín y nieve pura,
Al sol de mi esperanza desplegando, 15
Pasaban ¡ay! a mi alredor cantando.

Gorjeaban los dulces ruiseñores,
El sol iluminaba mi alegría,
El aura susurraba entre las flores,
El bosque mansamente respondía, 20
Las fuentes murmuraban sus amores . . .
¡Ilusiones[5] que llora el alma mía!
¡Oh! ¡cuán süave resonó en mi oído
El bullicio del mundo y su ruído!

Yo amaba todo: un noble sentimiento 25
Exaltaba mi ánimo, y sentía
En mi pecho un secreto movimiento,
De grandes hechos generoso guía:
La libertad con su inmortal aliento,
Santa diosa mi espíritu encendía, 30
Contino[6] imaginando en mi fe pura
Sueños de gloria al mundo[7] y de ventura.

[1] This canto has nothing whatever to do with the main theme of *El diablo mundo*. Espronceda himself inserted this note: *'Este canto es un desahogo de mi corazón; sáltelo el que no quiera leerlo sin escrúpulo, pues no está ligado de manera alguna con el poema.'* Why is this statement typically romantic?

[2] for

[3] The poet recalls the lovely dreams of his youth, which, like brilliantly colored butterflies, fluttered around him.

[4] seething, teeming

[5] youthful dreams

[6] Poetic for *continuo*. In l. 31, an adjective modifying *yo* in l. 25. Translate, constantly.

[7] in the world

El valor y la fe del caballero,[8]
Del trovador el arpa y los cantares,
Del gótico castillo el altanero 35
Antiguo torreón, do[9] sus pesares
Cantó tal vez con eco lastimero,
¡Ay! arrancada de sus patrios lares,[10]
Joven cautiva, al rayo de la luna,
Lamentando su ausencia y su fortuna:[11] 40

El dulce anhelo del amor que aguarda
Tal vez inquieto y con mortal recelo,
La forma bella que cruzó gallarda,
Allá en la noche, entre el medroso velo;[12]
La ansiada cita que en llegar se tarda 45
Al impaciente y amoroso anhelo,
La mujer y la voz de su dulzura,
Que inspira al alma celestial ternura;

A un tiempo mismo en rápida tormenta,
Mi alma alborotaban de contino,[6] 50
Cual[13] las olas que azota con violenta
Cólera, impetuoso torbellino:[14]
Soñaba al héroe ya, la plebe atenta
En mi voz escuchaba su destino,
Ya al caballero, al trovador soñaba, 55
Y de gloria y de amores suspiraba.

Yo desterrado en extranjera playa,
Con los ojos, extático seguía
La nave audaz que argentada raya[15]
Volaba al puerto de la patria mía: 60
Yo cuando en Occidente el sol desmaya,[16]
Solo y perdido en la arboleda umbría,
Oír pensaba el armonioso acento
De una mujer, al suspirar del viento.

¡Una mujer![17] En el templado rayo 65
De la mágica luna se colora,[18]
Del sol poniente al lánguido desmayo,
Lejos entre las nubes se evapora;[19]

[8] knight-at-arms. All the ideas expressed in this stanza and the next are thoughts which assaulted the young poet's mind and offered themselves as subjects for poems. Grammatically all these nouns are subjects of *alborotaban,* l. 50.
[9] Poetic for *donde*
[10] household gods, home
[11] bad fortune
[12] veil (of night)
[13] like
[14] Subject of *azota*
[15] silvery line; translate, along a foamy track
[16] to faint, swoon, disappear. Here present tense used for imperfect.
[17] This is a purely fantastic woman (cf. ll. 75–6) whose presence is felt by Espronceda in all the beauties of nature. She represents a longed-for, perfect being; hence the perfect beauty of nature suggests her to his mind.
[18] Translate, she shows herself
[19] to disappear

Sobre las cumbres que florece[20] el mayo,
Brilla fugaz al despuntar la aurora, 70
Cruza tal vez por entre el bosque umbrío,
Juega en las aguas del sereno río.

¡Ay! aquella mujer, tan sólo aquélla
Tanto delirio[21] a realizar alcanza,
Y esa mujer tan cándida y tan bella, 75
Es mentida ilusión de la esperanza:
Es el alma que vívida destella[22]
Su luz al mundo cuando en él se lanza,
Y el mundo con su magia y galanura,
Es espejo no más de su hermosura: 80

¡Oh llama[23] santa! ¡celestial anhelo!
¡Sentimiento purísimo! memoria
Acaso triste de un perdido cielo,
¡Quizá esperanza de futura gloria!
¡Huyes y dejas llanto y desconsuelo! 85
¡Oh mujer! que en imagen ilusoria
Tan pura, tan feliz, tan placentera,
Brindó el amor a mi ilusión primera! . . .

¡Oh Teresa! ¡Oh dolor! Lágrimas mías,
¡Ah! ¡dónde estáis que no corréis a mares![24] 90
¿Por qué, por qué como en mejores días
No consoláis vosotras mis pesares?
¡Oh! los que no sabéis las agonías
De un corazón, que penas a millares
¡Ay! desgarraron, y que ya no llora, 95
¡Piedad tened de mi tormento ahora!

¿Quién pensara jamás, Teresa mía,
Que fuera eterno manantial de llanto,
Tanto inocente amor, tanta alegría,
Tantas delicias y delirio tanto? 100
¿Quién pensara jamás[25] llegase un día,
En que perdido el celestial encanto,
Y caída la venda de los ojos,
Cuanto diera placer causara enojos?

Aun parece, Teresa, que te veo 105
Aérea como dorada mariposa,
En sueño delicioso del deseo,
Sobre tallo gentil temprana rosa,

[20] to cover with flowers
[21] so much ecstatic dreaming (as the young poet had)
[22] to flash. The candid soul projects its purity into its imaginations; it expects the things of the world to have its own purity.
[23] flame (fire of idealistic love)
[24] Translate, in rivers
[25] Read, *que jamás*

Del amor venturoso devaneo,
Angélica, purísima y dichosa, 110
Y oigo tu voz dulcísima, y respiro
Tu aliento perfumado en tu suspiro.

Y aun miro aquellos ojos que robaron
A los cielos su azul, y las rosadas
Tintas sobre la nieve, que envidiaron 115
Las de mayo serenas alboradas;[26]
Y aquellas horas[27] dulces que pasaron
Tan breves ¡ay! como después lloradas,
Horas de confianza y de delicias,
De abandono, ye de amor, y de caricias. 120

Que así las horas rápidas pasaban,
Y pasaba a la par[28] nuestra ventura;
Y nunca nuestras ansias[29] las contaban,
Tú embriagada en mi amor, yo en tu hermosura:
Las horas[30] ¡ay! huyendo nos miraban, 125
Llanto tal vez vertiendo de ternura,
Que nuestro amor y juventud veían,
Y temblaban las horas que vendrían.

Los años ¡ay! de la ilusión pasaron;
Las dulces esperanzas que trajeron, 130
Con sus blancos[31] ensueños se llevaron[32]
Y el porvenir de oscuridad vistieron:
Las rosas del amor se marchitaron,
Las flores en abrojos convirtieron,
Y de afán tanto y tan soñada gloria, 135
Sólo quedó una tumba, una memoria.

¡Pobre Teresa! al recordarte siento
Un pesar tan intenso . . . ! embarga[33] impío
Mi quebrantada voz mi sentimiento,
Y suspira tu nombre el labio mío: 140
Para[34] allí su carrera el pensamiento,
Hiela mi corazón punzante frío,
Ante mis ojos la funesta losa,
Donde vil polvo tu beldad reposa.

Y tú feliz, que hallaste en la muerte 145
Sombra a que[35] descansar en tu camino,
Cuando llegabas mísera a perderte,

[26] dawn. Normal word order: *que las serenas alboradas de mayo envidiaron*
[27] Object of *miro*, l. 113
[28] *a la par*, at the same time
[29] yearning (of love)
[30] The hours (or Time) are now personified; they pity the lovers because they foresee their misfortunes.
[31] candid, pure
[32] Subject, *años*
[33] to check, hold back. Subject, *sentimiento*
[34] A verb
[35] shade in which

Y era llorar tu único destino:
Cuando en tu frente la implacable suerte
Grababa de los réprobos el sino[36] . . . ! 150
¡Feliz! la muerte te arrancó del suelo,
Y otra vez ángel te volviste al cielo.

Roída de recuerdos de amargura,
Árido el corazón sin ilusiones,
La delicada flor de tu hermosura 155
Ajaron del dolor los Aquilones:
Sola, y envilecida, y sin ventura,
Tu corazón secaron las pasiones,
Tus hijos ¡ay! de ti se avergonzaran,[37]
Y hasta el nombre de madre[38] te negaran. 160

Los ojos escaldados de tu llanto,
Tu rostro cadavérico y hundido,
Único desahogo en tu quebranto,
El histérico ¡ay! de tu gemido:
¿Quién, quién, pudiera en infortunio tanto, 165
Envolver tu desdicha en el olvido,
Disipar tu dolor y recogerte
En su seno de paz? ¡Sólo la muerte!

¡Oh! ¡cruel! ¡muy cruel! . . . ¡Ah! yo entretanto
Dentro del pecho mi dolor oculto, 170
Enjugo de mis párapados el llanto
Y doy al mundo el exigido culto:[39]
Yo escondo con vergüenza mi quebranto,
Mi propia pena con mi risa insulto,
Y me divierto en arrancar del pecho 175
Mi mismo corazón pedazos hecho.

Gozemos sí; la cristalina esfera
Gira bañada en luz: ¡bella es la vida!
¿Quién a parar alcanza la carrera
Del mundo hermoso que al placer convida? 180
Brilla radiante el sol, la primavera
Los campos pinta en la estación florida:
Truéquese en risa mi dolor profundo . . .
¡Que haya un cadáver más, qué importa al mundo![40]

[36] Poetic license for *signo*

[37] The r-form of the imperfect subjunctive is used here for the pluperfect indicative, a literary construction.

[38] After breaking with Espronceda, Teresa left her two children—one by her husband and the other by our poet and eventually became a woman of the streets.

[39] *doy . . . culto,* freely, I behave the way people expect me to

[40] An oft quoted verse which well illustrates the violent antithesis between life and death often employed by romantic writers.

Mariano José de Larra

WHEN at the age of twenty-eight Larra (1809–37) committed suicide in desperation over a tragic life and an unhappy love affair, he was looked on mainly as a promising young man. Today he is generally regarded as the most representative Spanish romantic author, the *hombre-cumbre* of the movement.

The tragedy of his life dates from his childhood. An unwanted child of a young mother and an old father, he was loved by neither. His father, a doctor and a sympathizer of the French, went into exile in 1813, along with the deposed Joseph Bonaparte. The precocious youngster studied in French schools in Bordeaux and probably in Paris from 1813 to 1818, completely forgetting his Spanish during this time. The event which finished the formation of his character was a tragic love affair in Valladolid when he was sixteen years old. Although we are inadequately informed about this episode of his life, we know that it was a terrific shock to the youth and caused his immediate departure from his family to gain an independent living in Madrid. There he lived a bohemian existence, gradually attaining literary prestige and achieving success first as a dramatist, then as a journalist. For the newspapers and magazines of the time he wrote criticism on the theater, political satires, and *cuadros de costumbres,* which latter represent the best of his production. They are little familiar essays, describing some characteristic phase of Spanish life, generally satirical in tone, with the reform of national customs in view. His marriage in 1829 was unhappy from the beginning; the very next year he was engaged in an illicit love affair which was to terminate with his suicide in 1837. The last three years of his life saw him grow more and more bitter. At his funeral, which was attended by all the literary figures of the day, Zorrilla read some impassioned verses which brought him his first recognition.

Larra's tragedy was fundamentally one of inner contradiction. His French education had taught him to believe in logic and progress, qualities which he hoped to bring into Spain, but whose introduction he always found blocked by elements inherent in Spanish character itself. He shared this character and, along with it, a profound love for Spain. Consequently he found himself often wanting progress which would do away with the very things he most intimately loved. His logic forced him to criticize many traits of Spanish nature and gave him a reputation among his contemporaries as an acid critic, even anti-Spanish in his attacks. They refer to his *'tristeza y amargura'* and his *'sarcástica sonrisa.'* But underneath, Larra's real desire was to better Spain. He was not content with inferior things; and part of his desperation derived from the fact that his country was not realizing the great possibilities he felt lay in it. Despite his reputation for sarcasm, under this protective armor he was really a timid man, anxious for friendship and love.

Larra's reputation depends partly on the fascination of his life, partly on the fact that he foreshadows the very ideas concerning Spain which have been in vogue in the twentieth century, and partly on the intrinsic artistic worth of his productions. Larra is both a thinker and a master of self-expression. Because of these two qualities, his popularity has risen in recent years to the point of a veritable cult.

Mariano José de Larra

La sociedad

Es cosa generalmente reconocida que el hombre es *animal social,* y yo, que no concibo que las cosas puedan ser sino del modo que son, yo, que no creo que pueda suceder sino lo que sucede, no trato, por consiguiente, de negarlo. Puesto que vive en sociedad, social es sin duda. No pienso adherirme a la opinión de los escritores malhumorados que han querido probar que el hombre habla por una aberración, que su verdadera posición es la de los cuatro pies, y que comete un grave error en buscar y fabricarse todo género de comodidades, cuando pudiera pasar pendiente de las bellotas de una encina el mes, por ejemplo, en que vivimos.[1]

Hanse[2] apoyado para fundar semejante opinión en que la sociedad le roba parte de su libertad,[3] si no toda: pero tanto valdría decir que el frío no es cosa natural, porque incomoda. Lo más que concederemos a los abogados[4] de la vida salvaje es que la sociedad es de todas las necesidades de la vida la peor: eso sí. Ésta es una desgracia, pero en el mundo feliz que habitamos casi todas las desgracias son verdad; razón por la cual nos admiramos siempre que vemos tantas investigaciones para buscar ésta.[5] A nuestro modo de ver no hay nada más fácil que encontrarla: allí donde está el mal, allí está la verdad. Lo malo es lo cierto. Sólo los bienes son ilusión.[6]

. . .

Pero como no basta estar convencidos de las cosas para convencer de

[1] This *cuadro de costumbres* was published in January 1835. Of course, this would be an especially bad month in which to live a 'natural' life.

[2] *se han*

[3] Rousseau and his followers declared that the natural man was free, good, and happy; but that living in a civilized social group robbed mankind of these qualities. Larra refers to them and answers them neatly in the next line.

[4] champion, advocate

[5] *la verdad*

[6] A good expression of Larra's bitter attitude.

ellas a los demás, inútilmente hacía yo las anteriores reflexiones a un primo mío que quería entrar en el mundo[7] hace tiempo, joven, vivaracho, inexperto, y por consiguiente alegre. Criado en el colegio, y versado en los autores clásicos, traía al mundo llena la cabeza de las virtudes que en los poemas y comedias se encuentran. Buscaba un Pílades;[8] toda amante le parecía una Safo,[9] y estaba seguro de encontrar una Lucrecia[10] el día que la necesitase. Desengañarle era una crueldad. ¿Por qué no había de ser feliz mi primo unos días como lo hemos sido todos? Pero además hubiera sido imposible. Limitéme, pues, a tomar sobre mí el cuidado de introducirle en el mundo, dejando a los demás el de desengañarle de él.

Después de haber presidido[11] al cúmulo de pequeñeces indispensables, al lado de las cuales nada es un corazón recto, un alma noble, ni aun una buena figura, es decir, después de haberse proporcionado unos cuantos fraques y cadenas, pantalones, colán[12] y mi colán,[13] reloj, sortijas y media docena de onzas[14] siempre en el bolsillo, primeras virtudes en sociedad, introdújelo por fin en las casas de mejor tono. Un poco de presunción, un personal[15] excelente, suficiente atolondramiento para no quedarse nunca sin conversación, un modo de bailar semejante al de una persona que anda sin gana, un bonito frac, seis apuestas de a[16] onza en el écarté,[17] y todo el desprecio posible de las mujeres, hablando con los hombres, le granjearon el afecto y la amistad verdadera de todo el mundo. Es inútil decir que quedó contento de su introducción.

—Es encantadora—me dijo—la sociedad. ¡Qué alegría! ¡Qué generosidad! ¡Ya tengo amigos, ya tengo amante!!!

A los quince días conocía a todo Madrid; a los veinte, no hacía caso ya de su antiguo consejero. Alguna vez llegó a mis oídos que afeaba mi filosofía y mis descabelladas ideas, como las llamaba.

—Preciso es que sea muy malo mi primo—decía—para pensar tan mal de los demás.

A lo cual solía yo responder para mí:

—Preciso es que sean muy malos los demás para haberme obligado a pensar tan mal de ellos.

Cuatro años habían pasado desde la introducción de mi primo en la sociedad: habíale perdido ya de vista, porque yo hago con el mundo lo que se hace con las pieles en verano: voy de cuando en cuando, para que no entre el olvido en mis relaciones, como se sacan aquéllas tal cual vez[18] al aire para que no se albergue en sus pelos la polilla. Había, sí, sabido mil aventuras suyas de estas que, por una contradicción inexplicable, honran mientras sólo las sabe todo el mundo en confianza, y que desacreditan cuando las llega a saber alguien de oficio:[19] pero nada más. Ocurrióme en esto[20] noches pasadas[21] ir a matar a una casa la polilla de mi relación; y a pocos pasos encontréme con mi primo. Parecióme no tener todo el buen humor que en otros tiempos le había visto; no sé si me buscó él a mí, si le busqué yo a él; sólo sé que a pocos minutos paseábamos el salón de bracero,[22] y alimentando el siguiente diálogo:

—¿Tú en el mundo? —me dijo.

[7] social world, high society
[8] A character noted for his faithful friendship; hence, a friend
[9] A poetess and charming lady
[10] A model wife
[11] Subject, *yo*
[12] French *collant*, tight-fitting
[13] moderately tight
[14] gold coin worth about $8
[15] personality
[16] *de a*, at the rate of
[17] A card game
[18] *tal cual vez*, once in a while
[19] officially
[20] *en esto*, at this point in the matter
[21] a few nights ago
[22] arm in arm

—Sí, de cuando en cuando vengo: cuando veo que se amortigua mi odio, cuando me siento inclinado a pensar bien, cuando empiezo a echarle menos, me presento una vez, y me curo para otra temporada. Pero, ¿tú no bailas?

—Es ridículo: ¿quién va a bailar en un baile?

—Sí por cierto . . . ¡Si fuera en otra parte! Pero observo desde que falto a esta casa multitud de caras nuevas . . . que no conozco . . .

—Es decir, que faltas a todas las casas de Madrid . . . porque las caras son las mismas; las casas son las diferentes; y por cierto que no vale la pena de variar de casa para no variar de gente.

—Así es —respondí—, que falto a todas. Quisiera, por tanto, que me instruyeses . . . ¿Quién es, por ejemplo, esa joven . . .? Linda por cierto . . . Baila muy bien . . . Parece muy amable . . .

—Es la baroncita viuda de * * *. Es una señora que, a fuerza de ser hermosa y amable, a fuerza de gusto en el vestir, ha llegado a ser aborrecida de todas las demás mujeres. Como su trato es harto fácil, y no abriga más malicia que la que cabe en veintidós años, todos los jóvenes que la ven se creen con derecho a ser correspondidos; y como al llegar a ella se estrellan, desgraciadamente, los más de sus cálculos en su virtud (porque aunque la ves tan loca al parecer, en el fondo es virtuosa), los unos han dado en llamar coquetería su amabilidad; los otros, por venganza, le dan otro nombre peor. Unos y otros hablan infamias de ella; debe, por consiguiente, a su mérito y a su virtud el haber perdido la reputación. ¿Qué quieres? ¡Ésa es la sociedad!

—¿Y aquélla de aquel aspecto grave, que se remilga tanto cuando un hombre se la acerca? Parece que teme que la vean los pies según se baja el vestido a cada momento.

—Ésa ha entendido mejor el mundo. Ésa responde con bufidos[23] a todo galán. Una casualidad rarísima me ha hecho descubrir dos relaciones que ha tenido en menos de un año; nadie las sabe sino yo; es casada, pero como brilla poco su lujo, como no es una hermosura de primer orden, como no se pone en evidencia, nadie habla mal de ella. Pasa por la mujer más virtuosa de Madrid. Entre las dos se pudiera hacer una maldad completa: la primera tiene las apariencias y ésta la realidad. ¿Qué quieres? ¡En la sociedad siempre triunfa la hipocresía! Mira, apartémonos: quiero evitar el encuentro de ese que se dirige hacia nosotros: me encuentra en la calle y nunca me saluda; pero en sociedad es otra cosa: como es tan desairado estar de pie, sin hablar con nadie, aquí me habla siempre. Soy su amigo para estos recursos, para los momentos de fastidio: también en el Prado[24] se me suele agregar cuando no ha encontrado ningún amigo más íntimo. Ésa es la sociedad.

—Pero observo que huyendo de él nos hemos venido al écarté. ¿Quién es aquel que juega a la derecha?

—¿Quién ha de ser? Un amigo mío íntimo, cuando yo jugaba. Ya se ve, ¡perdía[25] con tan buena fe! Desde que no juego no me hace caso. ¡Ay! Éste viene a hablarnos.

Efectivamente, llegósenos un joven con aire marcial y muy amistoso.

—¿Cómo le tratan a usted? . . .—le preguntó mi primo.

—Pícaramente; diez onzas he perdido. ¿Y a usted?

—Peor todavía; adiós.

Ni siquiera nos contestó el perdidoso.[26]

[23] snort (of indignation)
[24] The fashionable promenade of Madrid
[25] Subject, *yo*
[26] loser

—Hombre, si no has jugado—le dije a mi primo—, ¿cómo dices . . .?

—Amigo, ¿qué quieres? Conocí que me venía a preguntar si tenía suelto.[27] En[28] su vida ha tenido diez onzas; la sociedad es para él una especulación: lo que no gana lo pide . . .

—Pero ¿y qué inconveniente había en prestarle? Tú que eres tan generoso . . .

—Sí, hace cuatro años; ahora no presto ya hasta que no me paguen lo que me deben; es decir, que ya no prestaré nunca. Ésa es la sociedad. Y, sobre todo, ese que nos ha hablado . . .

—¡Ah, es cierto! Recuerdo que era antes tu amigo íntimo: no os separabais.

—Es verdad, y yo le quería: me lo encontré a mi entrada en el mundo; teníamos nuestros amores en una misma casa,[29] y yo tuve la torpeza de creer simpatía lo que era comunidad de intereses. Le hice todo el bien que pude, ¡inexperto de mí![30] Pero de allí a poco puso los ojos en mi bella, me perdió[31] en su opinión y nos hizo reñir. Él no logró nada, pero desbarató mi felicidad. Por mejor decir, me hizo feliz; me abrió los ojos.

—¿Es posible?

—Ésa es la sociedad. Era mi amigo íntimo. Desde entonces no tengo más que amigos; íntimos, estos pesos duros[32] que traigo en el bolsillo; son los únicos que no venden; al revés, compran.

—¿Y tampoco has tenido más amores?

—¡Oh, eso sí! De eso he tardado más en desengañarme. Quise a una que me quería sin duda por vanidad, porque a poco de quererla me sucedió un fracaso que me puso en ridículo, y me dijo que no podía arrostrar el ridículo; luego quise frenéticamente a una casada; ésa sí, creí que me quería sólo por mí; pero hubo hablillas, que promovió precisamente aquella fea que ves allí, que como no puede tener amores, se complace en desbaratar los ajenos; hubieron de llegar a oídos del marido; que empezó a darla mala vida: entonces mi apasionada me dijo que empezaba el peligro y que debía concluirse el amor; su tranquilidad era lo primero. Es decir, que amaba más a su comodidad que a mí. Ésa es la sociedad.

—¿Y no has pensado nunca en casarte?

—Muchas veces; pero a fuerza de conocer maridos, también me he desengañado.

—Observo que no llegas a hablar a las mujeres.

—¿Hablar a las mujeres en Madrid? Como en general no se sabe hablar de nada, sino de intrigas amorosas; como no se habla de artes, de ciencias, de cosas útiles; como ni de política se entiende, no se puede uno dirigir ni sonreír tres veces a una mujer; no se puede ir dos veces a su casa sin que digan: «Fulano hace el amor a mengana.» Esta expresión pasa a sospecha, y dicen con una frase, por cierto bien poco delicada: «¿Si estará metido con fulana?»[33] Al día siguiente esta sospecha es ya una realidad, un compromiso. Luego hay mujeres que porque han tenido una desgracia o una flaqueza, que se ha hecho pública por este hermoso sistema de sociedad, están siempre acechando la ocasión de encontrar cómplices o imitadoras que las disculpen, las cuales ahogan la vergüenza en la murmurmación. Si hablas a una bonita, la pierdes; si das conversación a una fea, quieres atrapar

[27] small change, coins
[28] Supply *nunca* before *en*.
[29] Here, family
[30] Translate, inexperienced as I was
[31] to ruin, lower
[32] *pesos duros,* dollars; cf. the proverb: *No hay más amigo que Dios y un duro en el bolsillo.*
[33] *Si . . . fulana,* suppose he's carrying on with so and so

su dinero. Si gastas chanzas con la parienta de un ministro, quieres un empleo. En una palabra, en esta sociedad de ociosos y habladores nunca se concibe la idea de que puedas hacer nada inocente, ni con buen fin, ni aun sin fin.

Al llegar aquí no pude menos de recordar a mi primo sus expresiones de hacía cuatro años: «Es encantadora la sociedad: ¡qué alegría! ¡Qué generosidad! ¡Ya tengo amigos, ya tengo amante!!!»

Un apretón de manos me convenció de que me había entendido.

—¿Qué quieres? —me añadió de allí a un rato—; nadie quiere creer sino en la experiencia: todos entramos buenos en el mundo, y todo andaría bien si nos buscáramos los de una edad; pero nuestro amor propio nos pierde: a los veinte años queremos encontrar amigos y amantes en las personas de treinta, es decir, en las que han llevado el chasco[34] antes que nosotros, y en los que ya no creen: como es natural, le llevamos entonces nosotros, y se le pegamos luego a los que vienen detrás. Ésa es la sociedad; una reunión de víctimas y de verdugos. ¡Dichoso aquel que no es verdugo y víctima a un tiempo! ¡Pícaros, necios, inocentes! ¡Más dichoso aún, si hay excepciones, el que puede ser excepción![35]

La Nochebuena de 1836

Yo y mi criado: Deliro filosófico

El número 24 me es fatal: si tuviera que probarlo diría que en día 24 nací.[1] Doce veces al año amanece sin embargo un día 24: soy supersticioso, porque el corazón del hombre necesita creer algo, y cree mentiras cuando no encuentra verdades que creer; sin duda por esa razón creen los amantes, los casados y los pueblos, a sus ídolos, a sus consortes y a sus gobiernos; y una de mis supersticiones consiste en creer que no puede haber para mí un día 24 bueno. El día 23 es siempre en mi calendario víspera de desgracia, y a imitación de aquel jefe de policía ruso que mandaba tener prontas las bombas las vísperas de incendios, así yo desde el 23 me prevengo para el siguiente día de sufrimiento y de resignación, y en dando[2] las doce ni tomo vaso en mi mano por no romperle, ni apunto carta[3] por no perderla, ni enamoro a mujer porque no me diga que sí, pues en punto a amores tengo otra superstición: imagino que la mayor desgracia que a un hombre le puede suceder es que una mujer le diga que le quiere. Si no la cree es un tormento, y si la cree . . . ¡Bienaventurado aquél a quien la mujer dice *no quiero,* porque ése a lo menos oye la verdad![4]

El último día 23 del año 1836 aca-

[34] *llevar un chasco,* to be disappointed

[35] We see that Larra has no hope of reforming society; he merely satirizes it and gives us to understand that the man who really knows social life is always disillusioned about it. Thus a note of hopeless bitterness runs through this essay.

[1] Larra was born on March 24, 1809.

[2] *en dando,* modern Spanish, *al dar*

[3] *apuntar carta,* to bet on a card

[4] Larra's marriage had gone on the rocks; his extra-marital affair with another man's wife was becoming more and more disappointing and embittered. Only a month and a half after writing this essay he committed suicide, after a final rupture with his paramour.

baba de expirar en la muestra de mi péndola,[5] y consecuente en mis principios supersticiosos ya estaba yo agachado esperando el aguacero[6] y sin poder conciliar el sueño. Así pasé las horas de la noche, más largas para el triste desvelado que una guerra civil;[7] hasta que por fin la mañana vino con paso de intervención, es decir, lentísimamente, a teñir de púrpura y rosa las cortinas de mi estancia.

El día anterior había sido hermoso, y no sé por qué me daba el corazón que el día 24 había de ser *día de agua*.[8] Fue peor todavía; amaneció nevando. Miré el termómetro, y marcaba muchos grados bajo cero; como el crédito del estado.[9]

Resuelto a no moverme . . . , incliné la frente, cargada como el cielo, de nubes frías, [y] apoyé los codos en mi mesa. Ora vagaba mi vista sobre la multitud de artículos y folletos que yacen empezados y no acabados ha más de seis meses[10] sobre mi mesa, y de que sólo existen los títulos, como esos nichos preparados en los cementerios[11] que no aguardan más que el cadáver; comparación exacta, porque en cada artículo entierro una esperanza o una ilusión. Ora volvía los ojos a los cristales[12] de mi balcón; veíalos empañados y como llorosos por dentro: los vapores condensados se deslizaban a manera de lágrimas a lo largo del diáfano cristal; así se empaña la vida, pensaba; así el frío exterior del mundo condensa las penas en el interior del hombre, así caen gota a gota las lágrimas sobre el corazón. Los que ven de fuera los cristales, los ven tersos y brillantes; los que ven sólo los rostros, los ven alegres y serenos . . .

Haré merced a mis lectores de las más de mis meditaciones; no hay periódicos bastantes en Madrid,[13] acaso no hay lectores bastantes tampoco. Dichoso el que tiene oficina, dichoso el empleado aún sin sueldo o sin cobrarlo,[14] que es lo mismo: al menos no está obligado a pensar, puede fumar, puede leer la gaceta!![15]

¡Las cuatro! ¡La comida! me dijo una voz de criado, una voz de entonación servil y sumisa; en el hombre que sirve hasta la voz parece pedir permiso para sonar. Esta palabra me sacó de mi estupor e involuntariamente iba a exclamar como don Quijote: «Come, Sancho hijo, come, tú que no eres caballero andante y que naciste para comer»[16] porque al fin los filósofos, es decir, los desgraciados, podemos no

[5] *la muestra de mi péndola,* the face of my clock

[6] *agachado esperando el aguacero,* squatting down awaiting the shower; here figuratively, hunched up waiting for the blow

[7] Larra compares his protracted wakefulness to the civil war which had been dragging on for three years when he wrote this essay.

[8] *día de agua,* a rainy day. Just before Larra has said that the dawn had colored his curtains; now he will say that it is snowing. It seems that the allusion to the colors of the sunrise is merely an ironical reference to the conventional pastoral verses, which Larra frequently satirizes.

[9] The thermometer was of the Centigrade system where zero is at 32 degrees Fahrenheit. The allusion to the credit of the state refers to the sagging prices of government bonds.

[10] *ha más de seis meses,* more commonly, *hace más de seis meses*

[11] In many Spanish cemeteries, the coffins are not buried, but slid into long narrow niches in walls surounding courtyards. Of course, when a new section of a cemetery is built, the empty niches await the new coffins.

[12] *cristal,* window pane

[13] Understand, enough newspapers to contain all my gloomy thoughts. Remember that Larra's essays appeared in newspapers.

[14] The government often skipped salary payments to its employees; another evidence of its low credit. See note 9.

[15] In the government offices the employees did little work, but passed the day talking, smoking, drinking coffee, and reading the official newspaper (*La Gaceta*).

[16] Larra has apparently confused two passages from the *Quijote,* one in which Quijote tells Sancho to sleep (Part I, Chap. 20) and another where he tells him to eat (Part II, Chap. 59).

comer, pero los criados de los filósofos!!! Una idea más luminosa me ocurrió: era día de Navidad.[17] Me acordé de que en sus famosas saturnales[18] los romanos trocaban los papeles y que los esclavos podían decir la verdad a sus amos. Costumbre humilde, digna del cristianismo. Miré a mi criado y dije para mí: esta noche me dirás la verdad. Saqué de mi gaveta[19] unas monedas; tenían el busto de los monarcas de España; cualquiera diría que son retratos; sin embargo eran artículos de periódico.[20] Las miré con orgullo: «come y bebe de mis artículos», añadí con desprecio: sólo en esa forma, sólo por medio de ese estratagema se pueden meter los artículos en el cuerpo de ciertas gentes. Una risa estúpida se dibujó en la fisonomía de aquel ser que los naturalistas han tenido la bondad de llamar racional sólo porque lo han visto hombre.[21] Mi criado se rió. Era aquella risa el demonio de la gula[22] que reconocía su campo.

Tercié la capa, calé el sombrero y en la calle.

¿Qué es un aniversario? Acaso un error de fecha. Si no se hubiera compartido el año en trescientos sesenta y cinco días ¿qué sería de nuestros aniversarios? Pero al pueblo le han dicho: hoy es un aniversario: y el pueblo ha respondido: «pues si es un aniversario, comamos, y comamos doble», ¿Por qué come hoy más que ayer? O ayer pasó hambre, u hoy pasará indigestión. Miserable humanidad destinada siempre a quedarse más acá o a ir más allá.[23]

Hace mil ochocientos treinta y seis años nació el Redentor del mundo, nació el que no reconoce principio; y el que no reconoce fin, nació para morir. Sublime misterio.

¿Hay misterio que celebrar? Pues comamos, dice el hombre; no dice: reflexionemos. El vientre es el encargado de cumplir con las grandes solemnidades. El hombre tiene que recurrir a la materia para pagar las deudas del espíritu. ¡Argumento terrible en favor del alma!

Para ir desde mi casa al teatro es preciso pasar por la plaza[24] tan indispensablemente como es preciso pasar por el dolor para ir desde la cuna al sepulcro. Montones de comestibles acumulados, risa y algazara, compra y venta, sobras por todas partes y alegría . . .

¡Las cinco! hora del teatro: el telón se levanta a la vista de un pueblo palpitante y bullicioso. Dos comedias de circunstancias, o yo estoy loco.[25] Una representación en que los hombres son mujeres y las mujeres hombres. He aquí nuestra época y nuestras costumbres. Los hombres ya no saben sino hablar como las mujeres, en congresos y en corrillos. Y las mujeres son hombres, ellas son las únicas que conquistan. Segunda comedia; un novio que no ve el logro de su esperanza: ese novio es el pueblo español: no se casa con un solo gobierno con quien

[17] Although not actually Christmas Day, the celebration of Christmas has begun. Spaniards traditionally have a feast on Christmas Eve, either before or after the midnight mass (*Misa de gallo*).

[18] The Roman Saturnalia was a festival lasting from December 17 to December 24 which had many similarities to our Christmas, such as religious ceremonies, exchange of gifts, feasting and gaiety, in which all classes, even slaves, were included. The festival came to be known especially for its licentiousness.

[19] *gaveta,* money drawer

[20] The coins were 'newspaper articles' because they were received in payment for Larra's journalistic work.

[21] *lo han visto hombre,* they have seen that he was a man

[22] *gula,* gluttony

[23] *a quedarse más acá o a ir más allá,* to fall short or to go too far

[24] Larra alludes to the *Plaza Mayor* where stands are put up before Christmas to sell food, toys, and candies.

[25] *comedia de circunstancias,* play based on an involved plot; *o yo estoy loco,* Larra wagers that he has guessed correctly the trite nature of the plays, or if not, you may call him crazy

no tenga que reñir al día siguiente.[26] Es el matrimonio repetido al infinito.

Pero las orgías llaman a los ciudadanos. Ciérranse las puertas, ábrense las cocinas. Dos horas, tres horas, y yo rondo de calle en calle a merced de mi pensamiento. La luz que ilumina los banquetes viene a herir mis ojos por las rendijas de los balcones, el ruido de los panderos[27] y de la bacanal que estremece los pisos y las vidrieras se abre paso hasta mis sentidos, y entra en ellos como cuña a mano,[28] rompiendo y desbaratando.

Las doce van a dar: las campanas . . . citan a los cristianos al oficio divino. ¿Qué es esto? ¿Va a espirar el 24 y no me ha ocurrido en él más contratiempo que mi mal humor de todos los días? Pero mi criado me espera en mi casa; como espera la cuba al catador,[29] llena de vino; mis artículos, hechos moneda, mi moneda hecha mosto se ha apoderado del imbécil como imaginé, y el asturiano[30] ya no es un hombre; es todo verdad.[31] . . . La verdad me esperaba en él y era preciso oírla de sus labios impuros. La verdad es como el agua filtrada, que no llega a los labios sino al través del cieno. Me abrió mi criado, y no tardé en reconocer su estado.

—Aparta, imbécil, exclamé empujando suavemente aquel cuerpo sin alma que en uno de sus columpios[32] se venía sobre mí. ¡Oiga! está ebrio. ¡Pobre muchacho! ¡Da lástima!

Me entré de rondón[33] a mi estancia; pero el cuerpo me siguió con un rumor sordo e interrumpido: una vez dentro los dos, su aliento desigual y sus movimientos violentos apagaron la luz; una bocanada de aire, colada por la puerta al abrirme, cerró la de mi habitación, y quedamos dentro casi a oscuras yo y mi criado, es decir, la verdad y Fígaro,[34] aquella en figura de hombre beodo[35] arrimado[36] a los pies de mi cama para no vacilar, y yo a su cabecera, buscando inútilmente un fósforo que nos iluminase.

Dos ojos brillaban como dos llamas fatídicas enfrente de mí: no sé por qué misterio mi criado encontró entonces, y de repente, voz y palabras, y habló y raciocinó: misterios más raros se han visto acreditados: los fabulistas hacen hablar a los animales ¿por qué no he de hacer yo hablar a mi criado? Oradores conozco yo de quienes hace algún tiempo no hubiera hecho yo una pintura más favorable que de mi astur,[37] y que han roto sin embargo a hablar, y los oye el mundo y los escucha, y nadie se admira.

En fin, yo cuento un hecho: tal me ha pasado: yo no escribo para los que dudan de mi veracidad: el que no quiera creerme puede doblar la hoja: ése se ahorrará tal vez de fastidio: pero una voz salió de mi criado y entre ella

[26] Ministries never lasted very long in Spain, but Larra probably had something more specific in mind. A few months before writing this essay, he had been elected *diputado* for Ávila, the city where his paramour was then living. But six days later a revolution deposed the ministry and nullified Larra's election. (One of the leaders of Larra's party was the Duque de Rivas.)

[27] *pandero,* tambourine. Many noise-makers are still used in Spanish Christmas festivities.

[28] *cuña a mano,* wedge

[29] *como espera la cuba al catador,* as the vat waits for the taster

[30] *asturiano,* a man from Asturias, on the northern coast. Asturians and Gallegos were frequently servants in other parts of Spain.

[31] An allusion to the famous Latin proverb: *In vino veritas.*

[32] *columpio,* swing; here, swaying motion

[33] *de rondón,* abruptly

[34] *Fígaro,* Larra's pen name, taken from the play by Beaumarchais, *Le Barbier de Seville.* Larra was thinking of a passage in the play where the count asks Fígaro what has given him such a gay philosophy. Fígaro answers: "My habitual griefs. I hasten to laugh at everything from fear of being obliged to weep about it."

[35] *beodo,* drunk

[36] *arrimar,* to approach; *arrimar a* (*una cosa*), to lean on (something)

[37] *astur,* Asturian

y la mía se estableció el siguiente diálogo.

—Lástima, dijo la voz, repitiendo mi piadosa exclamación.[38] ¿Y por qué me has de tener lástima, escritor? Yo a ti, ya lo entiendo.

¿Tú a mí? pregunté sobrecogido ya por un terror supersticioso: y es que la voz empezaba a decir verdad.

—Escucha: tú vienes triste como de costumbre: yo estoy más alegre que suelo.[39] ¿Por qué ese color pálido, ese rostro deshecho, esas hondas y verdes ojeras que ilumino con mi luz al abrirte todas las noches? ¿Por qué esa distracción constante y esas palabras vagas e interrumpidas de que sorprendo todos los días fragmentos errantes sobre tus labios? ¿Por qué te vuelves y te envuelves en tu mullido lecho[40] como un criminal, acostado con su remordimiento, en tanto que yo ronco sobre mi tosca tarima?[41] ¿Quién debe tener lástima a quién? No pareces criminal; la justicia no prende sino a los pequeños criminales, a las que roban con ganzúas,[42] o a los que matan con puñal; pero a los que arrebatan el sosiego de una familia seduciendo a la mujer casada o a la hija honesta, a los que roban con los naipes en la mano, a los que matan una existencia con una palabra dicha al oído, con una carta cerrada,[43] a ésos ni los llama la sociedad criminales, ni la justicia los prende, porque la víctima no arroja sangre, ni manifiesta herida, sino agoniza lentamente consumida por el veneno de la pasión que su verdugo le ha propinado. ¡Qué de tísicos[44] han muerto asesinados por una infiel, por un ingrato, por un calumniador! Los entierran; dicen que la cura no ha alcanzado y que los médicos no la entendieron. Pero la puñalada hipócrita alcanzó e hirió el corazón. Tú acaso eres de esos criminales y hay un acusador dentro de ti, y ese frac elegante y esa media de seda, y ese chaleco de tisú de oro que yo te he visto, son tus armas maldecidas.

—Silencio, hombre borracho.

—No; has de oír al vino, una vez que habla. Acaso ese oro que a fuer de[45] elegante has ganado en tu sarao[46] y que vuelcas[47] con indiferencia sobre tu tocador, es el precio del honor de una familia. Acaso ese billete que desdoblas es un anónimo embustero que va a separar de ti para siempre la mujer que adorabas; acaso es una prueba de la ingratitud de ella o de su perfidia. Más de uno[48] te he visto morder y despedazar con tus uñas y tus dientes en los momentos en que el buen tono cede el paso a la pasión y a la saciedad.

Tú buscas la felicidad en el corazón humano, y para eso le destrozas, hozando[49] en él, como quien remueve la tierra en busca de un tesoro. Yo nada busco, y el desengaño no me espera a la vuelta de[50] la esperanza. Tú eres literato y escritor, y qué tormentos no te hace pasar tu amor propio, ajado diariamente por la indiferencia de unos, por la envidia de otros, por el rencor de muchos. Preciado de gracioso, harías reír a costa de un amigo, si amigos hubiera, y no quieres tener remordimiento. Hombre de partido,[51] haces la guerra a otro partido: o cada vencimiento es una

[38] The last thing Larra said, four paragraphs before, was "Da lástima."
[39] *soler,* to be accustomed
[40] *mullido lecho,* downy couch
[41] *tarima,* pallet
[42] *ganzúa,* skeleton key
[43] *carta cerrada,* letter
[44] *qué de tísicos,* how many consumptives
[45] *a fuer de,* in the manner of
[46] *sarao,* party, entertainment (from the French *soirée*). Gambling was common at parties in Larra's time.
[47] *volcar,* to pour; to upset
[48] *uno* has *billete* as its antecedent.
[49] *hozar,* to root (like a pig)
[50] *a la vuelta de,* around the corner from
[51] *partido,* political party; *hombre de partido,* a party man

humillación, o compras la victoria demasiado cara para gozar de ella. Ofendes y no quieres tener enemigos. ¡A mí quién me calumnia! ¿quién me conoce? Tú me pagas un salario bastante a cubrir mis necesidades; a ti te paga el mundo como paga a los demás que le sirven . . . Despedazado siempre por la sed de gloria, inconsecuencia rara, despreciarás acaso a aquéllos para quienes escribes y reclamas con el incensario en la mano su adulación: adulas a tus lectores para ser de ellos adulado, y eres también despedazado por el temor, y no sabes si mañana irás a coger tus laureles a las Baleares o a un calabozo.[52]

—¡Basta, basta!

—Concluyo; yo en fin no tengo necesidades: tú, a pesar de tus riquezas, acaso tendrás que someterte mañana a un usurero para un capricho innecesario, porque vosotros tragáis oro, o para un banquete de vanidad en que cada bocado es un tósigo. Tú lees día y noche buscando la verdad en los libros hoja por hoja, y sufres de no encontrarla ni escrita.[53] Ente ridículo, bailas sin alegría; tu movimiento turbulento es el movimiento de la llama, que sin gozar ella, quema. Cuando yo necesito de mujeres echo mano de[54] mi salario, y las encuentro, fieles por más de un cuarto de hora; tú echas mano de tu corazón y vas, y lo arrojas a los pies de la primera que pasa, y no quieres que lo pise y lo lastime, y le entregas ese depósito sin conocerla. Confías tu tesoro a cualquiera por su linda cara, y crees porque quieres; y si mañana tu tesoro desaparece, llamas ladrón al depositario, debiendo llamarte imprudente y necio a ti mismo.

—Por piedad, déjame, voz del infierno.

—Concluyo: inventas palabras y haces de ellas sentimientos, ciencias, artes, objetos de existencia. Política, gloria, saber, poder, riqueza, amistad, amor. Y cuando descubres que son palabras, blasfemas y maldices. En tanto el pobre asturiano come, bebe y duerme, y nadie le engaña, y si no es feliz, no es desgraciado, no es al menos hombre de mundo,[55] ni ambicioso, ni elegante, ni literato ni enamorado. Ten lástima ahora al pobre asturiano.[56] Tú me mandas, pero no te mandas a ti mismo. Ténme lástima, literato. Yo estoy ebrio de vino, es verdad; pero tú lo estás de deseos y de impotencia . . . !!

Un ronco sonido terminó el diálogo; el cuerpo cansado del esfuerzo había caído al suelo; el órgano de la providencia había callado; y el asturiano roncaba. ¡Ahora te conozco, exclamé, día 24!

Una lágrima preñada de horror y de desesperación surcaba mi mejilla ajada ya por el dolor. A la mañana amo y criado yacían, aquél en el lecho, éste en el suelo. El primero tenía todavía abiertos los ojos y los clavaba con delirio y con delicia en una caja amarilla, donde se leía *mañana.* ¿Llegará ese *mañana* fatídico? ¿Qué encerraba la caja? En tanto la *Nochebuena* era pasada y el mundo todo, a mis barbas,[57] cuando hablaba de ella la seguía llamando Noche buena.

[52] After the many violent changes of government in Spain the opponents of the regime in power were often exiled to some distant part of the country, such as the Balearic Islands, or put in jail. A politician had to fear such a possible outcome of his career.

[53] *ni escrita,* here, anywhere at all

[54] *echar mano de,* to draw on, to appeal to

[55] *hombre de mundo,* a society man, man of the world

[56] The servant comes back to his starting point, that is, Larra's exclamation of pity for him. The whole harangue of the Asturian has been based on the idea that Larra is more to be pitied than his servant. Since the whole dialogue takes place in the dark and since the servant talks with unusual eloquence, Larra leaves us with the impression that the servant's words are merely projections of his own thoughts.

[57] *a mis barbas,* right to my face

José Zorrilla

ZORRILLA (1817–93) was one of the few romantic poets to live a long life. As a young man he ran away from his family to Madrid, where he lived a bohemian existence for several years. He attained sudden fame at the age of twenty for his verses to Larra, read at the latter's funeral. Perhaps this meteoric rise was due as much to the impassioned way in which he read them as to their intrinsic worth, for he himself tells us that he broke down when halfway through the poem and had to hand the manuscript to a friend to finish. Zorrilla's greatest literary success was the play *Don Juan Tenorio* (1844).[1] His marriage was unhappy, and he left Madrid, partly to escape his wife, to live in Paris (1850–54) and in Mexico (1854–66). He was a favorite of the emperor Maximilian. After his return to Spain he found that he belonged to a forgotten generation. During his last years he suffered constantly from poverty.

There is an apparent contradiction in Zorrilla's make-up for, despite his romantic escapades as a young man and his life-long adherence to the romantic school in literature, fundamentally Zorrilla was a conservative. The two great sources of his inspiration always were religion and the fatherland. He himself tells us: *'Al publicar el segundo* [*tomo*] *he tenido presentes dos cosas, la Patria en que nací y la Religión en que vivo. Español, he buscado en nuestro suelo mis inspiraciones. Cristiano, he creído que mi religión encierra más poesía que el paganismo.'* This conservative credo was written only one year after Larra's death, and marks Zorrilla's shift from the romantic revolt to the romantic revival. We can understand that he came later to look on the verses that he wrote for Larra as morally wrong, for Larra's suicide branded him as sacrilegious to the Catholic Zorrilla:

Broté como una hierba corrompida
Al borde de la tumba de un malvado
Y mi primer cantar fué a un suicida
¡Agüero fué, por Dios, bien desdichado!
(Introduction to *Obras completas,* 1884)

Zorrilla's best poetic works are those in which he seeks inspiration in his fatherland, goes back into the legendary past of the nation, and brings in

[1] See Vol. I, p. 138.

the religious traditions and popular beliefs of the people. These poems, most of which run to several hundred lines and combine lyric feeling with dramatic elements in their presentation, he calls *Leyendas.* Zorrilla was a man of the people—another reason why the *leyenda,* an essentially popular form, should be his best mode of expression.

Zorrilla wrote poetry almost as easily as he talked; hence he has the advantage of spontaneity, but the disadvantage of writing entirely too much. There is little intensity of feeling or condensation of emotion in his productions. On the other hand he is a master of musical, flowing verse and beautiful imagery.

José Zorrilla

A buen juez, mejor testigo[1]

(Tradición de Toledo)

I

Entre pardos nubarrones
Pasando la blanca luna,
Con resplandor fugitivo,
La baja tierra no alumbra.
Tal vez[2] un pálido rayo 5
La opaca atmósfera cruza,[3]
Y unas en otras las sombras
Confundidas se dibujan.
Reverberan los cristales[4]
La trémula llama turbia, 10
Y un instante entre las rocas
Riëla la fuente oculta.
Los álamos de la vega
Parecen en la espesura
De fantasmas apiñados 15
Medrosa y gigante turba;
Y alguna vez desprendida
Gotea pesada lluvia,
Que no despierta a quien duerme,
Ni a quien medita importuna. 20
Yace Toledo en el sueño
Entre las sombras confusas,
Y el Tajo a sus pies pasando
Con pardas ondas lo arrulla.
¡Qué dulce es dormir en calma 25
Cuando a lo lejos susurran
Los álamos que se mecen,
Las aguas que se derrumban!
Se sueñan bellos fantasmas
Que el sueño del triste endulzan, 30
Y en tanto que sueña el triste,
No le aqueja su amargura.
Tan en calma y tan sombría
Como la noche[5] que enluta
La esquina en que desemboca 35
Una callejuela oculta,
Se ve de un hombre que aguarda
La vigilante figura,
Y tan a la sombra vela
Que entre las sombras se ofusca.[6] 40
Frente por frente a sus ojos
Un balcón a poca altura
Deja escapar por los vidrios
La luz que dentro le alumbra;
Mas ni en el claro aposento, 45
Ni en la callejuela oscura
El silencio de la noche

[1] For a good judge, a better witness
[2] *tal vez,* once in a while
[3] *cruzar,* here, to pierce
[4] *reverberan los cristales,* the window panes reflect
[5] The comparison is to the *figura* (l. 38) which is as quiet and gloomy as the night.
[6] *ofuscar,* to dazzle; to confuse; here, to blend into the shadows

Rumor sospechoso turba.
Pasó así tan largo tiempo,
Que pudiera haberse duda 50
De si es hombre, o solamente
Mentida[7] ilusión nocturna;
Pero es hombre, y bien se ve,
Porque con planta segura
Ganando el centro a la calle 55
Resuelto y audaz pregunta:
—¿Quién va?— y a corta distancia
El igual compás se escucha
De un caballo que sacude[8]
Las sonoras herraduras. 60
—¿Quién va?— repite, y cercana
Otra voz menos robusta
Responde: —Un hidalgo, ¡calle![9]—
Y el paso el bulto[10] apresura.
—Téngase el hidalgo— el hombre 65
Replica, y la espada empuña.
—Ved más bien si me haréis calle
(Repitieron[11] con mesura)
Que hasta hoy a nadie se tuvo[12]
Ibán de Vargas y Acuña. 70
—Pase el Acuña y perdone—
Dijo el mozo en faz de fuga,[13]
Pues teniéndose el embozo[14]
Sopla un silbato, y se oculta.
Paró el jinete a una puerta, 75
Y con precaución difusa[15]
Salió una niña al balcón
Que llama interior alumbra.
—¡Mi padre!— clamó en voz baja
Y el viejo en la cerradura 80
Metió la llave pidiendo
A sus gentes que le acudan.
Un negro por ambas bridas
Tomó la cabalgadura,
Cerróse detrás la puerta 85
Y quedó la calle muda.
En esto desde el balcón,
Como quien tal acostumbra,
Un mancebo por las rejas
De la calle se asegura.[16] 90
Asió el brazo al que apostado
Hizo cara a Ibán de Acuña,
Y huyeron, en el embozo
Velando la catadura.[17]

II

Clara, apacible y serena 95
Pasa la siguiente tarde,
Y el sol tocando su ocaso
Apaga su luz gigante:
Se ve la imperial Toledo
Dorada por los remates,[18] 100
Como una ciudad de grana[19]
Coronada de cristales.
El Tajo por entre rocas
Sus anchos cimientos lame,
Dibujando en las arenas 105
Las ondas con que las bate.[20]
Y la ciudad se retrata
En las ondas desiguales,
Como en prenda de que el río
Tan afanoso la bañe.[21] 110
A lo lejos en la vega[22]
Tiende galán por sus márgenes,
De sus álamos y huertos
El pintoresco ropaje,
Y porque[23] su altiva gala 115
Más a los ojos halague,
La salpica con escombros
De castillos y de alcázares.
Un recuerdo es cada piedra
Que toda una historia vale, 120
Cada colina un secreto

[7] *mentida,* false
[8] *sacudir,* to shake; to pound, beat
[9] *calle,* here, make way! (Let me have the street. Remember that many streets of Toledo are extremely narrow.)
[10] *bulto,* vague figure, half-seen object
[11] *repitieron,* equivalent to *se repitió*
[12] *a nadie se tuvo,* has not stopped for anyone
[13] *en faz de fuga,* with the appearance of fleeing
[14] *teniéndose el embozo,* keeping his face muffled up (in his cape)
[15] *difuso,* here, elaborate, great
[16] *de la calle se asegura,* here, makes sure that the street is safe
[17] *catadura,* countenance
[18] *remate,* end; here, steeples, pinnacles
[19] *grana,* scarlet
[20] Leaving on the sandy beaches the traces of the waves that wash up on them
[21] *Como en prenda . . . la bañe,* as if giving [its reflection] as a pledge that the river will bathe it so eagerly
[22] *vega.* Below Toledo, the valley of the Tajo opens out into a fertile plain, *la vega.*
[23] *porque* (with subjunctive, *halague*) so that

De príncipes o galanes.[24]
Aquí se bañó la hermosa
Por quien dejó un rey culpable
Amor, fama, reino y vida 125
En manos de musulmanes.[25]
Allí recibió Galiana[26]
A su receloso amante
En esa cuesta que entonces
Era un plantel de azahares. 130
Allá por aquella torre,[27]
Que hicieron puerta los árabes,
Subió el Cid sobre Babieca
Con su gente y su estandarte.
La sombra en este momento[28] 135
Tiende sus turbios cendales
Por todas esas memorias
De las pasadas edades,
Y del Cambrón y Visagra[29]
Los caminos desiguales, 140
Camino a los toledanos
Hacia las murallas abren.
Los labradores se acercan
Al fuego de sus hogares,
Cargados con sus aperos, 145
Cansados de sus afanes.
Los ricos y sedentarios
Se tornan con paso grave,
Calado el ancho sombrero,
Abrochados los gabanes, 150
Y los clérigos y monjes
Y los prelados y abades
Sacudiendo el leve polvo
De capelos y sayales.
Quédase sólo un mancebo 155
De impetuosos ademanes,
Que se pasea ocultando
Entre la capa el semblante.
Los que pasan le contemplan
Con decisión de evitarle, 160
Y él contempla a los que pasan
Como si a alguien aguardase.
Los tímidos aceleran
Los pasos al divisarle,
Cual[30] temiendo de seguro 165
Que les proponga un combate;
Y los valientes le miran
Cual si sintieran dejarle
Sin que libres sus estoques,
En riña sonora dancen. 170
Una mujer también sola
Se viene el llano adelante,[31]
La luz del rostro escondida
En tocas y tafetanes.
Mas en lo leve del paso 175
Y en lo flexible del talle
Puede, a través de los velos,
Una hermosa adivinarse.[32]
Vase derecha al que aguarda
Y él al encuentro le sale, 180
Diciendo . . . cuanto se dicen
En las citas los amantes.
Mas ella, galanterías
Dejando severa aparte,
Así al mancebo interrumpe, 185
En voz decisiva y grave:
—Abreviemos de razones,
Diego Martínez; mi padre,
Que un hombre ha entrado en su
ausencia,
Dentro mi aposento sabe; 190

[24] Zorrilla loved to collect legends. When he was seventeen he enrolled in the now defunct University of Toledo. Instead of attending lectures, he spent his time wandering through the narrow streets, sketching the old ruins of castles, mosques, and synagogues, and listening to the legends associated with the city. His father, highly dissatisfied with his progress in his studies, did not allow him to return to Toledo after his first year.

[25] Lines 123 to 126 allude to the legend of Rodrigo, the last Visigothic king, who saw Count Julian's daughter bathing in the river and violated her. The count's revenge was to invite the Musulmans to invade Spain.

[26] Galiana, a Moorish princess, was the mistress of Charlemagne according to a legend with no foundation in history. A ruined building on the bank of the Tajo is still called *el palacio de la Galiana.*

[27] The tower and gate are the still existing *Puerta del Sol,* through which, according to legend, the Cid entered Toledo on his charger, Babieca.

[28] The author now shifts our attention back to the afternoon he has been describing from l. 95 on.

[29] Cambrón and Visagra are two gates of Toledo, on opposite sides of the city. The author means that all the inhabitants of Toledo, from one gate to the other, are taking their afternoon walk.

[30] *cual,* as if

[31] *el llano adelante,* across the plain

[32] One can conclude that she is a beautiful woman.

Y así, quien mancha mi honra
Con la suya me la lave;[33]
O dadme mano de esposo,
O libre de vos dejadme.
Miróla Diego Martínez 195
Atentamente un instante,
Y echando a un lado el embozo,
Repuso palabras tales:
—Dentro de un mes, Inés mía,
Parto a la guerra de Flandes; 200
Al año estaré de vuelta
Y contigo en los altares.
Honra que yo te desluzca,
Con honra mía se lave,
Que por honra vuelven honra 205
Hidalgos que en honra nacen.
—Júralo— exclamó la niña.
—Más que mi palabra vale
No te valdrá un juramento.
—Diego, la palabra es aire. 210
—¡Vive Dios que estás tenaz!
Dalo por jurado y baste.[34]
—No me basta, que olvidar
Puedes la palabra en Flandes.
—¡Voto a Dios!, ¿qué más pretendes? 215
—Que a los pies de aquella imagen
Lo jures como cristiano
Del santo Cristo delante.
Vaciló un poco Martínez;
Mas, porfiando que jurase, 220
Llevóle Inés hacia el templo[35]
Que en medio la vega yace.
Enclavado en un madero,
En duro y postrero trance,
Ceñida la sien de espinas, 225
Descolorido el semblante,
Veíase allí un crucifijo[36]
Teñido de negra sangre,
A quien Toledo, devota,
Acude hoy en sus azares. 230
Ante sus plantas divinas
Llegaron ambos amantes,
Y haciendo Inés que Martínez
Los sagrados pies tocase,
Preguntóle:
—Diego, ¿juras 235
A tu vuelta desposarme?
Contestó el mozo:
—¡Sí, juro!
Y ambos del templo se salen.

III

Pasó un día y otro día
Un mes y otro mes pasó, 240
Y un año pasado había;
Mas de Flandes no volvía
Diego, que a Flandes partió.[37]
Lloraba la bella Inés
Su vuelta aguardando en vano; 245
Oraba un mes y otro mes
Del crucifijo a los pies
Do puso el galán su mano.
Todas las tardes venía
Después de traspuesto el sol, 250
Y a Dios llorando pedía
La vuelta del español,
Y el español no volvía.
Y siempre al anochecer,
Sin dueña y sin escudero, 255
En un manto una mujer
El campo salía a ver
Al alto del *Miradero*.[38]
Dos años al fin pasaron
En esperar y gemir, 260
Y las guerras acabaron,
Y los de Flandes tornaron
A sus tierras a vivir.
Pasó un día y otro día,
Un mes y otro mes pasó, 265
Y el tercer año corría;
Diego a Flandes se partió,

[33] The spot on her honor can be washed by his honor, and he can give her his honor by marrying her. This is her wish.

[34] consider it as already sworn and let that be enough.

[35] The temple in question is the basilica of Santa Leocadia.

[36] The original image, about which several miracles were told, was destroyed by the French during the Napoleonic invasion. The modern image, which is the same one that Zorrilla saw, has little or no artistic worth. It is, as we shall see, made of wood.

[37] *partió,* here, had departed. The verse form has changed from *romance* to the five-line stanzas called *quintillas.*

[38] Miradero, a public walk from which a long stretch of road can be seen. Inés is watching for Diego's return.

Mas de Flandes no volvía.
  Era una tarde serena;
Doraba el sol de Occidente 270
Del Tajo la vega amena,
Y apoyada en una almena
Miraba Inés la corriente.
  Así la niña lloraba
El rigor de su fortuna, 275
Y así la tarde pasaba
Y al horizonte trepaba
La consoladora luna.
  A lo lejos, por el llano,
En confuso remolino, 280
Vió de hombres tropel lejano
Que en pardo polvo liviano
Dejan envuelto el camino.
  Bajó Inés del torreón,
Y, llegando recelosa 285
A las puertas del Cambrón,
Sintió latir, zozobrosa,
Más inquieto el corazón.
  Tan galán como altanero,
Dejó ver la escasa luz 290
Por bajo el arco primero
Un hidalgo caballero
En un caballo andaluz.
  Vienen tras este jinete,
Sobre potros jerezanos,[39] 295
De lanceros hasta siete,
Y en la adarga y coselete
Diez peones castellanos.
  Asióse a su estribo Inés,
Gritando: —¿Diego, eres tú? 300
Y él, viéndola de través,[40]
Dijo: —¡Voto a Belcebú,[41]
Que no me acuerdo quién es!
  Dió la triste un alarido
Tal respuesta al escuchar, 305
Y a poco[42] perdió el sentido,
Sin que más voz ni gemido
Volviera en tierra a exhalar.
  Frunciendo ambas a dos[43] cejas,
Encomendóla a su gente 310
Diciendo; —¡Malditas viejas
Que a las mozas malamente
Enloquecen con consejas!
  Y aplicando el capitán
A su potro las espuelas, 315
El rostro a Toledo dan,
Y a trote cruzando van
Las oscuras callejuelas.

IV

  Así por sus altos fines
Dispone y permite el cielo 320
Que puedan mudar al hombre
Fortuna, poder y tiempo.
A Flandes partió Martínez
De soldado aventurero,
Y por su suerte y hazañas 325
Allí capitán le hicieron.
Según alzaba en honores,
Alzábase en pensamientos,
Y tanto ayudó en la guerra
Con su valor y altos hechos, 330
Que el mismo rey a su vuelta
Le armó en Madrid caballero,
Tomándole a su servicio
Por capitán de lanceros.
Y otro no fué que Martínez, 335
Quien a poco[44] entró en Toledo,
Tan orgulloso y ufano
Cual salió humilde y pequeño.
Ni es otro a quien se dirige,
Cobrado el conocimiento, 340
La amorosa Inés de Vargas,
Que vive por él muriendo.
En vano porfiaba Inés
Con amenazas y ruegos;
Cuanto más ella importuna, 345
Está Martínez severo.
Y así llamando a su gente,
De amor y piedad ajeno,
Mandóles que a Inés llevaran
De grado o de valimiento.[45] 350
Mas ella, antes que la asieran,
Cesando un punto[46] en su duelo,
Así habló, el rostro lloroso

[39] *potro jerezano,* young horse from Jerez
[40] *viéndola de través,* looking at her obliquely
[41] *Belcebú,* the Devil
[42] *a poco,* immediately
[43] *ambas a dos,* both. An archaism to preserve the rhythm.
[44] *a poco,* recently
[45] that they take Inés away, either willingly or by force
[46] *un punto,* a bit, an instant

Hacia Martínez volviendo:
—Contigo se fué mi honra, 355
Conmigo tu juramento;[47]
Pues buenas prendas son ambas,
En buen fiel[48] las pesaremos.
Y la faz descolorida
En la mantilla envolviendo, 360
A pasos desatentados[49]
Salióse del aposento.

V

Era entonces de Toledo
Por el rey gobernador
El justiciero y valiente 365
Don Pedro Ruiz de Alarcón.
Muchos años por su patria
El buen viejo peleó;
Cercenado tiene un brazo,
Mas entero el corazón. 370
La mesa tiene delante,
Los jueces en derredor,
Los corchetes[50] a la puerta
Y en la derecha el bastón.[51]
Está, como presidente 375
Del tribunal superior,
Entre un dosel y una alfombra,
Reclinado en un sillón,
Escuchando con paciencia
La casi asmática voz 380
Con que un tétrico escribano
Solfea una apelación.
Los asistentes bostezan
Al murmullo arrullador;
Los jueces, medio dormidos, 385
Hacen pliegues al ropón;[52]
Los escribanos repasan
Sus pergaminos al sol;
Los corchetes a una moza
Guiñan en un corredor, 390
Y abajo, en Zocodover,[53]
Gritan en discorde son
Los que en el mercado venden
Lo vendido y el valor.[54]
Una mujer en tal punto, 395
En faz de[55] gran aflicción,
Rojos de llorar los ojos,
Ronca de gemir la voz,
Suelto el cabello y el manto,
Tomó plaza en el salón 400
Diciendo a gritos: —¡Justicia,
Jueces; justicia, señor!
Y a los pies se arroja, humilde,
De don Pedro de Alarcón,
En tanto que los curiosos 405
Se agitan al derredor.
Alzóla cortés don Pedro
Calmando la confusión
Y el tumultuoso murmullo
Que esta escena ocasionó, 410
Diciendo:
—Mujer, ¿qué quieres?
—Quiero justicia, señor.
—¿De qué?
—De una prenda hurtada.
—¿Qué prenda?
—Mi corazón.
—¿Tú le diste?
—Le presté. 415
—¿Y no te le han vuelto?
—No.
—¿Tienes testigos?
—Ninguno.
—¿Y promesa?
—¡Sí, por Dios!
Que al partirse de Toledo
Un juramento empeñó. 420
—¿Quién es él?
—Diego Martínez.
—¿Noble?
—Y capitán, señor.
—Presentadme al capitán,
Que cumplirá si juró.—
Quedó en silencio la sala, 425
Y a poco en el corredor
Se oyó de botas y espuelas
El acompasado son.
Un portero, levantando
El tapiz, en alta voz 430

[47] Supply the understood verb *se quedó.*
[48] *el fiel,* balance, scales
[49] *desatentado,* thoughtless, disordered; here, staggering
[50] *corchete,* constable
[51] *bastón,* staff. The symbol of his authority.
[52] *ropón,* cloak, mantle
[53] *Zocodover,* the principal square and market place of Toledo
[54] *lo vendido y el valor,* what they are selling and the price
[55] *en faz de,* with the appearance of

Dijo: —El capitán don Diego.
Y entró luego en el salón
Diego Martínez, los ojos
Llenos de orgullo y furor.
—¿Sois el capitán don Diego 435
—Díjole don Pedro—vos?[56]
Contestó, altivo y sereno,
Diego Martínez:
—Yo soy.
—¿Conocéis a esa muchacha?
—Ha tres años, salvo error.[57] 440
—¿Hicísteisla juramento
De ser su marido?
—No.
—¿Juráis no haberlo jurado?
—Sí juro.
—Pues id con Dios.
—¡Miente! —clamó Inéz, llorando 445
De despecho y de rubor.
—Mujer, ¡piensa lo que dices!
—Digo que miente: juró.
—¿Tienes testigos?
—Ninguno.
—Capitán, idos con Dios, 450
Y dispensad que, acusado,
Dudara de vuestro honor.
Tornó Martínez la espalda
Con brusca satisfacción,
E Inés, que le vió partirse, 455
Resuelta y firme gritó:
—Llamadle, tengo un testigo.
Llamadle otra vez, señor.
Volvió el capitán don Diego,
Sentóse Ruiz de Alarcón, 460
La multitud aquietóse
Y la de Vargas siguió:
—Tengo un testigo a quien nunca
Faltó verdad ni razón.
—¿Quién?
—Un hombre que de lejos 465
Nuestras palabras oyó,
Mirándonos desde arriba.
—¿Estaba en algún balcón?
—No, que estaba en un suplicio
Donde ha tiempo que expiró. 470
—¿Luego es muerto?
—No, que vive.
—Estáis loca, ¡vive Dios!
¿Quién fué?
—El Cristo de la Vega
A cuya faz perjuró.[58]
Pusiéronse en pie los jueces 475
Al nombre del Redentor,
Escuchando con asombro
Tan excelsa apelación.
Reinó un profundo silencio
De sorpresa y de pavor, 480
Y Diego bajó los ojos
De vergüenza y confusión.
Un instante con los jueces
Don Pedro en secreto habló,
Y levantóse diciendo 485
Con respetuosa voz:
—La ley es ley para todos;
Tu testigo es el mejor;
Mas para tales testigos
No hay más tribunal que Dios. 490
Haremos . . . lo que sepamos;[59]
Escribano: al caer el sol,
Al Cristo que está en la vega
Tomaréis declaración.

VI

Es una tarde serena, 495
Cuya luz tornasolada
Del purpurino horizonte
Blandamente se derrama.
Allá por el *Miradero,*
Por el Cambrón y Visagra, 500
Confuso tropel de gente
Del Tajo a la vega baja.
Vienen delante don Pedro
De Alarcón, Ibán de Vargas,
Su hija Inés, los escribanos, 505
Los corchetes y los guardias;
Y detrás monjes, hidalgos,
Mozas, chicos y canalla.
Otra turba de curiosos
En la vega les aguarda, 510
Cada cual comentariando[60]

[56] *vos,* the subject of the verb *sois,* is the archaic pronoun of formal address, used by Zorrilla to recreate the atmosphere of the Golden Age.
[57] *salvo error,* if I'm not mistaken
[58] in whose presence he swore
[59] *lo que sepamos* (*hacer*), whatever we can do
[60] *comentariar,* to comment on. The usual word is *comentar.*

El caso según le cuadra.
Entre ellos está Martínez
En apostura bizarra,
Calzadas espuelas de oro, 515
Valona[61] de encaje blanca,
Bigote a la borgoñesa,[62]
Melena desmelenada,[63]
El sombrero guarnecido
Con cuatro lazos de plata, 520
Un pie delante del otro,
Y el puño en el de la espada.[64]
Los plebeyos de reojo
Le miran de entre las capas:
Los chicos, al uniforme, 525
Y las mozas, a la cara.
Llegado el gobernador
Y gente que le acompaña
Entraron todos al claustro
Que iglesia y patio separa. 530
Encendieron ante el Cristo
Cuatro cirios[65] y una lámpara,
Y de hinojos un momento
Le rezaron en voz baja.
Está el Cristo de la Vega, 535
La cruz en tierra posada,
Los pies alzados del suelo
Poco menos de una vara;
Hacia la severa imagen
Un notario se adelanta, 540
De modo que con el rostro
Al pecho santo llegaba.
A un lado tiene a Martínez;
A otro lado, a Inés de Vargas;
Detrás, el gobernador 545
Con sus jueces y sus guardias.
Después de leer dos veces
La acusación entablada,
El notario a Jesucristo
Así demandó en voz alta: 550
—Jesús, Hijo de María,
Ante nos esta mañana
Citado como testigo
Por boca de Inés de Vargas,
¿Juráis ser cierto que un día 555
A vuestras divinas plantas
Juró a Inés Diego Martínez
Por su mujer desposarla?
Asida a un *brazo* desnudo
Una *mano* atarazada[66] 560
Vino a posar en los autos[67]
La seca y hendida palma,
Y allá en los aires "¡Sí juro!",
Clamó una voz más que humana.
Alzó la turba medrosa 565
La vista a la imagen santa . . .
Los labios tenía abiertos
Y una mano desclavada.

CONCLUSIÓN

Las vanidades del mundo
Renunció allí mismo Inés, 570
Y espantado de sí propio,
Diego Martínez también.
Los escribanos, temblando,
Dieron de esta escena fe,[68]
Firmando como testigos 575
Cuantos hubieron poder.[69]
Fundóse un aniversario
Y una capilla con él,
Y don Pedro de Alarcón
El altar ordenó hacer, 580
Donde hasta el tiempo que corre,
Y en cada año una vez,
Con la mano desclavada
El crucifijo se ve.

[61] *valona,* ruff, collar
[62] *a la borgoñesa,* in the fashion of Burgundy
[63] *melena,* mane, (long) hair; *desmelenado,* dishevelled
[64] *el puño en el de la espada, puño,* fist, hand; pummel (of sword)
[65] *cirio,* candle
[66] *atarazado,* torn, wounded
[67] *auto,* here, legal document
[68] *dar fe,* to certify
[69] *hubieron poder,* had the right

The Romantic Drama and the Duque de Rivas

A SERIES of important dramas appeared in the first years following the introduction of romanticism into Spain (see p. 260). These works have always attracted considerable attention, perhaps even more than they merit on the basis of their intrinsic worth, because they stand as symbols of the revolt against worn-out classicism. All these plays have a common characteristic in the fact that they break all classic rules, and since the number of classic restrictions in this genre was particularly great, it was natural that the romanticists chose it as a field in which to show their rebellious spirit. They set out to undo the earlier restraints so systematically and thoroughly that this breaking of rules became practically a new set of rules in itself. Thus it was indispensable for the play to have a setting which shifted from place to place, and its action had to cover a period of several years. Many duels, murders, and suicides had to take place on the stage, simply because they were prohibited in the classic drama. A mixture of prose and verse, and elaborately detailed stage settings were also used because the older school would not tolerate them.

There is also a certain atmosphere common to all these plays—an atmosphere of immense and fatal passion, great sacrifices, bitter vengeance, impenetrable mystery, cruel murders, and tragic suidices. All this melodramatic element is taken in deadly earnest, although secondary comic scenes are brought in to relieve the gloom of the principal action, again in open contradiction to the classic precepts. The fundamental plot is always tragic; there is no such thing as a romantic comedy. We must admit that occasionally we like to escape from humdrum existence to this fantastic, tortured world, but that as a steady diet its lack of variety soon satiates our appetite.

Aside from the freedom it brought, the romantic drama had certain good points which were to remain as a part of theatrical technique to the present day. Chief among these was the use of realistic settings, which, combined with realistic minor characters, formed a sharp contrast with the unreality of the main plot. We shall see in *Don Álvaro* that the scenes at the water-seller's booth, in the inn, and in the monastery when alms are being distributed are picturesque little *cuadros de costumbres* skilfully woven into the plot. These same scenes also sparkle with delicious humor.

Not only are the settings realistic; they are picturesque. In the case of *Don Álvaro,* the fact that the Duque de Rivas was himself a painter made him see his settings as a series of tableaux and made him realize that one element—light—was of the greatest importance in producing a picturesque effect. We shall see in *Don Álvaro* that practically none of the scenes takes place in full daylight. The stage directions almost always indicate moonlight, sunset, a dark, stormy night, et cetera. So the use of light and the use of Nature to convey moods (another romantic innovation) are in his case practically one and the same thing.

Against this picturesque background stalks the romantic hero with somber majesty. He is the same person in all romantic plays, for the individualistic traits he receives from one play to another are almost negligible. Gallant, generous, and brave, he attracts to himself, as if by predestination, the heroine's love and makes of passion the very mainspring of his existence. But in every case he is separated from the heroine by a fatal mystery. He is an outcast from society because of his obscure origin. Of course he always turns out to be of the highest nobility, but this revelation comes when Fate has already sealed his and his beloved's doom. He knows or instinctively feels his nobility and inherent greatness and longs for a role in society and a marriage at the level of his aspirations; but as uncomprehending society refuses to take him at his own value, he is plunged in a frustrated melancholy. He feels that the only reason he does not occupy the high station of which he dreams is that a malignant and adverse Fate is always working against him.

The question of Fate has never been more discussed than in the case of *Don Álvaro,* whose very sub-title is *La fuerza del sino.* We must admit, however, that the Duque de Rivas probably never guessed that Fate in his drama would be a matter of debate. He was simply working out a dramatic and animated theme in which Fate was expected to play a role. We usually think of Fate in the drama as the inevitable. The misfortunes which it brings on are inescapable. Try as the hero may, he finds himself blocked at every turn by some new calamity. But in *Don Álvaro* Fate takes on much more the appearance of Chance. A gun goes off and, as if by accident, kills a man; or the characters meet in unexpected places, apparently by mere coincidence. Thus, the comparison of Don Álvaro with Oedipus, the outstanding victim of Fate in the Greek theater, does not make sense. Furthermore, the Duque de Rivas makes it clear to us that Don Álvaro is essentially Christian, and for a Christian the denial of free will, implicit in Fatalism, is heresy.

Another theory is that Don Álvaro is a bad Christian and that all of his sufferings spring from an initial sin, his attempted elopement with the heroine. If this were so, instead of Fate we should be confronted with Divine Justice. Yet we must not forget that Don Álvaro's intentions were perfectly honorable and that, although he was overriding the social law of parental authority, he intended to fulfil punctiliously the religious law of marriage.

We believe that Don Álvaro, like all the romantic heroes, is merely deluding himself. Feeling that he deserves a higher place in life than society is willing to give him, and being essentially a weak man, he proclaims that his lack of success is due not to himself but to Fate.

The author of *Don Álvaro,* ÁNGEL DE SAAVEDRA (1791–1865), who later inherited the title of Duque de Rivas, presents in his life one of those contrasts so peculiarly Spanish. As a young man he fought bravely for the liberal cause and suffered ten years' exile for his political beliefs, but adhered to a strictly conservative, classical point of view in his poetry and plays. Shortly after his return to Spain, when he had just won a reputation as one of the leading romantic writers, he inherited his title and immediately reversed the position of his youth. He was now a conservative in politics (being a member of the *senado* and holding positions as minister and ambassador) but liberal (romantic) in literature.

The deciding factor in his change from classicism to romanticism was the five years of exile spent in Malta, where one of his friends, Sir John Hookham Frere, a former British ambassador to Portugal and Spain, introduced him not only to the English romanticists but to Spanish literature of the Middle Ages and Golden Age. It was during his stay in Malta that he began to write *El moro expósito,* published immediately after his return to Madrid (1834), and generally considered the first work of Spanish romanticism, although in reality some romantic novels had been published earlier. *El moro expósito* is a long half-epic, half-lyric reworking of the story of the *Siete infantes de Lara* (see Vol. I, p. 14). However, Rivas treats the legend very freely, making Mudarra, the Moorish half-brother of the Infantes, the central figure and converting him into a typical romantic hero. A secondary theme of the poem is the contrast between the brilliant, warm, Moorish civilization of Córdoba (Rivas's native city) and the cold, puritanical, Christian civilization of Burgos. This theme is announced in the subtitle, *Córdoba y Burgos en el siglo décimo.* Finally, the prologue of the work, written by Rivas's friend Alcalá Galiano, was a manifesto, although a mild and restrained one, of the Spanish romantic school.

One year after the publication of *El moro expósito,* the Duque de Rivas's *Don Álvaro* was played in Madrid. Although not the first of the romantic dramas, it is certainly better than any except Zorrilla's *Don Juan*

Tenorio. Yet its animated, picturesque scenes and gloomy grandeur achieved only a mild success; in fact the play ran only eleven nights in the first year. It was originally written in prose while Rivas was in France during the latter part of his exile and was to be translated into French for production in Paris. From this rough draft, Rivas, after his return to Madrid, produced the play as we know it in the remarkably short period of two weeks.

One final work of Rivas remains to be described. In 1841 he brought out the *Romances históricos*, a series of eighteen independent ballads, most of which deal with historical figures, such as the medieval king, Pedro el Cruel, Columbus, Cortés, or Carlos V. Some critics believe that Rivas reaches his peak in these *romances*.

We must not look in Rivas for any philosophical or political thought, such as we found in Larra. Rivas is first and foremost a literary man and his one ambition is to create works of beauty. In this he excelled because of his gift as a versifier, his warm Andalusian spirit, and his artist's appreciation of the picturesque and colorful.

Duque de Rivas

Don Álvaro o La fuerza del sino[1]

Drama original en cinco jornadas en prosa y verso[2]

PERSONAJES

DON ÁLVARO
EL MARQUÉS DE CALATRAVA
DON CARLOS DE VARGAS, *su hijo*
DON ALFONSO DE VARGAS, *idem*
DOÑA LEONOR, *idem*
CURRA, *criada*
PRECIOSILLA, *gitana*
UN CANÓNIGO
EL PADRE GUARDIÁN DEL CONVENTO DE LOS ÁNGELES
EL HERMANO MELITÓN, *portero del mismo*
PEDRAZA Y OTROS OFICIALES
UN CIRUJANO DE EJÉRCITO
UN CAPELLÁN DE REGIMIENTO
UN ALCALDE
UN ESTUDIANTE
UN MAJO
MESONERO
MESONERA
LA MOZA DEL MESÓN
EL TÍO TRABUCO, *arriero*
EL TÍO PACO, *aguador*
EL CAPITÁN PREBOSTE
UN SARGENTO
UN ORDENANZA A CABALLO
DOS HABITANTES DE SEVILLA
SOLDADOS ESPAÑOLES, ARRIEROS, LUGAREÑOS Y LUGAREÑAS

Los trajes son los que se usaban a mediados del siglo pasado.

[1] Verdi, on making our play into an opera, used the title, *La forza del destino*.

[2] See Vol. II, p. 366, n. 40.

Jornada Primera

La escena es en Sevilla y sus alrededores.

La escena[3] representa la entrada del antiguo puente de barcas de Triana, el que estará practicable a la derecha. En primer término, al mismo lado, un aguaducho o barraca de tablas y lonas, con un letrero que diga: *Agua de Tomares:* dentro habrá un mostrador rústico con cuatro grandes cántaros, macetas de flores, vasos, un anafre con una cafetera de hoja de lata y una bandeja con azucarillos. Delante del aguaducho habrá bancos de pino. Al fondo se descubrirá de lejos parte del arrabal de Triana, la huerta de los Remedios con sus altos cipreses, el río y varios barcos en él, con flámulas y gallardetes. A la izquierda se verá en lontananza la Alameda. Varios habitantes de Sevilla cruzarán en todas direcciones durante la escena. El cielo demonstrará el ponerse el sol en una tarde de Julio, y al descorrerse el telón aparecerán: EL TÍO[4] PACO detrás del mostrador en mangas de camisa; EL OFICIAL, bebiendo un vaso de agua y de pie; PRECIOSILLA, a su lado templando una guitarra; EL MAJO y los DOS HABITANTES DE SEVILLA sentados en los bancos.

Escena Primera

OFICIAL

Vamos, Preciosilla, cántanos la rondeña. Pronto, pronto: ya está bien templada.

PRECIOSILLA

Señorito, no sea su merced tan súpito. Déme antes esa mano, y le diré la buenaventura.

OFICIAL

Quita, que no quiero tus zalamerías. Aunque efectivamente tuvieras la habilidad de decirme lo que me ha de suceder, no quisiera oírtelo . . . Sí, casi siempre conviene el ignorarlo.

MAJO (*Levantándose.*)

Pues yo quiero que me diga la buenaventura esta prenda. He aquí mi mano.

5 PRECIOSILLA

Retire usted allá esa porquería . . . Jesús, ni verla quiero, no sea que se encele aquella niña de los ojos grandes.

MAJO (*Sentándose.*)

10 ¡Qué se ha de encelar de ti, pendón![5]

PRECIOSILLA

Vaya, saleroso, no se cargue usted de estera,[6] convídeme a alguna cosita.

[3] The stage setting emphasizes picturesque elements: the water-stand (*aguaducho*) in the foreground, the river with its ancient pontoon bridge and ships in the middle distance, and the quaint suburb of Triana against the sunset in the background. The human beings also represent types noted for their picturesqueness and their connection with Sevilla, the most animated city of Andalucía. The bull-fighting popular dandy (*majo*), the Gipsy fortune-teller and singer (*Preciosilla*), the army officer (*oficial*), with gruff but hale language, are all part of the local color. Furthermore, the naming of various places within or near Sevilla (*Tomares* and *Utrera,* small towns near by; *la Alameda,* a promenade in the city; *la Borcinería,* a quarter of the city) serves to heighten the same impression.

Certainly the first glimpse of the stage would suffice to tell the audience that this is not a classical play.

[4] 'Old' Paco

[5] How could she be jealous of you, you miserable creature!

[6] *no . . . estera,* don't get upset

MAJO

Tío Paco, déle usted un vaso de agua a esta criatura, por mi cuenta.

PRECIOSILLA

¿Y con panal?

OFICIAL

Sí, y después que te refresques el garguero y que te endulces la boca, nos cantarás las corraleras.
(*El aguador sirve un vaso de agua con panal a* PRECIOSILLA, *y el* OFICIAL *se sienta junto al* MAJO.)

HABITANTE 1.°

¡Hola! Aquí viene el señor canónigo.

ESCENA II

CANÓNIGO

Buenas tardes, caballeros.

HABITANTE 2.°

Temíamos no tener la dicha de ver a su merced esta tarde, señor canónigo.

CANÓNIGO

(*Sentándose y limpiándose el sudor.*) ¿Qué persona de buen gusto, viviendo en Sevilla, puede dejar de venir todas las tardes de verano a beber la deliciosa agua de Tomares, que con tanta limpieza y pulcritud nos da el tío Paco, y a ver un ratito este puente de Triana, que es lo mejor del mundo?

HABITANTE 1.°

Como ya se está poniendo el sol . . .

CANÓNIGO

Tío Paco, un vasito de la fresca.

TÍO PACO

Está usía muy sudado; en descansando[7] un poquito le daré el refrigerio.

MAJO

Dale a su señoría agua templada.

CANÓNIGO

No, que hace mucho calor.

5 MAJO

Pues yo templada la he bebido, para tener el pecho suave,[8] y poder entonar el rosario por el barrio de la Borcinería, que a mí me toca esta noche.

10 OFICIAL

Para suavizar el pecho, mejor es un trago de aguardiente.

MAJO

El aguardiente es bueno para sosegarlo
15 después de haber cantado la letanía.

OFICIAL

Yo lo tomo antes y después de mandar el ejercicio.[9]

PRECIOSILLA

20 (*Habrá estado punteando la guitarra y dirá al* MAJO:)
Oiga usted, rumboso, ¿y cantará usted esta noche la letanía delante del balcón de aquella persona? . . .

25 CANÓNIGO

Las cosas santas se han de tratar santamente. Vamos. ¿Y qué tal los toros de ayer?

MAJO

30 El toro berrendo de Utrera salió un buen bicho,[10] muy pegajoso[11] . . . Demasiado.

HABITANTE 1.°

Como que se me figura que le tuvo
35 usted asco.[12]

[7] after resting (an antiquated construction)
[8] to have my throat clear
[9] military drill
[10] 'critter,' beast
[11] pugnacious
[12] *tener asco,* to be sickened by, be repelled by

MAJO

Compadre, alto allá, que yo soy muy duro de estómago[13] . . . Aquí está mi capa (*Enseña un desgarrón.*) diciendo por esta boca[14] que no anduvo muy lejos.

HABITANTE 2.°

No fué la corrida tan buena como la anterior.

PRECIOSILLA

Como que ha faltado en ella don Álvaro[15] el indiano,[16] que a caballo y a pie es el mejor torero que tiene España.

MAJO

Es verdad que es todo un hombre, muy duro con el ganado y muy echado adelante.

PRECIOSILLA

Y muy buen mozo.

HABITANTE 1.°

¿Y por qué no se presentaría ayer en la plaza?

OFICIAL

Harto tenía que hacer con estarse llorando el mal fin de sus amores.

MAJO

Pues qué, ¿lo ha plantado ya la hija del señor Marqués? . . .

OFICIAL

No: doña Leonor no lo ha plantado a él, pero el Marqués la ha trasplantado a ella.

HABITANTE 2.°

¿Cómo? . . .

HABITANTE 1.°

Amigo, el Sr. Marqués de Calatrava
5 tiene mucho copete[17] y sobrada vanidad para permitir que un advenedizo sea su yerno.

OFICIAL

¿Y qué más podía apetecer su señoría
10 que el ver casada a su hija (que con todos sus pergaminos[18] está muerta de hambre) con un hombre riquísimo, y cuyos modales están pregonando que es un caballero?

15 PRECIOSILLA

¡Si los señores de Sevilla son vanidad y pobreza todo en una pieza! Don Álvaro es digno de ser marido de una emperadora . . . ¡Qué gallardo! . . .
20 ¡Qué formal y qué generoso! . . . Hace pocos días que le dije la buenaventura (y por cierto no es buena[19] la que le espera si las rayas de la mano no mienten), y me dió una onza de oro
25 como un sol de mediodía.

TÍO PACO

Cuantas veces viene aquí a beber, me pone sobre el mostrador una peseta columnaria.[20]

30 MAJO

¡Y vaya un hombre valiente! Cuando en la Alameda Vieja le salieron acquella noche los siete hombres más duros que tiene Sevilla, metió mano[21]
35 y me[22] los acorraló a todos contra las tapias del picadero.

[13] I have a strong stomach

[14] rip (The rip from the bull's horn indicates a close call and bespeaks valor.)

[15] From here to the end of the scene the author builds up our interest in Don Álvaro and characterizes him for us. He took part in the bull fights as an amateur, as did many noblemen of former times.

[16] A Spaniard who returned to Spain from America was known as an *indiano,* since America was generally called *las Indias. Indianos* was traditionally rich and often mysterious.

[17] *tener copete,* to be haughty, proud

[18] parchments, i.e. patents of nobility

[19] The first inkling of the evil Fate which awaits our hero.

[20] A silver coin, made in America, which had two columns on one side

[21] Supply: to his sword

[22] The dative of interest; omit in translating.

OFICIAL

Y en el desafío que tuvo con el capitán de artillería se portó como un caballero.[23]

PRECIOSILLA

El Marqués de Calatrava es un vejete tan ruin, que por no aflojar la mosca,[24] y por no gastar . . .

OFICIAL

Lo que debía hacer don Álvaro era darle una paliza que . . .

CANÓNIGO

Paso, paso,[25] señor militar. Los padres tienen derecho de casar a sus hijas con quien les convenga.

OFICIAL

¿Y por qué no le ha de convenir don Álvaro? ¿Porque no ha de nacido en Sevilla? . . . Fuera de Sevilla nacen también caballeros.

CANÓNIGO

Fuera de Sevilla nacen también caballeros, sí señor; pero . . . ¿lo es don Álvaro? . . . Sólo sabemos que ha venido de Indias hace dos meses, y que ha traído dos negros y mucho dinero . . . ¿Pero quién es? . . .

HABITANTE 1.°

Se dicen tantas y tales cosas de él . . .

HABITANTE 2.°

Es un ente muy misterioso.[26]

TÍO PACO

La otra tarde estuvieron aquí unos señores hablando de lo mismo, y uno de ellos dijo que el tal don Álvaro había hecho sus riquezas siendo pirata . . .

MAJO

¡Jesucristo!

TÍO PACO

Y otro, que don Álvaro era hijo bas-
5 tardo de un grande de España y de una reina mora . . .

OFICIAL

¡Qué disparate!

TÍO PACO

10 Y luego dijeron que no, que era . . . no lo puedo declarar . . . finca . . . o brinca . . . una cosa así . . . así como . . . una cosa muy grande allá de la otra banda.[27]

15 OFICIAL

¿Inca?

TÍO PACO

Sí, señor, eso, Inca . . . Inca.

CANÓNIGO

20 Calle usted, tío Paco, no diga sandeces.

TÍO PACO

Yo nada digo, ni me meto en honduras;[28] para mí cada uno es hijo de sus obras, y en siendo buen cristiano y
25 caritativo . . .

PRECIOSILLA

Y generoso y galán.

OFICIAL

El vejete roñoso del Marqués de Cala-
30 trava hace muy mal en negarle su hija.

CANÓNIGO

Señor militar, el señor Marqués hace muy bien. El caso es sencillísimo. Don Álvaro llegó hace dos meses; nadie
35 sabe quién es. Ha pedido en casa-

[23] Notice how each person praises Don Álvaro according to his own character and interests.
[24] *aflojar la mosca,* to loosen his purse-strings
[25] slowly, take it easy
[26] One of the indispensable characteristics of the romantic hero
[27] the other side (of the ocean)
[28] *meter en honduras,* to get in deep water

miento a doña Leonor, y el Marqués, no juzgándolo buen partido para su hija, se le ha negado. Parece que la señorita estaba encaprichadilla, fascinada, y el padre la ha llevado al campo, a la hacienda que tiene en el Aljarafe, para distraerla. En todo lo cual el señor Marqués se ha portado como persona prudente.[29]

OFICIAL

¿Y don Álvaro, qué hará?

CANÓNIGO

Para acertarlo debe buscar otra novia: porque si insiste en sus descabelladas pretensiones, se expone a que los hijos del señor Marqués vengan, el uno de la Universidad, y el otro del regimiento, a sacarle de los cascos los amores de doña Leonor.

OFICIAL

Muy partidario soy de don Álvaro, aunque no le he hablado en mi vida, y sentiría verlo empeñado en un lance con don Carlos, el hijo mayorazgo del Marqués. Le he visto el mes pasado en Barcelona, y he oído contar los dos últimos desafíos que ha tenido ya: y se le puede ayunar.[30]

CANÓNIGO

Es uno de los oficiales más valientes del regimiento de Guardias Españolas, donde no se chancea en esto de lances de honor.

HABITANTE 1.°

Pues el hijo segundo del señor Marqués, el don Alfonso, no le va en zaga.[31] Mi primo, que acaba de llegar de Salamanca, me ha dicho que es el coco[32] de la Universidad, más espadachín que estudiante, y que tiene 5 metidos en un puño[33] a los matones sopistas.

MAJO

¿Y desde cuándo está fuera de Sevilla la señorita doña Leonor?

10 OFICIAL

Hace cuatro días que se la llevó el padre a su hacienda, sacándola de aquí a las cinco de la mañana, después de haber estado toda la noche hecha 15 la casa un infierno.

PRECIOSILLA

¡Pobre niña! . . . ¡Qué linda que es y qué salada![34] . . . Negra suerte le espera . . . Mi madre le dijo la buen-20 aventura, recién nacida, y siempre que la nombra se le saltan las lágrimas[35] . . . Pues el generoso don Álvaro . . .

HABITANTE 1.°

25 En nombrando el ruin de Roma, luego asoma[36] . . . allí viene don Álvaro.

ESCENA III

(*Empieza a anochecer, y se va obscureciendo el teatro.* DON ÁLVARO *sale* 30 *embozado en una capa de seda, con un gran sombrero blanco, botines y espuelas; cruza lentamente la escena mirando con dignidad y melancolía a todos lados, y se va por el puente.* 35 *Todos lo observan en gran silencio.*[37])

[29] The Canon, who we discover is a friend of the Marqués, states the latter's objections against Don Álvaro; but in a larger sense he represents the antagonism of the respectable middle class towards the romantic hero, who was always an outcast, at odds with staid respectability.

[30] *se le puede ayunar,* one can get along without (fighting) him

[31] *no le va en zaga,* doesn't trail behind him; is as good as he

[32] bogeyman

[33] *tiene metidos en un puño,* he has under his thumb

[34] charming

[35] A premonition of the adverse Fate which hangs over Leonor too

[36] Proverb: Speaking of the devil . . .

[37] Don Álvaro's silent passage across the stage, after so careful a preparation, serves to incite our curiosity all the more. The situation is tensely dramatic.

Escena IV

MAJO

¿Adónde irá a estas horas?

CANÓNIGO

A tomar el fresco al Altozano.

TÍO PACO

Dios vaya con él.

MILITAR

¿A que[38] va al Aljarafe?

TÍO PACO

Yo no sé, pero como estoy siempre aquí de día y de noche, soy un vigilante centinela de cuanto pasa por esta[39] puente . . . Hace tres días que a media tarde pasa por ella hacia allá un negro con dos caballos de mano, y que don Álvaro pasa a estas horas; y luego a las cinco de la mañana vuelve a pasar hacia acá, siempre a pie, y como media hora después pasa el negro con los mismos caballos llenos de polvo y de sudor.

CANÓNIGO

¿Cómo? . . . ¿Qué me cuenta usted, tío Paco? . . .

TÍO PACO

Yo nada, digo lo que he visto; y esta tarde ya ha pasado el negro, y hoy no lleva dos caballos, sino tres.

HABITANTE 1.°

Lo que es[40] atravesar el puente hacia allá a estas horas, he visto yo a don Álvaro tres tardes seguidas.

MAJO

Y yo he visto ayer a la salida de Triana al negro con los caballos.

HABITANTE 2.°

Y anoche, viniendo yo de San Juan de Alfarache, me paré en medio del olivar a apretar las cinchas a mi caballo, y pasó a mi lado, sin verme y a escape,[41] don Álvaro, como alma que llevan los demonios, y detrás iba el negro. Los conocí por la jaca torda, que no se puede despintar . . . ¡Cada relámpago que daban las herraduras![42] . . .

CANÓNIGO (*Levantándose y aparte.*)

¡Hola! ¡hola![43] . . . Preciso es dar aviso al señor Marqués.

MILITAR

Me alegrara de que la niña traspusiese[44] una noche con su amante, y dejara al vejete pelándose las barbas.[45]

CANÓNIGO

Buenas noches, caballeros; me voy, que empieza a ser tarde. (*Aparte yéndose.*) Sería faltar a la amistad no avisar al instante al Marqués de que don Álvaro le ronda la hacienda. Tal vez podemos evitar una desgracia.

Escena V

(El teatro representa una sala colgada de damasco, con retratos de familia, escudos de armas y los adornos que se estilaban en el siglo pasado, pero todo deteriorado, y habrá dos balcones,[46] uno cerrado y otro abierto y practicable, por el que se verá un cielo puro, iluminado por la luna, y algunas copas de árboles. Se pondrá en medio una mesa con tapete de damasco, y sobre ella habrá una guitarra, vasos chinescos con flores, y dos candeleros de plata con velas, únicas luces que alumbrarán la escena. Junto a la

[38] What do you bet that
[39] Modern Spanish: *el puente*
[40] *Lo que es,* As for
[41] at full speed
[42] What sparks their shoes gave forth!
[43] Well, well!
[44] *trasponer,* to run away
[45] *pelarse las barbas,* to pull out one's beard
[46] window

mesa habrá un sillón. Por la izquierda entrará el MARQUÉS DE CALATRAVA *con una palmatoria en la mano, y detrás de él* DOÑA LEONOR, *y por la derecha entra la* CRIADA.)

MARQUÉS

(*Abrazando y besando a su hija.*)

Buenas noches, hija mía;
Hágate una santa el cielo.
Adiós, mi amor, mi consuelo,
Mi esperanza, mi alegría.
No dirás que no es galán
Tu padre. No descansara
Si hasta aquí no te alumbrara
Todas las noches . . . Están
Abiertos estos balcones, (*Los cierra.*)
Y entra relente . . . Leonor . . .
¿Nada me dice tu amor?
¿Por qué tan triste te pones?

DOÑA LEONOR

(*Abatida y turbada.*)[47]
Buenas noches, padre mío.

MARQUÉS

Allá para Navidad
Iremos a la ciudad,
Cuando empiece el tiempo frío.
Y para entonces traeremos
Al estudiante, y también
Al capitán. Que les den
Permiso a los dos haremos.
¿No tienes gran impaciencia
Por abrazarlos?

DOÑA LEONOR

¿Pues no?
¿Qué más puedo anhelar yo?

MARQUÉS

Los dos lograrán licencia.
Ambos tienen mano franca,
Condición[48] que los abona,[49]
Y Carlos, de Barcelona,
Y Alfonso, de Salamanca,
Ricos presentes te harán.
Escríbeles tú, tontilla,
5 Y algo que no haya en Sevilla
Pídeles, y lo traerán.

DOÑA LEONOR

Dejarlo será mejor
A su gusto delicado.

10 MARQUÉS

Lo tienen, y muy sobrado:
Como tú quieras, Leonor.

CURRA

Si como a usted, señorita,
15 Carta blanca[50] se me diera,
A don Carlos le pidiera
Alguna bata bonita
De Francia. Y una cadena
Con su broche de diamante
20 Al señorito estudiante,
Que en Madrid la hallará buena.

MARQUÉS

Lo que gustes, hija mía.
Sabes que el ídolo eres
25 De tu padre . . . ¿No me quieres?
(*La abraza y besa tiernamente.*)

DOÑA LEONOR

¡Padre! . . . ¡Señor! . . . (*Afligida.*)

MARQUÉS

30 La alegría
Vuelva a ti, prenda del alma;
Piensa que tu padre soy,
Y que de continuo estoy
Soñando tu bien . . . La calma
35 Recobra, niña . . . En verdad
Desde que estamos aquí
Estoy contento de ti.
Veo la tranquilidad
Que con la campestre vida
40 Va renaciendo en tu pecho,

[47] From the beginning of this scene Leonor is overwrought; she knows what is planned for this very night. Her disturbance increases in proportion to the kindness her father shows to her, for she becomes more reluctant to hurt him. So in this scene we have the motivation for her hesitance in the next one.

[48] trait, character

[49] to bring credit to

[50] *carte blanche,* a free hand

Y me tienes satisfecho;
Sí, lo estoy mucho, querida.
Ya se me ha olvidado todo;
Eres muchacha obediente,
Y yo seré diligente
En darte un buen acomodo.[51]
Sí, mi vida . . . ¿quién mejor
Sabrá lo que te conviene,
Que un tierno padre, que tiene
Por ti el delirio mayor?

DOÑA LEONOR

(*Echándose en brazos de su padre con gran desconsuelo.*)
¡Padre amado! . . . ¡Padre mío!

MARQUÉS

Basta, basta . . . ¿Qué te agita?

(*Con gran ternura.*)

Yo te adoro, Leonorcita;
No llores . . . ¡Qué desvarío!

DOÑA LEONOR

¡Padre! . . . ¡Padre!

MARQUÉS

(*Acariciándola y desasiéndose de sus brazos.*)
Adiós, mi bien.
A dormir, y no lloremos.
Tus cariñosos extremos
El cielo bendiga, amén.
(*Vase el* MARQUÉS, *y queda* LEONOR *muy abatida y llorosa sentada en el sillón.*)

ESCENA VI

(CURRA *va detrás del* MARQUÉS, *cierra la puerta por donde aquél se ha ido, y vuelve cerca de* LEONOR.)

CURRA

¡Gracias a Dios! . . . Me temí
Que todito se enredase,
Y que Señor[52] se quedase
Hasta la mañana aquí.
¡Qué listo cerró el balcón! . . .
Que por el del palomar[53]
5 Vamos las dos a volar,
Le dijo su corazón.
Abrirlo sea lo primero; (*Ábrelo.*)
Ahora lo segundo es
Cerrar las maletas. Pues
10 Salgan ya de su agujero.
(*Saca* CURRA *unas maletas y ropa, y se pone a arreglarlo todo sin que en ello repare* DOÑA LEONOR.)

DOÑA LEONOR

15 ¡Infeliz de mí! . . . ¡Dios mío!
¿Por qué un amoroso padre,
Que por mí tanto desvelo
Tiene, y cariño tan grande,
Se ha de oponer tenazmente
20 (¡Ay, el alma se me parte! . . .)
A que yo dichosa sea,
Y puedo feliz llamarme? . . .
¿Cómo, quien tanto me quiere,
Puede tan crüel mostrarse?
25 Más dulce mi suerte fuera
Si aun me viviera mi madre.

CURRA

¿Si viviera la señora? . . .
Usted está delirante.
30 Más vana que Señor era;
Señor al cabo es un ángel.
¡Pero ella! . . . Un genio tenía
Y un copete . . . Dios nos guarde.
Los señores de esta tierra
35 Son todos de un mismo talle.
Y si alguna señorita
Busca un novio que le cuadre,
Como no esté en pergaminos
Envuelto,[54] levantan tales
40 Alaridos . . . ¿Mas qué importa
Cuando hay decisión bastante . . . ?
Pero no perdamos tiempo;
Venga usted, venga a ayudarme,
Porque yo no puedo sola . . .

[51] match, marriage [52] *Señor* is the Marqués.
[53] the window of the dovecot, i.e. of our little nest
[54] *Como no esté en pergaminos envuelto,* if he isn't wrapped in parchments; i.e. if he isn't of an old noble line

DOÑA LEONOR

¡Ay, Curra! . . . ¡Si penetrases
Cómo tengo el alma! Fuerza
Me falta hasta para alzarme
De esta silla . . . ¡Curra amiga!
Lo confieso, no lo extrañes:
No me resuelvo, imposible . . .
Es imposible. ¡Ah! . . . ¡Mi padre!
Sus palabras cariñosas,
Sus extremos, sus afanes,
Sus besos y sus abrazos,
Eran agudos puñales
Que el pecho me atravesaban.
Si se queda un solo instante
No hubiera más resistido . . .
Ya iba a sus pies a arrojarme,
Y confundida, aterrada,
Mi proyecto a revelarle;
Y a morir, ansiando sólo
Que su perdón me acordase.[55]

CURRA

¡Pues hubiéramos quedado
Frescas, y echado un buen lance![56]
Mañana vería usted
Revolcándose en su sangre,
Con la tapa de los sesos
Levantada, al arrogante,
Al enamorado, al noble
Don Álvaro. O arrastrarle[57]
Como un malhechor, atado,
Por entre estos olivares
A la cárcel de Sevilla;
Y allá para Navidades
Acaso, acaso en la horca.

DOÑA LEONOR

¡Ay, Curra! . . . El alma me partes.

CURRA

Y todo esto, señorita,
Porque la desgracia grande
Tuvo el infeliz de veros,
Y necio[58] de enamorarse
De quien no le corresponde,
Ni resolución bastante
Tiene para . . .

DOÑA LEONOR

5 Basta, Curra;
No mi pecho despedaces.
¿Yo a su amor no correspondo?
Que le correspondo sabes . . .
Por él mi casa y familia,
10 Mis hermanos y mi padre
Voy a abandonar, y sola . . .

CURRA

Sola no, que yo soy alguien,
Y también Antonio va,
15 Y nunca en ninguna parte
La dejaremos . . . ¡Jesús![59]

DOÑA LEONOR

¿Y mañana?

CURRA

20 Día grande.
Usted la adorada esposa
Será del más adorable,
Rico y lindo caballero
Que puede en el mundo hallarse,
25 Y yo la mujer de Antonio:
Y a ver tierras muy distantes
Iremos ambas . . . ¡Qué bueno!

DOÑA LEONOR

¿Y mi anciano y tierno padre?

30 CURRA

¿Quién? . . . ¿Señor? . . . Rabiará un poco,
Pateará, contará el lance
Al Capitán general
35 Con sus pelos y señales;[60]
Fastidiará al Asistente[61]
Y también a sus compadres
El canónigo, el jurado

[55] to accord, give
[56] *Pues . . . lance,* Well, we would have been in a fine fix and have acted very cleverly (if we had followed your plan)!
[57] Or [you would see them] dragging him
[58] and [being] foolish [enough] to
[59] What an idea!
[60] *Con sus pelos y señales,* with all its details
[61] governor (He will ask the governor to send the police after the elopers.)

Y los vejetes maestrantes;
Saldrán mil requisitorias
Para buscarnos en balde,
Cuando nosotras estemos
Ya seguritas en Flandes.
Desde allí escribirá usted,
Y comenzará a templarse
Señor, y a los nueve meses,
Cuando sepa hay un infante[62]
Que tiene sus mismos ojos,
Emperzará a consolarse.
Y nosotras chapurrando,[63]
Que no nos entienda nadie,
Volveremos de allí a poco,
A que con festejos grandes
Nos reciban, y todito
Será banquetes y bailes.

DOÑA LEONOR

¿Y mis hermanos del alma?

CURRA

¡Toma! ¡toma! . . . Cuando agarren
Del generoso cuñado,
Uno con que hacer alarde[64]
De vistosos uniformes,
Y con que rendir beldades;
Y el otro para libracos,
Merendonas y truhanes,
Reventarán de algería.

DOÑA LEONOR

No corre en tus venas sangre.
¡Jesús, y qué cosas tienes!

CURRA

Porque digo las verdades.[65]

DOÑA LEONOR

¡Ay desdichada de mí!

CURRA

Desdicha por cierto grande
El ser adorado dueño[66]
Del mejor de los galanes.
Pero vamos, señorita,
Ayúdeme usted, que es tarde.

DOÑA LEONOR

5 Sí, tarde es, y aún no parece
Don Álvaro . . . ¡Oh, si faltase
Esta noche! . . . ¡Ojalá! . . . ¡Cielos! . . .
Que jamás estos umbrales
Hubiera pisado, fuera
10 Mejor . . . No tengo bastante
Resolución . . . Lo confieso.
Es tan duro el alejarse
Así de su casa . . . ¡Ay triste!
(*Mira el reloj y sigue en inquietud.*)
15 Las doce han dado . . . ¡Qué tarde
Es ya, Curra! No, no viene.
¿Habrá en esos olivares
Tenido algún mal encuentro?
Hay siempre en el Aljarafe
20 Tan mala gente . . . ¿Y Antonio
Estará alerta?

CURRA

Indudable
Es que está de centinela . . .

25 DOÑA LEONOR

¡Curra! . . . ¿Qué suena? . . . ¿Escuchaste?
(*Con gran sobresalto.*)

CURRA

30 Pisadas son de caballos.

DOÑA LEONOR

¡Ay! él es . . . (*Corre al balcón.*)

CURRA

Si que faltase
35 Era imposible . . .[67]

DOÑA LEONOR

¡Dios mío! (*Muy agitada.*)

[62] baby
[63] to talk brokenly a foreign language
[64] *hacer alarde,* to make a show
[65] The servant girl regards the whole escapade as a lark; but the sensitive, high-bred heroine foresees misfortune, which to a considerable extent originates in her very character.
[66] *Desdicha . . . dueño,* It certainly is a great misfortune to be the adored possessor
[67] Word order: *Si era imposible que faltase*

CURRA

Pecho al agua,[68] y adelante.

ESCENA VII

(DON ÁLVARO *en cuerpo,*[69] *con una jaquetilla de mangas perdidas sobre una rica chupa de majo, redecilla, calzón de ante,*[70] *etc., entra por el balcón y se echa en brazos de* LEONOR.)

DON ÁLVARO

(*Con gran vehemencia.*)

¡Ángel consolador del alma mía! . . .
¿Van ya los santos cielos
A dar corona eterna a mis desvelos? . . .
Me ahoga la alegría . . .
¿Estamos abrazados
Para no vernos nunca separados? . . .
Antes, antes la muerte,
Que de ti separame y que perderte.

DOÑA LEONOR

¡Don Álvaro! (*Muy agitada.*)

DON ÁLVARO

Mi bien, mi Dios, mi todo.
¿Qué te agita y te turba de tal modo?
¿Te turba el corazón ver que tu amante
Se encuentra en este instante
Más ufano que el sol? . . . ¡Prenda adorada!

DOÑA LEONOR

Es ya tan tarde . . .

DON ÁLVARO

¿Estabas enojada
Porque tardé en venir? De mi retardo
No soy culpado, no, dulce señora;
Hace más de una hora
Que despechado aguardo
Por estos rededores
La ocasión de llegar, y ya temía
Que de mi adversa estrella los rigores
Hoy deshicieran la esperanza mía.
5 Mas no, mi bien, mi gloria, mi consuelo;
Protege nuestro amor el santo cielo,
Y una carrera eterna de ventura,
Próvido[71] a nuestras plantas asegura.
10 El tiempo no perdamos.
¿Está ya todo listo? Vamos, vamos.

CURRA

Sí: bajo del balcón, Antonio, el guarda,
15 Las maletas espera;
Las echaré al momento. (*Va hacia el balcón.*)

DOÑA LEONOR

(*Resuelta.*)

20 Curra, aguarda,
Deténte . . . ¡Ay Dios! ¿No fuera,
Don Álvaro, mejor? . . .

DON ÁLVARO

¿Qué, encanto mío? . . .
25 ¿Por qué tiempo perder? La jaca torda,
La que, cual dices tú, los campos borda,[72]
La que tanto te agrada
Por su obediencia y brío,
30 Para ti está, mi dueño, enjaezada,
Para Curra el overo,
Para mí el alazán gallardo y fiero . . .
¡Oh, loco estoy de amor y de alegría!
En San Juan de Alfarache, preparado
35 Todo, con gran secreto, lo he dejado.
El sacerdote en el altar espera;
Dios nos bendecirá desde su esfera;
Y cuando el nuevo sol en el Oriente,
Protector de mi estirpe soberana
40 Numen eterno en la región indiana,[73]
La regia pompa de su trono ostente,

[68] Proverbial expression: Courage!
[69] in indoor dress
[70] *una jaquetilla . . . ante,* a short jacket with sleeves open from the shoulder over a fancy waistcoat such as worn by the local dandies, a hairnet, buckskin breeches

[71] benevolent (modifies *cielo*)
[72] embroiders, i.e. traverses daintily
[73] The sun was the god of the Incas and the ancestor of their royal line. What are we to understand when Don Álvaro says: *protector de mi estirpe?*

Monarca de la luz, padre del día,
Yo tu esposo seré, tú esposa[74] mía.

DOÑA LEONOR

Es tan tarde . . . ¡Don Álvaro!

DON ÁLVARO (*A* CURRA.)

Muchacha,
¿Qué te detiene ya? Corre, despacha:
Por el balcón esas maletas, luego . . .

DOÑA LEONOR

¡Curra, Curra, deténte! (*Fuera de si.*)
¡Don Álvaro!

DON ÁLVARO

¡Leonor!!!

DOÑA LEONOR

¡Dejadlo os ruego
Para mañana!

DON ÁLVARO

¿Qué?

DOÑA LEONOR

Más fácilmente . . .

DON ÁLVARO

(*Demudado y confuso.*)
¿Qué es esto, qué, Leonor? ¿Te falta ahora
Resolución? . . . ¡Ay, yo desventurado![75]

DOÑA LEONOR

¡Don Álvaro! ¡Don Álvaro!!!

DON ÁLVARO

¡Señora!

DOÑA LEONOR

¡Ay! Me partís el alma . . .

DON ÁLVARO

Destrozado
Tengo yo el corazón . . . ¿Dónde está, dónde,
5 Vuestro amor, vuestro firme juramento?
Mal con vuestra palabra corresponde
Tanta irresolución en tal momento.
Tan súbita mudanza . . .
10 No os conozco, Leonor. ¿Llevóse el viento
De mi delirio toda la esperanza?
Sí, he cegado en el punto
En que alboraba[76] el más risueño día.
15 Me sacarán difunto
De aquí, cuando inmortal salir creía.
Hechicera engañosa,
¿La perspectiva hermosa
Que falaz me ofreciste así deshaces?
20 ¡Pérfida! ¿Te complaces
En levantarme al trono del Eterno
Para después hundirme en el infierno? . . .
¡Sólo me resta ya![77] . . .

25 DOÑA LEONOR

(*Echándose en sus brazos.*)
No, no, te adoro.
¡Don Álvaro! . . . ¡Mi bien! . . . Vamos, sí, vamos.

30 DON ÁLVARO

¡Oh mi Leonor! . . .

CURRA

El tiempo no perdamos.

DON ÁLVARO

35 ¡Mi encanto! ¡Mi tesoro!
(DOÑA LEONOR, *muy abatida, se apoya en el hombro de* DON ÁLVARO, *con muestras de desmayarse.*)

[74] Don Álvaro's intention is to comply with religious law by marrying Leonor. Remember that in Catholic Spain marriage is a sacrament of the church. Don Álvaro is not so much of a rebel as many romanticists, for example Espronceda.

[75] unhappy me!

[76] Poetic for *alboreaba*

[77] Some such word as *morir* would complete this fragmentary sentence.

Mas ¿qué es esto? ¡Ay de mí! ¡Tu mano yerta!
Me parece la mano de una muerta . . .
Frío está tu semblante,
Como la losa de un sepulcro helado . . .

DOÑA LEONOR

¡Don Álvaro!

DON ÁLVARO

¡Leonor! (*Pausa.*) Fuerza bastante
Hay para todo en mí . . .[78] ¡Desventurado!
La conmoción conozco que te agita,
Inocente Leonor. Dios no permita
Que por debilidad en tal momento
Sigas mis pasos y mi esposa seas.
Renuncio a tu palabra y juramento;
Hachas de muerte las nupciales teas
Fueran para los dos . . . Si no me amas,
Como yo te amo a ti . . . Si arrepentida . . .

DOÑA LEONOR

Mi dulce esposo, con el alma y vida
Es tuya tu Leonor; mi dicha fundo
En seguirte hasta el fin del ancho mundo.
Vamos; resuelta estoy, fijé mi suerte;
Separarnos podrá sólo la muerte.
(*Van hacia el balcón, cuando de repente se oye ruido, ladridos, y abrir y cerrar puertas.*)

DOÑA LEONOR

¡Dios mío! ¿Qué ruido es éste? ¡Don Álvaro!!!

CURRA

Parece que han abierto la puerta del patio . . . y la de la escarera . . .

DOÑA LEONOR

¿Se habrá puesto malo mi padre? . . .

[78] He has strength enough even to give up Leonor.

CURRA

¡Qué! No, señora; el ruido viene de otra parte.

DOÑA LEONOR

5 ¿Habrá llegado alguno de mis hermanos?

DON ÁLVARO

Vamos, vamos, Leonor, no perdamos ni un instante.
10 (*Vuelve hacia el balcón, y de repente se ve por él el resplandor de hachones de viento, y se oye galopar caballos.*)

DOÑA LEONOR

¡Somos perdidos! . . . Estamos descu-
15 biertos . . . Imposible es la fuga.

DON ÁLVARO

Serenidad es necesario en todo caso.

CURRA

¡La Virgen del Rosario nos valga y las
20 ánimas benditas! . . . ¿Qué será de mi pobre Antonio? (*Se asoma al balcón y grita.*) ¡Antonio! ¡Antonio!

DON ÁLVARO

¡Calla, maldita! no llames la atención
25 hacia este lado; entorna el balcón.
(*Se acerca el ruido de puertas y pisadas.*)

DOÑA LEONOR

¡Ay desdichada de mí! Don Álvaro,
30 escóndete . . . aquí . . . en mi alcoba . . .

DON ÁLVARO (*Resuelto.*)

No, yo no me escondo . . . No te abandono en tal conflicto. (*Prepara
35 una pistola.*) Defenderte y salvarte es mi obligación.

DOÑA LEONOR

(*Asustadísima.*)
¿Qué intentas? ¡Ay! Retira esa pistola, que me hiela la sangre . . . ¡Por Dios, suéltala! . . . ¿La dispararás contra mi buen padre? . . . ¿Contra alguno de mis hermanos? . . . ¿Para matar a alguno de los fieles y antiguos criados de esta casa?

DON ÁLVARO

(*Profundamente confuso.*)
No, no, amor mío . . . La emplearé en dar fin a mi desventurada vida.

DOÑA LEONOR

¡Qué horror! ¡Don Álvaro!

ESCENA VIII

(*Ábrese la puerta con estrépito, después de varios golpes en ella, y entra el* MARQUÉS, *en bata y gorro, con un espadín desnudo en la mano, y detrás dos criados mayores con luces.*)

MARQUÉS (*Furioso.*)

¡Vil seductor! . . . ¡Hija infame!

DOÑA LEONOR

(*Arrojándose a los pies de su padre.*)
¡Padre!!! ¡Padre!!!

MARQUÉS

No soy tu padre . . . Aparta . . . Y tú, vil advenedizo . . .

DON ÁLVARO

Vuestra hija es inocente . . . Yo soy el culpado . . . Atravesadme el pecho. (*Hinca una rodilla.*)

MARQUÉS

Tu actitud suplicante manifiesta lo bajo de tu condición . . .

DON ÁLVARO (*Levantándose.*)

¡Señor Marqués! . . . ¡Señor Marqués! . . .

MARQUÉS (*A su hija.*)

5 Quita, mujer inicua. (*A* CURRA, *que le sujeta el brazo.*) ¿Y tú, infeliz . . . osas tocar a tu señor? (*A los criados.*) Ea, echaos sobre ese infame, sujetadle,
10 atadle . . .

DON ÁLVARO (*Con dignidad.*)

Desgraciado del que[79] me pierda el respeto.
15 (*Saca una pistola y la monta.*)

DOÑA LEONOR

(*Corriendo hacia* DON ÁLVARO.)
¡Don Álvaro! . . . ¿Qué vais a hacer?

MARQUÉS

20 Echaos sobre él al punto.

DON ÁLVARO

¡Ay de vuestros criados si se mueven! Vos sólo tenéis derecho para atrave-
25 sarme el corazón.

MARQUÉS

¿Tú morir a manos de un caballero? No; morirás a las del verdugo.

DON ÁLVARO

30 ¡Señor Marqués de Calatrava! Mas ¡ah! no: tenéis derecho para todo . . . Vuestra hija es inocente . . . Tan pura como el aliento de los ángeles que rodean el trono del Altísimo. La
35 sospecha a que puede dar origen mi presencia aquí a tales horas concluya con mi muerte; salga envolviendo mi cadáver como si fuera mi mortaja[80] . . . Sí, debo morir . . . , pero a
40 vuestras manos. (*Pone una rodilla en tierra.*) Espero resignado el golpe, no lo resistiré; ya me tenéis desarmado.

[79] Woe upon the one who
[80] *salga . . . mortaja,* may it [the suspicion] leave [this house] shrouding my corpse as if it were my winding sheet

(*Tira la pistola, que al dar en tierra se dispara y hiere al* MARQUÉS, *que cae moribundo en los brazos de su hija y de los criados, dando un alarido.*)

MARQUÉS

Muerto soy . . . ¡Ay de mí! . . .

DON ÁLVARO

¡Dios mío! ¡Arma funesta![81] ¡Noche terrible!

DOÑA LEONOR

¡Padre, padre!!!

MARQUÉS

Aparta; sacadme de aquí . . . , donde muera sin que esta vil me contamine con tal nombre . . .

5

DOÑA LEONOR

¡Padre! . . .

MARQUÉS

Yo te maldigo.[82]

(*Cae* DOÑA LEONOR *en brazos de* DON
10 ÁLVARO, *que la arrastra hacia el balcón.*)

JORNADA SEGUNDA

La escena es en la villa de Hornachuelos y sus alrededores.

ESCENA PRIMERA

(*Es de noche, y el teatro representa la cocina de un mesón de la villa de Hornachuelos. Al frente estará la chimenea y el hogar. A la izquierda la* 15 *puerta de entrada; a la derecha dos puertas practicables. A un lado una mesa largo de pino, rodeada de asientos toscos, y alumbrado todo por un gran candilón. El* MESONERO *y el* ALCALDE *aparecerán sentados grave-* 20 *mente al fuego. La* MESONERA, *de rodillas guisando. Junto a la mesa, el* ESTUDIANTE *cantando y tocando la guitarra. El* ARRIERO *que habla, cribando cebada en el fondo del teatro.* 25 *El* TÍO TRABUCO, *tendido en primer término sobre sus jalmas. Los* DOS LUGAREÑOS, *las* DOS LUGAREÑAS, *la* MOZA *y uno de los* ARRIEROS, *que no habla, estarán bailando seguidillas. El otro* 30 ARRIERO, *que no habla, estará sentado junto al* ESTUDIANTE *y jaleando a las que bailan. Encima de la mesa habrá una bota de vino, unos vasos y un frasco de aguardiente.*[83]

ESTUDIANTE

(*Cantando en voz recia al son de la guitarra, y las tres parejas bailando con gran algazara.*)

Poned en estudiantes
vuestro cariño,
que son, como discretos,
agradecidos.
Viva Hornachuelos,
vivan de sus muchachas
los ojos negros.
Dejad a los soldados,
que es gente mala,
y así que dan el golpe
vuelven la espalda.[84]
Viva Hornachuelos,
vivan de sus muchachas
los ojos negros.

[81] Fatal weapon! (Don Álvaro feels that Fate is acting against him, cf. p. 303, l. 3b, where many people would see nothing but Chance. But does not Fate work through chance events? Still, in the workings of Fate we expect a certain inevitability which is lacking here.

[82] The curse which the Marqués places upon his daughter with his dying breath adds more gloom to her already unhappy prospects.

[83] Again we have a setting and a group of minor characters which are very picturesque. Notice how the latter again bring in the exposition of the act.

[84] *y así . . . espalda,* as soon as they get their way, they turn elsewhere

MESONERA

(*Poniendo una sartén sobre la mesa.*) Vamos, vamos, que se enfría . . . (*A la criada.*) Pepa, al avío.

ARRIERO (*El del cribo.*)

Otra coplita.

ESTUDIANTE

(*Dejando la guitarra.*) Abrenuntio.[85] Antes de todo, la cena.

MESONERA

Y si después quiere la gente seguir bailando y alborotando, váyanse al corral o la calle, que hay una luna clara como de día. Y dejen en silencio el mesón, que si unos quieren jaleo, otros quieren dormir. Pepa, Pepa . . . ¿no digo que basta ya de zangoloteo? . . .

TÍO TRABUCO

(*Acostado en sus arreos.*) Tía Colasa, usted está en lo cierto. Yo por mí, quiero dormir.

MESONERO

Sí, ya basta de ruido. Vamos a cenar. Señor Alcalde, eche su merced la bendición, y venga a tomar una presita.

ALCALDE

Se agradece, señor Monipodio.

MESONERA

Pero acérquese su merced.

ALCALDE

Que eche la bendición el señor licenciado.

ESTUDIANTE

Allá voy, y no seré largo, que huele el bacalao a gloria. *In nomine Patris et Filii et Spiritus Sancti.*

TODOS

Amén.

(*Se van acomodando alrededor de la mesa todos menos* TRABUCO.)

MESONERA

Tal vez el tomate no estará bastante cocido, y el arroz estará algo duro . . . Pero con tanta babilonia no se puede. . .

ARRIERO

Está diciendo comedme, comedme.[86]

ESTUDIANTE

(*Comiendo con ansia.*) Está exquisito . . . especial; parece ambrosía . . .

MESONERA

Alto allá, señor bachiller; la tía Ambrosia[87] no me gana a mí a guisar, ni sirve para descalzarme el zapato; no, señor.

ARRIERO

La tía Ambrosia es más puerca que una telaraña.

MESONERO

La tía Ambrosia es un guiñapo, es un paño de aporrear moscas;[88] se revuelven las tripas de[89] entrar en su mesón, y compararla con mi Colasa no es regular.[90]

[85] I renounce, I give up (a Latin word, appropriate for a student)
[86] The food is saying: 'Eat me.'
[87] This scene serves as comic relief from the heavy tragedy of the main plot. The peasants confuse *ambrosía* (ambrosia, food of the gods) with *Ambrosia,* a rival innkeeper.
[88] a cloth for swatting flies, i.e. a foul creature
[89] *se . . . de,* one's insides are upset by
[90] proper

ESTUDIANTE

Ya sé yo que la señora Colasa es pulcra, y no lo dije por tanto.[91]

ALCALDE

En toda la comarca de Hornachuelos no hay una persona más limpia que la señora Colasa, ni un mesón como el del señor Monipodio.

MESONERA

Como que cuantas comidas de boda se hacen en la villa pasan por estas manos que ha de comer la tierra. Y de las bodas de señores, no le parezca, a usted,[92] señor bachiller . . . Cuando se casó el escribano[93] con la hija del regidor . . .

ESTUDIANTE

Con que se le puede decir a la señora Colasa, *tu das mihi epulis accumbere divum.*[94]

MESONERA

Yo no sé latín, pero sé guisar . . . Señor Alcalde, moje siquiera una sopa . . .[95]

ALCALDE

Tomaré, por no despreciar, una cucharadita de gazpacho, si es que lo hay.

MESONERO

¿Cómo que si lo hay?

MESONERA

¿Pues había de faltar donde yo estoy? . . . ¡Pepa! (*A la* MOZA.) Anda a traerlo. Está sobre el brocal del pozo, desde media tarde, tomando el fresco. (*Vase la* MOZA.)

ESTUDIANTE

(*Al arriero, que está acostado.*) ¡Tío Trabuco, hola, Tío Trabuco! ¿No viene usted a hacer la razón?[96]

TÍO TRABUCO

No ceno.

ESTUDIANTE

¿Ayuna usted?

TÍO TRABUCO

Sí, señor, que es viernes.

MESONERO

Pero un traguito . . .

TÍO TRABUCO

Venga. (*Le alarga el* MESONERO *la bota, y bebe un trago el* TÍO TRABUCO.) ¡Jú! Esto es zupia. Alárgueme usted, tío Monipodio, el frasco del aguardiente para enjuagarme la boca. (*Bebe y se acurruca.*)

(*Entra la* MOZA *con una fuente de gazpacho.*)

MOZA

Aquí está la gracia de Dios.[97]

TODOS

Venga, venga.

ESTUDIANTE

Parece, señor Alcalde, que esta noche hay mucha gente forastera en Hornachuelos.

ARRIERO

Las tres posadas están llenas.

ALCALDE

Como es el jubileo de la Porciúncula,[98] y el convento de San Francisco de los

[91] *no . . . tanto,* I wasn't speaking seriously
[92] *no le parezca a usted,* I want you to know
[93] The humor lies in the class of people the hostess considers as *señores.*
[94] Latin: You allow me to recline at the banquets of the gods. From Virgil's *Aeneid.*
[95] *moje . . . sopa,* dip in at least one sop
[96] *hacer la razón,* to eat
[97] *la gracia de Dios,* the food
[98] A festival commemorating the foundation of the Franciscan order at the Porziuncula sanctuary in Italy. Many persons visit Franciscan monasteries on this date (August 2) to receive plenary indulgence.

Ángeles, que está aquí en el desierto, a media legua corta, es tan famoso . . . viene mucha gente a confesarse con el padre Guardián, que es un siervo de Dios. 5

MESONERA

Es un santo.

MESONERO

(*Toma la bota y se pone de pie.*) Jesús; por la buena compañía, y que 10 Dios nos dé salud y pesetas en esta vida, y la gloria en la eterna. (*Bebe.*)

TODOS

Amén. (*Pasa la bota de mano en mano.*) 15

ESTUDIANTE (*Después de beber.*)

Tío Trabuco, Tío Trabuco, ¿está usted con los angelitos?[99]

TÍO TRABUCO

Con las malditas pulgas y con sus voces 20 de usted, ¿quién puede estar sino con los demonios?

ESTUDIANTE

Queríamos saber, Tío Trabuco, si esa personilla de alfeñique,[100] que ha ve- 25 nido con usted y que se ha escondido de nosotros, viene a ganar el jubileo.

TÍO TRABUCO

Yo no sé nunca a lo que van ni vienen 30 los que viajan conmigo.

ESTUDIANTE

Pero . . . ¿es gallo, o gallina?

TÍO TRABUCO

Yo de los viajeros no miro más que la moneda, que ni es hembra ni es macho.

ESTUDIANTE

Sí, es género epiceno, como si dijéramos hermafrodita . . . Pero veo que es usted muy taciturno, Tío Trabuco.

TÍO TRABUCO

Nunca gasto saliva en lo que no me importa; y buenas noches, que se me va quedando la lengua dormida, y quiero guardarle el sueño; sonsoniche.[101]

ESTUDIANTE

Pues, señor, con el Tío Trabuco no hay emboque.[102] Dígame usted, nostrama[103] (*A la* MESONERA.), ¿por qué no ha venido a cenar el tal caballerito?

MESONERA

Yo no sé.

ESTUDIANTE

Pero, vamos, ¿es hembra o varón?

MESONERA

Que sea lo que sea, lo cierto es que le vi el rostro, por más que se lo recataba, cuando se apeó del mulo, y que lo tiene como un sol; y eso que traía los ojos, de llorar y de polvo, que daba compasión.

ESTUDIANTE

¡Oiga!

MESONERA

Sí, señor; y en cuanto se metió en ese cuarto, volviéndome siempre la espalda, me preguntó cuánto había de aquí al convento de los Ángeles, y yo se lo enseñé desde la ventana, que, 35 como está tan cerca, se ve clarito, y . . .

ESTUDIANTE

¡Hola, con que es pecador que viene al jubileo!

[99] *con los angelitos,* asleep
[100] a sweetmeat; here, a delicate person
[101] be quiet (thieves' slang)
[102] a narrow entrance; hence, you can't worm your way into his confidence
[103] Popular speech for *nuestra ama*

MESONERA

Yo no sé; luego, se acostó; digo, se echó en la cama, vestido, y bebió antes un vaso de agua con unas gotas de vinagre.

ESTUDIANTE

Ya, para refrescar el cuerpo.

MESONERA

Y me dijo que no quería luz, ni cena, ni nada, y se quedó como rezando el Rosario entre dientes. A mí me parece que es persona muy . . .

MESONERO

Charla, charla . . . ¿Quién diablos te mete en hablar de los huéspedes? . . . ¡Maldita sea tu lengua!

MESONERA

Como el señor licenciado quería saber . . .

ESTUDIANTE

Sí, señora Colasa; dígame usted . . .

MESONERO (*A su mujer.*)

¡Chitón![104]

ESTUDIANTE

Pues, señor, volvamos al Tío Trabuco. Tío Trabuco, Tío Trabuco!

(*Se acerca a él y le despierta.*)

TÍO TRABUCO

¡Malo! . . . ¿Me quiere usted dejar en paz?

ESTUDIANTE

Vamos, dígame usted, esa persona ¿cómo viene en el mulo, a mujeriegas o a horcajadas?

TÍO TRABUCO

¡Ay, qué sangre! . . . De cabeza.

[104] Sh! not a word!

ESTUDIANTE

Y dígame usted, ¿de dónde salió usted esta mañana, de Posadas o de Palma?

TÍO TRABUCO

5 Yo no sé sino que tarde o temprano voy al cielo.

ESTUDIANTE

¿Por qué?

TÍO TRABUCO

10 Porque ya me tiene usted en el purgatorio.

ESTUDIANTE (*Se ríe.*)

¡Ah, ah, ah! . . . ¿Y va usted a Extremadura?

15 TÍO TRABUCO

(*Se levanta, recoge sus jalmas y se va con ellas muy enfadado.*)
No, señor, a la caballeriza, huyendo de usted, y a dormir con mis mulos, que
20 no saben latín ni son bachilleres.

ESTUDIANTE (*Se ríe.*)

¡Ah, ah, ah! Se atufó . . . ¡Hola, Pepa, salerosa! ¿Y no has visto tú al escondido?

25 MOZA

Por la espalda.

ESTUDIANTE

¿Y en qué cuarto está?

MOZA

30 (*Señala la primera puerta de la derecha.*)
En ése . . .

ESTUDIANTE

Pues ya que es lampiño, vamos a pin-
35 tarle unos bigotes con tizne . . . Y cuando se despierte por la mañana reiremos un poco.
(*Se tizna los dedos y va hacia el cuarto.*)

ALGUNOS

Sí . . ., sí.

MESONERO

No, no.

ALCALDE (*Con gravedad.*)

Señor estudiante, no lo permitiré yo, pues debo proteger a los forasteros que llegan a esta villa, y administrarles justicia como a los naturales de ella.

ESTUDIANTE

No lo dije por tanto,[105] señor Alcalde . . .

ALCALDE

Yo sí. Y no fuera malo saber quién es el señor licenciado, de dónde viene y adónde va, pues parece algo alegre de cascos.

ESTUDIANTE

Si la justicia me lo pregunta de burlas o de veras, no hay inconveniente en decirlo, que aquí se juega limpio. Soy el bachiller Pereda, graduado por Salamanca, *in utroque,*[106] y hace ocho años que curso sus escuelas, aunque pobre, con honra, y no sin fama. Salí de allí hace más de un año, acompañando a mi amigo y protector el señor licenciado Vargas,[107] y fuimos a Sevilla, a vengar la muerte de su padre el marqués de Calatrava, y a indagar el paradero de su hermana, que se escapó con el matador. Pasamos allí algunos meses, donde también estuvo su hermano mayor, el actual marqués, que es oficial de Guardias. Y como no lograron su propósito, se separaron jurando venganza. Y el licenciado y yo nos vinimos a Córdoba, donde dijeron que estaba la hermana. Pero no la hallamos tampoco, y allí supimos que había muerto en la refriega que armaron los criados del Marqués, la noche de su muerte, con los del robador y asesino, y que éste se había vuelto a América. Con lo que marchamos a Cádiz, donde mi protector, el licenciado Vargas, se ha embarcado para buscar allá al enemigo de su familia. Y yo me vuelvo a mi universidad a desquitar el tiempo perdido y a continuar mis estudios; con los que, y la ayuda de Dios, puede ser que me vea algún día gobernador del Consejo o arzobispo de Sevilla.

ALCALDE

Humos[108] tiene el señor bachiller, y ya basta; pues se ve en su porte y buena explicación que es hombre de bien y que dice verdad.

MESONERA

Dígame usted, señor estudiante, ¿y qué, mataron a ese marqués?

ESTUDIANTE

Sí.

MESONERA

¿Y lo mató el amante de su hija y luego la robó? . . . ¡Ay! Cuéntenos su merced esa historia, que será muy divertida; cuéntela su merced . . .

MESONERO

¿Quién te mete a ti en saber vidas ajenas? ¡Maldita sea tu curiosidad! Pues que ya hemos cenado, demos gracias a Dios, y a recogerse.
(*Se ponen todos en pie, y se quitan el sombrero como que rezan.*)
Eh, buenas noches; cada mochuelo a su olivo.[109]

[105] See note 91
[106] Latin: in both [subjects], i.e. civil and canon law
[107] Leonor's brother
[108] vanity, high ambition
[109] Proverbial expression: Every owl to his olive tree, i.e. everyone to his bed.

ALCALDE

Buenas noches, y que haya juicio y silencio.

ESTUDIANTE

Pues me voy a mi cuarto.
(*Se va a meter en el del viajero incógnito.*)

MESONERO

¡Hola! No es ése; el de más allá.

ESTUDIANTE

Me equivoqué.
(*Vanse el* ALCALDE *y los* LUGAREÑOS; *entra el* ESTUDIANTE *en su cuarto; la* MOZA, *el* ARRIERO *y la* MESONERA *retiran la mesa y bancos, dejando la escena desembarazada. El* MESONERO *se acerca al hogar, y queda todo en silencio y solos el* MESONERO *y* MESONERA.)

ESCENA II

MESONERO

Colasa, para medrar
En nuestro oficio, es forzoso
Que haya en la casa reposo
Y a ninguno incomodar.
Nunca meterse a oliscar
Quiénes los huéspedes son;
No gastar conversación
Con cuantos llegan aquí;
Servir bien, decir *no* o *sí*,
Cobrar la mosca,[110] y chitón.

MESONERA

No, por mí no lo dirás;
Bien sabes que callar sé.
Al bachiller pregunté . . .

MESONERO

Pues eso estuvo de más.

MESONERA

También ahora extrañarás
Que entre en ese cuarto a ver
Si el huésped ha menester
Alguna cosa, marido;
Pues es, sí, lo he conocido,
Una afligida mujer.
5 (*Toma un candil y entra la* MESONERA *muy recatadamente en el cuarto.*)

MESONERO

Entra, que entrar es razón,
Aunque temo, a la verdad,
10 Que vas por curiosidad,
Más bien que por compasión.

MESONERA

(*Saliendo muy asustada.*)
¡Ay, Dios mío! Vengo muerta;
15 Desapareció la dama;
Nadie he encontrado en la cama,
Y está la ventana abierta.

MESONERO

¿Cómo? ¿cómo? . . . ¡Ya lo sé! . . .
20 La ventana al campo da,
Y como tan baja está,
Sin gran trabajo se fué.

(*Andando hacia el cuarto donde entró la mujer, quedándose él a la puerta.*)
25 Quiera Dios no haya cargado[111]
Con la colcha nueva.

MESONERA (*Dentro.*)

Nada,
Todo está aquí . . . ¡Desdichada!
30 Hasta dinero ha dejado . . .
Sí, sobre la mesa un duro.

MESONERO

Vaya entonces en buen hora.

MESONERA

35 (*Saliendo a la escena.*)
No hay duda: es una señora
Que se encuentra en grande apuro.

MESONERO

Pues con bien[112] la lleve Dios,
40 Y vámonos a acostar,

[110] to collect the cash
[111] to run off with
[112] with good fortune

Y mañana no charlar,
Que esto quede entre los dos.
Echa un cuarto en el cepillo[113]
De las ánimas, mujer;
Y el duro véngame a ver;
Échamelo en el bolsillo.

ESCENA III

(*El teatro representa una plataforma en la ladera de una áspera montaña. A la izquierda precipicios y derrumbaderos. Al frente un profundo valle atravesado por un riachuelo, en cuya margen se ve, a lo lejos, la villa de Hornachuelos, terminando el fondo en altas montañas. A la derecha, la fachada del convento*[114] *de los Ángeles, de pobre y humilde arquitectura. La gran puerta de la iglesia, cerrada, pero practicable, y sobre ella una claraboya de medio punto*[115] *por donde se verá el resplandor de las luces interiores; más hacia el proscenio, la puerta de la portería, también practicable y cerrada; en medio de ella una mirilla o gatera, que se abre y se cierra, y al lado el cordón de una campanilla. En medio de la escena habrá una gran cruz de piedra tosca y corroída por el tiempo, puesta sobre cuatro gradas que puedan servir de asiento. Estará todo iluminado por una luna clarísima. Se oirá dentro de la iglesia el órgano, y cantar maitines al coro de frailes, y saldrá como subiendo por la izquierda* DOÑA LEONOR, *muy fatigada y vestida de hombre con un gabán de mangas, sombrero gacho y botines.*)

DOÑA LEONOR

Sí . . . ya llegué . . . Dios mío,
Gracias os doy rendida.
(*Arrodíllase al ver el convento.*)
En ti, Virgen Santísima, confío;
Sed el amparo de mi amarga vida.
Este refugio es sólo
El que puedo tener de polo a polo.
(*Álzase.*)
No me queda en la tierra
Más asilo y resguardo
5 Que los áridos riscos de esta sierra:
En ella estoy . . . ¿Aún tiemblo y me acobardo? . . .
(*Mira hacia el sitio por donde ha*
10 *venido.*)
¡Ah! . . . Nadie me ha seguido,
Ni mi fuga veloz notada ha sido.
No me engañé; la horrenda historia mía
15 Escuché referir en la posada . . .
Y ¿quién, cielos, sería
Aquel que la contó? ¡Desventurada!
Amigo dijo ser de mis hermanos . . .
¡Oh cielos soberanos! . . .
20 ¿Voy a ser descubierta?
Estoy de miedo y de cansancio muerta.
(*Se sienta mirando en rededor y luego al cielo.*)
¡Qué asperezas! ¡Qué hermosa y clara
25 luna!
¡La misma que hace un año
Vió la mudanza atroz de mi fortuna,
Y abrirse los infiernos en mi daño!
(*Pausa larga.*)
30 No fué ilusión . . . Aquel que de mí hablaba
Dijo que navegaba
Don Álvaro, buscando nuevamente
Los apartados climas de Occidente.
35 ¡Oh Dios! ¿Y será cierto?
Con bien arribe de su patria al puerto.
(*Pausa.*)
¿Y no murió la noche desastrada
En que yo, yo . . . manchada
40 Con la sangre infeliz del padre mío,
Le seguí . . . le perdí? . . . ¿Y huye el impío?
¿Y huye el ingrato? . . . ¿Y huye y me abandona?[116]
45 (*Cae de rodillas.*)
¡Oh Madre santa de piedad! Perdona,

[113] alms-box for masses in behalf of the souls in purgatory
[114] monastery
[115] *una . . . punto,* a semicircular window
[116] Despite her resolution to take up a hermit's life, the eternal feminine in her is resentful at Álvaro's neglect.

Perdona, le olvidé. Sí, es verdadera,
Lo es mi resolución. Dios de bondades,
Con penitencia austera,
Lejos del mundo en estas soledades
El furor expiaré de mis pasiones. 5
¡Piedad, piedad, Señor, no me abandones!
(*Queda en silencio y como en profunda meditación, recostada en las gradas de la cruz, y después de una* 10 *larga pausa continúa:*)
Los sublimes acentos de ese coro
De bienaventurados,
Y los ecos pausados
Del órgano sonoro, 15
Que cual[117] de incienso vaporosa nube
Al trono santo del eterno sube,
Difunden en mi alma
Bálsamo dulce de consuelo y calma.
(*Se levanta resuelta.*) 20
¿Qué[118] me detengo, pues? . . . Corro al tranquilo . . .
Corro al sagrado asilo . . .
(*Va hacia el convento y se detiene.*)
Mas ¿cómo a tales horas? . . . ¡Ah! . . . 25 No puedo
Ya dilatarlo más; hiélame el miedo
De encontrarme aquí sola. En esa aldea
Hay quien mi historia sabe.
En lo posible cabe 30
Que descubierta con la aurora sea.
Este santo prelado
De mi resolución está informado,
Y de mis infortunios . . . Nada temo.
Mi confesor de Córdoba hace días 35
Que las desgracias mías
Le escribió largamente . . .
Sé de su caridad el noble extremo;
Me acogerá indulgente.
¿Qué dudo, pues, qué dudo? . . . 40
Sed, oh Virgen santísima, mi escudo.
(*Llega a la portería y toca la campanilla.*)

ESCENA IV

(*Se abre la mirilla que está en la puerta, y por ella sale el resplandor de* 45 *un farol que da de pronto en el rostro de* DOÑA LEONOR, *y ésta se retira como asustada. El* HERMANO MELITÓN *habla toda esta escena dentro.*)

HERMANO MELITÓN

¿Quién es?

DOÑA LEONOR

Una persona a quien interesa mucho, mucho, ver al instante al reverendo padre Guardián.

HERMANO MELITÓN

¡Buena hora de ver al padre Guardián! . . . La noche está clara y no será ningún caminante perdido. Si viene a ganar el jubileo, a las cinco se abrirá la iglesia; vaya con Dios; él le ayude.

DOÑA LEONOR

Hermano, llamad al padre Guardián. Por caridad.

HERMANO MELITÓN

¡Qué caridad a estas horas! El padre Guardián está en el coro.

DOÑA LEONOR

Traigo para su reverencia un recado muy urgente del padre Cleto, definidor[119] del convento de Córdoba, quien ya le ha escrito sobre el asunto de que vengo a hablarle.

HERMANO MELITÓN

¡Hola! . . . ¿Del padre Cleto, el definidor del convento de Córdoba? Eso es distinto . . . Iré, iré a decírselo al padre Guardián. Pero dígame, hijo: ¿el recado y la carta, son sobre aquel asunto con el padre General,[120] que está pendiente allá en Madrid?

DOÑA LEONOR

Es una cosa muy interesante.

[117] like
[118] For *por qué*
[119] A member of the governing body of the monastery
[120] Head of the religious order

HERMANO MELITÓN

Pero ¿para quién?

DOÑA LEONOR

Para la criatura más infeliz del mundo.

HERMANO MELITÓN

¡Mala recomendación! . . . Pero, bueno, abriré la portería, aunque es contra regla, para que entréis a esperar.

DOÑA LEONOR

No, no, no puedo entrar . . . ¡¡Jesús!!

HERMANO MELITÓN

Bendito sea su santo nombre . . . ¿Pero sois algún excomulgado? . . . Si no, es cosa rara preferir el esperar al raso.[121] En fin, voy a dar el recado, que probablemente no tendrá respuesta. Si no vuelvo, buenas noches; ahí a la bajadita[122] está la villa, y hay un buen mesón: el de la tía Colasa. (*Ciérrase la ventanilla, y* DOÑA LEONOR *queda muy abatida.*)

ESCENA V

DOÑA LEONOR

¿Será tan negra y dura
Mi suerte miserable,
Que este santo prelado
Socorro y protección no quiera darme?
La rígida aspereza
Y las dificultades
Que ha mostrado el portero
Me pasman de terror, hielan mi sangre.
Mas no; si da el aviso
Al reverendo padre,
Y éste es tan dulce y bueno
Cual dicen todos, volará a ampararme.
¡Oh Soberana Virgen,
De desdichados Madre!
Su corazón ablanda
Para que venga pronto a consolarme.

(*Queda en silencio: da la una el reloj del covento: se abre la portería, en la que aparecen el* PADRE GUARDIÁN *y el* HERMANO MELITÓN *con un farol; éste se queda en la puerta y aquél sale a la escena.*)

ESCENA VI

PADRE GUARDIÁN

¿El que me busca quién es?

DOÑA LEONOR

Yo soy, Padre, que quería . . .

PADRE GUARDIÁN

Ya se abrió la portería;
Entrad en el claustro, pues.

DOÑA LEONOR

(*Muy sobresaltada.*)
¡Ah! . . . Imposible, padre, no.

PADRE GUARDIÁN

¡Imposible! . . . ¿Qué decís? . . .

DOÑA LEONOR

Si que os hable permitís,
Aquí sólo puedo yo.

PADRE GUARDIÁN

Si os envía el padre Cleto,
Hablad, que es mi grande amigo.

DOÑA LEONOR

Padre, que sea sin testigo,
Porque me importa el secreto.

PADRE GUARDIÁN

¿Y quién? . . . Mas ya os entendí.
Retiraos, fray Melitón,
Y encajad ese portón;
Dejadnos solos aquí.

HERMANO MELITÓN

¿No lo dije? Secretitos.
Los misterios ellos solos,

[121] in the open air

[122] *a la bajadita,* right at the foot of the hill

Que los demás somos bolos[123]
Para estos santos benditos.

PADRE GUARDIÁN

¿Qué murmura?

HERMANO MELITÓN

Que está tan
Premiosa[124] esta puerta . . . y luego . . .

PADRE GUARDIÁN

Obedezca, hermano lego.

HERMANO MELITÓN

Ya me la echó de guardián.[125]
(*Ciérrase la puerta y vase.*)

Escena VII

PADRE GUARDIÁN

(*Acercándose a* LEONOR.)
Ya estamos, hermano, solos.
¿Mas por qué tanto misterio?
¿No fuera más conveniente
Que entrarais en el convento?
No sé qué pueda impedirlo . . . 25
Entrad, pues, que yo os lo ruego;
Entrad, subid a mi celda;
Tomaréis un refrigerio,
Y después . . .

DOÑA LEONOR

No, padre mío. 30

PADRE GUARDIÁN

¿Qué os horroriza? . . . No entiendo 35
. . .

DOÑA LEONOR

(*Muy abatida.*)
Soy una infeliz mujer.

PADRE GUARDIÁN

(*Asustado.*)
¡Una mujer! . . . ¡Santo cielo! 40
¡Una mujer! . . . . A estas horas,
En este sitio . . . ¿Qué es esto?

DOÑA LEONOR

Una mujer infelice,[126]
5 Maldición del universo,
Que a vuestras plantas rendida
(*Se arrodilla.*)
Os pide amparo y remedio,
Pues vos podéis libertarla
10 De este mundo y del infierno.

PADRE GUARDIÁN

Señora, alzad. Que son grandes
(*La levanta.*)
Vuestros infortunios creo,
15 Cuando os miro en este sitio
Y escucho tales lamentos.
¿Pero qué apoyo, decidme,
Qué amparo prestaros puedo
Yo, un humilde religioso,
20 Encerrado en estos yermos?

DOÑA LEONOR

¿No habéis, padre, recibido
La carta que el padre Cleto . . .

PADRE GUARDIÁN

(*Recapacitando.*)
¿El padre Cleto os envía? . . .

DOÑA LEONOR

A vos, cual solo[127] remedio
De todos mis infortunios;
Si benigno[128] los intentos
Que a estos montes me conducen
Permitís tengan efecto.

PADRE GUARDIÁN

(*Sorprendido.*)
¿Sois doña Leonor de Vargas? . . .
¿Sois por dicha? . . . ¡Dios eterno!

DOÑA LEONOR

(*Abatida.*)
¡Os horroriza el mirarme!

[123] stupid
[124] hard to close
[125] He has put on the airs of an Abbot.
[126] Poetic form for *infeliz* [127] as the only
[128] Modifies the understood subject of *permitís*

PADRE GUARDIÁN

(*Afectuoso.*)
No, hija mía, no por cierto,
Ni permita Dios que nunca
Tan duro sea mi pecho,
Que a los desgraciados niegue
La compasión y el respeto.

DOÑA LEONOR

¡Yo lo[129] soy tanto!

PADRE GUARDIÁN

Señora,
Vuestra agitación comprendo.
No es extraño, no. Seguidme,
Venid. Sentaos un momento
Al pie de esta cruz; su sombra
Os dará fuerza y consuelos.
(*Lleva el* GUARDIÁN *a* DOÑA LEONOR, *y se sientan al pie de la cruz.*)

DOÑA LEONOR

¡No me abandonéis, oh, padre! 20

PADRE GUARDIÁN

No, jamás; contad conmigo.

DOÑA LEONOR

De este santo monasterio
Desde que el término piso,
Más tranquila tengo el alma,
Con más libertad respiro.
Ya no me cercan, cual hace
Un año, que hoy se ha cumplido,
Los espectros y fantasmas 30
Que siempre en redor[130] he visto.
Ya no me sigue la sombra
Sangrienta del padre mío,
Ni escucho sus maldiciones,
Ni su horrenda herida miro,
Ni . . .

PADRE GUARDIÁN

!Oh, no lo dudo, hija mía!
Libre estáis en este sitio
De esas vanas ilusiones,
Aborto de los abismos.
Las insidias del demonio,
Las sombras a que da brío
Para conturbar al hombre,
No tienen aquí dominio. 5

DOÑA LEONOR

Por eso aquí busco ansiosa
Dulce consuelo y auxilio,
Y de la Reina del cielo
Bajo el regio manto abrigo. 10

PADRE GUARDIÁN

Vamos despacio, hija mía;
El padre Cleto me ha escrito
La resolución tremenda
Que al desierto os ha traído;
Pero no basta. 15

DOÑA LEONOR

Sí basta;
Es inmutable . . . lo fío,
Es inmutable.

PADRE GUARDIÁN

¡Hija mía!

DOÑA LEONOR

Vengo resuelta, lo he dicho,
A sepultarme por siempre
En la tumba de estos riscos. 25

PADRE GUARDIÁN

¡Cómo!

DOÑA LEONOR

¿Seré la primera? . . .
No lo seré, padre mío.
Mi confesor me ha informado
De que en este santo sitio,
Otra mujer infelice 35
Vivió muerta para el siglo.[131]
Resuelta a seguir su ejemplo
Vengo en busca de su asilo:
Dármelo sin duda puede
La gruta que le dió abrigo, 40
Vos la protección y amparo

129 Antecedent: *desgraciada*
130 *en redor,* poetic for *alrededor*

131 the secular world

Que para ello necesito,
Y la soberana Virgen
Su santa gracia y su auxilio.

PADRE GUARDIÁN

No os engañó el padre Cleto,
Pues diez años ha vivido
Una santa penitente
En este yermo tranquilo,
De los hombres ignorada,
De penitencias prodigio.
En nuestra iglesia sus restos
Están, y yo los estimo
Como la joya más rica
De esta casa que, aunque indigno,
Gobierno en el santo nombre
De mi padre San Francisco.
La gruta que fué su albergue,
Y a que reparos precisos
Se le hicieron, está cerca,
En ese hondo precipicio.
Aun existen en su seno
Los humildes utensilios
Que usó la santa; a su lado
Un arroyo cristalino
Brota apacible.

DOÑA LEONOR

Al momento
Llevadme allá, padre mío.

PADRE GUARDIÁN

¡Oh, doña Leonor de Vargas!
¿Insistís?

DOÑA LEONOR

Sí, padre, insisto.
Dios me manda . . .

PADRE GUARDIÁN

Raras veces
Dios tan grandes sacrificios
Exige de los mortales.
Y ¡ay de aquel que de un delirio
En el momento, hija mía,
Tal vez se engaña a sí mismo!
Todas las tribulaciones
De este mundo fugitivo,
Son, señora, pasajeras,
Al cabo encuentran alivio.
Y al Dios de bondad se sirve,
Y se le aplaca lo mismo
5 En el claustro, en el desierto,
De la corte en el bullicio,
Cuando se le entrega el alma
Con fe viva y pecho limpio.

10 DOÑA LEONOR

No es un acaloramiento,
No un instante de delirio,
Quien me sugirió la idea
Que a buscaros me ha traído.
15 Desengaños de este mundo,
Y un año ¡ay Dios! de suplicios,
De largas meditaciones,
De continuados peligros,
De atroces remordimientos,
20 De reflexiones conmigo,
Mi intención han madurado
Y esfuerzo me han concedido
Para hacer voto solemne
De morir en este sitio.
25 Mi confesor venerable,
Que ya mi historia os ha escrito,
El Padre Cleto, a quien todos
Llaman santo, y con motivo,
Mi resolución aprueba;
30 Aunque, cual vos, al principio
Trató de desvanecerla
Con sus doctos raciocinios:
Y a vuestras plantas me envía
Para que me deis auxilio.
35 No me abandonéis, oh Padre;
Por el cielo os lo suplico;
Mi resolución es firme,
Mi voto inmutable y fijo,
Y no hay fuerza en este mundo
40 Que me saque de estos riscos.

PADRE GUARDIÁN

Sois muy joven, hija mía;
¿Quién lo que el cielo propicio
45 Aun nos puede guardar sabe?

DOÑA LEONOR

Renuncio a todo, lo he dicho.

PADRE GUARDIÁN

Acaso aquel caballero . . .

DOÑA LEONOR

¿Qué pronunciáis? . . . ¡oh martirio!
Aunque inocente, manchado
Con sangre del padre mío
Está, y nunca, nunca . . .

PADRE GUARDIÁN

Entiendo,
Mas de vuestra casa el brillo,
Vuestros hermanos . . .

DOÑA LEONOR

Mi muerte
Sólo anhelan vengativos.

PADRE GUARDIÁN

¿Y la bondadosa tía
Que en Córdoba os ha tenido
Un año oculta?

DOÑA LEONOR

No puedo,
Sin ponerla en compromiso,
Abusar de sus bondades.

PADRE GUARDIÁN

Y qué, ¿más seguro asilo
No fuera, y más conveniente,
Con las esposas de Cristo,
En un convento? . . .

DOÑA LEONOR

No, Padre;
Son tantos los requisitos
Que para entrar en el claustro
Se exigen . . . y . . . ¡oh! no, Dios, mío,
Aunque me encuentro inocente,
No puedo, tiemblo al decirlo,
Vivir sino donde nadie
Viva y converse conmigo.
Mi desgracia en toda España
Suena de modo distinto,
Y una alusión, una seña,
Una mirada, suplicios
Pudieran ser que me hundieran
Del despecho en el abismo.
No, jamás . . . Aquí, aquí sólo;
Si no me acogéis benigno,
Piedad pediré a las fieras
5 Que habitan en estos riscos,
Alimento a estas montañas,
Vivienda a estos precipicios.
No salgo de este desierto;
Una voz hiere mi oído,
10 Voz del cielo, que me dice:
Aquí, aquí; y aquí respiro.
(*Se abraza con la cruz.*)
No, no habrá fuerzas humanas
Que me arranquen de este sitio.

15 PADRE GUARDIÁN

(*Levantándose y aparte.*)
¡Será verdad, Dios eterno!
¿Será tan grande y tan alta
La protección que concede
20 Vuestra Madre Soberana[132]
A mí, pecador indigno,
Que cuando soy de esta casa
Humilde prelado, venga
Con resolución tan santa
25 Otra mujer penitente
A ser luz de estas montañas?
¡Bendito seáis, Dios eterno,
Cuya omnipotencia narran
Esos cielos estrellados,
30 Escabel de vuestras plantas!
¿Vuestra vocación es firme? . . .
¿Sois tan bienaventurada? . . .

DOÑA LEONOR

Es inmutable, y cumplirla
35 La voz del cielo me manda.

PADRE GUARDIÁN

Sea, pues, bajo el amparo
De la Virgen Soberana.
40 (*Extiende una mano sobre ella.*)

DOÑA LEONOR

(*Arrojándose a las plantas del* PADRE GUARDIÁN.)
45 ¿Me acogéis? . . . ¡Oh Dios! . . . ¡Oh dicha!

[132] the Virgin Mary

¡Cuán feliz vuestras palabras
Me hacen en este momento! . . .

PADRE GUARDIÁN

(*Levantándola*)
Dad a la Virgen las gracias.
Ella es la que asilo os presta
A la sombra de su casa.
No yo, pecador protervo,
Vil gusano, tierra, nada. (*Pausa.*)

DOÑA LEONOR

Y vos, tan sólo vos, oh Padre mío,
Sabréis que habito en estas asperezas,
Ningún otro mortal.

PADRE GUARDIÁN

Yo solamente
Sabré quién sois. Pero que avise es fuerza
A la comunidad de que la ermita
Está ocupada y de que vive en ella
Una persona penitente. Y nadie,
Bajo precepto santo de obediencia,
Osará aproximarse de cien pasos,
Ni menos penetrar la humilde cerca
Que a gran distancia la circunda en torno.
La mujer santa, antecesora vuestra,
Sólo fué conocida del prelado,
También mi antecesor. Que mujer era,
Lo supieron los otros religiosos,
Cuando se celebraron sus exequias.
Ni yo jamás he de volver a veros:
Cada semana, sí, con gran reserva,
Yo mismo os dejaré junto a la fuente
La escasa provisión: de recogerla
Cuidaréis vos . . . Una pequeña esquila,
Que está sobre la puerta con su cuerda,
Calando a lo interior, tocaréis sólo
De un gran peligro en la ocasión extrema,
O en la hora de la muerte. Su sonido,
A mí, o al que cual yo prelado sea,
Avisará, y espiritual socorro
Jamás os faltará . . . No, nada tema.
La Virgen de los Ángeles os cubre
Con su manto, será vuestra defensa
El ángel del Señor.

DOÑA LEONOR

5 Mas mis hermanos . . .
O bandidos tal vez . . .

PADRE GUARDIÁN

Y ¿quién pudiera
10 Atreverse, hija mía, sin que al punto
Sobre él tronara la venganza eterna?
Cuando vivió la penitente antigua
En este mismo sitio, adonde os lleva
Gracia especial del brazo omnipotente,
15 Tres malhechores, con audacia ciega,
Llegar quisieron al albergue santo;
Al momento una horrísona tormenta
Se alzó, enlutando el indignado cielo,
Y un rayo desprendido de la esfera
20 Hizo ceniza a dos de los bandidos,
Y el tercero, temblando, a nuestra iglesia
Acogióse, vistió el escapulario,
Abrazando contrito nuestra regla,
25 Y murió a los dos meses.

DOÑA LEONOR

Bien: ¡oh Padre!
30 Pues que encontré donde esconderme pueda
A los ojos del mundo, conducidme;
Sin tardanza llevadme . . .

PADRE GUARDIÁN

35 Al punto sea,
Que ya la luz del alba se avecina.
Mas antes entraremos en la iglesia;
Recibiréis mi absolución, y luego
40 El pan de vida y de salud eterna.[133]
Vestiréis el sayal de San Francisco,
Y os daré avisos que importaros puedan
Para la santa y penitente vida,
45 A que con gloria tanta estáis resuelta.

[133] *El pan . . . eterna,* communion wafer

Escena VIII

PADRE GUARDIÁN

¡Hola! . . . Hermano Melitón.
¡Hola! . . . despierte le digo;
De la iglesia abra el postigo.

HERMANO MELITÓN (*Dentro.*)

Pues qué, ¿ya las cinco son? . . .
(*Sale bostezando.*)
Apostaré a que no han dado. (*Bosteza.*)

PADRE GUARDIÁN

La iglesia abra.

HERMANO MELITÓN

No es de día.

PADRE GUARDIÁN

¿Replica? . . . Por vida mía . . .

HERMANO MELITÓN

¿Yo? . . . en mi vida[134] he replicado.
Bien podía el penitente
Hasta las cinco esperar;
5 Difícil será encontrar
Un pecador tan urgente.
(*Vase, y en seguida se oye descorrer el cerrojo de la puerta de la iglesia, y se la ve abrirse lentamente.*)

PADRE GUARDIÁN

10 (*Conduciendo a* LEONOR *hacia la iglesia.*)
Vamos al punto, vamos.
En la casa de Dios, hermana, entremos,
Su nombre bendigamos,
En su misericordia confiemos.
15

Jornada Tercera

La escena es en Italia, en Veletri y sus alrededores.

Escena Primera

(*El teatro representa una sala corta,*[135] *alojamiento de oficiales calaveras. En las paredes estarán colgados en desorden uniformes, capotes, sillas* 20 *de caballos, armas, etc.; en medio habrá una mesa con tapete verde, dos candeleros de bronce con velas de sebo; cuatro oficiales alrededor, uno de ellos con la baraja en la mano: algu-* 25 *nas sillas desocupadas.*)[136]

PEDRAZA (*Entra muy de prisa.*)

¡Qué frío está esto!

OFICIAL 1.°

Todos se han ido en cuanto me han 30 desplumado:[137] no he conseguido tirar ni una buena talla.[138]

PEDRAZA

Pues precisamente va a venir un gran punto,[139] y si ve esto tan desierto y frío . . .

OFICIAL 1.°

¿Y quién es el pájaro?

TODOS

¿Quién?

PEDRAZA

El ayudante del General, ese teniente coronel que ha llegado con la orden de que al amanecer estemos sobre las armas.[140] Es gran aficionado, tiene mucho rumbo,[141] y a lo que parece es blanquito.[142] Hemos cenado juntos en

[134] never. Again Melitón introduces comic relief reminiscent of Shakespeare's gatekeeper in *Macbeth*.

[135] A setting occupying only the front of the stage, so that another set can be ready behind it.

[136] Once more the act starts with a picturesque scene serving to bring in suspense with respect to the main plot.

[137] to clean one out

[138] hand

[139] clever fellow (said ironically). Perhaps a play on words is intended, for *punto* can mean a 'better' in gambling. Compare the English word 'punter,' meaning 'better.'

[140] under arms

[141] *tener mucho rumbo,* to make a great splurge

[142] an easy mark (*blanco* means *target*)

casa de la coronela, a quien ya le está echando requiebros, y el taimado de nuestro capellán[143] lo marcó por suyo. Le convidó con que viniera a jugar, y ya lo trae hacia aquí.

OFICIAL 1.°

Pues, señores, ya es éste otro cantar. Ya vamos a ser todos unos . . .[144] ¿Me entienden ustedes?

TODOS

Sí, sí, muy bien pensado.

OFICIAL 2.°

Como que es de plana mayor,[145] y será contrario de los pobres pilíes.[146]

OFICIAL 4.°

A él, y duro.

OFICIAL 1.°

Pues para jugar con él tengo baraja preparada, más obediente que un recluta y más florida[147] que el mes de Mayo . . . (*Saca una baraja del bolsillo.*) Y aquí está.

OFICIAL 3.°

¡Qué fino es usted, camarada!

OFICIAL 1.°

No hay que jugar ases ni figuras.[148] Y al avío,[149] que ya suena gente en la escalera. Tiro,[150] tres a la derecha, nueve a la izquierda.

ESCENA II

(*Entran* DON CARLOS DE VARGAS *y el* CAPELLÁN.)

CAPELLÁN

Aquí viene, compañeros,
Un rumboso aficionado.

5 TODOS

Sea, pues, muy bien llegado.
(*Levantándose y volviéndose a sentar.*)

DON CARLOS

Buenas noches, caballeros.
10 ¡Qué casa tan indecente! (*Aparte.*)
Estoy, vive Dios, corrido
De verme comprometido
A alternar con esta gente.

OFICIAL 1.°

15 Sentaos.
(*Se sienta* DON CARLOS, *haciéndole todos lugar.*)

CAPELLÁN

Señor capitán, (*Al banquero.*)
20 ¿Y el concurso?

OFICIAL 1.°

Se afufó (*Barajando.*)
En cuanto me desbancó.
Toditos repletos van.
25 Se declaró un juego eterno
Que no he podido quebrar,
Y siempre salió a ganar
Una sota del infierno.[151]
Veintidós veces salió
30 Y jamás a la derecha.

OFICIAL 2.°

El que nunca se aprovecha
De tales gangas[152] soy yo.

OFICIAL 3.°

35 Y yo en el juego contrario
Me empeñé, que nada vi,

[143] *el taimado . . . capellán,* our sly chaplain
[144] Complete the sentence with some word such as *santos* (said ironically).
[145] *plana mayor,* general staff
[146] A word not in the dictionaries, probably military slang for *ordinary officers.*
[147] flowery; but figuratively, select, carefully chosen
[148] picture cards
[149] *al avío,* begin the preparations
[150] I deal
[151] *una . . . infierno,* a cursed jack
[152] easy pickings

Y ya sólo estoy aquí
Para rezar el rosario.

CAPELLÁN

Vamos.

PEDRAZA

Vamos.

OFICIAL 1.°

Tiro.

DON CARLOS

Juego.

OFICIAL 1.°

Tiro, a la derecha el as,
Y a la izquierda la sotita.

OFICIAL 2.°

Ya salió la muy maldita.
Por vida de Barrabás . . .

OFICIAL 1.°

Rey a la derecha, nueve
A la izquierda.

DON CARLOS

Yo lo gano.

OFICIAL 1.°

¡Tengo apestada la mano! (*Paga.*)
Tres onzas, nada se debe.
A la derecha la sota.

OFICIAL 4.°

Ya quebró.[153]

OFICIAL 3.°

Pegarle fuego.[154]

OFICIAL 1.°

A la izquierda siete.

DON CARLOS

Juego.

OFICIAL 2.°

Sólo el verla me rebota. 5

DON CARLOS

Copo.[155]

CAPELLÁN

¿Con carta tapada?[156]

OFICIAL 1.°

10 Tiro, a la derecha el tres.

PEDRAZA

¡Qué bonita carta es!

OFICIAL 1.°

15 Cuando sale descargada.[157]
A la izquierda el cinco.

DON CARLOS

(*Levantándose y sujetando la mano del que talla.*)
No,
20 Con tiento, señor banquero,
(*Vuelve su carta.*)
Que he ganado mi dinero,
Y trampas no sufro yo.

OFICIAL 1.°

25 ¿Cómo trampas? . . . ¿Quién osar . . . ?

DON CARLOS

Yo: pegado tras del cinco
Está el caballo; buen brinco
Le hicisteis, amigo, dar.[158]

OFICIAL 1.°

30 Soy hombre pundonoroso,
Y esto una casualidad . . .

[153] At last it has broken [its streak of falling on the left].
[154] Burn it up!; Curse it!
[155] I cover [the entire amount of the bank].
[156] With a card still to be dealt?
[157] Probably a metaphor comparing the card to an unloaded (*descargado*) gun, hence harmless.
[158] The dealer slipped the *caballo* (queen) behind the five.

DON CARLOS

Ésta es una iniquidad;
Vos un taimado tramposo.

PEDRAZA

Sois un loco, un atrevido.

DON CARLOS

Vos un vil, y con la espada . . .

TODOS

Ésta es una casa honrada.

CAPELLÁN

Por Dios, no hagamos ruído.

DON CARLOS

(*Echando a rodar la mesa.*)
Abreviemos de razones.

TODOS (*Tomando las espadas.*)
¡Muera, muera el insolente!

DON CARLOS

(*Sale defendiéndose.*)
¿Qué puede con un valiente
Una cueva de ladrones?
(*Salen de la estancia acuchillándose, y dos o tres soldados retiran la mesa, las sillas y desembarazan la escena.*)

ESCENA III

(*El teatro representa una selva en noche muy obscura. Aparece al fondo* DON ÁLVARO, *solo, vestido de capitán de granaderos; se acerca lentamente, y dice con gran agitación.*)

DON ÁLVARO *solo.*[159]

¡Qué carga tan insufrible
Es el ambiente vital,
Para el mezquino mortal
Que nace en signo terrible!
¡Qué eternidad tan horrible
La breve vida! ¡Este mundo,
5 Qué calabozo profundo
Para el hombre desdichado,
A quien mira el cielo airado
Con su ceño furibundo!
Parece, sí, que a medida
10 Que es más dura y más amarga,
Más extiende, más alarga
El destino nuestra vida.
Si nos está concedida
Sólo para padecer,
15 Y debe muy breve ser
La[160] del feliz, como en pena
De que su objeto no llena,[161]
¡Terrible cosa es nacer!
Al que tranquilo, gozoso
20 Vive entre aplausos y honores,
Y de inocentes amores
Apura el cáliz sabroso,
Cuando[162] es más fuerte y brioso,
La muerte sus dichas huella[163]
25 Sus venturas atropella;
Y yo que infelice soy,
Yo que buscándola voy,
No puedo encontrar con ella.
¿Mas cómo la he de obtener,
30 ¡Desventurado de mí!
Pues cuando infeliz nací,
Nací para envejecer?
Si aquel día de placer
(Que uno sólo he disfrutado)
35 Fortuna hubiese fijado,[164]
¡Cuán pronto muerte precoz
Con su guadaña feroz
Mi cuello hubiera segado!
Para engalanar mi frente,
40 Allá en la abrasada zona,
Con la espléndida corona
Del imperio de Occidente,
Amor y ambición ardiente

[159] This famous soliloquy is Don Álvaro's first revelation of his intimate feelings. Up to this point, almost half-way through the play, he has only appeared briefly, yet he has dominated the play. Now he meditates on the cruel Fate which has ruled his existence.

[160] Supply: *vida*

[161] *como . . . llena,* as if in retribution for not fulfilling its [Life's] objective [of suffering]

[162] at the very time that

[163] to trample underfoot

[164] Fortune had stopped its wheel, i.e. had allowed me to remain happy with Leonor

Me engendraron de concierto;[165]
Pero con tal desacierto,
Con tan contraria fortuna,
Que una cárcel fué mi cuna,
Y fué mi escuela el desierto.
Entre bárbaros crecí,
Y en la edad de la razón,
A cumplir la obligación
Que un hijo tiene, acudí:
Mi nombre ocultando fuí
(Que es un crimen) a salvar
La vida, y así pagar
A los que a mí me la dieron.[166]
Que un trono soñando vieron
Y un cadalso al despertar.
Entonces risueño un día,
Uno sólo, nada más,
Me dió el destino; quizás
Con intención más impía.
Así[167] en la cárcel sombría
Mete una luz el sayón,
Con la tirana intención
De que un punto el preso vea
El horror que lo rodea
En su espantosa mansión.
¡Sevilla!!! ¡Guadalquivir!!![168]
¡Cuál atormentáis mi mente! . . .
Noche en que vi de repente
Mis breves dichas huir!
¡Oh qué carga es el vivir! . . .
¡Cielos, saciad el furor! . . .
Socórreme, mi Leonor,
Gala del suelo andaluz,
Que ya eres ángel de luz
Junto al trono del Señor.[169]
Mírame desde tu altura
Sin nombre en extraña tierra,
Empeñado en una guerra
Por ganar mi sepultura.
¿Qué me importa, por ventura,
Que triunfe Carlos o no?
5 ¿Qué tengo de Italia en pro?
¿Qué tengo? ¡Terrible suerte!
Que en ella reina la muerte,
Y a la muerte busco yo.
¡Cuánto, oh Dios, cuánto se engaña
10 El que elogia mi ardor ciego,
Viéndome siempre en el fuego
De esta extranjera campaña!
Llámanme la prez de España,
Y no saben que mi ardor
15 Sólo es falta de valor,
Pues busco ansioso el morir
Por no osar el resistir
De los astros el furor.
Si el mundo colma de honores
20 Al que mata a su enemigo,
El que lo[170] lleva consigo
¿Por qué no puede . . .?
(*Óyese ruido de espadas.*)

DON CARLOS (*Dentro.*)

25 ¡Traidores!!![171]

VOCES (*Dentro.*)

¡Muera!

30 DON CARLOS (*Dentro.*)

¡Viles!

DON ÁLVARO (*Sorprendido.*)

¡Qué clamores!

35 DON CARLOS (*Dentro.*)

¡Socorro!!!

[165] Another hint about his parentage, implying that he was heir to the Empire of the Incas.

[166] The first light on the central mystery of the play. We have wondered why Don Álvaro didn't tell the Marqués de Calatrava who he was. But now we see that even telling his name is a crime. Furthermore, Don Álvaro's parents are in mortal danger, and his trip to Spain is an attempt to save them.

[167] just so

[168] Remember that Rivas was an exile from his beloved Andalucía when he penned these lines. In his lyric poetry he frequently inserts passages in praise of his native region.

[169] He believes that Leonor is dead just as she originally thought that Don Álvaro was killed on the night of their elopement.

[170] *Lo* refers to *enemigo;* the one who is his own enemy. Why can't he [take his own life]? Don Álvaro is again Christian (as he was in the matter of marriage) in his refusal to commit suicide. Again he differs from the general run of romantic characters and authors.

[171] The interrupting of Don Álvaro's meditation by some of the most violent action of the play is a clever dramatic device. The soliloquy could not be allowed to peter out to a weak ending.

DON ÁLVARO

(*Desenvainando la espada.*)
Dárselo quiero,
Que oigo crujir el acero;
Y si a los peligros voy
Porque desgraciado soy,
También voy por caballero.
(*Éntrase; suena ruido de espadas; atraviesan dos hombres la escena como fugitivos, y vuelven a salir* DON ÁLVARO 10 *y* DON CARLOS.)

ESCENA IV

DON ÁLVARO

Huyeron . . . ¿Estáis herido?

DON CARLOS

Mil gracias os doy, señor;
Sin vuestro heroico valor
De cierto estaba perdido;
Y no fuera maravilla:
Eran siete contra mí,
Y cuando grité, me vi
En tierra ya una rodilla.

DON ÁLVARO

¿Y herido estáis?

DON CARLOS (*Reconociéndose.*)[172]

Nada siento.
(*Envainan.*)

DON ÁLVARO

¿Quiénes eran?

DON CARLOS

Asesinos.

DON ÁLVARO

¿Cómo osaron tan vecinos
De un militar campamento? . . .

DON CARLOS

Os lo diré francamente:
Fué contienda sobre el juego.
Entré sin pensarlo, ciego,
En un casuco indecente . . .

DON ÁLVARO

5 Ya caigo, aquí, á mano diestra . . .

DON CARLOS

Sí.

DON ÁLVARO

Que extrañe perdonad,
Que un hombre de calidad,
Cual vuestro esfuerzo demuestra,
Entrara en tal gazapón,
15 Donde sólo va la hez,
La canalla más soez,
De la milicia borrón.[173]

DON CARLOS

Sólo el ser recién llegado
20 Puede, señor, disculparme;
Vinieron a convidarme,
Y accedí desalumbrado.

DON ÁLVARO

¿Con que ha poco estáis aquí?

25 DON CARLOS

Diez días ha que llegué
A Italia; dos sólo que
Al cuartel general fuí.
Y esta tarde al campamento
30 Con comisión especial
Llegué de mi general,
Para el reconocimiento
De mañana. Y si no fuera
Por vuestra espada y favor,
35 Mi carrera sin honor
Ya terminada estuviera.
Mi gratitud sepa, pues,
A quién la vida he debido,
Porque el ser agradecido
40 La obligación mayor es
Para el hombre bien nacido.

DON ÁLVARO (*Con indiferencia.*)

Al acaso.[174]

[172] feeling himself
[173] stain. Word order: *borrón de la milicia*

[174] [You owe your life] to chance.

DON CARLOS (*Con expresión.*)

Que me deis
Vuestro nombre a suplicaros
Me atrevo. Y para obligaros,
Primero el mío sabréis.
(Siento no decir verdad) (*Aparte.*)
Soy don Félix de Avendaña,
Que he venido a esta campaña
Sólo por curiosidad.
Soy teniente coronel,
Y del general Briones
Ayudante: relaciones
Tengo de sangre con él.

DON ÁLVARO (*Aparte.*)

¡Qué franco es y qué expresivo!
Me cautiva el corazón.

DON CARLOS

Me parece que es razón
Que sepa yo por quién vivo,
Pues la gratitud es ley.

DON ÁLVARO

Soy . . . don Fadrique de Herreros,
Capitán de granaderos
Del regimiento del Rey.

DON CARLOS

(*Con grande admiración y entusiasmo.*)
¿Sois . . . ¡grande dicha es la mía!
Del ejército español
La gloria, el radiante sol
De la hispana valentía?

DON ÁLVARO

Señor . . .

DON CARLOS

Desde que llegué
A Italia, sólo elogiaros
Y prez de España llamaros
Por donde quiera escuché.
Y de español tan valiente
Anhelaba la amistad.

DON ÁLVARO

Con ella, señor, contad,
Que me honráis muy altamente.
Y según os he encontrado
5 Contra tantos combatiendo
Bizarramente, comprendo
Que seréis muy buen soldado.
Y la gran cortesanía
Que en vuestro trato mostráis,
10 Dice a voces que gozáis
De aventajada hidalguía.
(*Empieza a amanecer.*)
Venid, pues, a descansar
A mi tienda.

DON CARLOS

15 Tanto honor,
Será muy corto, señor,
Que el alba empieza a asomar.
(*Se oye a lo lejos tocar generala a las bandas de tambores.*[175])

20 DON ÁLVARO

Y por todo el campamento,
De los tambores el son
Convoca a la formación.
Me voy a mi regimiento.

DON CARLOS

25 Yo también, y a vuestro lado
Asistiré en la pelea,
Donde os admire y os vea
Como a mi ejemplo y dechado.

DON ÁLVARO

30 Favorecedor y amigo,
Si sois cual cortés valiente,[176]
Yo de vuestro arrojo ardiente
Seré envidioso testigo. (*Vanse.*)

ESCENA V

(*El teatro representa un risueño*
35 *campo de Italia, al amanecer; se verá a lo lejos el pueblo de Veletri y varios puestos militares; algunos cuerpos de tropa cruzan la escena, y luego sale una compañía de infantería con el*

[175] *tocar . . . tambores,* the drum corps beat the call to arms

[176] *Si . . . valiente,* If you are [as] brave as [you are] courteous

CAPITÁN, *el* TENIENTE *y el* SUBTENIENTE: DON CARLOS *sale a caballo con una ordenanza detrás y coloca la compañía a un lado, avanzando una guerrilla al fondo del teatro.*)

DON CARLOS

Señor capitán, permaneceréis aquí hasta nueva orden; pero si los enemigos arrollan[177] las guerrillas y se dirigen a esa altura donde está la compañía de Cantabria, marchad a socorrerla a todo trance.

CAPITÁN

Está bien: cumpliré con mi obligación. (*Vase* DON CARLOS.)

ESCENA VI

CAPITÁN

Granaderos, en su lugar, descanso. Parece que lo entiende este ayudante. (*Salen los oficiales de las filas y se reúnen, mirando con un anteojo hacia donde suena rumor de fusilería.*)

TENIENTE

Se va galopando al fuego como un energúmeno y la acción se empeña[178] más y más.

SUBTENIENTE

Y me parece que ha de ser muy caliente.

CAPITÁN

(*Mirando con el anteojo.*)
Bien combaten los granaderos del Rey.

TENIENTE

Como que llevan a la cabeza a la prez de España, al valiente don Fadrique de Herreros, que pelea como un desesperado.

SUBTENIENTE

(*Tomando el anteojo y mirando con él.*)
Pues los alemanes cargan[179] a la bayoneta y con brío; adiós, que nos desalojan de aquel puesto. (*Se aumenta el tiroteo.*)

CAPITÁN (*Toma el anteojo.*)

A ver, a ver . . . ¡Ay! Si no me engaño, el capitán de granaderos del Rey ha caído o muerto o herido; lo veo claro, muy claro.

TENIENTE

Yo distingo que se arremolina la compañía . . . y creo que retrocede.

SOLDADOS

¡A ellos, a ellos!

CAPITÁN

Silencio. Firmes. (*Vuelve a mirar con el anteojo.*) Las guerrillas también retroceden.

SUBTENIENTE

Uno corre a caballo hacia allá.

CAPITÁN

Sí, es el ayudante . . . Está reuniendo la gente y carga . . . ¡con qué denuedo! . . . nuestro es el día.

TENIENTE

Sí, veo huir a los alemanes.

SOLDADOS

¡A ellos!

CAPITÁN

Firmes, granaderos. (*Mira con el anteojo.*) El ayudante ha recobrado el puesto, la compañía del Rey carga a la bayoneta y lo arrolla todo.

[177] to crush
[178] to become violent
[179] to charge

TENIENTE

A ver, a ver. (*Toma el anteojo y mira.*) Sí, cierto. Y el ayudante se apea del caballo y retira en sus brazos al capitán don Fadrique. No debe de estar más que herido; se lo llevan hacia Veletri.

TODOS

Dios nos le conserve, que es la flor del ejército.

CAPITÁN

Pero por este lado no va tan bien. Teniente, vaya usted a reforzar con la mitad de la compañía las guerrillas que están en esa cañada; que yo voy a acercarme a la compañía de Cantabria; vamos, vamos.

SOLDADOS

¡Viva España! ¡Viva España! ¡Viva Nápoles![180]
(*Marchan.*)

ESCENA VII

(*El teatro representa el alojamiento de un oficial superior; al frente estará la puerta de la alcoba practicable y con cortinas. Entra* DON ÁLVARO *herido y desmayado en una camilla, llevada por cuatro granaderos, el* CIRUJANO *a un lado y* DON CARLOS *a otro, lleno de polvo y como muy cansado; un soldado traerá la maleta de* DON ÁLVARO *y la pondrá sobre una mesa; colocarán la camilla en medio de la escena, mientras los granaderos entran en la alcoba a hacer la cama.*)

DON CARLOS

Con mucho, mucho cuidado,
Dejadle aquí, y al momento
Entrad a arreglar mi cama.
(*Vanse a la alcoba dos de los soldados y quedan otros dos.*)

CIRUJANO

Y que haya mucho silencio. 5

DON ÁLVARO

(*Volviendo en sí.*)
¿Dónde estoy? ¿Dónde? 10

DON CARLOS

(*Con mucho cariño.*)
En Veletri,
A mi lado, amigo excelso. 15
Nuestra ha sido la victoria,
Tranquilo estad.

DON ÁLVARO

¡Dios eterno! 20
¡Con salvarme de la muerte,
Qué gran daño me habéis hecho!

DON CARLOS

No digáis tal, don Fadrique,
Cuando tan vano[181] me encuentro 25
De que salvaros la vida
Me haya concedido el cielo.

DON ÁLVARO

¡Ay, don Félix de Avendaña, 30
Qué grande mal me habéis hecho!
(*Se desmaya.*)

CIRUJANO

Otra vez se ha desmayado: 35
Agua y vinagre.

DON CARLOS

(*A uno de los soldados.*)
Al momento. 40
¿Está de mucho peligro? (*Al* CIRUJANO.)

[180] Naples was once a viceroyalty of Spain. In the eighteenth century it became a separate kingdom under Spanish protection. At the time of the play there was a real battle (1744) at Velletri, near Rome, between the Neopolitans and Spaniards on one side and the Austrians on the other. King Carlos of Naples, mentioned soon, later became Carlos III of Spain, noted for his enlightened policies.

[181] proud

CIRUJANO

Este balazo del pecho,
En donde aun tiene la bala,
Me da muchísimo miedo;
Lo que es las otras heridas
No presentan tanto riesgo.

DON CARLOS

(*Con gran vehemencia.*)
Salvad su vida, salvadle;
Apurad todos los medios
Del arte, y os aseguro
Tal galardón . . .

CIRUJANO

Lo agradezco:
Para cumplir con mi oficio
No necesito de cebo,[182]
Que en salvar a este valiente
Interés muy grande tengo.
(*Entra el soldado con un vaso de agua y vinagre. El* CIRUJANO *le rocía el rostro y le aplica un pomito a las narices.*)

DON ÁLVARO (*Vuelve en sí.*)

¡Ay!

DON CARLOS

Ánimo, noble amigo,
Cobrad ánimo y aliento:
Pronto, muy pronto curado
Y restablecido y bueno
Volveréis a ser la gloria,
El norte de los guerreros.
Y a vuestras altas hazañas
El Rey dará todo el premio
Que merecen. Sí, muy pronto
Lozano otra vez, cubierto
De palmas inmarchitables
Y de laureles eternos,
Con una rica encomienda[183]
Se adornará vuestro pecho
De Santiago o Calatrava.[184]

DON ÁLVARO (*Muy agitado.*)

¿Qué escucho? ¿Qué? ¡Santo cielo!
¡Ah! . . . no, no de Calatrava:
Jamás, jamás . . . ¡Dios eterno!

5 CIRUJANO

Ya otra vez se desmayó:
Sin quietud y sin silencio
No habrá forma de curarlo.
Que no le habléis más os ruego.
10 (*A* DON CARLOS.—*Vuelvo a darle agua y a aplicarle el pomito a las narices.*)

DON CARLOS

(*Suspenso, aparte.*)
El nombre de Calatrava
15 ¿Qué tendrá, qué tendrá . . . tiemblo,
De terrible a sus oídos? . . .[185]

CIRUJANO

No puede esperar más tiempo.
¿Aun no está lista la cama?

20 DON CARLOS

(*Mirando a la alcoba.*)
Ya lo está.
(*Salen los dos soldados.*)

CIRUJANO

25 (*A los cuatro soldados.*)
Llevadle luego.

DON ÁLVARO

¡Ay de mí! (*Volviendo en sí.*)

30 CIRUJANO

Llevadle.

DON ÁLVARO

35 (*Haciendo esfuerzos.*)
Esperen.

[182] bait; figuratively, incentive
[183] cross; honorary decoration carrying with it important duties and rewards
[184] The Knights of Santiago and Calatrava were similar to the Knights of the Temple (Templars), originally half-monks, half-fighting men. In Spain these military orders were founded in the Middle Ages to aid against the Moors; in later times they were mainly honorary (cf. the Orders of the Bath and of the Garter in present-day England).
[185] Don Álvaro's violent reaction to the word *Calatrava* (to him the title of the dead Marqués) sows suspicion in Don Carlos's mind.

Poco, por lo que en mí siento,
Me queda ya de este mundo,
Y en el otro pensar debo.
Mas antes de desprenderme
De la vida, de un gran peso 5
Quiero descargarme. Amigo,
(*A* DON CARLOS.)
Un favor tan sólo anhelo.

CIRUJANO

Si habláis, señor, no es posible . . .

DON ÁLVARO

No volver a hablar prometo.
Pero sólo una palabra,
Y a él solo, que decir tengo.

DON CARLOS

(*Al* CIRUJANO *y soldados.*)
Apartad, démosle gusto;
Dejadnos por un momento.
(*Se retira el* CIRUJANO *y los asistentes a un lado.*)

DON ÁLVARO

Don Félix, vos solo, solo, (*Dale la mano.*)
Cumpliréis con lo que quiero
De vos exigir. Juradme
Por la fe de caballero
Que haréis cuanto aquí os encargue,
Con inviolable secreto.

DON CARLOS

Yo os lo juro, amigo mío;
Acabad, pues.
(*Hace un esfuerzo* DON ÁLVARO *como para meter la mano en el bolsillo y no puede.*)

DON ÁLVARO

¡Ah! . . . no puedo.
Meted en este bolsillo,
Que tengo aquí al lado izquierdo
Sobre el corazón, la mano.
(*Lo hace* DON CARLOS.)
¿Halláis algo en él?

DON CARLOS

Sí, encuentro
Una llavecita . . .

DON ÁLVARO

Es ésa.
(*Saca* DON CARLOS *la llave.*)
Con ella abrid, yo os lo ruego, 10
A solas y sin testigos,
Una caja que en el centro
Hallaréis de mi maleta.
En ella con sobre y sello
Un legajo hay de papeles; 15
Custodiadlos con esmero,
Y al momento que yo expire
Los daréis, amigo, al fuego.

DON CARLOS

¿Sin abrirlos? 20

DON ÁLVARO

(*Muy agitado.*)
Sin abrirlos,
Que en ellos hay un misterio
Impenetrable . . . ¿Palabra
Me dais, don Félix, de hacerlo? 25

DON CARLOS

Yo os la doy con toda el alma.

DON ÁLVARO 30

Entonces tranquilo muero.
Dadme el postrimer abrazo,
Y ¡adiós, adiós!

CIRUJANO (*Enfadado.*) 35

Al momento
A la alcoba. Y vos, don Félix,
Si es que tenéis tanto empeño
En que su vida se salve,
Haced que guarde silencio: 40
Y excusad también que os vea,
Pues se conmueve en extremo.
(*Llévanse los soldados la camilla; entra también el* CIRUJANO, *y* DON CARLOS *queda pensativo y lloroso.*) 45

ESCENA VIII

DON CARLOS

¿Ha de morir . . . ¡qué rigor!
Tan bizarro militar?
Si no lo puedo salvar
Será eterno mi dolor.
Puesto que él me salvó á mi,
Y desde el momento aquel
Que guardó mi vida él,
Guardar la suya ofrecí. (*Pausa.*)
Nunca vi tanta destreza
En las armas, y jamás
Otra persona de más
Arrogancia y gentileza.
Pero es hombre singular;
Y en el corto tiempo que
Le trato, rasgos noté
Que son dignos de extrañar. (*Pausa.*)
¿Y de Calatrava el nombre
Por qué así le horrorizó
Cuando pronunciarlo oyó? . . .
¿Qué hallará en él que le asombre?
¡Sabrá que está deshonrado! . . .
Será un hidalgo andaluz . . .
¡Cielos! . . . ¡Qué rayo de luz
Sobre mí habéis derramado
En este momento! . . . Sí.
¿Podrá ser éste el traidor,
De mi sangre deshonor,
El que a buscar vine aquí?
(*Furioso y empuñando la espada.*)
¿Y aun respira? . . . No, ahora mismo
A mis manos . . .
(*Corre hacia la alcoba y se detiene.*)
¿Dónde estoy? . . .
¿Ciego a despeñarme voy
De la infamia en el abismo?
¿A quien mi vida salvó,
Y que muribundo está,
Matar inerme podrá
Un caballero cual yo? (*Pausa.*)
¿No puede falsa salir
Mi sospecha? . . . Sí . . . ¿Quién sabe? . . .
Pero ¡cielos! esta llave
Todo me lo va a decir.
(*Se acerca a la maleta, la abre precipitado y saca la caja, poniéndola sobre la mesa.*)
Salid, caja misteriosa,
5 Del destino urna fatal,
A quien[186] con sudor mortal
Toca mi mano medrosa:
Me impide abrirte el temblor
Que me causa el recelar
10 Si en tu centro voy a hallar
Los pedazos de mi honor.
(*Resuelto y abriendo.*)
Mas no, que en ti mi esperanza,
La luz que me da el destino,
15 Está para hallar[187] camino
Que me lleve a la venganza.
(*Abre y saca un legajo sellado.*)
Ya el legajo tengo aquí.
¿Qué tardo el sello en romper? . . .
20 (*Se contiene.*)
¡Oh cielos! ¡Qué voy a hacer!
¿Y la palabra que di?
¿Mas si la suerte me da
Tan inesperado medio
25 De dar a mi honor remedio,
El perderlo qué será?
Si a Italia sólo he venido
A buscar al matador
De mi padre y de mi honor,
30 Con nombre y porte[188] fingido,
¿Qué importa que el pliego abra,
Si lo que vine a buscar
A Italia voy a encontrar? . . .
Pero no, di mi palabra.
35 Nadie, nadie aquí lo ve . . .
¡Cielos! lo estoy viendo yo.
Mas si él mi vida salvó,
También la suya salvé.
Y si es el infame indiano,
40 El seductor asesino,
¿No es bueno cualquier camino
Por donde venga a mi mano?
Rompo esta cubierta, sí,
Pues nadie lo ha de saber . . .
45 Mas ¡cielos! ¿qué voy a hacer?
¿Y la palabra que di? (*Suelta el legajo.*)
No, jamás. ¡Cuán fácilmente

[186] which. Carlos is personifying the box; hence, he uses *a quien.*

[187] *Está para hallar,* is about to find

[188] bearing; here, way of life

Nos pinta nuestra pasión
Una infame y vil acción
Como acción indiferente!
A Italia vine anhelando
Mi honor manchado lavar;
¿Y mi empresa he de empezar
El honor amancillando?
Queda, oh secreto, escondido,
Si en este legajo estás;
Que un medio infame, jamás
Lo usa el hombre bien nacido.[189]
(*Registrando la maleta.*)
Si encontrar aquí pudiera
Algún otro abierto indicio
Que, sin hacer prejüicio
A mi opinión,[190] me advirtiera . . .
(*Sorprendido.*)
¡Cielos! . . . lo hay . . . esta cajilla,
(*Saca una cajita como de retrato.*)
Que algún retrato contiene,
(*Reconociéndola.*)
Ni sello ni sobre tiene,
Tiene sólo una aldabilla.
Hasta sin ser indiscreto
Reconocerla me es dado;
Nada de ella me han hablado,
Ni rompo ningún secreto.
Ábrola, pues, en buen hora,
Aunque un basilisco[191] vea,
Aunque para el mundo sea
Caja fatal de Pandora.
(*La abre, y exclama muy agitado.*)
¡Cielos! . . . no . . . no me engañé,
Ésta es mi hermana Leonor . . .
¿Para qué prueba mayor? . . .
Con la más clara encontré.
Ya está todo averiguado;
Don Álvaro es el herido.
Brújula el retrato ha sido
Que mi norte[192] me ha marcado.
5 ¿Y a la infame . . . me atribulo,
Con él en Italia tiene? . . .
Descubrirlo me conviene
Con astucia y disimulo.
¡Cuán feliz será mi suerte
10 Si la venganza y castigo
Sólo de un golpe consigo,[193]
A los dos dando la muerte! . . .
Mas . . . ¡ah! . . . no me precipite
Mi honra ¡cielos! ofendida.
15 Guardad a este hombre la vida
Para que yo se la quite.
(*Vuelve a colocar los papeles y el retrato en la maleta. Se oye ruido, y queda suspenso.*)
20

Escena IX

(*El* CIRUJANO *sale muy contento.*)

CIRUJANO
25
Albricias pediros quiero;
Ya le he sacado la bala, (*Se la enseña.*)
Y no es la herida tan mala
Cual me pareció primero.
30
DON CARLOS

(*Le abraza fuera de sí.*)
¿De veras? . . . Feliz me hacéis:
Por ver bueno al capitán,
35 Tengo, amigo, más afan
Del que imaginar podéis.[194]

[189] Since we know that the letters will shed light on Don Álvaro's parentage and his reasons for hiding his identity, we cannot help wishing that Don Carlos would look at them. We suspect that once the latter knows who Don Álvaro is, the chances of settling their differences peacefully are much greater. But through the irony of Fate, the noble sentiment of honor prohibits this solution.

[190] reputation, honor

[191] A fabulous beast, the basilisk, which killed merely by looking at its victim

[192] course, path

[193] *Sólo . . . consigo,* I get with just one blow

[194] Carlos' sense of honor is exactly like that of the heroes of the dramas of the Golden Age. In addition to honor, *Don Álvaro* resembles the older plays in many ways—the amount of action, the duels, the disguises, etc.

JORNADA CUARTA

La escena es en Veletri.

ESCENA PRIMERA

(*El teatro representa una sala corta, de alojamiento militar.* DON ÁLVARO *y* DON CARLOS.)

DON CARLOS

Hoy que vuestra cuarentena[195]
Dichosamente cumplís,
¿De salud cómo os sentís?
¿Es completamente buena? . . . 10
¿Reliquia alguna notáis
De haber tanto padecido?
¿Del todo restablecido,
Y listo y fuerte os halláis?

DON ÁLVARO

Estoy como si tal cosa;[196]
Nunca tuve más salud,
Y a vuestra solicitud
Debo mi cura asombrosa. 20
Sois excelente enfermero;
Ni una madre por un hijo
Muestra un afán más prolijo,
Tan gran cuidado y esmero.

DON CARLOS

En extremo interesante
Me era la vida salvaros.[197]

DON ÁLVARO

¿Y con qué, amigo, pagaros
Podré interés semejante?
Y aunque gran mal me habéis hecho
En salvar mi amarga vida,
Será eterna y sin medida
La gratitud de mi pecho.

DON CARLOS

¿Y estáis tan repuesto y fuerte
Que sin ventaja pudiera
Un enemigo cualquiera?[198] . . .

DON ÁLVARO

Estoy, amigo, de suerte
Que en casa del coronel
He estado ya a presentarme,
5 Y de alta acabo de darme[199]
Ahora mismo en el cuartel.

DON CARLOS

¿De veras?

DON ÁLVARO

¿Os enojáis
Porque ayer no os dije acaso
Que iba hoy a dar este paso?
15 Como tanto me cuidáis,
Que os opusierais temí;
Y estando sano, en verdad,
Vivir en la ociosidad
No era honroso para mí.

DON CARLOS

¿Conque ya no os duele nada,
Ni hay asomo de flaqueza
En el pecho, en la cabeza,
25 Ni en el brazo de la espada?

DON ÁLVARO

No . . . Pero parece que
Algo, amigo, os atormenta,
30 Y que acaso os descontenta
El que yo tan bueno esté.

DON CARLOS

¡Al contrario! . . . Al veros bueno,
35 Capaz de entrar en acción,
Palpita mi corazón
Del placer más alto lleno.
Solamente no quisiera
Que os engañara el valor,
40 Y que el personal vigor
En una ocasión[200] cualquiera . . .

[195] convalescence
[196] *Estoy . . . cosa,* I'm in the pink
[197] Word order: *Me era en extremo interesante* [*importante*] *salvaros la vida.*
[198] *Que sin . . . cualquiera,* that any enemy might [fight you] without having an advantage over you
[199] *dar de alta,* to release [from hospital], to declare cured
[200] danger, quarrel

DON ÁLVARO

¿Queréis pruebas?

DON CARLOS

(*Con vehemencia.*)
Las deseo.

DON ÁLVARO

A la descubierta vamos
De mañana, y enredamos
Un rato de tiroteo.[201]

DON CARLOS

La prueba se puede hacer,
Pues que estáis fuerte, sin ir
Tan lejos a combatir,
Que no hay tiempo que perder.

DON ÁLVARO

(*Confuso.*)
No os entiendo . . .

DON CARLOS

¿No tendréis,
Sin ir a los imperiales,[202]
Enemigos personales
Con quien probaros podréis?

DON ÁLVARO

¿A quién le faltan? . . . Mas no
Lo que me decís comprendo.

DON CARLOS

Os lo está a voces diciendo
Más la conciencia que yo.
Disimular fuera en vano . . .
Vuestra turbación es harta . . .
¿Habéis recibido carta
De don Álvaro el indiano?

DON ÁLVARO

(*Fuera de sí.*)
¡Ah, traidor! . . . ¡Ah, fementido! . . .
Violaste infame un secreto,
Que yo débil, yo indiscreto,
Moribundo . . . inadvertido . . .

DON CARLOS

¿Qué osais pensar? . . . Respeté
5 Vuestros papeles sellados,
Que los que nacen honrados
Se portan cual me porté.
El retrato de la infame
Vuestra cómplice os perdió,
10 Y sin lengua me pidió
Que el suyo y mi honor reclame.
Don Carlos de Vargas soy,
Que por vuestro crimen es
De Calatrava marqués:
15 Temblad, que ante vos estoy.

DON ÁLVARO

No sé temblar . . . Sorprendido,
Sí, me tenéis . . .

20 DON CARLOS

No lo extraño.

DON ÁLVARO

¿Y usurpar con un engaño
25 Mi amistad honrado ha sido?
¡Señor Marqués! . . .

DON CARLOS

De esa suerte
No me permito llamar,
30 Que sólo he de titular[203]
Después de daros la muerte.

DON ÁLVARO

Aconteceros pudiera
35 Sin el título morir.

DON CARLOS

Vamos pronto a combatir,
Quedemos o dentro o fuera.[204]
Vamos donde mi furor . . .

[201] *A la descubierta . . . tiroteo,* We'll go reconnoitering in the morning and get involved in a little shooting.
[202] The troops of the Austrian Empire
[203] take my title
[204] *Quedemos . . . fuera,* whether it be indoors or out.

DON ÁLVARO

Vamos, pues, señor don Carlos,
Que si nunca fuí a buscarlos,
No evito lances de honor.
Mas esperad, que en el alma
Del que goza de hidalguía,
No es furia la valentía,
Y ésta obra siempre con calma.
Sabéis que busco la muerte,
Que los riesgos solicito,
Pero con vos necesito
Comportarme de otra suerte;
Y explicaros . . .

DON CARLOS

Es perder
Tiempo toda explicación.

DON ÁLVARO

No os neguéis a la razón,
Que suele funesto ser.
Pues trataron las estrellas
Por raros modos de hacernos
Amigos, ¿a qué oponernos
A lo que buscaron ellas?[205]
Si nos quisieron unir
De mutuos y altos servicios
Con los vínculos propicios,
No fué, no, para reñir.
Tal vez fué para enmendar
La desgracia inevitable
De que no fuí yo culpable.[206]

DON CARLOS

¿Y me la osáis recordar?

DON ÁLVARO

¿Teméis que vuestro valor
Se disminuya y se asombre,
Si halla en su contrario un hombre
De nobleza y pundonor?

DON CARLOS

5 ¡Nobleza un aventurero!
¡Honor un desconocido!
¡Sin padre, sin apellido,
Advenedizo, altanero! . . .

DON ÁLVARO

10
¡Ay, que ese error a la muerte,
Por más que lo evité yo,
A vuestro padre arrastró![207] . . .
No corráis la misma suerte.[208]
15 Y que infundados agravios
E insultos no ofenden, muestra
El que[209] está ociosa mi diestra
Sin arrancaros los labios.
Si un secreto misterioso
20 Romper hubiera podido,
¡Oh! . . . cuán diferente sido[210] . . .

DON CARLOS

Guardadlo, no soy curioso.
25 Que sólo anhelo venganza
Y sangre.

DON ÁLVARO

¿Sangre? .. . La habrá.

30

DON CARLOS

Salgamos al campo ya.

DON ÁLVARO

35 Salgamos sin más tardanza. (*Deteniéndose.*)
Mas, don Carlos . . . ¡Ah! ¿Podréis
Sospecharme con razón
De falta de corazón?

[205] We have now reached the climax of the play where the two forces (Don Álvaro's desire for happiness and his adverse Fate, personified now in Don Carlos) are in exact balance. It even seems that Fate has relented momentarily. Either a tragic or a happy outcome seems possible, although obviously the author has been preparing us for the former.

[206] Don Álvaro feels that Fate killed the Marqués; see p. 338, l. 14a.

[207] The central mystery of the play, Don Álvaro's origin, led the Marqués to refuse Leonor to our hero. It is the great obstacle which Fate has placed between Álvaro and Leonor (see 6 lines below). The mention of it, despite Álvaro's early refusal to take insult, is one reason why he kills Carlos. Had the latter shown belief in Álvaro's claims to nobility and had he inquired about his origin, it is probable that the mystery would be revealed at this point and that the play could achieve a happy denouement (see p. 338, ll. 2–9a).

[208] risk

[209] *El que,* the fact that

[210] how different [would have] been [the outcome of my love for Leonor]

No, no, que me conocéis.
Si el orgullo, principal
Y tan poderoso agente
En las acciones del ente
Que se dice racional,
Satisfecho tengo ahora,
Esfuerzos no he de omitir
Hasta aplacar conseguir
Ese furor que os devora.[211]
Pues mucho repugno yo
El desnudar el acero
Con el hombre que primero
Dulce amistad me inspiró.
Yo a vuestro padre no herí,
Le hirió sólo su destino.
Y yo, a aquel ángel divino,
Ni seduje, ni perdí.
Ambos nos están mirando
Desde el cielo; mi inocencia
Ven, esa ciega demencia
Que os agita, condenando.

DON CARLOS (*Turbado.*)

Pues qué, ¿mi hermana? . . . ¿Leonor? . . .
(Que con vos aquí no está
Lo tengo aclarado ya.)
¿Mas cuándo ha muerto? . . . ¡Oh furor!

DON ÁLVARO

Aquella noche terrible
Llevándola yo a un convento,
Exánime, y sin aliento,
Se trabó[212] un combate horrible
Al salir del olivar
Entre mis fieles criados
Y los vuestros irritados,
Y no la pude salvar.
Con tres heridas caí,
Y un negro de puro fiel
(Fidelidad bien crüel),
Veloz me arrancó de allí,
Falto de sangre y sentido;
Tuve en Gelves larga cura,
Con accesos de locura;
Y apenas restablecido
Ansioso empecé a indagar
De mi único bien la suerte,
Y supe ¡ay Dios! que la muerte
En el obscuro olivar . . . 5

DON CARLOS (*Resuelto.*)

¡Basta, imprudente impostor!
¿Y os preciáis de caballero? . . .
¿Con embrollo tan grosero
10 Queréis calmar mi furor?
Deponed tan necio engaño:
Después del funesto día,
En Córdoba, con su tía,
Mi hermana ha vivido un año.
15 Dos meses ha que fuí yo
A buscarla, y no la hallé.
Pero de cierto indagué
Que al verme llegar huyó.
Y el perseguirla he dejado,
20 Porque sabiendo yo allí
Que vos estabais aquí,
Me llamó mayor cuidado.

DON ÁLVARO (*Muy conmovido.*)

25 ¡Don Carlos! . . . ¡Señor! . . . ¡Amigo!
¡Don Félix! . . . ¡ah! . . . tolerad
Que el nombre que en amistad
Tan tierna os unió conmigo
Use en esta situación.
30 ¡Don Félix! . . . soy inocente;
Bien lo podéis ver patente
En mi nueva agitación.
¡Don Félix! . . . ¡Don Félix! . . . ¡ah! . . .
35 ¿Vive? . . . ¿vive? . . . ¡oh justo Dios!

DON CARLOS

Vive; ¿y qué os importa a vos?
Muy pronto no vivirá. 40

DON ÁLVARO

Don Félix, mi amigo; sí.
Pues que vive vuestra hermana,
La satisfacción es llana
45 Que debéis tomar en mí.
A buscarla juntos vamos;
Muy pronto la encontraremos,

[211] If you satisfy my pride, I shall explain my conduct, thus satisfying your honor. This is the offer implied in these words. Word order: *conseguir aplacar*

[212] Here, to begin

Y en santo nudo estrechemos
La amistad que nos juramos.
¡Oh! . . . Yo os ofrezco, yo os juro
Que no os arrepentiréis
Cuando a conocer lleguéis
Mi origen excelso y puro.
Al primer grande español
No le cedo en jerarquía;
Es más alta mi hidalguía
Que el trono del mismo sol.[213]

DON CARLOS

¿Estáis, don Álvaro, loco?
¿Qué es lo que pensar osáis?
¿Qué proyectos abrigáis?
¿Me tenéis a mí en tan poco?
Ruge entre los dos un mar
De sangre . . . ¿Yo al matador
De mi padre y de mi honor
Pudiera hermano llamar?
¡Oh afrenta! Aunque fuerais rey.
Ni la infame ha de vivir.
No, tras de vos va a morir,
Ques es de mi venganza ley.
Si a mí vos no me matáis,
Al punto la buscaré,
Y la misma espada que
Con vuestra sangre tiñáis,
En su corazón . . .

DON ÁLVARO

Callad.
Callad . . . ¿delante de mí
Osasteis? . . .

DON CARLOS

Lo juro, sí;
Lo juro . . .

DON ÁLVARO

¿El qué[214] . . . Continuad.

DON CARLOS

La muerte de la malvada,
En cuanto acabe con vos.

DON ÁLVARO

Pues no será, vive Dios,
Que tengo brazo y espada.
Vamos . . . Libertarla anhelo
5 De su verdugo. Salid.

DON CARLOS

A vuestra tumba venid.

10

DON ÁLVARO

Demandad perdón al cielo.[215]

ESCENA II

15

(*El teatro representa la plaza principal de Veletri; a un lado y otro se ven tiendas y cafés; en medio, puestos de frutas y verduras; al fondo, la*
20 *guardia del Principal,*[216] *y el centinela paseándose delante del armero; los oficiales en grupos a una parte y otra, y la gente del pueblo cruzando en todas direcciones. El* TENIENTE, SUB-
25 TENIENTE *y* PEDRAZA *se reunirán a un lado de la escena, mientras los* OFICIALES 1.°, 2.°, 3.°*y* 4.° *hablan entre sí, después de leer un edicto que está fijado en una esquina y que llama la*
30 *atención de todos.*)

OFICIAL 1.°

El rey Carlos de Nápoles no se chancea; pena de muerte nada menos.

OFICIAL 2.°

35 ¿Cómo pena de muerte?

OFICIAL 3.°

Hablamos de la ley que se acaba de publicar, y que allí está para que nadie la ignore, sobre desafíos.

40

OFICIAL 2.°

Ya, ciertamente es un poco dura.

[213] See n. 73 [214] What?
[215] Álvaro has been seeking death, but now that he knows Leonor is alive he wants to live. Furthermore, he must now kill Carlos to save her as well as to satisfy his wounded honor.
[216] the guard-house of the military police

OFICIAL 3.°

Yo no sé cómo un Rey tan valiente y joven puede ser tan severo contra los lances de honor.

OFICIAL 1.°

Amigo, es que cada uno arrima el ascua a su sardina;[217] y como siempre los desafíos suelen ser entre españoles y napolitanos, y éstos llevan lo peor, el rey, que al cabo es Rey de Nápoles . . . 10

OFICIAL 2.°

No, ésas son fanfarronadas; pues hasta ahora no han llevado siempre lo peor los napolitanos; acordaos del mayor 15 Caraciolo, que despabiló[218] a dos oficiales.

TODOS

Eso fué una casualidad.

OFICIAL 1.°

Lo cierto es que la ley es dura; pena de muerte por batirse; pena de muerte por ser padrino; pena de muerte por llevar cartas;[219] qué sé yo. Pues el primero que caiga . . .

OFICIAL 2.°

No, no es tan rigurosa.

OFICIAL 1.°

¿Cómo no? Vean ustedes. Leamos otra vez.
(*Se acercan a leer el edicto, y se adelantan en la escena los otros.*)

SUBTENIENTE

¡Hermoso día!

TENIENTE

Hermosísimo. Pero pica mucho el sol.

PEDRAZA

Buen tiempo para hacer la guerra.

TENIENTE

Mejor es para los heridos convalecientes. Yo me siento hoy enteramente bueno de mi brazo.

SUBTENIENTE 5

También me parece que el valiente capitán de granaderos del Rey está enteramente restablecido. ¡Bien pronto se ha curado!

PEDRAZA

¿Se ha dado ya de alta?

TENIENTE

Sí, esta mañana. Está como si tal cosa; un poco pálido, pero fuerte. Hace un rato que lo encontré; iba como hacia la Alameda a dar un paseo con su 20 amigote el ayudante don Félix de Avendaña.

SUBTENIENTE

Bien puede estarle agradecido, pues 25 además de haberlo sacado del campo de batalla, le ha salvado la vida con su prolija y esmerada asistencia.

TENIENTE

30 También puede dar gracias a la habilidad del doctor Pérez, que se ha acreditado de ser el mejor cirujano del ejército.

SUBTENIENTE 35

Y no lo perderá; pues, según dicen, el ayudante, que es muy rico y generoso, le va a hacer un gran regalo.

PEDRAZA

40 Bien puede; pues según me ha dicho un sargento de mi compañía, andaluz, el tal don Félix está aquí con nombre supuesto, y es un Marqués riquísimo de Sevilla.

[217] *cada uno . . . sardina,* each one rakes the coals near his own sardine, i.e. each one looks out for his own interests

[218] to snuff out

[219] a written challenge

TODOS

¿De veras?
(*Se oye ruido, y se arremolinan todos mirando hacia el mismo lado.*)

TENIENTE

¡Hola! ¿Qué alboroto es aquél?

SUBTENIENTE

Veamos . . . Sin duda algún preso. Pero ¡Dios mío! ¿qué veo?

PEDRAZA

¿Qué es aquello?

TENIENTE

¿Estoy soñando? . . . ¿No es el capitán de granaderos del Rey el que traen preso?

TODOS

No hay duda, es el valiente don Fadrique.
(*Se agrupan todos sobre el primer bastidor de la derecha, por donde sale el capitán preboste y cuatro granaderos, y en medio de ellos preso, sin espada ni sombrero,* DON ÁLVARO; *y atravesando la escena, seguidos por la multitud, entran en el cuerpo de guardia,*[220] *que está al fondo; mientras tanto se desembaraza el teatro.—Todos vuelven a la escena, menos* PEDRAZA, *que entra en el cuerpo de guardia.*)

TENIENTE

Pero, señor, ¿qué será esto? ¿Preso el militar más valiente, más exacto que tiene el ejército?

SUBTENIENTE

Ciertamente es cosa muy rara.

TENIENTE

Vamos a averiguar . . .

SUBTENIENTE

Ya viene aquí Pedraza, que sale del cuerpo de guardia, y sabrá algo. Hola, Pedraza, ¿qué ha sido?

PEDRAZA

(*Señalando al edicto, y se reúne más gente a los cuatro oficiales.*)
Muy mala causa tiene. Desafío . . . El primero que quebranta la ley; desafío y muerte.

TODOS

¡Cómo!!! ¿Y con quién?

PEDRAZA

¡Caso extrañísimo! El desafío ha sido con el teniente coronel Avendaña.

TODOS

¡Imposible! . . . ¡Con su amigo!

PEDRAZA

Muerto le deja de una estocada ahí detrás del cuartel.

TODOS

¡Muerto!

PEDRAZA

Muerto.

OFICIAL 1.°

Me alegro, que era un botarate.

OFICIAL 2.°

Un insultante.

TENIENTE

¡Pues, señores, la ha hecho buena! Mucho me temo que va a estrenar aquella ley.

TODOS

¡Qué horror!

[220] guard-house; see n. 216

SUBTENIENTE

Será una atrocidad. Debe haber alguna excepción a favor de oficial tan valiente y benemérito.

PEDRAZA

Sí, ya esá fresco.[221]

TENIENTE

El capitán Herreros es, con razón, el ídolo del ejército. Y yo creo que el general y el coronel, y los jefes todos, tanto españoles como napolitanos, hablarán al Rey . . . , y tal vez . . .

SUBTENIENTE

El rey Carlos es tan testarudo . . . , y como éste es el primer caso que ocurre, el mismo día que se ha publicado la ley . . . No hay esperanza. Esta noche misma se juntará el Consejo de guerra, y antes de tres días le arcabucean . . . Pero, ¿sobre qué habrá sido el lance?

PEDRAZA

Yo no sé, nada me han dicho. Lo que es[222] el capitán tiene malas pulgas,[223] y su amigote era un poco caliente de lengua.

OFICIALES 1.° Y 4.°

Era un charlatán, un fanfarrón.

SUBTENIENTE

En el café han entrado algunos oficiales del regimiento del Rey; sabrán sin duda todo el lance. Vamos a hablar con ellos.

TODOS

Sí, vamos.

Escena III

(El teatro representa el cuarto de un oficial de guardia; se verá a un lado el tabladillo y el colchón, y en medio habrá una mesa y sillas de paja. Entran en la escena DON ÁLVARO *y el* CAPITÁN.)

CAPITÁN

5 Como la mayor desgracia
Juzgo, amigo y compañero,
El estar hoy de servicio
Para ser alcaide vuestro.
Resignación, don Fadrique,
10 Tomad una silla os ruego.
(Se sienta DON ÁLVARO.)
Y mientras yo esté de guardia
No miréis este aposento
Como prisión . . . Mas es fuerza,
15 Pues orden precisa tengo,
Que dos centinelas ponga
De vista . . .

DON ÁLVARO

20 Yo os agradezco,
Señor, tal cortesanía.
Cumplid, cumplid al momento
Con lo que os tienen mandado,
Y los centinelas luego
25 Poned . . . Aunque más seguro
Que de hombres y armas en medio,
Está el oficial de honor
Bajo su palabra[224] . . . ¡Oh cielos!
(Coloca el CAPITÁN *dos centinelas;*
30 *un soldado entra*[225] *luces, y se sientan el* CAPITÁN *y* DON ÁLVARO *junto a la mesa.)*
¿Y en Veletri qué se dice?
¿Mil necedades diversas
35 Se esparcirán, procurando
Explicar mi suerte adversa?

CAPITÁN

En Veletri, ciertamente,
No se habla de otra materia.
40 Y aunque de aquí separarme
No puedo, como está llena
Toda la plaza de gente,
Que gran interés demuestra
Por vos, a algunos he hablado . . .

[221] he's in a fine fix
[222] See n. 40
[223] *tener malas pulgas*, to be irritable, short-tempered
[224] Word order: *bajo su palabra de honor*
[225] to bring in

DON ÁLVARO

Y bien, ¿qué dicen? ¿qué piensan?

CAPITÁN

La amistad íntima todos,
Que os enlazaba, recuerdan,
Con don Félix . . . Y las causas
Que la hicieron tan estrecha,
Y todos dicen . . .

DON ÁLVARO

Entiendo.
Que soy un monstruo, una fiera.
Que a la obligación más santa
He faltado. Que mi ciega
Furia ha dado muerte a un hombre,
A cuyo arrojo y nobleza
Debí la vida en el campo;
Y a cuya nimia asistencia
Y esmero debí mi cura,
Dentro de su casa mesma.[226]
Al que como tierno hermano . . .
¡Como hermano! . . . ¡Suerte horrenda!
¿Como hermano? . . . ¡Debió serlo!
Yace convertido en tierra
Por no serlo . . . ¡Y yo respiro!
¿Y aun el suelo me sustenta? . . .
¡Ay! ¡ay de mí![227]
(*Se da una palmada en la frente, y queda en la mayor agitación.*)

CAPITÁN

Perdonadme
Si con mis noticias necias . . .

DON ÁLVARO

Yo lo amaba . . . ¡Ah, cual me aprieta
El corazón una mano[228]
De hierro ardiente! La fuerza
Me falta . . . ¡Oh Dios! ¡Qué bizarro,
Con qué noble gentileza
Entre un diluvio de balas
Se arrojó, viéndome en tierra,
A salvarme de la muerte!
¡Con cuánto afán y terneza
Pasó las noches y días
5 Sentado a mi cabecera! (*Pausa.*)

CAPITÁN

Anuló sin duda tales
Servicios con un agravio.
10 Diz[229] que era un poco altanero,
Picajoso, temerario;
Y un hombre cual vos . . .

15 DON ÁLVARO

No, amigo;
Cuanto de él se diga es falso.
Era un digno caballero
De pensamientos muy altos.
20 Retóme con razón harta,
Y yo también le he matado
Con razón. Sí, si aun viviera,
Fuéramos de nuevo al campo,
Él a procurar mi muerte,
25 Yo a esforzarme por matarlo.
O él o yo sólo en el mundo.
Pero imposible en él ambos.

CAPITÁN

30 Calmaos, señor don Fadrique:
Aun no estáis del todo bueno
De vuestras nobles heridas,
Y que os pongáis malo temo.

35 DON ÁLVARO

¿Por qué no quedé en el campo
De batalla como bueno?
Con honra acabado[230] hubiera,
Y ahora, oh Dios . . . , la muerte anhelo,
40 Y la tendré . . . pero ¿cómo?
En un patíbulo horrendo,

[226] For *misma* to preserve assonance

[227] Lest the audience lose its good opinion of Don Álvaro for having killed his friend, Rivas makes his present words especially noble. After the officers have found fault with Carlos, in the previous scene, Álvaro's taking of all the blame on himself and defending Carlos against other people's accusations (see his speech below beginning "No, amigo; . . .") win back any esteem he may have lost.

[228] *cual . . . mano,* it is as if a hand were crushing my heart

[229] They say (archaic form occasionally found in writing)

[230] to die

Por infractor de las leyes,
De horror o de burla objeto.

CAPITÁN

¿Qué decís? . . . No hemos llegado,
Señor, a tan duro extremo;
Aun puede haber circunstancias
Que justifiquen el duelo,
Y entonces . . .

DON ÁLVARO

No, no hay ninguna.
Soy homicida, soy reo.

CAPITÁN

Mas, según tengo entendido
(Ahora de mi regimiento
Me lo ha dicho el Ayudante),
Los generales, de acuerdo
Con todos los coroneles,
Han ido sin perder tiempo
A echarse a los pies del Rey,
Que es benigno, aunque severo,
Para pedirle . . .

DON ÁLVARO (*Conmovido.*)

¿De veras?
Con el alma lo agradezco,
Y el interés de los jefes
Me honra y me confunde a un tiempo.
Pero ¿por qué han de empeñarse
Militares tan excelsos,
En que una excepción se haga
A mi favor de un decreto
Sabio, de una ley tan justa,
A que yo falté el primero?
Sirva mi pronto castigo
Para saludable ejemplo.
¡Muerte, es mi destino, muerte,
Porque la muerte merezco,
Porque es para mí la vida
Aborrecible tormento!
Mas ¡ay de mí sin ventura!
¿Cuál es la muerte que espero?
La del criminal, sin honra,
¡En un patíbulo!! . . . ¡Cielos!!!
(*Se oye un redoble.*)

ESCENA IV

(*Entra el* SARGENTO.)

SARGENTO

5 Mi Capitán . . .

CAPITÁN

¿Qué se ofrece?

SARGENTO

10 El Mayor . . .

CAPITÁN

Voy al momento. (*Vase.*)

ESCENA V

15

DON ÁLVARO

¡Leonor! ¡Leonor! Si existes, desdichada,
¡Oh, qué golpe te espera,
20 Cuando la nueva fiera
Te llegue adonde vives retirada,
De que la misma mano,
La mano ¡ay triste! mía,
Que te privó de padre y de alegría,
25 Acaba de privarte de un hermano!
No; te ha librado, sí, de un enemigo,
De un verdugo feroz, que por castigo
De que diste en tu pecho
Acogida a mi amor, verlo[231] deshecho,
30 Y roto, y palpitante,
Preparaba anhelante,
Y con su brazo mismo,
De su venganza hundirte en el abismo.
¡Respira, sí, respira,
35 Que libre estás de su tremenda ira!
(*Pausa.*)
¡Ay de mí! Tú vivías,
Y yo, lejos de ti, muerte buscaba,
Y sin remedio las desgracias mías
40 Despechado juzgaba;
Mas tú vives, ¡mi cielo!
Y aun aguardo un instante de consuelo.
¿Y qué espero? ¡Infeliz! De sangre un
45 río,

[231] *Lo* stands for *tu pecho*

Que yo no derramé, serpenteaba
Entre los dos; mas ahora el brazo mío
En mar inmenso de tornarlo[232] acaba.
¡Hora de maldición, aciaga hora
Fué aquélla en que te vi la vez primera 5
En el soberbio templo de Sevilla,
Como un ángel bajado de la esfera
En donde el trono del Eterno brilla!
¡Qué porvenir dichoso
Vió mi imaginación por un momento, 10
Que huyó tan presuroso
Como al soplar de repentino viento
Las torres de oro, y montes argentinos,
Y colosos y fúlgidos follajes
Que forman los celajes[233] 15
En otoño a los rayos matutinos!
(*Pausa.*)
¡Mas en qué espacio vago, en qué regiones
Fantásticas! ¿Qué espero? 20
¡Dentro de breves horas,
Lejos de las mundanas afecciones,
Vanas y engañadoras,
Iré de Dios al tribunal severo! (*Pausa.*)
¿Y mis padres? . . . Mis padres desdichados 25
Aun yacen encerrados
En la prisión horrenda de un castillo[234] . . . ,
Cuando con mis hazañas y proezas 30
Pensaba restaurar su nombre y brillo
Y rescatar sus míseras cabezas.
No me espera más suerte
Que, como criminal, infame muerte.[235]
(*Queda sumergido en el despecho.*) 35

ESCENA VI

(*Entra el* CAPITÁN.)

CAPITÁN

¡Hola, amigo y compañero! . . .

DON ÁLVARO

¿Vais a darme alguna nueva?
¿Para cuándo convocado
Está el Consejo de guerra?

CAPITÁN

5 Dicen que esta noche misma
Debe reunirse a gran priesa . . .
De hierro,[236] de hierro tiene
El rey Carlos la cabeza.

DON ÁLVARO

10 ¡Es un valiente soldado!
¡Es un gran Rey!

CAPITÁN

Mas pudiera
15 No ser tan tenaz y duro;
Pues nadie, nadie lo apea[237]
En diciendo no.

DON ÁLVARO

20 En los reyes
La debilidad es mengua.

CAPITÁN

Los jefes y generales
25 Que hoy en Veletri se encuentran,
Han estado en cuerpo a verle
Y a rogarle[238] suspendiera
La ley en favor de un hombre
Que tantos méritos cuenta . . .
30 Y todo sin fruto. Carlos,
Aun más duro que una peña,
Ha dicho que no, resuelto,
Y que la ley se obedezca;
Mandando que en esta noche
35 Falle el Consejo de guerra.
Mas aun quedan esperanzas;
Puede ser que el fallo sea . . .

DON ÁLVARO

Según la ley. No hay remedio;
40 Injusta otra cosa fuera.

CAPITÁN

Pero ¡qué pena tan dura,
Tan extraña, tan violenta! . . .

[232] has just changed it [the river]
[233] which the clouds of the sky form
[234] Another ray of light shed on the key mystery.
[235] This second soliloquy is much softer and more resigned in tone than the first. It is a farewell to life, while the first was a diatribe against it.
[236] unbending, stubborn
[237] to dissuade
[238] Supply: *que*

DON ÁLVARO

La muerte. Como cristiano[239]
La sufriré: no me aterra.
Dármela Dios no ha querido,
Con honra y con fama eterna,
En el campo de batalla,
Y me la da con afrenta
En un patíbulo infame . . .
Humilde la aguardo . . . Venga.

CAPITÁN

No será acaso . . . Aun veremos . . .
Puede que se arme una gresca . . .
El ejército os adora . . .
Su agitación es extrema,
Y tal vez un alboroto . . .

DON ÁLVARO

Basta . . . ¿Qué decís? ¿Tal piensa
Quien de militar blasona?[240]
¿El ejército pudiera
Faltar a la disciplina,
Ni yo deber mi cabeza
A una rebelión? . . . No, nunca;
Que jamás, jamás suceda
Tal desorden por mi causa.[241]

CAPITÁN

¡La ley es atroz, horrenda!

DON ÁLVARO

Yo la tengo por muy justa;
Forzoso remediar era
Un abuso . . .
(*Se oye un tambor y dos tiros.*)

CAPITÁN

¿Qué?

DON ÁLVARO

¿Escuchasteis?

CAPITÁN

El desorden ya comienza.
(*Se oye gran ruido; tiros, confusión y cañonazos, que van en aumento hasta* 5 *el fin del acto.*)

ESCENA VII

(*Los mismos y el* SARGENTO, *que entra muy presuroso.*) 10

SARGENTO

¡Los alemanes! ¡Los enemigos están en Veletri! ¡Estamos sorprendidos!

15 VOCES (*Dentro*)

¡A las armas! ¡A las armas!
(*Sale el oficial un instante, se aumenta el ruido, y vuelve con la espada des-* 20 *nuda.*)

CAPITÁN

Don Fadrique, escapad; no puedo guardar más vuestra persona: andan 25 los nuestros y los imperiales mezclados por las calles; arde el palacio del Rey; hay una confusión espantosa; tomad vuestro partido.[242] Vamos, hijos, a abrirnos paso como valientes, o a 30 morir como españoles.[243]
(*Vanse el* CAPITÁN, *los centinelas y el* SARGENTO.)

ESCENA VIII

35 DON ÁLVARO

Denme una espada: volaré a la muerte,
Y si es vivir mi suerte,
Y no la[244] logro en tanto desconcierto,
Yo os hago, eterno Dios, voto profundo
40 De renunciar al mundo
Y de acabar mi vida en un desierto.[245]

[239] Don Álvaro reaffirms his essential Christianity.
[240] *Quien . . . blasona,* one who prides himself on being a soldier
[241] In the first place, Álvaro wants to die; in the second, he is too noble to think in selfish terms.
[242] take your own course, make your own way
[243] The author has not prepared us for Don Álvaro's escape. In technical language, it is *unmotivated,* hence *melodramatic.* The use of such unexpected solutions is common in the romantic drama.
[244] *la* for *muerte*
[245] i.e. to become a monk or a hermit

JORNADA QUINTA

La escena es en el convento de los Ángeles y sus alrededores.

ESCENA PRIMERA

(*El teatro representa lo interior del claustro bajo del convento de los Ángeles, que debe ser una galería mezquina, alrededor de un patiecillo con naranjos, adelfas y jazmines. A la izquierda se verá la portería; a la derecha la escalera. Debe de ser decoración corta,*[246] *para que detrás estén las otras por su orden.—Aparecen el* PADRE GUARDIÁN *paseándose gravemente por el proscenio y leyendo en su breviario; el* HERMANO MELITÓN *sin manto, arremangado, y repartiendo con un cucharón, de un gran caldero, la sopa, al* VIEJO, *al* COJO, *al* MANCO, *a la* MUJER *y al grupo de pobres que estará apiñado en la portería.*)

HERMANO MELITÓN

Vamos, silencio y orden, que no están en ningún figón.

MUJER

Padre, ¡a mí, a mí!

VIEJO

¿Cuántas raciones quiere, Marica?

COJO

Ya le han dado tres, y no es regular . . .

HERMANO MELITÓN

Callen, y sean humildes, que me duele la cabeza.

MANCO

Marica ha tomado tres raciones.

MUJER

Y aun voy a tomar cuatro, que tengo seis chiquillos.

HERMANO MELITÓN

¿Y por qué tiene seis chiquillos? . . . Sea su alma.[247]

MUJER

Porque me los ha dado Dios.

HERMANO MELITÓN

Sí . . . Dios . . . Dios . . . No los tendría si se pasara las noches, como yo, rezando el rosario, o dándose disciplina.

PADRE GUARDIÁN

(*Con gravedad.*)
¡Hermano Melitón! . . . ¡Hermano Melitón! . . . ¡Válgame Dios!

HERMANO MELITÓN

Padre nuestro, si estos desarrapados tienen una fecundidad que asombra.

COJO

¡A mí, padre Melitón, que tengo ahí fuera a mi madre baldada!

HERMANO MELITÓN

¡Hola! . . . ¿También ha venido hoy la bruja? Pues no nos falta nada.

PADRE GUARDIÁN

¡Hermano Melitón! . . .

MUJER

Mis cuatro raciones.

MANCO

A mí antes.

VIEJO

A mí.

[246] Same as *sala corta,* n. 135

[247] Supply: cursed

TODOS

A mí, a mí . . .

HERMANO MELITÓN

Váyanse noramala,[248] y tengan modo[249] . . . ¿A que les doy[250] con el cucharón? . . .

PADRE GUARDIÁN

¡Caridad, hermano, caridad, que son hijos de Dios!

HERMANO MELITÓN

(*Sofocado.*)
Tomen, y váyanse . . .

MUJER

Cuando nos daba la guiropa[251] el padre Rafael lo hacía con más modo y con más temor de Dios.

HERMANO MELITÓN

Pues llamen al padre Rafael . . . , que no los pudo aguantar ni una semana.

VIEJO

Hermano, ¿me quiere dar otro poco de bazofia? . . .

HERMANO MELITÓN

¡Galopo! . . . ¿Bazofia llama a la gracia de Dios?[252] . . .

PADRE GUARDIÁN

Caridad y paciencia, hermano Melitón; harto trabajo tienen los pobrecitos.

HERMANO MELITÓN

Quisiera yo ver a Vuestra Reverendísima lidiar con ellos un día, y otro, y otro.

COJO

El padre Rafael . . .

HERMANO MELITÓN

No me jeringuen[253] con el padre 5 Rafael . . . y . . . tomen las arrebañaduras. (*Les reparte los restos del caldero, y lo echa a rodar de una patada*), y a comerlo al sol.

10 MUJER

Si el padre Rafael quisiera bajar a decirle los Evangelios a mi niño, que tiene sisiones[254] . . .

HERMANO MELITÓN

15 Tráigalo mañana, cuando salga a decir misa el padre Rafael.

COJO

20 Si el padre Rafael quisiera venir a la villa, a curar a mi compañero, que se ha caído . . .

HERMANO MELITÓN

25 Ahora no es hora de ir a hacer milagros: por la mañanita, por la mañaita, con la fresca.

MANCO

30 Si el padre Rafael . . .

HERMANO MELITÓN

(*Fuera de sí.*)
Ea, ea, fuera . . . Al sol . . . ¡Cómo cunde la semilla de los perdidos! 35 Horrio[255] . . . ¡afuera!

(*Los va echando con el cucharón y cierra la portería, volviendo luego muy sofocado y cansado donde está el* 40 GUARDIÁN.)

[248] *en hora mala,* and bad luck to you
[249] good manners
[250] *A . . . doy,* What do you bet that I'll hit you
[251] stew (a local word of Andalucía)
[252] See n. 97
[253] to molest, bother
[254] An Andalusian pronunciation for *ciciones,* fever
[255] Away!

ESCENA II

HERMANO MELITÓN

No hay paciencia que baste, padre nuestro.

PADRE GUARDIÁN

Me parece, hermano Melitón, que no os ha dotado el Señor con gran cantidad de ella. Considere que en dar de comer a los pobres de Dios desempeña un ejercicio de que se honraría un ángel.

HERMANO MELITÓN

Yo quisiera ver a un ángel en mi lugar siquiera tres días . . . Puede ser que de cada guantada[256] . . .

PADRE GUARDIÁN

No diga disparates.

HERMANO MELITÓN

Pues si es verdad. Yo lo hago con mucho gusto, eso es otra cosa. Y bendito sea el Señor, que nos da bastante para que nuestras sobras sirvan de sustento a los pobres. Pero es preciso enseñarles los dientes. Viene entre ellos mucho pillo . . . Los que están tullidos y viejos, vengan en hora buena, y les daré hasta mi ración, el día que no tenga mucha hambre; pero jastiales[257] que pueden derribar a puñadas un castillo, váyanse a trabajar. Y hay algunos tan insolentes . . . Hasta llaman bazofia a la gracia de Dios . . . Lo mismo que restregarme siempre por los hocicos al padre Rafael; toma si[258] nos daba más, daca si[258] tenía mejor modo, torna si[259] no metía tanta prisa. Pues a fe, a fe, que el bendito padre Rafael a los ocho días se hartó de pobres y de guiropa, y se metió en su celda, y aquí quedó el hermano Melitón. Y por cierto, no sé por qué esta canalla dice que tengo mal genio. Pues el padre Rafael también tiene su piedra en el rollo,[260] y sus prontos,[261] y sus ratos de murria como cada cual.

PADRE GUARDIÁN

Basta, hermano, basta. El padre Rafael no podía, teniendo que cuidar del altar y que asistir al coro, entender en el repartimiento de la limosna, ni éste ha sido nunca encargo de un religioso antiguo, sino incumbencia del portero . . . ¿Me entiende . . . ? Y, hermano Melitón, tenga más humildad y no se ofenda cuando prefieran al padre Rafael, que es un siervo de Dios a quien todos debemos imitar.

HERMANO MELITÓN

Yo no me ofendo de que prefieran al padre Rafael. Lo que digo es que tiene su genio.[262] Y a mí me quiere mucho, padre nuestro, y echamos nuestras manos[263] de conversación. Pero tiene de cuando en cuando unas salidas, y se da unas palmadas en la frente . . . y habla solo, y hace visajes como si viera algún espíritu.

PADRE GUARDIÁN

Las penitencias, los ayunos . . .

HERMANO MELITÓN

Tiene cosas muy raras. El otro día estaba cavando en la huerta, y tan pálido y tan desemejado, que le dije en broma: Padre, parece un mulato; y me echó una mirada, y cerró el puño, y aun lo enarboló de modo que parecía que me iba a tragar. Pero se contuvo,

[256] slap. The implication is that even the angel would not turn the other cheek.
[257] rough country fellows
[258] *toma si, daca si;* now that . . . now that
[259] *torna si, vuelta si;* next that . . . then that

[260] *su . . . rollo,* his touchy side
[261] fits of temper
[262] moments of bad temper
[263] short period, bit

se echó la capucha y desapareció; digo, se marchó de allí a buen paso.

PADRE GUARDIÁN

Ya.

HERMANO MELITÓN

Pues el día que fué a Hornachuelos a auxiliar al alcalde, cuando estaba en toda su furia aquella tormenta, en que nos cayó la centella sobre el campanario, al verlo yo salir sin cuidarse del aguacero ni de los truenos que hacían temblar estas montañas, le dije por broma que parecía entre los riscos un indio bravo,[264] y me dió un berrido que me aturulló . . . Y como vino al convento de un modo tan raro, y nadie lo viene nunca a ver, ni sabemos dónde nació . . .

PADRE GUARDIÁN

Hermano, no haga juicios temerarios. Nada tiene de particular eso, ni el modo con que vino a esta casa el padre Rafael es tan raro como dice. El padre limosnero, que venía de Palma, se lo encontró muy mal herido en los encinares de Escalona, junto al camino de Sevilla, víctima, sin duda, de los salteadores, que nunca faltan en semejante sitio, y lo trajo al convento, donde Dios, sin duda, le inspiró la vocación de tomar nuestro santo escapulario, como lo verificó en cuanto se vió restablecido, y pronto hará cuatro años. Esto no tiene nada de particular.

HERMANO MELITÓN

Ya, eso sí . . . Pero, la verdad, siempre que lo miro me acuerdo de aquello que Vuestra Reverendísima nos ha contado muchas veces, y también se nos ha leído en el refectorio, de cuando se hizo fraile de nuestra orden el demonio,[265] y que estuvo allá en un convento algunos meses. Y se me ocurre si el padre Rafael será alguna cosa así . . . ; pues tiene unos repentes,[266] una fuerza y un mirar de ojos . . .

PADRE GUARDIÁN

Es cierto, hermano mío; así consta de nuestras crónicas y está consignado en nuestros archivos. Pero además de que rara vez se repiten tales milagros, entonces el Guardián de aquel convento en que ocurrió el prodigio tuvo una revelación que le previno de todo. Y lo que es[267] yo, hermano mío, no he tenido hasta ahora ninguna. Con que tranquilícese y no caiga en la tentación de sospechar del padre Rafael.

HERMANO MELITÓN

Yo nada sospecho.

PADRE GUARDIÁN

Le aseguro que no he tenido revelación.

HERMANO MELITÓN

Ya, pues entonces . . . Pero tiene muchas rarezas el padre Rafael.

PADRE GUARDIÁN

Los desengaños del mundo, las tribulaciones . . . Y luego el retiro con que vive, las continuas penitencias . . . (*Suena la campanilla de la portería.*) Vaya a ver quién llama.

HERMANO MELITÓN

¿A que son otra vez los pobres? Pues ya está limpio el caldero . . . (*Suena otra vez la campanilla.*) No hay más limosna; se acabó por hoy, se acabó. (*Suena otra vez la campanilla.*)

PADRE GUARDIÁN

Abra, hermano, abra la puerta. (*Vase.*) (*Abre el lego la portería.*)

[264] wild Indian

[265] An old legend, half religious and half superstitious, of the type which appealed to the romanticists.

[266] bursts of anger

[267] See n. 40

Escena III

(DON ALFONSO *vestido de monte, que sale embozado.*)

DON ALFONSO

(*Con muy mal modo y sin desembozarse.*)
De esperar me he puesto cano.
¿Sois vos, por dicha, el portero?

HERMANO MELITÓN

(Tonto es este caballero.) (*Aparte.*)
Pues que abrí la puerta, es llano. (*Alto.*)
Y aunque de portero estoy,
No me busque las cosquillas,[268]
Que padre de campanillas[269]
Con olor de santo soy.

DON ALFONSO

¿El Padre Rafael está?
Tengo que verme con él.

HERMANO MELITÓN

(¡Otro Padre Rafael!) (*Aparte.*)
Amostazándome va.

DON ALFONSO

Responda pronto.

HERMANO MELITÓN

(*Con miedo.*)
Al momento.
Padres Rafaeles . . . hay dos.
¿Con cuál queréis hablar vos?

DON ALFONSO

Para mí más que haya ciento.[270]
El Padre Rafael . . . (*Muy enfadado.*)

HERMANO MELITÓN

¿El gordo?
¿El natural de Porcuna?
No os oirá cosa ninguna,
Que es como una tapia sordo.
Y desde el pasado invierno
En la cama está tullido;
Noventa años ha cumplido.
5 El otro es . . .

DON ALFONSO

El del infierno.

HERMANO MELITÓN

10 Pues ahora caigo en quién es:
El alto, adusto, moreno,
Ojos vivos, rostro lleno . . .

DON ALFONSO

15 Llevadme a su celda, pues.

HERMANO MELITÓN

Daréle aviso primero,
Porque si está en oración,
Disturbarle no es razón . . .
20 Y ¿quién diré?

DON ALFONSO

Un caballero.

HERMANO MELITÓN

25 (*Yéndose hacia la escalera muy lentamente, dice aparte.*)
¡Caramba! . . . ¡Qué raro gesto![271]
Me da malísima espina,
Y me huele a chamusquina[272] . . .

30 DON ALFONSO

(*Muy irritado.*)
¿Qué aguarda? Subamos presto.
(*El* HERMANO *se asusta y sube la escalera, y detrás de él* DON ALFONSO.)
35

Escena IV

(*El teatro representa la celda de un franciscano. Una tarima con una es-*
40 *tera a un lado; un vasar con una jarra y vasos; un estante con libros,*

[268] *No . . . cosquillas,* don't make me lose patience
[269] important, 'with bells on'; or, who answers the bells (a pun)

[270] *Para . . . ciento,* What's it to me if there are a hundred?
[271] As usually, 'expression,' not 'gesture'
[272] to smell like a quarrel; literally, of scorching

estampas, disciplinas y cilicios colgados. Una especie de oratorio pobre, y en su mesa una calavera;[273] DON ÁLVARO, *vestido de fraile francisco, aparece de rodillas en profunda oración mental.*)

HERMANO MELITÓN

¡Padre, Padre! (*Dentro.*)[274]

DON ÁLVARO

(*Levantándose.*)
¿Qué se ofrece?
Entre, Hermano Melitón.

HERMANO MELITÓN

Padre, aquí os busca un matón,
(*Entra.*)
Que muy ternejal parece.

DON ÁLVARO

(*Receloso.*)
¿Quién, hermano? . . . ¿A mí? . . . 20
¿Su nombre?

HERMANO MELITÓN

Lo ignoro; muy altanero
Dice que es un caballero,
Y me parece un mal hombre.
Él muy bien portado viene,
Y en un andaluz rocín;
Pero un genio muy rüin,
Y un tono muy duro tiene.

DON ÁLVARO

Entre al momento quien sea.

HERMANO MELITÓN

No es un pecador contrito.
(Se quedará tamañito[275] (*Aparte.*)
Al instante que lo vea.) (*Vase.*)

ESCENA V

DON ÁLVARO

¿Quién podrá ser? . . . No lo acierto.
Nadie, en estos cuatro años,
Que huyendo de los engaños
Del mundo, habito el desierto,
Con este sayal cubierto,
Ha mi quietud disturbado.
5 ¿Y hoy un caballero osado
A mi celda se aproxima?
¿Me traerá nuevas de Lima?[276]
¡Santo Dios! . . . ¡qué he recordado!

ESCENA VI

10 (DON ÁLVARO *y* DON ALFONSO, *que entra sin desembozarse, reconoce en un momento la celda, y luego cierra la puerta por dentro y echa el pestillo.*)

15 DON ALFONSO

¿Me conocéis?

DON ÁLVARO

No, señor.

DON ALFONSO

¿No veis en mis ademanes
Rasgo alguno que os recuerde
De otro tiempo y de otros males?
¿No palpita vuestro pecho,
25 No se hiela vuestra sangre,
No se anonada y confunde
Vuestro corazón cobarde
Con mi presencia? . . . O, por dicha,
¿Es tan sincero, es tan grande,
30 Tal vuestro arrepentimiento,
Que ya no se acuerda el padre
Rafael, de aquel indiano
Don Álvaro, del constante
Azote de una familia
35 Que tanto en el mundo vale?
¿Tembláis y bajáis los ojos?
Alzadlos, pues, y miradme.
(*Descubriéndose el rostro y mostrándoselo.*)

40 DON ÁLVARO

¡Oh Dios! . . . ¡Qué veo! . . . ¡Dios mío!

[273] skull. A frequent decoration of a monk's cell, in order to keep one's thoughts on death.
[274] offstage, within [the wings]
[275] so big (said with a gesture of the thumb and index finger indicating a minute quantity)
[276] Lima in Perú, the heart of the Inca's empire

¿Pueden mis ojos burlarme?
¡Del Marqués de Calatrava
Viendo estoy la viva imagen!

DON ALFONSO

Basta, que está dicho todo.
De mi hermano y de mi padre
Me está pidiendo venganza
En altas voces la sangre.
Cinco años ha que recorro,
Con dilatados vïajes,
El mundo para buscaros;
Y aunque ha sido todo en balde,
El cielo (que nunca impunes
Deja las atrocidades
De un monstruo, de un asesino,
De un seductor, de un infame)
Por un imprevisto acaso
Quiso por fin indicarme
El asilo donde a salvo
De mi furor os juzgaste.
Fuera el mataros inerme
Indigno de mi linaje.
Fuiste valiente, robusto
Aun estáis para un combate;
Armas no tenéis, lo veo;
Yo dos espadas iguales
Traigo conmigo: son éstas;
(*Se desemboza y saca dos espadas.*)
Elegid la que os agrade.

DON ÁLVARO

(*Con gran calma, pero sin orgullo.*)
Entiendo, joven, entiendo,
Sin que escucharos me pasme,
Porque he vivido en el mundo
Y apurado sus afanes.
De los vanos pensamientos
Que en este punto en vos arden,
También el juguete he sido;
Quiera el Señor perdonarme.
Víctima de mis pasiones,
Conozco todo el alcance
De su influjo, y compadezco
Al mortal a quien combaten.
Mas ya sus borrascas miro,
Como el náufrago que sale
Por un milagro a la orilla,
Y jamás torna a[277] embarcarse.
5 Este sayal que me viste,
Esta celda miserable,
Este yermo, adonde acaso
Dios por vuestro bien os trae,
Desengaños os presentan
10 Para calmaros bastantes;
Y más os responden mudos
Que pueden labios mortales.
Aquí de mis muchas culpas,
Que son ¡ay de mí! harto grandes,
15 Pido a Dios misericordia;
Que la consiga dejadme.[278]

DON ALFONSO

¿Dejaros? . . . ¿Quién? . . . ¿Yo dejaros
20 Sin ver vuestra sangre impura
Vertida por esta espada
Que arde en mi mano desnuda?
Pues esta celda, el desierto,
Ese sayo, esa capucha,
25 Ni a un vil hipócrita guardan,
Ni a un cobarde infame escudan.

DON ÁLVARO

¿Qué decís? . . . ¡Ah! . . . (*Furioso.*)
30 (*Reportándose.*) ¡No, Dios mío! . . .
En la garganta se anuda
Mi lengua . . . ¡Señor! . . . esfuerzo
Me dé vuestra santa ayuda.
Los insultos y amenazas (*Repuesto.*)
35 Que vuestros labios pronuncian,
No tienen para conmigo[279]
Poder ni fuerza ninguna.
Antes, como caballero,
Supe vengar las injurias;
40 Hoy, humilde religioso,
Darles perdón y disculpa.
Pues veis cuál es ya mi estado,
Y, si sois sagaz, la lucha
Que conmigo estoy sufriendo,
45 Templad vuestra saña injusta.

[277] Same as *volver a*
[278] Word order: *dejadme que la consiga.* Don Álvaro's calm seems to spring from a true religious vocation. If this were so, a peaceful (although undramatic) solution of the play would be possible. But his susceptible character (or his Fate?) drives him towards a tragic outcome.
[279] *para commigo,* for me

Respetad este vestido,
Compadeced mis angustias,
Y perdonad generoso
Ofensas que están en duda.
(*Con gran conmoción.*)
¡Sí, hermano, hermano!

DON ALFONSO

¿Qué nombre
Osáis pronunciar? . . .

DON ÁLVARO

¡Ah! . . .

DON ALFONSO

Una
Sola hermana me dejasteis
Perdida y sin honra . . . ¡Oh furia!

DON ÁLVARO

¡Mi Leonor! ¡Ah! No sin honra,[280]
Un religioso os lo jura.
¡Leonor . . . ¡ay! la que absorbía
Toda mi existencia junta![281] (*En delirio.*)
La que en mi pecho por siempre . . .
Por siempre, sí, sí . . . que aun dura . . .
Una pasión . . . Y qué,[282] ¿vive?
¿Sabéis vos noticias suyas? . . .
Decid que me ama y matadme.
Decidme . . . ¡Oh Dios! . . . ¿Me rehusa
(*Aterrado.*)
Vuestra[283] gracia sus auxilios?
¿De nuevo el triunfo asegura
El infierno, y se desploma
Mi alma en su sima profunda?
¡Misericordia! . . . Y vos, hombre
O ilusión, ¿sois, por ventura,
Un tentador que renueva
Mis criminales angustias
Para perderme? . . . ¡Dios mío!

DON ALFONSO (*Resuelto.*)

De estas dos espadas, una
Tomad, don Álvaro, luego;[284]
Tomad, que en vano procura
5 Vuestra infame cobardía
Darle treguas a mi furia.
Tomad . . .

DON ÁLVARO (*Retirándose.*)

10 No, que aun fortaleza
Para resistir la lucha
De las mundanas pasiones
Me da Dios con bondad suma.
¡Ah! Si mis remordimientos,
15 Mis lágrimas, mis confusas
Palabras no son bastante
Para aplacaros; si escucha
Mi arrepentimiento humilde
Sin caridad vuestra furia,
20 (*Arrodíllase.*)
Prosternado a vuestras plantas
Vedme, cual persona alguna
Jamás me vió . . .

DON ALFONSO

25
(*Con desprecio.*)
Un caballero
No hace tal infamia nunca.
Quien sois bien claro publica
30 Vuestra actitud, y la inmunda
Mancha que hay en vuestro escudo.

DON ÁLVARO

35 (*Levantándose con furor.*)
¿Mancha? . . . y ¿cuál? . . . ¿cuál? . . .[285]

DON ALFONSO

¿Os asusta?

40

DON ÁLVARO

Mi escudo es como el sol limpio,
Como el sol.

[280] [She isn't] dishonored
[281] *junta* reinforces *toda:* every bit of
[282] what about her?
[283] i.e. God's, for Álvaro suddenly becomes contrite again and begins to pray
[284] immediately
[285] Once again the mystery of his origin arouses Álvaro where all other means fail.

DON ALFONSO

¿Y no lo anubla
Ningún cuartel de mulato?
¿De sangre mezclada, impura?

DON ÁLVARO

(*Fuera de sí.*)
¡Vos mentís, mentís, infame![286]
Venga el acero; mi furia
(*Toca el pomo de una de las espadas.*)
Os arrancará la lengua,
Que mi clara estirpe insulta.
Vamos.

DON ALFONSO

Vamos.

DON ÁLVARO

(*Reportándose.*)
No . . . no triunfa
Tampoco con esta industria[287]
De mi constancia el infierno.[288]
Retiraos, señor.

DON ALFONSO

(*Furioso.*)
¿Te burlas
De mí, inicuo? Pues cobarde
Combatir conmigo excusas,
No excusarás mi venganza.
Me basta la afrenta tuya:
Toma. (*Le da una bofetada.*)

DON ÁLVARO

(*Furioso y recobrando toda su energía.*)
¿Qué hiciste? . . . ¡Insensato!!!
Ya tu sentencia es segura:
Hora es de muerte, de muerte.
El infierno me confunda.
(*Salen ambos precipitados.*)

ESCENA VII

5 (*El teatro representa el mismo claustro bajo que en las primeras escenas de esta jornada. El* HERMANO MELITÓN *saldrá por un lado: y como bajando la escalera,* DON ÁLVARO *y* DON ALFONSO,
10 *embozado en su capa, con gran precipitación.*)

HERMANO MELITÓN

(*Saliéndole al paso.*)
15 ¿Adónde bueno?[289]

DON ÁLVARO

(*Con voz terrible.*)
Abra la puerta.

20 HERMANO MELITÓN

La tarde está tempestuosa, va a llover a mares.

DON ÁLVARO

25 Abra la puerta.

HERMANO MELITÓN

(*Yendo hacia la puerta.*)
¡Jesús! Hoy estamos de marea alta.[290]
30 Ya voy . . . ¿Quiere que le acompañe? . . . ¿Hay algún enfermo de peligro en el cortijo? . . .

DON ÁLVARO

35 La puerta, pronto.

[286] Although strictly speaking Álvaro's blood is *mestizo* (Indian and white) not mulatto, his furious denial of the accusation (which is after all true) and his willingness to fight in order to do away with the man who knows this secret make us believe that we have at last reached the heart of the mystery he has so carefully guarded. To be sure, he speaks later of the dishonor sullying his name because of the imprisonment of his parents, but that motive seems to be his rationalization of the situation. In a similar way, he converts his subconscious shame at his mixed blood into an unusually great family pride (especially pride in the very Inca ancestors whom Spanish society disdains) and a certain touchiness in matters of personal honor and pride. We see now why he, like all romantic heroes, feels himself an outcast.

[287] trick

[288] Word order: *el infierno no triunfa tampoco de mi constancia con esta industria*

[289] Where are you off to?

[290] *estamos . . . alta,* we've got the wind up, we're in bad humor

HERMANO MELITÓN

(*Abriendo la puerta.*)
¿Va el padre a Hornachuelos?

DON ÁLVARO

(*Saliendo con* DON ALFONSO.)
Voy al infierno.
(*Queda el* HERMANO MELITÓN *asustado.*)

ESCENA VIII

HERMANO MELITÓN

¡Al infierno! . . . ¡Buen vïaje!
También que era del infierno
Dijo, para mi gobierno,[291]
Aquel nuevo personaje.
¡Jesús, y qué caras tan . . . !
Me temo que mis sospechas
Han de quedar satisfechas.
Voy a ver por dónde van.
(*Se acerca a la portería y dice como admirado:*)
¡Mi gran Padre San Francisco
Me valga! . . . Van por la sierra,
Sin tocar con el pie en tierra,
Saltando de risco en risco.
Y el jaco los sigue en pos
Como un perillo faldero.
Calla[292] . . . , hacia el despeñadero
De la ermita van los dos.
(*Asomándose a la puerta con gran afán: a voces.*)
¡Hola . . . hermanos . . . hola! . . .
¡Digo! . . .
No lleguen al paredón,
Miren que hay excomunión.
Que Dios les va a dar castigo.
(*Vuelve a la escena.*)
No me oyen, vano es gritar.
Demonios son, es patente.
Con el santo penitente
Sin duda van a cargar.[293]
¡El padre, el padre Rafael! . . .
Si quien piensa mal, acierta.[294]
Atrancaré bien la puerta . . .
Pues tengo un miedo crüel.
(*Cierra la puerta.*)
Un olorcillo han dejado
De azufre . . . Voy a tocar
Las campanas.
(*Vase por un lado, y luego vuelve por otro como con gran miedo.*)
Avisar
Será mejor al prelado.
Sepa que en esta ocasión,
Aunque refunfuñe luego,
No el padre Guardián, el lego
Tuvo la revelación. (*Vase.*)

ESCENA IX

(*El teatro representa un valle rodeado de riscos inaccesibles y de malezas, atravesado por un arroyuelo. Sobre un peñasco accesible con dificultad, y colocado al fondo, habrá una medio gruta, medio ermita con puerta practicable, y una campana que pueda sonar y tocarse desde dentro: el cielo representará el ponerse el sol de un día borrascoso, se irá obscureciendo lentamente la escena y aumentándose los truenos y relámpagos;* DON ÁLVARO *y* DON ALFONSO *salen por un lado.*)

DON ALFONSO

De aquí no hemos de pasar.

DON ÁLVARO

No, que tras de estos tapiales,
Bien sin ser vistos, podemos
Terminar nuestro combate.
Y aunque en hollar este sitio
Cometo un crimen muy grande,
Hoy es de crímenes día,
Y todos han de apurarse.
De uno de los dos la tumba
Se está abriendo en este instante.

DON ALFONSO

Pues no perdamos más tiempo,
Y que las espadas hablen.

[291] for my information [292] Why! [293] See n. 111. [294] A proverb

DON ÁLVARO

Vamos: mas antes es fuerza
Que un gran secreto os declare,
Pues que de uno de nosotros
Es la muerte irrevocable:
Y si yo caigo es forzoso
Que sepáis en este trance
A quién habéis dado muerte,
Que puede ser importante.

DON ALFONSO

Vuestro secreto no ignoro.
Y era el mejor de mis planes
(Para la sed de venganza
Saciar que en mis venas arde),
Después de heriros de muerte
Daros noticias tan grandes,
Tan impensadas y alegres,
De tan feliz desenlace,
Que al despecho de saberlas,
De la tumba en los umbrales,
Cuando no hubiese remedio,
Cuando todo fuera en balde,
El fin espantoso os diera
Digno de vuestras maldades.

DON ÁLVARO

Hombre, fantasma o demonio,
Que ha tomado humana carne
Para hundirme en los infiernos,
Para perderme . . . ¿qué sabes? . . .

DON ALFONSO

Corrí el Nuevo Mundo . . . ¿Tiemblas?
Vengo de Lima . . . esto baste.

DON ÁLVARO

No basta, que es imposible
Que saber quién soy lograses.

DON ALFONSO

De aquel Virrey fementido
Que (pensando aprovecharse
De los trastornos y guerras,
5 De los disturbios y males
Que la sucesión al trono[295]
Trajo a España) formó planes
De tornar su virreinato
En imperio, y coronarse,
10 Casando con la heredera
Última de aquel linaje
De los Incas (que en lo antiguo,
Del mar del Sur a los Andes
Fueron los emperadores),
15 Eres hijo.[296] De tu padre
Las traiciones descubiertas,
Aun a tiempo de evitarse,
Con su esposa, en cuyo seno
Eras tú ya peso grave,
20 Huyó a los montes, alzando
Entre los indios salvajes
De traición y rebeldía
El sacrílego estandarte.
No los ayudó fortuna,
25 Pues los condujo a la cárcel
De Lima, do tú naciste . . .
(*Hace extremos de indignación y sorpresa* DON ÁLVARO.)
Oye . . . espera hasta que acabe.
30 El triunfo del rey Felipe
Y su clemencia notable,
Suspendieron la cuchilla
Que ya amagaba a tus padres;
Y en una prisión perpetua
35 Convirtió el suplicio infame.
Tú entre los indios creciste,
Como fiera te educaste,
Y viniste ya mancebo
Con oro y con favor grande,
40 A buscar completo indulto
Para tus traidores padres.[297]

[295] The reference is to the Wars of the Spanish Succession (1701–13). When Carlos II, the last Hapsburg monarch, was going to die without an heir, he was persuaded to leave the throne of Spain to a grandson of Louis XIV of France, who became Felipe V of Spain (1700). England, Holland, and Austria supported the claims of another candidate, Charles, an Austrian Hapsburg.

[296] Word order: *Eres hijo de aquel Virrey,* etc. (in the first line of this speech)

[297] Don Álvaro has done absolutely nothing to alleviate his parents' situation in the years he has been in Europe. This is another reason to believe that their imprisonment is not the real reason he cannot reveal the truth about his birth, even though he deludes himself into thinking that this is the cause.

Mas no, que viniste sólo
Para asesinar cobarde,
Para seducir inicuo,
Y para que yo te mate.

DON ÁLVARO (*Despechado.*)

Vamos a probarlo al punto.

DON ALFONSO

Ahora tienes que escucharme.
Que has de apurar ¡vive el cielo!
Hasta las heces el cáliz.
Y si, por ser mi destino,
Consiguieses el matarme,
Quiero allá en tu aleve pecho
Todo un infierno dejarte.
El Rey, benéfico, acaba
De perdonar a tus padres.
Ya están libres y repuestos
En honras y dignidades.
La gracia alcanzó tu tío,
Que goza favor notable,
Y andan todos tus parientes
Afanados por buscarte
Para que tenga heredero . . .

DON ÁLVARO

(*Muy turbado y fuera de sí.*)
Ya me habéis dicho bastante . . .
No sé dónde estoy ¡oh cielos! . . .
Si es cierto, si son verdades
Las noticias que dijisteis . . .
(*Enternecido y confuso.*)
¡Todo puede repararse!
Si Leonor existe, todo:
¿Veis lo ilustre de mi sangre? . . .
¿Veis? . . .

DON ALFONSO

Con sumo gozo veo
Que estáis ciego y delirante.
¿Qué es reparación?[298] . . . Del mundo
Amor, gloria, dignidades
No son para vos . . . Los votos
Religiosos e inmutables
Que os ligan a este desierto,
Esa capucha, ese traje,
Capucha y traje que encubren
5 A un desertor, que al infame
Suplicio escapó en Italia,
De todo incapaz os hacen.
Oye cuál truena indignado (*Truena.*)
Contra ti el cielo . . . Esta tarde
10 Completísimo es mi triunfo.
Un sol hermoso y radiante
Te he descubierto, y de un soplo
Luego he sabido apagarle.

15 DON ÁLVARO

(*Volviendo al furor.*)
¿Eres monstruo del infierno,
Prodigio de atrocidades?

20 DON ALFONSO

Soy un hombre rencoroso
Que tomar venganza sabe.
Y porque sea más completa,
Te digo que no te jactes
25 De noble . . . eres un mestizo,[299]
Fruto de traiciones . . .

DON ÁLVARO

(*En el extremo de la desesperación.*)
30 Baste.
¡Muerte y exterminio! ¡Muerte
Para los dos! Yo matarme
Sabré, en teniendo[300] el consuelo
De beber tu inicua sangre.
35 (*Toma la espada, combaten y cae herido* DON ALFONSO.)

DON ALFONSO

Ya lo conseguiste . . . ¡Dios mío!
40 ¡Confesión![301] Soy cristiano . . . Perdonadme . . . salva mi alma . . .

DON ÁLVARO

(*Suelta la espada y queda como petri-*
45 *ficado.*)

[298] What do you mean, all can be amended? (referring to l. 34a)

[299] Once more the supreme taunt, with the same extreme reaction from Don Álvaro.

[300] while having

[301] confession, without which he would be damned

¡Cielos! . . . ¡Dios mío! . . . ¡Santa madre de los Ángeles! . . . ¡Mis manos tintas en sangre . . . en sangre de Vargas! . . .

DON ALFONSO

¡Confesión! ¡Confesión! . . . Conozco mi crimen y me arrepiento . . . Salvad mi alma, vos que sois ministro del Señor . . .

DON ÁLVARO (*Aterrado.*)

¡No, yo no soy más que un réprobo, presa infeliz del demonio! Mis palabras sacrílegas aumentarían vuestra condenación. Estoy manchado de sangre, estoy irregular[302] . . . Pedid a Dios misericordia . . . Y . . . esperad . . . cerca vive un santo penitente . . . podrá absolveros . . . Pero está prohibido acercarse a su mansión . . . ¿Qué importa? Yo que he roto todos los vínculos, que he hollado todas las obligaciones . . .

DON ALFONSO

¡Ah! Por caridad, por caridad . . .

DON ÁLVARO

Sí; voy a llamarlo . . . al punto . . .

DON ALFONSO

Apresuraos, padre . . . ¡Dios mío! (DON ÁLVARO *corre a la ermita y golpea la puerta.*)

DOÑA LEONOR (*Dentro.*)

¿Quién se atreve a llamar a esta puerta?
Respetad este asilo.

DON ÁLVARO

Hermano, es necesario salvar un alma, socorrer a un moribundo: venid a darle el auxilio espiritual.

DOÑA LEONOR (*Dentro.*)

Imposible, no puedo, retiraos.

[302] impure

DON ÁLVARO

Hermano, por el amor de Dios.

DOÑA LEONOR (*Dentro.*)

No, no, retiraos.

DON ÁLVARO

Es indispensable, vamos. (*Golpea fuertemente la puerta.*)

DOÑA LEONOR

(*Dentro tocando la campanilla.*) ¡Socorro! ¡Socorro!

ESCENA X

(*Los mismos y* DOÑA LEONOR, *vistida con un saco, y esparcidos los cabellos, pálida y desfigurada, aparece a la puerta de la gruta, y se oye repicar a lo lejos las campanas del convento.*)

DOÑA LEONOR

Huid, temerario; temed la ira del cielo.

DON ÁLVARO

(*Retrocediendo horrorizado por la montaña abajo.*) ¡Una mujer! . . . ¡Cielos! . . . ¡Qué acento! . . . ¡Es un espectro! . . . Imagen adorada . . . ¡Leonor! ¡Leonor!

DON ALFONSO

(*Como queriéndose incorporar.*[303]) ¡Leonor! . . . ¿Qué escucho? ¡Mi hermana!

DOÑA LEONOR

(*Corriendo detrás de* DON ÁLVARO.) ¡Dios mío! ¿Es don Álvaro? . . . Conozco su voz . . . Él es . . . ¡Don Álvaro!

DON ALFONSO

¡Oh furia! Ella es . . . ¡Estaba aquí con su seductor! . . . ¡Hipócritas! . . . ¡Leonor!!!

[303] As if trying to sit up.

DOÑA LEONOR

¡Cielos! . . . ¡Otra voz conocida! . . . Mas ¿qué veo? . . .
(*Se precipita hacia donde ve a* DON ALFONSO.)

DON ALFONSO

¡Ves al último de tu infeliz familia!

DOÑA LEONOR

(*Precipitándose en los brazos de su hermano.*)
¡Hermano mío . . . ¡Alfonso!

DON ALFONSO

(*Hace un esfuerzo, saca un puñal y hiere de muerte a* LEONOR.)
Toma, causa de tantos desastres, recibe el premio de tu deshonra . . . Muero vengado.
(*Muere.*)

DON ÁLVARO

¡Desdichado! . . . ¿Qué hiciste? . . . ¡Leonor! ¿Eras tú? . . . ¿Tan cerca de mí estabas? . . . ¡Ay! (*Se inclina hacia el cadáver de ella.*) Aún respira . . . , aún palpita aquel corazón todo mío . . . Ángel de mi vida . . . vive,[304] vive; yo te adoro . . . ¡Te hallé, por fin . . . sí, te hallé . . . muerta!
(*Queda inmóvil.*)

ESCENA ÚLTIMA

(*Hay un rato de silencio; los truenos resuenan más fuertes que nunca, crecen los relámpagos, y se oye cantar a lo lejos el* Miserere *a la comunidad, que se acerca lentamente.*)

VOZ (*Dentro.*)

Aquí, aquí. ¡Qué horror!
(DON ÁLVARO *vuelve en sí, y luego huye hacia la montaña.—Sale el* PADRE GUARDIÁN *con la comunidad, que queda asombrada.*)

PADRE GUARDIÁN

¡Dios mío! . . . ¡Sangre derramada! ¡Cadáveres! . . . ¡La mujer penitente!

TODOS LOS FRAILES

¡Una mujer! . . . ¡Cielos!

PADRE GUARDIÁN

¡Padre Rafael!

DON ÁLVARO

(*Desde un risco, con sonrisa diabólica, todo convulso, dice:*)
Busca, imbécil, al padre Rafael . . . Yo soy un enviado del infierno, soy el demonio exterminador . . . Huid, miserables.

TODOS

¡Jesús, Jesús!

DON ÁLVARO

Infierno, abre tu boca y trágame. Húndase el cielo, perezca la raza humana; exterminio, destrucción . . .[305]
(*Sube a lo más alto del monte y se precipita.*)

EL PADRE GUARDIAN Y LOS FRAILES

(*Aterrados y en actitudes diversas.*)
¡Misericordia, Señor! ¡Misericordia!

[304] An imperative

[305] Rivas undoubtedly is trying to convey the impression of insanity; therefore these expressions are not to be taken too literally.

Ramón de Mesonero Romanos

MESONERO ROMANOS (1803–82) opens his memoirs of his boyhood with a picture of family prayers, showing his well-to-do, stern, old-fashioned father leading the family and the servants in their evening devotions. Here we have the whole background of this author—money, solid respectability, middle-class comfort. When he was sixteen years old, he was suddenly given the responsibilities of the head of a family by the death of his father. He ran extensive business interests for thirteen years, then, content with his fortune, sold out his holdings to devote his long life to literature, philanthropy, and municipal reforms.

Above all a bourgeois, Mesonero stands for what is both good and bad in the character of the middle class. In a period of violent passions in politics and literature, he is an outstanding and exceptional moderate, refusing to take part in partisan quarrels in either sphere. Sometimes he even showed himself timid through his desire not to hurt anyone or to avoid violence at all costs. But, on the positive side, this moderation manifested itself in a constant friendliness, affability, and good humor. Why should he not be good-humored? He was well satisfied with himself, with his status in life, and with his environment. His intense love for his native city led him to write its first guide book, which he later expanded into a history of Madrid under the title *El antiguo Madrid.* But he also showed the lack of creative imagination which we associate with the moneyed middle classes, and was content to write simply short sketches or essays on the things he saw about him. These pictorial essays, similar in form to those of Larra, were also known as *cuadros de costumbres* and may consist of a short description of a part of Madrid (*La calle de Toledo*), of a custom (*La empleomanía*—the mania of the Spaniards for having a government job), or a criticism of something which the author believes should be reformed (*Tengo lo que me basta*—criticizing the Spaniards' little fondness for work). A note of satire runs through some of these little scenes, although Mesonero is careful not to paint definite persons but to apply his criticism to whole classes of people. Furthermore he is always, benign and gentle in his desire to correct. While he seeks reforms in Madrid, they are always little, practical reforms, such as paving of streets, street lighting, sanitation, et cetera. Never do we find in him the cutting, sweeping satire of the passionate Larra. Through his excellent, straightforward style, his animated dialogues, and constant good humor, Mesonero raises his essays to the rank of great literature, comparable to the works of Addison and Steele, his English counterparts.

Ramón de Mesonero Romanos

El romanticismo y los románticos

«Señales son del juicio
Ver que todos lo perdemos,
Unos por carta de más
Y otros por carta de menos.»[1]

LOPE DE VEGA

Si fuera posible reducir a un solo eco las voces todas de la actual generación europea, apenas cabe ponerse en duda que la palabra *romanticismo* parecería ser la dominante desde el Tajo al Danubio, desde el mar del Norte al estrecho de Gibraltar.

Y sin embargo (¡cosa singular!), esta palabra, tan favorita, tan cómoda, que así aplicamos a las personas como a las cosas, a las verdades de la ciencia como a las ilusiones de la fantasía; esta palabra, que todas las plumas adoptan, que todas las lenguas repiten, todavía carece de una definición exacta, que fije distintamente su verdadero sentido.[2]

. . .

El escritor osado, que acusa a la sociedad de[3] corrompida, al mismo tiempo que contribuye a corromperla más con la inmoralidad de sus escritos; el político, que exagera todos los sistemas, todos los desfigura y contradice, y pretende reunir en su doctrina el feudalismo y la república; el historiador, que poetiza la Historia; el poeta, que finge un sociedad fantástica, y se queja de ella porque no reconoce su retrato; el artista, que pretende pintar a la naturaleza aún más hermosa que en su original; todas estas manías, que en cualesquiera épocas han debido existir, y sin duda en siglos anteriores habrán podido pasar por extravíos de la razón o debilidades de la humana especie, el siglo actual, más adelantado y perspicuo, las ha calificado de *romanticismo puro.*

«La necedad se pega»[4]—ha dicho un autor célebre. No es esto afirmar que lo que hoy se entiende por romanticismo sea necedad,[5] sino que todas las cosas exageradas suelen degenerar en necias; y bajo este aspecto, la romántico-manía se pega también. Y no sólo se pega, sino que, al revés de otras enfermedades contagiosas, que a medida que[6] se transmiten pierden en

[1] *Señales . . . menos,* It is characteristic of good sense to see that we all lose it, some by going too far and some by not going far enough.

[2] A concise definition of romanticism never has been and never can be given.

[3] Supply, being

[4] *pegarse,* to be contagious

[5] Mesonero is careful not to offend the romanticists too much. As a matter of fact, he read this essay to the *Liceo,* a literary group containing both romanticists and classicists. After some hesitation on their part about how to take the essay, Mesonero's good humor and tact carried the day and all laughed with him.

[6] *a medida que,* in proportion as

grado de intensidad, ésta, por el contrario, adquiere en la inoculación[7] tal desarrollo, que lo que en su origen pudo ser sublime, pasa después a ser ridículo; lo que en unos fué un destello del genio, en otros viene a ser un ramo de locura.

Y he[8] aquí por qué un muchacho que por los años de 1810 vivía en nuestra corte y su calle de la Reina, y era hijo del general francés *Hugo* y se llamaba *Víctor,* encontró el romanticismo donde menos podía esperarse, esto es, en el Seminario de Nobles;[9]—y el picaruelo conoció[10] lo que nosotros no habíamos sabido apreciar, y teníamos enterrado hace dos siglos con Calderón;[11]—y luego regresó a París, extrayendo de entre nosotros esta primera materia,[12] y la confeccionó a la francesa, y provisto, como de costumbre, con su patente de invención,[13] abrió su almacén, y dijo que él era el Mesías de la literatura, que venía a redimirla de la esclavitud de las reglas;—y acudieron ansiosos los noveleros; y la manada de imitadores (*imitatores servum pecus,*[14] que dijo Horacio) se esforzaron en sobrepujarle y dejar atrás su exageración; y los poetas transmitieron el nuevo humor a los novelistas; éstos a los historiadores; éstos a los políticos; éstos a todos los demás hombres; éstos a todas las mujeres,—y luego salió de Francia aquel virus ya bastardeado,[15] y corrió toda la Europa, y vino, en fin, a España; y llegó a Madrid (de donde había salido puro), y de una en otra pluma, de una en otra cabeza, vino a dar en la cabeza y en la pluma de mi sobrino, de aquel sobrino de que ya en otro tiempo creo haber hablado a mis lectores; y tal llegó a sus manos, que ni el mismo Víctor Hugo le conocería, ni el Seminario de Nobles tampoco.

La primera aplicación que mi sobrino creyó deber hacer de adquisición tan importante, fué a su propia física personal, esmerándose en poetizarla por medio del romanticismo aplicado al tocador.

Porque (decía él) la fachada de un romántico debe ser gótica, ojiva,[16] piramidal y emblemática.

Para ello comenzó a revolver cuadros y libros viejos, y a estudiar los trajes del tiempo de las Cruzadas; y cuando en un códice roñoso y amarillento acertaba a encontrar un monigote formando alguna letra inicial de capítulo, o rasguñado al margen por infantil e inexperta mano, daba por[17] bien empleado su desvelo, y luego poníase a formular en su persona aquel trasunto de la Edad Media.

Por resultado de estos experimentos llegó muy luego[18] a ser considerado como la estampa más *romántica* de todo Madrid, y a servir de modelo a todos los jóvenes aspirantes a esta nueva, no sé si diga[19] ciencia o arte. —Sea dicho en verdad; pero si yo hubiese mirado el negocio sólo por el lado económico, poco o nada podía pesarme de ello; porque mi sobrino, procediendo a simplificar su traje,

[7] transmission
[8] behold. Translate, this is why
[9] Victor Hugo attended this school as a small boy, but Mesonero's statement that he learned romanticism there is of course pure whimsy. Hugo's first works were in the classical vein, so he did not learn romanticism until after his return to France and his début as an author. However, some of the Spanish romanticists did attend the *Seminario de Nobles,* but after Hugo had left it. The chief influence of Spain on Hugo was in the Spanish setting of some of his plays.
[10] to recognize
[11] The last exponent of the drama of the Golden Age, which in many ways resembled romanticism. See Vol. II, pp. 259–60.
[12] raw material
[13] *patente de invención,* patent
[14] Latin, the servile band of imitators
[15] degenerated
[16] ogive, pointed arch as in Gothic cathedrals and castles, of which romantic authors often spoke
[17] *dar por,* to consider
[18] soon, immediately
[19] whether I should say

llegó a alcanzar tal rigor ascético, que un ermitaño daría más que hacer a los *Utrillas* y *Rougets*.[20]

Por de pronto eliminó el frac, por considerarle del tiempo de la decadencia; y aunque no del todo conforme con la levita, hubo de transigir con ella, como más análoga a la sensibilidad de la expresión. Luego suprimió el chaleco, por redundante; luego el cuello de la camisa, por inconexo; luego las cadenas y relojes, los botones y alfileres, por minuciosos y mecánicos; después los guantes, por embarazosos; luego las aguas de olor, los cepillos, el barniz de las botas, y las navajas de afeitar, y otros mil adminículos que los que no alcanzamos la perfección romántica creemos indispensables y de todo rigor.[21]

Quedó, pues, reducido todo el atavío de su persona a un estrecho pantalón, que designaba la musculatura pronunciada de aquellas piernas; una levitilla de menguada faldamenta y abrochada tenazmente hasta la nuez de la garganta;[22] un pañuelo negro descuidadamente anudado en torno de ésta, y un sombrero de misteriosa forma, fuertemente introducido[23] hasta la ceja izquierda. Por bajo de él descolgábanse de entrambos lados de la cabeza dos guedejas de pelo negro y barnizado, que formando un doble bucle convexo, se introducían por bajo de las orejas, haciendo desaparecer éstas de la vista del espectador; las patillas, la barba y el bigote, formando una continuación de aquella espesura, daban con dificultad permiso para blanquear[24] a dos mejillas lívidas, dos labios mortecinos, una afilada nariz, dos ojos grandes, negros y de mirar sombrío, una frente triangular y *fatídica*.[25]—Tal era la *vera efigies*[26] de mi sobrino; y no hay que decir que tan uniforme tristura ofrecía no sé qué[27] de siniestro e inanimado; de suerte que no pocas veces, cuando, cruzado de brazos y la barba sumida en el pecho, se hallaba abismado en sus tétricas reflexiones, llegaba yo a dudar si era él mismo o sólo su traje colgado de una percha, y acontecióme más de una ocasión el ir a hablarle por la espalda, creyendo verle de frente, o darle una palmada en el pecho, juzgando dársela en el lomo.

Ya que vió romantizada su persona, toda su atención se convirtió a romantizar igualmente sus ideas, su carácter y sus estudios.—Por de pronto, me declaró rotundamente su resolución contraria a seguir ninguna de las carreras que le propuse, asegurándome que encontraba en su corazón algo de volcánico y sublime, incompatible con la exactitude matemática[28] o con las fórmulas del foro; y después de largas disertaciones, vine a sacar en consecuencia que la carrera que le parecía más análoga a sus circunstancias era la carrera de poeta, que, según él, es la que guía derechita[29] al templo de la inmortalidad.

En busca de sublimes inspiraciones, y con el objeto sin duda de formar su carácter tétrico y sepulcral, recorrió día y noche los cementerios y escuelas anatómicas; trabó amistosa relación con los enterradores y fisiólogos; aprendió el lenguaje de los buhos y de las lechuzas; encaramóse a las peñas escarpadas, y se perdió en la espesura de los bosques; interrogó a las ruinas de los monasterios y de las ventas (que él tomaba por góticos castillos); examinó la ponzoñosa virtud de las plan-

[20] Fashionable tailors of the day
[21] *de todo rigor*, indispensable, necessary
[22] Adam's apple
[23] to pull down
[24] to show their paleness
[25] fateful. The word *fate* is forever appearing in romantic works.
[26] Latin, true image
[27] *no sé qué*, something or other
[28] Supply, of engineering
[29] right straight

tas, e hizo experiencia en algunos animales del filo de su cuchilla y de los convulsos movimientos de la muerte.[30] —Trocó los libros que yo le recomendaba, los Cervantes, los Solís, los Quevedos, los Saavedras, los Moretos, Meléndez y Moratines, por los Hugos y Dumas, los Balzacs, los Sands y Souliés;[31] rebutió su mollera de todas las encantadoras fantasías de lord Byron y de los tétricos cuadros de d'Arlincourt; no se le escapó uno solo de los abortos teatrales de Ducange, ni de los fantásticos ensueños de Hoffman; y en los ratos en que menos propenso estaba a la melancolía, entreteníase en estudiar la *Craneoscopia* del doctor Gall, o las *Meditaciones* de Volney.[32]

Fuertemente pertrechado con toda esta diabólica erudición, se creyó ya en estado de dejar correr su pluma, y rasguñó unas cuantas docenas de *fragmentos* en prosa poética, y concluyó algunos *cuentos* en verso prosaico; y todos empezaban con puntos suspensivos,[33] y concluían en *¡maldición¡*; y unos y otros estaban atestados de *figuras de capuz,* y de *siniestros bultos;* y de *hombres gigantes,* y de *sonrisa infernal;* y de *almenas altísimas,* y de *profundos fosos;* y de *buitres carnívoros,* y de *copas*[34] *fatales;* y de *ensueños fatídicos,* y de *velos transparentes;* y de *aceradas mallas,* y de *briosos corceles,* y de *flores amarillas,* y de *fúnebre cruz.*—Generalmente todas estas composiciones *fugitivas* solían llevar sus títulos tan incomprensibles y vagos como ellas mismas; v. gr.: *¡¡¡Qué será!!!—¡¡¡ . . . No . . . !!!—¡Más allá . . . !—Puede ser.—¿Cuando?—¡Acaso . . . !—¡Oremus!*[35]

Esto en cuanto a la forma de sus composiciones; en cuanto al fondo de sus pensamientos, no sé qué decir, sino que unas veces me parecía mi sobrino un gran poeta, y otras un loco de atar;[36]—en algunas ocasiones me estremecía al oírle cantar el suicidio, o discurrir dudosamente sobre la inmortalidad del alma; y otras teníale por un santo, pintando la celestial sonrisa de los ángeles o haciendo tiernos apóstrofes a la Madre de Dios.—Yo no sé a punto fijo[37] qué pensaba él sobre todo esto; pero creo que lo más seguro es que no pensaba nada, ni él mismo entendía lo que quería decir.

Sin embargo, el muchacho con estos *raptos* consiguió al fin verse admirado por una turba de aprendices del delirio, que le escuchaban enternecidos cuando él con voz monótona y sepulcral les recitaba cualquiera de sus composiciones; y siempre le aplaudían en aquellos rasgos más extravagantes y oscuros, y sacaban copias nada escrupulosas, y las aprendían de memoria, y luego esforzábanse a imitarlas, y sólo acertaban a imitar los defectos, y de ningún modo las bellezas originales que podían recomendarlas.

Todos estos encomios y adulaciones de amistad lisonjeaban muy poco el altivo deseo de mi sobrino, que era nada menos que atraer hacia sí la atencion y el entusiasmo de todo el país.—Y convencido de que para llegar al templo de la inmortalidad (partiendo de Madrid) es cosa indispensable el

[30] Mesonero is poking fun at the romanticists' melancholy, their feeling of the futility of life, and their interest in death.

[31] He exchanged time-tested Spanish authors for recent romantic French ones. The Saavedra that Mesonero includes as one of the reputable Spanish authors is probably Diego Saavedra Fajardo, 1584–1648, for Ángel de Saavedra, the Duque de Rivas, was best known for two romantic works.

[32] Gall, a German physiologist (d. 1828) who studied the nervous system and the brain. Count de Volney (d. 1820), a free-thinker, interested in Oriental languages and civilization, who wrote *Les ruines, ou méditations sur les révolutions des empires.*

[33] dots to indicate suspended thought

[34] goblet; figuratively, drink, potion

[35] Latin, let us pray

[36] *loco de atar,* stark mad

[37] *a punto fijo,* precisely

pasarse por la calle del Príncipe,[38] quiero decir, el componer una obra para el teatro, he aquí la razón por qué reunió todas sus fuerzas intelectuales; llamó a concurso su fatídica estrella, sus recuerdos, sus lecturas; evocó las sombras de los muertos para preguntarles sobre diferentes puntos; martirizó las historias y tragó el polvo de los archivos; interpeló a su calenturienta musa, colocándose con ella en la región aérea donde se forman las románticas tormentas; y mirando desde aquella altura esta sociedad terrena, reducida por la distancia a una pequeñez microscópica, aplicado al ojo izquierdo el catalejo romántico, que todo lo abulta, que todo lo descompone, inflamóse al fin su fosfórica fantasía y compuso un drama.

¡Válgame Dios! ¡Con qué placer haría yo a mis lectores el mayor de los 5 regalos posibles dándoles *in integrum*[39] esta composición sublime, práctica explicación del sistema romántico, en que, según la medicina homeopática, que consiste en curar las enfermedades 10 con sus semejantes, se intenta, a fuerza de crímenes, corregir el crimen mismo! Mas ni la suerte ni mi sobrino me han hecho poseedor de aquel tesoro, y únicamente la memoria, depositaria infiel 15 de secretos, ha conservado en mi imaginación el título y personajes del drama. Helos aquí:

¡¡ELLA . . . !!! Y ¡¡ÉL . . . !!!

Drama Romántico Natural,

Emblemático-Sublime, Anónimo, Sinónimo, Tétrico y Espasmódico;

Original, en diferentes prosas[40]
y versos, en seis actos y
catorce cuadros.

Por . . .

Aquí había una nota que decía: (*Cuando el público pida el nombre del autor*),
y seguía más abajo:

Siglos IV y V.—La escena pasa en toda Europa y dura unos cien años.[41]

INTERLOCUTORES.

La mujer (todas las mujeres, toda la mujer).
El marido (*todos los maridos*).
Un hombre salvaje (el amante).
El Dux de Venecia.
El tirano de Siracusa.
El doncel.
La Archiduquesa de Austria.
Un espía.
Un favorito.
20 Un verdugo.
Un boticario.
La Cuádruple Alianza
El sereno del barrio.
Coro de monjas carmelitas.
25 Coro de padres agonizantes.[42]
Un hombre del pueblo.
Un pueblo de hombres.

[38] The principal theater of Madrid was the *Teatro del Príncipe,* located in the street of the same name.

[39] Latin, in full

[40] The classicists wrote their plays all in *one* verse form; the romanticists prided themselves on using both prose and various verse meters, so Mesonero goes them one better and has his nephew write in several kinds of prose!

[41] Notice how thoroughly he breaks the unities of place and time. Not infrequently the romanticists seem to go almost out of their way in order to break classic rules.

[42] Priests who devote themselves to caring for dying persons

Un espectro que habla.
Otro ídem que agarra.
Un demandadero de la Paz y Caridad.
Un judío.
Cuatro enterradores.
Músicos y danzantes.
Comparsas de tropa, brujas, gitanos, frailes y gente ordinaria.

—Los títulos de las jornadas (porque cada una llevaba el suyo, a manera de código) eran, si mal no me acuerdo, los siguientes:—1.ª *Un crimen.*—2.ª *El veneno.*—3.ª *Ya es tarde.*—4.ª *El panteón.*—5.ª *¡Ella!*—6.ª *¡Él!*—y las decoraciones eran las seis obligadas en todos los dramas románticos, a saber: *Salón de baile; Bosque; La capilla; Un subterráneo; La alcoba* y *El cementerio.*

Con tan buenos elementos confeccionó mi sobrino su admirable composición, en términos, que si yo recordase una sola escena para estamparla aquí, peligraba[43] el sistema nervioso de mis lectores; con que, así no hay sino dejarlo en tal punto y aguardar a que llegue día en que la fama nos las[44] transmita en toda su integridad; día que él retardaba, aguardando a que *las masas* (las masas somos nosotros) se hallen (o nos hallemos) en el caso de digerir esta comida, que él modestamente llamaba un *poco fuerte.*

De esta manera mi sobrino caminaba a la inmortalidad por la senda de la muerte; quiero decir, que con tales fatigas cumplía lo que él llamaba *su misión sobre la tierra.*[45] Empero la continuación de las vigilias y el obstinado combate de sentimientos tan hiperbólicos habíanle reducido a una situación tan lastimosa de cerebro, que cada día me temía encontrarle consumido a impulsos de su fuego celestial.

Y aconteció que, para acabar de rematar lo poco que en él quedaba de seso, hubo de ver una tarde por entre los mal labrados hierros de su balcón a cierta Melisendra[46] de diez y ocho abriles, más pálida que una noche de luna, y más mortecina que lámpara sepulcral; con sus luengos cabellos trenzados a la veneciana, y sus mangas a la María Tudor, y su blanquísimo vestido aéreo a la Straniera, y su cinturón a la Esmeralda, y su cruz de oro al cuello a la huérfana de Underlach.[47]

Hallábase a la sazón meditabunda, los ojos elevados al cielo, la mano derecha en la apagada mejilla, y en la izquierda sosteniendo débilmente un libro abierto . . . libro que, según el forro[48] amarillo, su tamaño y demás proporciones, no podía ser otro, a mi entender, que el *Han de Islandia* o el *Bug-Jargal.*[49]

No fué menester más para que la chispa eléctrico-romántica atravesase instantáneamente la calle, y pasase desde el balcón de la doncella sentimental al otro frontero donde se hallaba mi sobrino, viniendo a inflamar súbitamente su corazón. Miráronse pues, y creyeron adivinarse;[50] luego se hablaron, y concluyeron por no entenderse; esto es, por entregarse a aquel sentimiento vago, ideal, fantástico, frenético, que no sé bien cómo designar aquí, sino es ya que me valga de la consabida calificación de . . . *romanticismo puro.*

Pero al cabo, el sujeto[51] en cuestión era mi sobrino, y el bello objeto de sus arrobamientos, una señorita, hija de

[43] Imperfect tense used for a conditional for greater emphasis
[44] Antecedent, *escenas*
[45] Romantic poets often spoke of their 'mission' to lead mankind toward a better life.
[46] A name common in the Spanish ballads for a young heroine
[47] *María Tudor,* a play by Victor Hugo (1833); *La Straniera,* an opera by Bellini (1829); *Esmeralda,* the heroine of Hugo's *Notre Dame de Paris* (1831); *la huérfana de Underlach,* the heroine of d'Arlincourt's *Solitaire* (1821).
[48] cover
[49] Two novels by Victor Hugo
[50] to comprehend each other instinctively
[51] individual

un honrado vecino mío, procurador del número[52] y clásico por todas sus coyunturas.[53] A mí no me desagradó la idea de que el muchacho se inclinase a la muchacha (siempre llevando por delante la más sana intención), y con el deseo también de distraerle de sus melancólicas tareas, no sólo le introduje en la casa, sino que favorecí (Dios me lo perdone) todo lo posible el desarrollo de su inclinación.

Lisonjeábame, pues, con la idea de un desenlace natural y espontáneo, sabiendo que toda la familia de la niña participaba de mis sentimientos, cuando una noche me hallé sorprendido con la vuelta repentina de mi sobrino, que en el estado más descompuesto y atroz corrió a encerrarse en su cuarto gritando desaforadamente: —«¡Asesino! . . . ¡Asesino! . . . ¡Fatalidad! ¡Maldición! . . .»

—¿Qué demonios es esto?—Corro al cuarto del muchacho, pero había cerrado por dentro y no me responde; vuelo a casa del vecino por si[54] alcanzo a averiguar la causa de aquel desorden, y me encuentro en otro no menos terrible a toda la familia: la chica accidentada y convulsa, la madre llorando, el padre fuera de sí . . .[55]

—¿Qué es esto, señores? ¿qué es lo que hay?

—¿Qué ha de ser?[56] (me contestó el buen hombre), ¿qué ha de ser? sino que el demonio en persona se ha introducido en mi casa con su sobrino de usted . . . Lea usted, lea usted qué proyectos son los suyos; qué ideas de amor y de religión . . . —Y me entregó unos papeles, que por lo visto había sorprendido[57] a los amantes.

Recorrílos rápidamente, y me encontré diversas composiciones de éstas de tumba y hachero, que yo estaba tan acostumbrado a escuchar a mi sobrino. —En todas ellas venía a decir a su amante, con la mayor ternura, que era preciso que se muriesen para ser felices; que se matara ella, y luego él iría a derramar flores sobre su sepulcro, y luego se moriría también y los enterrarían bajo una misma losa . . . Otras veces la proponía que para huir de la tiranía del hombre—«este *hombre* soy yo», decía el pobre procurador,—se escurriese con él a los bosques o a los mares, y que se irían a una caverna a vivir con las fieras, o se harían piratas o bandoleros; en unas ocasiones la suponía ya difunta y la cantaba el responso en bellísimas quintillas y coplas de pie quebrado;[58] en otras llenábala de maldiciones por haberle hecho probar la ponzoña del amor.

—Y a todo esto (añadía el padre), nada de boda, ni nada de solicitar un empleo para mantenerla . . . Vea usted, vea usted: por ahí ha de estar . . .; oiga usted cómo se explica en este punto . . .; ahí, en esas coplas o seguidillas,[59] o lo que sean, en que la dice lo que tiene que esperar de él . . .

Y en tan fiera esclavitud,
Sólo puede darte mi alma
Un suspiro . . . y una palma . . .
Una tumba . . . y una cruz . . .

—Pues cierto que son buenos adminículos para llenar una carta de dote[60] . . .; no, sino échelos[61] usted en el puchero y verá qué caldo sale . . . Y no es esto lo peor (continuaba el buen hombre), sino que la muchacha se ha vuelto tan loca como él, y ya

[52] *procurador del número,* a lawyer of the guild
[53] joint. Translate, a dyed-in-the-wool classicist [54] Translate, to see if
[55] *fuera de sí,* beside himself
[56] What can it be?; what do you suppose it is? *Haber de* stands for a future of probability.
[57] to take by surprise
[58] Kinds of verse usually employed for light or even jocular compositions
[59] Popular dance tunes and poems
[60] *carta de dote,* a dowry contract, marriage contract
[61] Translate, just try throwing them

habla de féretros y letanías, y dice que está deshojada y que es un tronco carcomido, con otras mil barbaridades, que no sé cómo no la mato . . . y a lo mejor nos asusta por las noches, despertando despavorida y corriendo por toda la casa, diciendo que la persigue la sombra de no sé qué Astolfo[62] o Ingolfo *el exterminador;* y nos llama tiranos a su madre y a mí; y dice que tiene guardado un veneno, no sé bien si para ella o para nosotros; y entre tanto las camisas no se cosen, y la casa no se barre, y los libros malditos me consumen todo el caudal.

—Sosiéguese usted, señor don Cleto, sosiéguese usted.

Y llamándole aparte, le hice una explicación del carácter de mi sobrino, componiéndolo de suerte que, si no lo convencí de que podía casar a su hija con un tigre, por menos le determiné a casarla con un loco.

Satisfecho con tan buenas nuevas, regresé a mi casa para tranquilizar el espíritu del joven amante; . . . Me pareció conveniente poner un término a tan grotesca escena, entrando a recoger a mi moribundo sobrino y encerrarle bajo de llave en su cuarto; y al reconocer[63] cuidadosamente y separar todos los objetos con que pudiera ofenderse,[64] hallé sobre la mesa una carta sin fecha, dirigida a mí, y copiada de la *Galería fúnebre,*[65] la cual estaba concebida en términos tan alarmantes, que me hizo empezar a temer de veras sus proyectos y el estado infeliz de su cabeza. Conocí, pues, que no había más que un medio que adoptar, y era el arrancarle con mano fuerte a sus lecturas, a sus amores y a sus reflexiones, haciéndole emprender una carrera activa, peligrosa y varia; ninguna me pareció mejor que la militar, a la que él también mostraba alguna inclinación; hícele poner una charretera[66] al hombro izquierdo y le vi partir con alegría a reunirse a sus banderas.[67]

Un año ha trascurrido desde entonces, y hasta hace pocos días no le había vuelto a ver; y pueden considerar mis lectores el placer que me causaría al contemplarle robusto y alegre, la charretera a la derecha[68] y una cruz[69] en el lado izquierdo, cantando perpetuamente zorcicos y rondeñas, y por toda biblioteca en la maleta la *Ordenanza militar* y la *Guía del oficial en campaña.*

Luego que ya le vi en estado que no peligraba, le entregué la llave de su escritorio; y era cosa de ver el oírle repetir a carcajadas sus fúnebres composiciones; deseoso, sin duda, de probarme su nuevo humor, quiso entregarlas al fuego; pero yo, celoso de su fama póstuma, me opuse fuertemente a esta resolución; únicamente consentí en hacer un escrupuloso escrutinio, dividiéndolas, no en clásicas y románticas,[70] sino en tontas y no tontas, sacrificando aquéllas, y poniendo éstas sobre la niñas[71] de mis ojos.—En cuanto al drama, no fué posible encontrarle, por haberle prestado mi sobrino a otro poeta novel, el cual le comunicó a varios aprendices del oficio, y éstos le adoptaron por tipo, y repartieron entre sí las bellezas de que abundaba, usurpando de este modo, ora los

[62] Astolfo, a character of Ariosto's *Orlando furioso,* had a magic trumpet whose sound alone was enough to conquer his enemies.

[63] to reconnoitre

[64] to harm oneself

[65] A book in 12 volumes, published in 1831, dealing with ghosts and supernatural apparitions.

[66] epaulet. Only one is worn on the left shoulder by the lowest commissioned officers.

[67] Here, his regiment

[68] Signifying a rise in rank

[69] medal

[70] Once again Mesonero shows himself to be a partisan of moderation. This attitude was to become more and more important in Spain. It is often called *eclecticism,* that is, a selection of elements from all preceding literary schools.

[71] apple (of eye)

aplausos, ora los silbidos que a mi sobrino correspondían, y dando al público en mutilados trozos el esqueleto de tan gigantesca composición.

La lectura, en fin, de sus versos, trajo a la memoria del joven militar un recuerdo de su vaporosa deidad; preguntóme por ella con interés, y aun llegué a sospechar que estaba persuadido de que se habría evaporado de puro amor; pero yo procuré tranquilizarle con la verdad del caso; y era que la abandonada Ariadna[72] se había conformado con su suerte: ítem más, se había pasado al género clásico, entregando su mano, y aun no sé si su corazón, a un honrado mercader de la calle de Postas . . . ¡Ingratitud notable de mujeres! . . . bien es la verdad que él por su parte no la había hecho, según me confesó, sino unas catorce o quince infidelidades en el año transcurrido. De este modo concluyeron unos amores que, si hubieran seguido su curso natural habrían podido dar a los venideros Shakespeares materia sublime para otro nuevo *Romeo.*

[72] Ariadne, the abandoned lover of Theseus

Gustavo Adolfo Bécquer

A DREAMY young man, who suffered from poverty and delicate health, who never found satisfaction for his yearnings for love and glory, and who died of a mysterious illness at the age of thirty-four, is now regarded as Spain's greatest poet of the nineteenth century.

Gustavo Adolfo Bécquer (1836–70) was left an orphan at the age of nine. He went to Madrid from his native Sevilla when he was eighteen, but achieved no literary recognition until about 1860, his twenty-fourth year. With his beloved brother Valeriano, he struggled to make a living by writing and by painting. All of his work was accomplished in just ten years. Because of his poor health, he retired with his brother to live for a year in a ruined monastery on the slopes of the Moncayo, a mountain about fifty miles west of Zaragoza. Later the brothers spent several months in Toledo, where they hoped to establish permanent residence. Bécquer had married impetuously after being disdained in another love affair, but found no happiness in this union, although he loved his two children tenderly. Valeriano's death, just three months before Gustavo's, robbed the latter of his most sympathetic and understanding comrade.

This poet's total production consists of seventy-nine *rimas* and a handful of legends in poetic prose. The *rimas* are all very short, some no longer than four lines, and almost all deal with various aspects of one central theme, love, shown in all its multifold aspects—sometimes as a yearning after the ideal woman, sometimes as disillusionment, sometimes as bitter, death-seeking despair. Love is the sun around which Bécquer's soul revolves, and the poems are merely an exposition of the states of his soul as it basks in light or plunges into darkness.

Not that all these poems relate to real love affairs. Bécquer himself tells that *'Me cuesta trabajo saber qué cosas he soñado y cuáles me han sucedido. Mis afectos se reparten entre fantasmas de la imaginación y personajes reales. Mi memoria clasifica, revueltos, nombres y fechas de mujeres y días que han muerto o han pasado, con los días y mujeres que no han existido sino en mi mente.'* The intensity of Bécquer's imaginative life was such that he created beings for his delight out of his own mind. To such an extent were his thoughts centered on love that he felt it to be a mysterious force animating all nature and pervading the whole world.

What we have told of Bécquer's life is sufficient to indicate that we are dealing with a romantic poet. His works, too, lead us to the same conclusion, but a great change took place between the romantic period and the decade (1860–70) during which Bécquer composed his works. While we find the melancholy, the yearnings, and the passion of the romantic poet, a new and equally important element lies in the deliberate vagueness which permeates his poems and which, in turn, depends upon a new concept of poetry. Bécquer believes that poetry, like love, pervades everything, lies all about us, and that the poet merely suggests it to his reader. He does not deal with concrete forms, persons, and sentiments, except as symbols of the states of his soul. In trying to convey to us the delicate nuances of his feelings he often has to express himself indirectly by a series of metaphors. There are no precise words for the things which Bécquer wishes to name; he can merely say that they are like this or like that. Or again his words, chosen for their indistinct emotional connotations, are such as to *suggest* to the reader emotions which he shares with the poet and which cannot be named directly. As one critic has said: 'Bécquer's poems begins when the verse ends.'

Another feature tending also towards the same end is the almost constant use of assonance instead of consonantal rhyme. Less obtrusive than the latter, assonance does not mark out the verse structure so sharply and gives the poem a hazy outline. Bécquer's harmonies are as subtle as his thoughts and both share the same self-imposed vagueness.

In his legends Bécquer loves to take us into a fantastic world of the Middle Ages. He constantly uses supernatural beings, and his heroes are almost always poetic, romantic young men. He excels especially in lyrical descriptions of nature.

Bécquer stands between the romantic school and the new poetry of suggestion which dominated the literatures of the world during the last fifty years of the nineteenth century and the first third of the twentieth. He is one of the earliest to conceive this new idea of poetry. But even more than for this originality, Bécquer deserves our admiration and our sympathy for his tragic life and his melodious, heartfelt verses.

Another poet whose work has some of the qualities of Bécquer's is Rosalía de Castro. A native of Galicia, she loved and was inspired by the natural beauty of her homeland. Much of her poetry is written in Galician dialect. A second theme of her verse is her profound melancholy, a feeling which she owed partly to her illegitimate birth and partly to the misfortunes of her life—the death of loved ones and her impossible love affairs. These feelings she expresses in tenderly lyrical, haunting verses.

Gustavo Adolfo Bécquer

Los ojos verdes

Hace mucho tiempo que tenía ganas de escribir cualquier cosa con este título.

Hoy, que se me ha presentado ocasión, lo he puesto con letras grandes en la primera cuartilla de papel, y luego he dejado a capricho volar la pluma.

Yo creo que he visto unos ojos como los que he pintado en esta leyenda. No sé si en sueños, pero yo los he visto.[1] De seguro no los podré describir tales cuales[2] ellos eran: luminosos, transparentes como las gotas de la lluvia que se resbalan sobre las hojas de los árboles después de una tempestad de verano. De todos modos, cuento con la imaginación de mis lectores[3] para hacerme comprender en este que pudiéramos llamar boceto de un cuadro que pintaré algun día.

I

—Herido va el ciervo . . . herido va; no hay duda. Se ve el rastro de la sangre entre las zarzas del monte, y al saltar uno de esos lentiscos[4] han flaqueado sus piernas . . . Nuestro joven señor comienza por donde otros acaban . . . en cuarenta años de montero no he visto mejor golpe . . . Pero, ¡por San Saturio, patrón de Soria!,[5] cortadle el paso por esas carrascas,[6] azuzad los perros, soplad en esas trompas hasta echar los hígados,[7] y hundidle a los corceles una cuarta de hierro[8] en los ijares. ¿No veis que se dirige hacia la fuente de los álamos,[9] y si la salva antes de morir podemos darle por perdido?

Las cuencas del Moncayo[10] repitieron de eco en eco el bramido de las trompas, el latir de la jauría desencadenada, y las voces de los pajes resonaron con nueva furia, y el confuso tropel de hombres, caballos y perros se dirigió al punto que Íñigo, el montero mayor[11] de los marqueses de Almenar, señalara[12] como el más propósito para cortarle el paso a la res.

Pero todo fué inútil. Cuando el más ágil de los lebreles llegó a las carrascas jadeante y cubiertas las fauces de espuma, ya el ciervo, rápido como una saeta, las había salvado de un solo brinco, perdiéndose entre los matorrales de una trocha que conducía a la fuente.

—¡Alto! . . . ¡Alto todo el mundo!—gritó Íñigo entonces—; estaba de Dios que había de marcharse.[13]

Y la cabalgata se detuvo, y enmudecieron las trompas, y los lebreles dejaron refunfuñando la pista a la voz de los cazadores.

En aquel momento se reunía a la comitiva el héroe de la fiesta, Fernando de Argensola, el primogénito de Almenar.

[1] Here we see how intense an imagination Bécquer possessed, as he cannot divide his real and imaginative lives.
[2] *tales cuales,* just as
[3] This bears out what we have said about Bécquer's *suggesting* his mood to the reader, who must use his imagination and help in the creation of the artistic work.
[4] mastic tree
[5] An old city in eastern Castilla, near Bécquer's monastery retreat
[6] swamp oak
[7] *hasta echar los hígados;* translate, until you burst
[8] *una . . . hierro,* literally, a span of iron; here, spurs
[9] poplar tree
[10] A mountain near Soria
[11] chief, head
[12] Imperfect subjunctive used for pluperfect indicative
[13] Here, to get away

—¿Qué haces?—exclamó dirigiéndose a su montero, y en tanto, ya se pintaba el asombro en sus facciones, ya ardía la cólera en sus ojos—. ¿Qué haces, imbécil? ¡Ves que la pieza[14] está herida, que es la primera que cae por mi mano, y abandonas el rastro y la dejas perder para que vaya a morir en el fondo del bosque! ¿Crees acaso que he venido a matar ciervos para festines de lobos?

—Señor—murmuró Íñigo entre dientes—, es imposible pasar de este punto.

—¡Imposible! ¿y por qué?

—Porque esa trocha—prosiguió el montero—conduce a la fuente de los álamos; la fuente de los álamos, en cuyas aguas habita un espírtu del mal. El que osa enturbiar su corriente,[15] paga caro su atrevimiento. Ya la res habrá salvado sus márgenes; ¿cómo la salvaréis vos[16] sin atraer sobre vuestra cabeza alguna calamidad horrible? Los cazadores somos reyes del Moncayo, pero reyes que pagan un tributo. Pieza que se refugia en esa fuente misteriosa, pieza perdida.

—¡Pieza perdida! Primero perderé yo el señorío de mis padres, y primero perderé el ánima en manos de Satanás, que permitir que se me escape ese ciervo, el único que ha herido mi venablo, la primicia de mis excursiones de cazador . . . ¿Lo ves? . . . ¿lo ves? . . . Aún se distingue a intervalos desde aquí . . . las piernas le faltan, su carrera se acorta;[17] déjame . . . déjame . . . suelta esa brida o te revuelco en el polvo . . . ¿Quién sabe si no le daré lugar[18] para que llegue a la fuente? Y si llegase, al diablo ella, su limpidez y sus habitadores. ¡Sus!, ¡Relámpago!, ¡sus, caballo mío!, si lo alcanzas, mando engarzar los diamantes de mi joyel en tu serreta de oro.

Caballo y jinete partieron como un huracán.

Íñigo los siguió con la vista hasta que se perdieron en la maleza; después volvió los ojos en derredor suyo; todos, como él, permanecían inmóviles y consternados.

El montero exclamó al fin:

—Señores, vosotros lo habéis visto; me he expuesto a morir entre los pies de su caballo por detenerle. Yo he cumplido con mi deber. Con el diablo no sirven valentías. Hasta aquí llega el montero con su ballesta; de aquí adelante, que pruebe a pasar el capellán con su hisopo.[19]

II

—Tenéis la color quebrada;[20] andáis mustio y sombrío; ¿qué os sucede? Desde el día, que yo siempre tendré por fuenesto, en que llegasteis a la fuente de los álamos en pos de[21] la res herida, diríase que una mala bruja os ha encanijado con sus hechizos.

Ya no vais a los montes precedido de la ruidosa jauría, ni el clamor de vuestras trompas despierta sus ecos. Solo con esas cavilaciones que os persiguen, todas las mañanas tomáis la ballesta para enderezaros a la espesura y permanecer en ella hasta que el sol se esconde. Y cuando la noche obscurece y volvéis pálido y fatigado al castillo, en balde[22] busco en la bandolera los despojos de la caza. ¿Qué os ocupa tan largas horas lejos de los que más os quieren?

Mientras Íñigo hablaba, Fernando, absorto en sus ideas, sacaba maquinalmente astillas de su escaño de ébano con el cuchillo de monte.

[14] Here, game
[15] The *fuente* is not only the *spring,* but the *stream* which flows from it.
[16] Old Spanish for *vosotros* (used to give an archaic flavor to the text)
[17] Translate, it is slowing down
[18] *dar lugar,* to give [him] time
[19] sprinkler for holy water (which would drive away evil spirits)
[20] altered
[21] *en pos de,* after
[22] *en balde,* in vain

Después de un largo silencio, que sólo interrumpía el chirrido de la hoja[23] al resbalarse sobre la pulimentada madera, el joven exclamó dirigiéndose a su servidor, como si no hubiera escuchado una sola de sus palabras:

—Íñigo, tú que eres viejo, tú que conoces todas las guaridas del Moncayo, que has vivido en sus faldas[24] persiguiendo a las fieras, y en tus errantes excursiones de cazador subiste más de una vez a su cumbre, dime: ¿has encontrado por acaso una mujer que vive entre sus rocas?

—¡Una mujer!—exclamó el montero con asombro y mirándole de hito en hito.[25]

—Sí—dijo el joven—; es una cosa extraña lo que me sucede, muy extraña . . . Creí poder guardar ese secreto eternamente, pero no es ya posible; rebosa en mi corazón y asoma a mi semblante. Voy, pues, a revelártelo . . . Tú me ayudarás a desvanecer el misterio que envuelve a esa criatura, que al parecer sólo para mí existe, pues nadie la conoce, ni la ha visto, ni puede darme razón[26] de ella.

El montero, sin despegar los labios, arrastró su banquillo hasta colocarlo junto al escaño de su señor, del que no apartaba un punto los espantados ojos. Éste, después de coordinar sus ideas, prosiguió así.

—Desde el día en que a pesar de tus funestas predicciones llegué a la fuente de los álamos, y atravesando sus aguas recobré el ciervo que vuestra superstición hubiera dejado huir, se llenó mi alma del deseo de la soledad.

Tú no conoces aquel sitio. Mira, la fuente brota escondida en el seno de una peña, y cae resbalándose gota a gota por entre las verdes y flotantes hojas de las plantas que crecen al borde de su cuna. Aquellas gotas que al desprenderse brillan como puntos de oro y suenan como las notas de un instrumento, se reúnen entre los céspedes, y susurrando, susurrando, con un ruido semejante al de las abejas que zumban en torno de las flores, se alejan por entre las arenas, y forman un cauce, y luchan con los obstáculos que se oponen a su camino, y se repliegan sobre sí mismas, y saltan, y huyen, y corren, unas veces con risa, otras con suspiros, hasta caer en un lago. En el lago caen con un rumor indescriptible. Lamentos, palabras, nombres, cantares, yo no sé lo que he oído en aquel rumor cuando me he sentado solo y febril sobre el peñasco, a cuyos pies saltan las aguas de la fuente misteriosa para estancarse en una balsa profunda, cuya inmóvil superficie apenas riza el viento de la tarde.

Todo es allí grande. La soledad, con sus mil rumores desconocidos, vive en aquellos lugares y embriaga el espíritu en su inefable melancolía. En las plateadas hojas de los álamos, en los huecos de las peñas, en las ondas del agua, parece que nos hablan los invisibles espíritus de la Naturaleza, que reconocen un hermano en el inmortal espíritu del hombre.

Cuando al despuntar la mañana me veías tomar la ballesta y dirigirme al monte, no fué nunca para perderme entre sus matorrales en pos de la caza, no; iba a sentarme al borde de la fuente, a buscar en sus ondas . . . no sé qué, ¡una locura! El día en que salté sobre ella con mi Relámpago, creí haber visto brillar en su fondo una cosa extraña . . . muy extraña . . . los ojos de una mujer.

Tal vez sería un rayo de sol que serpeó fugitivo entre su espuma; tal vez una de esas flores que flotan entre las algas de su seno, y cuyos cálices parecen esmeraldas . . . no sé: yo creí ver una

[23] blade
[24] slopes
[25] *de hito en hito,* fixedly
[26] Here, an account

mirada que se clavó en la mía; una mirada que encendió en mi pecho un deseo absurdo, irrealizable: el de encontrar una persona con unos ojos como aquéllos.

En su busca fuí un día y otro[27] a aquel sitio.

Por último, una tarde . . . yo me creí juguete de un sueño . . . ; pero no, es verdad: la he hablado ya muchas veces, como te hablo a ti ahora . . . ; una tarde encontré sentada en mi puesto, y vestida con unas ropas que llegaban hasta las aguas y flotaban sobre su haz, una mujer hermosa sobre toda ponderación. Sus cabellos eran como el oro; sus pestañas brillaban como hilos de luz, y entre las pestañas volteaban[28] inquietas unas pupilas que yo había visto . . . sí; porque los ojos de aquella mujer eran los ojos que yo tenía clavados en la mente; unos ojos de un color imposible; unos ojos . . .

—¡Verdes!—exclamó Íñigo con un acento de profundo terror e incorporándose de un salto en su asiento.

Fernando le miró a su vez[29] como asombrado de que concluyese lo que iba a decir, y le preguntó con una mezcla de ansiedad y de alegría:

—¿La conoces?

—¡Oh, no!—dijo el montero—. ¡Líbreme Dios de conocerla! Pero mis padres, al prohibirme llegar hasta esos lugares, me dijeron mil veces que el espíritu, trasgo, demonio o mujer que habita en sus aguas, tiene los ojos de ese color. Yo os conjuro, por los que más améis en la tierra, a no volver a la fuente de los álamos. Un día u otro os alcanzará su venganza, y expiaréis muriendo el delito de haber encenagado sus ondas.

—¡Por los que más amo! . . .— murmuró el joven con una triste sonrisa.

—Sí—prosiguió el anciano—: por vuestros padres, por vuestros deudos, por las lágrimas de la que el cielo destina para vuestra esposa, por las de un servidor que os ha visto nacer . . .

—¿Sabes tú lo que más amo en este mundo? ¿Sabes tú por qué[30] daría yo el amor de mi padre, los besos de la que me dió la vida, y todo el cariño que pueden atesorar todas las mujeres de la tierra? Por una mirada, por una sola mirada de esos ojos . . . ¡Cómo podré yo dejar de buscarlos!

Dijo Fernando estas palabras con tal acento, que la lágrima que temblaba en los párpados de Íñigo se resbaló silenciosa por su mejilla, mientras exclamó con acento sombrío: ¡Cúmplase la voluntad del cielo!

III

—¿Quién eres tú? ¿Cuál es tu patria? ¿En dónde habitas? Yo vengo un día y otro en tu busca, y ni veo el corcel que te trae a estos lugares, ni a los servidores que conducen tu litera. Rompe de una vez el misterioso velo en que te envuelves como en una noche profunda. Yo te amo, y, noble o villana, seré tuyo, tuyo siempre . . .

El sol había traspuesto la cumbre del monte; las sombras bajaban a grandes pasos por su falda; la brisa gemía entre los álamos de la fuente, y la niebla,[31] elevándose poco a poco de la superficie del lago, comenzaba a envolver las rocas de su margen.

Sobre una de estas rocas, sobre una que parecía próxima a desplomarse en el fondo de las aguas, en cuya superficie se retrataba temblando, el primogénito de Almenar, de rodillas a los pies de su misteriosa amante, procuraba en vano arrancarle el secreto de su existencia.

Ella era hermosa, hermosa y pálida, como una estatua de alabastro. Uno

[27] *un día y otro,* day after day
[28] Here, to rove
[29] *a su vez,* in his turn
[30] for what
[31] mist

de sus rizos caía sobre sus hombros, deslizándose entre los pliegues del velo, como un rayo de sol que atraviesa las nubes, y en el cerco[32] de sus pestañas rubias brillaban sus pupilas, como dos esmeraldas sujetas en una joya de oro.

Cuando el joven acabó de hablarle, sus labios se removieron como para pronunciar algunas palabras; pero sólo exhalaron un suspiro, un suspiro débil, doliente, como el de la ligera onda que empuja una brisa al morir entre los juncos.

—¡No me respondes!—exclamó Fernando al ver burlada su esperanza—; ¿querrás que dé crédito a lo que de ti me han dicho? ¡Oh, no! . . . Háblame; yo quiero saber si me amas; yo quiero saber si puedo amarte, si eres una mujer . . .

—O un demonio . . . ¿Y si lo fuese?

El joven vaciló un instante; un sudor frío corrió por sus miembros; sus pupilas se dilataron al fijarse con más intensidad en las de aquella mujer, y fascinado por su brillo fosfórico, demente casi, exclamó en un arrebato de amor:

—Si lo fueses . . . te amaría . . . te amaría, como te amo ahora, como es mi destino amarte, hasta más allá de esta vida, si hay algo más allá de ella.

—Fernando—dijo la hermosa entonces con una voz semejante a una música—; yo te amo más aún que tú me amas; yo que desciendo hasta un mortal, siendo un espíritu puro. No soy una mujer como las que existen en la tierra; soy una mujer digna de ti, que eres superior a los demás hombres. Yo vivo en el fondo de estas aguas; incorpórea como ellas, fugaz y transparente, hablo con sus rumores y ondulo con sus pliegues. Yo no castigo al que osa turbar la fuente donde moro;[33] antes le premio con mi amor, como a un mortal superior a las supersticiones del vulgo, como a un amante capaz de comprender mi cariño extraño y misterioso.

Mientras ella hablaba así, el joven, absorto en la contemplación de su fantástica hermosura, atraído como por una fuerza desconocida, se aproximaba más y más al borde de la roca. La mujer de los ojos verdes prosiguió así:

—¿Ves, ves el límpido fondo de ese lago, ves esas plantas de largas y verdes hojas que se agitan en su fondo? . . . Ellas nos darán un lecho de esmeraldas y corales . . . y yo . . . yo te daré una felicidad sin nombre, esa felicidad que has soñado en tus horas de delirio, y que no puede ofrecerte nadie . . . Ven, la niebla del lago flota sobre nuestras frentes como un pabellón de lino . . . las ondas nos llaman con sus voces incomprensibles, el viento empieza entre los álamos sus himnos de amor; ven . . . ven . . .

La noche comenzaba a extender sus sombras, la luna rielaba en la superficie del lago, la niebla se arremolinaba al soplo del aire, y los ojos verdes brillaban en la obscuridad como los fuegos fatuos[34] que corren sobre el haz de las aguas infectas . . . Ven . . . ven . . . Estas palabras zumbaban en los oídos de Fernando como un conjuro. Ven . . . y la mujer misteriosa le llamaba al borde del abismo donde estaba suspendida, y parecía ofrecerle un beso . . . un beso . . .

Fernando dió un paso hacia ella . . . otro . . . y sintió unos brazos delgados y flexibles que se liaban a su cuello, y una sensación fría en sus labios ardorosos, un beso de nieve[35] . . . y vaciló . . . y perdió pie, y cayó al agua con un rumor sordo y lúgubre.

Las aguas saltaron en chispas de luz, y se cerraron sobre su cuerpo, y sus círculos de plata fueron ensanchándose, ensanchándose hasta expirar en las orillas.

[32] hedge; here, border [33] *morar,* to dwell [34] *fuego fatuo,* will-o'-the-wisp [35] an icy kiss

Rimas

IV

No digáis que agotado su tesoro,
  De asuntos falta,[1] enmudeció la lira.[2]
Podrá no haber poetas; pero siempre
  Habrá poesía.[3]

Mientras las ondas de la luz al beso[4] 5
  Palpiten encendidas;
Mientras el sol las desgarradas nubes
  De fuego y oro vista;

Mientras el aire en su regazo lleve
  Perfumes y armonías; 10
Mientras haya en el mundo primavera,
  ¡Habrá poesía!

Mientras la ciencia a descubrir no alcance
  Las fuentes de la vida,
Y en el mar o en el cielo haya un abismo 15
  Que al cálculo resista;

Mientras la humanidad siempre avanzando
  No sepa a dó[5] camina;
Mientras haya un misterio para el hombre,
  ¡Habrá poesía! 20

Mientras sintamos que se alegra el alma,
  Sin que los labios rían;
Mientras se llore, sin que el llanto acuda
  A nublar la pupila;

Mientras el corazón y la cabeza 25
  Batallando prosigan;
Mientras haya esperanzas y recuerdos,
  ¡Habrá poesía!

Mientras haya unos ojos que reflejen
  Los ojos que los miran; 30
Mientras responda el labio suspirando
  Al labio que suspira;

Mientras sentirse puedan en un beso
  Dos almas confundidas;

[1] *falta de,* lacking
[2] lyre; i.e., poetry
[3] Bécquer believes that poetry is every where, even if there are no poets to catch it and transmit it to less sensitive souls. He is going to tell us the particular places where poetry most commonly resides: in Nature, the mysteries of life, the emotions (especially love) all things which man can never completely fathom.
[4] Read, *al beso de la luz*
[5] Poetic for *dónde*

Mientras exista una mujer hermosa, 35
¡Habrá poesía!

XV

Cendal[6] flotante de leve bruma,
Rizada cinta de blanca espuma,
Rumor sonoro
De arpa de oro,
Beso del aura, onda de luz: 5
Eso eres tú.

Tú, sombra aérea, que cuantas veces
Voy a tocarte, te desvaneces
Como la llama, como el sonido,
Como la niebla, como el gemido 10
Del lago azul.

En mar sin playas onda sonante,
En el vacío cometa errante,
Largo lamento
Del ronco viento, 15
Ansia perpetua de algo mejor:
Eso soy yo.[7]

¡Yo, que a tus ojos en mi agonía
Los ojos vuelvo de noche y día;
Yo, que incansable corro y demente 20
Tras una sombra, tras la hija ardiente
De una visión!

XXI

¿Qué es poesía dices mientras clavas
En mi pupila[8] tu pupila azul;
¿Qué es poesía? ¿Y tú me lo preguntas?
¡Poesía . . . eres tú!

XXXIII

Es cuestión de palabras, y no obstante,
Ni tú ni yo jamás,
Después de lo pasado, convendremos
En quién la culpa está.

¡Lástima que el amor un diccionario 5
No tenga donde hallar
Cuando el orgullo es simplemente orgullo,
Y cuando es dignidad!

[6] delicate cloth; translate, scarf

[7] Notice how Bécquer uses a series of metaphors to express his feeling about the two persons of this poem. An example of deliberate vagueness and suggestion.

[8] Translate, eyes

XLI

Tú eras el huracán, y yo la alta
Torre que desafía su poder:
¡Tenías que estrellarte o abartirme! . . .
¡No pudo ser!

Tú eras el océano, y yo la enhiesta 5
Roca que firme aguarda su vaivén:
¡Tenías que romperte o que arrancarme!
¡No pudo ser!

Hermosa tú, yo altivo; acostumbrados
Uno a arrollar, el otro a no ceder: 10
La senda estrecha, inevitable el choque . . .
¡No pudo ser!

XLVII

Yo me he asomado a las profundas simas
De la tierra y del cielo,
Y les he visto el fin o con los ojos,
O con el pensamiento.

Mas ¡ay! de un corazón llegué al abismo, 5
Y me incliné por verlo,
Y mi alma y mis ojos se turbaron:
¡Tan hondo era y tan negro!

LI

De lo poco de vida que me resta
Diera con gusto los mejores años,
Por saber lo que a otros
De mí has hablado.

Y esta vida mortal . . . y de la eterna 5
Lo que me toque, si me toca algo,
Por saber lo que a solas
De mí has pensado.

LIII

Volverán las oscuras golondrinas
En tu balcón sus nidos a colgar,
Y, otra vez, con el ala a sus cristales
Jugando llamarán;[9]

Pero aquellas que el vuelo refrenaban 5
Tu hermosura y mi dicha a contemplar,

[9] to knock

[10] *Ésas* are the same as *aquellas*. By changing to *ésas* the poet implies that they are now a mental image in the lady's mind.

Aquellas que aprendieron nuestros nombres . . .
Ésas[10] . . . ¡no volverán!

Volverán las tupidas madreselvas
De tu jardín las tapias a escalar, 10
Y otra vez a la tarde, aun más hermosas,
Sus flores se abrirán;

Pero aquéllas cuajadas[11] de rocío,
Cuyas gotas mirábamos temblar
Y caer, como lágrimas del día . . . 15
Ésas . . . ¡no volverán!

Volverán del amor en tus oídos
Las palabras ardientes a sonar;
Tu corazón de sus profundo sueño
Tal vez despertará; 20

Pero mudo y absorto y de rodillas,
Como se adora a Dios ante su altar,
Como yo te he querido . . . desengáñate,
¡Así no te querrán!

Rosalía de Castro

Las campanas

Yo las amo, yo las oigo,
cual oigo el rumor del viento,
el murmurar de la fuente
o el balido del cordero.

Como los pájaros, ellas, 5
tan pronto asoma en los cielos
el primer rayo del alba,
le saludan con sus ecos.

Y en sus notas, que van prolongándose
por los llanos y los cerros, 10
hay algo de candoroso,
de apacible y de halagüeño.

Si por siempre enmudecieran,
¡qué tristeza en el aire y el cielo!
¡qué silencio en las iglesias! 15
¡qué extrañeza entre los muertos!

[11] Here, drenched

Dicen que no hablan las plantas

Dicen que no hablan las plantas, ni las fuentes, ni los pájaros,
Ni el onda con sus rumores, ni con su brillo los astros,
Lo dicen, pero no es cierto, pues siempre cuando yo paso
De mí murmuran y exclaman:
—Ahí va la loca, soñando 5
Con la eterna primavera de la vida y de los campos,
Y ya bien pronto, bien pronto, tendrá los cabellos canos,
Y ve temblando, aterida, que cubre la escarcha el prado.

Hay canas en mi cabeza, hay en los prados escarcha,
Mas yo prosigo soñando, pobre, incurable sonámbula, 10
Con la eterna primavera de la vida que se apaga
Y la perenne frescura de los campos y las almas,
Aunque los unos se agostan y aunque las otras se abrasan.

Astros y fuentes y flores, no murmuréis de mis sueños:
Sin ellos, ¿cómo admiraros, ni cómo vivir sin ellos? 15

Realism in the Novel

THROUGHOUT Europe the novel was the greatest literary success of the nineteenth century. Yet in Spain the novel did not attain importance until romanticism had vanished and realism had taken its place. It is true that during the romantic period many romantic novels were written, some by the authors whom we have studied, but none of these is highly regarded today. However, realism had already asserted itself in the *cuadros de costumbres* and out of these very *cuadros* was to be formed the realistic novel of Spain.

A woman, CECILIA BÖHL VON FABER (1796–1877), writing under the pen name of Fernán Caballero, gave the novel a new start and a direction which it followed throughout the century. In 1849 she produced *La Gaviota, novela de costumbres,* by stringing together on the thread of a plot a number of sketches of contemporary life. She herself says: *'Lo que escribo no son novelas de fantasía sino una reunión de escenas de la vida real, de descripciones, de retratos y reflexiones.'* Her declared objective was, then, to give a realistic description of customs in Andalucía, her home province. Since customs differ in the different regions of Spain, her novel necessarily had to deal with some one district. Therefore, we sometimes speak of the type as the 'regional novel.' These two qualities, realism and regionalism, appeared in most of the subsequent authors. Even Fernán Caballero's fault, excessive moralization—in her case in defense of the traditional way of life—crops out in the propagandistic tendencies of almost all her followers.

Realism as a literary term means an exact photographic reproduction of a scene or character. The term has taken on in some countries a further meaning, since their realistic authors deliberately sought out the less attractive aspects of life; but the term never had this implication in Spain. And, moreover, realism of this pictorial type is nothing new in Spain but has always been found in every period of Spanish literature.

The great masters of the novel, Valera, Galdós, and Pereda, whom we shall analyze in detail in following chapters, all owe much to Fernán Caballero, but for the time being we shall mention only two of her followers not taken up elsewhere.

PEDRO DE ALARCÓN (1833–91) vacillated between liberalism and conservatism and between romanticism and realism. He tried writing all kinds of novels, but never attained much success except as a realist. In his masterpiece, *El sombrero de tres picos* (1874), he depicts with characteristic humor and inimitable skill in handling an elaborate plot, the life and customs of a small Andalusian city.

ARMANDO PALACIO VALDÉS (1853–1938) attained his first success with a novel of liberal tendencies, *Marta y María* (1883), and continued to produce regional novels up to the 1930's. He describes his native region, Asturias, in his masterpiece, *La aldea perdida,* which shows the bad effects of progress when miners invade and spoil a charming village, and in *José,* a delightful idyll of the life of fisher folk. He also showed an unusual ability for assimilating the local color of other regions, as in *La hermana San Sulpicio,* set in Andalucía, and *La alegría del capitán Ribot,* which takes place in Valencia.

Juan Valera

JUAN VALERA (1824–1905) belonged to a family of the upper social stratum. His father owned estates in Andalucía and was an officer in the navy, and his mother was of noble blood. After taking his college degree, he devoted most of his life to the diplomatic service, only giving over to literature two short periods (1868–81 and 1895–1905). In his youth he was sent to the consulate at Naples, where he had as his chief the Duque de Rivas and where he became thoroughly imbued with classical art and literature, studying Greek with a charming and witty Rumanian lady. In rapid succession he held posts in Portugal, Brazil, Germany, and Russia. The political upheavals of 1868 left him without a position and he retired to his Andalusian estate. Here he devoted himself to writing, producing his first and most famous novel, *Pepita Jiménez,* in 1874. Between 1881 and 1895 he was Spanish Minister to Lisbon, Washington, Brussels, and Vienna. The last ten years of his life were devoted largely to critical writing.

Valera's character is a very unusual one for a Spaniard. We may call him an elegant pagan, understanding by paganism that worship of life and physical beauty which we associate with the ancient Greeks. Valera never made the distinction between the flesh and the spirit, the one bad and the other good, which so often appears in Christianity, but which never formed an element of Greek thought. For him, as for them, earthly love, material beauty, and refined sensualism were commingled with and undivided from beauty of mind and soul.

In his novels, Valera always seems to be an Olympian figure, urbane, well-bred, and aloof from the literary theories and quarrels of his time. His emotions are always deliberately held in restraint. But we know from his letters—of which several thousand still exist—that he was subject to emotional disturbances—boredom, ambition, love. His work is always well-proportioned, and always gives great stress to form. Hence Valera is one of the few Spaniards to catch the true classic spirit, not in the narrow sense of the literary 'rules,' but in the broader sense of moderation, proportion, and restraint. His studies of Greek and Latin and his travels in Italy prepared him for this point of view.

Valera did not copy anyone in literature, but formed a literary code based on his own preferences. In opposition to almost all the writers of his century, he believed that art should avoid social and political quarrels and should not strive to teach or to propagandize. But, since Valera was a very subtle person we sometimes detect a hidden didactic note in his novels. However, the main purpose of his art was beauty; therefore, Valera's code can be summed up in the phrase, 'Art for Art's sake.' He did not insist on an exact copying of nature. Although most of his novels are set in Andalucía, they are not strictly regional and contain little of the *costumbrista* element, which is so typical of most of the novels of the nineteenth century. Valera tends to idealize the scene, and his classical feeling makes it more universal (capable of being anywhere) than specifically Andalusian (regional). However, he believed that the psychological reality of the characters must be faithfully observed, although through personal preference he always chose to write about beautiful persons, never sordid or base ones. In his best novels he delicately analyzes the minds of his characters, showing himself to be a consummate psychologist.

While Valera was never truly popular with the masses, his artistic perfection will always find him readers among the cultivated public.*

Juan Valera

Pepita Jiménez (abridged)

Nescit labi virtus.[1]

El señor Deán de la catedral de ***, muerto pocos años ha, dejó entre sus papeles un legajo, que rodando de unas manos en otras, ha venido a dar en las mías, sin que, por extraña fortuna, se haya perdido uno solo de los documentos de que constaba . . .

Contiene el legajo tres partes. La primera dice: *Cartas de mi sobrino;* la segunda, *Paralipómenos,*[2] y la tercera, *Epílogo.—Cartas de mi hermano* . . .

Las cartas que la primera parte contiene parecen escritas por un joven de pocos años, con algún conocimiento teórico, pero con ninguna práctica de las cosas del mundo, educado al lado del señor Deán, su tío, y en el Seminario, y con gran fervor religioso y empeño decidido de ser sacerdote.

A este joven llamaremos D. Luis de Vargas.

El mencionado *manuscrito,* fielmente trasladado a la estampa, es como sigue:

I. *Cartas de mi Sobrino*

22 de marzo.

Querido tío y venerado maestro: Hace cuatro días que llegué con toda

* List of important books:

Pepita Jiménez
Doña Luz
Las ilusiones del Dr. Faustino
El comendador Mendoza
Juanita la larga

besides many volumes of critical works.

[1] Latin: Virtue cannot be overcome.

[2] The books of the Chronicles in the Old Testament. Since these books supplement the preceding Books of the Kings, their name indicates 'a supplementary account' (from the Greek 'left aside').

felicidad a este lugar de mi nacimiento, donde he hallado bien de salud a mi padre, al señor Vicario y a los amigos y parientes. El contento de verlos y de hablar con ellos, después de tantos años de ausencia, me ha embargado el ánimo y me ha robado el tiempo, de suerte que hasta ahora no he podido escribir a usted.

Usted me lo perdonará.

Como salí de aquí tan niño y he vuelto hecho un hombre, es singular la impresión que me causan todos estos objetos que guardaba en la memoria. Todo me parece más chico, mucho más chico, pero también más bonito que el recuerdo que tenía. La casa de mi padre, que en mi imaginación era inmensa, es sin duda una gran casa de un rico labrador, pero más pequeña que el Seminario. Lo que ahora comprendo y estimo mejor es el campo de por aquí.[3] Las huertas, sobre todo, son deliciosas. ¡Qué sendas tan lindas hay entre ellas! A un lado, y tal vez a ambos, corre el agua cristalina con grato murmullo. Las orillas de las acequias están cubiertas de hierbas olorosas y de flores de mil clases. En un instante puede uno coger un gran ramo de violetas. Dan sombra a estas sendas pomposos y gigantescos nogales, higueras y otros árboles, y forman los vallados la zarzamora, el rosal, el granado y la madreselva.

Es portentosa la multitud de pajarillos que alegran estos campos y alamedas.

Yo estoy encantado con las huertas, y todas las tardes me paseo por ellas un par de horas.

Mi padre quiere llevarme a ver sus olivares, sus viñas, sus cortijos; pero nada de esto hemos visto aún. No he salido del lugar y de las amenas huertas que le circundan.

Es verdad que no me dejan parar con tanta visita.

Hasta cinco mujeres han venido a verme,[4] que todas han sido mis amas y me han abrazado y besado.

Todos me llaman Luisito o el niño de D. Pedro, aunque tengo ya veintidós años cumplidos. Todos preguntan a mi padre por el niño cuando no estoy presente.

Se me figura que son inútiles los libros que he traído para leer, pues ni un instante me dejan solo.

La dignidad de cacique, que yo creía cosa de broma, es cosa harto seria. Mi padre es el cacique del lugar.

Apenas hay aquí quien acierte a comprender lo que llaman mi manía de hacerme clérigo, y esta buena gente me dice, con un candor selvático, que debo ahorcar los hábitos,[5] que el ser clérigo está bien para los pobretones; pero que yo, que soy un rico heredero, debo casarme y consolar la vejez de mi padre, dándole media docena de hermosos y robustos nietos.

Para adularme y adular a mi padre, dicen hombres y mujeres que soy un real mozo, muy salado, que tengo mucho ángel,[6] que mis ojos son muy pícaros y otras sandeces que me afligen, disgustan y avergüenzan, a pesar de que no soy tímido y conozco las miserias y locuras de esta vida, para no escandalizarme ni asustarme de nada.

El único defecto que hallan en mí es el de que estoy muy delgadito a fuerza de estudiar. Para que engorde se proponen no dejarme estudiar ni leer un papel mientras aquí permanezca, y además hacerme comer cuantos primores de cocina y de repostería se confeccionan en el lugar. Está visto: quieren cebarme. No hay familia conocida que no me haya enviado algún

[3] *de por aquí,* around here; or, of this region [4] Supply: *diciendo*
[5] Literally, to hang up the robes; figuratively, to give up studying for the priesthood
[6] *tener mucho ángel,* to have the gift of pleasing

obsequio. Ya me envían una torta de bizcocho, ya un cuajado, ya una pirámide de piñonate, ya un tarro de almíbar.

Los obsequios que me hacen no son sólo estos presentes enviados a casa, sino que también me han convidado a comer tres o cuatro personas de las más importantes del lugar.

Mañana como en casa de la famosa Pepita Jiménez, de quien usted habrá oído hablar, sin duda alguna. Nadie ignora aquí que mi padre la pretende.

Mi padre, a pesar de sus cincuenta y cinco años, está tan bien, que puede poner envidia a los más gallardos mozos del lugar. Tiene, además, el atractivo poderoso, irresistible para algunas mujeres, de sus pasadas conquistas, de su celebridad, de haber sido una especie de Don Juan Tenorio.

No conozco aún a Pepita Jiménez. Todos dicen que es muy linda. Yo sospecho que será una beldad lugareña y algo rústica. Por lo que de ella se cuenta, no acierto a decir si es buena o mala moralmente; pero sí que es de gran despejo natural. Pepita tendrá veinte años; es viuda; sólo tres años estuvo casada. Era hija de doña Francisca Gálvez, viuda, como usted sabe, de un capitán retirado.

Que le dejó a su muerte
Sólo su honrosa espada por herencia,

según dice el poeta. Hasta la edad de diez y seis años, vivió Pepita con su madre en la mayor estrechez, casi en la miseria.

Tenía un tío llamado D. Gumersindo, poseedor de un mezquinísimo mayorazgo, de aquellos que en tiempos antiguos una vanidad absurda fundaba. Cualquiera persona regular hubiera vivido con las rentas de este mayorazgo en continuos apuros, llena tal vez de trampas, y sin acertar a darse el lustre y decoro propios de su clase; pero D. Gumersindo era un ser extraordinario; el genio de la economía. No se podía decir que crease riqueza; pero tenía una extraordinaria facultad de absorción con respecto a la de los otros, y en punto a[7] consumirla, será difícil hallar sobre la tierra persona alguna en cuyo mantenimiento, conservación y bienestar hayan tenido menos que afanarse la madre naturaleza y la industria humana. No se sabe cómo vivió; pero el caso es que vivió hasta la edad de ochenta años, ahorrando sus rentas íntegras y haciendo crecer su capital por medio de préstamos muy sobre seguro.[8] Nadie por aquí le critica de usurero, antes bien le califican de caritativo, porque siendo moderado en todo, hasta en la usura lo era, y no solía llevar más de un 10 por 100[9] al año, mientras que en toda esta comarca llevan un 20 y hasta un 30 por 100, y aun parece poco . . .

Las prendas de su sencillo vestuario estaban algo raídas, pero sin una mancha y saltando de limpias,[10] aunque de tiempo inmemorial se le conocía la misma capa, el mismo chaquetón y los mismos pantalones y chaleco. A veces se interrogaban en balde las gentes unas a otras a ver si alguien le había visto estrenar una prenda.

Con todos estos defectos, que aquí y en otras partes muchos consideran virtudes, aunque virtudes exageradas, D. Gumersindo tenía excelentes cualidades: era afable, servicial, compasivo, y se desvivía por complacer y ser útil a todo el mundo, aunque le costase trabajos, desvelos y fatiga, con tal que no le costase un real. Alegre y amigo de chanzas y de burlas, se hallaba en todas las reuniones y fiestas, cuando

[7] *en punto a,* with respect to
[8] *muy sobre seguro,* very secure
[9] per cent
[10] *saltar de limpias,* to be spotlessly clean

no eran a escote,[11] y las regocijaba con la amenidad de su trato y con su discreta, aunque poco ática, conversacion. Nunca había tenido inclinación alguna amorosa a una mujer determinada; pero inocentemente, sin malicia, gustaba de todas, y era el viejo más amigo de requebrar a las muchachas y que más las hiciese reír que había en diez leguas a la redonda.

Ya he dicho que era tío de la Pepita. Cuando frisaba en los ochenta años, iba ella a cumplir los diez y seis. Él era poderoso; ella pobre y desvalida.

La madre de ella era una mujer vulgar, de cortas luces y de instintos groseros. Adoraba a su hija, pero continuamente y con honda amargura se lamentaba de los sacrificios que por ella hacía, de las privaciones que sufría y de la desconsolada vejez y triste muerte que iba a tener en medio de tanta pobreza . . .

En tan angustiosa situación empezó D. Gumersindo a frecuentar la casa de Pepita y de su madre y a requebrar a Pepita con más ahinco y persistencia que solía requebrar a otras. Era, con todo, tan inverosímil y tan desatinado el suponer que un hombre que había pasado ochenta años sin querer casarse pensase en tal locura cuando ya tenía un pie en el sepulcro, que ni la madre de Pepita, ni Pepita mucho menos, sospecharon jamás los en verdad atrevidos pensamientos de D. Gumersindo. Así es que un día ambas se quedaron atónitas y pasmadas cuando, después de varios requiebros, entre burlas y veras, D. Gumersindo soltó con la mayor formalidad, y a boca de jarro,[12] la siguiente categórica pregunta:

—Muchacha, ¿quieres casarte conmigo?

Pepita, aunque la pregunta venía después de mucha broma y pudiera tomarse por broma, y aunque inexperta de las cosas del mundo, por cierto instinto adivinatorio que hay en las mujeres, y sobre todo en las mozas, por cándidas que sean, conoció que aquello iba por lo serio,[13] se puso colorada como una guinda y no contestó nada. La madre contestó por ella.

—Niña, no seas mal criada;[14] contesta a tu tío lo que debes contestar: Tío, con mucho gusto; cuando usted quiera.

Este *Tío, con mucho gusto; cuando usted quiera,* entonces y varias veces después, dicen que salió casi mecánicamente de entre los trémulos labios de Pepita, cediendo a las amonestaciones, a los discursos, a las quejas y hasta al mandato imperioso de su madre.

Veo que me extiendo demasiado en hablar a usted de esta Pepita Jiménez y de su historia; pero me interesa, y supongo que debe interesarle, pues si es cierto lo que aquí aseguran, va a ser cuñada de usted y madrastra mía. Procuraré, sin embargo, no detenerme en pormenores, y referir, en resumen, cosas que acaso usted ya sepa, aunque hace tiempo que falta de aquí.

Pepita Jiménez se casó con D. Gumersindo.

La envidia se desencadenó contra ella en los días que precedieron a la boda, y algunos meses después.

En efecto, el valor moral de este matrimonio es harto discutible; mas para la muchacha, si se atiende a los ruegos de su madre, a sus quejas, hasta a su mandato; si se atiende a que ella creía por este medio proporcionar a su madre una vejez descansada . . . fuerza es confesar que merece atenuación la censura. Por otra parte, ¿cómo penetrar en lo íntimo del corazón, en el secreto escondido de la mente juve-

[11] Dutch-treat, each one paying his own scot
[12] *a boca de jarro,* point-blank
[13] was in earnest
[14] *mal criada,* impolite

nil de una doncella, criada tal vez con recogimiento exquisito e ignorante de todo, y saber qué idea podía ella formarse del matrimonio? Tal vez entendió que casarse con aquel viejo era consagrar su vida a cuidarle, a ser su enfermera, a dulcificar los últimos años de su vida, a no dejarle en soledad y abandono, cercado sólo de achaques y asistido por manos mercenarias, y a iluminar y dorar, por último, sus postrimerías con el rayo esplendente y suave de su hermosura y de su juventud, como ángel que toma forma humana. Si algo de esto o todo esto pensó la muchacha, y en su inocencia no penetró en otros misterios, salva queda la bondad de lo que hizo.

Como quiera que sea, dejando a un lado estas investigaciones psicológicas que no tengo derecho a hacer, pues no conozco a Pepita Jiménez, es lo cierto que ella vivió en santa paz con el viejo durante tres años; que el viejo parecía más feliz que nunca; que ella le cuidaba y regalaba con esmero admirable, y que en su última y penosa enfermedad le atendió y veló con infatigable y tierno afecto, hasta que el viejo murió en sus brazos dejándola heredera de una gran fortuna.

Aunque hace más de dos años que perdió a su madre, y más de año y medio que enviudó, Pepita lleva aún el luto de viuda. Su compostura, su vivir retirado y su melancolía son tales, que cualquiera pensaría que llora la muerte del marido como si hubiera sido un hermoso mancebo. Tal vez alguien presume o sospecha que la soberbia de Pepita y el conocimiento cierto que tiene hoy de los poco poéticos medios con que se ha hecho rica, traen su conciencia alterada y más que escrupulosa; y que, avergonzada a sus propios ojos y a los de los hombres, busca en la austeridad y en el retiro consuelo y reparo a la herida de su corazón . . .

Pepita, pues, con dinero y siendo además hermosa, y haciendo, como dicen todos, buen uso de su riqueza, se ve en el día considerada y respetada extraordinariamente. De este pueblo y de todos los de las cercanías han acudido a pretenderla los más brillantes partidos, los mozos mejor acomodados. Pero ella los desdeña a todos con extremada dulzura, procurando no hacerse ningún enemigo, y se supone que tiene llena el alma de la más ardiente devoción, y que su constante pensamiento es consagrar su vida a ejercicios de caridad y de piedad religiosa.

Mi padre no está más adelantado ni ha salido mejor librado, según dicen, que los demás pretendientes; pero Pepita, para cumplir el refrán de que no quita lo cortés a lo valiente,[15] se esmera en mostrarle la amistad más franca, afectuosa y desinteresada. Se deshace con él en obsequios y atenciones; y siempre que mi padre trata de hablarle de amor, le pone a raya[16] echándole un sermón dulcísimo, trayéndole a la memoria sus pasadas culpas, y tratando de desengañarle del mundo y de sus pompas vanas.

Confieso a usted que empiezo a tener curiosidad de conocer a esta mujer; tanto oigo hablar de ella. No creo que mi curiosidad carezca de fundamento, tenga nada de vano ni de pecaminoso; yo mismo siento lo que dice Pepita;[17] yo mismo deseo que mi padre, en su edad provecta, venga a mejor vida, olvide y no renueve las agitaciones y pasiones de su mocedad, y llegue a una vejez tranquila, dichosa y honrada. Sólo difiero del sentir de Pepita

[15] *no quita lo cortés a lo valiente,* being brave does not keep one from being courteous

[16] *poner a raya,* to check

[17] I regret what Pepita says; that is, that she rejects my father's advances

en una cosa: en creer que mi padre, mejor que quedándose soltero, conseguiría esto casándose con una mujer digna, buena y que le quisiese. Por esto mismo deseo conocer a Pepita y ver si ella puede ser esta mujer, pesándome[18] ya algo, y tal vez entre en esto cierto orgullo de familia, que si es malo quisiera desechar, los desdenes, aunque melifluos y afectuosos, de la mencionada joven viuda.

Si tuviera yo otra condición, preferiría que mi padre se quedase soltero. Hijo único entonces, heredaría todas sus riquezas, y como si dijéramos[19] nada menos que el cacicato de este lugar; pero usted sabe bien lo firme de mi resolución.

Aunque indigno y humilde, me siento llamado al sacerdocio, y los bienes de la tierra hacen poco mella[20] en mi ánimo. Si hay algo en mí del ardor de la juventud y de la vehemencia de las pasiones propias de dicha edad, todo habrá de emplearse en dar pábulo a una caridad activa y fecunda. Hasta los muchos libros que usted me ha dado a leer, y mi conocimiento de la historia de las antiguas civilizaciones de los pueblos del Asia, unen en mí la curiosidad científica al deseo de propagar la fe, y me convidan y excitan a irme de misionero al remoto Oriente.[21] Yo creo que no bien salga de este lugar, donde usted mismo me envía a pasar algún tiempo con mi padre, y no bien me vea elevado a la dignidad del sacerdocio, y aunque ignorante y pecador como soy, me sienta revestido por don sobrenatural y gratuito, merced a la soberana bondad del Altísimo, de la facultad de perdonar los pecados y de la misión de enseñar a las gentes, y reciba[22] el perpetuo y milagroso favor de traer a mis manos impuras al mismo Dios humanado, dejaré a España y me iré a tierras distantes a predicar el Evangelio.

. . . usted me ha enseñado a analizar lo que el alma siente, a buscar su origen bueno o malo, a escudriñar los más hondos senos del corazón, a hacer, en suma, un escrupuloso examen de conciencia . . .

Digo todo esto porque quiero hablar a usted de un asunto tan delicado, tan vidrioso, que apenas hallo términos con que expresarle. En resolución, yo me pregunto a veces: este propósito[23] mío, ¿tendrá por fundamento, en parte al menos, el carácter de mis relaciones con mi padre? En el fondo de mi corazón, ¿he sabido perdonarle su conducta con mi pobre madre, víctima de sus liviandades?[24]

Lo examino detenidamente y no hallo un átomo de rencor en mi pecho. Muy al contrario, la gratitud lo llena todo. Mi padre me ha criado con amor; ha procurado honrar en mí la memoria de mi madre, y se diría que al criarme, al cuidarme, al mimarme, al esmerarse conmigo cuando pequeño, trataba de aplacar su irritada sombra, si la sombra, si el espíritu de ella, que era un ángel de bondad y de mansedumbre, hubiera sido capaz de ira. Repito, pues, que estoy lleno de gratitud hacia mi padre; él me ha reconocido, y además, a la edad de diez años me envió con usted, a quien debo cuanto soy.

Si hay en mi corazón algún germen de virtud; si hay en mi mente algún principio de ciencia; si hay en mi vo-

[18] *pesándome* has *los desdenes* as its subject

[19] *y . . . dijéramos,* and we might say

[20] *hacer poca mella,* to make little impression

[21] Our first glimpse of the romantic nature of our hero. In his mind being a priest is joined with travels in distant and mysterious lands.

[22] Depends on *no bien,* seven lines above

[23] i.e. his plan of leaving Spain for distant missions

[24] The implication here and later is that Luis's father had not married his mother.

luntad algún honrado y buen propósito, a usted lo debo . . .

Adiós, tío: en adelante escribiré a usted a menudo y tan por extenso como me tiene encargado, si bien no tanto como hoy, para no pecar de prolijo.

28 de marzo.

Me voy cansando de mi residencia en este lugar, y cada día siento más deseo de volverme con usted y de recibir las órdenes; pero mi padre quiere acompañarme, quiere estar presente en esa gran solemnidad y exige de mí que permanezca aquí con él dos meses por lo menos. Está[25] tan afable, tan cariñoso conmigo, que sería imposible no darle gusto en todo. Permaneceré, pues, aquí el tiempo que él quiera. Para complacerle me violento y procuro aparentar que me gustan las diversiones de aquí, las jiras campestres y hasta la caza, a todo lo cual le acompaño. Procuro mostrarme más alegre y bullicioso de lo que naturalmente soy. Como en el pueblo, medio de burla, medio en son de elogio, me llaman el *santo,* yo por modestia trato de disimular estas apariencias de santidad o de suavizarlas y humanarlas con la virtud de la eutrapelia,[26] ostentando una alegría serena y decente, la cual nunca estuvo reñida ni con la santidad ni con los santos. Confieso, con todo, que las bromas y fiestas de aquí, que los chistes groseros y el regocijo estruendoso, me cansan . . .

Hace tres días tuvimos el convite, de que hablé a usted, en casa de Pepita Jiménez. Como esta mujer vive tan retirada, no la conocí hasta el día del convite; me pareció, en efecto, tan bonita como dice la fama, y advertí que tiene con mi padre una afabilidad tan grande, que le da alguna esperanza, al menos miradas las cosas someramente, de que al cabo ceda y acepte su mano.

Como es posible que sea mi madrastra, la he mirado con detención y me parece una mujer singular, cuyas condiciones morales no atino a determinar con certidumbre. Hay en ella un sosiego, una paz exterior, que puede provenir de frialdad de espíritu y de corazón, de estar muy sobre sí[27] y de calcularlo todo, sintiendo poco o nada, y pudiera provenir también de otras prendas que hubiera en su alma; de la tranquilidad de su conciencia, de la pureza de sus aspiraciones y del pensamiento de cumplir en esta vida con los deberes que la sociedad impone, fijando la mente, como término, en esperanzas más altas. Ello es lo cierto que,[28] o bien porque en esta mujer todo es cálculo, sin elevarse su mente a superiores esferas, o bien porque enlaza la prosa del vivir y la poesía de sus ensueños en una perfecta armonía, no hay en ella nada que desentone del cuadro general en que está colocada, y, sin embargo, posee una distinción natural, que la levanta y separa de cuanto la rodea. No afecta vestir traje aldeano ni se viste tampoco según la moda de las ciudades: mezcla ambos estilos en su vestir, de modo que parece una señora, pero una señora de lugar. Disimula mucho, a lo que yo presumo, el cuidado que tiene de su persona; no se advierten en ella ni cosméticos ni afeites; pero la blancura de sus manos, las uñas tan bien cuidadas y acicaladas, y todo el aseo y pulcritud con que está vestida, denotan que cuida de estas cosas más de lo que pudiera creerse en una persona que vive en un pueblo y que además dicen que desdeña las vanidades del mundo y sólo piensa en las cosas del cielo.

Tiene la casa limpísima y todo en

[25] *Está* instead of the usual *es* because the reference is to one particular period, not to his habitual characteristic.

[26] moderation

[27] *sobre sí,* sure of herself

[28] *Ello . . . que,* The fact is that

un orden perfecto. Los muebles no son artísticos ni elegantes; pero tampoco se advierte en ellos nada de pretencioso y de mal gusto. Para poetizar su estancia, tanto en el patio como en las salas y galerías, hay multitud de flores y plantas. No tiene, en verdad, ninguna planta rara ni ninguna flor exótica; pero sus plantas y sus flores, de lo más común que hay por aquí, están cuidadas con extraordinario mimo.

Varios canarios en jaulas doradas animan con sus trinos toda la casa. Se conoce que el dueño de ella necesita seres vivos en quien poner algún cariño; y, a más de algunas criadas, que se diría que ha elegido con empeño, pues no puede ser mera casualidad el que[29] sean todas bonitas, tiene, como las viejas solteronas, varios animales que le hacen compañía: un loro, una perrita de lanas muy lavada y dos o tres gatos, tan mansos y sociables, que se le ponen a uno encima.[30]

En un extremo de la sala principal hay algo como oratorio, donde resplandece un Niño Jesús de talla, blanco y rubio,[31] con ojos azules y bastante guapo. Su vestido[32] es de raso blanco, con manto azul lleno de estrellitas de oro, y todo él está cubierto de dijes y de joyas. El altarito en que está el Niño Jesús se ve adornado de flores, y alrededor macetas de brusco y lauréola, y en el altar mismo, que tiene gradas o escaloncitos, mucha cera ardiendo.

Al ver todo esto, no sé qué pensar; pero más a menudo me inclino a creer que la viuda se ama a sí misma sobre todo, y que para recreo y para efusión de este amor tiene los gatos, los canarios, las flores y al propio Niño Jesús, que en el fondo de su alma tal vez no esté muy por encima de los canarios y de los gatos . . .

Asistieron al convite el médico, el escribano y el señor Vicario, grande 5 amigo de la casa y padre espiritual de Pepita.

El señor Vicario debe de tener un alto concepto de ella, porque varias veces me habló aparte de su caridad, 10 de las muchas limosnas que hacía, de lo compasiva[33] y buena que era para todo el mundo; en suma, me dijo que era una santa.

Oído el señor Vicario, y fiándome 15 en su juicio, yo no puedo menos de desear que mi padre se case con la[34] Pepita. Como mi padre no es a propósito para hacer vida penitente, éste sería el único modo de que cambiase 20 su vida, tan agitada y tempestuosa hasta aquí, y de que viniese a parar a un término, si no ejemplar, ordenado y pacífico.

Cuando nos retiramos de casa de Pe- 25 pita Jiménez y volvimos a la nuestra, mi padre me habló resueltamente de su proyecto: me dijo que él había sido un gran calavera, que había llevado una vida muy mala y que no veía me- 30 dio de enmendarse, a pesar de sus años, si aquella mujer, que era su salvación, no le quería y se casaba con él. Dando ya por supuesto[35] que iba a quererle y a casarse, mi padre me habló de inte- 35 reses: me dijo que era muy rico y que me dejaría mejorado, aunque tuviese varios hijos más.

Yo le respondí que para los planes y fines de mi vida necesitaba harto poco 40 dinero, y que mi mayor contento sería verle dichoso con mujer e hijos, olvidado de sus antiguos devaneos. Me habló luego mi padre de sus esperanzas amorosas, con un candor y con una

[29] the fact that
[30] *se . . . encima,* they climb all over one
[31] *de talla, blanco y rubio,* of carved wood, painted white and gold
[32] In Spain it is customary to dress holy images in clothes.
[33] *de lo compasiva,* of how compassionate
[34] The article before a woman's name indicates familiarity and often, as here, a little scorn.
[35] *Dando . . . supuesto,* Assuming

vivacidad tales, que se diría que yo era el padre y el viejo, y él un chico de mi edad o más joven. Para ponderarme el mérito de la novia y la dificultad del triunfo, me refirió las condiciones y excelencias de los quince o veinte novios que Pepita había tenido, y que todos habían llevado calabazas.[36] En cuanto a él, según me explicó, hasta cierto punto las había también llevado; pero se lisonjeaba de que no fuesen definitivas, porque Pepita le distinguía tanto y le mostraba tan grande afecto, que, si aquello no era amor, pudiera fácilmente convertirse en amor con el largo trato y con la persistente adoración que él le consagraba . . .

Tales son, querido tío, las preocupaciones y ocupaciones de mi padre en este pueblo, y las cosas tan extrañas para mí y tan ajenas a mis propósitos y pensamientos de que me habla con frecuencia, y sobre las cuales quiere que dé mi voto.

No parece sino que la excesiva indulgencia de usted para conmigo ha hecho cundir aquí mi fama de hombre de consejo; paso por un pozo de ciencia; todos me refieren sus cuitas y me piden que les muestre el camino que deben seguir. Hasta el bueno del señor Vicario, aun exponiéndose a revelar algo como secretos de confesión, ha venido ya a consultarme sobre varios casos de conciencia que se le han presentado en el confesionario.

Mucho me ha llamado la atención uno de estos casos, que me ha sido referido por el Vicario, como todos, con profundo misterio y sin decirme el nombre de la persona interesada. Cuenta el señor Vicario que una hija suya de confesión tiene grandes escrúpulos porque se siente llevada, con irresistible impulso, hacia la vida solitaria y contemplativa; pero teme, a veces, que este fervor de devoción no venga acompañado de una verdadera humildad, sino que en parte le promueva y excite el mismo demonio del orgullo . . .

Sobre este caso de conciencia, harto alambicado y sutil para que así preocupe a una lugareña, ha venido a consultarme el padre Vicario. Yo he querido excusarme de decir nada, fundándome en mi inexperiencia y pocos años; pero el señor Vicario se ha obstinado de tal suerte, que no he podido menos de discurrir sobre el caso. He dicho, y mucho me alegraría de que usted aprobase mi parecer, que lo que importa a esta hija de confesión atribulada es mirar con mayor benevolencia a los hombres que la rodean, y en vez de analizar y desentrañar sus[37] faltas con el escalpelo de la crítica, tratar de cubrirlas con el manto de la caridad, haciendo resaltar todas las buenas cualidades de ellos y ponderándolas mucho, a fin de amarlos y estimarlos; que debe esforzarse por ver en cada ser humano un objeto digno de amor, un verdadero prójimo, un igual suyo, un alma en cuyo fondo hay un tesoro de excelentes prendas y virtudes, un ser hecho, en suma, a imagen y semejanza de Dios . . .

Si, como sospecho, es Pepita Jiménez la que ha consultado al señor Vicario sobre estas dudas y tribulaciones, me parece que mi padre no puede lisonjearse todavía de ser muy querido; pero si el Vicario acierta a darla mi consejo, y ella le acepta y pone en práctica, o vendrá a hacerse una María de Ágreda[38] o cosa por el estilo, o, lo que es más probable, dejará a un lado misticismos y desvíos, y se conformará y contentará con aceptar la mano y el corazón de mi padre, que en nada es inferior a ella.

[36] *llevar calabazas,* to be rejected
[37] their
[38] A Franciscan nun of the seventeenth century, noted for her mystic visions, often consulted on matters of policy by Felipe IV.

4 de abril.

La monotonía de mi vida en este lugar empieza a fastidiarme bastante, y no porque la vida mía en otras partes haya sido más activa físicamente; antes al contrario, aquí me paseo mucho a pie y a caballo, voy al campo, y por complacer a mi padre concurro a casinos[39] y reuniones; en fin, vivo como fuera de mi centro y de mi modo de ser; pero mi vida intelectual es nula: no leo un libro ni apenas me dejan un momento para pensar y meditar sosegadamente; y como el encanto de mi vida estribaba en estos pensamientos y meditaciones, me parece monótona la que hago ahora. Gracias a la paciencia que usted me ha recomendado para todas las ocasiones, puedo sufrirla.

Otra causa de que mi espíritu no esté completamente tranquilo es el anhelo, que cada día siento más vivo, de tomar el estado a que resueltamente me inclino desde hace años. Me parece que en estos momentos, cuandos se halla tan cercana la realización del constante sueño de mi vida, es como una profanación distraer la mente hacia otros objetos. Tanto me atormenta esta idea y tanto cavilo sobre ella, que mi admiración por la belleza de las cosas creadas, por el cielo tan lleno de estrellas en estas serenas noches de primavera y en esta región de Andalucía; por estos alegres campos, cubiertos ahora de verdes sembrados, y por estas frescas y amenas huertas con tan lindas y sombrías alamedas, con tantos mansos arroyos y acequias, con tanto lugar[40] apartado y esquivo, con tanto pájaro que le da música, y con tantas flores y hierbas olorosas: esta admiración y entusiasmo mío, repito, que en otro tiempo me parecían avenirse por completo con el sentimiento religioso que llenaba mi alma, excitándole y sublimándole en vez de debilitarle, hoy casi me parecen pecaminosa distracción e imperdonable olvido de lo eterno por lo temporal, de lo increado y suprasensible por lo sensible y creado . . . Harto sé que no peco amando las cosas por el amor de Dios, lo cual es amarlas por ellas con rectitud; porque, ¿qué son ellas más que la manifestación, la obra del amor de Dios? Y, sin embargo, no sé qué extraño temor, qué singular escrúpulo, qué apenas perceptible e indeterminado remordimiento me atormenta ahora, cuando tengo, como antes, como en otros días de mi juventud, como en la misma niñez, alguna efusión de ternura, algún rapto de entusiasmo, al penetrar en una enramada frondosa, al oír el canto del ruiseñor en el silencio de la noche, al escuchar el pío de las golondrinas, al sentir el arrullo enamorado de la tórtola, al ver las flores o al mirar las estrellas. Se me figura a veces que hay en todo esto algo de delectación sensual, algo que me hace olvidar, por un momento al menos, más altas aspiraciones[41] . . . Porque yo me digo: si amo la hermosura de las cosas terrenales tales como ellas son, y si la amo con exceso, es idoltría: debo amarla como signo, como representación de una hermosura oculta y divina, que vale mil veces más, que es incomparablemente superior en todo.

Hace pocos días cumplí veintidós años. Tal ha sido hasta ahora mi fervor religioso, que no he sentido más amor que el inmaculado amor de Dios mismo y de su santa religión, que quisiera difundir y ver triunfante en todas las regiones de la tierra. Confieso que algún sentimiento profano se ha

[39] The *casino* of a Spanish town is a club open to all men of some social standing.
[40] Translate by the plural.
[41] Valera makes skillful use of Nature throughout this book. Luis's growing admiration for it parallels his increasing concern with Pepita Jiménez, in which Nature is also playing its role.

mezclado con esta pureza de afecto. Usted lo sabe, se lo he dicho mil veces; y usted, mirándome con su acostumbrada indulgencia, me ha contestado que el hombre no es un ángel, y que sólo pretender tanta perfección es orgullo; que debo moderar esos sentimientos y no empeñarme en ahogarlos del todo. El amor a la ciencia, el amor a la propia gloria, adquirida por la ciencia misma, hasta el formar uno de sí propio no desventajoso concepto; todo ello, sentido con moderación, velado y mitigado por la humilidad cristiana y encaminado a buen fin, tiene, sin duda, algo de egoísta; pero puede servir de estímulo y apoyo a las más firmes y nobles resoluciones. No es, pues, el escrúpulo que me asalta hoy el de mi orgullo, el de tener sobrada confianza en mí mismo, el de ansiar gloria mundana, o el de ser sobrado curioso de ciencia: no es nada de esto; nada que tenga relación con el egoísmo, sino en cierto modo lo contrario. Siento una dejadez, un quebranto, un abandono de la voluntad, una facilidad tan grande para las lágrimas; lloro tan fácilmente de ternura al ver una florecilla bonita o al contemplar el rayo misterioso, tenue y ligerísimo de una remota estrella, que casi tengo miedo.[42]

Dígame usted qué piensa de estas cosas; si hay algo de enfermizo en esta disposición de mi ánimo.

8 de abril.

Siguen las diversiones campestres, en que tengo que intervenir muy a pesar mío.

He acompañado a mi padre a ver casi todas sus fincas, y mi padre y sus amigos se pasman de que yo no sea completamente ignorante de las cosas del campo. No parece sino que para ellos el estudio de la teología, a que me he dedicado, es contrario del todo al conocimiento de las cosas naturales. ¡Cuánto han admirado mi erudición al verme distinguir en las viñas, donde apenas empiezan a brotar los pámpanos, la cepa Pedro-Jiménez[43] de la baladí y de la de Don Bueno![43] ¡Cuánto han admirado también que en los verdes sembrados sepa yo distinguir la cebada del trigo y el anís de las habas; que conozca muchos árboles frutales y de sombra, y que, aun de las hierbas que nacen espontáneamente en el campo, acierte yo con varios nombres y refiera bastantes condiciones y virtudes!

Pepita Jiménez, que ha sabido por mi padre lo mucho que me gustan las huertas de por aquí, nos ha convidado a ver una que posee a corta distancia del lugar, y a comer las fresas tempranas que en ella se crían. Este antojo de Pepita de obsequiar tanto a mi padre, quien la pretende y a quien desdeña, me parece a menudo que tiene su poco de coquetería, digna de reprobación; pero cuando veo a Pepita después, y la hallo tan natural, tan franca y tan sencilla, se me pasa el mal pensamiento e imagino que todo lo hace candorosamente y que no la lleva otro fin que el de conservar la buena amistad que con mi familia la liga.

Sea como sea, anteayer tarde fuimos a la huerta de Pepita. Es hermoso sitio, de lo más ameno y pintoresco que pueda imaginarse. El riachuelo que riega casi todas estas huertas, sangrado por mil acequias, pasa al lado de la que visitamos; se forma allí una presa, y cuando se suelta el agua sobrante del riego, cae en un hondo barranco poblado en ambas márgenes de álamos blancos y negros, mimbrones, adelfas floridas y otros árboles frondosos. La

[42] Valera delicately reveals to us the psychological state of one who without realizing it is on the brink of falling in love. His condition is that of one who is 'in love with love,' not with any specific person.

[43] Names of kinds of grapevines

cascada, de agua limpia y transparente, se derrama en el fondo, formando espuma, y luego sigue su curso tortuoso por un cauce que la naturaleza misma ha abierto, esmaltando sus orillas de mil hierbas y flores, y cubriéndolas ahora de multitud de violetas. Las laderas que hay en un extremo de la huerta están llenas de nogales, higueras, avellanos y otros árboles de fruta. Y en la parte llana hay cuadros de hortalizas, de fresas, de tomates, patatas, judías y pimientos, y su poco de jardín,[44] con grande abundancia de flores, de las que por aquí más comúnmente se crían. Los rosales, sobre todo, abundan, y los hay de mil diferentes especies. La casilla del hortelano es más bonita y limpia de lo que en esta tierra se suele ver, y al lado de la casilla hay otro pequeño edificio reservado para el dueño de la finca, y donde nos agasajó Pepita con una espléndida merienda, a la cual dió pretexto el comer las fresas, que era el principal objeto que allí nos llevaba. La cantidad de fresas fué asombrosa para lo temprano de la estación, y nos fueron servidas con leche de algunas cabras que Pepita también posee.

Asistimos a esta jira el médico, el escribano, mi tía doña Casilda, mi padre y yo; sin faltar el indispensable señor Vicario, padre espiritual, y más que padre espiritual, admirador y encomiador perpetuo de Pepita.

Por un refinamiento algo sibarítico, no fué el hortelano, ni su mujer, ni el chiquillo del hortelano, ni ningún otro campesino quien nos sirvió la merienda, sino dos lindas muchachas, criadas y como confidentas de Pepita, vestidas a lo rústico, si bien con suma pulcritud y elegancia. Llevaban trajes de percal de vistosos colores, cortos y ceñidos al cuerpo, pañuelo de seda cubriendo las espaldas, y descubierta la cabeza, donde lucían abundantes y lustrosos cabellos negros, trenzados y atados luego, formando un moño en figura de martillo, y por delante rizos sujetos con sendas horquillas, por acá llamados *caracoles*. Sobre el moño o castaña ostentaba cada una de estas doncellas un ramo de frescas rosas.

Salvo la superior riqueza de la tela y su color negro, no era más cortesano el traje de Pepita. Su vestido de merino tenía la misma forma que el de las criadas, y, sin ser muy corto, no arrastraba ni recogía suciamente el polvo del camino. Un modesto pañolito de seda negra cubría también, al uso del lugar, su espalda y su pecho, y en la cabeza no ostentaba tocado, ni flor, ni joya, ni más adorno que el de sus propios cabellos rubios. En la única cosa que noté por parte de Pepita cierto esmero, en que se apartaba de los usos aldeanos, era en llevar guantes. Se conoce que cuida mucho sus manos y que tal vez pone alguna vanidad en tenerlas muy blancas y bonitas, con unas uñas lustrosas y sonrosadas; pero si tiene esta vanidad, es disculpable en la flaqueza humana, y al fin, si yo no estoy trascordado, creo que Santa Teresa[45] tuvo la misma vanidad cuando era joven, lo cual no le impidió ser una santa tan grande.

En efecto, yo me explico, aunque no disculpo, esta pícara vanidad. ¡Es tan distinguido, tan aristocrático, tener una linda mano! Hasta se me figura, a veces, que tiene algo de simbólico. La mano es el instrumento de nuestras obras, el signo de nuestra nobleza, el medio por donde la inteligencia reviste de forma sus pensamientos artísticos, y da ser a las creaciones de la voluntad, y ejerce el imperio que Dios concedió al hombre sobre todas las criaturas . . . Imposible parece que el que tiene manos como Pepita tenga pensamiento

[44] flower garden
[45] Santa Teresa de Ávila, the great Spanish saint and mystic author of the sixteenth century.

impuro, ni idea grosera, ni proyecto ruin que esté en discordancia con las limpias manos que deben ejecutarle.

No hay que decir que mi padre se mostró tan embelesado como siempre de Pepita, y ella tan fina y cariñosa con él, si bien con un cariño más filial de lo que mi padre quisiera . . . Apenas si se atreve decir a Pepita «buenos ojos tienes;»[46] y en verdad que si lo dijese no mentiría, porque los tiene grandes, verdes como los de Circe,[47] hermosos y rasgados; y lo que más mérito y valor les da es que no parece sino que ella no lo sabe, pues no se descubre en ella la menor intención de agradar a nadie ni de atraer a nadie con lo dulce de sus miradas. Se diría que cree que los ojos sirven para ver y nada más que para ver. Lo contrario de lo que yo, según he oído decir, presumo que creen la mayor parte de las mujeres jóvenes y bonitas, que hacen de los ojos un arma de combate y como un aparato eléctrico y fulmíneo para rendir corazones y cautivarlos. No son así, por cierto, los ojos de Pepita, donde hay una serenidad y una paz como del cielo. Ni por eso se puede decir que miren con fría indiferencia. Sus ojos están llenos de caridad y de dulzura. Se posan con afecto en un rayo de luz, en una flor, hasta en cualquier objeto inanimado; pero con más afecto aún, con muestras de sentir más blando, humano y benigno, se posan en el prójimo, sin que el prójimo, por joven, gallardo y presumido que sea, se atreva a suponer nada más que caridad y amor al prójimo, y cuando más,[48] predilección amistosa en aquella serena y tranquila mirada . . .

Ello es que la fiesta en la huerta fué apaciblemente divertida; se habló de flores, de frutos, de injertos, de plantaciones y de otras mil cosas relativas a la labranza, luciendo Pepita sus conocimientos agrónomos en competencia con mi padre, conmigo y con el señor Vicario, que se queda con la boca abierta cada vez que habla Pepita, y jura que en los setenta y pico de años que tiene de edad, y en sus largas peregrinaciones, que le han hecho recorrer casi toda la Andalucía, no ha conocido mujer más discreta ni más atinada en cuanto piensa y dice.

Cuando volvemos a casa, de cualquiera de estas expediciones, vuelvo a insistir con mi padre en mi ida con usted, a fin de que llegue el suspirado momento de que yo me vea elevado al sacerdocio; pero mi padre está tan contento de tenerme a su lado y se siente tan a gusto en el lugar, cuidando de sus fincas, ejerciendo mero y mixto[49] imperio como cacique, y adorando a Pepita y consultándoselo todo como a su ninfa Egeria,[50] que halla siempre y hallará aún, tal vez durante algunos meses, fundado pretexto para retenerme aquí. Ya tiene que clarificar el vino de yo no sé cuántas pipas de la candiotera; ya tiene que trasegar otro; ya es menester binar los majuelos; ya es preciso arar los olivares y cavar los pies a los olivos: en suma, me retiene aquí contra mi gusto; aunque no debiera yo decir «contra mi gusto,» porque le tengo muy grande en vivir con un padre que es para mí tan bueno.

Lo malo es que con esta vida temo materializarme demasiado: me parece sentir alguna sequedad de espíritu durante la oración; mi fervor religioso disminuye; la vida vulgar va penetrando y se va infiltrando en mi naturaleza. Cuando rezo padezco dis-

[46] i.e. a single word, the simplest compliment

[47] Circe, the mythological woman with whom Ulysses fell in love while returning home from Troy.

[48] *cuando más,* at the most

[49] *mero* refers to *natural* law, *mixto* to law which is both *natural* and *civil,* translate, all embracing power.

[50] A mythological goddess endowed with prophetic foresight

tracciones; no pongo en lo que digo a mis solas,[51] cuando el alma debe elevarse a Dios, aquella atención profunda que antes ponía. En cambio, la ternura de mi corazón, que no se fija en un objeto condigno, que no se emplea y consume en lo que debiera, brota y como que rebosa en ocasiones por objetos y circunstancias que tienen mucho de pueriles, que me parecen ridículos, y de los cuales me avergüenzo. Si me despierto en el silencio de la alta noche y oigo que algún campesino enamorado canta, al son de su guitarra mal rasgueada, una copla de fandango o de rondeñas, ni muy discreta, ni muy poética, ni muy delicada, suelo enternecerme como si oyera la más celestial melodía. Una compasión loca, insana, me aqueja a veces. El otro día cogieron los hijos del aperador de mi padre un nido de gorriones, y al ver yo los pajarillos sin plumas aún y violentamente separados de la madre cariñosa, sentí suma angustia, y, lo confieso, se me saltaron las lágrimas. Pocos días antes trajo del campo un rústico una ternerita que se había perniquebrado; iba a llevarla al matadero y venía a decir[52] a mi padre qué quería de ella para su mesa: mi padre pidió unas cuantas libras de carne, la cabeza y las patas; yo me conmoví al ver a la ternerita, y estuve a punto, aunque la vergüenza lo impidió, de comprársela al hombre, a ver si la curaba y conservaba viva. En fin, querido tío, menester es tener la gran confianza que tengo yo con usted para contarle estas muestras de sentimiento extraviado y vago, y hacerle ver con ellas que necesito volver a mi antigua vida, a mis estudios, a mis altas especulaciones, y acabar por ser sacerdote para dar al fuego que devora mi alma el alimento sano y bueno que debe tener.

14 de abril.

Sigo haciendo la misma vida de siempre y detenido aquí a ruegos de mi padre.

El mayor placer de que disfruto, después del de vivir con él, es el trato y conversación del señor Vicario, con quien suelo dar a solas largos paseos. Imposible parece que un hombre de su edad, que debe tener muy cerca de ochenta años, sea tan fuerte, ágil y andador. Antes me canso yo que él, y no queda vericueto ni lugar agreste, ni cima de cerro escarpado en estas cercanías, adonde no lleguemos.

El señor Vicario me va reconciliando mucho con el clero español, a quien algunas veces he tildado yo, hablando con usted, de poco ilustrado. ¡Cuánto más vale, me digo a menudo, este hombre, lleno de candor y de buen deseo, tan afectuoso e inocente, que cualquiera que haya leído muchos libros y en cuya alma no arda con tal viveza como en la suya el fuego de la caridad unido a la fe más sincera y más pura! No crea usted que es vulgar el entendimiento del señor Vicario: es un espíritu inculto, pero despejado y claro. A veces imagino que pueda provenir la buena opinión que de él tengo, de la atención con que me escucha; pero si no es así, me parece que todo lo entiende con notable perspicacia y que sabe unir al amor entrañable de nuestra santa religión el aprecio de todas las cosas buenas que la civilización moderna nos ha traído.[53] Me encantan, sobre todo, la sencillez, la sobriedad en hiperbólicas manifestaciones de sentimentalismo, la naturalidad, en suma, con que el señor Vicario

[51] *a mis solas,* by myself

[52] Here, to ask

[53] The vicar shows the moderation characteristic of Valera himself. In the great social quarrel of the nineteenth century, in which religion and progress were generally opposed, he reconciles the two extremes and succeeds in uniting the best of each side. This is one of the few allusions Valera makes to contemporary problems.

ejerce las más penosas obras de caridad. No hay desgracia que no remedie, ni infortunio que no consuele, ni humillación que no procure restaurar, ni pobreza a que no acuda solícito con un socorro.

Para todo esto, fuerza es confesarlo, tiene un poderoso auxiliar en Pepita Jiménez, cuya devoción y natural compasivo siempre está él poniendo por las nubes.

El carácter de esta especie de culto que el Vicario rinde a Pepita va sellado, casi se confunde con el ejercicio de mil buenas obras: con las limosnas, el rezo, el culto público y el cuidado de los menesterosos. Pepita no da sólo para los pobres, sino también para novenas, sermones y otras fiestas de iglesia. Si los altares de la parroquia brillan a veces adornados de bellísimas flores, estas flores se deben a la munificencia de Pepita, que las ha hecho traer de su huerta. Si en lugar del antiguo manto, viejo y raído, que tenía la Virgen de los Dolores, luce hoy un flamante y magnífico manto de terciopelo negro bordado de plata, Pepita es quien le ha costeado. Estos y otros tales beneficios, el Vicario está siempre decantándolos y ensalzándolos. Así es que cuando no hablo yo de mis miras, de mi vocación, de mis estudios, lo cual embelesa en extremo al señor Vicario, y le trae suspenso de mis labios; cuando es él quien habla y yo quien escucho, la conversación, después de mil vueltas y rodeos, viene a parar siempre en hablar de Pepita Jiménez. Y al cabo ¿de quién me ha de hablar el señor Vicario? Su trato con el médico, con el boticario, con los ricos labradores de aquí, apenas da motivo para tres palabras de conversación. Como el señor Vicario posee la rarísima cualidad en un lugareño de no ser amigo de contar vidas ajenas ni lances escandalosos, de nadie tiene que hablar sino de la mencionada mujer, a quien visita con frecuencia, y con quien, según se desprende de lo que dice, tiene los más íntimos coloquios . . .

Por lo que relata el padre Vicario, entreveo que en el alma de Pepita Jiménez, en medio de la serenidad y calma que aparenta, hay clavado un agudo dardo de dolor; hay un amor de pureza contrariado por su vida pasada. Pepita amó a don Gumersindo como a su compañero, como a su bienhechor, como al hombre a quien todo se lo debía; pero la atormenta, la avergüenza el recuerdo de que don Gumersindo fué su marido.

En su devoción a la Virgen se descubre un sentimiento de humillación dolorosa, un torcedor, una melancolía que influye en su mente el recuerdo de su matrimonio indigno y estéril.

Hasta en su adoración al Niño Dios, representado en la preciosa imagen de talla que tiene en su casa, interviene el amor maternal que busca ese objeto en un ser no nacido de pecado y de impureza.

El padre Vicario dice que Pepita adora al Niño Jesús como a su Dios, pero que le ama con las entrañas maternales con que amaría a un hijo, si le tuviese, y si en su concepción no hubiera habido cosa de que tuviera ella que avergonzarse. El padre Vicario nota que Pepita sueña con la madre ideal y con el hijo ideal, inmaculados ambos, al rezar a la Virgen Santísima, y al cuidar a su lindo Niño Jesús de talla . . .

Veo que distraídamente voy cayendo en el mismo defecto que en el padre Vicario censuro, y que no hablo a usted sino de Pepita Jiménez. Pero esto es natural. Aquí no se habla de otra cosa. Se diría que todo el lugar está lleno del espíritu, del pensamiento, de la imagen de esta singular mujer, que yo no acierto aún a determinar si es un ángel o una refinada coqueta llena de *astucia instintiva,* aunque los términos parezcan contradictorios. Porque lo que es[54] con plena conciencia estoy convencido de que esta mujer no es coqueta ni sueña en ganarse voluntades para satisfacer su vanagloria.

Hay sinceridad y candor en Pepita Jiménez. No hay más que verla para creerlo así. Su andar airoso y reposado, su esbelta estatura, lo terso y despejado de su frente, la suave y pura luz de sus miradas, todo se concierta en un ritmo adecuado, todo se une en perfecta armonía, donde no se descubre nota que disuene.

¡Cuánto me pesa de haber venido por aquí y de permanecer aquí tan largo tiempo! Había pasado la vida en su casa de usted y en el Seminario; no había visto ni tratado más que a mis compañeros y maestros; nada conocía del mundo sino por especulación y teoría;[55] y de pronto, aunque sea en un lugar, me veo lanzado en medio del mundo, y distraído de mis estudios, meditaciones y oraciones por mil objetos profanos.

20 de abril.

Las últimas cartas de usted, queridísimo tío, han sido de grata consolación, para mi alma. Benévolo como siempre, me amonesta usted y me ilumina con advertencias útiles y discretas . . .

Hay mucha soberbia en mí, y yo he de procurar humillarme a mis propios ojos, a fin de que el espíritu del mal no me humille, permitiéndolo Dios, en castigo de mi presunción y de mi orgullo.

No creo, a pesar de todo, como usted me advierte, que es tan fácil para mí una fea y no pensada caída. No confío en mí: confío en la misericordia de Dios y en su gracia, y espero que no sea.

Con todo, razón tiene usted que le sobra en aconsejarme que no me ligue mucho en amistad con Pepita Jiménez; pero yo disto bastante de estar ligado con ella . . .

Lleno de un provechoso temor de Dios, y con debida desconfianza de mi flaqueza, no olvidaré los consejos y prudentes amonestaciones de usted, rezando con fervor mis oraciones y meditando en las cosas divinas para aborrecer las mundanas en lo que tienen de aborrecibles; pero aseguro a usted que hasta ahora, por más que ahondo en mi conciencia y registro con suspicacia sus más escondidos senos, nada descubro que me haga temer lo que usted teme.

Si de mis cartas anteriores resultan encomios para el alma de Pepita Jiménez, culpa es de mi padre y del señor Vicario y no mía, porque al principio, lejos de ser favorable a esta mujer, estaba yo prevenido contra ella con prevención injusta.

En cuanto a la belleza y donaire corporal de Pepita, crea usted que lo he considerado todo con entera limpieza de pensamiento. Y aunque me sea costoso el decirlo, y aunque a usted le duela un poco, le confesaré que si alguna leve mancha ha venido a empañar el sereno y pulido espejo de mi alma en que Pepita se reflejaba, ha sido la ruda sospecha de usted, que casi me ha llevado por un instante a que yo mismo sospeche.

Pero no: ¿qué he pensado yo, qué he mirado, qué he celebrado en Pepita, por donde nadie pueda colegir que propendo a sentir por ella algo que no sea amistad y aquella inocente y limpia admiración que inspira una obra de arte, y más si la obra es del

[54] the fact is

[55] It is interesting to see that Luis is now aware of his lack of worldly knowledge, while in his first letters he considered himself thoroughly sophisticated.

Artífice soberano y nada menos que su templo? . . .

No lo dude usted: yo veo en Pepita Jiménez una hermosa criatura de Dios, y por Dios la amo como a hermana. Si alguna predilección siento por ella, es por las alabanzas que de ella oigo a mi padre, al señor Vicario y a casi todos los de este lugar.

Por amor a mi padre desearía yo que Pepita desistiese de sus ideas y planes de vida retirada y se casase con él; pero prescindiendo de esto, y si yo viese que mi padre sólo tenía un capricho y no una verdadera pasión, me alegraría de que Pepita permaneciese firme en su casta viudez, y cuando yo estuviese muy lejos de aquí, allá en la India o en el Japón, o en algunas misiones más peligrosas, tendría un consuelo en escribirle algo sobre mis peregrinaciones y trabajos. Cuando, ya viejo, volviese yo por este lugar también gozaría mucho en intimar con ella, que estaría ya vieja, y en tener con ella coloquios espirituales y pláticas por el estilo de las que tiene ahora el padre Vicario.[56] Hoy, sin embargo, como soy mozo, me acerco poco a Pepita; apenas la hablo. Prefiero pasar por encogido, por tonto, por mal criado y arisco, a dar la menor ocasión, no ya a la realidad de sentir por ella lo que no debo, pero ni a la sospecha ni a la maledicencia.

En cuanto a Pepita, ni remotamente convengo en lo que usted deja entrever como vago recelo. ¿Qué plan ha de formar respecto a un hombre que va a ser clérigo dentro de dos o tres meses? Ella, que ha desairado a tantos, ¿por qué había de prendarse de mí? Harto me conozco y sé que no puedo, por fortuna, inspirar pasiones. Dicen que no soy feo, pero soy desmañado, torpe, corto de genio, poco ameno; tengo trazas de lo que soy: de un estudiante humilde. ¿Qué valgo yo al lado de los gallardos mozos, aunque algo rústicos, que han pretendido a Pepita: ágiles jinetes, discretos y regocijados en la conversación, cazadores como Nembrot,[57] diestros en todos los ejercicios de cuerpo, cantadores finos y celebrados en todas las ferias de Andalucía, y bailarines apuestos, elegantes y primorosos? Si Pepita ha desairado todo esto, ¿cómo ha de fijarse ahora en mí y ha de concebir el diabólico deseo y más diabólico proyecto de turbar la paz de mi alma, de hacerme abandonar mi vocación, tal vez de perderme? No, no es posible. Yo creo buena a Pepita, y a mí, lo digo sin mentida modestia, me creo insignificante. Ya se entiende que me creo insignificante para enamorarla, no para ser su amigo; no para que ella me estime y llegue a tener un día cierta predilección por mí, cuando yo acierte a hacerme digno de esta predilección con una santa y laboriosa vida.

Perdóneme usted si me defiendo con sobrado calor de ciertas reticencias de la carta de usted, que suenan a acusaciones y a fatídicos pronósticos.

Yo no me quejo de esas reticencias; usted me da avisos prudentes, gran parte de los cuales acepto y pienso seguir. Si va usted más allá de lo justo en el recelar, consiste sin duda en el interés que por mí se toma y que yo de todo corazón le agradezco.

4 de mayo.

Extraño es que en tantos días yo no haya tenido tiempo para escribir a usted; pero tal es la verdad. Mi padre no me deja parar y las visitas me asedian . . .

La vida de aquí tiene cierto en-

[56] Pepita now has a part in Luis's dreams of his future life, despite his recent denials of anything but simple friendship towards her.

[57] Nimrod, 'a mighty hunter before Jehovah,' according to the Bible (Genesis 10. 9).

canto.[58] Para quien no sueña con la gloria, para quien nada ambiciona, comprendo que sea muy descansada y dulce vida. Hasta la soledad puede lograrse aquí haciendo un esfuerzo. Como yo estoy aquí por una temporada, no puedo ni debo hacerlo; pero si yo estuviese de asiento,[59] no hallaría dificultad, sin ofender a nadie, en encerrarme y retraerme durante muchas horas o durante todo el día, a fin de entregarme a mis estudios y meditaciones.

Su nueva y más reciente carta de usted me ha afligido un poco. Veo que insiste usted en sus sospechas, y no sé qué contestar para justificarme sino lo que ya he contestado.

Dice usted que la gran victoria en cierto género de batallas consiste en la fuga; que huir es vencer. ¿Cómo he de negar yo lo que el Apóstol y tantos santos Padres y Doctores han dicho? Con todo, de sobra sabe usted que el huir no depende de mi voluntad. Mi padre no quiere que me vaya; mi padre me retiene a pesar mío; tengo que obedecerle.[60] Necesito, pues, vencer por otros medios, y no por el de la fuga.

Para que usted se tranquilice, repetiré que la lucha apenas está empeñada; que usted ve las cosas más adelantadas de lo que están.[61]

No hay el menor indicio de que Pepita Jiménez me quiera. Y aunque me quisiese, sería de otro modo que como querían las mujeres que usted cita para mi ejemplar escarmiento. Una señora bien educada y honesta, en nuestros días, no es tan inflamable y desaforada como esas matronas de que están llenas las historias antiguas . . .

En estos últimos días he tenido ocasión de ejercitar mi paciencia en grande y de mortificar mi amor propio del modo más cruel.

Mi padre quiso pagar a Pepita el obsequio de la huerta, y la convidó a visitar su quinta del Pozo de la Solana. La expedición fué el 22 de abril. No se me olvidará esta fecha.

El Pozo de la Solana dista más de dos leguas de este lugar, y no hay hasta allí sino camino de herradura.[62] Tuvimos todos que ir a caballo. Yo, como jamás he aprendido a montar, he acompañado a mi padre en todas las anteriores excursiones en una mulita de paso,[63] muy mansa, y que, según la expresión de Dientes, el mulero, es más noble que el oro y más serena que un coche. En el viaje al Pozo de la Solana fuí en la misma cabalgadura.

Mi padre, el escribano, el boticario y mi primo Currito iban en buenos caballos. Mi tía doña Casilda, que pesa más de diez arrobas, en una enorme y poderosa burra con sus jamugas. El señor Vicario, en una mula mansa y serena como la mía.

En cuanto a Pepita Jiménez, que imaginaba yo que vendría también en burra con jamugas, pues ignoraba que montase, me sorprendió, apareciendo en un caballo tordo muy vivo y fogoso, vestida de amazona, y manejando el caballo con destreza y primor notables.

Me alegré de ver a Pepita tan gallarda a caballo; pero, desde luego, presentí y empezó a mortificarme el desairado papel que me tocaba hacer al lado de la robusta tía doña Casilda y del padre Vicario, yendo nosotros a retaguardia, pacíficos, y *serenos* como

[58] Contrast this statement with the repeated expressions of boredom in the early letters.

[59] *de asiento,* permanently

[60] Luis rationalizes, throwing the blame for his stay on his father. Another bit of penetrating psychology.

[61] Here Luis admits indirectly that he loves Pepita. Valera shows his skill as a narrator by this subtle revelation, so unobtrusive that the reader scarcely notices it.

[62] *camino de herradura,* bridle-path

[63] a slow mule

en coche, mientras que la lucida cabalgata caracolearía, correría, trotaría y haría mil evoluciones y escarceos.

Al punto se me antojó que Pepita me miraba compasiva, al ver la facha lastimosa que sobre la mula debía yo de tener. Mi primo Currito me miró con sonrisa burlona, y empezó en seguida a embromarme y atormentarme.

Aplauda usted mi resignación y mi valerosa paciencia. A todo me sometí de buen talante, y pronto hasta las bromas de Currito acabaron al notar cuán invulnerable yo era. Pero ¡cuánto sufrí por dentro! Ellos corrieron, galoparon, se nos adelantaron a la ida y a la vuelta. El Vicario y yo permanecimos siempre *serenos,* como las mulas, sin salir del paso y llevando a doña Casilda en medio.

Ni siquiera tuve el consuelo de hablar con el padre Vicario, cuya conversación me es tan grata, ni de encerrarme dentro de mí mismo y fantasear y soñar, ni de admirar a mis solas la belleza del terreno que recorríamos. Doña Casilda es de una locuacidad abominable, y tuvimos que oírla. Nos dijo cuanto hay que saber de chismes del pueblo, y nos habló de todas sus habilidades, y nos explicó el modo de hacer salchichas, morcillas de sesos, hojaldres y otros mil guisos y regalos. Nadie la vence en negocios de cocina y de matanza de cerdos, según ella, sino Antoñona, la nodriza de Pepita Jiménez, y hoy su ama de llaves y directora de su casa. Yo conozco ya a la tal Antoñona, pues va y viene a casa con recados, y, en efecto, es muy lista: tan parlanchina como la tía Casilda, pero cien mil veces más discreta.

El camino hasta el Pozo de la Solana es delicioso; pero yo iba tan contrariado que no acerté a gozar de él. Cuando llegamos a la casería y nos apeamos, se me quitó de encima un gran peso, como si fuese yo quien hubiese llevado a la mula y no la mula a mí.

Ya a pie, recorrimos la posesión, que es magnífica, variada y extensa. Hay allí más de ciento veinte fanegas de viña añeja y majuelo, todo bajo una linde: otro tanto o más de olivar, y, por último, un bosque de encinas de las más corpulentas que aun quedan en pie en toda Andalucía. El agua del Pozo de la Solana forma un arroyo claro y abundante, donde vienen a beber todos los pajarillos de las cercanías, y donde se cazan a centenares por medio de espartos con liga, o con red, en cuyo centro se colocan el cimbel y el reclamo. Allí recordé mis diversiones de la niñez y cuántas veces había ido yo a cazar pajarillos de la manera expresada.

Siguiendo el curso del arroyo, y sobre todo en las hondonadas, hay muchos álamos y otros árboles altos que, con las matas y hierbas, crean un intrincado laberinto y una sombría espesura. Mil plantas silvestres y olorosas crecen allí de un modo espontáneo, y por cierto que es difícil imaginar nada más esquivo, agreste y verdaderamente solitario, apacible y silencioso que aquellos lugares. Se concibe allí en el fervor del mediodía, cuando el sol vierte a torrentes la luz desde un cielo sin nubes, en las calurosas y reposadas siestas, el mismo terror misterioso de las horas nocturnas. Se concibe allí la vida de los antiguos patriarcas y de los primitivos héroes y pastores, y las apariciones y visiones que tenían de ninfas, de deidades y de ángeles, en medio de la claridad meridiana.

Andando por aquella espesura, hubo un momento en el cual, no acierto a decir cómo, Pepita y yo nos encontramos solos: yo al lado de ella. Los demás se habían quedado atrás.

Entonces sentí por todo mi cuerpo un estremecimiento. Era la primera vez que me veía a solas con aquella mujer y en sitio tan apartado, y cuando yo pensaba en las apariciones meridianas, ya siniestras, ya dulces y siempre sobrenaturales, de los hombres de las edades remotas.

Pepita había dejado en la casería la larga falda de montar, y caminaba con un vestido corto que no estorbaba la graciosa ligereza de sus movimientos. Sobre la cabeza llevaba un sombrerillo andaluz, colocado con gracia. En la mano, el látigo, que se me antojó como varita de virtudes,[64] con que pudiera hechizarme aquella maga.

No temo repetir aquí los elogios de su belleza. En aquellos sitios agrestes se me pareció más hermosa. La cautela, que recomiendan los ascetas, de pensar en ella afeada por los años y por las enfermedades, de figurármela muerta, llena de hedor y podredumbre y cubierta de gusanos, vino, a pesar mío, a mi imaginación; y digo *a pesar mío,* porque no entiendo que[65] tan terrible cautela fuese indispensable. Ninguna idea mala en lo material, ninguna sugestión del espíritu maligno turbó entonces mi razón ni logró inficionar mi voluntad y mis sentidos.

Lo que sí se me ocurrió fué un argumento para invalidar, al menos en mí, la virtud de esa cautela. La hermosura, obra de un arte soberano y divino, puede ser caduca, efímera, desaparecer en el instante; pero su idea es eterna, y en la mente del hombre vive vida inmortal, una vez percibida. La belleza de esta mujer, tal como hoy se manifiesta, desaparecerá dentro de breves años: ese cuerpo elegante, esas formas esbeltas, esa noble cabeza, tan gentilmente erguida sobre los hombros, todo será pasto de gusanos inmundos; pero si la materia ha de transformarse, la forma, el pensamiento artístico, la hermosura misma, ¿quién la destruirá? ¿No está en la mente divina? Percibida y conocida por mí, ¿no vivirá en mi alma, vencedora de la vejez y aun de la muerte?

Así meditaba yo, cuando Pepita y yo nos acercamos. Así serenaba yo mi espíritu y mitigaba los recelos que usted ha sabido infundirme. Yo deseaba y no deseaba a la vez que llegasen los otros. Me complacía y me afligía al mismo tiempo de estar solo con aquella mujer.

La voz argentina de Pepita rompió el silencio, y, sacándome de mis meditaciones, dijo:

—¡Qué callado y qué triste está usted, señor don Luis! Me apesadumbra el pensar que tal vez por culpa mía, en parte al menos, da a usted hoy un mal rato su padre trayéndole a estas soledades, y sacándole de otras más apartadas, donde no tendrá usted nada que le distraiga de sus oraciones y piadosas lecturas.

Yo no sé lo que contesté a esto. Hube de contestar alguna sandez porque estaba turbado; y ni quería hacer un cumplimiento a Pepita diciendo galanterías profanas, ni quería tampoco contestar de un modo grosero.

Ella prosiguió:

—Usted me ha de perdonar si soy maliciosa; pero se me figura que, además del disgusto de verse usted separado hoy de sus ocupaciones favoritas, hay algo más que contribuye poderosamente a su mal humor.

—¿Qué es ese algo más—dije yo—, pues usted lo descubre todo o cree descubrirlo?

—Ese algo más—replicó Pepita—no es sentimiento propio de quien va a ser sacerdote tan pronto, pero sí lo es de un joven de veintidós años.

Al oír esto, sentí que la sangre me subía al rostro y que el rostro me ardía. Imaginé mil extravagancias, me creí presa de una obsesión. Me juzgué provocado por Pepita, que iba a darme

[64] *varita de virtudes,* magic wand

[65] why

a entender que conocía que yo gustaba de ella.[66] Entonces mi timidez se trocó en atrevida soberbia, y la miré de hito en hito. Algo de ridículo hubo de haber en mi mirada, pero, o Pepita no lo advirtió, o lo disimuló con benévola prudencia, exclamando del modo más sencillo:

—No se ofenda usted porque yo le descubra alguna falta. Ésta que he notado me parece leve. Usted está lastimado de las bromas de Currito y de hacer (hablando profanamente) un papel poco airoso montado en una mula mansa, como el señor Vicario, con sus ochenta años, y no en un brioso caballo, como debiera un joven de su edad y circunstancias. La culpa es del señor Deán, que no ha pensado en que usted aprenda a montar. La equitación no se opone a la vida que usted piensa seguir, y yo creo que su padre de usted, ya que está usted aquí, debiera en pocos días enseñarle. Si usted va a Persia o a China, allí no hay ferrocarriles aún, y hará usted una triste figura cabalgando mal. Tal vez se desacredite el misionero entre aquellos bárbaros, merced a esta torpeza, y luego sea más difícil de lograr el fruto de las predicaciones.

Estos y otros razonamientos más adujo Pepita para que yo aprendiese a montar a caballo, y quedé tan convencido de lo útil que es la equitación para un misionero, que le prometí aprender en seguida, tomando a mi padre por maestro.

—En la primera nueva expedición que hagamos—le dije—, he de ir en el caballo más fogoso de mi padre, y no en la mulita de paso en que voy ahora.

—Mucho me alegraré—replicó Pepita con una sonrisa de indecible suavidad.

En esto llegaron todos al sitio en que estábamos, y yo me alegré en mis adentros, no por otra cosa, sino por temor de no acertar a sostener la conversación, y de salir con doscientas mil simplicidades por mi poca o ninguna práctica de hablar con mujeres.

Después del paseo, sobre la fresca hierba y en el más lindo sitio junto al arroyo, nos sirvieron los criados de mi padre una rústica y abundante merienda. La conversación fué muy animada, y Pepita mostró mucho ingenio y discreción. Mi primo Currito volvió a embromarme sobre mi manera de cabalgar y sobre la mansedumbre de mi mula: me llamó *teólogo* y me dijo que sobre aquella mula parecía que iba yo repartiendo bendiciones. Esta vez, ya con el firme propósito de hacerme jinete, contesté a las bromas con desenfado picante. Me callé, con todo,[67] el compromiso contraído de aprender la equitación. Pepita, aunque en nada habíamos convenido, pensó sin duda, como yo, que importaba el sigilo para sorprender luego cabalgando bien, y nada dijo de nuestra conversación. De aquí provino, natural y sencillamente, que existiera un secreto entre ambos; lo cual produjo en mi ánimo extraño efecto.

Nada más occurió aquel día que merezca contarse.

Por la tarde volvimos al lugar como habíamos venido. Yo, sin embargo, en mi mula mansa y al lado de la tía Casilda, no me aburrí ni entristecí a la vuelta como a la ida. Durante todo el viaje oí a la tía sin cansancio referir sus historias, y por momentos me distraje en vagas imaginaciones.[68]

Nada de lo que en mi alma pasa debe ser un misterio para usted. Declaro que la figura de Pepita era como el centro, o mejor dicho, como el nú-

[66] that I *liked* her
[67] withal, nevertheless
[68] One of the distinctive traits of Luis's romantic young nature is his propensity to daydreaming. He has already mentioned it on p. 404, l. 24a.

cleo y el foco de estas imaginaciones vagas . . .

Aquella noche dije a mi padre mi deseo de aprender a montar. No quise ocultarle que Pepita me había excitado a ello. Mi padre tuvo una alegría extraordinaria.[69] Me abrazó, me besó y me dijo que ya no era usted solo mi maestro, que él también iba a tener el gusto de enseñarme algo. Me aseguró, por último, que en dos o tres semanas haría de mí el mejor caballista de toda Andalucía; capaz de ir a Gibraltar por contrabando y de volver de allí, burlando al resguardo, con una coracha de tabaco y con un buen alijo de algodones; apto, en suma, para pasmar a todos los jinetes que se lucen en las ferias de Sevilla y de Mairena,[70] y para oprimir los lomos de Babieca,[71] de Bucéfalo[72] y aun de los propios caballos del Sol, si por acaso bajaban a la tierra y podía yo asirlos de la brida.

Ignoro qué pensará usted de este arte de la equitación que estoy aprendiendo; pero presumo que no le tendrá por malo.

¡Si viera usted qué gozoso está mi padre y cómo se deleita enseñándome! Desde el día siguiente al de la expedición que he referido, doy[73] dos lecciones diarias. Día hay[74] durante el cual la lección es perpetua, porque nos lo pasamos a caballo. La primera semana fueron las lecciones en el corralón de casa, que está desempedrado y sirvió de picadero.

Ya salimos al campo, pero procurando que nadie nos vea. Mi padre no quiere que me muestre en público hasta que pasme por lo bien plantado, según él dice. Si su vanidad de padre no le engaña, esto será muy pronto, porque tengo una disposición maravillosa para ser buen jinete.

—¡Bien se ve que eres mi hijo!—exclama mi padre con júbilo al contemplar mis adelantos . . .

Ayer fué día de la Cruz y estuvo el lugar muy animado. En cada calle hubo seis o siete cruces de mayo llenas de flores, si bien ninguna tan bella como la que puso Pepita en la puerta de su casa. Era un mar de flores el que engalanaba la cruz.[75]

Por la noche tuvimos fiesta en casa de Pepita. La cruz, que había estado en la calle, se colocó en una gran sala baja, donde hay piano, y nos dió Pepita un espectáculo sencillo y poético que yo había visto cuando niño, aunque no le recordaba.

De la cabeza de la cruz pendían siete listones o cintas anchas, dos blancas, dos verdes y tres encarnadas, que son los colores simbólicos de las virtudes teologales. Ocho niños de cinco o seis años, representando los siete Sacramentos, asidos de las siete cintas que pendían de la cruz, bailaron a modo de una contradanza muy bien ensayada. El Bautismo era un niño vestido de catecúmeno con su túnica blanca; el Orden, otro niño de sacerdote; la Confirmación, un obispito; la Extremaunción, un peregrino con bordón y esclavina llena de conchas; el Matrimonio, un novio y una novia, y un Nazareno con cruz y corona de espinas, la Penitencia.[76]

El baile, más que baile, fué una serie de reverencias, pasos, evoluciones y genuflexiones al compás de una música no mala, de algo como marcha, que el organista tocó en el piano con bastante destreza.

[69] Does the father's remarkable demonstration of joy come only from his desire to teach his son to ride? Does he suspect the truth of the situation?

[70] Town near Sevilla [71] The Cid's horse

[72] Alexander the Great's horse

[73] I take [74] There are days

[75] On the third of May the Spaniards set up crosses covered with flowers. The children dance around the cross holding ribbons in their hands, just as our children do around the Maypole.

[76] Luis omits the sacrament of communion in his description.

Los niños, hijos de criados y familiares de la casa de Pepita, después de hacer su papel, se fueron a dormir muy regalados y agasajados.

La tertulia continuó hasta las doce, y hubo refresco, esto es, tacillas de almíbar, y, por último, chocolate con torta de bizcocho y agua con azucarillos.

El retiro y la soledad de Pepita van olvidándose desde que volvió la primavera, de lo cual mi padre está muy contento. De aquí en adelante Pepita recibirá todas las noches, y mi padre quiere que yo sea de la tertulia.

Pepita ha dejado el luto, y está ahora más galana y vistosa con trajes ligeros y casi de verano, aunque siempre muy modestos.

Tengo la esperanza de que lo más que mi padre me retendrá ya por aquí será todo este mes. En junio nos iremos juntos a esa ciudad, y ya usted verá cómo, libre de Pepita, que no piensa en mí ni se acordará de mí para malo ni para bueno, tendré el gusto de abrazar a usted y de lograr la dicha de ser sacerdote.

7 de mayo.

Todas las noches, de nueve a doce, tenemos, como ya indiqué a usted, tertulia en casa de Pepita. Van cuatro o cinco señoras y otras tantas señoritas del lugar, contando con la tía Casilda, y van también seis o siete caballeritos, que suelen jugar a juegos de prendas con las niñas. Como es natural, hay tres o cuatro noviazgos.

La gente formal de la tertulia es la de siempre. Se compone, como si dijéramos, de los altos funcionarios: de mi padre, que es el cacique; del boticario, del médico, del escribano y del señor Vicario.

Pepita juega al tresillo con mi padre, con el señor Vicario y con algún otro.

Yo no sé de qué lado ponerme. Si me voy con la gente joven, estorbo con mi gravedad en sus juegos y enamoramientos. Si me voy con el estado mayor, tengo que hacer el papel de mirón en una cosa que no entiendo. Yo no sé más juego de naipes que el burro ciego, el burro con vista y un poco de tute o brisca cruzada.

Lo mejor sería que yo no fuese a la tertulia, pero mi padre se empeña en que vaya. Con no ir, según él, me pondría en ridículo.

Muchos extremos de admiración hace mi padre al notar mi ignorancia de ciertas cosas. Esto de que yo no sepa jugar al tresillo, siquiera al tresillo, le tiene maravillado.

—Tu tío te ha criado—me dice—debajo de un fanal,[77] haciéndote tragar teología y más teología, y dejándote a obscuras de lo demás que hay que saber. Por lo mismo que vas a ser clérigo y que no podrás bailar ni enamorar en las reuniones, necesitas jugar al tresillo. Si no, ¿qué vas a hacer, desdichado?

A estos y otros discursos por el estilo he tenido que rendirme, y mi padre me está enseñando en casa a jugar al tresillo, para que, no bien le sepa, le juegue en la tertulia de Pepita. También . . . ha querido enseñarme la esgrima, y después, a fumar y a tirar a la pistola y la barra; pero en nada de esto he consentido yo.

—¡Qué diferencia—exclama mi padre—entre tu mocedad y la mía!

Y luego añade riéndose:

—En substancia, todo es lo mismo. Yo también tenía mis horas canónicas en el cuartel de Guardias de Corps;[78] el cigarro era el incensario, la baraja el libro de coro, y nunca me faltaban otras devociones y ejercicios más o menos espirituales . . .

Sigue mi padre contentísimo de mí

[77] under a glass bell (as certain special melons are raised); very protected

[78] Royal Body Guard

como discípulo de equitación. Dentro de cuatro o cinco días asegura que podré ya montar y montaré en Lucero, caballo negro, hijo de un caballo árabe y de una yegua de la casta de Guadalcázar, saltador, corredor, lleno de fuego y adiestrado en todo linaje de corvetas.

—Quien eche a Lucero los calzones encima—dice mi padre—, ya puede apostarse a montar con los propios centauros; y tú le echarás los calzones encima dentro de poco.

Aunque me paso todo el día en el campo a caballo, en el casino y en la tertulia, robo algunas horas al sueño, ya voluntariamente, ya porque me desvelo, y medito en mi posición y hago examen de conciencia. La imagen de Pepita está siempre presente en mi alma. ¿Será esto amor?, me pregunto . . .

Toda otra consideración, toda otra forma, no destruye la imagen de esta mujer. Entre el Crucifijo y yo se interpone, entre la imagen devotísima de la Virgen y yo se interpone, sobre la página del libro espiritual que leo viene también a interponerse.

No creo, sin embargo, que estoy herido de lo que llaman amor en el siglo.[79] Y aunque lo estuviera, yo lucharía y vencería.

La vista diaria de esa mujer y el oír cantar sus alabanzas de continuo, hasta al padre Vicario, me tienen preocupado; divierten mi espíritu hacia lo profano y le alejan de su debido recogimiento; pero no, yo no amo a Pepita todavía. Me iré y la olvidaré.

Mientras aquí permanezca, combatiré con valor. Combatiré con Dios, para vencerle por el amor y el rendimiento. Mis clamores llegarán a Él como inflamadas saetas, y derribarán el escudo con que se defiende y oculta a los ojos de mi alma. Yo pelearé como Israel, en el silencio de la noche, y Dios me llagará en el muslo y me quebrantará en ese combate, para que yo sea vencedor siendo vencido.[80]

12 de mayo.

Antes de lo que yo pensaba, querido tío, me decidió mi padre a que montase en Lucero. Ayer, a las seis de la mañana, cabalgaba en esta hermosa fiera como le llama mi padre, y me fuí con mi padre al campo. Mi padre iba caballero en una jaca alazana.

Lo hice tan bien, fuí tan seguro y apuesto en aquel soberbio animal, que mi padre no pudo resistir a la tentación de lucir a su discípulo, y después de reposar en un cortijo que tiene a media legua de aquí, y a eso de las once, me hizo volver al lugar y entrar por lo más concurrido y céntrico, metiendo mucha bulla y desempedrando[81] las calles. No hay que afirmar que pasamos por la de Pepita, quien de algún tiempo a esta parte[82] se va haciendo algo ventanera y estaba a la reja, en una ventana baja, detrás de la verde celosía.

No bien sintió Pepita el ruido y alzó los ojos y nos vió, se levantó, dejó la costura que traía entre manos y se puso a mirarnos. Lucero, que, según he sabido después, tiene ya la costumbre de hacer piernas cuando pasa por delante de la casa de Pepita, empezó a retozar y a levantarse un poco de manos. Yo quise calmarle, pero como extrañase[83] las mías y también extrañase al jinete, despreciándole tal vez, se alborotó más y más y empezó a dar resoplidos, a hacer corvetas y aun a dar algunos botes; yo me tuve firme y sereno, mostrándole que era su amo, castigándole con la espuela, tocándole

[79] See p. 318, n. 131.

[80] Jacob wrestled all night with an angel, being wounded in the thigh during the struggle. In the morning the angel bestowed on him a new name, Israel. See Genesis 32.

[81] Literally, unpaving the streets, tearing up the pavement (due to the pawing and cavorting of the horse)

[82] *de algún tiempo a esta parte,* for some time

[83] he was not used to

con el látigo en el pecho y reteniéndole por la brida. Lucero, que casi se había puesto de pies sobre los cuartos traseros, se humilló entonces hasta doblar mansamente las rodillas haciendo una reverencia.

La turba de curiosos, que se había agrupado alrededor, rompió en estrepitosos aplausos. Mi padre dijo:

—¡Bien por los mozos crudos y de arrestos![84]

Y notando después que Currito, que no tiene otro oficio que el de paseante, se hallaba entre el concurso, se dirigió a él con estas palabras:

—Mira, arrastrado; mira al *teólogo* ahora, y, en vez de burlarte, quédate patitieso de asombro.

En efecto, Currito estaba con la boca abierta, inmóvil, verdaderamente asombrado.

Mi triunfo fué grande y solemne, aunque impropio de mi carácter. La inconveniencia de este triunfo me infundió vergüenza. El rubor coloró mis mejillas. Debí ponerme encendido como la grana, y más aun cuando advertí que Pepita me aplaudía y me saludaba cariñosa, sonriendo y agitando sus lindas manos.

En fin, he ganado la patente de hombre recio y de jinete de primera calidad.

Mi padre no puede estar más satisfecho y orondo; asegura que está completando mi educación; que usted le ha enviado en mí un libro muy sabio, pero en borrador y desencuadernado, y que él está poniéndome en limpio y encuadernándome.

El tresillo, si es parte de la encuadernación y de la limpieza, también está ya aprendido.

Dos noches he jugado con Pepita.

La noche que siguió a mi hazaña ecuestre, Pepita me recibió entusiasmada, e hizo lo que nunca había querido ni se había atrevido a hacer conmigo: me alargó la mano.

No crea usted que no recordé lo que recomiendan tantos y tantos moralistas y ascetas; pero, allá en mi mente, pensé que exageraban el peligro. Aquello del Espíritu Santo[85] de que el que echa mano a una mujer se expone como si cogiera un escorpión, me pareció dicho en otro sentido. Sin duda que en los libros devotos, con la más sana intención, se interpretan harto duramente ciertas frases y sentencias de la Escritura. ¿Cómo entender, si no, que la hermosura de la mujer, obra tan perfecta de Dios, es causa de perdición siempre? ¿Cómo entender, en sentido general y constante, que la mujer es más amarga que la muerte? ¿Cómo entender que el que toca a una mujer, en toda ocasión y con cualquier pensamiento que sea, no saldrá sin mancha?

En fin, respondí rápidamente dentro de mi alma a éstos y a otros avisos, y tomé la mano que Pepita cariñosamente me alargaba y la estreché en la mía. La suavidad de aquella mano me hizo comprender mejor su delicadeza y primor, que hasta entonces no conocía sino por los ojos.

Según los usos del siglo, dada ya la mano una vez, la debe uno dar siempre, cuando llega y cuando se despide. Espero que en esta ceremonia, en esta prueba de amistad, en esta manifestación de afecto, si se procede con pureza y sin el menor átomo de liviandad, no verá usted nada malo ni peligroso.

Como mi padre tiene que estar muchas noches con el aperador y con otra gente de campo, y hasta las diez y media o las once suele no verse libre, yo le sustituyo en la mesa del tresillo

[84] *Bien . . . arrestos,* Hurray for rough and daring lads!

[85] Eight well-known Spanish monks, most of them writers on theological subjects, took this name in religion. Probably the one here referred to is Tomás del Espíritu Santo, who died a martyr in Japan in 1622.

al lado de Pepita. El señor Vicario y el escribano son casi siempre los otros tercios. Jugamos a décimo de real, de modo que un duro o dos es lo más que se atraviesa en la partida.

Mediando, como media, tan poco interés en el juego, le interrumpimos continuamente con agradables conversaciones y hasta con discusiones sobre puntos extraños al mismo juego, en todo lo cual demuestra siempre Pepita una lucidez de entendimiento, una viveza de imaginación y una tan extraordinaria gracia en el decir, que no pueden menos de maravillarme.

No hallo motivo suficiente para variar de opinión respecto a lo que ya he dicho a usted, contestando a sus recelos de que Pepita pueda sentir cierta inclinación hacia mí. Me trata con el afecto natural que debe tener al hijo de su pretendiente, don Pedro de Vargas, y con la timidez y encogimiento que inspira un hombre en mis circunstancias, que no es sacerdote aun, pero que pronto va a serlo.

Quiero y debo, no obstante, decir a usted, ya que le escribo siempre como si estuviese de rodillas delante de usted a los pies del confesionario, una rápida impresión que he sentido dos o tres veces; algo que tal vez sea una alucinación o un delirio, pero que he notado.

Ya he dicho a usted en otras cartas que los ojos de Pepita, verdes como los de Circe, tienen un mirar tranquilo y honestísimo. Se diría que ella ignora el poder de sus ojos, y no sabe que sirven más que para ver. Cuando fija en alguien la vista, es tan clara, franca y pura la dulce luz de su mirada, que, en vez de hacer nacer ninguna mala idea, parece que crea pensamientos limpios; que deja en reposo grato a las almas inocentes y castas, y mata y destruye todo incentivo en las almas que no lo son. Nada de pasión ardiente, nada de fuego hay en los ojos de Pepita. Como la tibia luz de la luna, es el rayo de su mirada.

Pues bien, a pesar de esto, yo he creído notar dos o tres veces un resplandor instantáneo, un relámpago, una llama fugaz y devoradora en aquellos ojos que se posaban en mí. ¿Será vanidad ridícula sugerida por el mismo demonio?

Me parece que sí; quiero creer y creo que sí.

Lo rápido, lo fugitivo de la impresión, me induce a conjeturar que no ha tenido nunca realidad extrínseca; que ha sido un ensueño mío.

La calma del cielo, el frío de la indiferencia amorosa,[86] si bien templado por la dulzura de la amistad y de la caridad, es lo que descubro siempre en los ojos de Pepita.

Me atormenta, no obstante, este ensueño, esta alucinación de la mirada extraña y ardiente.

Mi padre dice que no son los hombres sino las mujeres las que toman la iniciativa, y que la toman sin responsabilidad, y pudiendo negar y volverse atrás cuando quieren. Según mi padre, la mujer es quien se declara por medio de miradas fugaces, que ella misma niega más tarde a su propia conciencia, si es menester, y de las cuales, más que leer, logra el hombre a quien van dirigidas adivinar el significado. De esta suerte, casi por medio de una conmoción eléctrica, casi por medio de una sutilísima e inexplicable intuición, se percata el que es amado de que es amado, y luego, cuando se resuelve a hablar, va ya sobre seguro y con plena confianza de la correspondencia.

¿Quién sabe si estas teorías de mi padre, oídas por mí, porque no puedo menos de oírlas, son las que me han calentado la cabeza y me han hecho imaginar lo que no hay?[87]

De todos modos, me digo a veces,

[86] indifference in respect to love

[87] Here, to exist

¿sería tan absurdo, tan imposible que lo hubiera? Y si lo hubiera, si yo agradase a Pepita de otro modo que como amigo, si la mujer a quien mi padre pretende se prendase de mí, ¿no sería espantosa mi situación?

Desechemos estos temores fraguados, sin duda, por la vanidad. No hagamos de Pepita una Fedra y de mí un Hipólito.[88]

Lo que sí empieza a sorprenderme es el descuido y plena seguridad de mi padre. Perdone usted, pídale a Dios que perdone mi orgullo; de vez en cuando me pica y enoja la tal seguridad. Pues qué, me digo, ¿soy tan adefesio para que mi padre no tema que, a pesar de mi supuesta santidad, o por mi misma supuesta santidad, no pueda yo enamorar, sin querer, a Pepita? . . .

Sería una falta de respeto, pecaría yo de presumido e insolente si advirtiese a mi padre del peligro que no ve. No hay medio de que yo le diga nada. Además, ¿qué había yo de decirle? ¿Que se me figura que una o dos veces Pepita me ha mirado de otra manera que como suele mirar? ¿No puede ser esto ilusión mía? No, no tengo la menor prueba de que Pepita desee siquiera coquetear conmigo.

¿Qué es, pues, lo que entonces podría yo decir a mi padre? ¿Había de decirle que yo soy quien está enamorado de Pepita, que yo codicio el tesoro que ya él tiene por suyo? Esto no es verdad; y sobre todo, ¿cómo declarar esto a mi padre, aunque fuera verdad por mi desgracia y por mi culpa?

Lo mejor es callarme; combatir en silencio, si la tentación llega a asaltarme de veras, y tratar de abandonar cuanto antes este pueblo y de volverme con usted.

19 de mayo.

Gracias a Dios y a usted por las nuevas cartas y nuevos consejos que me envía. Hoy los necesito más que nunca . . .

Es cierto; ya no puedo negárselo a usted. Yo no debí poner los ojos con tanta complacencia en esta mujer peligrosísima.

No me juzgo perdido, pero me siento conturbado.

Como el corzo sediento desea y busca el manantial de las aguas, así mi alma busca a Dios todavía.[89] A Dios se vuelve para que le dé reposo, y anhela beber en el torrente de sus delicias, cuyo ímpetu alegra el Paraíso, y cuyas ondas claras ponen más blanco que la nieve; pero un abismo llama a otro abismo, y mis pies se han clavado en el cieno que está en el fondo.

Sin embargo, aun me quedan voz y aliento para clamar con el Salmista: ¡Levántate, gloria mía![90] Si te pones de mi lado, ¿quién prevalecerá contra mí? . . .

Las mortificaciones, el ayuno, la oración y la penitencia serán las armas de que me revista para combatir y vencer con el auxilio divino.

No era sueño, no era locura; era realidad. Ella me mira a veces con la ardiente mirada de que ya he hablado a usted. Sus ojos están dotados de una atracción magnética inexplicable. Me atrae, me seduce, y se fijan en ella los míos. Mis ojos deben arder entonces, como los suyos, con una llama funesta; como los de Amón[91] cuando se fijaban

[88] Phaedra fell in love with her stepson, Hippolytus. When he refused her advances, she told her husband Theseus that his son was making love to her. Theseus gave Hippolytus up to the mercy of Neptune, who brought about his death. In remorse, Phaedra hanged herself.

[89] See Psalms 42. I:

'As the hart panteth after the water brooks,
So panteth my soul after thee. O God.'

The wording of this entire paragraph is full of Biblical reminiscences.

[90] Psalms 57. 8.

[91] Amnon, who fell in love with his sister, Tamar (II Samuel, 13. 1).

en Tamar; como los de príncipe de Siquén[92] cuando se fijaban en Dina.

Al mirarnos así, hasta de Dios me olvido. La imagen de ella se levanta en el fondo de mi espíritu, vencedora de todo. Su hermosura resplandece sobre toda hermosura; los deleites del cielo me parecen inferiores a su cariño; una eternidad de penas creo que no paga la bienaventuranza infinita que vierte sobre mí en un momento con una de estas miradas, que pasan cual relámpago.

Cuando vuelvo a casa, cuando me quedo solo en mi cuarto, en el silencio de la noche, reconozco todo el horror de mi situación y formo buenos propósitos, que luego se quebrantan.

Me prometo a mí mismo fingirme enfermo, buscar cualquier otro pretexto para no ir a la noche siguiente a casa de Pepita, y sin embargo voy.

Mi padre, confiado hasta lo sumo, sin sospechar lo que pasa en mi alma, me dice cuando llega la hora:

—Vete a la tertulia. Yo iré más tarde, luego que despache al aperador.

Yo no atino con la excusa, no hallo el pretexto y en vez de contestar: —No puedo ir—, tomo el sombrero y voy a la tertulia.

Al entrar, Pepita y yo nos damos la mano, y al dárnosla me hechiza. Todo mi ser se muda. Penetra hasta mi corazón un fuego devorante, y ya no pienso más que en ella. Tal vez soy yo mismo quien provoca las miradas si tardan en llegar. La miro con insano ahinco, por un estímulo irresistible, y a cada instante creo descubrir en ella nuevas perfecciones. Ya los hoyuelos de sus mejillas cuando sonríe, ya la blancura sonrosada de la tez, ya la forma recta de la nariz, ya la pequeñez de la oreja, ya la suavidad de contornos y admirable modelado de la garganta.

Entro en su casa, a pesar mío, como evocado por un conjuro; y, no bien entro en su casa, caigo bajo el poder de su encanto; veo claramente que estoy dominado por una maga cuya fascinación es ineluctable.

No es ella grata a mis ojos solamente, sino que sus palabras suenan en mis oídos como la música de las esferas, revelándome toda la armonía del universo, y hasta imagino percibir una sutilísima fragancia que su limpio cuerpo despide, y que supera al olor de los mastranzos que crecen a orillas de los arroyos y al aroma silvestre del tomillo que en los montes se cría.

Excitado de esta suerte, no sé cómo juego al tresillo, ni hablo, ni discurro con juicio, porque estoy todo en ella. Cada vez que se encuentran nuestras miradas se lanzan en ellas nuestras almas, y en los rayos que se cruzan se me figura que se unen y compenetran. Allí se descubren mil inefables misterios de amor, allí se comunican sentimientos que por otro medio no llegarían a saberse, y se citan poesías que no caben en lengua humana, y se cantan canciones que no hay voz que exprese ni acordada cítara que module.

Desde el día en que vi a Pepita en el Pozo de la Solana, no he vuelto a verla a solas. Nada le he dicho ni me ha dicho, y, sin embargo, nos lo hemos dicho todo.

Cuando me sustraigo a la fascinación, cuando estoy solo por la noche en mi aposento, quiero mirar con frialdad el estado en que me hallo, y veo abierto a mis pies el precipicio en que voy a sumirme, y siento que me resbalo y que me hundo.

Me recomienda usted que piense en la muerte; no en la de esta mujer, sino en la mía. Me recomienda usted que piense en lo instable, en lo inseguro de nuestra existencia y en lo que hay más allá. Pero esta consideración y esta

[92] Prince Shechem forced his attentions on Dinah (Genesis 34).

meditación ni me atemorizan ni me arredran. ¿Cómo he de temer la muerte cuando deseo morir? El amor y la muerte son hermanos. Un sentimiento de abnegación se alza de las profundidades de mi ser, y me llama a sí, y me dice que todo mi ser debe darse y perderse por el objeto amado. Ansío confundirme en una de sus miradas; diluir y evaporar toda mi esencia en el rayo de luz que sale de sus ojos, quedarme muerto mirándola, aunque me condene.

Lo que es aún eficaz en mí contra el amor, no es el temor, sino el amor mismo. Sobre este amor determinado, que ya veo con evidencia que Pepita me inspira, se levanta en mi espíritu el amor divino en consurrección poderosa. Entonces todo se cambia en mí, y aun me prometo la victoria. El objeto de mi amor superior se ofrece a los ojos de mi mente como el sol que todo lo enciende y alumbra, llenando de luz los espacios; y el objeto de mi amor, más bajo, como átomo de polvo que vaga en el ambiente y que el sol dora. Toda su beldad, todo su resplandor y todo su atractivo no es más que el reflejo de ese sol increado, no es más que la chispa brillante, transitoria, inconsistente de aquella infinita y perenne hoguera.

Mi alma, abrasada de amor, pugna por criar alas, y tender el vuelo, y subir a esa hoguera, y consumir allí cuanto hay en ella de impuro.

Mi vida, desde hace algunos días, es una lucha constante. No sé cómo el mal que padezco no me sale a la cara. Apenas me alimento; apenas duermo. Si el sueño cierra mis párpados, suelo despertar azorado, como si me hallase peleando en una batalla de ángeles rebeldes y de ángeles buenos. En esta batalla de la luz contra las tinieblas, yo combato por la luz; pero tal vez imagino que me paso al enemigo, que soy un desertor infame; y oigo la voz del águila de Patmos[93] que dice: «Y los hombres prefirieron las tinieblas a la luz;» y entonces me lleno de terror y me juzgo perdido.

No me queda más recurso que huir. Si en lo que falta para terminar el mes mi padre no me da su venia y no viene conmigo, me escapo como un ladrón; me fugo sin decir nada.

23 de mayo.

Soy un vil gusano, y no un hombre; soy el oprobio y la abyección de la humanidad; soy un hipócrita.

Me han circundado dolores de muerte, y torrentes de iniquidad me han conturbado.

Vergüenza tengo de escribir a usted, y no obstante le escribo. Quiero confesárselo todo.

No logro enmendarme. Lejos de dejar de ir a casa de Pepita, voy más temprano todas las noches. Se diría que los demonios me agarran de los pies y me llevan allá sin que yo quiera.

Por dicha, no hallo sola nunca a Pepita. No quisiera hallarla sola. Casi siempre se me adelanta el excelente padre Vicario, que atribuye nuestra amistad a la semejanza de gustos piadosos, y la funda en la devoción, como la amistad inocentísima que él le profesa.

El progreso de mi mal es rápido. Como piedra que se desprende de lo alto del templo y va aumentando su velocidad en la caída, así mi espíritu ahora.

Cuando Pepita y yo nos damos la mano, no es ya como al principio. Ambos hacemos un esfuerzo de voluntad y nos transmitimos, por nuestras diestras enlazadas, todas las palpitaciones del corazón. Se diría que, por arte diabólico, obramos una transfusión y mez-

[93] Saint John, the author of the Apocalypse or the book of Revelation, lived on the island of Patmos, near the west coast of Asia Minor (Revelation 1. 9).

cla de lo más sutil de nuestra sangre. Ella debe de sentir circular mi vida por sus venas, como yo siento en las mías la suya . . .

Todas las noches salgo de su casa diciendo: «Ésta será la última noche que vuelvo aquí,» y vuelvo a la noche siguiente.

Cuando habla, y estoy a su lado, mi alma queda como colgada de su boca; cuando sonríe, se me antoja que un rayo de luz inmaterial se me entra en el corazón y le alegra.

A veces, jugando al tresillo, se han tocado por acaso nuestras rodillas, y he sentido un indescriptible sacudimiento.

Sáqueme usted de aquí. Escriba usted a mi padre que me dé licencia para irme. Si es menester, dígaselo todo. ¡Socórrame usted! ¡Sea usted mi amparo!

30 de mayo.

Dios me ha dado fuerzas para resistir y he resistido.

Hace días que no pongo los pies en casa de Pepita, que no la veo.

Casi no tengo que pretextar una enfermedad, porque realmente estoy enfermo. Estoy pálido y ojeroso; y mi padre, lleno de afectuoso cuidado, me pregunta qué padezco y me muestra el interés más vivo.

El reino de los cielos cede a la violencia, y yo quiero conquistarle. Con violencia llamo a sus puertas para que se me abran.

Con ajenjo me alimenta Dios para probarme, y en balde le pido que aparte de mí ese cáliz de amargura; pero he pasado y paso en vela muchas noches entregado a la oración, y ha venido a endulzar lo amargo del cáliz una inspiración amorosa del espíritu consolador y soberano.

He visto con los ojos del alma la nueva patria,[94] y en lo más íntimo de mi corazón ha resonado el cántico nuevo de la Jerusalén celeste.

Si al cabo logro vencer, será gloriosa la victoria; pero se la deberé a la Reina de los Ángeles, a quien me encomiendo. Ella es mi refugio y mi defensa; torre y alcázar de David, de que penden mil escudos y armaduras de valerosos campeones; cedro del Líbano, que pone en fuga a las serpientes.[95]

En cambio, a la mujer que me enamora de un modo mundanal procuro menospreciarla y abatirla en mi pensamiento, recordando las palabras del Sabio[96] y aplicándoselas.

Eres lazo de cazadores, la digo; tu corazón es red engañosa, y tus manos redes que atan: quien ama a Dios huirá de ti, y el pecador será por ti aprisionado.

Meditando sobre el amor, hallo mil motivos para amar a Dios y no amarla.

Siento en el fondo de mi corazón una inefable energía que me convence de que yo lo despreciaría todo por el amor de Dios: la fama, la honra, el poder y el imperio. Me hallo capaz de imitar a Cristo; y si el enemigo tentador me llevase a la cumbre de la montaña y me ofreciese todos los reinos de la tierra porque doblase ante él la rodilla,[97] yo no la doblaría; pero cuando me ofrece a esta mujer, vacilo aún y no le rechazo. ¿Vale más esta mujer a mis ojos que todos los reinos de la tierra; más que la fama, la honra, el poder y el imperio? . . .

6 de junio.

La nodriza de Pepita, hoy su ama de llaves, es, como dice mi padre, una buena pieza de arrugadillo;[98] picotera, alegre y hábil como pocas . . .

[94] Luis has seen Heaven in a mystic vision.

[95] A series of epithets given the Virgin Mary in mystic prayers.

[96] Solomon

[97] Christ underwent this form of temptation (Matthew 4).

[98] *pieza de arrugadillo,* a smart one

Antoñona, que así se llama, tiene o se toma la mayor confianza con todo el señorío. En todas las casas entra y sale como en la suya. A todos los señoritos y señoritas de la edad de Pepita, o de cuatro o cinco años más, los tutea, los llama niños y niñas, y los trata como si los hubiera criado a sus pechos.

A mí me habla de mira,[99] como a los otros. Viene a verme, entra en mi cuarto, y ya me ha dicho varias veces que soy un ingrato, y que hago mal en no ir a ver a su señora.

Mi padre, sin advertir nada, me acusa de extravagante; me llama buho, y se empeña también en que vuelva a la tertulia. Anoche no pude ya resistirme a sus repetidas instancias, y fuí muy temprano, cuando mi padre iba a hacer las cuentas con el aperador.

¡Ojalá no hubiera ido!

Pepita estaba sola. Al vernos, al saludarnos, nos pusimos los dos colorados. Nos dimos la mano con timidez, sin decirnos palabra.

Yo no estreché la suya; ella no estrechó la mía, pero las conservamos unidas un breve rato.

En la mirada que Pepita me dirigió, nada había de amor, sino de amistad, de simpatía, de honda tristeza.

Había adivinado toda mi lucha interior; presumía que el amor divino había triunfado en mi alma; que mi resolución de no amarla era firme e invencible.

No se atrevía a quejarse de mí; conocía que la razón estaba de mi parte. Un suspiro, apenas perceptible, que se escapó de sus frescos labios entreabiertos, manifestó cuánto lo deploraba.

Nuestras manos seguían unidas aún. Ambos mudos. ¿Cómo decirle que yo no era para ella ni ella para mí; que importaba separarnos para siempre?

Sin embargo, aunque no se lo dije con palabras, se lo dije con los ojos. Mi severa mirada confirmó sus temores; la persuadió de la irrevocable sentencia.

De pronto se nublaron sus ojos; todo su rostro hermoso, pálido ya de una palidez traslúcida, se contrajo con una bellísima expresión de melancolía. Parecía la madre de los dolores.[100] Dos lágrimas brotaron lentamente de sus ojos y empezaron a deslizarse por sus mejillas.

No sé lo que pasó en mí. ¿Ni cómo describirlo aunque lo supiera?

Acerqué mis labios a su cara para enjugar el llanto, y se unieron nuestras bocas en un beso.

Inefable embriaguez, desmayo fecundo en peligros invadió todo mi ser y el ser de ella. Su cuerpo desfallecía y lo sostuve entre mis brazos.

Quiso el cielo que oyésemos los pasos y la tos del padre Vicario que llegaba, y nos separamos al punto.

Volviendo en mí, y reconcentrando todas las fuerzas de mi voluntad, pude entonces llenar con estas palabras, que pronuncié en voz baja e intensa, aquella terrible escena silenciosa:

—¡El primero y el último!

Yo aludía al beso profano; mas, como si hubieran sido mis palabras una evocación, se ofreció en mi mente la visión apocalíptica en toda su terrible majestad. Vi al que es por cierto el primero y el último, y con la espada de dos filos que salía de su boca me hería en el alma, llena de maldades, de vicios y de pecados.[101]

[99] with great familarity. *Mira,* 'see here' or 'listen,' is a common way of beginning a familiar conversation.

[100] The statue of the Virgin representing her as weeping for her Son's suffering with her heart transfixed with seven daggers, symbolical of her seven sorrows.

[101] In Revelation 2. 16–17, John saw the figure of the Son of God (who is of course first and last, Alpha and Omega) with a sword protruding from his mouth, smiting the sinful.

Toda aquella noche la pasé en un frenesí, en un delirio interior, que no sé cómo disimulaba.

Me retiré de casa de Pepita muy temprano.

En la soledad fué mayor mi amargura.

Al recordarme de aquel beso y de aquellas palabras de despedida, me comparaba yo con el traidor Judas, que vendía besando; y con el sanguinario y alevoso asesino Joab,[102] cuando al besar a Amasá, le hundió el hierro agudo en las entrañas.

Había incurrido en dos traiciones y en dos falsías.

Había faltado a Dios y a ella.

Soy un ser abominable.

11 de junio.

Aun es tiempo de remediarlo todo. Pepita sanará de su amor y olvidará la flaqueza que ambos tuvimos.

Desde aquella noche no he vuelto a su casa.

Antoñona no parece por la mía.

A fuerza de súplicas he logrado de mi padre la promesa formal de que partiremos de aquí el 25, pasado el día de San Juan, que aquí se celebra con fiestas lucidas, y en cuya víspera hay una famosa velada.[103]

Lejos de Pepita me voy serenando y creyendo que tal vez ha sido una prueba este comienzo de amores . . .

Sí, la imagen profana de esa mujer saldrá definitivamente y para siempre de mi alma. Yo haré un azote durísimo de mis oraciones y penitencias, y con él la arrojaré de allí como Cristo arrojó del templo a los condenados mercaderes.

18 de junio.

Ésta será la última carta que yo escriba a usted.

El 25 saldré de aquí sin falta. Pronto tendré el gusto de dar a usted un abrazo.

Cerca de usted estaré mejor. Usted me infundirá ánimo y me prestará la energía de que carezco.

Una tempestad de encontradas afecciones combate ahora en mi corazón.

El desorden de mis ideas se conocerá en el desorden de lo que estoy escribiendo.

Dos veces he vuelto a casa de Pepita. He estado frío, severo, como debía estar; pero ¡cuánto me ha costado!

Ayer me dijo mi padre que Pepita está indispuesta y que no recibe.

En seguida me asaltó el pensamiento de que su amor mal pagado podría ser la causa de la enfermedad.

¿Por qué la he mirado con las mismas miradas de fuego con que ella me miraba? ¿Por qué la he engañado vilmente? ¿Por qué la[104] he hecho creer que la quería? ¿Por qué mi boca infame buscó la suya y se abrasó y la abrasó con las llamas del infierno?

Pero, no: mi pecado no ha de traer como indefectible consecuencia otra pecado.

Lo que ya fué no puede dejar de haber sido, pero puede y debe remediarse.

El 25, repito, partiré sin falta.

La desenvuelta Antoñona acaba de entrar a verme.

Escondí esta carta, como si fuera una maldad escribir a usted.

Sólo un minuto ha estado aquí Antoñona.

Yo me levanté de la silla para hablar con ella de pie y que la visita fuera corta.

En tan corta visita, me ha dicho mil locuras que me afligen profundamente.

[102] II Samuel 20. 10 tells how Joab murdered Amasa while giving him a kiss of greeting.

[103] Saint John's Day (June 24) is a Christian holiday which retains traces of the pagan midsummer's festival of fertility. On its eve many bonfires are lit, and there is much courting and merrymaking. We shall soon learn of other customs of the day.

[104] *La* for *le,* as often in spoken Spanish.

Por último, ha exclamado al despedirse, en su jerga medio gitana:

—¡Anda, fullero de amor, *indinote,* maldecido seas; *malos chuqueles te tagelen el drupo,*[105] que has puesto enferma a la niña y con tus retrecherías la estás matando!

Dicho esto, la endiablada mujer me aplicó, de una manera indecorosa y plebeya, por bajo de las espaldas, seis o siete feroces pellizcos, como si quisiera sacarme a túrdigas el pellejo. Después se largó echando chispas.[106]

No me quejo, merezco esta broma brutal, dado que sea broma. Merezco que me atenacen los demonios con tenazas hechas ascuas.[107]

¡Dios mío, haz que Pepita me olvide; haz, si es menester, que ame a otro y sea con él dichosa!

¿Puedo pedirte más, Dios mío?

Mi padre no sabe nada, no sospecha nada. Más vale así.

Adiós. Hasta dentro de pocos días, que nos veremos y abrazaremos.

¡Qué mudado va usted a encontrarme! ¡Qué lleno de amargura mi corazón! ¡Cuán perdida la inocencia! ¡Qué herida y qué lastimada mi alma!

II. *Paralipómenos*[108]

No hay más cartas de don Luis de Vargas que las que hemos transcrito. Nos quedaríamos, pues, sin averiguar el término que tuvieron estos amores, y esta sencilla y apasionada historia no acabaría, si un sujeto, perfectamente enterado de todo, no hubiese compuesto la relación que sigue . . .

A los cinco días de la fecha de la última carta que hemos leído, empieza nuestra narración.

Eran las once de la mañana. Pepita estaba en una sala alta al lado de su alcoba y de su tocador, donde nadie, salvo Antoñona, entraba jamás sin que llamase ella.

Los muebles de aquella sala eran de poco valor, pero cómodos y aseados. Las cortinas y el forro de los sillones, sofás y butacas eran de tela de algodón pintada de flores; sobre una mesita de caoba había recado de escribir y papeles; y en un armario, de caoba también, bastantes libros de devoción y de historia. Las paredes se veían adornadas con cuadros, que eran estampas de asuntos religiosos; pero con el buen gusto, inaudito, raro, casi inverosímil en un lugar de Andalucía, de que dichas estampas no fuesen malas litografías francesas, sino grabados de nuestra Calcografía,[109] como el *Pasmo de Sicilia,* de Rafael; el *San Ildefonso y la Virgen,* la *Concepción,* el *San Bernardo* y los dos medios puntos, de Murillo.[110]

Sobre una antigua mesa de roble, sostenida por columnas salomónicas,[111] se veía un contadorcillo o papelera con embutidos de concha, nácar, marfil y bronce, y muchos cajoncitos donde

[105] *Anda . . . drupo,* Go on, you love cheat, you awful wicked person, curses on you; may bad dogs gnaw your bones . . . (*indinote,* popular for *indigno* plus augmentative; *chuqueles,* dogs; *drupo,* body; *tagelar,* to eat. All Andalusian slang)

[106] *echando chispas,* with eyes flashing; very angry

[107] red hot; literally, made into glowing coals

[108] See n. 2.

[109] Government engraving office

[110] *Pasmo de Sicilia . . . Murillo;* el *Pasmo de Sicilia* is a picture originally painted for a monastery in Palermo, Sicily, and is now in the Museo del Prado, Madrid. It represents an episode of the 'Via Crucis,' when Christ, bearing his cross to Calvary, stumbles and falls. *San Ildefonso y la Virgen* is a picture in the Prado which shows the saint receiving a vestment from the hands of the Virgin. Murillo painted several versions of the Immaculate Conception, always representing the Virgin standing on clouds and the crescent moon, surrounded by cherubim. *La visión de San Bernardo* depicts the occasion on which the Virgin appeared before the saint. The *medios puntos* are semi-circular paintings, one in Madrid and the other in Cádiz.

[111] twisted columns

guardaba Pepita cuentas y otros documentos. Sobre la misma mesa había dos vasos de porcelana con muchas flores. Colgadas en la pared había, por último, algunas macetas de loza de la Cartuja[112] sevillana con geranio-hiedra y otras plantas, y tres jaulas doradas con canarios y jilgueros.

Aquella sala era el retiro de Pepita, donde no entraban de día sino el médico y el padre Vicario, y donde a prima noche entraba sólo el aperador a dar sus cuentas. Aquella sala era y se llamaba el despacho.

Pepita estaba sentada, casi recostada en un sofá, delante del cual había un velador pequeño con varios libros.

Se acababa de levantar, y vestía una ligera bata de verano. Su cabello rubio mal peinado aún, parecía más hermoso en su mismo desorden. Su cara, algo pálida y con ojeras, si bien llena de juventud, lozanía y frescura, parecía más bella con el mal que le robaba colores.

Pepita mostraba impaciencia; aguardaba a alguien.

Al fin llegó, y entró sin anunciarse la persona que aguardaba, que era el padre Vicario.

Después de los saludos de costumbre, y arrellanado el padre Vicario en una butaca al lado de Pepita, se entabló la conversación.

—Me alegro, hija mía, de que me hayas llamado; pero sin que te hubieras molestado en llarmarme, ya iba yo a venir a verte. ¡Qué pálida estás! ¿Qué padeces? ¿Tienes algo importante que decirme?

A esta serie de preguntas cariñosas empezó a contestar Pepita con un hondo suspiro. Después dijo:

—¿No adivina usted mi enfermedad? ¿No descubre usted la causa de mi padecimiento?

El Vicario se encogió de hombros, y miró a Pepita con cierto susto porque nada sabía, y le llamaba la atención la vehemencia con que ella se expresaba.

Pepita prosiguió:

—Padre mío, yo no debí llamar a usted, sino ir a la iglesia y hablar con usted en el confesionario, y allí confesar mis pecados. Por desgracia, no estoy arrepentida; mi corazón se ha endurecido en la maldad, y no he tenido valor ni me he hallado dispuesta para hablar con el confesor, sino con el amigo.

—¿Qué dices de pecados ni de dureza de corazón? ¿Estás loca? ¿Qué pecados han de ser los tuyos, si eres tan buena?

—No, padre, yo soy mala. He estado engañando a usted, engañándome a mí misma, queriendo engañar a Dios.

—Vamos, cálmate, serénate; habla con orden y con juicio para no decir disparates.

—¿Y cómo no decirlos cuando el espíritu del mal me posee?

—¡Ave María Purísima! Muchacha, no desatines. Mira, hija mía: tres son los demonios más temibles que se apoderan de las almas, y ninguno de ellos, estoy seguro, se puede haber atrevido a llegar hasta la tuya. El uno es Leviatán, o el espíritu de soberbia; el otro Mamon, o el espíritu de la avaricia; el otro Asmodeo, o el espíritu de los amores impuros.[113]

—Pues de los tres soy víctima; los tres me dominan.

—¡Qué horror! . . . Repito que te calmes. De lo que tú eres víctima es de un delirio.

—¡Pluguiese[114] a Dios que así fuera!

[112] A monastery of the Carthusian Order. This order, which in France distilled the famous Chartreuse liqueur, apparently manufactured pottery in Sevilla.

[113] Leviathan is the spirit of pride (Job 41. 1–34): 'Canst thou draw out leviathan with a fish-hook . . . He is king over all the sons of pride.' Mammon is avarice (Matthew 6. 24). 'Ye cannot serve God and mammon.' Asmodaeus is the demon of lust, originally the evil demon of the Persians.

[114] Imperfect subjunctive of *placer*

Es, por mi culpa, lo contrario. Soy avarienta, porque poseo cuantiosos bienes y no hago las obras de caridad que debiera hacer; soy soberbia, porque he despreciado a muchos hombres, no por virtud, no por honestidad, sino porque no los hallaba acreedores[115] a mi cariño. Dios me ha castigado; Dios ha permitido que este tercer enemigo, de que usted habla, se apodere de mí.

—¿Cómo es eso, muchacha? ¿Qué diablura se te ocurre? ¿Estás enamorada quizás? Y si lo estás, ¿qué mal hay en ello? ¿No eres libre? Cásate, pues, y déjate de tonterías. Seguro estoy de que mi amigo don Pedro de Vargas ha hecho el milagro. ¡El demonio es el tal don Pedro! Te declaro que me asombra. No juzgaba yo el asunto tan mollar y tan maduro como estaba.

—¡Pero si[116] no es de don Pedro de Vargas de quien estoy enamorada!

—¿Pues de quién entonces?

Pepita se levantó de su asiento; fué hacia la puerta; la abrió; miró para ver si alguien escuchaba desde fuera; la volvió a cerrar; se acercó luego al padre Vicario, y toda acongojada, con voz trémula, con lágrimas en los ojos, dijo casi al oído del buen anciano:

—Estoy perdidamente enamorada de su hijo.

—¿De qué hijo?—interrumpió el padre Vicario, que aun no quería creerlo.

—¿De qué hijo ha de ser? Estoy perdida, frenéticamente enamorada de don Luis.

La consternación, la sorpresa más dolorosa se pintó en el rostro del cándido y afectuoso sacerdote.

Hubo un momento de pausa. Después dijo el Vicario:

—Pero ése es un amor sin esperanza, un amor imposible. Don Luis no te querrá.

Por entre las lágrimas que nublaban los hermosos ojos de Pepita brilló un alegre rayo de luz; su linda y fresca boca, contraída por la tristeza, se abrió con suavidad, dejando ver las perlas de sus dientes y formando una sonrisa.

—Me quiere—dijo Pepita con un ligero y mal disimulado acento de satisfacción y de triunfo, que se alzaba por cima de su dolor y de sus escrúpulos.

Aquí subieron de punto[117] la consternación y el asombro del padre Vicario. Si el santo de su mayor devoción hubiera sido arrojado del altar y hubiera caído a sus pies, y se hubiera hecho cien mil pedazos, no se hubiera el Vicario consternado tanto. Todavía miró a Pepita con incredulidad como dudando de que aquello fuese cierto, y no una alucinación de la vanidad mujeril. Tan de firme creía en la santidad de don Luis y en su misticismo.

—¡Me quiere!—dijo otra vez Pepita, contestando a aquella incrédula mirada.

—¡Las mujeres son peores que pateta![118]—dijo el Vicario—. Echáis la zancadilla[119] al mismísimo mengue.[120]

—¿No se lo decía yo a usted? ¡Yo soy muy mala!

—¡Sea todo por Dios! Vamos, sosiégate. La misericordia de Dios es infinita. Cuéntame lo que ha pasado.

—¿Qué ha de haber pasado? Que le quiero, que le amo, que le adoro; que él me quiere también, aunque lucha por sofocar su amor y tal vez lo consiga; y que usted, sin saberlo, tiene mucha culpa de todo.

—¡Pues no faltaba más! ¿Cómo es eso de que tengo yo mucha culpa?

[115] Here, worthy
[116] Here, indeed
[117] *subir de punto,* to increase
[118] 'the dickens'
[119] *echar la zancadilla,* to trip up
[120] Familiar for the devil, 'old Nick'

—Con la extremada bondad que le es propia, no ha hecho usted más que alabarme a don Luis, y tengo por cierto que a don Luis le habrá usted hecho de mí mayores elogios aun, si bien harto menos merecidos. ¿Qué había de suceder? ¿Soy yo de bronce? ¿Tengo yo más de veinte años?[121]

—Tienes razón que te sobra. Soy un mentecato. He contribuído poderosamente a esta obra de Lucifer.

El padre Vicario era tan bueno y tan humilde, que al decir las anteriores frases estaba confuso y contrito, como si él fuese el reo y Pepita el juez.

Conoció Pepita el egoísmo rudo con que había hecho cómplice y punto menos que[122] autor principal de su falta al padre Vicario, y le habló de esta suerte:

—No se aflija usted, padre mío; no se aflija usted, por amor de Dios. ¡Mire usted si soy perversa! ¡Cometo pecados gravísimos y quiero hacer responsable de ellos al mejor y más virtuoso de los hombres! No han sido las alabanzas que usted me ha hecho de don Luis, sino mis ojos y mi poco recato los que me han perdido. Aunque usted no me hubiera hablado jamás de las prendas de don Luis, de su saber, de su talento y de su entusiasta corazón, yo lo hubiera descubierto todo oyéndole hablar, pues al cabo no soy tan tonta ni tan rústica. Me he fijado además en la gallardía de su persona, en la natural distinción y no aprendida elegancia de sus modales, en sus ojos llenos de fuego y de inteligencia, en todo él, en suma, que me parece amable y deseable. Los elogios de usted han venido sólo a lisonjear mi gusto, pero no a despertarle. Me han encantado porque coincidían con mi parecer y eran como el eco adulador, harto amortiguado y debilísimo, de lo que yo pensaba. El más elocuente encomio que me ha hecho usted de don Luis no ha llegado, ni con mucho,[123] al encomio que sin palabras me hacía yo de él a cada minuto, a cada segundo, dentro del alma.

—¡No te exaltes, hija mía!—interrumpió el padre Vicario.

Pepita continuó con mayor exaltación:

—Pero, ¡qué diferencia entre los encomios de usted y mis pensamientos! Usted veía y trazaba en don Luis el modelo ejemplar del sacerdote, del misionero, del varón apostólico; ya predicando el Evangelio en apartadas regiones y convirtiendo infieles, ya trabajando en España para realzar la cristiandad, tan perdida hoy por la impiedad de los unos y la carencia de virtud, de caridad y de ciencia de los otros. Yo, en cambio, me le representaba galán, enamorado, olvidando a Dios por mí, consagrándome su vida, dándome su alma, siendo mi apoyo, mi sostén, mi dulce compañero. Yo anhelaba cometer un robo sacrílego. Soñaba con robársele a Dios y a su templo, como el ladrón, enemigo del cielo, que roba la joya más rica de la venerada Custodia. Para cometer este robo he desechado los lutos de la viudez y de la orfandad y me he vestido galas profanas; he abandonado mi retiro y he buscado y llamado a mí a las gentes; he procurado estar hermosa; he cuidado con infernal esmero de todo este cuerpo miserable, que ha de hundirse en la sepultura y ha de convertirse en polvo vil, y he mirado, por último, a don Luis con miradas provocantes, y, al estrechar su mano, he querido transmitir de mis venas a las suyas este fuego inextinguible en que me abraso.

—¡Ay, niña, niña! ¡Qué pena me

[121] Pepita excuses herself by throwing the blame on the innocent vicar, a very natural psychological process. Compare with n. 60.

[122] *punto menos que,* almost

[123] *no ha llegado, ni con mucho,* hasn't reached or come anywhere near

da lo que te oigo! ¡Quién lo hubiera podido imaginar siquiera!

—Pues hay más todavía—añadió Pepita—. Logré que don Luis me amase. Me lo declaraba con los ojos. Sí; su amor era tan profundo, tan ardiente como el mío. Su virtud, su aspiración a los bienes eternos, su esfuerzo varonil trataban de vencer esta pasión insana. Yo he procurado imperdirlo. Una vez, después de muchos días que faltaba de esta casa, vino a verme y me halló sola. Al darle la mano lloré; sin hablar me inspiró el infierno una maldita elocuencia muda, le di a entender mi dolor porque me desdeñaba, porque no me quería, porque prefería a mi amor otro amor sin mancilla.[124] Entonces no supo él resistir a la tentación y acercó su boca a mi rostro para secar mis lágrimas. Nuestras bocas se unieron. Si Dios no hubiera dispuesto que llegase usted en aquel instante, ¿qué hubiera sido de mí?

—¡Qué vergüenza, hija mía! ¡Qué vergüenza!—dijo el padre Vicario.

Pepita se cubrió el rostro con entrambas manos y empezó a sollozar como una Magdalena. Las manos eran, en efecto, tan bellas, más bellas que lo que don Luis había dicho en sus cartas. Su blancura, su transparencia nítida, lo afilado de los dedos, lo sonrosado, pulido y brillante de las uñas de nácar, todo era para volver loco a cualquier hombre.

El virtuoso Vicario comprendió, a pesar de sus ochenta años, la caída o tropiezo de don Luis.

—¡Muchacha—exclamó—no seas extremosa! ¡No me partas el corazón! Tranquilízate. Don Luis se ha arrepentido, sin duda, de su pecado. Arrepiéntete tú también, y se acabó. Dios os perdonará y os hará unos santos. Cuando don Luis se va pasado mañana, clara señal es de que la virtud ha triunfado en él, y huye de ti, como debe, para hacer penitencia de su pecado, cumplir su promesa y acudir a su vocación.

—Bueno está eso—replicó Pepita—; cumplir su promesa . . . acudir a su vocación . . . ¡y matarme a mí antes! ¿Por qué me ha querido, por qué me ha engreído, por qué me ha engañado? Su beso fué marca, fué hierro candente con que me señaló y selló como a su esclava. Ahora, que estoy marcada y esclavizada, me abandona, y me vende, y me asesina. ¡Feliz principio quiere dar a sus misiones, predicaciones y triunfos evangélicos! ¡No será! ¡Vive Dios[125] que no será!

Este arranque de ira y de amoroso despecho aturdió al padre Vicario.

Pepita se había puesto de pie. Su ademán, su gesto tenían una animación trágica. Fulguraban sus ojos como dos puñales; relucían como dos soles. El Vicario callaba y la miraba casi con terror. Ella recorrió la sala a grandes pasos. No parecía ya tímida gacela, sino iracunda leona.

—Pues qué—dijo, encarándose de nuevo con el padre Vicario—, ¿no hay más que burlarse de mí, destrozarme el corazón, humillármele, pisoteármele después de habérmele robado por engaño? ¡Se acordará de mí! ¡Me la pagará! Si es tan santo, si es tan virtuoso, ¿por qué me miró prometiéndomelo todo con su mirada? Si ama tanto a Dios, ¿por qué hace mal a una pobre criatura de Dios? ¿Es esto caridad? ¿Es religión esto? No; es egoísimo sin entrañas.

La cólera de Pepita no podía durar mucho. Dichas las últimas palabras, se trocó en desfallecimiento. Pepita se dejó caer en una butaca llorando más que antes, con una verdadera congoja.

El Vicario sintió la más tierna compasión; pero recobró su brío al ver que el enemigo se rendía.

—Pepita, niña—dijo—, vuelve en ti;

[124] i.e. the love of God

[125] By heavens!

no te atormentes de ese modo. Considera que él habrá luchado mucho para vencerse; que no te ha engañado; que te quiere con toda el alma, pero que Dios y su obligación están antes. Esta vida es muy breve y pronto se pasa. En el cielo os reuniréis y os amaréis como se aman los ángeles. Dios aceptará vuestro sacrificio y os premiará y recompensará con usura. Hasta tu amor propio debe estar satisfecho. ¡Qué no valdrás tú cuando has hecho vacilar y aun pecar a un hombre como don Luis! ¡Cuán honda herida no habrás logrado hacer en su corazón! Bástete con esto. ¡Sé generosa, sé valiente! Compite con él en firmeza. Déjale partir; lanza de tu pecho el fuego del amor impuro; ámale como a tu prójimo, por el amor de Dios. Guarda su imagen en tu mente, pero como la de criatura predilecta, reservando al Creador la más noble parte del alma. No sé lo que te digo, hija mía, porque estoy muy turbado; pero tú tienes mucho talento y mucha discreción, y me comprendes por medias palabras. Hay, además, motivos mundanos poderosos que se opondrían a estos absurdos amores, aunque la vocación y promesa de don Luis no se opusieran. Su padre te pretende: aspira a tu mano, por más que[126] tú no le ames. ¿Estará bien visto que salgamos ahora con que el hijo es rival del padre? ¿No se enojará el padre contra el hijo por amor tuyo? Mira cuán horrible es todo esto, y domínate por Jesús Crucificado y por su bendita madre María Santísima.

—¡Qué fácil es dar consejos!—contestó Pepita sosegándose un poco—. ¡Qué difícil me es seguirlos, cuando hay como una fiera y desencadenada tempestad en mi cabeza! ¡Si[127] me da miedo de volverme loca!

—Los consejos que te doy son por tu bien. Deja que don Luis se vaya. La ausencia es gran remedio para el mal de amores. Él sanará de su pasión entregándose a sus estudios y consagrándose al altar. Tú, así que esté lejos don Luis, irás poco a poco serenándote, y conservarás de él un grato y melancólico recuerdo, que no te hará daño. Será como una hermosa poesía que dorará con su luz tu existencia . . .

—¡Padre mío! ¡Padre mío! ¡Qué bueno es usted! Sus santas palabras me prestan valor. Yo me dominaré; yo me venceré. Sería bochornoso, ¿no es verdad que sería bochornoso que don Luis supiera dominarse y vencerse, y yo fuera liviana y no me venciera? Que se vaya. Se va pasado mañana. Vaya bendito de Dios. Mire usted su tarjeta. Ayer estuvo a despedirse con su Padre y no le he recibido. Ya no le veré más. No quiero conservar ni el recuerdo poético de que usted habla. Estos amores han sido una pesadilla. Yo la arrojaré lejos de mí.

—¡Bien, muy bien! Así te quiero yo, enérgica, valiente.

—¡Ay, padre mío! Dios ha derribado mi soberbia con este golpe; mi engreimiento era insolentísimo y han sido indispensables los desdenes de ese hombre para que sea yo todo lo humilde que debo. ¿Puedo estar más postrada ni más resignada? Tiene razón don Luis: yo no le merezco. ¿Cómo, por más esfuerzos que hiciera, habría yo de elevarme hasta él, y comprenderle, y poner en perfecta comunicación mi espíritu con el suyo? Yo soy zafia aldeana, inculta, necia; él no hay ciencia que no comprenda, ni arcano que ignore, ni esfera encumbrada del mundo intelectual adonde no suba. Allá se remonta en alas de su genio, y a mí, pobre y vulgar mujer, me deja por acá, en este bajo suelo, incapaz de seguirle ni siquiera con

[126] *por más que,* however much that, despite the fact that

[127] indeed, why

una levísima esperanza y con mis desconsolados suspiros.

—Pero, Pepita, por los clavos de Cristo, no digas eso ni lo pienses. ¡Si don Luis no te desdeña por zafia, ni porque es muy sabio y tú no le entiendes, ni por esas majaderías que ahí estás ensartando! Él se va porque tiene que cumplir con Dios; y tú debes alegrarte de que se vaya porque sanarás del amor, y Dios te dará el premio de tan grande sacrificio.

Pepita, que ya no lloraba y que se había enjugado las lágrimas con el pañuelo, contestó tranquila:

—Está bien, padre; yo me alegraré; casi me alegro ya de que se vaya. Deseando estoy que pase el día de mañana, y que pasado venga Antoñana a decirme cuando yo despierte: «Ya se fué don Luis.» Usted verá cómo renacen entonces la calma y la serenidad antigua en mi corazón.

—Así sea—dijo el padre Vicario; y convencido de que había hecho un prodigio y de que había curado casi el mal de Pepita, se despidió de ella y se fué a su casa, sin poder resistir ciertos estímulos de vanidad al considerar la influencia que ejercía sobre el noble espíritu de aquella preciosa muchacha.

Pepita, que se había levantado para despedir al padre Vicario, no bien volvió a cerrar la puerta y quedó sola, de pie, en medio de la estancia, permaneció un rato inmóvil, con la mirada fija, aunque sin fijarla en ningún objeto, y con los ojos sin lágrimas. Hubiera recordado a un poeta o a un artista la figura de Ariadna,[128] como la describe Catulo, cuando Teseo la abandonó en la isla de Naxos. De repente, como si lograse desatar un nudo que le apretaba la garganta, como si quebrase un cordel que la ahogaba, rompió Pepita en lastimeros gemidos, vertió un raudal de llanto, y dió con su cuerpo[129] tan lindo y delicado, sobre las losas frías del pavimento. Allí, cubierta la cara con las manos, desatada la trenza de sus cabellos y en desorden la vestidura, continuó en sus sollozos y en sus gemidos.

Así hubiera seguido largo tiempo, si no llega[130] Antoñona. Antoñona la oyó gemir, antes de entrar y verla, y se precipitó en la sala. Cuando la vió tendida en el suelo, hizo Antoñona mil extremos de furor.

—¡Vea usted—dijo—, ese zángano, pelgar, vejete, tonto, qué maña se da para consolar a sus amigas! Habrá largado alguna barbaridad, algún buen par de coces a esta criaturita de mi alma, y me la ha dejado aquí medio muerta, y él se ha vuelto a la iglesia, a preparar lo conveniente para cantarle el gorigori,[131] y rociarla con el hisopo y enterrámela si más ni más[132] . . .

Aunque Pepita no fuese una paja, Antoñona la alzó del suelo en sus brazos, como si lo[133] fuera, y la puso con mucho tiento sobre el sofá, como quien coloca la alhaja más frágil y primorosa para que no se quiebre.

—¿Qué soponcio es éste?—preguntó Antoñona—. Apuesto cualquier cosa a que ese zanguango de Vicario te ha echado un sermón de acíbar y te ha destrozado el alma a pesadumbres.

[128] Ariadne, daughter of Minos, helped Theseus out of the labyrinth by giving him the thread to follow. Later Theseus abandoned her on the Island of Naxos, while she was asleep. Catullus, Latin poet of the first century B.C., describes her dismay on awakening and seeing Theseus' ship already far from shore. (See his *Epithalamium for Peleus and Thetis,* l. 52 ff.)

[129] *dió . . . cuerpo,* let herself fall

[130] Present tense for conditional perfect to give great vividness

[131] An onomatopoetic imitation of a Latin chant

[132] *sin más ni más,* without more ado

[133] *lo* refers to the idea 'light as a straw,' not to the definite word *paja*

Pepita seguía llorando y sollozando, sin contestar.

—¡Ea! Déjate de llanto y dime lo que tienes. ¿Qué te ha dicho el Vicario?

—Nada me ha dicho que pueda ofenderme—contestó al fin Pepita.

Viendo luego que Antoñona aguardaba con interés a que ella hablase, y deseando desahogarse con quien simpatizaba mejor con ella y más *humanamente* la comprendía, Pepita habló de esta manera:

—El padre Vicario me amonesta con dulzura para que me arrepienta de mis pecados; para que deje partir en paz a don Luis; para que me alegre de su partida; para que le olvide. Yo he dicho que sí a todo. He prometido alegrarme de que don Luis se vaya. He querido olvidarle y hasta aborrecerle. Pero mira, Antoñona, no puedo; es un empeño superior a mis fuerzas. Cuando el Vicario estaba aquí, juzgué que tenía yo bríos para todo, y no bien se fué, como si Dios me dejara de su mano, perdí los bríos y me caí en el suelo desolada. Yo había soñado una vida venturosa al lado de este hombre que me enamora; yo me veía ya elevada hasta él por obra milagrosa del amor; mi pobre inteligencia en comunión perfectísima con su inteligencia sublime; mi voluntad siendo una con la suya; con el mismo pensamiento ambos; latiendo nuestros corazones acordes. ¡Dios me le quita y se le lleva, y yo me quedo sola, sin esperanza ni consuelo! ¿No es verdad que es espantoso? Las razones del padre Vicario son justas, discretas . . . Al pronto me convencieron. Pero se fué, y todo el valor de aquellas razones me parece nulo; vano juego de palabras; mentiras, enredos y argucias. Yo amo a don Luis, y esta razón es más poderosa que todas las razones. Y si él me ama, ¿por qué no lo deja todo y me busca, y se viene a mí y quebranta promesas y anula compromisos? No sabía yo lo que era amor. Ahora lo sé: no hay nada más fuerte en la tierra y en el cielo. ¿Qué no haría yo por don Luis? Y él por mí nada hace. Acaso no me ama. No. Don Luis no me ama. Yo me engañé: la vanidad me cegó. Si don Luis me amase, me sacrificaría sus propósitos, sus votos, su fama, sus aspiraciones a ser un santo y a ser una lumbrera de la Iglesia; todo me lo sacrificaría. Dios me lo perdone . . . es horrible lo que voy a decir, pero lo siento aquí en el centro del pecho; me arde aquí, en la frente calenturienta: yo por él daría hasta la salvación de mi alma.

—¡Jesús, María y José!—interrumpió Antoñona.

—¡Es cierto; Virgen Santa de los Dolores, perdonadme, perdonadme . . . , estoy loca . . . , no sé lo que digo y blasfemo!

—Sí, hija mía, ¡estás algo empecatada! ¡Válgame Dios y cómo te ha trastornado el juicio ese teólogo pisaverde! Pues si yo fuera que[134] tú, no la tomaría contra[135] el cielo, que no tiene la culpa, sino contra el mequetrefe del colegial, y me las pagaría o me borraría el nombre que tengo. Ganas me dan de ir a buscarle y traértele aquí de una oreja, y obligarle a que te pida perdón y a que te bese los pies de rodillas.

—No, Antoñona. Veo que mi locura es contagiosa y que tú deliras también. En resolución, no hay más recurso que hacer lo que me aconseja el padre Vicario. Lo haré aunque me cueste la vida. Si muero por él, él me amará, él guardará mi imagen en su memoria, mi amor en su corazón; y Dios, que es tan bueno, hará que yo vuelva a verle en el cielo; con los ojos del alma,

[134] Omit in translating

[135] *tomar contra,* to bear a grudge against, to complain against

y que allí nuestros espíritus se amen y se confundan.

Antoñona, aunque era recia de veras y nada sentimental, sintió al oír esto, que se le saltaban las lágrimas.

—Caramba, niña—dijo Antoñona—, vas a conseguir que suelte yo el trapo a llorar[136] y que berree como una vaca. Cálmate, y no pienses en morirte, ni de chanza. Veo que tienes muy excitados los nervios. ¿Quieres que traiga una taza de tila?

—No, gracias. Déjame . . . , ya ves cómo estoy sosegada.

—Te cerraré las ventanas, a ver si duermes. Si no duermes hace días, ¿cómo has de estar? ¡Mal haya el tal don Luis y su manía de meterse cura! ¡Buenos supiripandos[137] te cuesta!

Pepita había cerrado los ojos; estaba en calma y en silencio, harta ya del coloquio con Antoñona.

Ésta, creyéndola dormida, o deseando que durmiera, se inclinó hacia Pepita, puso con lentitud y suavidad un beso sobre su blanca frente, le arregló y plegó el vestido sobre el cuerpo, entornó las ventanas para dejar el cuarto a media luz, y se salió de puntillas, cerrando la puerta sin hacer el menor ruido.

Mientras que ocurrían estas cosas en casa de Pepita, no estaba más alegre y sosegado en la suya el señor don Luis de Vargas.

Su padre, que no dejaba casi ningún día de salir al campo a caballo, había querido llevarle en su compañía; pero don Luis se había excusado con que le dolía la cabeza, y don Pedro se fué sin él. Don Luis había pasado solo toda la mañana, entregado a sus melancólicos pensamientos, y más firme que roca en su resolución de borrar de su alma la imagen de Pepita, y de consagrarse a Dios por completo.

No se crea, con todo, que no amaba a la joven viuda. Ya hemos visto por las cartas la vehemencia de su pasión; pero él seguía enfrenándola con los mismos afectos piadosos y consideraciones elevadas de que en las cartas da larga muestra, y que podemos omitir aquí para no pecar de prolijos.

Tal vez, si profundizamos con severidad en este negocio, notaremos que contra el amor de Pepita no luchaban sólo en el alma de don Luis el voto hecho ya en su interior, aunque no confirmado; el amor de Dios, el respeto a su padre, de quien no quería ser rival, y la vocación, en suma, que sentía por el sacerdocio. Había otros motivos de menos depurados quilates y de más baja ley.

Don Luis era pertinaz, era terco: tenía aquella condición que, bien dirigida, constituye lo que se llama firmeza de carácter, y nada había que le rebajase más a sus propios ojos que el variar de opinión y de conducta. El propósito de toda su vida, lo que había sostenido y declarado ante cuantas personas le trataban, su figura moral, en una palabra, que era ya la de un aspirante a santo, la de un hombre consagrado a Dios, la de un sujeto imbuído en las más sublimes filosofías religiosas, todo esto no podía caer por tierra sin gran mengua de don Luis, como caería, si se dejase llevar del amor de Pepita Jiménez. Aunque el precio era sin comparación mucho más subido, a don Luis se le figuraba que si cedía iba a remedar a Esaú, y a vender su primogenitura[138] y a deslustrar su gloria . . .

Cuando don Luis reflexionaba sobre todo esto, se elevaba su espíritu, se encumbraba por encima de las nubes en la región empírea, y la pobre Pepita Jiménez quedaba allá muy lejos, y apenas si él la veía.

[136] *soltar el trapo a llorar,* to burst into tears
[137] Popular for *suspiros*

[138] Esau sold his birthright for a mess of pottage.

Pero pronto se abatía el vuelo de su imaginación, y el alma de don Luis tocaba a la tierra y volvía a ver a Pepita, tan graciosa, tan joven, tan candorosa y tan enamorada, y Pepita combatía dentro de su corazón contra sus más fuertes y arraigados propósitos, y don Luis temía que diese al traste con[139] ellos.

Así se atormentaba don Luis con encontrados[140] pensamientos, que se daban guerra, cuando entró Currito en su cuarto sin decir oxte ni moxte.[141]

Currito, que no estimaba gran cosa a su primo mientras no fué más que teólogo, le veneraba, le admiraba y formaba de él un concepto sobrehumano desde que le había visto montar tan bien en Lucero . . .

—Vengo a buscarte—le dijo—para que me acompañes al casino, que está animadísimo hoy y lleno de gente. ¿Qué haces aquí solo, tonteando y hecho un papamoscas?[142]

Don Luis, casi sin replicar y como si fuera mandato, tomó su sombrero y su bastón, y diciendo: «Vámonos donde quieras,» siguió a Currito, que se adelantaba, tan satisfecho de aquel dominio que ejercía.

El casino, en efecto, estaba de bote en bote,[143] gracias a la solemnidad del día siguiente, que era el día de San Juan. A más de[144] los señores del lugar había muchos forasteros, que habían venido de los lugares inmediatos para concurrir a la feria y velada de aquella noche . . .

Currito llevó a don Luis, y don Luis se dejó llevar, a la sala donde estaba la flor y nata[145] de los elegantes, *dandies* y *cocodés*[146] del lugar y de toda la comarca. Entre ellos descollaba el Conde de Genazahar, de la vecina ciudad de ***Era un personaje ilustre y respetado. Había pasado en Madrid y en Sevilla largas temporadas, y se vestía con los mejores sastres, así de majo[147] como de señorito. Había sido diputado dos veces, y había hecho una interpelación al Gobierno sobre un atropello de un alcalde-corregidor.

Tendría el Conde de Genazahar treinta y tantos años; era buen mozo y lo sabía, y se jactaba además de tremendo en paz y en lides, en desafíos y en amores. El Conde, no obstante, y a pesar de haber sido uno de los más obstinados pretendientes de Pepita, había recibido las confitadas calabazas[148] que ella solía propinar a quienes la requebraban y aspiraban a su mano.

La herida que aquel duro y amargo confite había abierto en su endiosado corazón, no estaba cicatrizada todavía. El amor se había vuelto odio, y el conde se desahogaba a menudo poniendo a Pepita como chupa de dómine.[149]

En este ameno ejercicio se hallaba el Conde cuando quiso la mala ventura que don Luis y Currito llegasen y se metiesen en el corro, que se abrió para recibirlos, de los que oían el extraño sermón de honras. Don Luis, como si el mismo diablo lo hubiera dispuesto, se encontró cara a cara con el Conde, que decía de este modo:

—No es mala pécora la tal Pepita Jiménez.[150] Con más fantasía y más humos que la infanta Micomicona,[151] quiere hacernos olvidar que nació y

[139] *dar al traste con,* to upset, spoil
[140] conflicting, opposite
[141] *sin decir oxte ni moxte,* without saying a word
[142] *hecho un papamoscas,* like an idiot
[143] *de bote en bote,* packed
[144] *A más de,* besides
[145] the flower and cream; the elite group
[146] French, *cocodès;* dandy, fop
[147] *de majo,* in the regional dress, contrasted with *de señorito,* in city styles
[148] *las . . . calabazas,* the sweet refusal
[149] *poner como chupa de dómine,* to slander, speak ill of
[150] *No . . . Jiménez,* Pepita Jiménez is a sly one.
[151] An imaginary character of high lineage in the *Quijote.*

vivió en la miseria hasta que se casó con aquel pelele, con aquel vejestorio, con aquel maldito usurero, y le cogió los ochavos. La única cosa buena que ha hecho en su vida la tal viuda es concertarse con Satanás para enviar pronto al infierno a su galopín de marido, y librar la tierra de tanta infección y de tanta peste. Ahora le ha dado a Pepita por[152] la virtud y por la castidad. ¡Bueno estará todo ello! Sabe Dios si estará enredada de ocultis[153] con algún gañán, y burlándose del mundo como si fuese la reina Artemisa[154] . . .

Don Luis . . . se quedó herido como por un rayo, cuando vió al insolente Conde arrastrar por el suelo, mancillar y cubrir de inmundo lodo la honra de la mujer que amaba.

¿Cómo defenderla, no obstante? No se le ocultaba que, si bien no era marido, ni hermano, ni pariente de Pepita, podía sacar la cara[155] por ella como caballero; pero veía el escándalo que esto causaría cuando no había allí ningún profano que defendiese a Pepita; antes bien, todos reían al Conde la gracia.[156] Él, casi ministro ya de un Dios de paz, no podía dar un mentís y exponerse a una riña con aquel desvergonzado.

Don Luis estuvo por enmudecer e irse; pero no lo consintió su corazón, y pugnando por revestirse de una autoridad que ni sus años juveniles, ni su rostro, donde había más bozo que barbas, ni su presencia en aquel lugar consentían, se puso a hablar con verdadera elocuencia contra los maldicientes y a echar en rostro al Conde, con libertad cristiana y con acento severo, la fealdad de su ruin acción. Fué predicar en desierto, o peor que predicar en desierto. El Conde contestó con pullas y burletas a la homilía; la gente, entre la que había no pocos forasteros, se puso del lado del burlón, a pesar de ser don Luis el hijo del cacique; el propio Currito, que no valía para nada y era un blandengue, aunque no se rió, no defendió a su amigo, y éste tuvo que retirarse, vejado y humillado bajo el peso de la chacota.

—¡Esta flor le faltaba al ramo¡[157]— murmuró entre dientes el pobre don Luis cuando llegó a su casa, y volvió a meterse en su cuarto, mohino y maltratado por la rechifla, que él se exageraba y figuraba insufrible. Se echó de golpe en un sillón, abatido y descorazonado, y mil ideas contrarias asaltaron su mente.

La sangre de su padre, que hervía en sus venas, le despertaba la cólera y le excitaba a ahorcar los hábitos, como al principio le aconsejaban en el lugar, y dar luego su merecido al señor Conde; pero todo el porvenir que se había creado se deshacía al punto, y veía al Deán que renegaba de él; y hasta el Papa, que había enviado ya la dispensa pontificia para que se ordenase antes de la edad, y el prelado diocesano, que había apoyado la solicitud de la dispensa en su probada virtud, ciencia sólida y firmeza de vocación, se le aparecían para reconvenirle . . .

En estas y otras meditaciones por el estilo transcurrieron las horas hasta que dieron las tres, y don Pedro, que acababa de volver del campo, entró en el cuarto de su hijo para llamarle a comer. La alegre cordiali-

[152] *le . . . por,* Pepita has gone in for
[153] on the sly
[154] A queen who raised a great funeral monument to her husband Mausolos (hence the word mausoleum) and who is regarded as a model of wives, faithful to her husband even after his death.
[155] *sacar la cara,* come out (in her defense)
[156] *reían . . . gracia,* laughed at the wit of the Count
[157] *Esta . . . ramo,* This is the last straw!

dad del padre, sus chistes, sus muestras de afecto, no pudieron sacar a don Luis de la melancolía ni abrirle el apetito. Apenas comió; apenas habló en la mesa.

Si bien disgustadísimo con la silenciosa tristeza de su hijo, cuya salud, aunque robusta, pudiera resentirse, como don Pedro era hombre que se levantaba al amanecer y bregaba mucho durante el día, luego que acabó de fumar un buen cigarro habano de sobremesa, acompañándole con su taza de café y su copita de aguardiente de anís doble, se sintió fatigado, y según costumbre, se fué a dormir sus dos o tres horas de siesta.

Don Luis tuvo muy buen cuidado de no poner en noticia de su padre, la ofensa que le había hecho el Conde de Genazahar. Su padre, que no iba a cantar misa y que tenía una índole poco sufrida, se hubiera lanzado al instante a tomar la venganza que él no tomó.

Solo ya, don Luis, dejó el comedor para no ver a nadie, y volvió al retiro de su estancia para abismarse más profundamente en sus ideas.

Abismado en ellas estaba hacía largo rato, sentado junto al bufete, los codos sobre él y en la derecha mano apoyada la mejilla, cuando sintió cerca ruido. Alzó los ojos y vió a su lado a la entrometida Antoñona, que había penetrado como una sombra, aunque tan maciza, y que le miraba con atención y con cierta mezcla de piedad y de rabia.

Antoñona se había deslizado hasta allí sin que nadie lo advirtiese, aprovechando la hora en que comían los criados y don Pedro dormía, y había abierto la puerta del cuarto y la había vuelto a cerrar tras sí con tal suavidad, que don Luis, aunque no hubiera estado tan absorto, no hubiera podido sentirla.

Antoñona venía resuelta a tener una conferencia muy seria con don Luis; pero no sabía a punto fijo lo que iba a decirle. Sin embargo, había pedido, no se sabe si al cielo o al infierno, que desatase su lengua y que le diese habla,[158] y habla no chabacana y grotesca, como la que usaba por lo común, sino culta, elegante e idónea para las nobles reflexiones y bellas cosas que ella imaginaba que le convenía expresar.

Cuando don Luis vió a Antoñona arrugó el entrecejo, mostró bien en el gesto lo que le contrariaba aquella visita, y dijo con tono brusco:

—¿A qué vienes aquí? Vete.

—Vengo a pedirte cuenta de mi niña —contestó Antoñona sin turbarse—, y no me he de ir hasta que me la des.

En seguida acercó una silla a la mesa, y se sentó enfrente de don Luis con aplomo y descaro.

Viendo don Luis que no había remedio, mitigó el enojo, se armó de paciencia y, ya con acento menos cruel, exclamó:

—Di lo que tengas que decir.

—Tengo que decir—prosiguió Antoñona—que lo que estás maquinando contra mi niña es una maldad. Te estás portando como un tuno. La has hechizado; la has dado un bebedizo maligno. Aquel angelito se va a morir. No come, ni duerme, ni sosiega por culpa tuya. Hoy ha tenido dos o tres soponcios sólo de pensar en que te vas. Buena hacienda[159] dejas hecha antes de ser clérigo. Dime, condenado, ¿por qué viniste por aquí y no te quedaste por allá con tu tío? Ella, tan libre, tan señora de su voluntad, avasallando la de todos y no dejándose cautivar de ninguno, ha venido a caer en tus traidoras redes . . .

—Antoñona—contestó don Luis—, déjame en paz. Por Dios, no me atormentes. Yo soy un malvado, lo con-

[158] A noun; speech, the gift of speech

[159] deeds

fieso. No debí mirar a tu ama. No debí darle a entender que la amaba; pero yo la amaba y la amo aún con todo mi corazón, y no le he dado bebedizo, ni filtro, sino el mismo amor que la tengo. Es menester, sin embargo, desechar, olvidar este amor . . .

Yo no puedo remediar el mal de tu dueña. ¿Qué he de hacer?

—¿Qué has de hacer?—interrumpió Antoñona, ya más blanda y afectuosa y con voz insinuante—. Yo te diré lo que has de hacer. Si no remediares el mal de mi niña, le aliviarás al menos. ¿No eres tan santo? Pues los santos son compasivos, y, además, valerosos. No huyas como un cobardón grosero, sin despedirte. Ven a ver a mi niña, que está enferma. Haz esta obra de misericordia.

—¿Y qué conseguiré con esa visita? Agravar el mal en vez de sanarle.

—No será así; no estás en el busilis.[160] Tú irás allí, y con esa cháchara que gastas y esa labia que Dios te ha dado, le infundirás en los cascos la resignación y la dejarás consolada; y si le dices que la quieres y que por Dios sólo la dejas, al menos su vanidad de mujer no quedará ajada.

—Lo que me propones es tentar a Dios, es peligroso para mí y para ella.

—¿Y por qué ha de ser tentar a Dios? Pues si Dios ve la rectitud y la pureza de tus intenciones, ¿no te dará su favor y su gracia para que no te pierdas en esta ocasión en que te pongo con sobrado motivo? ¿No debes volar a librar a mi niña de la desesperación y a traerla al buen camino? Si se muriera de pena por verse así desdeñada, o si rabiosa agarrase un cordel y se colgase de una viga, créeme, tus remordimientos serían peores que las llamas de pez y azufre de las calderas de Lucifer.

—¡Qué horror! No quiero que se desespere. Me revestiré de todo mi valor; iré a verla.

—¡Bendito seas! ¡Si[161] me lo decía el corazón! ¡Si eres bueno!

—¿Cuándo quieres que vaya?

—Esta noche a las diez en punto. Yo estaré en la puerta de la calle aguardándote y te llevaré donde está.

—¿Sabe ella que has venido a verme?

—No lo sabe. Ha sido todo ocurrencia mía; pero yo la prepararé con buen arte, a fin de que tu visita, la sorpresa, el inesperado gozo, no la hagan caer en un desmayo. ¿Me prometes que irás?

—Iré.

—Adiós. No faltes. A las diez de la noche en punto. Estaré a la puerta.

Y Antoñona echó a correr, bajó la escalera de dos en dos ecalones y se plantó en la calle . . .

Volvió, pues, Antoñona a casa de su dueña, muy satisfecha de sí misma y muy resuelta a disponer las cosas con tino para que el remedio que había buscado no fuese inútil, o no agravase el mal de Pepita en vez de sanarle.

A Pepita no pensó ni determinó prevenirla sino a lo último, diciéndole que don Luis espontáneamente le había pedido hora para hacerle una visita de despedida, y que ella había señalado las diez.

A fin de que no se originasen habladurías, si en la casa veían entrar a don Luis, pensó en que no le viesen entrar, y para ello era también muy propicia la hora y la disposición de la casa. A las diez estaría llena de gente la calle con la velada, y por lo mismo repararían menos en don Luis cuando pasase por ella. Penetrar en el zaguán sería obra de un segundo; y ella, que estaría allí aguardando, llevaría a don Luis hasta el despacho sin que nadie le viese.

Todas o la mayor parte de las casas

[160] *no estás en el busilis,* you don't see the point

[161] See n. 127.

de los ricachos lugareños de Andalucía son como dos casas en vez de una, y así era la casa de Pepita. Cada casa tiene su puerta. Por la principal se pasa al patio enlosado y con columnas, a las salas y demás habitaciones señoriles; por la otra, a los corrales, caballeriza y cochera, cocinas, molino, lagar, graneros, trojes donde se conserva la aceituna hasta que se muele; bodegas donde se guarda el aceite, el mosto, el vino de quema, el aguardiente y el vinagre en grandes tinajas; y candioteras o bodegas donde está en pipas y toneles el vino bueno y ya hecho o rancio. Esta segunda casa o parte de casa, aunque esté en el centro de una población de veinte o veinticinco mil almas, se llama casa de campo. El aperador, los capataces, el mulero, los trabajadores principales y más constantes en el servicio del amo se juntan allí por la noche; en invierno, en torno de una enorme chimenea de una gran cocina, y en verano, al aire libre o en algún cuarto muy ventilado y fresco, y están holgando y de tertulia hasta que los señores se recogen.[162]

Antoñona imaginó que el coloquio y la explicación que ella deseaba que tuviesen su niña y don Luis, requerían sosiego y que no viniesen a interrumpirlos, y así determinó que aquella noche, por ser la velada de San Juan, las chicas que servían a Pepita vacasen en todos sus quehaceres y oficios, y se fuesen a solazar a la casa de campo, armando con los rústicos trabajadores un *jaleo probe,*[163] de fandango, lindas coplas, repiqueteo de castañuelas, brincos y mudanzas.

De esta suerte, la casa señoril quedaría casi desierta y silenciosa, sin más habitantes que ella y Pepita, y muy a propósito para la solemnidad, trascendencia y no turbado sosiego que eran necesarios en la entrevista que ella tenía preparada, y de la que dependía quizás, o de seguro, el destino de dos personas de tanto valer . . .

Don Luis confortó su espíritu con la esperanza de que iba a tener mucha serenidad y de que Dios iba a poner en sus labios un raudal de elocuencia, por donde persuadiría a Pepita, que era tan buena, de que ella misma le impulsase a cumplir con su vocación, sacrificando el amor mundanal y haciéndose semejante a las santas mujeres que ha habido, las cuales, no ya han desistido de unirse con un novio o con un amante, sino hasta de unirse con el esposo, viviendo con él como con un hermano, según se refiere, por ejemplo, en la vida de San Eduardo, rey de Inglaterra.[164] Y después de pensar en esto, se sentía don Luis más consolado y animado, y ya se figuraba que él iba a ser como San Eduardo, y que Pepita era como la reina Edita, su mujer; y bajo la forma y condición de la tal reina, virgen a par de[165] esposa, le parecía Pepita, si cabe, mucho más gentil, elegante y poética.

No estaba, sin embargo, don Luis todo lo seguro y tranquilo que debiera estar después de haberse resuelto a imitar a San Eduardo. Hallaba aún cierto no sé qué de criminal en aquella visita que iba a hacer sin que su padre lo supiese, y estaba por ir a despertarle de su siesta y descubrírselo todo. Dos o tres veces se levantó de su silla y empezó a andar en busca de su padre; pero luego se detenía y creía aquella revelación indigna, la creía una vergonzosa chiquillada. Él podía revelar sus secretos; pero revelar los de Pepita para ponerse bien con su padre, era

[162] We have here a bit of *costumbrista* material, which, as we have noted, is not nearly so common in Valera's works as in those of his contemporaries.

[163] a servants' party (*probe* is an Andalusianism for *pobre*)

[164] Edward the Confessor, king of England from 1042–66. [165] *a par de*, at the same time as

bastante feo. La fealdad y lo cómico y miserable de la acción se aumentaban, notando que el temor de no ser bastante fuerte para resistir era lo que a hacerla le movía. Don Luis se calló, pues, y no reveló nada a su padre . . .

Por último, si bien tenía abierto el balcón por ser verano, le parecía que iba a ahogarse allí por falta de aire, y que el techo le pesaba sobre la cabeza, y que para respirar necesitaba de toda la atmósfera, y para andar de todo el espacio sin límites, y para alzar la frente y exhalar sus suspiros y encumbrar sus pensamientos, de no tener sobre sí, sino la inmensa bóveda del cielo.

Aguijoneado de esta necesidad, tomó su sombrero y su bastón y se fué a la calle. Ya en la calle, huyendo de toda persona conocida y buscando la soledad, se salió al campo y se internó por lo más frondoso y esquivo de las alamedas, huertas y sendas que rodean la población y hacen un paraíso de sus alrededores en un radio de más de media legua.

Poco hemos dicho hasta ahora de la figura de don Luis. Sépase, pues, que era un buen mozo en toda la extensión de la palabra: alto, ligero, bien formado, cabello negro, ojos negros también y llenos de fuego y de dulzura. La color trigueña, la dentadura blanca, los labios finos, aunque relevados, lo cual le daba un aspecto desdeñoso; y algo de atrevido y varonil en todo el ademán, a pesar del recogimiento y de la mansedumbre clericales. Había, por último, en el porte y continente de don Luis aquel indescriptible sello de distinción y de hidalguía que parece, aunque no lo sea siempre, privativa calidad y exclusivo privilegio de las familias aristocráticas.

Al ver a don Luis, era menester confesar que Pepita Jiménez sabía de estética por instinto.

Corría, que no[166] andaba, don Luis por aquellas sendas, saltando arroyos y fijándose apenas en los objetos, casi como toro picado del tábano. Los rústicos con quienes se encontró, los hortelanos que le vieron pasar, tal vez le tuvieron por loco.

Cansado ya de caminar sin propósito, se sentó al pie de una cruz de piedra, junto a las ruinas de un antiguo convento de San Francisco de Paula, que dista más de tres kilómetros del lugar, y allí se hundió en nuevas meditaciones, pero tan confusas, que ni él mismo se daba cuenta de lo que pensaba . . .

El sol acababa de ocultarse detrás de los picos gigantescos de las sierras cercanas, haciendo que las pirámides, agujas y rotos obeliscos de la cumbre se destacasen sobre un fondo de púrpura y tópacio, que tal parecía el cielo, dorado por el sol poniente. Las sombras empezaban a extenderse sobre la vega, y en los montes opuestos a los montes por donde el sol se ocultaba, relucían las peñas más erguidas, como si fueran de oro o de cristal hecho ascua . . .

Una poesía melancólica inspiraba a la naturaleza, y con la música callada que sólo el espíritu acierta a oír, se diría que todo entonaba un himno al Creador. El lento son de las campanas, amortiguado y semiperdido por la distancia, apenas turbaba el reposo de la tierra, y convidaba a la oración sin distraer los sentidos con rumores. Don Luis se quitó su sombrero, se hincó de rodillas al pie de la cruz, cuyo pedestal le había servido de asiento, y rezó con profunda devoción el *Angelus Domini*.

Las sombras nocturnas fueron pronto ganando terreno . . . La luna plateaba las copas de los árboles y se reflejaba en la corriente de los arroyos . . . Entre la espesura de la arbo-

[166] *que no,* rather than

leda cantaban los ruiseñores. Las hierbas y flores vertían más generoso perfume. Por las orillas de las acequias, entre la hierba menuda y las flores silvestres, relucían como diamantes o carbunclos los gusanillos de luz en multitud innumerable . . . Muchos árboles frutales, en flor todavía; muchas acacias y rosales sin cuento embalsamaban el ambiente, impregnándole de suave fragancia.

Don Luis se sintió dominado, seducido, vencido por aquella voluptuosa naturaleza, y dudó de sí.[167] Era menester, no obstante, cumplir la palabra dada y acudir a la cita.

Aunque dando un largo rodeo, aunque recorriendo otras sendas, aunque vacilando a veces, . . . don Luis, a paso lento y pausado, se dirigió hacia la población.

. . . aun se hallaba a alguna distancia del pueblo, cuando sonaron las diez, hora de la cita, en el reloj de la parroquia. Las diez campanadas fueron como diez golpes que le hirieron el corazón. Allí le dolieron materialmente, si bien con un dolor y con un sobresalto mixtos de traidora inquietud y de regalada dulzura.

Don Luis apresuró el paso a fin de no llegar muy tarde, y pronto se encontró en la población.

El lugar estaba animadísimo. Las mozas solteras venían a la fuente del ejido a lavarse la cara, para que fuese fiel el novio a la que le tenía, y para que a la que no le tenía le saltase novio. Mujeres y chiquillos, por acá y por allá, volvían de coger verbena, ramos de romero u otras plantas, para hacer sahumerios mágicos. Las guitarras sonaban por varias partes. Los coloquios de amor y las parejas dichosas y apasionadas se oían y se veían a cada momento. La noche y la mañanita de San Juan, aunque fiesta católica, conservan no sé qué resabios del paganismo y naturalismo antiguos.[168] Tal vez sea por la coincidencia aproximada de esta fiesta con el solsticio de verano. Ello es que todo era profano, y no religioso. Todo era amor y galanteo. En nuestros viejos romances y leyendas siempre roba el moro a la linda infantina cristiana y siempre el caballero cristiano logra su anhelo con la princesa mora, en la noche o en la mañanita de San Juan, y en el pueblo se diría que conservaban la tradición de los viejos romances.

Las calles estaban llenas de gente. Todo el pueblo estaba en las calles, y además los forasteros. Hacían asimismo muy difícil el tránsito la multitud de mesillas de turrón, arropía y tostones, los puestos de fruta, las tiendas de muñecos y juguetes, y las buñolerías, donde gitanas jóvenes y viejas, ya freían la masa, infestando el aire con el olor del aceite, ya pesaban y servían los buñuelos, ya respondían con donaire a los piropos de los galanes que pasaban, y decían la buena ventura.

Don Luis procuraba no encontrar a los amigos y, si los veía de lejos, echaba por otro lado. Así fué llegando poco a poco, sin que le hablasen ni detuviesen, hasta cerca del zaguán de casa de Pepita. El corazón empezó a latirle con violencia, y se paró un instante para serenarse. Miró el reloj: eran cerca de las diez y media.

—¡Válgame Dios!—dijo—, hará cerca de media hora que me estará aguardando.

Entonces se precipitó y penetró en el zaguán. El farol que le alumbraba de

[167] Nature has now reached its point of greatest beauty and fertility. Valera has cleverly timed his plot so that Luis's love reaches its climax at just this time.

[168] See n. 103. *Naturalismo* here means worship of Nature.

diario,[169] daba poquísima luz aquella noche.

No bien entró don Luis en el zaguán, una mano, mejor diremos, una garra, le asió por el brazo derecho. Era Antoñona, que dijo en voz baja:

—¡Diantre de colegial, ingrato, desaborido, mostrenco! Ya imaginaba yo que no venías. ¿Dónde has estado *peal*? ¿Cómo te atreves a tardar, haciéndote de pencas,[170] cuando toda la sal de la tierra se está derritiendo por ti, y el sol de la hermosura te aguarda?

Mientras Antoñona expresaba estas quejas, no estaba parada, sino que iba andando y llevando en pos de sí, asido siempre del brazo, al colegial atortolado y silencioso. Salvaron la cancela, y Antoñona la cerró con tiento y sin ruido; atravesaron el patio, subieron por la escalera, pasaron luego por unos corredores y por dos salas, y llegaron a la puerta del despacho, que estaba cerrada.

En toda la casa reinaba maravilloso silencio. El despacho estaba en lo interior y no llegaban a él los rumores de la calle. Sólo llegaban, aunque confusos y vagos, el resonar de las castañuelas y el son de la guitarra, y un leve murmullo, causado todo por los criados de Pepita, que tenían su *jaleo probe* en la casa de campo.

Antoñona abrió la puerta del despacho, empujó a don Luis para que entrase, y al mismo tiempo le anunció diciendo:

—Niña, aquí tienes al señor don Luis, que viene a despedirse de ti.

Hecho el anuncio con la formalidad debida, la discreta Antoñona se retiró de la sala, dejando a sus anchas al visitante y a la niña, y volviendo a cerrar la puerta . . .

Mucho queremos nosotros a Pepita; pero la verdad es antes que todo, y la hemos de decir, aunque perjudique a nuestra heroína. A las ocho le dijo Antoñona que don Luis iba a venir, y Pepita que hablaba de morirse, que tenía los ojos encendidos y los párpados un poquito inflamados de llorar, y que estaba bastante despeinada, no pensó desde entonces sino en componerse y arreglarse para recibir a don Luis. Se lavó la cara con agua tibia para que el estrago del llanto desapareciese hasta el punto preciso de no afear, mas no para que no quedasen huellas de que había llorado; se compuso el pelo de suerte que no denunciaba estudio cuidadoso, sino que demostraba cierto artístico y gentil descuido, sin rayar en desorden, lo cual hubiera sido poco decoroso; se pulió las uñas, y como no era propio recibir de bata a don Luis, se vistió un traje sencillo de casa. En suma, miró instintivamente a que todos los pormenores de tocador concurriesen a hacerla parecer más bonita y aseada, sin que se trasluciera el menor indicio del arte, del trabajo y del tiempo gastado en aquellos perfiles,[171] sino que todo ello resplandeciera como obra natural y don gratuito; como algo que persistía en ella, a pesar del olvido de sí misma causado por la vehemencia de los afectos.

Según hemos llegado a averiguar, Pepita empleó más de una hora en estas faenas de tocador, que habían de sentirse sólo por los efectos. Después se dió el postrer retoque y vistazo al espejo con satisfacción mal disimulada. Y por último, a eso de las nueve y media, tomando una palmatoria, bajó a la sala donde estaba el Niño Jesús. Encendió primero las velas del altarito, que estaban apagadas; vió con cierta pena que las flores yacían marchitas; pidió perdón a la devota imagen por haberla tenido desatendida

[169] *de diario,* ordinarily

[170] *hacerse de pencas,* to consent reluctantly to do something; to come so reluctantly

[171] Here, adornments

mucho tiempo; y, postrándose de hinojos, y a solas, oró con todo su corazón y con aquella confianza y franqueza que inspira quien está de huésped en casa desde hace muchos años . . . Pepita le pidió que le dejase a don Luis; que no se le llevase; porque él, tan rico y tan abastado de todo, podía sin gran sacrificio desprenderse de aquel servidor y concedérsele a ella.

Terminados estos preparativos, que nos será lícito clasificar y dividir en cosméticos, indumentarios y religiosos, Pepita se instaló en el despacho, aguardando la venida de don Luis con febril impaciencia.

Atinada anduvo Antoñona en no decir que iba a venir sino hasta poco antes de la hora. Aun así, gracias a la tardanza del galán, la pobre Pepita estuvo deshaciéndose, llena de ansiedad y de angustia, desde que terminó sus oraciones y súplicas con el Niño Jesús hasta que vió dentro del despacho al otro niño.

La visita empezó del modo más grave y ceremonioso. Los saludos de fórmula se pronunciaron maquinalmente de una parte y de otra; y don Luis, invitado a ello, tomó asiento en una butaca, sin dejar el sombrero ni el bastón, y a no corta distancia de Pepita. Pepita estaba sentada en el sofá. El velador se veía al lado de ella con libros y con la palmatoria, cuya luz iluminaba su rostro. Una lámpara ardía además sobre el bufete. Ambas luces, con todo, siendo grande el cuarto, como lo era, dejaban la mayor parte de él en la penumbra. Una gran ventana que daba a un jardincillo interior, estaba abierta por el calor, y si bien sus hierros[172] eran como la trama de un tejido de rosas-enredaderas y jazmines, todavía por entre la verdura y las flores se abrían camino los claros rayos de la luna, penetraban en la estancia y querían luchar con la luz de la lámpara y de la palmatoria. Penetraban, además, por la ventana-verjel el lejano y confuso rumor del jaleo de la casa de campo, que estaba al otro extremo, el murmullo monótono de una fuente que había en el jardincillo, y el aroma de los jazmines y de las rosas que tapizaban la ventana, mezclado con el de los dompedros, albahacas y otras plantas que adornaban los arriates al pie de ella.[173]

Hubo una larga pausa, un silencio tan difícil de sostener como de romper . . .

—Al fin se dignó usted venir a despedirse de mí antes de su partida—dijo Pepita—. Yo había perdido ya la esperanza . . .

—Su queja de usted es injusta . . . He estado aquí a despedirme de usted con mi padre, y como no tuvimos el gusto de que usted nos recibiese, dejamos tarjetas. Nos dijeron que estaba usted algo delicada de salud, y todos los días hemos enviado recado para saber de usted. Grande ha sido nuestra satisfacción al saber que estaba usted aliviada. ¿Y ahora se encuentra usted mejor?

—Casi estoy por decir a usted que no me encuentro mejor—replicó Pepita—; pero como veo que viene usted de embajador de su padre, y no quiero afligir a un amigo tan excelente, justo será que diga a usted, y que usted repita a su padre, que siento bastante alivio. Singular es que haya venido usted solo. Mucho tendrá que hacer don Pedro cuando no le ha acompañado.

—Mi padre no me ha acompañado, señora, porque no sabe que he venido a ver a usted. Yo he venido solo, porque mi despedida ha de ser solemne,

[172] bars (of grating)

[173] Notice how our author emphasizes the appeals to the senses of sight, hearing, and smell.

grave, para siempre quizá, y la suya es de índole harto diversa. Mi padre volverá por aquí dentro de unas semanas; yo es posible que[174] no vuelva nunca, y si vuelvo, volveré muy otro del que soy ahora.

Pepita no pudo contenerse. El porvenir de felicidad con que había soñado se desvanecía como una sombra. Su resolución inquebrantable de vencer a toda costa a aquel hombre, único que había amado en la vida, único que se sentía capaz de amar, era una resolución inútil. Don Luis se iba. La juventud, la gracia, la belleza, el amor de Pepita no valían para nada. Estaba condenada, con veinte años de edad y tanta hermosura, a la viudez perpetua, a la soledad, a amar a quien no la amaba. Todo otro amor era imposible para ella. El carácter de Pepita, en quien los obstáculos recrudecían y avivaban más los anhelos; en quien una determinación, una vez tomado, lo arrollaba todo hasta verse cumplida, se mostró entonces con notable violencia y rompiendo todo freno. Era menester morir o vencer en la demanda . . . Su alma, con cuanto había en ella de apasionado, tomó forma sensible en sus palabras, y sus palabras no sirvieron para envolver su pensar y su sentir, sino para darle cuerpo. No habló como hubiera hablado una dama de nuestros salones, con ciertas pleguerías[175] y atenuaciones en la expresión, sino con la desnudez idílica con que Cloe hablaba a Dafnis[176] y con la humildad y el abandono completo con que se ofreció a Booz la nuera de Noemí.[177]

Pepita dijo:

—¿Persiste usted, pues, en su propósito? ¿Está usted seguro de su vocación? ¿No teme usted ser un mal clérigo? . . . Aquí hay hechos que se pueden comentar de dos modos. Con ambos comentarios queda usted mal. Expondré mi pensamiento. Si la mujer[178] que con sus coqueterías, no por cierto muy desenvueltas, casi sin hablar a usted palabra, a los pocos días de verle y tratarle, ha conseguido provocar a usted, moverle a que la mire con miradas que auguraban amor profano, y hasta ha logrado que le dé usted una muestra de cariño, que es una falta, un pecado en cualquiera, y más en un sacerdote; si esta mujer es, como lo es en realidad, una lugareña ordinaria, sin instrucción, sin talento y sin elegancia, ¿qué no se debe temer de usted cuando trate y vea y visite en las grandes ciudades a otras mujeres mil veces más peligrosas? . . . Si usted ha cedido a una zafia aldeana, hallándose en vísperas de la ordenación, con todo el entusiasmo que debe suponerse, y, si ha cedido impulsado por capricho fugaz,[179] ¿no tengo razón en prever que va usted a ser un clérigo detestable, impuro, mundanal y funesto, y que cederá a cada paso? En esta suposición,[180] créame usted, señor don Luis, y no se me ofenda, ni siquiera vale usted para marido de una mujer honrada. Si usted ha estrechado las manos con el ahinco y la ternura del más frenético amante; si usted ha mirado con miradas que prometían un cielo, una eternidad de amor, y si usted ha . . . besado a una mujer que nada le inspiraba sino algo que para mí no tiene nombre, vaya usted con Dios, y no se case usted con esa mujer. Si ella es buena, no le querrá a usted para

[174] Word order: *es posible que yo*
[175] twist, roundabout phrase
[176] Daphnis and Chloe, not the mythological characters, but the hero and heroine of a Greek pastoral novel by Longus, written in the fourth century A.D. Their love affair formed a charming idyll.
[177] Ruth, the daughter-in-law of Naomi, offered herself ingenuously to her protector, Boaz (Ruth 3. 9).
[178] Pepita is referring to herself.
[179] If, in other words, Luis doesn't really love Pepita and has just been flirting.
[180] in this case

marido, ni siquiera para amante; pero, por amor de Dios, no sea usted clérigo tampoco. La Iglesia ha menester de otros hombres más serios y más capaces de virtud para ministros del Altísimo. Por el contrario, si usted ha sentido una gran pasión por esta mujer de que hablamos, aunque ella sea poco digna, ¿por qué abandonarla y engañarla con tanta crueldad? Por indigna que sea, si es que ha inspirado esa gran pasión, ¿no cree usted que la compartirá y que será víctima de ella? . . . ¿Y cómo no temer por ella si usted la abandona? ¿Tiene ella la energía varonil, la constancia que infunde la sabiduría que los libros encierran, el aliciente de la gloria, la multitud de grandiosos proyectos, y todo aquello que hay en su cultivado y sublime espíritu de usted para distraerle y apartarle, sin desgarradora violencia, de todo otro terrenal afecto? ¿No comprende usted que ella morirá de dolor, y que usted, destinado a hacer incruentos sacrificios, empezará por sacrificar despiadadamente a quien más le ama? . . .

—Voy a contestar a los extremos del cruel dilema que ha forjado usted en mi daño. Aunque me ha criado al lado de mi tío y en el Seminario, donde no he visto mujeres, no me crea usted tan ignorante ni tan pobre de imaginación que no acertase a representármelas en la mente todo lo bellas,[181] todo lo seductoras que pueden ser. Mi imaginación, por el contrario, sobrepujaba a la realidad en todo eso. Excitada por la lectura de los cantores bíblicos y de los poetas profanos, se fingía mujeres más elegantes, más graciosas, más discretas que las que por lo común se hallan en el mundo real. Yo conocía, pues, el precio del sacrificio que hacía, y hasta le exageraba, cuando renuncié al amor de esas mujeres, pensando elevarme a la dignidad del sacerdocio . . . Todo esto me lo figuraba yo con tal viveza y lo leía con tal hermosura, que, no lo dude usted, si yo llego a ver y a tratar a esas mujeres de que usted me habla, lejos de caer en la adoración y en la locura que usted predice, tal vez sea un desengaño lo que reciba, al ver cuánta distancia media de lo soñado a lo real y de lo vivo a lo pintado.[182]

—¡Éstos de usted sí que son sofismas! —interrumpió Pepita—. ¿Cómo negar a usted que lo que usted se pinta en la imaginación es más hermoso que lo que existe realmente? Pero, ¿cómo negar tampoco que lo real tiene más eficacia seductora que lo imaginado y soñado? Lo vago y aéreo de un fantasma, por bello que sea, no compite con lo que mueve materialmente los sentidos. Contra los ensueños mundanos comprendo que venciesen en su alma de usted las imágenes devotas; pero temo que las imágenes devotas no habían de vencer a las mundanas realidades.

—Pues no lo tema usted, señora— replicó don Luis—. Mi fantasía es más eficaz en lo que crea que todo el universo, menos usted, en lo que por los sentidos me transmite.

—¿Y por qué *menos yo?* Esto me hace caer en otro recelo. ¿Será quizás la idea que usted tiene de mí, la idea que ama, creación de esa fantasía tan eficaz, ilusión en nada conforme conmigo?

—No, no lo es; tengo fe de que esta idea es en todo conforme con usted; pero tal vez es ingénita en mi alma; tal vez está en ella desde que fué creada por Dios; tal vez es parte de su esencia; tal vez es lo más puro y rico de su ser, como el perfume en las flores.

—¡Bien me lo temía yo! Usted me lo confiesa ahora. Usted no me ama.

[181] *todo lo bellas;* just as beautiful

[182] *y de . . . pintado,* and between the living being and the imaginary creation

Eso que ama usted es la esencia, el aroma, lo más puro de su alma, que ha tomado una forma parecida a la mía.[183]

—No, Pepita; no se divierta usted en atormentarme. Esto que yo amo es usted, y usted tal cual es; pero es tan bello, tan limpio, tan delicado esto que yo amo, que no me explico que pase todo por los sentidos de un modo grosero y llegue así hasta mi mente. Supongo, pues, y creo, y tengo por cierto, que estaba antes en mí. Es como la idea de Dios, que estaba en mí, que ha venido a magnificarse y desenvolverse en mí, y que, sin embargo, tiene su objeto real, superior, infinitamente superior a la idea. Como creo que Dios existe, creo que existe usted y que vale usted mil veces más que la idea que de usted tengo formada.

—Aun me queda una duda. ¿No pudiera ser la mujer en general, y no yo singular y exclusivamente, quien ha despertado esa idea?

—No, Pepita: la magia, el hechizo de una mujer, bella de alma y de gentil presencia, habían, antes de ver a usted, penetrado en mi fantasía. No hay duquesa ni marquesa en Madrid, ni emperatriz en el mundo, ni reina ni princesa en todo el orbe, que valgan lo que valen las ideales y fantásticas criaturas con quienes yo he vivido, porque se aparecían en los alcázares y camarines, estupendos de lujo, buen gusto y exquisito ornato, que yo edificaba en mis espacios imaginarios, desde que llegué a la adolescencia . . . Sobre todos los ensueños de mi juvenil imaginación ha venido a sobreponerse y entronizarse la realidad que en usted he visto; sobre todas mis ninfas, reinas y diosas, usted ha descollado; por cima de mis ideales creaciones, derribadas, rotas, deshechas por el amor divino, se levantó en mi alma la imagen fiel, la copia exactísima de la viva hermosura que adorna, que es la esencia de ese cuerpo y de esa alma. Hasta algo de misterioso, de sobrenatural, puede haber intervenido en esto, porque amé a usted desde que la vi, casi antes de que la viera. Mucho antes de tener conciencia de que la amaba a usted, ya la amaba. Se diría que hubo en esto algo de fatídico; que estaba escrito; que era una predestinación.

—Y si es una predestinación, si estaba escrito—interrumpió Pepita—, ¿por qué no someterse, por qué resistirse todavía? Sacrifique usted sus propósitos a nuestro amor. ¿Acaso no he sacrificado yo mucho? Ahora mismo, al rogar, al esforzarme por vencer los desdenes de usted, ¿no sacrifico mi orgullo, mi decoro y mi recato? Yo también creo que amaba a usted antes de verle. Ahora amo a usted con todo mi corazón, y sin usted no hay felicidad para mí. Cierto es que en mi humilde inteligencia no puede usted hallar rivales tan poderosos como yo tengo en la de usted . . . Con alguien, no obstante, más bello, entendido, poético y amoroso que los hombres que me han pretendido hasta ahora; con un amante más distinguido y cabal que todos mis adoradores de este lugar y de los lugares vecinos, soñaba yo para que me amara y para que yo le amase y le rindiese mi albedrío. Ese alguien era usted. Lo presentí cuando me dijeron que usted había llegado al lugar; lo reconocí cuando vi a usted por vez primera. Pero como mi imaginación es tan estéril, el retrato que yo de usted me había trazado no valía, ni con mucho, lo que usted vale. Yo también he leído algunas historias y poesías, pero de todos los elementos

[183] A not uncommon idea in poetry and philosophy. Luis may love not Pepita, but what he imagines Pepita to be. Hence what he loves is his own idea, springing from himself, not her.

que de ellas guardaba mi memoria, no logré nunca componer una pintura que no fuese muy inferior en mérito a lo que veo en usted y comprendo en usted desde que le conozco. Así es que estoy rendida y vencida y aniquilada desde el primer día . . . ¿Es acaso que para avasallar y rendir un alma pequeña, cuitada y débil como la mía, basta un pequeño amor, y para avasallar la de usted, cuando tan altos y fuertes pensamientos la velan y custodian, se necesita de amor más poderoso, que yo no soy digna de inspirar, ni capaz de compartir, ni hábil para comprender siquiera?

—Pepita—contestó don Luis—, no es que su alma de usted sea más pequeña que la mía, sino que está libre de compromisos, y la mía no lo está. El amor que usted me ha inspirado es inmenso; pero luchan contra él mi obligación, mis votos, los propósitos de toda mi vida, próximos a realizarse. ¿Por qué no he de decirlo, sin temor de ofender a usted? Si usted logra en mí su amor, usted no se humilla. Si yo cedo a su amor de usted, me humillo y me rebajo. Dejo al Creador por la criatura, destruyo la obra de mi constante voluntad, rompo la imagen de Cristo, que estaba en mi pecho, y el hombre nuevo, que a tanta costa había yo formado en mí, desaparece para que el hombre antiguo renazca. ¿Por qué, en vez de bajar yo hasta el suelo, hasta el siglo, hasta la impureza del mundo, que antes he menospreciado, no se eleva usted hasta mí por virtud de ese mismo amor que me tiene, limpiándole de toda escoria? ¿Por qué no nos amamos entonces sin vergüenza y sin pecado y sin mancha? Dios, con el fuego purísimo y refulgente de su amor, penetra las almas santas y las llena por tal arte, que así como un metal que sale de la fragua, sin dejar de ser metal reluce y deslumbra, y es todo fuego, así las almas se hinchen de Dios, y en todo son Dios, penetradas por dondequiera[184] de Dios, en gracia del amor divino. Estas almas se aman y se gozan entonces, como si amaran y gozaran a Dios, amándole y gozándole, porque Dios son ellas. Subamos, juntos en espíritu, esta mística y difícil escala; asciendan a la par nuestras almas a esta bienaventuranza, que aun en la vida mortal es posible; mas para ello es fuerza que nuestros cuerpos se separen; que yo vaya adonde me llama mi deber, mi promesa y la voz del Altísimo, que dispone de su siervo y le destina al culto de sus altares.[185]

—¡Ay, señor don Luis!—replicó Pepita toda desolada y compungida— . . . Soy una pecadora infernal. Mi espíritu grosero e inculto no alcanza esas sutilezas, esas distinciones, esos refinamientos de amor. Mi voluntad rebelde se niega a lo que usted propone. Yo ni siquiera concibo a usted sin usted. Para mí es usted su boca, sus ojos, sus negros cabellos, que deseo acariciar con mis manos; su dulce voz y el regalado acento de sus palabras, que hieren y encantan materialmente mis oídos; toda su forma corporal, en suma, que me enamora y seduce, y al través de la cual, y sólo al través de la cual se me muestra el espíritu invisible, vago y lleno de misterios. Mi alma, reacia e incapaz de esos raptos maravillosos, no acertará a seguir a usted nunca a las regiones donde quiere llevarla. Si usted se eleva hasta ellas, yo me quedaré sola, abandonada, sumida en la mayor aflicción. Prefiero morirme . . . Máteme usted antes para que nos amemos así . . . Pero viva, no puede ser. Yo amo en usted, no ya sólo el alma, sino el cuerpo, y la sombra del cuerpo, y el reflejo del cuerpo en los espejos y en el agua,

[184] *por dondequiera,* everywhere, throughout
[185] Luis is thinking of a mystical, spiritual companionship such as that of Saint Edward and his wife.

y el nombre y el apellido, y la sangre, y todo aquello que le determina como tal don Luis de Vargas; el metal de la voz, el gesto, el modo de andar y no sé qué más diga. Repito que es menester matarme. Máteme usted sin compasión. No; yo no soy cristiana, sino idólatra materialista.[186]

Aquí hizo Pepita una larga pausa. Don Luis no sabía qué decir y callaba. El llanto bañaba las mejillas de Pepita, la cual prosiguió sollozando:

—Lo conozco: usted me desprecia y hace bien en despreciarme. Con ese justo desprecio me matará usted mejor que con un puñal, sin que se manche de sangre ni su mano ni su conciencia. Adiós. Voy a libertar a usted de mi presencia odiosa. Adiós para siempre.

Dicho esto, Pepita se levantó de su asiento, y sin volver la cara inundada de lágrimas, fuera de sí, con precipitados pasos se lanzó hacia la puerta que daba a las habitaciones interiores. Don Luis sintió una invencible ternura, una piedad funesta. Tuvo miedo de que Pepita muriese. La siguió para detenerla, pero no llegó a tiempo. Pepita pasó la puerta. Su figura se perdió en la obscuridad. Arrastrado don Luis como por un poder sobrehumano, impulsado como por una mano invisible, penetró en pos de Pepita en la estancia sombría.

El despacho quedó solo.

El baile de los criados debía de haber concluído, pues no se oía el más leve rumor. Sólo sonaba el agua de la fuente del jardincillo.

Ni un leve soplo de viento interrumpía el sosiego de la noche y la serenidad del ambiente. Penetraban por la ventana el perfume de las flores y el resplandor de la luna.

Al cabo de un largo rato, don Luis apareció de nuevo, saliendo de la obscuridad. En su rostro se veía pintado el terror; algo de la desesperación de Judas.

5 Se dejó caer en una silla; puso ambos puños cerrados en su cara y en sus rodillas ambos codos, y así permaneció más de media hora, sumido sin duda en un mar de reflexiones 10 amargas.

Cualquiera, si le hubiera visto, hubiera sospechado que acababa de asesinar a Pepita.

Pepita, sin embargo, apareció des-15 pués. Con paso lento, con actitud de profunda melancolía, con el rostro y la mirada inclinados al suelo, llegó hasta cerca de donde estaba don Luis, y dijo de este modo:

20 —Ahora, aunque tarde, conozco toda la vileza de mi corazón y toda la iniquidad de mi conducta. Nada tengo que decir en mi abono; mas no quiero que me creas más perversa de lo que 25 soy. Mira, no pienses que ha habido en mí artificio, ni cálculo, ni plan para perderte. Sí, ha sido una maldad atroz, pero instintiva; una maldad inspirada quizá por el espíritu del infierno, que 30 me posee. No te desesperes ni te aflijas, por amor de Dios. De nada eres responsable. Ha sido un delirio: la enajenación mental se apoderó de tu noble alma. No es en ti el pecado sino 35 muy leve. En mí es grave, horrible, vergonzoso. Ahora te merezco menos que nunca. Vete: yo soy ahora quien te pide que te vayas. Vete: haz penitencia. Dios te perdonará. Vete: que 40 un sacerdote te absuelva. Limpio de nuevo de culpa, cumple tu voluntad y sé ministro del Altísimo. Con tu vida trabajosa y santa no sólo borrarás hasta las últimas señales de esta caída, 45 sino que, después de perdonarme el mal que te he hecho, conseguirás del

[186] Let us recall here what we said in our introduction on Valera about his paganism, his inability (or unwillingness) to separate the flesh from the spirit, and his refined sensuousness. Pepita takes after her creator.

cielo mi perdón. No hay lazo alguno que conmigo te ligue; y si le hay, yo le desato o le rompo. Eres libre. Básteme el haber hecho caer por sorpresa al lucero de la mañana; no quiero, ni debo, ni puedo retenerle cautivo. Lo adivino, lo infiero de tu ademán, lo veo con evidencia; ahora me desprecias más que antes, y tienes razón en despreciarme. No hay honra, ni virtud, ni vergüenza en mí.

Al decir esto, Pepita hincó en tierra ambas rodillas, y se inclinó luego hasta tocar con la frente el suelo del despacho. Don Luis siguió en la misma postura que antes tenía. Así estuvieron los dos algunos minutos en desesperado silencio.

Con voz ahogada, sin levantar la faz de la tierra, prosiguió al cabo Pepita:

—Vete ya, Luis, y no por una piedad afrentosa permanezcas más tiempo al lado de esta mujer miserable. Yo tendré valor para sufrir tu desvío, tu olvido y hasta tu desprecio, que tengo tan merecido. Seré siempre tu esclava, pero lejos de ti, muy lejos de ti, para no traerte a la memoria la infamia de esta noche.

Los gemidos sofocaron la voz de Pepita al terminar estas palabras.

Don Luis no pudo más. Se puso en pie, llegó donde estaba Pepita y la levantó entre sus brazos, estrechándola contra su corazón, apartando blandamente de su cara los rubios rizos que en desorden caían sobre ella, y cubriéndola de apasionados besos.

—Alma mía—dijo por último don Luis—, vida de mi alma, prenda querida de mi corazón, luz de mis ojos, levanta la abatida frente y no te prosternes más delante de mí. El pecador, el flaco de voluntad, el miserable, el sandio y el ridículo soy yo, que[187] no tú. Los ángeles y los demonios deben reírse igualmente de mí y no tomarme por lo serio. He sido un santo postizo, que no he sabido resistir y desengañarte desde el principio, como hubiera sido justo, y ahora no acierto tampoco a ser un caballero, un galán, un amante fino, que sabe agradecer en cuanto valen los favores de su dama. No comprendo qué viste en mí para prendarte de ese modo. Jamás hubo en mí virtud sólida, sino hojarasca y pedantería de colegial, que había leído los libros devotos como quien lee novelas, y con ellos se había forjado su novela necia de misiones y contemplaciones. Si hubiera habido virtud sólida en mí, con tiempo te hubiera desengañado y no hubiéramos pecado ni tú ni yo. La verdadera virtud no cae tan fácilmente.[188] A pesar de toda tu hermosura, a pesar de tu talento, a pesar de tu amor hacia mí, yo no hubiera caído, si en realidad hubiera sido virtuoso, si hubiera tenido una vocación verdadera. Dios, que todo lo puede, me hubiera dado su gracia. Un milagro, sin duda, algo de sobrenatural se requería para resistir a tu amor; pero Dios hubiera hecho el milagro si yo hubiera sido digno objeto y bastante razón para que le hiciera. Haces mal en aconsejarme que sea sacerdote. Reconozco mi indignidad. No era más que orgullo lo que me movía. Era una ambición mundana como otra cualquiera. ¡Qué digo, como otra cualquiera! Era peor: una ambición hipócrita, sacrílega, simoníaca.[189]

[187] Omit in translating

[188] See n. 1.

[189] Suddenly Luis realizes that he has been a dreamy adolescent, reading religious books in order to project himself into the place of their heroes. In this respect he recalls Don Quijote or Mme Bovary. But now that he knows that his ambition was to be a famous man, not a good priest, he sees that he does not have to choose between love of God and love of Pepita. There was really no profound love of God, hence there was really no conflict. Yet, in another sense, there was a conflict between the pagan, natural way of life and the Christian training of both the protagonists.

—No te juzgues con tal dureza—replicó Pepita ya más serena y sonriendo a través de las lágrimas—. No deseo que te juzgues así, ni para que no me halles tan indigna de ser tu compañera; pero quiero que me elijas por amor, libremente, no para reparar una falta, no porque has caído en un lazo que pérfidamente puedes sospechar que te he tendido. Vete si no me amas, si sospechas de mí, si no me estimas. No exhalarán mis labios una queja si para siempre me abandonas y no vuelves a acordarte de mí.

La contestación de don Luis no cabía ya en el estrecho y mezquino tejido del lenguaje humano. Don Luis rompió el hilo del discuro de Pepita sellando los labios de ella con los suyos y abrazándola de nuevo.

Bastante más tarde, con previas toses y resonar de pies, entró Antoñona en el despacho, diciendo:

—¡Vaya una plática larga! Este sermón que ha predicado el colegial no ha sido el de las siete palabras,[190] sino que ha estado a punto de ser el de las cuarenta horas.[191] Tiempo es ya de que te vayas, don Luis. Son cerca de las dos de la mañana.

—Bien está—dijo Pepita—, se irá al momento.

Antoñona volvió a salir del despacho y aguardó fuera.

Pepita estaba transformada. . . .vencidos los obstáculos que se oponían a su dicha, viendo ya rendido a don Luis, teniendo su promesa espontánea de que la tomaría por mujer legítima, y creyéndose con razón amada, adorada, de aquél a quien amaba y adoraba tanto, brincaba y reía y daba otras muestras de júbilo, que, en medio de todo, tenían mucho de infantil y de inocente.

Era menester que don Luis partiera. Pepita fué por un peine y le alisó con amor los cabellos, besándoselos después.

Pepita le hizo mejor el lazo de la corbata.

—Adiós, dueño amado—le dijo—. Adiós, dulce rey de mi alma. Yo se lo diré todo a tu padre si tú no quieres atreverte. Él es bueno y nos perdonará.

Al cabo los dos amantes se separaron.

. . . don Luis bajó hasta el zaguán acompañado por Antoñona.

Antes de despedirse, dijo don Luis sin preparación ni rodeos:

—Antoñona, tú que lo sabes todo, dime quién es el Conde de Genazahar y qué clase de relaciones ha tenido con tu ama.

—Temprano empiezas a mostrarte celoso.

—No son celos; es curiosidad solamente.

—Mejor es así. Nada más fastidioso que los celos. Voy a satisfacer tu curiosidad. Ese Conde está bastante tronado. Es un perdido, jugador y mala cabeza; pero tiene más vanidad que don Rodrigo en la horca.[192] Se empeñó en que mi niña le quisiera y se casase con él, y como la niña le ha dado mil veces calabazas, está que trina.[193] Esto no impide que se guarde por allá más de mil duros, que hace años le prestó don Gumersindo, sin más hipoteca que un papelucho, por culpa y a ruegos de Pepita, que es mejor que el pan. El tonto del Conde creyó, sin duda, que Pepita, que fué tan buena de casada que hizo que le diesen dinero, había de ser de viuda tan re-

[190] The seven last words of Christ, the subject of sermons during Holy Week.

[191] A mission sermon during the time the Sacrament is exposed in the church for forty consecutive hours.

[192] Translate, proud as Lucifer. The Don Rodrigo in question was Don Rodrigo Calderón, a proud and haughty man who attained high position during the reign of Felipe III but who was hung at the death of this king (1621).

[193] *está que trina,* he is furious

buena para él, que le había de tomar por marido. Vino después el desengaño con la furia consiguiente.

—Adiós, Antoñona—dijo don Luis, y se salió a la calle, silenciosa ya y sombría.

Las luces de las tiendas y puestos de la feria se habían apagado y la gente se retiraba a dormir, salvo los amos de las tiendas de juguetes y otros pobres buhoneros, que dormían al sereno al lado de sus mercancías.

En algunas rejas seguían aún varios embozados, pertinaces e incansables, pelando la pava[194] con sus novias. La mayoría había desaparecido ya.

En la calle, lejos de la vista de Antoñona, don Luis dió rienda suelta a sus pensamientos. Su resolución estaba tomada, y todo acudía a su mente a confirmar su resolución. La sinceridad y el ardor de la pasión que había inspirado a Pepita; su hermosura; la gracia juvenil de su cuerpo y la lozanía primaveral de su alma, se le presentaban en la imaginación y le hacían dichoso.

Con cierta mortificación de la vanidad reflexionaba, no obstante, don Luis en el cambio que en él se había obrado. ¿Qué pensaría el Deán? ¿Qué espanto no sería el del Obispo? Y, sobre todo, ¿qué motivo tan grave de queja no había dado don Luis a su padre? Su disgusto, su cólera cuando supiese el compromiso que ligaba a Luis con Pepita, se ofrecían al ánimo de don Luis y le inquietaban sobremanera.

En cuanto a lo que él llamaba su caída antes de caer, fuerza es confesar que le parecía poco honda y poco espantosa después de haber caído. Su misticismo, bien estudiado con la nueva luz que acababa de adquirir, se le antojó que no había tenido ser ni consistencia; que había sido un producto artificial y vano de sus lecturas, de su petulancia de muchacho y de sus ternuras sin objeto de colegial inocente . . .

Don Luis apelaba a otro género de humildad cristiana para justificar a sus ojos lo que ya no quería llamar caída, sino cambio. Se confesaba indigno de ser sacerdote, y se allanaba a ser lego, casado, vulgar, un buen lugareño cualquiera,[195] cuidando de las viñas y los olivos, criando a sus hijos, pues ya los deseaba, y siendo modelo de maridos al lado de su Pepita.

Don Luis, cuando iba a ser clérigo, estuvo en su papel no defendiendo a Pepita de los groseros insultos del Conde de Genazahar sino con discursos morales, y no tomando venganza de la mofa y desprecio con que tales discursos fueron oídos. Pero, ahorcados ya los hábitos y teniendo que declarar en seguida que Pepita era su novia y que iba a casarse con ella, don Luis, a pesar de su carácter pacífico, de sus ensueños de humana ternura y de las creencias religiosas que en su alma quedaban íntegras, y que repugnaban todo medio violento, no acertaba a compaginar con su dignidad el absternerse de romper la crisma al Conde desvergonzado . . .

Decidido, pues, al lance, resolvió llevarle a cabo en seguida. Y pareciéndole feo y ridículo enviar padrinos y hacer que trajesen en boca el honor de Pepita, halló lo más razonable buscar camorra con cualquier otro pretexto.

Supuso además que el Conde, forastero y vicioso jugador, sería muy posible que estuviese[196] aún en el casino hecho un tahur, a pesar de lo avanzado de la noche, y don Luis se fué derecho al casino.

[194] *pelar la pava,* to flirt, court (through the window grating)

[195] Literally, any at all; here, ordinary

[196] Word order: *que sería muy posible que el Conde . . . estuviese.* Compare n. 174.

El casino permanecía abierto, pero las luces del patio y de los salones estaban casi todas apagadas. Sólo en un salón había luz. Allí se dirigió don Luis, y desde la puerta vió al Conde de Genazahar, que jugaba al monte, haciendo de banquero. Cinco personas nada más apuntaban: dos eran forasteros como el Conde; las otras tres eran el capitán de caballería encargado de la remonta,[197] Currito y el médico. No podían disponerse las cosas más al intento de don Luis. Sin ser visto, por lo afanados que estaban en el juego, don Luis los vió, y apenas los vió, volvió a salir del casino, y se fué rápidamente a su casa. Abrió un criado la puerta; preguntó don Luis por su padre, y sabiendo que dormía, para que no le sintiera ni se despertara, subió don Luis de puntillas a su cuarto con una luz, cogió unos tres mil reales que tenía de su peculio, en oro, y se los guardó en el bolsillo. Dijo después al criado que le volviese a abrir, y se fué al casino otra vez.

Entonces entró don Luis en el salón donde jugaban, dando taconazos recios, con estruendo y con aire de taco,[198] como suele decirse. Los jugadores se quedaron pasmados al verle.

—¡Tú por aquí a estas horas!—dijo Currito.

—¿De dónde sale usted, curita?—dijo el médico.

—¿Viene usted a echarme otro sermón?—exclamó el Conde.

—Nada de sermones—contestó don Luis con mucha calma—. El mal efecto que surtió el último que prediqué me ha probado con evidencia que Dios no me llama por ese camino, y ya he elegido otro. Usted, señor Conde, ha hecho mi conversión. He ahorcado los hábitos; quiero divertirme, estoy en la flor de la mocedad y quiero gozar de ella.

—Vamos, me alegro—interrumpió el Conde—; pero cuidado, niño, que si la flor es delicada, puede marchitarse y deshojarse temprano.

—Ya de eso cuidaré yo—replicó don Luis—. Veo que se juega. Me siento inspirado. Usted talla. ¿Sabe usted, señor Conde, que tendría chiste que yo le desbancase?

—Tendría chiste, ¿eh? ¡Usted ha cenado fuerte!

—He cenado lo que me ha dado la gana.

—Respondonzuelo se va haciendo el mocito.

—Me hago lo que quiero.

—Voto va . . . —dijo el Conde; y ya sentía venir la tempestad, cuando el capitán se interpuso y la paz se restableció por completo.

—Ea—dijo el Conde, sosegado y afable—; desembaúle usted los dinerillos y pruebe fortuna.

Don Luis se sentó a la mesa y sacó del bolsillo todo su oro. Su vista acabó de serenar al Conde, porque casi excedía aquella suma a la que tenía él de banca, y ya imaginaba que iba a ganársela al novato.

—No hay que calentarse mucho la cabeza[199] en este juego—dijo don Luis—. Ya me parece que le entiendo. Pongo dinero a una carta, y si sale la carta, gano, y si sale la contraria, gana usted.

—Así es, amiguito; tiene usted un entendimiento macho.[200]

—Pues lo mejor es que no tengo sólo macho el entendimiento, sino también la voluntad; y con todo, en el conjunto, disto bastante de ser un macho, como hay tantos por ahí.

[197] the raising or buying of horses for the military forces

[198] a swaggering air

[199] *calentarse mucho la cabeza*, to use one's brains very much

[200] *macho*, masculine, strong; as a noun, mule

—¡Vaya si viene usted parlanchín y si saca alicantinas![201]

Don Luis se calló: jugó unas cuantas veces, y tuvo tan buena fortuna, que ganó casi siempre.

El Conde comenzó a cargarse.

—¿Si me desplumará el niño?[202]—dijo—. Dios protege la inocencia.

Mientras que el Conde se amostazaba, don Luis sintió cansancio y fastidio y quiso acabar de una vez.[203]

—El fin de todo esto—dijo—es ver si yo me llevo esos dineros o si usted se lleva los míos. ¿No es verdad, señor Conde?

—Es verdad.

—Pues ¿para qué hemos de estar aquí en vela toda la noche? Ya va siendo tarde, y siguiendo su consejo de usted debo recogerme para que la flor de mi mocedad no se marchite.

—¿Qué es eso? ¿Se quiere usted largar? ¿Quiere usted tomar el olivo?[204]

—Yo no quiero tomar olivo ninguno. Al contrario. Curro, dime tú: aquí, en este montón de dinero, ¿no hay ya más que en la banca?

Currito miró, y contestó:

—Es indudable.

—¿Cómo explicaré—preguntó don Luis—que juego en un golpe cuanto hay en la banca contra otro tanto?

—Eso se explica—respondió Currito—diciendo: ¡copo!

—Pues, copo—dijo don Luis dirigiéndose al Conde—. Va el copo y la red[205] en este rey de espadas, cuyo compañero hará de seguro su epifanía antes que su enemigo el tres.

El Conde, que tenía todo su capital mueble en la banca, se asustó al verle comprometido de aquella suerte; pero no tuvo más que[206] aceptar.

Es sentencia del vulgo que los afortunados en amores son desgraciados al juego; pero más cierta parece la contraria afirmación. Cuando acude la 5 buena dicha, acude para todo, y lo mismo cuando la desdicha acude.

El Conde fué tirando cartas, y no salía ningún tres. Su emoción era grande, por más que[207] lo disimulaba. 10 Por último, descubrió por la pinta el rey de copas y se detuvo.

—Tire usted—dijo el capitán.

—No hay para qué. El rey de copas. ¡Maldito sea! El curita me ha despluma- 15 mado. Recoja usted el dinero.

El Conde echó con rabia la baraja sobre la mesa.

Don Luis recogió todo el dinero con indiferencia y reposo.

20 Después de un corto silencio habló el Conde:

—Curita, es menester que me dé usted el desquite.

—No veo la necesidad.

25 —¡Me parece que entre caballeros! . . .

—Por esa regla el juego no tiene término—observó don Luis—. Por esa regla lo mejor sería ahorrarse el tra- 30 bajo de jugar.

—Déme usted el desquite—replicó el Conde, sin atender a razones.

—Sea—dijo don Luis—. Quiero ser generoso.

35 El Conde volvió a tomar la baraja y se dispuso a echar nueva talla.

—Alto ahí—dijo don Luis—. Entendámonos antes. ¿Dónde está el dinero de la nueva banca de usted?

40 El Conde se quedó turbado y confuso.

Aquí no tengo dinero—contestó—; pero me parece que sobra con mi palabra.

[201] *Vaya . . . alicantinas,* You certainly are talkative and full of tricks!

[202] Suppose the boy should clean me out?

[203] *de una vez,* once and for all

[204] *tomar el olivo,* to go to bed. Cf. the saying *Cada mochuelo a su olivo,* Everyone to his bed

[205] a double pun, since as a noun *copo* means a small net and *red* means not only a net but an abundance. Translate, 'the whole works'

[206] *no tener más que,* not to be able to help

[207] See note 126.

Don Luis, entonces, con acento grave y reposado, dijo:

Señor Conde, yo no tendría inconveniente en fiarme de la palabra de un caballero y en llegar a ser su acreedor, si no temiese perder su amistad, que casi voy ya conquistando; pero desde que vi esta mañana la crueldad con que trató usted a ciertos amigos míos, que son sus acreedores, no quiero hacerme culpado para con usted del mismo delito. No faltaba más sino que yo voluntariamente incurriese en el enojo de usted prestándole dinero, que no me pagaría, como no ha pagado, sino con injurias, el que debe a Pepita Jiménez.

Por lo mismo que el hecho era cierto, la ofensa fué mayor. El Conde se puso lívido de cólera, y ya de pie, pronto a venir a las manos con el colegial, dijo con voz alterada:

—¡Mientes, deslenguado! ¡Voy a deshacerte entre mis manos, hijo de la grandísima . . . !

Esta última injuria, que recordaba a don Luis la falta de su nacimiento, y caía sobre el honor de la persona cuya memoria le era más querida y respetada, no acabó de formularse, no acabó de llegar a sus oídos.

Don Luis, por encima de la mesa, que estaba entre él y el Conde, con agilidad asombrosa y con tino y fuerza, tendió el brazo derecho, armado de un junco o bastoncillo flexible y cimbreante, y cruzó la cara de su enemigo, levantándole al punto un verdugón amoratado.

No hubo ni grito ni denuesto ni alboroto posterior. Cuando empiezan las manos suelen callar las lenguas. El Conde iba a lanzarse sobre don Luis para destrozarle si podía; pero la opinión había dado una gran vuelta desde aquella mañana, y entonces estaba en favor de don Luis. El capitán, el médico y hasta Currito, ya con más ánimo, contuvieron al Conde, que pugnaba y forcejeaba ferozmente por desasirse.

—Dejadme libre, dejadme que le mate—decía.

—Yo no trato de evitar un duelo—dijo el capitán—. El duelo es inevitable. Trato sólo de que no luchéis aquí como dos ganapanes. Faltaría a mi decoro si presenciase tal lucha.

—Que vengan armas—dijo el Conde—. No quiero retardar el lance ni un minuto . . . En el acto . . . , aquí.

—¿Queréis reñir al sable?—dijo el capitán.

—Bien está—respondió don Luis.

—Vengan los sables—dijo el Conde.

Todos hablaban en voz baja para que no se oyese nada en la calle. Los mismos criados del casino, que dormían en sillas, en la cocina y en el patio, no llegaron a despertar.

Don Luis eligió para testigos al capitán y a Currito. El Conde, a los dos forasteros. El médico quedó para hacer su oficio, y enarboló la bandera de la Cruz Roja.[208]

Era todavía de noche. Se convino en hacer campo de batalla de aquel salón, cerrando antes la puerta.

El capitán fué a su casa por los sables, y los trajo al momento debajo de la capa que para ocultarlos se puso.

Ya sabemos que don Luis no había empuñado en su vida un arma. Por fortuna, el Conde no era mucho más diestro en la esgrima, aunque nunca había estudiado teología ni pensado en ser clérigo.

Las condiciones del duelo se redujeron a que, una vez el sable en la mano, cada uno de los dos combatientes hiciera lo que Dios le diera a entender.

Se cerró la puerta de la sala.

Las mesas y las sillas se apartaron en un rincón para despejar el terreno.

[208] Figuratively speaking, of course

Las luces se colocaron de un modo conveniente. Don Luis y el Conde se quitaron levitas y chalecos, quedaron en mangas de camisa y tomaron las armas. Se hicieron a un lado[209] los testigos. A una señal del capitán, empezó el combate.

Entre dos personas que no sabían parar ni defenderse, la lucha debía de ser brevísima, y lo fué.

La furia del Conde, retenida por algunos minutos, estalló y le cegó. Era robusto; tenía unos puños de hierro, y sacudía con el sable una lluvia de tajos sin orden ni concierto. Cuatro veces tocó a don Luis, por fortuna siempre de plano. Lastimó sus hombros, pero no le hirió. Menester fué de todo el vigor del joven teólogo para no caer derribado a los tremendos golpes y con el dolor de las contusiones. Todavía tocó el Conde por quinta vez a don Luis, y le dió en el brazo izquierdo. Aquí la herida fué de filo, aunque de soslayo. La sangre de don Luis empezó a correr en abundancia. Lejos de contenerse un poco, el Conde arremetió con más ira para herir de nuevo: casi se metió bajo el sable de don Luis. Éste, en vez de prepararse a parar, dejó caer[210] el sable con brío y acertó con una cuchillada en la cabeza del Conde. La sangre salió con ímpetu, y se extendió por la frente y corrió sobre los ojos. Aturdido por el golpe, dió el Conde con su cuerpo en el suelo.

Toda la batalla fué negocio de algunos segundos.

Don Luis había estado sereno . . . pero, no bien miró a su contrario por tierra, bañado en sangre y como muerto, don Luis sintió una angustia grandísima y temió que le diese una congoja. Él, que no se creía capaz de matar un gorrión, acaso acababa de matar a un hombre. Él, que aun estaba resuelto a ser sacerdote, a ser misionero, a ser ministro y nuncio del Evangelio hacía cinco o seis horas, había cometido o se acusaba de haber cometido en nada de tiempo[211] todos los delitos, y de haber infringido todos los mandamientos de la ley de Dios. No había quedado pecado mortal de que no se contaminase.

El estado de don Luis, después de las agitaciones de todo aquel día, era el de un hombre que tiene fiebre cerebral.

Currito y el capitán, cada uno de un lado, le agarraron y le llevaron a su casa.

Don Pedro de Vargas se levantó sobresaltado cuando le dijeron que venía su hijo herido. Acudió a verle; examinó las contusiones y la herida del brazo, y vió que no eran de cuidado; pero puso el grito en el cielo diciendo que iba a tomar venganza de aquella ofensa, y no se tranquilizó hasta que supo el lance, y que don Luis había sabido tomar venganza por sí, a pesar de su teología.

El médico vino poco después a curar a don Luis, y pronosticó que en tres o cuatro días estaría don Luis para salir a la calle, como si tal cosa.[212] El Conde, en cambio, tenía para meses.[213] Su vida, sin embargo, no corría peligro. Había vuelto de su desmayo, y había pedido que le llevasen a su pueblo, que no dista más que una legua del lugar en que pasaron estos sucesos. Habían buscado un carricoche de alquiler y le habían llevado, yendo en su compañía su criado y los dos forasteros que le sirvieron de testigos.

A los cuatro días del lance se cumplieron, en efecto, los pronósticos del

[209] Here, to move to one side
[210] *dejó caer,* brought down
[211] *nada de tiempo,* no time at all
[212] *como . . . cosa,* as good as new, as if nothing had happened
[213] had [a wound which would incapacitate him] for months

doctor, y don Luis, aunque magullado de los golpes y con la herida abierta aún, estuvo en estado de salir, y prometiendo un restablecimiento completo en plazo muy breve.

El primer deber que don Luis creyó que necesitaba cumplir, no bien le dieron de alta,[214] fué confesar a su padre sus amores con Pepita, y declararle su intención de casarse con ella.

Don Pedro no había ido al campo ni se había empleado sino en cuidar a su hijo durante la enfermedad. Casi siempre estaba a su lado acompañándole y mimándole con singular cariño.

En la mañana del día 27 de junio, después de irse el médico, don Pedro quedó solo con su hijo; y entonces la tan difícil confesión para don Luis tuvo lugar del modo siguiente:

—Padre mío—dijo don Luis—; yo no debo seguir engañando a usted por más tiempo. Hoy voy a confesar a usted mis faltas y a desechar la hipocresía.

—Muchacho, si es confesión lo que vas a hacer mejor será que llames al padre Vicario. Yo tengo muy holgachón el criterio, y te absolveré de todo sin que mi absolución te valga para nada. Pero si quieres confiarme algún hondo secreto como a tu mejor amigo, empieza, que te escucho.

—Lo que tengo que confiar a usted es una gravísima falta mía, y me da vergüenza . . .

—Pues no tengas vergüenza con tu padre y di sin rebozo.

Aquí don Luis, poniéndose muy colorado y con visible turbación, dijo:

—Mi secreto es que estoy enamorado de . . . Pepita Jiménez, y que ella . . .

Don Pedro interrumpió a su hijo con una carcajada y continuó la frase:

—Y que ella está enamorada de ti, y que la noche de la velada de San Juan estuviste con ella en dulces coloquios hasta las dos de la mañana, y que por ella buscaste un lance con el Conde de Genazahar, a quien has roto la cabeza. Pues, hijo, bravo secreto me confías. No hay perro ni gato en el lugar que no esté ya al corriente de todo. Lo único que parecía posible ocultar era la duración del coloquio hasta las dos de la mañana, pero unas gitanas buñoleras te vieron salir de la casa, y no pararon hasta contárselo a todo bicho viviente. Pepita, además, no disimula cosa mayor; y hace bien, porque sería el disimulo de Antequera[215] . . . Desde que estás enfermo viene aquí Pepita dos veces al día, y otras dos o tres veces envía a Antoñona a saber de tu salud; y si no han entrado a verte, es porque yo me he opuesto, para que no te alborotes.

La turbación y el apuro de don Luis subieron de punto cuando oyó contar a su padre toda la historia en lacónico compendio.

—¡Qué sorpresa!—dijo—, ¡qué asombro habrá sido el de usted!

—Nada de sorpresa ni de asombro, muchacho. En el lugar sólo se saben las cosas hace cuatro días, y la verdad sea dicha, ha pasmado tu transformación . . . Pero a mí no me cogieron las noticias de susto, salvo tu herida. Los viejos sentimos crecer la hierba.[216] No es fácil que los pollos engañen a los recoveros.

—Es verdad: he querido engañar a usted. ¡He sido hipócrita!

—No seas tonto: no lo digo por mortejarte. Lo digo para darme tono de perspicaz. Pero hablemos con franqueza: mi jactancia es inmotivada. Yo sé punto por punto el progreso de tus amores con Pepita, desde hace más de dos meses; pero lo sé porque tu tío el Deán, a quien escribías tus impre-

[214] See p. 335, n. 199

[215] An attempt to conceal facts known to everybody

[216] We old people know what's going on.

siones, me lo ha participado todo. Oye la carta acusadora de tu tío, y oye la contestación que le di, documento importantísimo de que he guardado minuta.

. . . acabó don Pedro de leer su carta, y al volver a mirar a don Luis, vió que don Luis había estado escuchando con los ojos llenos de lágrimas.

El padre y el hijo se dieron un abrazo muy apretado y muy prolongado.

Al mes justo de esta conversación y de esta lectura, se celebraron las bodas de don Luis de Vargas y de Pepita Jiménez.

Temeroso el señor Deán de que su hermano le embromase demasiado con que el misticismo de Luisito había salido huero, y conociendo además que su papel iba a ser poco airoso en el lugar, donde todos dirían que tenía mala mano para sacar santos, dió por pretexto sus ocupaciones y no quiso venir, aunque envió su bendición y unos magníficos zarcillos, como presente para Pepita.

El padre Vicario tuvo, pues, el gusto de casarla con don Luis.

La novia muy bien engalanada, pareció hermosísima a todos y digna de trocarse por el cilicio y las disciplinas.

Aquella noche dió don Pedro un baile estupendo en el patio de su casa y salones contiguos. Criados y señores, hidalgos y jornaleros, las señoras y señoritas y las mozas del lugar asistieron y se mezclaron en él, como en la soñada primera edad del mundo, que no sé por qué llaman de oro. Cuatro diestros, o si no diestros, infatigables guitarristas, tocaron el fandango. Un gitano y una gitana, famosos cantadores, entonaron las coplas más amorosas y alusivas a las circunstancias. Y el maestro de escuela leyó un epitalamio en verso heroico . . .

Don Pedro estuvo hecho un cadete: bullicioso, bromista y galante . . . Bailó el fandango con Pepita, con sus más graciosas criadas y con otras seis o siete mozuelas. A cada una, al volverla a su asiento, cansada ya, le dió con efusión el correspondiente y prescrito abrazo, y a las menos serias, algunos pellizcos, aunque esto no formaba parte del ceremonial. Don Pedro llevó su galantería hasta el extremo de sacar a bailar a doña Casilda, que no pudo negarse, y que, con sus diez arrobas de humanidad y los calores de julio, vertía un chorro de sudor por cada poro. Por último, don Pedro atracó de tal suerte a Currito, y le hizo brindar tantas veces por la felicidad de los nuevos esposos, que el mulero Dientes tuvo que llevarle a su casa a dormir la mona,[217] terciado en una borrica como un pellejo de vino.

El baile duró hasta las tres de la madrugada; pero los novios se eclipsaron discretamente antes de las once y se fueron a casa de Pepita . . .

Aunque en el lugar es uso y costumbre, jamás interrumpida, dar una terrible cencerrada a todo viudo o viuda que contrae segundas nupcias, no dejándolos tranquilos con el resonar de los cencerros en la primera noche del consorcio, Pepita era tan simpática y don Pedro tan venerado y don Luis tan querido, que no hubo cencerros ni el menor conato de que resonasen aquella noche: caso raro, que se registra como tal en los anales del pueblo.

III. *Epílogo*

Cartas de mi hermano

La historia de Pepita y Luisito debiera terminar aquí. Este epílogo está

[217] *dormir la mona,* to sleep off one's drunkenness.

de sobra; pero el señor Deán lo tenía en el legajo, y ya que no le publiquemos por completo, publicaremos parte; daremos una muestra siquiera . . .

Todo prospera en casa. Luis y yo tenemos unas candioteras que no las hay mejores en España, si prescindimos de Jerez.[218] La cosecha de aceite ha sido este año soberbia. Podemos permitirnos todo género de lujos, y yo aconsejo a Luis y a Pepita que den un buen paseo por Alemania, Francia e Italia, no bien salga Pepita de su cuidado y se restablezca. Los chicos pueden, sin imprevisión ni locura, derrochar unos cuantos miles de duros en la expedición y traer muchos primores de libros, muebles y objetos de arte para adornar su vivienda.

Hemos aguardado dos semanas para que sea el bautizo el día mismo del primer aniversario de la boda. El niño es un sol de bonito y muy robusto. Yo he sido el padrino, y le hemos dado mi nombre. Yo estoy soñando con que Periquito hable y diga gracias . . .

Mis hijos han vuelto de su viaje bien de salud, y con Periquito muy travieso y precioso.

Luis y Pepita vienen resueltos a no volver a salir del lugar, aunque les dure más la vida que a Filemón y a Baucis.[219] Están enamorados como nunca el uno del otro.

Traen lindos muebles, muchos libros, algunos cuadros y no sé cuántas otras baratijas elegantes que han comprado por esos mundos y principalmente en París, Roma, Florencia y Viena . . .

Todo lo van mejorando y hermoseando para hacer de este retiro su edén.

No imagines, sin embargo, que la afición de Luis y de Pepita al bienestar 5 material haya entibiado en ellos, en lo más mínimo, el sentimiento religioso. La piedad de ambos es más profunda cada día, y en cada contento o satisfacción de que gozan o que pueden 10 proporcionar a sus semejantes ven un nuevo beneficio del cielo, por el cual se reconocen más obligados a demostrar su gratitud. Es más: esa satisfacción y ese contento no lo serían, no 15 tendrían precio, ni valor, ni sustancia para ellos, si la consideración y la firme creencia en las cosas divinas no se lo prestasen.

Luis no olvida nunca, en medio de 20 su dicha presente, el rebajamiento del ideal con que había soñado. Hay ocasiones en que su vida de ahora le parece vulgar, egoísta y prosaica, comparada con la vida de sacrificio, con 25 la existencia espiritual a que se creyó llamado en los primeros años de su juventud; pero Pepita acude solícita a disipar estas melancolías, y entonces comprende y afirma Luis que el hom-30 bre puede servir a Dios en todos los estados y condiciones, y concierta la viva fe y el amor de Dios, que llenan su alma, con este amor lícito de lo terrenal y caduco. Pero en todo ello 35 pone Luis como un fundamento divino, sin el cual, ni en los astros que pueblan el éter, ni en las flores y frutos que hermosean el campo, ni en los ojos de Pepita, ni en la inocencia y belleza 40 de Periquito, vería nada de amable . . .

En la casa de mis hijos hay, pues, algunas salas que parecen preciosas capillitas católicas o devotos oratorios; pero he de confesar que tienen ambos

[218] The town in which Jerez wine (called 'sherry' in English) is made.

[219] Philemon and Baucis, a married couple, symbols of conjugal love, entertained Jupiter and Mercury in their home when all their neighbors had refused them shelter. They asked as a reward that they might die at the same time. The gods gave them a long life and then converted them, one into a linden tree, the other into an oak.

también su poquito de paganismo, como poesía rústica amoroso-pastoril, la cual ha ido a refugiarse extramuros . . .

El merendero o cenador, donde comimos las fresas aquella tarde, que fué la segunda vez que Pepita y Luis se vieron y se hablaron, se ha transformado en un airoso templete, con pórtico y columnas de mármol blanco. Dentro hay una espaciosa sala con muy cómodos muebles. Dos bellas pinturas la adornan: una representa a Psiquis,[220] descubriendo y contemplando extasiada, a la luz de su lámpara, al Amor dormido en su lecho; otra representa a Cloe[221] cuando la cigarra fugitiva se le mete en el pecho, donde, creyéndose segura, y a tan grata sombra, se pone a cantar, mientras que Dafnis procura sacarla de allí.

Una copia hecha con bastante esmero en mármol de Carrara,[222] de la Venus de Médicis,[223] ocupa el preferente lugar, y como que preside en la sala. En el pedestal tiene grabados, en letras de oro, estos versos le Lucrecio:

Nec sine te quidquam dias in luminis oras
Exoritur, neque fit laetum, neque amabile quidquam.[224]

[220] Psyche was the nymph with whom Cupid fell in love. However, he wished to keep his identity from her and visited her only at night. Since an oracle had predicted she would marry a monster, one night Psyche took a lamp and looked at her companion while he was sleeping. Artists have frequently represented her surprise and joy on seeing a beautiful young god instead of the expected hideous creature. However, a drop of oil from the lamp fell on Cupid and awakened him; whereupon, in his anger, he abandoned her.

[221] See n. 176.

[222] The marble from this Italian town is especially prized by sculptors.

[223] Well-known statue of Venus in Florence, Italy. Its significance here is that it represents the pagan goddess of love, particularly the human, natural love which now fills Luis's life.

[224] From the invocation in Lucretius' *De rerum natura* to the goddess Venus: '. . . without thee nothing rises up into the goodly coasts of light, nor anything is joyous made nor lovely . . .' (Translated by Thomas Jackson)

Benito Pérez Galdós

THE life of Benito Pérez Galdós (1843–1920) is neither dramatic nor exciting. He devoted his mature years almost constantly to methodical work, interrupting his production only with brief periods of travel. But his seventy-seven novels and twenty-six plays are truly exciting and significant. Most critics place Galdós second only to Cervantes as a novelist.

Galdós was born in the Canary Islands and came to Madrid at the age of nineteen to study law. He soon abandoned serious university work and gave himself over to observation of Spanish life and to a wide range of reading. At the same time he wrote some unsuccessful plays and pursued a career as a journalist. Then, after a couple of promising novels of apprenticeship, he devoted himself to his first great plan—a series of historical novels depicting the life and politics of Spain in the early, formative years of the nineteenth century. Galdós felt that Spaniards needed to know the history of this period in order to understand their own times and to choose wisely the pathway of the future. Between 1873 and 1879 he wrote twenty novels under the general title of *Episodios Nacionales,* divided into two series of ten each, which covered Spanish history from 1805 to 1834. In each series Galdós traces the fortunes of a fictitious hero who takes part in many of the important historical events of the epoch. The heroes learn to love their fatherland and to believe in the moderate liberalism which Galdós thought necessary for the orderly progress of the country. We must not forget that he was writing these novels at a time when Spain was undergoing a civil war and other violent political upheavals.

Galdós had no intention of continuing the *Episodios Nacionales* after finishing the first twenty volumes in 1879. But much later, in 1898, he found himself in financial straits and returned to the *Episodios Nacionales,* which had always been best sellers. He wrote twenty-six more novels, carrying the history of Spain down to 1875, covering a period when he himself was a witness to many important events depicted in his work.

Despite their great popularity, none of the *Episodos Nacionales* can be considered a real masterpiece. Galdós's greatest achievements are all in another series of novels, the *Novelas Contemporáneas.* These were begun even while Don Benito was still working on the early series of *Episodios Nacionales,* in the 1870's. Throughout the *Novelas Contemporáneas* we can see Galdós gradually developing and refining his concept of realism. He moves from a somewhat allegorical vision of his characters as social forces (*Doña Perfecta,* 1876) to a naturalistic belief that people can be explained by their heredity and environment (*La desheredada,* 1881), then to a spiritualized naturalism (*Fortunata y Jacinta,* 4 vols., 1886–7) and finally to a period of spirituality, in which he sees the spirit as a motivating force for human conduct equal in power to physical drives (*Misericordia,* 1897). In these novels Galdós usually sets the action in Madrid, which he knew most intimately. His word pictures of numerous city types, his sympathetic humor, and his psychological profundity make many of the *Novelas Contemporáneas* truly outstanding creations.

We cannot talk so enthusiastically about his plays. Galdós did not begin to produce them until relatively late in life, the first, *Realidad,* being presented in 1892. Although Galdós did give a new realistic direction to the drama with this play, he became openly allegorical in his later theatrical works. The obviousness of his message frequently detracts from the dramatic illusion. He never felt really at home in the drama, but did achieve some remarkable successes, often because his play happened to coincide with some political or social crisis which could be related to the theme of the play.

Galdós was always a champion of liberalism—at first he supported a constitutional monarchy, but later, the republican cause. He loved the common people of Spain and felt that they were the great depository of Spanish virtues. He looked forward to a day when Spaniards would achieve a closer contact with reality, instead of living too frequently in a world of dreams, and when Spaniards would learn to love one another and work together to realize their great potential. Because of this vision of a greater Spain, Galdós continues to be one of the most widely read and respected Spanish authors.

Benito Pérez Galdós

Torquemada en la hoguera

I

Voy a contar cómo fué al quemadero el inhumano que tantas vidas infelices consumió en llamas;[1] . . . cómo vino el fiero sayón a ser víctima; cómo los odios que provocó se le volvieron lástima, y las nubes de maldiciones arrojaron sobre él lluvia de piedad. . . .

Mis amigos conocen ya, por lo que de él se me antojó referirles, a don Francisco Torquemada,[2] a quien algunos historiadores inéditos de estos tiempos llaman *Torquemada el Peor*. . . . Es Torquemada el habilitado de aquel infierno en que fenecen desnudos y fritos los deudores; hombres de más necesidades que posibles; empleados con más hijos que sueldo; otros ávidos de la nómina tras larga cesantía; militares trasladados de residencia, con familión y suegra de añadidura; personajes de flaco espíritu, poseedores de un buen destino, pero, con la carcoma de una mujercita que da tés y empeña el verbo para comprar las pastas; viudas lloronas que cobran del Montepío civil o militar y se ven en mil apuros; sujetos diversos que no aciertan a resolver el problema aritmético en que se funda la existencia social, y otros muy perdidos, muy faltones, muy destornillados de cabeza o rasos de moral, tramposos y embusteros.

Pues todos éstos, el bueno y el malo, 5 el desgraciado y el pillo, cada uno por su arte propio, pero siempre con su sangre y sus huesos, le amasaron al sucio de Torquemada una fortunita que ya la quisieran muchos que se dan 10 lustre en Madrid . . .

El año de la Revolucion,[3] compró Torquemada una casa de corredor[4] en la calle de San Blas, con vuelta a la de la Leche;[5] finca muy aprovechada, con 15 veinticuatro habitacioncitas, que daban, descontando insolvencias inevitables, reparaciones, contribución, etc., una renta de 1.300 reales al mes, equivalente a un siete o siete y medio 20 por ciento del capital. Todos los domingos se personaba en ella mi don Francisco para hacer la cobranza, los recibos en una mano, en otra el bastón con puño de asta de ciervo; y los 25 pobres inquilinos que tenían la desgracia de no poder ser puntuales, andaban desde el sábado por la tarde con el estómago descompuesto, porque la adusta cara, el carácter férreo del 30 propietario, no concordaban con la idea que tenemos del día de fiesta, del día del Señor, todo descanso y alegría.

[1] The allusion is, of course, to the Grand Inquisitor, Tomás de Torquemada, a Dominican monk who was first the confessor of Isabel la católica, then inquisitor-general of the Spanish Inquisition. It is estimated that 2,000 persons were executed during his 18 years as head of the organization. His severity caused him to be hated and brought censure upon him from the Pope.

[2] Torquemada had already appeared in several of Galdós's novels, always as a minor character. He was an astute and heartless moneylender.

[3] The revolution of 1868, when Isabel II was deposed and the liberals took over the government.

[4] *casa de corredor,* tenement house

[5] *calle de San Blas, calle de la Leche,* streets near the juncture of the *calle de Atocha* and the *Paseo del Prado;* a shabby district

El año de la Restauración,[6] ya había duplicado Torquemada la pella con que le cogió la *gloriosa,*[7] y el radical cambio político proporcionóle bonitos préstamos y anticipos. Situación nueva, nóminas frescas, pagas saneadas, negocio limpio. Los gobernadores flamantes que tenían que hacerse ropa, los funcionarios diversos que salían de la oscuridad, famélicos, le hicieron un buen Agosto. Toda la época de los conservadores fué regularcita; como que éstos le daban juego con las esplendideces propias de la dominación, y los liberales también con sus ansias y necesidades no satisfechas. Al entrar en el gobierno, en 1881,[8] los que tanto tiempo estuvieron sin catarlo, otra vez Torquemada en alza; préstamos de lo fino, adelantos de lo gordo, y vamos viviendo.[9] Total, que ya le estaba echando el ojo a otra casa, no de corredor, sino de buena vecindad, casi nueva, bien acondicionada para inquilinos modestos, y que si no rentaba más que un tres y medio a todo tirar,[10] en cambio su administración y cobranza no darían las jaquecas de la cansada finca dominguera.

Todo iba como una seda para aquella feroz hormiga, cuando de súbito le afligió el cielo con tremenda desgracia: se murió su mujer. Perdónenme mis lectores si les doy la noticia sin la preparación conveniente, pues sé que apreciaban a doña Silvia, como la apreciábamos todos los que tuvimos el honor de tratarla, y conocíamos sus excelentes prendas y circunstancias. Falleció de cólico miserere,[11] y he de decir, en aplauso de Torquemada, que no se omitió gasto de médico y botica para salvarle la vida a la pobre señora. Esta pérdida fué un golpe cruel para don Francisco, pues habiendo vivido el matrimonio en santa y laboriosa paz durante más de cuatro lustros, los caracteres de ambos cónyuges se habían compenetrado de un modo perfecto, llegando a ser ella otro él, y él como cifra y refundición de ambos. Doña Silvia no sólo gobernaba la casa con magistral economía, sino que asesoraba a su pariente en los negocios difíciles, auxilándole con sus luces y su experiencia para el préstamo. Ella defendiendo el céntimo en casa para que no se fuera a la calle, y él barriendo para adentro a fin de traer todo lo que pasara, formaron un matrimonio sin desperdicio, pareja que podría servir de modelo a cuantas hormigas hay debajo de la tierra y encima de ella.

Estuvo Torquemada el *Peor,* los primeros días de su viudez, sin saber lo que le pasaba, dudando que pudiera sobrevivir a su cara mitad. Púsose más amarillo de lo que comúnmente estaba, y le salieron algunas canas en el pelo y en la perilla. Pero el tiempo cumplió como suele cumplir siempre, endulzando lo amargo, limando con insensible diente las asperezas de la vida, y aunque el recuerdo de su esposa no se extinguió en el alma del usurero, el dolor hubo de calmarse; los días fueron perdiendo lentamente su fúnebre tristeza; despejóse el sol del alma, iluminando de nuevo las variadas combinaciones numéricas que en ella había; los negocios distrajeron al aburrido negociante, y a los dos años Torquemada parecía consolado; pero, entiéndase bien y repítase en honor suyo, sin malditas ganas de volver a casarse.

Dos hijos le quedaron: Rufinita,

[6] In 1875 the son of Isabel II, Alfonso XII, was restored to the throne of Spain.
[7] *la gloriosa,* the revolution of 1868
[8] The liberal party, under the leadership of Sagasta, won power in 1881. They had been out of power for six years.
[9] *y vamos viviendo,* freely, and everything is fine and dandy
[10] *un tres y medio a todo tirar,* three and a half per cent, stretching it to the utmost
[11] *cólico miserere,* severe abdominal pains, caused by a ruptured diaphragm

cuyo nombre no es nuevo para mis amigos;[12] y Valentinito, que ahora sale por primera vez. Entre la edad de uno y otro hallamos diez años de diferencia, pues a mi doña Silvia se le malograron más o menos prematuramente todas las crías intermedias, quedándole sólo la primera y la última. En la época en que cae lo que voy a referir, Rufinita había cumplido los veintidós, y Valentín andaba al ras de los doce. Y para que se vea la buena estrella de aquel animal de don Francisco, sus dos hijos eran, cada cual por su estilo, verdaderas joyas, o como bendiciones de Dios que llovían sobre él para consolarle en su soledad. Rufina había sacado todas las capacidades domésticas de su madre, y gobernaba el hogar casi tan bien como ella. Claro que no tenía el alto tino de los negocios, ni la consumada trastienda, ni el golpe de vista, ni otras aptitudes entre morales y olfativas de aquella insigne matrona; pero en formalidad, en honesta compostura y buen parecer, ninguna chica de su edad le echaba el pie adelante. No era presumida, ni tampoco descuidada en su persona; no se la podía tachar de desenvuelta, ni tampoco de huraña. Coqueterías, jamás en ella se conocieron. Un solo novio tuvo desde la edad en que apunta el querer hasta los días en que la presento; el cual, después de mucho rondar y suspiretear, mostrando por mil medios la rectitud de sus fines, fué admitido en la casa en los últimos tiempos de doña Silvia, y siguió después, con asentimiento del papá, en la misma honrada y amorosa costumbre. Era un *chico de Medicina,*[13] chico en toda la extensión de la palabra, pues levantaba del suelo lo menos que puede levantar un hombre; estudiosillo, inocente, bonísimo y manchego por más señas. Desde el cuarto año empezaron aquellas castas relaciones; y en los días de este relato, concluída ya la carrera y lanzado Quevedito (que así se llamaba) a la práctica de la facultad, tocaban ya a casarse. Satisfecho el *Peor* de la elección de la niña, alababa su discreción, su desprecio de las vanas apariencias, para atender sólo a lo sólido y práctico.

Pues digo, si de Rufina volvemos los ojos al tierno vástago de Torquemada, encontraremos mejor explicación de la vanidad que le infundía su prole, porque (lo digo sinceramente) no he conocido criatura más mona que aquel Valentín, ni precocidad tan extraordinaria como la suya. ¡Cosa más rara! No obstante el parecido con su antipático papá, era el chiquillo guapísimo, con tal expresión de intelgencia en aquella cara, que se quedaba uno embobado mirándole; con tales encantos en su persona y carácter, y rasgos de conducta tan superiores a su edad, que verle, hablarle y quererle vivamente, era todo uno. ¡Y qué hechicera gravedad la suya, no incompatible con la inquietud propia de la infancia! ¡Qué gracia mezclada de no sé qué aplomo inexplicable a sus años! ¡Qué rayo divino en sus ojos algunas veces, y otras qué misteriosa y dulce tristeza! Espigadillo de cuerpo, tenía las piernas delgadas, pero de buena forma; la cabeza más grande de lo regular, con alguna deformidad en el cráneo. En cuanto a su aptitud para el estudio, llamémosla verdadero prodigio, asombro de la escuela, y orgullo y gala de los maestros. De esto hablaré más adelante. Sólo he de afirmar ahora que el *Peor* no merecía tal joya, ¡qué había de merecerla! y que si fuese hombre capaz de alabar a Dios por los bienes con que le agraciaba, motivos tenía el muy tuno para estarse, como Moisés, tantísimas horas con los brazos

[12] Rufina appeared as a minor character in *Fortunata y Jacinta.*

[13] *chico de Medicina,* young fellow from the medical school

levantados al cielo.[14] No los levantaba, porque sabía que del cielo no había de caerle ninguna breva de las que a él le gustaban.

II

Vamos a otra cosa: Torquemada no era de esos usureros que se pasan la vida multiplicando caudales por el gustazo platónico de poseerlos; que viven sórdidamente para no gastarlos, y al morirse, quisieran, o bien llevárselos consigo a la tierra, o esconderlos donde alma viviente no los pueda encontrar. No: don Francisco habría sido así en otra época; pero no pudo eximirse de la influencia de esta segunda mitad del siglo XIX, que casi ha hecho una religión de las materialidades decorosas[1] de la existencia. Aquellos avaros de antiguo cuño, que afanaban riquezas y vivían como mendigos y se morían como perros en un camastro lleno de pulgas y de billetes de Banco metidos entre la paja, eran los místicos o metafísicos de la usura; su egoísmo se sutilizaba en la idea pura del negocio; adoraban la santísima, la inefable cantidad, sacrificando a ella su material existencia, las necesidades del cuerpo y de la vida, como el místico lo pospone todo a la absorbente idea de salvarse. Viviendo el *Peor* en una época que arranca de la desamortización,[2] sufrió, sin comprenderlo, la metamorfosis que ha desnaturalizado la usura metafísica, convirtiéndola en positivista, y si bien es cierto, como lo acredita la historia, que desde el 51 al 68, su verdadera época de aprendizaje, andaba muy mal trajeado y con afectación de pobreza, la cara y las manos sin lavar, rascándose a cada instante en brazos y piernas cual si llevase miseria,[3] el sombrero con grasa, la capa deshilachada; si bien consta también en las crónicas de la vecindad que en su casa se comía de vigilia casi todo el año, y que la señora salía a sus negocios con una toquilla agujereada y unas botas viejas de su marido, no es menos cierto que, alrededor del 70, la casa estaba ya en otro pie . . .

Pues en los últimos años de doña Silvia, la transformación acentuóse más. Por aquella época cató la familia los colchones de muelles; Torquemada empezó a usar chistera de cincuenta reales; disfrutaba dos capas, una muy buena, con embozos colorados; los hijos iban bien apañaditos; Rufina tenía un lavabo de los de mírame y no me toques,[4] con jofaina y jarro de cristal azul, que no se usaba nunca por no estropearlo; doña Silvia se engalanó con un abrigo de pieles que parecían de conejo, y dejaba bizca[5] a toda la calle de Tudescos y callejón del Perro[6] cuando salía con la *visita*[7] guarnecida de abalorio; en fin, que pasito a paso y a codazo limpio,[8] se habían ido metiendo en la clase media, en nuestra bonachona clase media, toda necesidades y pretensiones, y que

[14] In the battle against Amalek the action went in favor of the children of Israel as long as Moses held up his hands. But his hands became heavy; so Aaron and Hur held them up until the sun set. (Exodus 17. 8–13)

[1] *materialidades decorosas,* freely, comforts and luxuries

[2] *la desamortización,* the freeing of entailed lands. Many estates in Spain were entailed (that is, they could not be sold) and were inherited by the eldest son (*el mayorazgo*) of the family. Other entailed estates belonged to religious orders and churches, and still other lands were owned in common by villages. Many of these lands lay idle, an obstacle to the economic development of the country. In 1837 the government passed a law permitting their sale, which brought on a wave of speculation in lands.

[3] *miseria,* here, lice

[4] *de los de mírame y no me toques,* of the kind that is purely ornamental

[5] *dejaba bizca,* she had staring

[6] *calle de Tudescos y callejón del Perro,* streets in the north central section of Madrid, where Torquemada lived. As a young man Galdós lived for a short time in the *calle de Tudescos.* The *callejón del Perro* was destroyed by the opening of the Gran Vía.

[7] *visita,* visiting dress

[8] *a codazo limpio,* freely, elbowing their way

crece tanto, tanto, ¡ay dolor! que nos estamos quedando sin pueblo.[9]

Pues señor: revienta doña Silvia, y empuñadas por Rufina las riendas del gobierno de la casa, la metamorfosis se marca mucho más. A reinados nuevos, principios nuevos. Comparando lo pequeño con lo grande y lo privado con lo público, diré que aquello se me parecía a la entrada de los liberales, con su poquito de sentido revolucinario en lo que hacen y dicen. Torquemada representaba la idea conservadora; pero transigía, ¡pues no había de transigir! doblegándose a la lógica de los tiempos. Apechugó con la camisa limpia cada media semana; con el abandono de la capa número dos para del día,[10] relegándola al servicio nocturno; con el destierro absoluto del hongo número tres, que no podía ya con más sebo;[11] aceptó, sin viva protesta, la renovación de manteles entre semana[12] . . . y no tuvo nada que decir de las modestas galas de Rufina y de su hermanito, ni de la alfombra del gabinete, ni de otros muchos progresos que se fueron metiendo en la casa a modo de contrabando.[13]

Y vió muy pronto don Francisco que aquellas novedades eran buenas y que su hija tenía mucho talento, porque . . . vamos, parecía cosa del otro jueves[14] . . . echábase mi hombre a la calle y se sentía, con la buena ropa, más persona que antes; hasta le salían mejores negocios, más amigos útiles y explotables. Pisaba más fuerte, tosía más recio, hablaba más alto y atrevíase a levantar el gallo[15] en la tertulia del café, notándose con bríos para sustentar una opinión cualquiera, cuando antes, por efecto sin duda del mal pelaje[16] y de su rutinaria afectación de pobreza, siempre era de la opinión de los demás. Poco a poco llegó a advertir en sí los alientos propios de su capacidad social y financiera; se tocaba,[17] y el sonido le advertía que era propietario y rentista. Pero la vanidad no le cegó nunca. Hombre de composición homogénea, compacta y dura, no podía incurrir en la tontería de estirar el pie más del largo de la sábana.[18] En su carácter había algo de resistente a las mudanzas de forma impuestas por la época; y así como no varió nunca su manera de hablar, tampoco ciertas ideas y prácticas del oficio se modificaron. Prevaleció el amaneramiento de decir siempre que los tiempos eran muy malos, pero muy malos; el lamentarse de la desproporción entre sus míseras ganancias y su mucho trabajar; subsistió aquella melosidad de dicción y aquella costumbre de preguntar por la familia siempre que saludaba a alguien, y el decir que no andaba bien de salud, haciendo un mohín de hastío de la vida. Tenía ya la perilla amarillenta, el bigote más negro que blanco, ambos adornos de la cara tan recortaditos, que antes parecían pegados que nacidos allí. Fuera de la ropa, mejorada en calidad, si no en la manera de llevarla, era el mismo que conocimos en case de doña Lupe *la de los pavos;*[19] en su cara la propia confusión extraña de lo militar y lo eclesiástico, el color bilioso, los ojos negros y algo soñadores, el gesto y los modales expresando lo mismo afeminación que hipocresía, la calva

[9] *pueblo,* here, common people
[10] *para de día,* for daytime wear
[11] *que no podía ya con más sebo,* which couldn't possibly be more greasy
[12] *entre semana,* in the middle of the week
[13] *a modo de contrabando,* as if smuggled in
[14] *cosa del otro jueves,* an extraordinary thing
[15] *levantar el gallo,* to speak up
[16] *mal pelaje,* humble clothing
[17] *se tocaba,* freely, the bugle called
[18] *estirar el pie más del largo de la sábana,* to overreach himself
[19] *doña Lupe,* a character in *Fortunata y Jacinta* who was a moneylender, often involved in combinations with Torquemada. She had been a dealer in turkeys, hence the nickname, *la de los pavos.*

más despoblada y más limpia, y todo él craso, resbaladizo y repulsivo, muy pronto siempre, cuando se le saluda, a dar la mano, por cierto bastante sudada.

De la precoz inteligencia de Valentinito estaba tan orgulloso, que no cabía en su pellejo.[20] A medida que el chico avanzaba en sus estudios, don Francisco sentía crecer al amor paterno, hasta llegar a la ciega pasión. En honor del tacaño, debe decirse que, si se conceptuaba reproducido físicamente en aquel pedazo de su propia naturaleza, sentía la superioridad del hijo, y por esto se congratulaba más de haberle dado el ser. Porque Valentinito era el prodigio de los prodigios, un jirón excelso de la Divinidad caído en la tierra. Y Torquemada, pensando en el porvenir, en lo que su hijo había de ser, si viviera, no se conceptuaba digno de haberle engendrado, y sentía ante él la ingénita cortedad de lo que es materia frente a lo que es espíritu.[21]

En lo que digo de las inauditas dotes intelectuales de aquella criatura, no se crea que hay la más mínima exageración. Afirmo con toda ingenuidad que el chico era de lo más estupendo que se puede ver, y que se presentó en el campo de la enseñanza como esos extraordinarios ingenios que nacen de tarde en tarde destinados a abrir nuevos caminos a la humanidad. A más de la inteligencia, que en edad temprana despuntaba en él como aurora de un día espléndido, poseía todos los encantos de la infancia: dulzura, gracejo y amabilidad. El chiquillo, en suma, enamoraba y no es de extrañar que don Francisco y su hija estuvieran loquitos con él. Pasados los primeros años, no fué preciso castigarle nunca, ni aun siquiera reprenderle. Aprendió a leer por arte milagroso, en pocos días, como si lo trajera sabido ya del claustro[22] materno. A los cinco años, sabía muchas cosas que otros chicos aprenden difícilmente a los doce. Un día me hablaron de él dos profesores amigos míos que tienen colegio de primera y segunda enseñanza,[23] lleváronme a verle, y me quedé asombrado. Jamás vi precocidad semejante ni un apuntar de inteligencia tan maravilloso. Porque si algunas respuestas las endilgó de taravilla,[24] demostrando el vigor y riqueza de su memoria, en el tono con que decía otras se echaba de ver cómo comprendía y apreciaba el sentido.

La Gramática la sabía de carretilla; pero la Geografía la dominaba como un hombre. Fuera del terreno escolar, pasmaba ver la seguridad de sus respuestas y observaciones, sin asomos de arrogancia pueril. Tímido y discreto, no parecía comprender que hubiese mérito en las habilidades que lucía, y se asombraba de que se las ponderasen y aplaudiesen tanto. Contáronme que en su casa daba muy poco que hacer. Estudiaba las lecciones con tal rapidez y facilidad, que le sobraba tiempo para sus juegos, siempre muy sosos e inocentes. No le hablaran a él[25] de bajar a la calle para enredar con los chiquillos de la vecindad. Sus travesuras eran pacíficas, y consistieron, hasta los cinco años, en llenar

[20] *que no cabía en su pellejo,* freely, that he almost burst

[21] This sentence expresses the theme of the whole series of Torquemada novels. Besides *Torquemada en la hoguera* Galdós devoted three other novels to the development of the same character and throughout them all Torquemada is the materialist, who achieves great wealth and power, but for whom the realm of the spirit is closed.

[22] *claustro,* here, womb

[23] *colegio de primera y segunda enseñanza; colegio* is a private school, not a college.

[24] *las endilgó de taravilla,* he rattled them off from memory

[25] Understand, *No era necesario que le hablaran a él.*

de monigotes y letras el papel de las habitaciones o arrancarle algún cacho; en echar desde el balcón a la calle una cuerda muy larga con la tapa de una cafetera, arriándola hasta tocar el sombrero de un transeúnte, y recogiéndola después a toda prisa. A obediente y humilde no le ganaba ningún niño, y por tener todas las perfecciones, hasta maltrataba la ropa lo menos que maltratarse puede.

Pero sus inauditas facultades no se habían mostrado todavía: iniciáronse cuando estudió la Aritmética, y se revelaron más adelante en la segunda enseñanza. Ya desde sus primeros años, al recibir las nociones elementales de la ciencia de la cantidad, sumaba y restaba de memoria decenas altas y aun centenas. Calculaba con tino infalible, y su padre mismo, que era un águila para hacer, en el filo de la imaginación,[26] cuentas por la regla de interés, le consultaba no pocas veces. Comenzar Valentín el estudio de las matemáticas de Instituto[27] y revelar de golpe toda la grandeza de su numen aritmético, fué todo uno. No aprendía las cosas, las sabía ya, y el libro no hacía más que despertarle las ideas, abrírselas, digámoslo así, como si fueran capullos que al calor primaveral se despliegan en flores. Para él no había nada difícil, ni problema que le causara miedo. Un día fué el profesor a su padre y le dijo: «Ese niño es cosa inexplicable, señor Torquemada: o tiene el diablo en el cuerpo, o es el pedazo de Divinidad más hermoso que ha caído en la tierra. Dentro de poco no tendré nada que enseñarle. Es Newton resucitado, señor don Francisco; una organización excepcional para las matemáticas, un genio que sin duda se trae fórmulas nuevas debajo del brazo para ensanchar el campo de la ciencia. Acuérdese usted de lo que digo: cuando este chico sea hombre, asombrará y trastornará el mundo.»

Cómo se quedó Torquemada al oír esto, se comprenderá fácilmente. Abrazó al profesor, y la satisfacción le rebosaba por ojos y boca en forma de lágrimas y babas. Desde aquel día, el hombre no cabía en sí: trataba a su hijo, no ya con amor, sino con cierto respeto supersticioso. Cuidaba de él como de un ser sobrenatural, puesto en sus manos por especial privilegio. Vigilaba sus comidas, asustándose mucho si no mostraba apetito; al verle estudiando, recorría las ventanas para que no entrase aire,[28] se enteraba de la temperatura exterior antes de dejarle salir, para determinar si debía ponerse bufanda, o el *carrik* gordo, o las botas de agua; cuando dormía, andaba de puntillas; le llevaba a paseo los domingos, o al teatro; y si el angelito hubiese mostrado afición a juguetes extraños y costosos, Torquemada, vencida su sordidez, se los hubiera comprado. Pero el fenómeno aquél no mostraba afición sino a los libros: leía rápidamente y como por magia, enterándose de cada página en un abrir y cerrar de ojos. Su papá le compró una obra de viajes con mucha estampa de ciudades europeas y de comarcas salvajes. La seriedad del chico pasmaba a todos los amigos de la casa, y no faltó quien dijera de él que parecía un viejo. En cosas de malicia era de una pureza excepcional: no aprendía ningún dicho ni acto feo de los que saben a su edad los retoños desvergonzados de la presente generación. Su inocencia y celestial donosura casi nos permitían conocer a los ángeles como si los hubiéramos tratado, y su reflexión rayaba en lo maravilloso. Otros niños, cuando les preguntan lo que quieren ser, responden que obispos o generales si despuntan por la

[26] *en el filo de la imaginación,* here, mentally

[27] *Instituto,* (public) secondary school

[28] *aire,* here, draft

vanidad; los que pican por la destreza corporal, dicen que cocheros, atletas o payasos de circo; los inclinados a la imitación, actores, pintores . . . Valentinito, al oír la pregunta, alzaba los hombros y no respondía nada. Cuando más, decía «no sé,» y al decirlo, clavaba en su interlocutor una mirada luminosa y penetrante, vago destello del sinfín de ideas que tenía en aquel cerebrazo,[29] y que en su día habían de iluminar toda la tierra.

Mas el *Peor,* aun reconociendo que no había carrera a la altura de su milagroso niño, pensaba dedicarlo a ingeniero, porque la abogacía es cosa de charlatanes. Ingeniero; pero ¿de qué? ¿civil o militar? Pronto notó que a Valentín no le entusiasmaba la tropa, y que, contra la ley general de las aficiones infantiles, veía con indiferencia los uniformes. Pues ingeniero de caminos.[30] Por dictamen del profesor del colegio, fue puesto Valentín, antes de concluir los años del bachillerato,[31] en manos de un profesor de estudios preparatorios para carreras especiales, el cual, luego que tanteó su colosal inteligencia, quedóse atónito, y un día salió asustado, con las manos en la cabeza, y corriendo en busca de otros maestros de matemáticas superiores, les dijo: «Voy a presentarles a ustedes el monstruo[32] de la edad presente.» Y le presentó, y se maravillaron, pues fué el chico a la pizarra, y como quien garabatea por enredar y gastar tiza, resolvió problemas dificilísimos. Luego hizo de memoria diferentes cálculos y operaciones, que aun para los más peritos no son coser y cantar.[33] Uno de aquellos maestrazos, queriendo apurarle, le echó el cálculo de radicales numéricos, y como si le hubieran echado almendras. Lo mismo era para él la raíz *enésima*[34] que para otros dar un par de brincos. Los tíos aquéllos tan sabios se miraban absortos, declarando no haber visto caso ni remotamente parecido.

Era en verdad interesante aquel cuadro, y digno de figurar en los anales de la ciencia: cuatro varones de más de cincuenta años, calvos y medio ciegos de tanto estudiar, maestros de maestros, congregábanse delante de aquel mocoso que tenía que hacer sus cálculos en la parte baja del encerado, y la admiración les tenía mudos y perplejos, pues ya le podían echar dificultades al angelito, que se las bebía como agua. Otro de los examinadores puso las *homologías*[35] creyendo que Valentín estaba raso de ellas;[36] y cuando vieron que no, los tales no pudieron contener su entusiasmo: uno le llamó el Anticristo; otro le cogió en brazos y se lo puso a la pela,[37] y todos se disputaban sobre quién se le llevaría, ansiosos de completar la educación del primer matemático del siglo. Valentín les miraba sin orgullo ni cortedad, inocente y dueño de sí, como Cristo niño entre los doctores.[38]

[29] *cerebrazo,* great brain (augmentative of *cerebro*)
[30] *ingeniero de caminos,* civil engineer. The government school of civil engineering is called *Escuela de Ingenieros de Caminos, Canales y Puertos.*
[31] *bachillerato,* bachelor's degree given on graduation from the *Instituto.* It represents the equivalent of about two years' work in an American college.
[32] *monstruo,* phenomenon, miracle
[33] *coser y cantar,* here, like falling off a log
[34] *la raíz enésima,* the nth root
[35] *homologías,* homologies (corresponding sides of similar triangles)
[36] *estaba raso de ellas,* was ignorant of them
[37] *se lo puso a la pela,* set him on his shoulders
[38] See Luke 2. 41–51. A famous picture, painted by Paolo Veronese, of Jesus amid the learned priests of the Temple is in the Museo del Prado. Galdós may well have had this specific painting in mind as he wrote this passage, for not infrequently he compares his characters or scenes to specific portraits or pictorial compositions. Galdós was himself a good amateur painter and was well acquainted with the artistic productions of past times.

III

Basta de matemáticas, digo yo ahora, pues me urge apuntar que Torquemada vivía en la misma casa de la calle de Tudescos donde le conocimos cuando fué a verle la de Bringas[1] para pedirle no recuerdo qué favor, allá por el 68; y tengo prisa por presentar a cierto sujeto que conozco hace tiempo, y que hasta ahora nunca menté para nada: un don José Bailón, que iba todas las noches a la casa de nuestro don Francisco a jugar con él la partida de damas o de mus, y cuya intervención en mi cuento es necesaria ya para que se desarrolle con lógica. Este señor Bailón es un clérigo que ahorcó los hábitos[2] el 69, en Málaga, echándose a revolucionario y a librecultista con tan furibundo ardor, que ya no pudo volver al rebaño, ni aunque quisiera le habían de admitir.[3] Lo primero que hizo el condenado fué dejarse crecer las barbas,[4] despotricarse[5] en los clubs, escribir tremendas catilinarias contra los de su oficio, y, por fin, operando *verbo et gladio,*[6] se lanzó a las barricadas con un trabuco naranjero[7] que tenía la boca lo mismo que una trompeta. Vencido y dado a los demonios, le catequizaron los protestantes, ajustándole para predicar y dar lecciones en la capilla, lo que él hacía de malísima gana y sólo por el arrastrado garbanzo.[8] A Madrid vino cuando aquella gentil pareja, don Horacio y doña 5 Malvina,[9] puso establecimiento evangélico en Chamberí.[10] Por un regular estipendio, Bailón les ayudaba en los oficios, echando unos sermones agridulces, estrafalarios y fastidiosos. Pero 10 al año de estos tratos, yo no sé lo que pasó . . . ello fué cosa de algún atrevimiento apostólico de Bailón con las neófitas: lo cierto es que doña Malvina, que era persona muy mirada, le 15 dijo en mal español cuatro frescas; intervino don Horacio, denostando también a su coadjutor, y entonces, Bailón, que era hombre de muchísima sal[11] para tales casos, sacó una navaja 20 tamaña como[12] hoy y mañana, y se dejó decir que si no se quitaban de delante les echaba fuera el mondongo.[13] Fué tal el pánico de los pobres ingleses, que echaron a correr 25 pegando gritos y no pararon hasta el tejado. Resumen: que tuvo que abandonar Bailón aquel acomodo, y después de rodar por ahí dando sablazos,[14] fué a parar a la redacción de un 30 periódico muy atrevidillo; como que[15] su misión era echar chinitas de fuego[16] a toda autoridad: a los curas, a los obispos y al mismo Papa. Esto ocurría

[1] *la de Bringas,* the Bringas woman, the title character of an earlier Galdós novel, who, in financial straits caused by her craving for fine clothes, tries unsuccessfully to borrow money from Torquemada.

[2] *ahorcar los hábitos,* to hang up the robes, freely, to give up the priesthood

[3] *ni aunque . . . admitir,* not even if he had wanted, would they have admitted him

[4] *las barbas,* his beard. Since priests were almost the only clean-shaven group in the nineteenth century, he hastens to set himself apart from them.

[5] *despotricarse,* to rave. Political clubs were usually radical and offered a forum for the extreme liberals.

[6] *verbo et gladio,* (Latin) by word and sword, freely, by word and deed

[7] *un trabuco naranjero,* a great big blunderbuss (big enough to take bullets the size of oranges)

[8] *sólo por el arrastrado garbanzo,* just to get his confounded living. *Garbanzos,* chickpeas, are a common ingredient in Spanish cookery, hence, symbolically, *garbanzo* means "food" in general, then "livelihood, living."

[9] *don Horacio y doña Malvina,* English protestant missionaries whom Galdós had already described in *Fortunata y Jacinta*

[10] *Chamberí,* formerly a suburb, north of Madrid, now a part of the city

[11] *sal,* salt, figuratively, wit, cleverness; here the word is used very ironically.

[12] *tamaño como,* as big as

[13] *mondongo,* guts, tripe

[14] *dar sablazos,* to sponge off friends

[15] *como que,* because

[16] *echar chinitas de fuego,* to attack, literally, to throw red-hot pebbles

el 73, y de aquella época datan los opúsculos políticos de actualidad que publicó el clerizonte en el folletín, y de los cuales hizo tiraditas aparte; bobadas escritas en estilo bíblico, y que tuvieron, aunque parezca mentira, sus días de éxito. Como que se vendían bien, y sacaron a su endiablado autor de más de un apuro.

Pero todo aquello pasó, la fiebre revolucionaria, los folletos, y Bailón tuvo que esconderse, afeitándose para disfrazarse y poder huir al extranjero. A los dos años asomó por aquí otra vez, de bigotes larguísimos, aumentados con parte de la barba, como los que gastaba Víctor Manuel;[17] y por si traía o no traía chismes y mensajes de los emigrados, metiéronle mano y le tuvieron en el Saladero[18] tres meses. Al año siguiente, sobreseída la causa,[19] vivía el hombre en Chamberí, y según la cháchara del barrio muy a lo bíblico, amancebado con una viuda rica que tenía rebaño de cabras y además un establecimiento de burras de leche. Cuento todo esto como me lo contaron, reconociendo que en esta parte de la historia partriarcal de Bailón hay gran oscuridad. Lo público y notorio es que la viuda aquélla cascó,[20] que Bailón apareció al poco tiempo con dinero. El establecimiento y las burras y cabras le pertenecían. Arrendólo todo; se fué a vivir al centro de Madrid, dedicándose a *inglés,*[21] y no necesito decir más para que se comprenda de dónde vinieron su conocimiento y tratos con Torquemada, porque bien se ve que éste fué su maestro, le inició en los misterios del oficio, y le manejó parte de sus capitales como había manejado los de doña Lupe *la Magnífica,* más conocida por *la de los pavos.*

Era don José Bailón un animalote de gran alzada, atlético, de formas robustas y muy recalcado de facciones, verdadero y vivo estudio anatómico por su riqueza muscular. Últimamente había dado otra vez en afeitarse; pero no tenía cara de cura, ni de fraile, ni de torero. Era más bien un Dante echado a perder.[22] Dice un amigo mío, que por sus pecados[23] ha tenido que vérselas[24] con Bailón, que éste es el vivo retrato de las sibila de Cumas,[25] pintada por Miguel Ángel, con las demás señoras sibilas y los Profetas en el maravilloso techo de la Capilla Sixtina. Parece, en efecto, una vieja de raza titánica que lleva en su ceño todas las iras celestiales. El perfil de Bailón, y el brazo y pierna, como troncos añosos; el forzudo tórax, y las posturas que sabía tomar, alzando una pataza y enarcando el brazo, le asemejaban a esos figurones que andan por los techos de las catedrales, espatarrados sobre una nube. Lástima que no fuera moda que anduviéramos en cueros, para que luciese en toda su gallardía académica este ángel de cornisa.[26] En la época en que lo presento ahora, pasaba de los cincuenta años.

Torquemada lo estimaba mucho, porque en sus relaciones de negocios, Bailón hacía gala de gran formalidad

[17] *Victor Emmanuel,* king of Italy, was of liberal tendencies, hence, he was imitated by Bailón and other Spanish liberals.

[18] *el Saladero,* the prison of Madrid

[19] *sobreseída la causa,* the case having been dismissed

[20] *cascó,* she broke; here, kicked the bucket

[21] *inglés,* slang for moneylender

[22] He looked like a debauched Dante

[23] *por sus pecados,* to his misfortune

[24] *vérselas,* to have to do

[25] the sibyl (prophetess) of Cumae, whose books of prophecies were kept in a temple of ancient Rome. A painting by Michelangelo in the Sistine Chapel represents her with sunken cheeks and a hooked nose. Galdós had visited Rome three years before writing *Torquemada en la hoguera,* and, as we noted before, he was much interested in painting and sometimes took inspiration in his writing from a work of art.

[26] *ángel de cornisa,* an angel, such as would be sculptured on the cornice of a building; hence, a fine physical specimen

y aun de delicadeza. Y como el clérigo renegado tenía una historia tan variadita y dramática, y sabía contarla con mucho aquél,[27] adornándola con mentiras, don Francisco se embelesaba oyéndole, y en todas las cuestiones de un orden elevado le tenía por oráculo. Don José era de los que con cuatro ideas y pocas más palabras se las componen para aparentar que saben lo que ignoran y deslumbrar a los ignorantes sin malicia. El más deslumbrado era don Francisco, y además el único mortal que leía los folletos bailónicos[28] a los diez años de publicarse; literatura envejecida casi al nacer, y cuyo fugaz éxito no comprendemos sino recordando que la democracia sentimental, a estilo de Jeremías, tuvo también sus quince.[29]

Escribía Bailón aquellas necedades en parrafitos cortos, y a veces rompía con una cosa muy santa; verbigracia: «Gloria a Dios en las alturas y paz,» etc. . . . para salir luego por este registro:

«Los tiempos se acercan, tiempos de redención en que el hijo del Hombre será dueño de la tierra.

«El Verbo depositó hace dieciocho siglos la semilla divina. En noche tenebrosa fructificó. He aquí las flores.

«¿Cómo se llaman? Los derechos del pueblo.»

Y a lo mejor, cuando el lector estaba más descuidado, le soltaba ésta:

«He ahí al tirano. ¡Maldito sea!

«Aplicad el oído y decidme de dónde viene ese rumor vago, confuso, extraño.

«Posad la mano en la tierra y decidme por qué se ha estremecido.

«Es el hijo del Hombre que avanza, decidido a recobrar su primogenitura.

«¿Por qué palidece la faz del tirano? ¡Ah! el tirano ve que sus horas están contadas . . . »

Otras veces empezaba diciendo aquello de: «Joven soldado, ¿adónde vas?» Y por fin, después de mucho marear, quedábase el lector sin saber adónde iba el soldadito, como no fueran todos, autor y público, a Leganés.[30]

Todo esto le parecía de perlas a don Francisco, hombre de escasa lectura. Algunas tardes se iban a pasear juntos los dos tacaños, charla que te charla;[31] y si en negocios era Torquemada la sibila, en otra clase de conocimientos no había más sibila que el señor de Bailón. En política, sobre todo, el exclérigo se las echaba de muy entendido, principiando por decir que ya no le daba la gana de conspirar; como que tenía la olla asegurada y no quería exponer su pelleja para hacer el caldo gordo a cuatro silbantes.[32] Luego pintaba a todos los políticos, desde el más alto al más oscuro, como un atajo de pilletes, y les sacaba la cuenta, al céntimo, de cuanto habían rapiñado . . . Platicaban mucho también de reformas urbanas, y como Bailón había estado en París y Londres, podía comparar. La higiene pública les preocupaba a entrambos: el clérigo le echaba la culpa de todo a los miasmas, y formulaba unas teorías biológicas que eran lo que había que oír. De astronomía y música también se le alcanzaba algo, no era lego en botánica, ni en veterinaria, ni en el arte de escoger melones. Pero en nada lucía tanto su enciclopédico

[27] *aquél,* charm, wit

[28] *bailónico,* of Bailón

[29] *la democracia sentimental:* Bailón wrote his pamphlets in 1873 when the first Spanish republic existed; hence the allusion to democracy. *Tener sus quince,* to have its moment of triumph. (Fifteen was the winning number in a card game.)

[30] *Leganés,* a suburb of Madrid where the insane asylum was located

[31] *charla que te charla,* talking and talking

[32] *hacer el caldo gordo,* to thicken the broth, figuratively, to favor; *cuatro silbantes,* a few dissatisfied people. (*Silbar,* to hiss, to show dissatisfaction)

saber como en cosas de religión. Sus meditaciones y estudios le habían permitido sondear el grande y temerario problema de nuestro destino total. «¿Adónde vamos a parar cuando nos morimos? Pues volvemos a nacer: esto es claro como el agua. Yo me acuerdo —decía mirando fijamente a su amigo y turbándole con el tono solemne que daba a sus palabras—, yo me acuerdo de haber vivido antes de ahora. He tenido en mi mocedad un recuerdo vago de aquella vida, y ahora, a fuerza de meditar, puedo verla clara. Yo fuí sacerdote en Egipto, ¿se entera usted? allá por los años de qué sé yo cuántos . . . sí, señor, sacerdote en Egipto. Me parece que me estoy viendo con una sotana o vestimenta de color de azafrán, y unas al modo de orejeras que me caían por los lados de la cara. Me quemaron vivo, porque . . . verá usted . . . había en aquella iglesia, digo, templo, una sacerdotisita que me gustaba . . . de lo más barbián,[33] ¿se entera usted? . . . ¡y con unos ojos . . . así, y un golpe de caderas,[34] señor don Francisco . . . ! En fin, que aquello se enredó, y la diosa Isis y el buey Apis lo llevaron muy a mal. Alborotóse todo aquel cleriguicio, y nos quemaron vivos a la chavala y a mí . . . Lo que le cuento es verdad, como ése es sol. Fíjese usted bien, amigo; revuelva en su memoria; rebusque bien en el sótano y en los desvanes de su ser, y encontrará la certeza de que también usted ha vivido en tiempos lejanos. Su niño de usted, ese prodigio, debe de haber sido antes el propio Newton, o Galileo, o Euclides. Y por lo que hace a otras cosas, mis ideas son bien claras. Infierno y cielo no existen: papas simbólicas y nada más. Infierno y cielo están aquí. Aquí pagamos tarde o temprano todas las[35] que hemos hecho; aquí recibimos, si no hoy, mañana, nuestro premio, si lo merecemos, y quien dice mañana, dice el siglo que viene . . . Dios, ¡oh! la idea de Dios tiene mucho busilis . . . y para comprenderla hay que devanarse los sesos, como me los he devanado yo, dale que dale[36] sobre los libros, y meditando luego. Pues Dios . . . (poniendo unos ojazos muy reventones y haciendo con ambas manos el gesto expresivo de abarcar un grande espacio) es la Humanidad,[37] la Humanidad, ¿se entera usted? lo cual no quiere decir que deje de ser personal . . . ¿Qué cosa es personal? Fíjese bien. Personal es lo que es uno. Y el gran Conjunto, amigo don Francisco, el gran Conjunto . . . es uno, porque no hay más, y tiene los atributos de un ser infinitamente infinito. Nosotros, en montón, componemos la humanidad: somos los átomos que forman el gran todo; somos parte mínima de Dios, parte minúscula, y nos renovamos como en nuestro cuerpo se renuevan los átomos de la cochina materia . . . ¿se va usted enterando? . . .»

Torquemada no se iba enterando ni poco ni mucho; pero el otro se metía en un laberinto del cual no salía sino callándose. Lo único que don Francisco sacaba de toda aquella monserga, era que *Dios es la Humanidad,* y que la Humanidad es la que nos hace pagar nuestras picardías o nos premia por nuestras buenas obras. Lo demás no lo entendía así le ahorcaran.[38] El sentimiento católico de Tor-

[33] *barbián,* free and easy, forward
[34] *y un golpe de caderas,* and such hips!
[35] *todas las* [*maldades*] *que*
[36] *dale que dale,* literally, hitting and hitting, figuratively, constantly applying myself
[37] "God is Humanity" was the doctrine of some of the philosophical semi-religions of the nineteenth century. Galdós probably was thinking especially of the philosophy of Auguste Comte, who proclaimed "the religion of humanity." Bailón stands for ideas—such as the transmigration of souls—which had wide currency but which Galdós ridicules as extreme and bizarre.
[38] *así le ahorcaran,* even if they were to hang him

quemada no había sido nunca muy vivo. Cierto que en tiempos de doña Silvia iban los dos a misa, por rutina; pero nada más. Pues después de viudo, las pocas ideas del Catecismo que el *Peor* conservaba en su mente, como papeles o apuntes inútiles, las barajó con todo aquel fárrago de la Humanidad-Dios, haciendo un lío de mil demonios.

A decir verdad, ninguna de estas teologías ocupaba largo tiempo el magín del tacaño, siempre atento a la baja realidad de sus negocios. Pero llegó un día, mejor dicho, una noche en que tales ideas hubieron de posesionarse de su mente con cierta tenacidad, por lo que ahorita mismo voy a referir. Entraba mi hombre en su casa al caer de una tarde del mes de febrero, evacuadas mil diligencias con diverso éxito, discurriendo los pasos que daría al día siguiente, cuando su hija, que le abrió la puerta, le dijo estas palabras: «No te asustes, papá, no es nada . . . Valentín ha venido malo de la escuela.»

Las desazones del *monstruo* ponían a don Francisco en gran sobresalto. La que se le anunciaba podía ser insignificante, como otras. No obstante, en la voz de Rufina había cierto temblor, una veladura, un timbre extraño, que dejaron a Torquemada frío y suspenso.

—Yo creo que no es cosa mayor —prosiguió la señorita—. Parece que le dió un vahido. El maestro fué quien lo trajo . . . en brazos.

El *Peor* seguía clavado en el recibimiento, sin acertar a decir nada ni a dar un paso.

—Le acosté en seguida, y mandé un recado a Quevedo para que viniera a escape.

Don Francisco, saliendo de su estupor como si le hubiesen dado un latigazo, corrió al cuarto del chico, a quien vió en el lecho, con tanto abrigo encima que parecía sofocado. Tenía 5 la cara encendida, los ojos dormilones. Su quietud más era de modorra dolorosa que de sueño tranquilo. El padre aplicó su mano a las sienes del inocente monstruo, que abrasaban.

10 —Pero ese trasto de Quevedillo . . . Así reventara[39] . . . No sé en qué piensa . . . Mira, mejor será llamar otro médico que sepa más.

Su hija procuraba tranquilizarle; 15 pero él se resistía al consuelo. Aquel hijo no era un hijo cualquiera, y no podía enfermar sin que se alterara el orden del universo. No probó el afligido padre la comida; no hacía más 20 que dar vueltas por la casa, esperando al maldito médico, y sin cesar iba de su cuarto al del niño, y de aquí al comedor, donde se le presentaba ante los ojos, oprimiéndole el corazón, el 25 encerado en que Valentín trazaba con tiza sus problemas matemáticos. Aún subsistía lo pintado[40] por la mañana: garabatos que Torquemada no entendió, pero que casi le hicieron llorar 30 como una música triste: el signo de raíz, letras por arriba y por abajo, y en otra parte una red de líneas, formando como estrella de muchos picos con numeritos en las puntas.

35 Por fin, alabado sea Dios, llegó el dichoso Quevedito, y don Francisco le echó la correspondiente chillería, pues ya le trataba como a yerno. Visto y examinado el niño, no puso el médico 40 muy buena cara. A Torquemada se le podía ahogar con un cabello, cuando el doctorcillo, arrimándole contra la pared y poniéndole ambas manos en los hombros, le dijo: «No me gusta 45 nada esto; pero hay que esperar a mañana, a ver si brota alguna erupción.

[39] *Así reventara,* So may he burst, freely, May he come to no good

[40] *lo pintado,* here, what had been scribbled

La fiebre es bastante alta. Ya le he dicho a usted que tuviera mucho cuidado con este fenómeno del chico. ¡Tanto estudiar, tanto saber, un desarrollo cerebral disparatado! Lo que hay que hacer con Valentín es ponerle un cencerro al pescuezo, soltarle en el campo en medio de un ganado, y no traerle a Madrid hasta que esté bien bruto.»

Torquemada odiaba el campo y no podía comprender que en él hubiese nada bueno. Pero hizo propósito, si el niño se curaba, de llevarle a una dehesa a que bebiera leche a pasto[41] y respirase aires puros. Los aires puros, bien lo decía Bailón, eran cosa muy buena. ¡Ah! los malditos miasmas tenían la culpa de lo que estaba pasando. Tanta rabia sintió don Francisco, que si coge un miasma en aquel momento lo parte por el eje.[42] Fué la sibila aquella noche a pasar un rato con su amigo, y mira por donde se repitió la matraca[43] de la Humanidad, pareciéndole a Torquemada el clérigo más enigmático y *latero*[44] que nunca, sus brazos más largos, su cara más dura y temerosa. Al quedarse solo, el usurero no se acostó. Puesto que Rufina y Quevedo se quedaban a velar, él también velaría. Contigua a la alcoba del padre estaba la de los hijos, y en ésta el lecho de Valentín, que pasó la noche inquietísimo, sofocado, echando lumbre de su piel, los ojos atónitos y chispeantes, el habla insegura, las ideas desenhebradas, como cuentas de un rosario cuyo hilo se rompe.

IV

El día siguiente fué todo sobresalto y amargura. Quevedo opinó que la enfermedad era *inflamación de las meninges*,[1] y que el chico estaba en peligro de muerte. Esto no se lo dijo al padre, sino a Bailón para que le fuese preparando. Torquemada y él se encerraron, y de la conferencia resultó que por poco se pegan,[2] pues don Francisco, trastornado por el dolor, llamó a su amigo embustero y farsante. El desasosiego, la inquietud nerviosa, el desvarío del tacaño sin ventura, no se pueden describir. Tuvo que salir a varias diligencias de su penoso oficio, y a cada instante tornaba a casa, jadeante, con medio palmo de lengua fuera, el hongo echado hacia atrás. Entraba, daba un vistazo, vuelta a salir.[3] Él mismo traía las medicinas, y en la botica contaba toda la historia . . . «un vahido estando en clase; después calentura horrible . . . ¿para qué sirven los médicos?» Por consejo del mismo Quevedito, mandó venir a uno de los más eminentes, el cual calificó el caso de *meningitis aguda.*

La noche del segundo día, Torquemada, rendido de cansancio, se embutió en uno de los sillones de la sala, y allí se estuvo como media horita, dando vueltas a una pícara idea, ¡ay! dura y con muchas esquinas, que se le había metido en el cerebro. «He faltado a la Humanidad, y esa muy tal y cual[4] me la cobra ahora con los réditos atrasados . . . No: pues si Dios, o quienquiera que sea, me lleva mi hijo, ¡me voy a volver más malo, más perro . . . ! Ya verán entonces lo que es canela fina.[5] Pues no faltaba otra cosa . . . Conmigo no juegan . . . Pero no, ¡qué disparates digo! No me

[41] *a pasto,* abundantly
[42] *si coge . . . lo parte por el eje,* if he were to catch . . . he would break it right in two
[43] *mira por donde se repitió la matraca,* freely, and if he didn't repeat that twaddle
[44] *latero,* slang, annoying

[1] *inflamación de las meninges,* meningitis
[2] *por poco se pegan,* they almost came to blows
[3] *vuelta a salir,* and again he went out
[4] *esa muy tal y cual,* that great so-and-so
[5] *lo que es canela fina,* what is fine conduct (said very ironically)

le quitará, porque yo . . . Eso que dicen de que no he hecho bien a nadie, es mentira. Que me lo prueben . . . porque no basta decirlo. ¿Y los tantísimos a quien he sacado de apuros? . . . ¿pues y eso? Porque si a la Humanidad le han ido con cuentos de mí; que si aprieto, que si no aprieto . . . yo probaré . . . Ea, que ya me voy cargando:[6] si no he hecho ningún bien, ahora lo haré, ahora, pues por algo se ha dicho que nunca para el bien es tarde. Vamos a ver: ¿y si yo me pusiera ahora a rezar, qué dirían allá arriba? Bailón me parece a mí que está equivocado, y la Humanidad no debe de ser Dios, sino la Virgen . . . Claro, es hembra, señora . . . No, no, no . . . no nos fijemos en el materialismo de la palabra. La Humanidad es Dios, la Virgen y todos los santos juntos . . . Tente, hombre, tente, que te vuelves loco . . . Tan sólo saco en limpio que no habiendo buenas obras, todo es, como si dijéramos, basura . . . ¡Ay Dios, qué pena, qué pena . . . ! Si me pones bueno a mi hijo, yo no sé qué cosas haría; ¡pero qué cosas tan magníficas y tan . . . ! ¿Pero quién es el sinvergüenza que dice que no tengo apuntada ninguna buena obra? Es que me quieren perder, me quieren quitar a mi hijo, al que ha nacido para enseñar a todos los sabios y dejarles tamañitos.[7] Y me tienen envidia porque soy su padre, porque de estos huesos y de esta sangre salió aquella gloria del mundo . . . Envidia; pero ¡qué envidiosa es esta puerca Humanidad! Digo, la Humanidad no, porque es Dios . . . los hombres, los prójimos, nosotros, que somos todos muy pillos, y por eso nos pasa lo que nos pasa . . . Bien merecido nos está . . . bien merecido nos está.»

Acordóse entonces de que al día siguiente era domingo y no había extendido los recibos para cobrar los alquileres de su casa. Después de dedicar a esta operación una media hora, descansó algunos ratos, estirándose en el sofá de la sala. Por la mañana, entre nueve y diez, fué a la cobranza dominguera. Con el no comer y el mal dormir y la acerbísima pena que le destrozaba el alma, estaba el hombre *mismamente*[8] del color de una aceituna. Su andar era vacilante, y sus miradas vagaban inciertas, perdidas, tan pronto barriendo el suelo como disparándose a las alturas. Cuando el remendón,[9] que en el sucio portal tenía su taller, vió entrar al casero y reparó en su cara descompuesta y en aquel andar de beodo, asustóse tanto que se le cayó el martillo con que clavaba las tachuelas. La presencia de Torquemada en el patio, que todos los domingos era una desagradabilísma aparición, produjo aquel día verdadero pánico; y mientras algunas mujeres corrieron a refugiarse en sus respectivos aposentos, otras, que debían de ser malas pagadoras, y que observaron la cara que traía la fiera, se fueron a la calle. La cobranza empezó por los cuartos bajos, y pagaron sin chistar el albañil y las dos pitilleras, deseando que se les quitase de delante la aborrecida estampa de don Francisco. Algo desusado y anormal notaron en él, pues tomaba el dinero maquinalmente y sin examinarlo con roñosa nimiedad, como otras veces, cual si tuviera el pensamiento a cien leguas del acto importantísimo que estaba realizando; no se le oían aquellos refunfuños de perro mordelón, ni inspeccionó las habitaciones buscando el baldosín roto o el pedazo de revoco

[6] *me voy cargando,* I'm getting fed up

[7] *dejarles tamañitos,* to leave them so big, freely, to leave them far behind

[8] *mismamente,* substandard speech for *exactamente*

[9] *remendón,* shoe repairer. Shoe repair men often set up their benches in the wide entrance doors of buildings.

[10] *echar los tiempos,* to scold

caído, para echar los tiempos[10] a la inquilina.

Al llegar al cuarto de la Rumalda, planchadora, viuda, con su madre enferma en un camastro y tres niños menores que andaban en el patio enseñando las carnes por los agujeros de la ropa, Torquemada soltó el gruñido de ordenanza, y la pobre mujer, con afligida y trémula voz, cual si tuviera que confesar ante el juez un negro delito, soltó la frase de reglamento: «Don Francisco, por hoy no se puede. Otro día cumpliré.» No puedo dar idea del estupor de aquella mujer y de las dos vecinas, que presentes estaban, cuando vieron que el tacaño no escupió por aquella boca ninguna maldición ni herejía, cuando le oyeron decir con la voz más empañada y llorosa del mundo: «No, hija, si no te digo nada . . . si no te apuro . . . si no me ha pasado por la cabeza reñirte . . . ¡Qué le hemos de hacer, si no puedes . . . !»

—Don Francisco, es que . . . —murmuró la otra, creyendo que la fiera se expresaba con sarcasmo, y que tras el sarcasmo vendría la mordida.

—No, hija, si no he chistado[11] . . . ¿Cómo se han de decir las cosas? Es que a ustedes no hay quien las apee de[12] que yo soy un hombre, como quien dice, tirano . . . ¿De dónde sacáis que no hay en mí compasión, ni . . . ni caridad? En vez de agradecerme lo que hago por vosotras, me calumniáis . . . No, no: entendámonos. Tú, Rumalda, estate tranquila: sé que tienes necesidades, que los tiempos están malos . . . Cuando los tiempos están malos, hija, ¿qué hemos de hacer sino ayudarnos los unos a los otros?

Siguió adelante, y en el principal dió con una inquilina muy mal pagadora, pero de muchísimo corazón para afrontar a la fiera, y así que le vió llegar, juzgando por el cariz que venía más enfurruñado que nunca, salió al encuentro de su aspereza con estas arrogantes expresiones:

—Oiga usté,[13] a mí no me venga con apreturas. Ya sabe que no lo hay. *Ése* está sin trabajo. ¿Quiere que salga a un camino? ¿No ve la casa sin muebles, como un hespital prestao? ¿De dónde quiere que lo saque? . . . Maldita sea su alma . . .

—¿Y quién te dice a ti, grandísima tal,[14] deslenguada y bocona, que yo vengo a sofocarte? A ver si hay alguna tarasca de éstas que sostenga que yo no tengo humanidad. Atrévase a decírmelo . . .

Enarboló el garrote, símbolo de su autoridad y de su mal genio, y en el corrillo que se había formado sólo se veían bocas abiertas y miradas de estupefacción.

—Pues a ti y a todas les digo que no me importa un rábano que no me paguéis hoy. ¡Vaya! ¿Cómo lo he de decir para que lo entiendan? . . . ¡Conque estando tu marido sin trabajar te iba yo a poner el dogal al cuello? . . . Yo sé que me pagarás cuando puedas, ¿verdad? Porque lo que es intención de pagar, tú la tienes. Pues entonces, ¿a qué tanto enfurruñarse? . . . ¡Tontas, malas cabezas! (esforzándose en producir una sonrisa); ¡vosotras creyéndome a mí más duro que las peñas, y yo dejándooslo creer, porque me convenía, porque me convenía, claro, pues Dios manda que no echemos facha con[15] nuestra hu-

[11] *no he chistado,* I haven't said a word

[12] *no hay quien las apee de,* there's no one who can make you stop thinking

[13] In this speech Galdós imitates the language of the common people. *Usté* for *usted; ése* for *mi marido; hespital prestao* for *hospital prestado,* more commonly *hospital robado,* a poorly furnished dwelling. *¿Quiere que salga a un camino?* Do you want him to become a highway robber?

[14] *grandísima tal,* you great big so-and-so

[15] *que no echemos facha con,* that we shouldn't make a show of

manidad . . . ! Vaya, que sois todas unos grandísimos peines[16] . . . Abur, tú, no te sofoques. Y no creas que hago esto para que me eches bendiciones. Pero conste que no te ahogo; y para que veas lo bueno que soy . . .

Se detuvo y meditó un momento, llevándose la mano al bolsillo y mirando al suelo.

—Nada, nada . . . Quédate con Dios.

Y a otra. Cobró en las tres puertas siguientes sin ninguna dificultad. «Don Francisco, que me ponga usted piedra nueva en la hornilla, que aquí no se puede guisar . . .» En otras circunstancias, esta reclamación habría sido el principio de una chillería tremenda, verbigracia: «Pon el trasponTín en la hornilla, sinvergüenza, y arma el fuego encima» «Miren el tío manguitillas, así se le vuelvan veneno los cuartos.»[17] Pero aquel día todo era paz y concordia, y Torquemada concedía cuanto le demandaban.

—¡Ay, don Francisco! —le dijo otra en el número 11—, tenga los jeringados cincuenta reales. Para poderlos juntar, no hemos comido más que dos cuartos de gallineja y otros dos de hígado con pan seco . . . Pero por no verle el carácter de esa cara y no oírle, me mantendría yo con puntas de París.[18]

—Pues mira, eso es un insulto, una injusticia, porque si las he sofocado otras veces no ha sido por el materialismo del dinero, sino porque me gusta ver cumplir a la gente . . . para que no se diga . . . Debe haber dignidad en todos. ¡A fe que tienes buena idea de mí! . . . ¿Iba yo a consentir que tus hijos, estos borregos de Dios, tuviesen hambre? . . . Deja, déjate el dinero . . . O mejor, para que no lo tomes a desaire partámoslo y quédate con veinticinco reales . . . Ya me los darás otro día . . . ¡Bribonazas, cuando debíais confesar que soy para vosotras como un padre, me tacháis de inhumano y de qué sé yo qué! No, yo les aseguro a todas que respeto a la humanidad, que la considero, que la estimo, que ahora y siempre haré todo el bien que pueda y un poquito más . . . ¡Hala!

Asombro, confusión. Tras de él iba el parlero grupo, chismorreando así: «A este condenado le ha pasado algún desvío . . . Don Francisco no está bueno de la cafetera.[19] Mirad qué cara de patíbulo se ha traído. ¡Don Francisco con humanidad! Ahí tenéis por qué está saliendo todas las noches en el cielo esa estrella con rabo. Es que el mundo se va a acabar.»

En el número 16:

—Pero hija de mi alma, so tunanta,[20] ¿tenías a tu niña mala y no me habías dicho nada? ¿Pues para qué estoy yo en el mundo? Francamente, eso es un agravio que no te perdono, no te lo perdono. Eres una indecente; y en prueba de que no tienes ni pizca de sentido, ¿apostamos a que no adivinas lo que voy a hacer? ¿Cuánto va a que[21] no lo adivinas? . . . Pues voy a darte para que pongas un puchero . . . ¡ea! Toma, y dí ahora que yo no tengo humanidad. Pero sois tan mal agradecidas, que me pondréis como chupa de dómine,[22] y hasta puede que me echéis alguna maldición. Abur.

En el cuarto de la señá Casiana, una vecina se aventuró a decirle: «Don Francisco, a nosotras no nos la da usted[23] . . . A usted le pasa algo.

[16] *peine,* sly rascal

[17] *el tío manguitillas, así se le vuelvan veneno los cuartos,* the crafty old fellow, may his money turn to poison for him

[18] *puntas de París,* wire nails

[19] *cafetera,* coffee pot; slang for head

[20] *so tunanta,* you rascal. *So* reinforces an insult: *so animal, so bruto.*

[21] *¿Cuánto va a que,* how much do you bet?

[22] *poner como chupa de dómine,* to say all sorts of bad things about a person; to lay out in lavender

[23] *no nos la da usted,* you're not fooling us

¿Qué demonios tiene en esa cabeza o en ese corazón de cal y canto?»[24]

Dejóse el afligido casero caer en una silla, y quitándose el hongo se pasó la mano por la amarilla frente y la calva sebosa, diciendo tan sólo entre suspiros: «¡No es de cal y canto, puñales, no es de cal y canto!»

Como observasen que sus ojos se humedecían, y que, mirando al suelo, y apoyado con ambas manos en el bastón, cargaba sobre éste todo el peso del cuerpo, meciéndose, le instaron para que se desahogara; pero él no debió creerlas dignas de ser confidentes de su inmensa, desgarradora pena. Tomando el dinero, dijo con voz cavernosa: «Si no lo tuvieras, Casiana, lo mismo sería. Repito que yo no ahogo al pobre . . . como que yo también soy pobre . . . Quien dijese,[25] (levantándose con zozobra y enfado) que soy inhumano, miente más que la *Gaceta*.[26] Yo soy humano; yo compadezco a los desgraciados; yo les ayudo en lo que puedo, porque así nos lo manda la Humanidad; y bien sabéis todas que como faltéis a la Humanidad, lo pagaréis tarde o temprano, y que si sois buenas tendréis vuestra recompensa. Yo os juro por esa imagen de la Virgen de las Angustias con el Hijo muerto en los brazos (señalando una lámina), yo os juro que si no os he parecido caritativo y bueno, no quiere esto decir que no lo sea, ¡puñales! y que si son menester pruebas, pruebas se darán. Dale,[27] que no lo creen . . . pues váyanse todas con doscientos mil pares de demonios, que a mí, con ser bueno me basta . . . No necesito que nadie me dé bombo.[28] Piojosas, para nada quiero vuestras gratitudes . . . Me paso por las narices vuestras bendiciones.»[29]

Dicho esto salió de estampía. Todas le miraban por la escalera abajo, y por el patio adelante, y por el portal afuera, haciendo unos gestos tales que parecía el mismo demonio persignándose.

V

Corrió hacia su casa, y contra su costumbre (pues era hombre que comúnmente prefería despernarse a gastar una peseta), tomó un coche para llegar más pronto. El corazón dió en decirle que encontraría buenas noticias, el enfermo aliviado, la cara de Rufina sonriente al abrir la puerta; y en su impaciencia loca, parecíale que el carruaje no se movía, que el caballo cojeaba y que el cochero no sacudía bastantes palos[1] al pobre animal . . . «Arrea, hombre. ¡Maldito jaco! Leña en él[2]—le gritaba—. Mira que tengo mucha prisa.»

Llegó por fin; y al subir jadeante la escalera de su casa, razonaba sus esperanzas de esta manera: «No salgan ahora diciendo que es por mis maldades, pues de todo hay . . .» ¡Qué desengaño al ver la cara de Rufina tan triste, y al oír aquel *lo mismo, papá*, que sonó en sus oídos como fúnebre campanada! Acercóse de puntillas al enfermo y le examinó. Como el pobre niño se hallara en aquel momento amodorrado, pudo don Francisco observarle con relativa calma, pues cuando deliraba y quería echarse del lecho, revolviendo en torno los espantados ojos, el padre no tenía valor para presenciar tan doloroso espectáculo y huía de la alcoba trémulo y despa-

[24] *corazón de cal y canto,* flinty heart; *cal y canto,* literally, mortar and building stone
[25] *Quien dijese,* Whoever says
[26] *la Gaceta,* the Gazette, the official government newspaper, often suspected of altering facts to suit its policies
[27] *Dale,* Go on
[28] *dar bombo,* to build someone up, enhance one's reputation
[29] *Me paso por las narices vuestras bendiciones,* I don't give a hang for your blessings
[1] *no sacudía bastantes palos,* didn't whip [the animal] enough
[2] *Leña en él,* Give him the stick, Whip him

vorido. Era hombre que carecía de valor para afrontar penas de tal magnitud, sin duda por causa de su deficiencia moral; se sentía medroso, consternado, y como responsable de tanta desventura y dolor tan grande. Seguro de la esmeradísima asistencia de Rufina, ninguna falta hacía el afligido padre junto al lecho de Valentín: al contrario, más bien era estorbo, pues si le asistiera, de fijo, en su turbación, equivocaría las medicinas, dándole a beber algo que acelerara su muerte. Lo que hacía era vigilar sin descanso, acercarse a menudo a la puerta de la alcoba, y ver lo que ocurría, oír la voz del niño delirando o quejándose; pero si los ayes eran muy lastimeros y el delirar muy fuerte, lo que sentía Torquemada era un deseo instintivo de echar a correr y ocultarse con su dolor en el último rincón del mundo.

Aquella tarde le acompañaron un rato Bailón, el carnicero de abajo, el sastre del principal y el fotógrafo de arriba, esforzándose todos en consolarle con las frases de reglamento; mas no acertando Torquemada a sostener la conversación sobre tema tan triste les daba las gracias con desatenta sequedad. Todo se le volvía suspirar con bramidos, pasearse a trancos, beber buches de agua y dar algún puñetazo en la pared. ¡Tremendo caso aquél! ¡Cuántas esperanzas desvanecidas . . . ! ¡Aquella flor del mundo segada y marchita! Esto era para volverse loco. Más natural sería el desquiciamiento universal, que la muerte del portentoso niño que había venido a la tierra para iluminarla con el fanal de su talento . . . ¡Bonitas cosas hacía Dios, la Humanidad, o quienquiera que fuese el muy tal y cual que inventó el mundo y nos puso en él! Porque si habían de llevarse a Valentín, ¿para qué le trajeron acá, dándole a él, al buen Torquemada, el privilegio de engendrar tamaño prodigio? ¡Bonito negocio hacía la Providencia, la Humanidad, o el arrastrado Conjunto, como decía Bailón! ¡Llevarse al niño aquél, lumbrera de la ciencia, y dejar acá todos los tontos! ¿Tenía esto sentido común? ¿No había motivo para rebelarse contra los de arriba, ponerles como ropa de pascua y mandarles a paseo . . . ?[3] Si Valentín se moría, ¿qué quedaba en el mundo? Oscuridad, ignorancia. Y para el padre, ¡qué golpe! ¡Porque figurémonos todos lo que sería don Francisco cuando su hijo, ya hombre, empezase a figurar, a confundir a todos los sabios, a volver patas arriba[4] la ciencia toda . . . ! Torquemada sería en tal caso la segunda persona de la Humanidad: y sólo por la gloria de haber engendrado al gran matemático, sería cosa de plantarle en un trono. ¡Vaya un ingeniero que sería Valentín si viviese! Como que había de hacer unos ferrocarriles que irían de aquí a Pekín en cinco minutos, y globos para navegar por los aires, y barcos para andar por debajito del agua, y otras cosas nunca vistas ni siquiera soñadas. ¡Y el planeta se iba a perder estas gangas por una estúpida sentencia de los que dan y quitan la vida . . . ! Nada, nada, envidia pura, envidia. Allá arriba, en las invisibles cavidades de los altos cielos, alguien se había propuesto *fastidiar* a Torquemada. Pero . . . pero . . . ¿y si no fuese envidia, sino castigo? ¿Si se había dispuesto así para anonadar al tacaño cruel, al casero tiránico, al prestamista sin entrañas? ¡Ah! cuando esta idea entraba en turno, Torquemada sentía impulsos de correr hacia la pared más próxima y estrellarse contra ella.

[3] *ponerles como ropa de pascua y mandarles a paseo,* to give them a good bawling out and to tell them to beat it

[4] *volver patas arriba,* to turn upside down

Pronto se reaccionaba y volvía sobre sí. No, no podía ser castigo, porque él no era malo, y si lo fué, ya se enmendaría. Era envidia, tirria y malquerencia que le tenían, por ser autor de tan soberana eminencia. Querían truncarle su porvenir y arrebatarle aquella alegría y fortuna inmensa de sus últimos años . . . Porque su hijo, si viviese, había de ganar muchísimo dinero, pero muchísimo, y de aquí la celestial intriga. Pero él (lo pensaba lealmente) renunciaría a las ganancias pecuniarias del hijo, con tal que le dejaran la gloria, ¡la gloria! pues para negocios, le bastaba con los suyos propios . . . El último paroxismo de su exaltada mente fué renunciar a todo el *materialismo* de la ciencia del niño, con tal que le dejasen la gloria.

Cuando se quedó solo con él, Bailón le dijo que era preciso tuviese filosofía; y como Torquemada no entendiese bien el significado y aplicación de tal palabra, explanó la sibila su idea en esta forma: «Conviene resignarse, considerando nuestra pequeñez ante estas grandes evoluciones de la materia . . . pues, o substancia vital. Somos átomos, amigo don Francisco, nada más que unos tontos de átomos.[5] Respetemos las disposiciones del grandísimo Todo a que pertenecemos, y vengan penas. Para eso está la filosofía, o si se quiere, la religión: para hacer pecho a la adversidad. Pues si no fuera así, no podríamos vivir.» Todo lo aceptaba Torquemada menos resignarse. No tenía en su alma la fuente de donde tal consuelo pudiera salir, y ni siquiera lo comprendía. Como el otro, después de haber comido bien, insistiera en aquellas ideas, a don Francisco se le pasaron ganas de darle un par de trompadas, destruyendo en un punto el perfil más enérgico que dibujara[6] Miguel Ángel. Pero no hizo más que mirarle con ojos terroríficos, y el otro se asustó y puso punto en[7] sus teologías.

A prima noche, Quevedito y el otro médico hablaron a Torquemada en términos desconsoladores. Tenían poca o ninguna esperanza, aunque no se atrevían a decir en absoluto que la habían perdido, y dejaban abierta la puerta a las reparaciones de la naturaleza y a la misericordia de Dios. Noche horrible fué aquélla. El pobre Valentín se abrasaba en invisible fuego. Su cara encendida y seca, sus ojos iluminados por esplendor siniestro, su inquietud ansiosa, sus bruscos saltos en el lecho, cual si quisiera huir de algo que le asustaba, eran espectáculo tristísimo que oprimía el corazón. Cuando don Francisco, transido de dolor, se acercaba a la abertura de las entornadas batientes de la puerta y echaba hacia adentro una mirada tímida, creía escuchar, con la respiración premiosa del niño, algo como el chirrido de su carne tostándose en el fuego de la calentura. Puso atención a las expresiones incoherentes del delirio, y le oyó decir: «*Equis elevado al cuadrado, menos uno, partido por*[8] *dos, más cinco equis menos dos, partido por cuatro, igual equis por*[9] *equis más dos, partido por doce . . . Papá, papá, la característica del logaritmo de un entero tiene tantas unidades menos una como . . .*» Ningún tormento de la Inquisición iguala al que sufría Torquemada oyendo estas cosas. Eran las pavesas del asombroso entendimiento de su hijo, revolando sobre las llamas en que éste se consumía. Huyó de allí por no oír la dulce vocecita, y estuvo más de media hora echado en el sofá de la sala, agarrándose con ambas manos la cabeza como si se le quisiese escapar. De improviso se le-

[5] *unos tontos de átomos,* some dumb atoms
[6] *dibujara,* had drawn
[7] *puso punto en,* brought an end to
[8] *partido por,* divided by
[9] *por,* times

vantó, sacudido por una idea; fué al escritorio donde tenía el dinero; sacó un cartucho de monedas que debían de ser calderilla, y vaciándoselo en el bolsillo del pantalón, púsose capa y sombrero, cogió el llavín, y a la calle.

Salió como si fuera en persecución de un deudor. Después de mucho andar, parábase en una esquina, miraba con azoramiento a una parte y otra, y vuelta a correr calle adelante, con paso de inglés tras de su víctima. Al compás de la marcha, sonaba en la pierna derecha el retintín de las monedas . . . Grandes eran su impaciencia y desazón por no encontrar aquella noche lo que otras le salía tan a menudo al paso, molestándole y aburriéndole. Por fin . . . gracias a Dios . . . acercósele un pobre. «Toma hombre, toma: ¿dónde diablos os metéis esta noche? Cuando no hacéis falta, salís como moscas, y cuando se os busca para socorreros, nada . . .» Apareció luego uno de esos mendigos decentes que piden, sombrero en mano, con lacrimosa cortesía. «Señor, un pobre cesante.» — Tenga, tenga más. Aquí estamos los hombres caritativos para acudir a las miserias . . . Dígame: ¿no me pidió usted noches pasadas? Pues sepa que no le di porque iba muy de prisa. Y la otra noche y la otra, tampoco le di porque no llevaba suelto: lo que es voluntad la tuve, bien que la tuve. — Claro es que el cesante pordiosero se quedaba viendo visiones, y no sabía cómo expresar su gratitud. Más allá, salió de un callejón la fantasma. Era una mujer que pide en la parte baja de la calle de la Salud,[10] vestida de negro, con un velo espesísimo que le tapa la cara. «Tome, tome, señora . . . Y que me digan ahora que yo jamás he dado una limosna. ¿Le parece a usted qué calumnia?[11] Vaya, que ya habrá usted reunido bastantes cuartos esta noche. Como que hay quien dice que pidiendo así, y con ese velo por la cara, ha reunido usted un capitalito. Retírese ya, que hace mucho frío . . . y ruegue a Dios por mí.» En la calle del Carmen, en la de Preciados y Puerta del Sol, a todos los chiquillos que salían dió su perro por barba.[12] «¡Eh! niño, ¿tú pides o qué haces ahí, como un bobo?» Esto se lo dijo a un chicuelo que estaba arrimado a la pared, con las manos a la espalda, descalzos los pies, el pescuezo envuelto en una bufanda. El muchacho alargó la mano aterida. «Toma . . . Pues qué, ¿no te decía el corazón que yo había de venir a socorrerte? ¿Tienes frío y hambre? Toma más, y lárgate a tu casa, si la tienes. Aquí estoy yo para sacarte de un apuro; digo, para partir contigo un pedazo de pan, porque yo también soy pobre y más desgraciado que tú, ¿sabes? porque el frío, el hambre, se soportan; pero ¡ay! otras cosas . . .» Apretó el paso sin reparar en la cara burlona de su favorecido, y siguió dando, dando, hasta que le quedaron pocas piezas en el bolsillo. Corriendo hacia su casa, en retirada, miraba al cielo, cosa en él muy contraria a la costumbre, pues si alguna vez lo miró para enterarse del tiempo, jamás, hasta aquella noche, lo había contemplado. ¡Cuantísima estrella! Y qué claras y resplandecientes, cada una en su sitio, hermosas y graves, millones de millones de miradas que no aciertan a ver nuestra pequeñez. Lo que más suspendía el ánimo del tacaño era la idea de que todo aquel cielo estuviese indiferente a su gran dolor, o más bien ignorante de él. Por lo de-

[10] *calle de la Salud.* Torquemada is walking toward the center of the city, la Puerta del Sol. Galdós traces his route via streets between his home and the center.

[11] *¿Le parece a usted qué calumnia?* Don't you think that's a great slander?

[12] *perro por barba,* a penny apiece

más, como bonitas, ¡vaya si eran bonitas[13] las estrellas! Las había chicas, medianas y grandes; algo así como pesetas, medios duros y duros. Al insigne prestamista le pasó por la cabeza lo siguiente: «Como se ponga bueno, me ha de ajustar[14] esta cuenta: si acuñáramos todas las estrellas del cielo, ¿cuánto producirían al 5 por 100 de interés compuesto en los siglos que van desde que todo eso existe?»

Entró en su casa cerca de la una, sintiendo algún alivio en las congojas de su alma; se adormeció vestido, y a la mañana del día siguiente la fiebre de Valentín había remitido bastante. ¿Habría esperanzas? Los médicos no las daban sino muy vagas, y subordinando su fallo al recargo de la tarde. El usurero, excitadísimo, se abrazó a tan débil esperanza como el náufrago se agarra a la flotante astilla. Viviría, ¡pues no había de vivir!

—Papá—le dijo Rufina llorando—, pídeselo a la Virgen del Carmen, y déjate de Humanidades.

—¿Crees tú . . . ? Por mí no ha de quedar. Pero te advierto que no habiendo buenas obras no hay que fiarse de la Virgen. Y acciones cristianas habrá, cueste lo que cueste:[15] yo te lo aseguro. En las obras de misericordia está todo el intríngulis.[16] Yo vestiré desnudos, visitaré enfermos, consolaré tristes . . . Bien sabe Dios que ésa es mi voluntad, bien lo sabe . . . No salgamos después con la peripecia de que no lo sabía . . . Digo, como saberlo, lo sabe . . . Falta que quiera.

Vino por la noche el recargo, muy fuerte. Los calomelanos y revulsivos[17] no daban resultado alguno. Tenía el pobre niño las piernas abrasadas a sinapismos,[18] y la cabeza hecha una lástima con las embrocaciones[19] para obtener la erupción[20] artificial. Cuando Rufina le cortó el pelito por la tarde, con objeto de despejar el cráneo, Torquemada oía los tijeretazos como si se los dieran a él en el corazón. Fué preciso comprar más hielo para ponérselo en vejigas[21] en la cabeza, y después hubo que traer el iodoformo; recados que el *Peor* desempeñaba con ardiente actividad, saliendo y entrando cada poco tiempo. De vuelta a casa, ya anochecido, encontró, al doblar la esquina de la calle de Hita,[22] un anciano mendigo y haraposo, con pantalones de soldado, la cabeza al aire, un andrajo de chaqueta por los hombros, y mostrando el pecho desnudo. Cara más venerable no se podía encontrar sino en las estampas del *Año cristiano*.[23] Tenía la barba erizada y la frente llena de arrugas, como San Pedro; el cráneo terso, y dos rizados mechones blancos en las sienes. «Señor, señor —decía con el temblor de un frío intenso—, mire cómo estoy, míreme.» Torquemada pasó de largo, y se detuvo a poca distancia; volvió hacia atrás, estuvo un rato vacilando, y al fin siguió su camino. En el cerebro le fulguró esta idea: «Si conforme traigo la capa nueva, trajera la vieja . . .»[24]

VI

Y al entrar en su casa:

[13] *como bonitas, vaya si eran bonitas,* as for pretty, they certainly were pretty
[14] *me ha de ajustar,* he [Valentín] is going to have to calculate this account for me
[15] *cueste lo que cueste,* cost what it may
[16] *está todo el intríngulis,* is the whole heart of the matter
[17] *calomelanos y revulsivos,* calomels and revulsives (medicines)
[18] *sinapismo,* poultice
[19] *embrocación,* embrocation, lotion
[20] *erupción,* eruption, rash
[21] *vejiga,* bladder; here, ice bag
[22] *calle de Hita,* a short street leading into the *calle de Tudescos.* Torquemada is almost home.
[23] *Año cristiano,* an almanac which gives the saints' days and has sentimentally idealized pictures of saints
[24] *«Si conforme traigo la capa nueva, trajera la vieja,»* 'If, instead of my new cape, I were wearing my old one'

—¡Maldito de mí! No debí dejar escapar aquel acto de cristiandad.

Dejó la medicina que traía, y cambiando de capa, volvió a echarse a la calle. Al poco rato, Rufinita, viéndole entrar en cuerpo, le dijo asustada:

—Pero, papá, ¡cómo tienes la cabeza . . . ! ¿En dónde has dejado la capa?

—Hija de mi alma —contestó el tacaño bajando la voz y poniendo una cara muy compungida—, tú no comprendes lo que es un buen rasgo de caridad, de humanidad . . . ¿Preguntas por la capa? Ahí te quiero ver[1] . . . Pues se la he dado a un pobre viejo, casi desnudo y muerto de frío. Yo soy así: no ando con bromas cuando me compadezco del pobre. Podré parecer duro algunas veces; pero como me ablande . . . Veo que te asustas. ¿Qué vale un triste pedazo de paño?

—¿Era la nueva?

—No, la vieja . . . Y ahora, créemelo, me remuerde la conciencia por no haberle dado la nueva . . . y se me alborota también por habértelo dicho. La caridad no se debe pregonar.

No se habló más de aquello, porque de cosas más graves debían ambos ocuparse. Rendida de cansancio, Rufina no podía ya con su cuerpo:[2] cuatro noches hacía que no se acostaba; pero su valeroso espíritu la sostenía siempre en pie, diligente y amorosa como una hermana de la caridad. Gracias a la asistencia que tenían en casa, la señorita podía descansar algunos ratos; y para ayudar a la asistenta en los trabajos de la cocina, quedábase allí por las tardes la trapera de la casa, viejecita que recogía las basuras y los pocos desperdicios de la comida, *ab initio,*[3] o sea desde que Torquemada y doña Silvia se casaron, y lo mismo había hecho en la casa de los padres de doña Silvia. Llamábanla la *tía Roma,* no sé por qué (me inclino a creer que este nombre es corrupción de Jerónima), y era tan vieja, tan vieja y tan fea, que su cara parecía un puñado de telarañas revueltas con ceniza; su nariz de corcho ya no tenía forma; su boca redonda y sin dientes, menguaba o crecía, según la distensión de las arrugas que la formaban. Más arriba, entre aquel revoltijo de piel polvorosa, lucían los ojos de pescado, dentro de un cerco de pimentón húmedo. Lo demás de la persona desaparecía bajo un envoltorio de trapos y dentro de la remendada falda, en la cual había restos de un traje de la madre de doña Silvia, cuando era polla. Esta pobre mujer tenía gran apego a la casa, cuyas barreduras había recogido diariamente durante luengos años; tuvo en gran estimación a doña Silvia, la cual nunca quiso dar a nadie más que a ella los huesos, mendrugos y piltrafas sobrantes, y amaba entrañablemente a los niños, principalmente a Valentín, delante de quien se prosternaba con admiración supersticiosa. Al verle con aquella enfermedad tan mala, que era, según ella una reventazón del talento en la cabeza, la tía Roma no tenía sosiego: iba mañana y tarde a enterarse; penetraba en la alcoba del chico, y permanecía largo rato sentada junto al lecho, mirándole silenciosa, sus ojos como dos fuentes inagotables que inundaban de lágrimas los flaccidos pergaminos de la cara y pescuezo.

Salió la trapera del cuarto para volverse a la cocina, y en el comedor se encontró al amo que, sentado junto a la mesa y de bruces en ella, parecía entregarse a profundas meditaciones. La tía Roma, con el largo trato y su metimiento en la familia, se tomaba

[1] *Ahí te quiero ver,* I'd like to see you in my place

[2] *no podía ya con su cuerpo,* could hardly move

[3] *ab initio,* (Latin) from the beginning

confianzas con él . . . «Rece, rece—le dijo, poniéndose delante y dando vueltas al pañuelo con que pensaba enjugar el llanto caudaloso—, rece, que buena falta le hace . . . ¡Pobre hijo de mis entrañas, qué malito está . . . ! Mire, mire (señalando al encerado) las cosas tan guapas que escribió en ese bastidor negro. Yo no entiendo lo que dice . . . pero a cuenta que dirá[4] que debemos ser buenos . . . ¡Sabe más ese ángel . . . ! Como que por eso Dios no nos le quiere dejar . . .»

—¿Qué sabes tú, tía Roma? —dijo Torquemada poniéndose lívido—. Nos le dejará. ¿Acaso piensas tú que yo soy tirano y perverso, como creen los tontos y algunos perdidos, malos pagadores . . . ? Si uno se descuida, le forman la reputación más perra del mundo . . . Pero Dios sabe la verdad . . . Si he hecho o no he hecho caridades en estos días, eso no es cuenta de nadie: no me gusta que me averigüen y pongan en carteles mis buenas acciones . . . Reza tú también, reza mucho hasta que se te seque la boca, que tú debes de ser allá muy bien mirada, porque en tu vida[5] has tenido una peseta . . . Yo me vuelvo loco, y me pregunto qué culpa tengo yo de haber ganado algunos jeringados reales . . . ¡Ay, tía Roma, si vieras cómo tengo mi alma! Pídele a Dios que se nos conserve Valentín, porque si se nos muere, yo no sé lo que pasará: yo me volveré loco, saldré a la calle y mataré a alguien. Mi hijo es mío, ¡puñales! y la gloria del mundo. ¡Al que me le quite . . . !

—¡Ay qué pena! —murmuró la vieja ahogándose—. Pero quién sabe . . . puede que la Virgen haga el milagro . . . Yo se lo estoy pidiendo con muchísima devoción. Empuje usted por su lado, y prometa ser tan siquiera regular.[6]

—Pues por prometido no quedará . . . Tía Roma, déjame . . . déjame solo. No quiero ver a nadie. Me entiendo mejor solo con mi afán.

La anciana salió gimiendo, y don Francisco, puestas las manos sobre la mesa, apoyó en ellas su frente ardorosa. Así estuvo no sé cuánto tiempo, hasta que le hizo variar de postura su amigo Bailón, dándole palmadas en el hombro y diciéndole: «No hay que amilanarse. Pongamos cara de baqueta[7] a la desgracia, y no permitamos que nos acoquine la muy . . . Déjese para las mujeres la cobardía. Ante la Naturaleza, ante el sublime Conjunto, somos unos pedazos de átomos que no sabemos de la misa la media.»[8]

Váyase usted al rábano[9] con sus Conjuntos y sus papas,—le dijo Torquemada echando lumbre por los ojos.

Bailón no insistió; y juzgando que lo mejor era distraerle, apartando su pensamiento de aquellas sombrías tristezas, pasado un ratito le habló de cierto negocio que traía en la mollera. Como quiera que[10] el arrendatario de sus ganados asnales y cabríos hubiese rescindido el contrato, Bailón decidió explotar aquella industria en gran escala, poniendo un gran establecimiento de leches a estilo moderno con servicio puntual a domicilio, precios arreglados, local elegante, teléfono, etc. . . . Lo había estudiado, y . . . «Créame usted amigo don Francisco, es un negocio seguro, mayormente si añadimos el ramo de vacas, porque en Madrid las leches . . .»

—Déjeme usted a mí de leches y de . . . ¿Qué tengo yo que ver con burras ni con vacas? —gritó el *Peor* ponién-

[4] *a cuenta que dirá,* apparently he must say
[5] *en tu vida,* never in your life
[6] *tan siquiera regular,* at least reasonably good
[7] *cara de baqueta,* a stern face
[8] *no sabemos de la misa la media,* we don't know the half of it
[9] *Váyase usted al rábano,* Go to the dickens
[10] *Como quiera que,* As, Since

dose en pie y mirándole con desprecio—. Me ve cómo estoy, ¡puñales! muerto de pena, y me viene a hablar de la condenada leche . . . Hábleme de cómo se consigue que Dios nos haga caso cuando pedimos lo que necesitamos, hábleme de lo que . . . no sé cómo explicarlo . . . de lo que significa ser bueno y ser malo . . . porque, o yo soy un zote, o ésta es de las cosas que tienen más busilis[11] . . .

—¡Vaya si lo tienen, vaya si lo tienen, carambita! —dijo la sibila con expresión de suficiencia, moviendo la cabeza y entornando los ojos.

En aquel momento tenía el hombre actitud muy diferente de la de su similar en la Capilla Sixtina: sentado, las manos sobre el puño del bastón, éste entre las piernas, las piernas dobladas con igualdad, el sombrero caído para atrás,[12] el cuerpo atlético desfigurado dentro del gabán de solapas aceitosas, los hombros y cuello plagados de caspa. Y sin embargo de estas prosas, el muy arrastrado se parecía al Dante y ¡había sido sacerdote en Egipto! Cosas de la pícara humanidad . . .

—Vaya si lo tienen—repitió la sibila, preparándose a ilustrar a su amigo con una opinión cardinal—. ¡Lo bueno y lo malo . . . como quien dice, luz y tinieblas!

Bailón hablaba de muy distinta manera de como escribía. Esto es muy común. Pero aquella vez la solemnidad del caso exaltó tanto su magín, que se le vinieron a la boca los conceptos en la forma propia de su escuela literaria. «He aquí que el hombre vacila y se confunde ante el gran problema. ¿Qué es el bien? ¿Qué es el mal? Hijo mío, abre tus oídos a la verdad y tus ojos a la luz. El bien es amar a nuestros semejantes. Amemos y sabremos lo que es el bien, aborrezcamos y sabremos lo que es mal. Hagamos bien a los que nos aborrecen, y las espinas se nos volverán flores. Esto dijo el Justo, esto digo yo . . . Sabiduría de sabidurías, y ciencia de ciencia.»

—Sabidurías y armas al hombro[13]—gruñó Torquemada con abatimiento—. Eso ya lo sabía yo . . . pues lo de *al prójimo contra una esquina*[14] siempre me ha parecido una barbaridad. No hablemos más de eso . . . No quiero pensar en cosas tristes. No digo más sino que si se me muere el hijo . . . vamos, no quiero pensarlo . . . si se me muere, lo mismo me da lo blanco que lo negro . . .

En aquel momento oyóse un grito áspero, estridente, lanzado por Valentín, y que a entrambos los dejó suspensos de terror. Era el grito meníngeo, semejante al alarido del pavo real. Este extraño síntoma encefálico se había iniciado aquel día por la mañana, y revelaba el gravísimo y pavoroso curso de la enfermedad del pobre niño matemático. Torquemada se hubiera escondido en el centro de la tierra para no oír tal grito: metióse en su despacho sin hacer caso de las exhortaciones de Bailón, y dando a éste con la puerta en el hocico dantesco. Desde el pasillo le sintieron abriendo el cajón de su mesa, y al poco rato apareció guardando algo en el bolsillo interior de la americana. Cogió el sombrero, y sin decir nada se fué a la calle.

Explicaré lo que esto significa y adónde iba con su cuerpo[15] aquella tarde el desventurado don Francisco. El día mismo en que cayó malo Valentín, recibió su padre carta de un antiguo y sacrificado cliente o deudor suyo, pidiéndole préstamo con ga-

[11] *de las cosas que tienen más busilis,* one of the most crucial things (*busilis,* crux, key difficulty) [12] *caído para atrás,* tipped back

[13] *armas al hombro,* literally, shoulder arms! freely, get along with you!

[14] *lo de al prójimo contra una esquina,* that matter of always getting the best of the other fellow

[15] *iba con su cuerpo,* he went, he betook himself

rantía de los muebles de la casa. Las relaciones entre la víctima y el inquisidor databan de larga fecha, y las ganancias obtenidas por éste habían sido enormes, porque el otro era débil, muy delicado, y se dejaba desollar, freír y escabechar[16] como si hubiera nacido para eso. Hay personas así. Pero llegaron tiempos penosísimos, y el señor aquél no podía recoger su papel.[17] Cada lunes y cada martes,[18] el *Peor* le embestía, le mareaba, le ponía la cuerda al cuello y tiraba muy fuerte, sin conseguir sacarle ni los intereses vencidos. Fácilmente se comprenderá la ira del tacaño al recibir la cartita pidiendo un nuevo préstamo. ¡Qué atroz insolencia! Le habría contestado mandándole a paseo, si la enfermedad del niño no le trajera tan afligido y sin ganas de pensar en negocios. Pasaron dos días, y allá te va otra esquela angustiosa, de *in extremis,*[19] como pidiendo la Unción. En aquellas cortas líneas en que la víctima invocaba los *hidalgos sentimientos* de su verdugo, se hablaba de un compromiso de honor, proponíanse las condiciones más espantosas, se pasaba por todo[20] con tal de ablandar el corazón de bronce del usurero, y obtener de él la afirmativa. Pues cogió mi hombre la carta, y hecha pedazos la tiró a la cesta de papeles, no volviendo a acordarse más de semejante cosa. ¡Buena tenía él la cabeza para pensar en los compromisos y apuros de nadie, aunque fueran los del mismísimo verbo![21]

Pero llegó la ocasión aquélla antes descripta, el coloquio con la tía Roma y con don José, el grito de Valentín, y he aquí que al judío[22] le da como una corazonada, se le enciende en la mollera fuego de inspiración, trinca el sombrero y se va derecho en busca de su desdichado cliente. El cual era apreciable persona, sólo que de cortos alcances, con un familión sin fin, y una señora a quien le daba el hipo por[23] lo elegante. Había desempeñado el tal buenos destinos[24] en la Península, y en Ultramar, y lo que trajo de allá, no mucho, porque era hombre de bien,[25] se lo afanó el usurero en menos de un año. Después le cayó la herencia de un tío; pero como la señora tenía unos condenados *jueves*[26] para reunir y agasajar a la mejor sociedad, los cuartos de la herencia se escurrían de lo lindo, y sin saber cómo ni cuándo, fueron a parar al bolsón de Torquemada. Yo no sé qué demonios tenía el dinero de aquella casa, que era como un acero para correr hacia el imán del maldecido prestamista. Lo peor del caso es que aun después de hallarse la familia con el agua al pescuezo, todavía la tarasca aquella tan *fashionable* encargaba vestidos a París, invitaba a sus amigas para un *five o'clock tea,* o imaginaba cualquier otra majadería por el estilo.

Pues, señor, ahí va don Francisco hacia la casa del señor aquél, que, a juzgar por los términos aflictivos de la carta, debía de estar a punto de caer, con toda su elegancia y sus tés, en los tribunales, y de exponer a la burla y a la deshonra un nombre respetable. Por el camino sintió el tacaño que le tiraban de la capa. Volvióse . . . ¿y quién creéis que era? Pues una mujer que parecía la Magdalena por su cara dolorida y por su hermoso pelo, mal

[16] *desollar, freír y escabechar,* literally, skin, fry and pickle; freely, to be skinned, cheated and duped [17] *papel,* here, promissory notes

[18] *Cada lunes y cada martes,* Frequently, Quite often

[19] *de in extremis,* as from a dying man

[20] *se pasaba por todo,* one put up with any conditions

[21] *el mismísimo verbo,* the divine word itself

[22] *judío,* Jew; but here, moneylender

[23] *a quien le daba el hipo por,* who had a yen for

[24] *desempeñar buenos destinos,* to occupy good positions

[25] *hombre de bien,* an honest man

[26] *jueves,* open house every Thursday

encubierto con pañuelo de cuadros rojos y azules. El palmito[27] era de la mejor ley; pero muy ajado ya por fatigosas campañas. Bien se conocía en ella a la mujer que sabe vestirse, aunque iba en aquella ocasión hecha un pingo, casi indecente, con falda remendada, mantón de ala de mosca y unas botas . . . ¡Dios, qué botas, y cómo desfiguraban aquel pie tan bonito!

—¡Isidora[28] . . . ! —exclamó don Francisco, poniendo cara de regocijo, cosa en él muy desusada—. ¿Adónde va usted con ese ajetreado cuerpo?

—Iba a su casa, señor don Francisco, tenga compasión de nosotros . . . ¿Por qué es usted tan tirano y tan de piedra? ¿No ve cómo estamos? ¿No tiene tan siquiera un poquito de humanidad?

—Hija de mi alma, usted me juzga mal . . . ¿Y si yo le dijera ahora que iba pensando en usted . . . que me acordaba del recado que me mandó ayer por el hijo de la portera . . . y de lo que usted misma me dijo anteayer en la calle?

—¡Vaya, que no hacerse cargo de nuestra situación! —dijo la mujer echándose a llorar—. Martín muriéndose . . . el pobrecito . . . en aquel buhardillón helado . . . Ni cama, ni medicinas, ni con qué poner un triste puchero para darle una taza de caldo . . . ¡Qué dolor! Don Francisco, tenga cristiandad y no nos abandone. Cierto que no tenemos crédito; pero a Martín le quedan media docena de estudios[29] muy bonitos . . . Verá usted . . . el de la sierra de Guadarrama, precioso . . . el de La Granja, con aquellos arbolitos . . . también, y el de . . . qué sé yo qué. Todos muy bonitos. Se los llevaré . . . pero no sea malo y compadézcase del pobre artista . . .

—Eh . . . eh . . . no llore, mujer . . . Mire que yo estoy montado a pelo[30] . . . tengo una aflicción tal dentro de mi alma, Isidora, que . . . si sigue usted llorando, también yo soltaré el trapo.[31] Váyase a su casa, y espéreme allí. Iré dentro de un ratito . . . ¿Qué . . . duda de mi palabra?

—¿Pero de veras que va? No me engañe, por la Virgen Santísima.

—¿Pero la he engañado yo alguna vez? Otra queja podrá tener de mí; pero lo que es ésa . . .

—¿Le espero de verdad . . . ? ¡Qué bueno será usted si va y nos socorre . . . ! ¡Martín se pondrá más contento cuando se lo diga!

—Váyase tranquila . . . Aguárdeme, y mientras llego pídale a Dios por mí con todo el fervor que pueda.

VII

No tardó en llegar a la casa del cliente, la cual era un principal muy bueno, amueblado con mucho lujo y elegancia, con *vistas a San Bernardino*.[1] Mientras aguardaba a ser introducido, el *Peor* contempló el hermoso perchero y los soberbios cortinajes de la sala, que por la entornada puerta se alcanzaban a ver, y tanta magnificencia le sugirió estas reflexiones: «En lo tocante a los muebles, como buenos lo son . . . vaya si lo son.» Recibióle el amigo en su despacho; y apenas Torquemada le preguntó por la familia, dejóse caer en una silla con muestras de gran consternación. —¿Pero qué le pasa?—le dijo el otro.

[27] *palmito,* slang, (woman's) face

[28] *Isidora Rufete,* the heroine of Galdós's earlier novel, *La desheredada,* where the author traces the effects of her illusions of nobility on her character and her gradual decline and fall into a life of prostitution

[29] *estudios,* studies, here, paintings

[30] *estoy montado a pelo,* I'm on the ragged edge

[31] *yo soltaré el trapo,* I'll start bawling

[1] *con vistas a San Bernardino,* literally, with a view towards the poorhouse, freely, with the probability of soon ending in bankruptcy

—No me hable usted, no me hable usted, señor don Juan. Estoy con el alma en un hilo . . . ¡Mi hijo . . . !

—¡Pobrecito! Sé que está muy malo . . . ¿Pero no tiene usted esperanzas?

—No, señor . . . Digo, esperanzas, lo que se llama esperanzas . . . No sé; estoy loco; mi cabeza es un volcán . . .

—¡Sé lo que es eso! —observó el otro con tristeza—. He perdido dos hijos que eran mi encanto: el uno de cuatro años, el otro de once.

—Pero su dolor de usted no puede ser como el mío. Yo padre,[2] no me parezco a los demás padres, porque mi hijo no es como los demás hijos: es un milagro de sabiduría . . . ¡Ay, don Juan, don Juan de mi alma, tenga usted compasión de mí! Pues verá usted . . . Al recibir su carta primera, no pude ocuparme . . . La aflicción no me dejaba pensar . . . Pero me acordaba de usted y decía: «Aquel pobre don Juan, ¡qué amarguras estará pasando! . . .» Recibo la segunda esquela y entonces digo: «Ea, pues lo que es[3] yo no le dejo en ese pantano. Debemos ayudarnos los unos a los otros en nuestras desgracias.» Así pensé; sólo que con la batahola que hay en casa, no tuve tiempo de venir ni de contestar . . . Pero hoy, aunque estaba medio muerto de pena, dije: «Voy, voy al momento a sacar del purgatorio a ese buen amigo don Juan . . .» y aquí estoy para decirle que aunque me debe usted setenta y tantos mil reales, que hacen más de noventa con los intereses no percibidos, y aunque he tenido que darle varias prórrogas, y . . . francamente . . . me tema tener que darle alguna más, estoy decidido a hacerle a usted ese préstamo sobre los muebles para que evite la peripecia que se le viene encima.

—Ya está evitada—replicó don Juan, mirando al prestamista con la mayor frialdad—. Ya no necesito el préstamo.

—¡Que no lo necesita! —exclamó el tacaño desconcertado—. Repare usted una cosa don Juan. Se lo hago a usted . . . al doce por ciento.

Y viendo que el otro hacía signos negativos, levantóse, y recogiendo la capa, que se le caía, dió algunos pasos hacia don Juan, le puso la mano en el hombro y le dijo:

—Es que usted no quiere tratar conmigo, por aquello de si soy o no soy agarrado. ¡Me parece a mí que doce![4] ¿Cuándo las habrá visto usted más gordas?[5]

—Me parece muy razonable el interés; pero, lo repito, ya no me hace falta.

—¿Se ha sacado usted el premio gordo, por vida de . . . ? —exclamó Torquemada con grosería—. Don Juan no gaste usted bromas conmigo . . . ¿Es que duda de que le hable con seriedad? Porque eso de que no le hace falta . . . ¡rábano! . . . ¡a usted! que sería capaz de tragarse, no digo yo este pico,[6] sino la Casa de la Moneda enterita[7]. . . Don Juan, don Juan, sepa usted, si no lo sabe, que yo también tengo mi humanidad como cualquier hijo de vecino, que me intereso por el prójimo y hasta que favorezco a los que me aborrecen. Usted me odia, don Juan, usted me detesta, no me lo niegue, porque no me puede pagar: esto es claro. Pues bien: para que vea usted de lo que soy capaz, se lo doy al cinco . . . ¡al cinco!

Y como el otro repitiera con la cabeza los signos negativos, Torquemada se desconcertó más, y alzando los

[2] *Yo padre,* As a father
[3] *pues lo que es,* well the fact is
[4] *doce,* twelve [per cent]
[5] *¿Cuándo las habrá visto usted más gordas?* When have you ever seen a better deal?
[6] *pico,* here, bit (of money)
[7] *la Casa de la Moneda enterita,* the whole mint

brazos, con lo cual dicho se está que la capa fué a parar al suelo, soltó esta andanada:

—¡Tampoco al cinco! . . . Pues, hombre, menos que el cinco, ¡caracoles! . . . a no ser que quiera que le dé también la camisa que llevo puesta . . . ¿Cuándo se ha visto usted en otra?[8]. . . Pues no sé qué quiere el ángel de Dios[9] . . . De esta hecha,[10] me vuelvo loco. Para que vea, para que vea hasta dónde llega mi generosidad: se lo doy sin interés.

—Muchas gracias, amigo don Francisco. No dudo de sus buenas intenciones. Pero ya nos hemos arreglado. Viendo que usted no me contestaba, me fuí a dar con un pariente, y tuve ánimos para contarle mi triste situación. ¡Ojalá lo hubiera hecho antes!

—Pues aviado está el pariente . . . Ya puede decir que ha hecho un pan como unas hostias[11] . . . Con muchos negocios de ésos . . . En fin, usted no lo ha querido de mí, usted se lo pierde. Vaya diciendo ahora que no tengo buen corazón. Quien no lo tiene es usted . . .

—¿Yo? Esa sí que es salada.[12]

—Sí, usted, usted (con despecho). En fin, me las guillo,[13] que me aguardan en otra parte donde hago muchísima falta, donde me están esperando como agua de Mayo.[14] Aquí estoy de más. Abur . . .

Despidióle don Juan en la puerta y Torquemada bajó la escalera refunfuñando: "No se puede tratar con gente mal agradecida. Voy a entenderme con aquellos pobrecitos . . . ¡Qué será de ellos sin mí!"

No tardó en llegar a la otra casa, donde le aguardaban con tanta ansiedad. Era en la calle de la Luna,[15] edificio de buena apariencia, que albergaba en el principal a un aristócrata; más arriba familias modestas, y en el techo un enjambre de pobres. Torquemada recorrió el pasillo oscuro buscando una puerta. Los números de éstas eran inútiles, porque no se veían. La suerte fué que Isidora le sintió los pasos y abrió.

—¡Ah vivan los hombres de palabra.[16] Pase, pase.

Hallóse don Francisco dentro de una estancia, cuyo inclinado techo tocaba al piso por la parte contraria a la puerta; arriba un ventanón con algunos de sus vidrios rotos, tapados con trapos y papeles; el suelo de baldosín, cubierto a trechos de pedazos de alfombra; a un lado un baúl abierto, dos sillas, un anafre con lumbre; a otro una cama, sobre la cual, entre mantas y ropas diversas, medio vestido y medio abrigado, yacía un hombre como de treinta años, guapo, de barba puntiaguda, ojos grandes, frente hermosa, demacrado y con los pómulos ligeramente encendidos, en las sienes una depresión verdosa, y las orejas transparentes como la cera de los exvotos que se cuelgan en los altares. Torquemada le miró sin contestar al saludo, y pensaba así: «El pobre está más tísico que la Traviatta. ¡Lástima de muchacho![17] tan buen píntor y tan mala cabeza[18] . . . ¡Habría podido ganar tanto dinero!»

—Ya ve usted, don Francisco, cómo estoy . . . con este catarrazo que no me quiere dejar. Siéntese . . . ¡Cuanto le agradezco su bondad!

[8] *en otra,* in another so favorable deal
[9] *el ángel de Dios,* the dear fellow, i.e. don Juan
[10] *De esta hecha,* from this moment, beginning now
[11] *un pan como unas hostias,* a splendid deal (said ironically)
[12] That certainly is a clever idea
[13] *me las guillo,* I'll beat it
[14] *como agua de Mayo,* like rain in May, freely, like a blessing from heaven
[15] *calle de la Luna,* a street adjacent to the *calle de Tudescos,* hence near Torquemada's home
[16] *vivan los hombres de palabra,* hurray for men of their word
[17] *Lástima de muchacho,* Poor fellow
[18] *tan mala cabeza,* such a wild one

—No hay que agradecer nada . . . Pues no faltaba más. ¿No nos manda Dios vestir a los enfermos, dar de beber al triste, visitar al desnudo? . . . ¡Ay! todo lo trabuco. ¡Qué cabeza! . . . Decía que para aliviar las desgracias estamos los hombres de corazón blando . . . sí, señor.

Miró las paredes del buhardillón, cubiertas en gran parte por multitud de estudios de paisajes, algunos con el cielo para abajo, clavados en la pared o arrimados a ella.

—Bonitas cosas hay todavía por aquí.

—En cuanto suelte el constipado, voy a salir al campo—dijo el enfermo, los ojos iluminados por la fiebre—. ¡Tengo una idea, qué idea! . . . Creo que me pondré bueno de ocho a diez días si usted me socorre, don Francisco; y en seguida al campo, al campo . . .

«Al camposanto es adonde tú vas prontito»—pensó Torquemada; y luego en alta voz:

—Sí, eso es cuestión de ocho o diez días . . . nada más . . . Luego, saldrá usted por ahí . . . en un coche . . . ¿Sabe usted que la buhardilla es fresquecita? . . . ¡Caramba! Déjeme embozar en la capa.

—Pues asómbrese usted—dijo el enfermo incorporándose—. Aquí me he puesto algo mejor. Los últimos días que pasamos en el estudio . . . que se lo cuente a usted Isidora . . . estuve malísimo; como que nos asustamos, y . . .

Le entró tan fuerte golpe de tos, que parecía que se ahogaba. Isidora acudió a incorporarle, levantando las almohadas. Los ojos del infeliz parecía que se saltaban, sus deshechos pulmones agitábanse trabajosamente como fuelles rotos que no pueden expeler ni aspirar el aire; crispaba los dedos, quedando al fin postrado y como sin vida. Isidora le enjugó el sudor de la frente, puso en orden la ropa que por ambos lados del angosto lecho se caía, y le dió a beber un calmante.

—¡Pero qué pasmo tan atroz he cogido! . . . —exclamó el artista al reponerse del acceso.

—Habla lo menos posible—le aconsejó Isidora. Yo me enteré con don Francisco: verás cómo nos arreglamos. Este don Francisco es más bueno de lo que parece: es un santo disfrazado de diablo, ¿verdad?

Al reírse mostró su dentadura incomparable, una de las pocas gracias que le quedaban en su decadencia triste. Torquemada, echándoselas de bondadoso, la hizo sentar a su lado y le puso la mano en el hombro, diciéndole:

—Ya lo creo que nos arreglaremos . . . Como que con usted se puede entender uno fácilmente; porque usted, Isidorita, no es como esas otras mujeronas que no tienen educación. Usted es una persona decente que ha venido a menos, y tiene todo el aquél de mujer fina, como hija neta de marqueses . . . Bien lo sé . . . y que le quitaron la posición que le corresponde esos pillos de la curia . . .

—¡Ay, Jesús! —exclamó Isidora, exhalando en un suspiro todas las remembranzas tristes y alegres de su novelesco pasado—. No hablemos de eso . . . Pongámonos en la realidad. Don Francisco, ¿se ha hecho cargo de nuestra situación? A Martín le embargaron el estudio. Las deudas eran tantas, que no pudimos salvar más que lo que usted ve aquí. Después hemos tenido que empeñar toda su ropa y la mía para poder comer . . . No me queda más que lo puesto . . . ¡mire usted qué facha! y a él nada, lo que ve usted sobre la cama. Necesitamos desempeñar lo preciso; tomar una habitacioncita más abrigada, la del tercero, que está con papeles; encender lumbre, comprar medicinas, poner siquiera un buen cocido todos los días . . . Un señor de la beneficencia domiciliaria me trajo ayer dos bonos, y me mandó ir allá, adonde está la oficina; pero tengo vergüenza de presentarme con esta facha . . . Los que hemos nacido en cierta posición, señor don Francisco, por mucho que caigamos, nunca caemos hasta lo hondo . . . Pero vamos al caso: para todo eso que le he dicho, y para que Martín se reponga y pueda salir al campo, necesitamos tres mil reales . . . y no digo cuatro por que no se asuste. Es lo último. Sí, don Francisquito de mi alma, y confiamos en su buen corazón.

—¡Tres mil reales! —dijo el usurero poniendo la cara de duda reflexiva que para los casos de benevolencia tenía; cara que era ya en él como una fórmula dilatoria, de las que se usan en diplomacia—. ¡Tres mil realetes! . . . Hija de mi alma, mire usted.

Y haciendo con los dedos pulgar e índice una perfecta rosquilla, se la presentó a Isidora, y prosiguió así:

—No sé si podré disponer de los tres mil reales en el momento. De todos modos, me parece que podrían ustedes arreglarse con menos. Piénselo bien, y ajuste sus cuentas. Yo estoy decidido a protegerles y ayudarles para que mejoren de suerte . . . llegaré hasta el sacrificio y hasta quitarme el pan de la boca para que ustedes maten el hambre; pero . . . pero reparen que debo mirar también por mis intereses . . .

—Pongamos el interés que quiera, don Francisco—dijo con énfasis el enfermo, que por lo visto deseaba acabar pronto.

—No me refiero al materialismo del rédito del dinero, sino a mis intereses, claro, a mis intereses. Y doy por hecho que ustedes piensan pagarme algún día.

—Pues claro—replicaron a una[19] Martín e Isidora.

Y Torquemada para su coleto: «El día del Juicio por la tarde me pagaréis: ya sé que éste es dinero perdido.»

El enfermo se incorporó en su lecho, y con cierta exaltación dijo al prestamista:

—Amigo, ¿cree usted que mi tía, la que está en Puerto Rico, ha de dejarme en esta situación cuando se entere? Ya estoy viendo la letra de cuartrocientos o quinientos pesos que me ha de mandar. Le escribí por el correo pasado.

«Como no te mande tu tía quinientos puñales»—pensó Torquemada. Y en voz alta:

—Y alguna garantía me han de dar ustedes también . . . digo, me parece que . . .

—¡Toma! los estudios. Escoja los que quiera.

Echando en redondo una mirada pericial, Torquemada explanó su pensamiento en esta forma:

—Bueno, amigos míos: voy a decirles una cosa que les va a dejar turulatos. Me he compadecido de tanta miseria; yo no puedo ver una desgracia semejante sin acudir al instante a remediarla. ¡Ah! ¿qué idea teníais de mí? Porque otra vez me debieron un pico y les apuré y les ahogué, ¿creen que soy de mármol? Tontos, era porque entonces les vi triunfando y gastando, y francamente, el dinero que yo gano con tanto afán no es para tirado en francachelas. No me conocéis, os aseguro que no me conocéis. Comparen la tiranía de esos chupones que les embargaron el estudio y os dejaron en cueros vivos; comparen eso, digo, con mi generosidad, y con este corazón tierno que me ha dado Dios . . . Soy tan bueno, tan bueno, que yo mismo

[19] *a una,* at the same time

me tengo que alabar y darme las gracias por el bien que hago. Pues verán qué golpe. Miren . . .

Volvió a aparecer la rosquilla acompañada de estas graves palabras:

—Les voy a dar los tres mil reales, y se los voy a dar ahora mismo . . . pero no es eso lo más gordo, sino que se los voy a dar sin intereses . . . Qué tal, ¿es esto rasgo o no es rasgo?

—Don Francisco—exclamó Isidora con efusión,—déjeme que le dé un abrazo.

—Y yo le daré otro si viene acá —gritó el enfermo queriendo echarse fuera de la cama.

—Sí, vengan todos los cariños que queráis—dijo el tacaño, dejándose abrazar por ambos—. Pero no me alaben mucho, porque estas acciones son deber de toda persona que mire por la humanidad, y no tienen gran mérito . . . Abrácenme otra vez, como si fuera vuestro padre, y compadézcanme, que yo también lo necesito . . . En fin, que se me saltan las lágrimas si me descuido, porque soy tan compasivo . . . tan . . .

—Don Francisco de mis entretelas —declaró el tísico arropándose bien otra vez con aquellos andrajos—, es usted la persona más cristiana, más completa y más humanitaria que hay bajo el sol. Isidora, trae el tintero, la pluma y el papel sellado que compraste ayer, que voy a hacer un pagaré.

La otra le llevó lo pedido; y mientras el desgraciado joven escribía, Torquemada, meditabundo y con la frente apoyada en un solo dedo, fijaba en el suelo su mirar reflexivo. Al coger el documento que Isidora le presentaba, miró a sus deudores con expresión paternal, y echó el registro afeminado y dulzón de su voz para decirles:

—Hijos de mi alma, no me conocéis, repito que no me conocéis. Pensáis sin duda que voy a guardarme este pagaré . . . Sois unos bobalicones. Cuando yo hago una obra de caridad, allá te va de veras,[20] con el alma y con la vida. No os presto los tres mil reales, os los regalo, por vuestra linda cara. Mirad lo que hago: ras, ras . . .

Rompió el papel. Isidora y Martín lo creyeron porque lo estaban viendo; que si no, no lo hubieran creído.

—Eso se llama hombre cabal . . . Don Francisco, muchísimas gracias —dijo Isidora conmovida. Y el otro, tapándose la boca con las sábanas para contener el acceso de tos que se iniciaba:

—¡María Santísima, qué hombre tan bueno!

—Lo único que haré—dijo don Francisco levantándose y examinando de cerca los cuadros—, es aceptar un par de estudios, como recuerdo . . . Éste de las montañas nevadas y aquél de los burros pastando . . . Mire usted, Martín, también me llevaré, si le parece, aquella marinita y este puente con hiedra . . .

A Martín le había entrado el acceso y se asfixiaba. Isidora, acudiendo a auxiliarle, dirigió una mirada furtiva a las tablas y al escrutinio y elección que de ellas hacía el aprovechado prestamista.

—Los acepto como recuredo—dijo éste apartándolos—; y si les parece bien, también me llevaré este otro . . . Una cosa tengo que advertirles: si temen que con las mudanzas se estropeen estas pinturas, llévenmelas a casa, que allí las guardaré y pueden recogerlas el día que quieran . . . Vaya, ¿va pasando esta condenada tos? La semana que entra ya no toserá usted nada, pero nada. Irá usted al campo . . . allá por el puente de San Isidro . . . Pero ¡qué cabeza la mía . . . ! se

[20] *allá te va de veras,* freely, I go the whole way

me olvidaba lo principal, que es darles los tres mil reales . . . Venga acá, Isidorita, entérese bien . . . Un billete de cien pesetas, otro, otro . . . (Los iba contando y mojaba los dedos con saliva a cada billete, para que no se pegaran.) Setecientas pesetas . . . No tengo billete de cincuenta, hija. Otro día lo daré. Tienen ahí ciento cuarenta duros, o sean dos mil ochocientos reales . . .

VIII

Al ver el dinero, Isidora casi lloraba de gusto, y el enfermo se animó tanto que parecía haber recobrado la salud. ¡Pobrecillos, estaban tan mal, habían pasado tan horribles escaseces y miserias! Dos años antes se conocieron en casa de un prestamista que a entrambos los desollaba vivos. Se confiaron su situación respectiva, se compadecieron y se amaron: aquella misma noche durmió Isidora en el estudio. El desgraciado artista y la mujer perdida hicieron el pacto de fundir sus miserias en una sola, y de ahogar sus penas en el dulce licor de una confianza enteramente conyugal. El amor les hizo llevadera la desgracia. Se casaron en el ara del amancebamiento, y a los dos días de unión se querían de veras y hallábanse dispuestos a morirse juntos y a partir lo poco bueno y lo mucho malo que la vida pudiera traerles. Lucharon contra la pobreza, contra la usura, y sucumbieron sin dejar de quererse: él siempre amante, solícita y cariñosa ella; ejemplo ambos de abnegación, de esas altas virtudes que se esconden avergonzadas para que no las vean la ley y la religión, como el noble haraposo se esconde de sus iguales bien vestidos.[1]

Volvió a abrazarles Torquemada, diciéndoles con melosa voz:

—Hijos míos, sed buenos y que os aproveche el ejemplo que os doy. Favoreced al pobre, amad al prójimo, y así como yo os he compadecido, compadecedme a mí, porque soy muy desgraciado.

—Ya sé—dijo Isidora, desprendiéndose de los brazos del avaro—, que tiene usted al niño malo. ¡Pobrecito! Verá usted como se le pone bueno ahora . . .

—¡Ahora! ¿Por qué ahora? —preguntó Torquemada con ansiedad muy viva.

—Pues . . . qué sé yo . . . Me parece que Dios le ha de favorecer, le ha de premiar sus buenas obras . . .

—¡Oh! si mi hijo se muere—afirmó don Francisco con desesperación—, no sé qué va a ser de mí.

—No hay que hablar de morirse —gritó el enfermo, a quien la posesión de los santos cuartos había despabilado y excitado cual si fuera una toma del estimulante más enérgico—. ¿Qué es eso de morirse? Aquí no se muere nadie. Don Francisco, el niño no se muere. Pues no faltaba más. ¿Qué tiene? ¿Meningitis? Yo tuve una muy fuerte a los diez años; y ya me daban por muerto, cuando entré en reacción, y viví y aquí me tiene usted dispuesto a llegar a viejo, y llegaré, porque lo que es el catarro, ahora lo largo. Vivirá el niño, don Francisco, no tenga duda; vivirá.

—Vivirá—repitió Isidora—: yo se lo voy a pedir a la Virgencita del Carmen.

—Sí, hija, a la Virgen del Carmen —dijo Torquemada llevándose el pañuelo a los ojos—. Me parece muy bien. Cada uno empuje por su lado, a ver si entre todos . . .

El artista, loco de contento, quería communicárselo al atribulado padre,

[1] This paragraph is like a second more idealistic ending to the story of Isidora, since Galdós left her at the end of *La desheredada* in abject vice, untempered by the altruism she shows here.

y medio se echó de la cama para decirle:

—Don Francisco, no llore, que el chico vive . . . Me lo dice el corazón, me lo dice una voz secreta . . . Viviremos todos y seremos felices.

—¡Ay, hijo de mi alma—exclamó el *Peor;* y abrazándole otra vez—: Dios le oiga a usted. ¡Qué consuelo tan grande me da!

—También usted nos ha consolado a nosotros. Dios se lo tiene que premiar. Viviremos, sí, sí. Mire, mire: el día en que yo pueda salir, nos vamos todos al campo, el niño también, de merienda. Isidora nos hará la comida, y pasaremos un día muy agradable, celebrando nuestro restablecimiento.

—Iremos, iremos—dijo el tacaño con efusión, olvidándose de lo que antes había pensado respecto al *campo* a que iría Martín muy pronto—. Sí, y nos divertiremos mucho, y daremos limosnas a todos los pobres que nos salgan . . . ¡Qué alivio siento en mi interior desde que he hecho ese beneficio! . . . No, no me lo alaben . . . Pues verán: se me ocurre que aún les puedo hacer otro mucho mayor.

—¿Cuál? . . . A ver, don Francisquito.

—Pues se me ha ocurrido . . . no es idea de ahora, que la tengo hace tiempo . . . Se me ha ocurrido que si la Isidora conserva los papeles de su herencia y sucesión de la casa de Aransis,[2] hemos de intentar sacar eso . . .

Isidora le miró entre aturdida y asombrada.

—¿Otra vez eso? —fué lo único que dijo.

—Sí, sí, tiene razón don Francisco —afirmó el pobre tísico, que estaba de buenas,[3] entregándose con embriaguez a un loco optimismo—. Se intentará . . . Eso no puede quedar así.

—Tengo el recelo—añadió Torquemada—, de que los que intervinieron en la acción la otra vez no anduvieron muy listos, o se vendieron a la Marquesa vieja . . . Lo hemos de ver, lo hemos de ver.

—En cuantito que yo suelte el cacharro. Isidora, mi ropa; ve al momento a traer mi ropa, que me quiero levantar . . . ¡Qué bien me siento ahora! . . . Me dan ganas de ponerme a pintar, don Francisco. En cuanto el niño se levante de la cama quiero hacerle el retrato.

—Gracias, gracias . . . sois muy buenos . . . los tres somos muy buenos, ¿verdad? Venga otro abrazo, y pedid a Dios por mí. Tengo que irme, porque estoy con una zozobra que no puedo vivir.

—Nada, nada, que el niño está mejor, que se salva—repitió el artista cada vez más exaltado—. Si le estoy viendo, si no me puedo equivocar.

Isidora se dispuso a salir, con parte del dinero, camino de la casa de préstamos; pero al pobre artista le acometió la tos y disnea con mayor fuerza y tuvo que quedarse. Don Francisco se despidió con las expresiones más cariñosas que sabía y cogiendo los cuadritos salió con ellos debajo de la capa. Por la escalera iba diciendo: «¡Vaya, que es bueno ser bueno! . . . ¡Siento en mi interior una cosa, un consuelo . . . ! ¡Si tendrá razón Martín! ¡Si se me pondrá bueno aquel pedazo de mi vida! . . . Vamos corriendo allá. No me fío, no me fío. Este botarate tiene las ilusiones de los tísicos en último grado. Pero ¡quién sabe! se engaña de seguro respecto a sí mismo, y acierta en lo demás. Adonde

[2] Isidora had been suffering from the delusion that she was an illegitimate child of a girl of the noble Aransis family. Her pretensions to nobility had been her undoing, as she had scorned chances to marry industrious and honest suitors simply because they were not titled.

[3] *que estaba de buenas,* who was in a high mood

él va pronto es al nicho . . . Pero los moribundos suelen tener doble vista, y puede que haya *visto* la mejoría de Valentín . . . voy corriendo, corriendo. ¡Cuánto me estorban estos malditos cuadros! ¡No dirán ahora que soy tirano y judío, pues rasgos de éstos entran pocos en libra![4] . . . No me dirán que me cobro en pinturas, pues por estos apuntes, en venta, no me darían ni la mitad de lo que yo di. Verdad que si se muere valdrán más, porque aquí, cuando un artista está vivo, nadie le hace maldito caso, y en cuanto se muere de miseria o de cansancio, le ponen en las nubes, le llaman genio y qué sé yo qué . . . Me parece que no llego nunca a mi casa. ¡Qué lejos está, estando tan cerca!»

Subió de tres en tres peldaños la escalera de su casa, y le abrió la puerta la tía Roma, disparándole a boca de jarro estas palabras: Señor, el niño parece que está un poquito más tranquilo.» Oírlo don Francisco y soltar los cuadros y abrazar a la vieja, fué todo uno. La trapera lloraba, y el *Peor* le dió tres besos en la frente. Después fué derechito a la alcoba del enfermo y miró desde la puerta. Rufina se abalanzó hacia él para decirle: «Está desde mediodía más sosegado . . . ¿Ves? Parece que duerme el pobre ángel. Quién sabe . . . Puede que se salve. Pero no me atrevo a tener esperanzas, no sea que las perdamos esta tarde.»

Torquemada no cabía en sí de sobresalto y ansiedad. Estaba el hombre con los nervios tirantes, sin poder permanecer quieto ni un momento, tan pronto con ganas de echarse a llorar como de soltar la risa. Iba y venía del comedor a la puerta de la alcoba, de ésta a su despacho, y del despacho al gabinete. En una de estas volteretas, llamó a la tía Roma, y metiéndose con ella en la alcoba la hizo sentar, y le dijo:

—Tía Roma, ¿crees tú que se salva el niño?

—Señor, será lo que Dios quiera, y nada más. Yo se lo he pedido anoche y esta mañana a la Virgen del Carmen, con tanta devoción que más no puede ser, llorando a moco y baba.[5] ¿No me ve cómo tengo los ojos?

—¿Y crees tú . . . ?

—Yo tengo esperanza, señor. Mientras no sea cadáver, esperanzas ha de haber, aunque digan los médicos lo que dijeren.[6] Si la Virgen lo manda, los médicos se van a hacer puñales[7] . . . Otra:[8] anoche me quedé dormida rezando, y me pareció que la Virgen bajaba hasta delantito de mí y que me decía que sí con la cabeza . . . Otra: ¿no ha rezado usted?

—Sí, mujer; ¡qué preguntas haces! Voy a decirte una cosa importante. Verás.

Abrió un bargueño, en cuyos cajoncillos guardaba papeles y alhajas de gran valor que habían ido a sus manos en garantía de préstamos usurarios: algunas no eran todavía suyas; otras sí. Un rato estuvo abriendo estuches, y a la tía Roma, que jamás había visto cosa semejante, se le encandilaban los ojos de pez con los resplandores que de las cajas salían. Eran, según ella, esmeraldas como nueces, diamantes que arrojaban pálidos rayos, rubíes como pepitas de granada, y oro finísimo, oro de la mejor ley, que valía cientos de miles . . . Torquemada, después de abrir y cerrar estuches, encontró lo que buscaba: una perla enorme, del tamaño de una ave-

[4] *entran pocos en libra,* freely, are few and far between

[5] *llorando a moco y baba,* freely, crying for all I was worth

[6] *lo que dijeren,* whatever they may say. *Dijeren* is the future subjunctive.

[7] *hacer puñales,* freely, to be disappointed, to be wrong

[8] *Otra* for *otra cosa*

llana, de hermosísimo oriente; y cogiéndola entre los dedos, la mostró a la vieja.

—¿Qué te parece esta perla, tía Roma?

—Bonita de veras. Yo no lo entiendo. Valdrá miles de millones. ¿Verdá usté?[9]

—Pues esta perla—dijo Torquemada en tono triunfal—, es para la señora Virgen del Carmen. Para ella es, si pone bueno a mi hijo. Te la enseño, y pongo en tu conocimiento la intención, para que se lo digas. Si se lo digo yo, de seguro no me lo cree.

—Don Francisco (mirándole con profunda lástima), usted está malo de la jícara.[10] Dígame, por su vida, ¿para qué quiere ese requilorio la Virgen del Carmen?

—Toma, para que se lo pongan el día de su santo, el 16 de julio. ¡Pues no estará poco maja con esto! Fué regalo de boda de la excelentísima señora Marquesa de Tellería.[11] Créelo, como ésta hay pocas.

—Pero, don Francisco, ¡usted piensa que la Virgen le va a conceder . . . ! Paice[12] bobo . . . ¡Por ese piazo[13] de cualquier cosa!

—Mira qué oriente. Se puede hacer un alfiler y ponérselo a ella en el pecho, o al Niño.[14]

—¡Un rayo! ¡Valiente caso hace la Virgen de perlas y pindonguerías! . . . Créame a mí: véndala y déle a los pobres el dinero.

—Mira tú, no es mala idea—dijo el tacaño guardando la joya—. Tú sabes mucho. Seguiré tu consejo, aunque, si he de serte franco, eso de dar a los pobres viene a ser una tontería, porque cuanto les das se lo gastan en aguardiente. Pero ya lo arreglaremos de modo que el dinero de la perla no vaya a parar a las tabernas . . . Y ahora quiero hablarte de otra cosa. Pon muchísima atención: ¿te acuerdas de cuando mi hija, paseando una tarde por las afueras con Quevedo y las de Morejón, fué a dar allá, por donde tú vives, hacia los Tejares del Aragonés,[15] y entró en tu choza y vino contándome, horrorizada, la pobreza y escasez que allí vió? ¿Te acuerdas de eso? Contóme Rufina que tu vivienda es un cubil, una inmundicia hecha con adobes, tablas viejas y planchas de hierro, el techo de paja y tierra; me dijo que ni tú ni tus nietos tenéis cama, y dormís sobre un montón de trapos; que los cerdos y las gallinas que criáis con la basura son allí las personas; y vosotros los animales. Sí: Rufina me contó esto, y yo debí tenerte lástima y no te la tuve. Debí regalarte una cama, pues nos has servido bien, querías mucho a mi mujer, quieres a mis hijos, y en tantos años que entras aquí jamás nos has robado ni el valor de un triste clavo. Pues bien: si entonces no se me pasó por la cabeza socorrerte, ahora sí.

Diciendo esto, se aproximó al lecho y dió en él un fuerte palmetazo con ambas manos, como el que se suele dar para sacudir los colchones al hacer las camas.

—Tía Roma, ven acá, toca aquí. Mira qué blandura. ¿Ves este colchón de lana encima de un colchón de muelles? Pues es para ti, para ti, para

[9] *¿Verdá usté?* for *¿Verdad usted?, ¿No es verdad?*

[10] *jícara,* chocolate cup; slang, noddle, bean, head

[11] *Marquesa de Tellería,* a character who appears in other Galdosian novels, principally in *La familia de León Roch*

[12] *Paice* for *parece* [13] *piazo* for *pedazo*

[14] Notice how Torquemada thinks he can buy his son's life by a gift to the Virgin, just as he had hoped to buy it by his gifts to 'humanity.' Tía Roma's simple but profound belief makes a nice contrast to his attempt to bargain with God. As pointed out before (Chap. II, n. 21), Torquemada is always the materialist, for whom the realm of the spirit is closed.

[15] *los Tejares del Aragonés,* a place where tiles (*tejas*) are made on the outskirts of Madrid

que descanses tus huesos duros y te espatarres a tus anchas.

Esperaba el tacaño una explosión de gratitud por dádiva tan espléndida, y ya le parecía estar oyendo las bendiciones de la tía Roma, cuando ésta salió por un registro muy diferente. Su cara telarañosa se dilató, y de aquellas úlceras con vista que se abrían en el lugar de los ojos, salió un resplandor de azoramiento y susto, mientras volvía la espalda al lecho, dirigiéndose hacia la puerta.

—Quite, quite allá—dijo—: vaya con lo que se le ocurre . . . ¡Darme a mí los colchones, que ni tan siquiera caben por la puerta de mi casa! . . . Y aunque cupieran . . . ¡rayo! A cuenta que he vivido tantísimos años durmiendo en duro como una reina, y en estas blanduras no pegaría los ojos. Dios me libre de tenderme ahí. ¿Sabe lo que le digo? Que quiero morirme en paz. Cuando venga la de la cara fea[16] me encontrará sin una mota, pero con la conciencia como los chorros de la plata.[17] No, no quiero los colchones, que dentro de ellos está su idea . . . porque aquí duerme usted, y por la noche, cuando se pone a cavilar, las ideas se meten por la tela adentro y por los muelles, y ahí estarán como las chinches cuando no hay limpieza. ¡Rayo con el hombre, y la que me quería encajar![18] . . .

Accionaba la viejecilla de una manera gráfica, expresando tan bien, con el mover de las manos y de los flexibles dedos, cómo la cama del tacaño se contaminaba de sus ruines pensamientos, que Torquemada la oía con verdadero furor, asombrado de tanta ingratitud; pero ella, firme y arisca, continuó despreciando el regalo: «Pos vaya[19] un premio gordo que me caía, Santo Dios . . . ¡Pa[20] que yo durmiera en eso! Ni que estuviera boba, don Francisco. ¡Pa que a media noche me salga toda la gusanera de las ideas de usted, y se me meta por los oídos y por los ojos, volviéndome loca y dándome una mala muerte . . . ! Porque, bien lo sé yo . . . a mí no me la da usted[21] . . . ahí dentro, ahí dentro, están todos sus pecados, la guerra que le hace al pobre, su tacañería, los réditos que mama, y todos los números que le andan por la sesera para ajuntar dinero . . . Si yo me durmiera ahí, a la hora de la muerte me saldrían por un lado y por otro unos sapos con la boca muy grande, unos culebrones asquerosos que se me enroscarían en el cuerpo, unos diablos muy feos con bigotazos y con orejas de murciélago, y me cogerían entre todos para llevarme a rastras a los infiernos. Váyase al rayo,[22] y guárdese sus colchones, que yo tengo un camastro hecho de sacos de trapo, con una manta por encima, que es la gloria divina . . . Ya lo quisiera usted . . . Aquello sí que es rico para dormir a pierna suelta . . .»

—Pues dámelo, dámelo, tía Roma —dijo el avaro con aflicción—. Si mi hijo se salva, me comprometo a dormir en él lo que me queda de vida, y a no comer más que las bazofias que tú comes.

—A buenas horas y con sol.[23] Usted quiere ahora poner un puño en el cielo.[24] ¡Ay, señor, a cada paje su ropaje![25] A usted le sienta eso como

[16] *la de la cara fea,* i.e. death
[17] *como los chorros de la plata,* like a flood of silver, freely, as clear as crystal
[18] *Rayo con el hombre, y la que me quería encajar,* Curses on the man; what a deal he wanted to put over on me
[19] *Pos* for *Pues; vaya,* what a
[20] *Pa* for *para*
[21] See Chap. IV, n. 23.
[22] *Váyase al rayo,* Go to the dickens
[23] *A buenas horas y con sol,* A fine idea
[24] *poner un puño en el cielo,* to move heaven
[25] *a cada paje, su ropaje* (proverb), each person should stick to his own specialty; to each his own

a la burra las arracadas.[26] Y todo ello es porque está afligido; pero si se pone bueno el niño, volverá usted a ser más malo que Holofernes. Mire que ya va para viejo; mire que el mejor día se le pone delante la de la cara pelada,[27] y a ésa sí que no le da usted el timo.[28]

—¿Pero de dónde sacas tú, estampa de la basura—replicó Torquemada con ira, agarrándola por el pescuezo y sacudiéndola—, de dónde sacas tú que yo soy malo, ni lo he sido nunca?

—Déjeme, suélteme, no me menee, que no soy ninguna pandereta. Mire que soy más vieja que Jerusalén, y he visto mucho mundo, y le conozco a usted desde que se quiso casar con la Silvia. Y bien le aconsejé a ella que no se casara . . . y bien le anuncié las hambres que había de pasar. Ahora que está rico no se acuerda de cuando empezaba a ganarlo. Yo sí me acuerdo, y me paice que fué ayer cuando le contaba los garbanzos a la cuitada de Silvia y todo lo tenía usted bajo llave, y la pobre estaba descomida, trashijada y ladrando de hambre.[29] Como que si no es por mí, que le traía algún huevo de ocultis, se hubiera muerto cien veces. ¿Se acuerda de cuando se levantaba usted a media noche para registrar la cocina a ver si descubría algo de condumio, que la Silvia hubiera escondido para comérselo sola? ¿Se acuerda de cuando encontró un pedazo de jamón en dulce y un medio pastel que me dieron a mí en casa de la Marquesa, y que yo le traje a la Silvia para que se lo zampara ella sola, sin darle a usted ni tanto así?[30] ¿Recuerda que al otro día estaba usted hecho un león,[31] y que cuando entré me tiró al suelo y me estuvo pateando? Y yo no me enfadé, y volví, y todos los días le traía algo a la Silvia. Como usted era el que iba a la compra, no le podíamos sisar, y la infeliz no tenía una triste chambra que ponerse. Era una mártira,[32] don Francisco, una mártira; ¡y usted guardando el dinero y dándolo a peseta por duro al mes! Y mientre[33] tanto, no comían más que mojama cruda con pan seco y ensalada. Gracias que yo partía con ustedes lo que me daban en las casas ricas, y una noche, ¿se acuerda? traje un hueso de jabalí que lo estuvo usted echando en el puchero seis días seguidos, hasta que se quedó más seco que su alma puñalera.[34] Yo no tenía obligación de traer nada: lo hacía por la Silvia, a quien cogí en brazos cuando nació de señá Rufinica, la del callejón del Perro. Y lo que a usted le ponía furioso era que yo le guardase las cosas a ella y no se las diera a usted, ¡un rayo! Como si tuviera yo obligación de llenarle a usted el buche, perro, más que perro . . . Y dígame ahora, ¿me ha dado alguna vez el valor de un real? Ella sí me daba lo que podía, a la chita callando;[35] pero usted, el muy capigorrón, ¿qué me ha dado? Clavos torcidos, y las barreduras de la casa. ¡Véngase ahora con jipíos y farsa! . . . Valiente caso le van a hacer.

—Mira, vieja de todos los demonios —le dijo Torquemada furioso—, por respeto a tu edad no te reviento de una patada. Eres una embustera, una diabla, con todo el cuerpo lleno de mentiras y enredos. Ahora te da por

[26] That notion of yours is as becoming to you as earrings to a donkey

[27] *la de la cara pelada,* death

[28] and you certainly won't cheat it

[29] *descomida, trashijada y ladrando de hambre,* without food, lean, and howling with hunger (*Trashijada* is more commonly written *trasijada.*)

[30] *ni tanto así,* not even so much (said with a gesture indicating a tiny amount)

[31] *hecho un león,* like a roaring lion

[32] *mártira* for *mártir*

[33] *mientre* for *mientras*

[34] We remember that Torquemada's favorite oath has been *puñales.* Hence the appropriateness of the expression *su alma puñalera.*

[35] *a la chita callando,* on the sly

desacreditarme, después de haber estado más de veinte años comiendo mi pan. ¡Pero si te conozco, zurrón de veneno; si eso que has dicho nadie te lo va a creer: ni arriba ni abajo! El demonio está contigo, y maldita tú eres entre todas las brujas y esperpentos que hay en el cielo . . . digo, en el infierno.

IX

Estaba el hombre fuera de sí, delirante; y sin echar de ver[1] que la vieja se había largado a buen paso de la habitación, siguió hablando como si delante la tuviera. «Espantajo, madre de las telarañas, si te cojo, verás . . . ¡Desacreditarme así!» Iba de una parte a otra en la estrecha alcoba, y de ésta al gabinete, cual si le persiguieran sombras; daba cabezadas contra la pared, algunas tan fuertes que resonaban en toda la casa.

Caía la tarde, y la oscuridad reinaba ya en torno del infeliz tacaño, cuando éste oyó claro y distinto el grito de pavo real que Valentín daba en el paroxismo de su altísima fiebre. «¡Y decían que estaba mejor! . . . Hijo de mi alma . . . Nos han vendido, nos han engañado.»

Rufina entró llorando en la estancia de la fiera, y le dijo:

—¡Ay, papá, qué malito se ha puesto; pero qué malito!

—¡Ese trasto de Quevedo! —gritó Torquemada llevándose un puño a la boca y mordiéndoselo con rabia—. Le voy a sacar las entrañas . . . Él nos le ha matado.

—Papá, por Dios, no seas así . . . No te rebeles contra la voluntad de Dios . . . Si Él lo dispone . . .

—Yo no me rebelo, ¡puñales! yo no me rebelo. Es que no quiero, no quiero dar[2] a mi hijo, porque es mío, sangre de mi sangre y hueso de mis huesos . . .

—Resígnate, resígnate, y tengamos conformidad—exclamó la hija, hecha un mar de lágrimas.

—No puedo, no me da la gana de resignarme. Esto es un robo . . . Envidia, pura envidia. ¿Qué tiene que hacer Valentín en el cielo? Nada, digan lo que diejeran; pero nada . . . Dios, ¡cuánta mentira, cuánto embuste! Que si cielo, que si infierno, que si Dios, que si diablo, que si . . . tres mil rábanos. ¡Y la muerte, esa muy pindonga de la muerte,[3] que no se acuerda de tanto pillo, de tanto farsante, de tanto imbécil, y se le antoja mi niño, por ser lo mejor que hay en el mundo! . . . Todo está mal, y el mundo es un asco, una grandísima porquería.

Rufina se fué y entró Bailón, trayéndose una cara muy compungida. Venía de ver al enfermito, que estaba ya agonizando, rodeado de algunas vecinas y amigos de la casa. Disponíase el clerizonte a confortar al afligido padre en aquel trance doloroso, y empezó por darle un abrazo, diciéndole con empañada voz:

—Valor, amigo mío, valor. En estos casos se conocen las almas fuertes. Acuérdese usted de aquel gran filósofo que expiró en una cruz dejando consagrados los principios de la humanidad.

—¡Qué principios ni qué . . . ! ¿Quiere usted marcharse de aquí, so chinche? . . . Vaya que es de lo más pelmazo y cargante y apestoso que he visto. Siempre que estoy angustiado me sale con esos retruécanos.

—Amigo mío, mucha calma. Ante los designios de la Naturaleza, de la Humanidad, del Gran Todo, ¿qué puede el hombre? ¡El hombre! esa hormiga, menos aún, esa pulga . . . todavía mucho menos.

—Ese coquito . . . menos aún, ese . . . ¡puñales!—agregó Torquemada

[1] *echar de ver,* to notice
[2] *dar,* here, give up
[3] *esa muy pindonga de la muerte,* that good-for-nothing gadabout Death

con sarcasmo horrible, remedando la voz de la sibila y enarbolando después el puño cerrado—. Si no se calla le rompo la cara . . . Lo mismo me da a mí el grandísimo todo que la grandísima nada y el muy piojoso que la inventó. Déjeme, suélteme, por la condenada alma de su madre, o . . .

Entró Rufina otra vez, traída por dos amigas suyas para apartarla del tristísimo espectáculo de la alcoba. La pobre joven no podía sostenerse. Cayó de rodillas exhalando gemidos, y al ver a su padre forcejeando con Bailón, le dijo:

—Papá, por Dios, no te pongas así. Resígnate . . . yo estoy resignada, ¿no me ves? . . . El pobrecito . . . cuando yo entré . . . tuvo un instante ¡ay! en que recobró el conocimiento. Habló con voz clara, y dijo que veía a los ángeles que le estaban llamando.

—¡Hijo de mi alma, hijo de mi vida! —gritó Torquemada con toda la fuerza de sus pulmones, hecho un salvaje, un demente—no vayas, no hagas caso; que ésos son unos pillos que te quieren engañar . . . Quédate con nosotros . . .

Dicho esto, cayó redondo al suelo, estiró una pierna, contrajo la otra y un brazo. Bailón, con toda su fuerza no podía sujetarle, pues desarrollaba un vigor muscular inverosímil. Al propio tiempo soltaba de su fruncida boca un rugido feroz y espumarajos. Las contracciones de las extremidades y el pataleo eran en verdad horrible espectáculo: se clavaba las uñas en el cuello hasta hacerse sangre. Así estuvo largo rato, sujetado por Bailón y el carnicero, mientras Rufina, transida de dolor, pero en sus cinco sentidos, era consolada y atendida por Quevedito y el fotógrafo. Llenóse la casa de vecinos y amigos, que en tales trances suelen acudir compadecidos y serviciales. Por fin tuvo término el patatús de Torquemada, y caído en profundo sopor, que a la misma muerte, por lo quieto, se asemejaba, le cargaron entre cuatro y le arrojaron en su lecho. La tía Roma, por acuerdo de Quevedito, le daba friegas con un cepillo, rasca que te rasca,[4] como si le estuviera sacando lustre.[5]

Valentín había expirado ya. Su hermana, que quieras que no,[6] allá se fué, le dió mil besos, y, ayudada de las amigas, se dispuso a cumplir los últimos deberes con el pobre niño. Era valiente, mucho más valiente que su padre, el cual cuando volvió en sí de aquel tremendo síncope, y pudo enterarse de la completa extinción de sus esperanzas, cayó en profundísimo abatimiento físico y moral. Lloraba en silencio, y daba unos suspiros que se oían en toda la casa. Transcurrido un buen rato, pidió que le llevaran café con media tostada, porque sentía una debilidad horrible. La pérdida absoluta de la esperanza le trajo la sedación nerviosa, y la sedación, estímulos apremiantes de reparar el fatigado organismo. A media noche fué preciso administrarle un substancioso potingue, que fabricaron la hermana del fotógrafo de arriba y la mujer del carnicero de abajo, con huevos, Jerez y caldo de puchero. «No sé qué me pasa—decía el *Peor*—: pero ello es que parece que se me quiere ir la vida.» El suspirar hondo y el llanto comprimido le duraron hasta cerca del día, hora en que fué atacado de un nuevo paroxismo de dolor, diciendo que quería ver a su hijo; *resucitarle, costara lo que costase,* e intentaba salirse del lecho, contra los combinados esfuerzos de Bailón, del carnicero y de los demás amigos que contenerle y calmarle querían. Por fin lograron que

[4] *rasca que te rasca,* scratching and scratching, brushing and brushing

[5] *sacar lustre,* to polish

[6] *que quieras que no,* willy-nilly (in spite of her friends' advice to the contrary)

se estuviera quieto, resultado en que no tuvieron poca parte las filosóficas amonestaciones del clerigucho, y las sabias cosas que echó por aquella boca el canicero, hombre de pocas letras, pero muy buen cristiano. «Tienen razón—dijo don Francisco, agobiado y sin aliento—. ¿Qué remedio queda más que conformarse? ¡Conformarse! Es un viaje para el que no se necesitan alforjas. Vean de qué le vale a uno ser más bueno que el pan, y sacrificarse por los desgraciados, y hacer bien a los que no nos pueden ver ni en pintura . . . Total, que lo que pensaba emplear en favorecer a cuatro pillos . . . ¡mal empleado dinero, que había de ir a parar a las tabernas, a los garitos y a las casas de empeño! . . . digo que esos dinerales los voy a gastar en hacerle a mi hijo del alma, a esa gloria, a ese prodigio que no parecía de este mundo, el entierro más lucido que en Madrid se ha visto. ¡Ah, qué hijo! ¿No es dolor que me le hayan quitado? Aquello no era hijo: era un diosecito que engendramos a medias el Padre Eterno y yo . . . ¿No creen ustedes que debo hacerle un entierro magnífico? Ea, ya es de día. Que me traigan muestras de carros fúnebres . . . y vengan papeletas negras para convidar a todos los profesores.»

Con estos proyectos de vanidad, excitóse el hombre, y a eso de las nueve de la mañana, levantado y vestido, daba sus disposiciones con aplomo y serenidad. Almorzó bien, recibía a cuantos amigos llegaban a verle, y a todos les endilgaba la consabida historia: «Conformidad . . . ¡Qué le hemos de hacer! . . . Está visto: lo mismo da que usted se vuelva santo, que se vuelva usted Judas, para el caso de que le escuchen y le tengan misericordia . . . ¡Ah, misericordia!

Lindo anzuelo sin cebo para que se lo traguen los tontos.»

Y se hizo el lujoso entierro, y acudió a él mucha y lucida gente, lo que fué para Torquemada motivo de satisfacción y orgullo, único bálsamo de su hondísima pena. Aquella lúgubre tarde, después que se llevaron el cadáver del admirable niño, ocurrieron en la casa escenas lastimosas. Rufina, que iba y venía sin consuelo, vió a su padre salir del comedor con todo el bigote blanco, y se espantó creyendo que en un instante se había llenado de canas. Lo ocurrido fué lo siguiente: fuera de sí, y acometido de un espasmo de tribulación, el inconsolable padre fué al comedor y descolgó el encerado en que estaban aún escritos los problemas matemáticos, y tomándolo por retrato, que fielmente le reproducía las facciones del adorado hijo, estuvo larguísimo rato dando besos sobre la fría tela negra, y estrujándose la cara contra ella, con lo que la tiza se le pegó al bigote mojado de lágrimas, y el infeliz usurero parecía haber envejecido súbitamente. Todos los presentes se maravillaron de esto, y hasta se echaron a llorar. Llevóse don Francisco a su cuarto el encerado, y encargó a un dorador un marco de todo lujo para ponérselo, y colgarlo en el mejor sitio de aquella estancia.

Al día siguiente, el hombre fué acometido, desde que abrió los ojos, de la fiebre de los negocios terrenos. Como la señorita había quedado muy quebrantada por los insomnios y el dolor, no podía atender a las cosas de la casa: la asistenta y la incansable tía Roma la sustituyeron hasta donde sustituirla era posible. Y he aquí que cuando la tía Roma entró a llevarle el chocolate al gran inquisidor, ya estaba éste en planta, sentado a la mesa de su despacho, escribiendo números con mano febril. Y como la bruja aquélla tenía tanta confianza con el señor de la casa, permitiéndose tratarle como a igual, se llegó a él, le puso sobre el hombro su descarnada y fría mano, y le dijo: «Nunca aprende . . . Ya está otra vez preparando los trastos de ahorcar. Mala muerte va usted a tener, condenado de Dios, si no se enmienda.» Y Torquemada arrojó sobre 5 ella una mirada que resultaba enteramente amarilla, por ser en él de este color lo que en los demás humanos ojos es blanco, y le respondió de esta manera: «Yo hago lo que me da mi 10 santísima gana, so mamarracho, vieja más vieja que la Biblia. Lucido estaría si consultara con tu necedad lo que debo hacer.» Contemplando un momento el encerado de las matemáticas, exhaló un suspiro y prosiguió así: «Si preparo los trastos, eso no es cuenta tuya ni de nadie, que yo me sé cuanto 5 hay que haber de tejas abajo y aun de tejas arriba, ¡puñales! Ya sé que me vas a salir con el materialismo de la misericordia . . . A eso te respondo que si buenos memoriales eché, bue- 10 nas gordas calabazas me dieron. La misericordia que yo tenga, ! . . . ñales! que me la claven en la frente.»

Madrid, Febrero de 1889

José María de Pereda

PEREDA (1833–1906) was born, lived, and died in a small town, Polanco, near Santander. He seldom left his home except to go to Madrid as a student for two years and as a deputy representing the Carlist cause for one year.

As Galdós is the supreme champion of liberalism, so Pereda is the greatest representative of the traditional cause. Yet, strangely enough, these two men were always good friends. Pereda, by instinct and personal inclination, loved the old ways—in politics, religion, and even language. Even within his beloved native region, it was the remote and primitive village (Tablanca, in *Peñas arriba*) or the by-gone days (*old* Santander in *Sotileza*) of which he really approved. Consequently, Pereda's novels divide into two groups: those set in his native region, in which he expresses his love of the old-fashioned ways; and those, often set in Madrid, revealing his indignation at progressive ideas and materialistic city life. His outstanding successes were of the first type, not of the second.

Each one of his novels is really a gallery of pictures of people and landscapes. The plot is not emphasized, and the excellence of each individual scene distracts our attention from the novel as a whole. Moreover, all parts are equally interesting, so the work does not move to a climax. For this reason some critics have said that Pereda's most artistic work is in his collections of *cuadros de costumbres.*

Nevertheless, two novels, both of his native region, are considered Pereda's masterpieces—*Sotileza,* set among the fishermen of Santander, and especially *Peñas arriba,* which shows how a young man, corrupted by city life, is gradually won over to virtue and usefulness in society by contact with the simple existence of the country. Both these books lay great stress upon nature; the first upon the sea, the second, the mountains; and in both nature is conceived in its epic rather than idyllic aspect.

As a stylist, Pereda is usually ranked as the best of the nineteenth-century authors, and it is his sure mastery of a vast vocabulary and his skill in portraying characters or painting grand natural scenery which have given him his high rank in literature.

José María de Pereda

La buena gloria

Más de un lector, al pasar la vista por este cuadro, ha de pensar que es una invención mía, o que, cuando menos, está sacado de las viejas crónicas de la primitiva Santander. Conste que semejantes dudas ni me ofenden ni me extrañan.

Yo, que estoy viendo a estos marineros, embutidos materialmente en el laberinto de los modernos adelantos,[1] sin reparar siquiera en ellos; . . . yo que sé, en una palabra, hasta qué punto conservan las aficiones y las costumbres de sus abuelos, a pesar de haber invadido sus barrios la moderna sociedad con su nuevo carácter, me he resistido a creer en uso entre ellos, en la actualidad, escenas como las que voy a referir; y sólo después de haberlas palpado, como quien dice, he podido atreverme a asegurar, como aseguro, que no es la *Buena Gloria* una costumbre perdida ya entre los recuerdos de la antiquísima colonia de pescadores . . .

El siguiente histórico *ejemplar* es recentísimo.

Acababan de celebrarse en la iglesia de San Francisco las honras fúnebres por el alma de un pobre hombre que perteneció al Cabildo de mareantes de Abajo.[2] El cortejo, en el mismo orden en que había acompañado al cadáver a la iglesia, y de la iglesia al cementerio, volvió a la casa mortuoria:[3] delante los hombres, e inmediatamente después las mujeres, y todos en traje de día de fiesta. El de los primeros, compuesto de pantalón, chaleco y chaqueta de paño azul muy obscuro, corbata de seda negra . . . El de las mujeres, de saya de percalina[4] azul sobre refajo de bayeta[5] encarnada, jubón[6] de paño obscuro, mantilla de franela negra con anchos ribetes de panilla,[7] media azul y zapatos de paño negro.

La reciente viuda, con una mala saya de percal, desgarrada y sucia, en mangas de camisa, desgreñada y descalza, esperaba a la fúnebre comitiva, acurrucada en un rincón de la destartalada habitación en que había muerto su marido: sala, alcoba, pasadizo y comedor al mismo tiempo; pues aquella pieza y otra reducidísima y obscura que servía de cocina constituían toda la casa.[8] Alrededor de esta mujer había, sentados en el suelo, dos

[1] The modernization of Santander, especially the destruction of old houses and the filling in of part of the harbor to provide room for the railway, destroyed much of the area inhabited by fishermen. Pereda remembered every detail of the old city and complained bitterly that modern civilization was stamping out picturesque local customs.

[2] The fishermen were organized into two guilds: the *Cabildo de Abajo,* comprising those who lived in the *calle del Mar,* and the *Cabildo de Arriba,* or those who lived in the *calle Alta.* In other works Pereda describes the rivalry between the two groups.

[3] *la casa mortuoria,* the home of the deceased.

[4] *saya de percalina,* skirt of fancy cotton cloth

[5] *refajo de bayeta,* petticoat of baize (flannel)

[6] *jubón,* bodice, waist

[7] *ribetes de panilla,* borders of fine corduroy

[8] *casa,* here, apartment

chicos y una muchachuela, tan sucios y mal ataviados como ella, de quien eran dignos vástagos.

El cortejo fué penetrando acompasadamente en la sala. Los hombres formaron una línea contigua a las paredes, y las mujeres otra, algunos pasos más al centro. La viuda ocultó la cara entre las manos y lanzó un par de gemidos; su prole, sin cambiar de postura, miraba impasible la escena.

Como no había sillas en la casa, excusado es decir que el duelo permaneció de pie.

Una de las mujeres de él, la más autorizada por su vecindad y conexiones con aquella familia, se adelantó un paso a las demás personas de la comitiva.

—Por el eterno descanso del defunto, *Padre nuestro*—dijo con voz áspera y fuerte, aunque afectando emoción y compostura.[9]

A lo cual contestó la viuda con un tercer gemido, y el lúgubre cortejo con un *que estás en los cielos, santificado sea tu nombre,* etc., etc.

En seguida, la mujer se quitó la mantilla, la tendió en el suelo, se retiró un paso, y con la misma voz con que acababa de pedir una oración para el finado:[10]

—Para los dolientes, a cuatro cuartos[11]—dijo, mirando a todos.

—Eso es poco—contestó un hombre.

—Somos muchos—añadió otro.

—A rial[12]—volvió a decir la mujer.

—Curriente[13]—replicó el coro.

Y la que le dirigía levantó por el costado derecho su saya azul, metió la mano e nuna anchísima faltriquera que apareció encima del refajo encarnado, sacó cuatro piezas de a dos cuartos y las arrojó sobre la mantilla. En la misma operación la siguieron otras compañeras y algunos hombres; y en muy pocos instantes quedó la mantilla medio cubierta por las monedas de cobre.

—¡Alto! —gritó la mujer—; no lo metamos a barullo:[14] dir[15] echándolo poco a poco, que aquí hay anguno[16] que va a quedar bien con el dinero de los demás.

—Mientes—exclamaron algunas voces.

—Yo digo más verdá[17] que todos vusotros[18] juntos; y como sé lo que pasó en el intierro[19] de la mujer del tío Miterio[20] . . .

—Lo que allí pasó me lo sé yo mu retebién,[21] y lo callo porque no te salgan los colores a la cara.

—¿Quién es esa deslenguadona que me quiere prevocar?[22]

—¡A ver si vos calláis, condenás,[23] o dirvos[24] a reñir allá juera![25] . . . Dir echando los que falten, y cierre el pico la rigunión.[26]

Esta reprimenda, de un viejo pescador, puso en orden a las mujeres, que se disponían ya a hacer de las suyas.[27]

[9] *compostura,* restraint, control

[10] *el finado,* the deceased

[11] *a cuatro cuartos,* at [the rate of] four *cuartos* [apiece]. The *cuarto* was an old copper coin worth less than a cent. (The gift would be very small, but remember that the fishermen were very poor.)

[12] *rial,* for *real,* a coin worth about four cents. Pereda transcribes the speech of the common people, for which realistic device he was praised by contemporary critics. The standard forms will be given in the notes.

[13] *curriente* for *corriente,* agreed, O.K.

[14] *barullo,* confusion, disorder

[15] *dir* for *ir,* used for the command, *id*

[16] *anguno* for *alguno*

[17] *verdá* for *verdad*

[18] *vusotros* for *vosotros*

[19] *intierro* for *entierro*

[20] *Miterio* for *Emeterio.* Because one of the patron saints of the fishermen was named Emeterio, this name was frequent among the seafarers.

[21] *mu* for *muy; retebién,* very well. The prefixing of *re-* or of *rete-* to certain adverbs and adjectives intensifies their meaning.

[22] *prevocar* for *provocar*

[23] *condenás* for *condenadas*

[24] *dirvos* for *idos* (command)

[25] *juera* for *fuera*

[26] *rigunión* for *reunión,* the group, every body

[27] *hacer de las suyas,* to have one of their quarrels

—A rial para los dolientes—volvió a exclamar la voz de la presidenta, con la mayor tranquilidad.

Algunas piezas de a dos cuartos cayeron sobre la mantilla.

—A rial para los dolientes—añadió aún la mujer.

Pero esta petición no produjo ya resultado alguno.

—¿Cuántos semos?[28]—preguntó entonces aquélla.

Oyéronse en la sala fuertes murmullos por algunos instantes, y un marinero contestó después muy recio:

—Quince hombres y veinte mujeres.

—Enestonces,[29] debe haber en la mantilla . . . veinte y diez, treinta, y cinco, treinta y cinco . . . Treinta y cinco riales . . . menos treinta y cinco chavos.[30]

—Cabales . . .

La mujer contó los cuartos sobre la mantilla, redújolos a montones de a treinta y cuatro cada uno, y levantándose en seguida, dijo en alta voz, con cierto retintín:

—Aquí no hay más que veintiocho riales.

—Yo he echao . . . —Y yo . . . —Y yo . . . —Y yo . . . —fueron diciendo todas las personas de los dos corrillos.

—Es claro: ahora toos[31] han echao . . . ¡Como yo no sé lo que sucede en estas ocasiones! . . . ¡Y luego le dirán a una que falta a la verdá! . . .

—Vamos, mujer, no te consumas,[32] que ya sabemos lo que es contar dinero: a la más lista se le pega de los deos.[33]

—Estos diez[34] te voy a pegar en esa recancaneada jeta, ¡lambistona, embrolladora![35]. . .

—A mí me pegarás tú de lengua.[36]

—¡Malos peces vos coman, arrastrás![37] ¿No veis a esa probe[38] mujer que vos ascucha?[39]—gruñó el viejo pescador, interponiéndose entre las dos mujeres y señalando a la viuda.

¡Ayyy!—suspiró ésta al oírlo, limpiándose los ojos con las greñas.

—¿Falta dinero? Pus hacervos[40] la cuenta de que se lo tragó la tierra, y en paz . . . Vengan esos cuartos—añadió el viejo en tono brusco.

La mujer que los había contado recogió la mantilla y la desocupó en la gorra del pescador, murmurando hacia la que riñó con ella:

—Da gracias a la pena de esta infeliz, que si no . . .

—¿Qué se trae?—preguntó el pescador a la reunión.

—Queso . . . —Vino . . . —Aguardiente . . . —Pan . . .

—¿A quién hago caso yo? Toos piden a un tiempo . . . Que alcen el deo los que quieran vino . . . Uno, dos, tres . . . , seis, nueve . . . Nueve hombres y tres mujeres . . . Ahora que le alcen los que quieran aguardiente . . . ¡Ea!, no hay más que hablar: seis hombres y toas las mujeres, menos tres, dicen que no quieren vino . . . ¡Me alegro, me alegro, y que me alegro, ea! . . . Conque dempués[41] de gastar dos pesetas en queso y en un *guardia civil*,[42] lo demás pa *musolina*.[43] Vengo en un credo.[44]

El viejo salió de la sala, como si su comisión le hubiera quitado de en-

[28] *semos* for *somos*
[29] *enestonces* for *entonces*
[30] *chavo* for *ochavo*, a copper coin worth half a *cuarto*
[31] *toos* for *todos*
[32] *consumirse*, to burn up, to get excited
[33] *deos* for *dedos*
[34] Supply *dedos*.
[35] *recancaneada jeta, ¡lambistona, embrolladora!* exaggerated snout, you greedy woman, you trouble maker!
[36] *de lengua*, with your tongue, with words
[37] *arrastrás* for *arrastradas*, you low creatures
[38] *probe* for *pobre*
[39] *ascucha* for *escucha*
[40] *Pus hacervos* for *Pues haceos* (*haced* and *os*)
[41] *dempués* for *después*
[42] *guardia civil*, slang for a large loaf of bread
[43] *musolina*, slang for *aguardiente*
[44] *credo*, a moment (the time needed to say the creed)

cima la mitad del peso de sus años; y la presidenta del duelo, después de ponerse la mantilla y de dar a su fisonomía el aire de compunción de que la había despojado durante la última escena, cuadróse[45] en medio de la reunión, fijó la vista en el suelo y dijo en tono plañidero:

—Una *Salve* a la Santísima Virgen del Mar.

El coro la rezó por lo bajo.

—Por todos los fallecidos del cabildo, *Padre nuestro*.

Esta oración se rezó como la anterior.

—Para que Dios nuestro Señor tome en su miselicordia[46] los santos ufragios[47] que se acaban de hacer por el alma del defunto,[48] que en paz descanse, un *Credo*.

Y la reunión le rezó con el mayor recogimiento.

—En el nombre del Padre, del Hijo y del Espíritu Santo—dijo, santiguándose, la mujer.

—En el nombre del Padre, del Hijo y del Espíritu Santo—contestó, con la misma ceremonia, su auditorio.

II

—Amén—añadió el pescador de marras,[49] presentándose en la sala con una gran jarra de aguardiente y un vaso en una mano, un plato lleno de queso en la otra, y un *guardia civil* . . . o pan de seis libras, debajo del brazo.

La consabida mujer le salió al encuentro, después de haber tendido otra vez en el suelo su mantilla, y aceptó con cierta solemnidad la jarra y el vaso que el marinero le ofreció; en seguida colocó éste el pan y el queso sobre la mantilla, y sacó del bolsillo una navaja; calló de repente la concurrencia, lanzó el quinto gemido la mujer del *glorificado*, relamiéronse con fruición[50] sus tres hijos, y la que tenía la jarra llenó con admirable pulso, hasta los bordes, el primer vaso de aguardiente.

—Para la dolienta—dijo, levantándole en alto.

—Que gloria se le güelva[51]—contestó la reunión.

Sexto gemido de la viuda.

—¡Yo no puedo beber, que no puedo, que tengo un ñudo[52] en el pasapán![53] ¡Ay, mariduco mío de mi alma!

—Vaya, mujer, que ya no tien[54] remedio; y el perder tú la salú[55] no le ha de resucitar a él. Toma un trago, que tendrás el estómago aterecío[56] . . .

—No ha entrao[57] en él un bocao[58] desde antayer, créemelo, por mi salvación. ¡Ayyyy!

—Pus ahora comerás; y por de plonto,[59] échate eso al cuerpo *a la buena gloria del defunto*.

—¡Ay!, por eso no más lo hago; bien lo sabe Dios.

Y llevándose el vaso a los labios, le agotó sin resollar.

—¡Ay, compañero de mis entrañas! —exclamó en seguida, limpiándose la boca con la manga de la camisa.

El pescador se acercó a ella entonces, y la dió una gran rebanada de pan con un pedazo de queso encima.

Cada uno de los tres huérfanos recibió otra ración igual de pan y queso y medio vaso de aguardiente, previo el indispensable brindis «a la buena gloria del defunto.»

[45] *cuadrarse*, to stand erect
[46] *miselicordia* for *misericordia*
[47] *ufragios* for *sufragios*, suffrage, favor, support
[48] *defunto* for *difunto*
[49] *de marras*, before mentioned
[50] *relamiéronse con fruición*, licked their chops with relish
[51] *güelva* for *vuelva*. May it become happiness for her.
[52] *ñudo* for *nudo*
[53] *pasapán*, throat
[54] *tien* for *tiene*
[55] *salú* for *salud*
[56] *aterecio* for *atericido*, which stands for *aterido*, chilled
[57] *entrao* for *entrado*
[58] *bocao* for *bocado*, mouthful
[59] *plonto* for *pronto*

Y obsequiada ya de este modo la familia, el vaso, el pan y el queso comenzaron a circular por la reunión entre murmullos muy expresivos, oyéndose de vez en cuando aquí y allá, bien por la chillona voz de una mujer, bien por la ronca de un hombre, la frase consabida «a la buena gloria del defunto.»

La jarra volvió a presentarse otra vez delante de la viuda. Bebió ésta, bebieron sus hijos; y como al llegar a la mitad del corro faltase líquido, la escanciadora se retiró al centro de la sala, y exclamó en el tonillo de rigor:

—A rial para los dolientes.

—¡Para un rayo que te parta!—gritó la mujer que antes había reñido con ella—. ¿Adónde se han dío[60] dos azumbres de aguardiente que debía haber en la jarra?

—Pos al colaero[61] tuyo y al de otras tan borrachonas como tú—replicó la interpelada, con desgarro.[62]

—Oiga usté, desolladora,[63] ¿va eso conmigo?—dijo una tercera mujer.

—Usté lo sabrá . . . Y, por último, la que se pica, ajo ha comido.[64]

—Es que si fuera conmigo . . .

—Si fuera contigo te lo aguantarías.

—¡O no!

—¡O sí, te digo!

—¡Que no, y rete[65] que no!

—¡Que sí, y rete que sí! Y si has pensao que porque está aquí el tu[66] marido me he de morder yo la lengua y me he de amarrar[67] las manos, te llevas chasco . . . Mira, pa[68] él y pa ti.

Y la escanciadora del aguardiente, fingiendo una sonrisa de desprecio hasta alcanzarse las orejas con los extremos de su boca, escupió en medio del corro con la desenvoltura más provocativa. Pero su adversaria, no bien llegó la saliva al suelo, rugiendo como una pantera, saltó sobre la retadora, y asiéndola con todas sus fuerzas por el pelo, la hizo tocar el polvo[69] con las narices; en seguida, de otro tirón la metió la cabeza entre sus piernas; oprimiósela a su gusto; y tendido el cuerpo, sobre las espaldas de su víctima, alargó la mano izquierda hasta cogerle las sayas por la altura de las pantorillas; enarboló la diestra, trémula y amenazante . . . ; y a no acudir la viuda a detenerla, hubiera castigado delante de la reunión a su enemiga, con la ofensa más terrible que se puede hacer a estas mujeres: con una azotina *a telón corrido.*[70]

Detrás de la viuda acudieron algunos hombres, y a fuerza de sacudidas y porrazos,[71] lograron separar a aquellas dos furias, que parecían haberse adherido entre sí.

—¡Dolervos[72] de mis lágrimas!—gritaba la dolorida pescadora.

—¡Vaya usté mucho con Dios, zalamerona, cubijera![73]—la contestó, con un empellón, la vencedora.

—Deja, que yo la alcanzaré—bramó a su lado la mujer que estuvo a pique de ser azotada, levantando en alto la jarra vacía del aguardiente.

—¡No tires! . . . —gritaron algunos hombres, corriendo a detenerla.

—¡Quiero matarla!

Y con toda la intención de hacerlo así, despidió[74] la jarra, derecha a la

[60] *dío* for *ido*
[61] *colaero* for *coladero,* sieve, colander, here, gullet
[62] *desgarro,* impudence
[63] *desolladora,* skinner; evil-tongued woman
[64] A play on words: the one who feels a prickling, has eaten garlic, equivalent to 'If the shoe fits, wear it.' But *picarse* also means 'to get angry.'
[65] See n. 21.
[66] *el tu* for *tu*
[67] *amarrar,* to tie, here, to keep still
[68] *pa* for *para*
[69] *polvo,* dust, dirt. The floor of the apartment is trampled earth.
[70] *una azotina a telón corrido,* a spanking with the curtain (skirt) open
[71] *porrazo,* blow
[72] *Dolervos* for *doleos*
[73] *zalamerona,* you wheedler; *cubijera* for *cobijera,* you shelter-seeker
[74] *despidió,* she let fly

cara de su antagonista. Pero el marido de ésta, que pugnaba rato hacía por contenerla, al ver el proyectil, bajó instintivamente su cabeza, y cubriendo con ella la de su costilla,[75] recibió en medio del occipital[76] la jarra, que se hizo pedazos, como si chocado hubiera contra un muro. Saltó, rugiendo de ira, pero ileso, el marinero; llegó hasta la agresora, y bañándola en sangre la cara con una sonora bofetada, la tendió en el suelo cuan larga era.[77] Merced al desorden que este nuevo lance produjo en el *duelo*,[78] la viuda logró alcanzar con las uñas el pelo de su adversaria; zarandeóla un rato a su gusto, gritaron entrambas con horribles imprecaciones, terciaron los hombres en el asunto, hubo diferencias entre ellos, sacudiéronse el polvo[79] algunos; y en pocos instantes aquella mugrienta habitación se transformó en un campo de batalla, verdaderamente aterradora; batalla que hubiera costado mucha sangre, a no presentarse en la sala, muy a tiempo,[80] el Alcalde de mar.[81]

Uno de los chicuelos de la casa, después de ver el giro que tomaba la cuestión, había salido corriendo a la calle en busca de aquella autoridad, con tan buena estrella,[82] que la encontró al volver la esquina.

La presencia del Alcalde sofocó, como por encanto, los furores del combate; y eso que el tal personaje era ni más ni menos que un marinero como los demás. Pero estaba facultado para llevar a todo matriculado[83] ante el Capitán del puerto; y este señor cumplía la Ordenanza[84] al pie de la letra,[85] y la letra de la Ordenanza era capaz de amansar a una ballena.

Por buena compostura,[86] se desenlazó el drama marchando cada personaje por su lado, después de pagar entre todos la jarra hecha pedazos.

La viuda, al quedarse sola con sus hijos y el Alcalde, volvió a hacer pucheros[87] y a llorar por el difunto.

—Mira, embusterona—le dijo aquél—: si no quieres que te cruce las costillas con la vara, te callas la boca. Vete con esas lágrimas a onde[88] no te conozcan; que yo ya sé de qué pie cojeas.[89] ¡Hipocritona, borracha! . . . ¡A ver si te levantas de ese rincón y barres la casa y das de comer a esos muchachos!

—¿Qué he de darles, si no lo tengo?

—Bebe menos, y verás cómo lo encuentras.

Tras estas palabras y una mirada muy significativa, pero que nada tenía de dulce,[90] salió de la sala el Alcalde.

Entonces la contrariada mujer, mordiéndose los labios de coraje,[91] fijó maquinalmente su airada vista en los tres hijos que estaban a su lado, y dió un sopapo a cada uno.

—¡Largo de aquí![92]—les dijo con furor—; y si queréis comer, dir a garnarlo.

Después, excitada por la pelea y aturdida con el aguardiente que había bebido, se tendió en el suelo, mordiendo el polvo y mesándose las greñas.

III

No hace mucho tiempo llegó a mis manos un manuscrito rancio y ahu-

[75] *costilla,* rib, here, wife
[76] *occipital,* nape of the neck
[77] *cuan larga era,* full length [78] *duelo,* wake
[79] *sacudir el polvo,* to brush the dust off, here, to beat, hit
[80] *muy a tiempo,* just at the right time
[81] *Alcalde de mar,* the head of the fishermen's guilds
[82] *estrella,* star, fortune
[83] *matriculado,* member of the guild
[84] *Ordenanza,* the code of military laws
[85] *al pie de la letra,* literally
[86] *compostura,* compromise
[87] *hacer pucheros,* to blubber
[88] *onde* for *donde*
[89] *de qué pie cojeas,* what's the matter with you
[90] *que nada tenía de dulce,* which had nothing sweet about it [91] *coraje,* rage
[92] *¡Largo de aquí!* Get out of here!

mado, en cuya portada leí, en muy buenos caracteres, el siguiente rótulo: *Entremés de la buena gloria.*

Abríle con curiosidad, y vi que, en efecto, era un sainete, cuyo argumento se reducía a poner de relieve algunas escenas muy parecidas a las que acabo de referir. . . .

Se representó este sainete en Santander, según una nota que contiene, el año de 1783, en el día de los santos mártires Emeterio y Celedonio, es decir, el 30 de agosto. . . .

La *Buena Gloria,* cuyo origen se ignora, pero que es antiquísimo según el autor del sainete, y mucho más según uno de sus personajes, que dice, al echar el dinero sobre la capa,

> Ésta es una cirimonia[93]
> que *nuestros tatarabuelos*
> nos dejaron prevenío
> se observara con rispeto;[94]

la *Buena Gloria,* repito, continuó después en toda su escandalosa solemnidad, a despecho de sermones, de anatemas y del entremés citado; atravesó impávida épocas de tirantez e intolerancia, y sin que nada haya podido contra ella, logró aclimatarse en la moderna atmósfera de fósforo y vapor,[95] y aquí existen todavía en uso sus inconcebibles prácticas.*

[93] *cirimonia* for *ceremonia*

[94] *prevenío* for *prevenido; rispeto* for *respeto.* This is a ceremony which our great-great-grandparents handed down to us and which should be observed with respect.

[95] Pereda refers to the match and the steam engine as two great modern inventions.

* No me atrevería hoy a asegurar que se conserve en Santander esta costumbre tan arraigada como aun lo estaba cuando se publicó este cuadro por primera vez; pero tampoco me comprometo a afirmar que se ha desterrado enteramente. (*Nota del Autor en la edición de 1876.*)

Campoamor and Realism in Poetry

AFTER the romantic school had spent its force, lyric poetry declined in Spain. In the second half of the century we have very few real poets. Of course, Bécquer wrote from 1860 to 1870, but we have considered him as a late romanticist. Poetry became more and more regional in scope and restricted in ideas. We shall take up the one poet who achieved both popularity and prominence during this period, Ramón de Campoamor (1817–1901).

There is nothing poetic about the life of Campoamor. He lived a calm, unworried, bourgeois existence, playing a conservative role in politics, holding the office of governor of Alicante, and being several times a conservative deputy to the Cortes. He himself said that his only vices were reading and sleeping. He was also different from most other poets of his century in that he enjoyed great popularity with the reading public throughout his lifetime.

Although Campoamor aspired to be a philosopher and wrote several books on philosophical subjects, he is known for three collections of short poems, *Doloras* (1846), *Pequeños poemas* (1872–94), and *Humoradas* (1886–8). All of this verse is written in simple, everyday language and deals with subjects which could occur in everyday life. Hence in language and subject matter it falls within the scope of realism.

Behind each poem is an idea, often humorous or ironical, which serves as an example of, or a commentary on, some accepted value in life. Frequently the poems narrate a coincidence of the type we call 'irony of fate,' as when a young girl falls down and hurts herself while praying. This gives a sly dig at an accepted value, in this case, religion. Campoamor is constantly showing that everything depends upon the point of view and that in the case of most established truths more than one point of view is possible. Therefore, although a conservative in life and in politics, Campoamor in his writing is constantly undermining the most fundamental conservative beliefs, especially any form of idealism. It is evident that Campoamor's sly attacks on idealism tend to bring his readers back from an unreal world to the hard facts of the real world around us. Thus his philosophy is realistic, too. His view of life is disillusioned, seemingly that of an old man past his youthful enthusiasms.

His *Doloras* (a word he invented himself) are poems running from a few lines to two or three pages, which present an ironical contrast, often in dialogue form and emphasizing dramatic elements in their presentation. The *Pequeños poemas* are longer *Doloras,* but the *Humoradas* (another word of his invention) are very short, merely the kernel or the idea presented in its most economical form. Most of them have only two lines and seldom do they run to more than four.

Campoamor's popularity continues unabated to this day because of his clever ideas, simply expressed.

Ramón de Campoamor

Doloras

I

Rogad a tiempo[1]

Marchando con su madre, Inés resbala,
Cae al suelo, se hiere, y disputando
Se hablan así después las dos llorando:
—¡Si no fueras tan mala! . . . —No soy mala.
—¿Qué hacías al caer? . . . — ¡Iba rezando!

II

Cuestión de nombre

De una hermosa pagana la existencia
Salvó un cristiano, y, con fervor divino,
La pagana dió gracias al *Destino*
Y el cristiano alabó la *Providencia.*[2]

III

Cuestión de fe

Ya el amor los hastía
Y hablan de astronomía;
Y en tanto que él, impío,
Llama al cielo *el vacío,*
¡Ella, con santo celo,
Llama al vacío *el cielo!*

[1] Translate: Pray at the right time

[2] A beautiful illustration of two points of view. The pagan girl sees only Fate or Predestination, where the Christian sees the watchfulness and personal care of God. What it is depends on the person who is thinking about it. Hence Truth is relative; or there is no Absolute Truth. Again Campoamor is undermining an accepted belief. We can understand why he is so often called 'corrosive' by the Spaniards. Compare this poem with *Dolora* III and *Humorada* 5.

IV

Cosas del tiempo

Pasan veinte años; vuelve él,
Y al verse, exclaman él y ella:
(—¡Santo Dios! ¿y éste es aquél? . . .)
(—¡Dios mío! ¿y ésta es aquélla? . . .)[3]

V

¡Quién supiera escribir![4]

—Escribidme una carta, señor Cura.[5]
—Ya sé para quién es.
—¿Sabéis quién es, porque una noche oscura
Nos visteis juntos? —Pues.

—Perdonad; mas . . . —No extraño[6] ese tropiezo.[7] 5
La noche . . . la ocasión . . .
Dadme pluma y papel. Gracias. Empiezo:
Mi querido Ramón:

—¿Querido? . . . Pero, en fin, ya lo habéis puesto . . .
—Si no queréis . . . —¡Sí, sí! 10
—*¡Qué triste estoy!* ¿No es eso?—Por supuesto.
—*¡Qué triste estoy sin ti!*

Una congoja, al empezar me viene . . .
—¿Cómo sabéis mi mal? . . .
—Para un viejo, una niña siempre tiene 15
El pecho de cristal.

¿Qué es sin ti el mundo? Un valle de amargura.
¿Y contigo? Un edén.
—Haced la letra[8] clara, señor Cura;
Que lo entienda eso bien. 20

—*El beso aquel que de marchar a punto*[9]
Te di . . . —¿Cómo sabéis? . . .
—Cuando se va y se viene y se está junto,
Siempre . . . no os afrentéis.

Y si volver tu afecto no procura,[10] 25
Tanto me harás sufrir . . .

[3] This situation has been made into a charming one act play, entitled *Mañana de sol,* by the Quintero brothers.
[4] Translate: If I only knew how to write. (This is the best known of all Campoamor's works.)
[5] Notice that this poem is a dialogue between a priest and a charming but illiterate peasant girl. Remember the dashes indicate a change of speaker.
[6] to be surprised at
[7] slip, peccadillo
[8] writing, hand
[9] Read: *a punto de marchar*
[10] to try, find a way. Read: *si tu afecto no procura volver*

—¿Sufrir y nada más? No, señor Cura,
¡Que me voy a morir!

—¿Morir? ¿Sabéis que es ofender al cielo . . .
—Pues, sí, señor, ¡morir! 30
—Yo no pongo *morir*. —¡Qué hombre de hielo!
¡Quién supiera escribir!

¡Señor Rector, señor Rector! en vano
Me queréis complacer,
Si no encarnan los signos de la mano 35
Todo el ser de mi ser.

Escribidle, por Dios, que el alma mía
Ya en mí no quiere estar;
Que la pena no me ahoga cada día . . .
Porque puedo llorar. 40

Que mis labios, las rosas de su aliento,
No se saben abrir;
Que olvidan de la risa el movimiento
A fuerza de sentir.[11]

Que mis ojos, que él tiene por tan bellos, 45
Cargados con mi afán,
Como no tienen quien se mire en ellos,
Cerrados siempre están.

Que es, de cuantos tormentos he sufrido,
La ausencia el más atroz; 50
Que es un perpetuo sueño de mi oído
El eco de su voz . . .

Que siendo por su causa, el alma mía
¡Goza tanto en sufrir! . . .
Dios mío, ¡cuántas cosas le diría 55
Si supiera escribir! . . .

Epílogo

—Pues señor, ¡bravo amor! Copio y concluyo;
A don Ramón . . . En fin,
Que es inútil saber para esto arguyo
Ni el griego ni el latín.[12] 60

[11] Translate, feeling sad

[12] The ironical contrast which is the basis of this poem is the constant opposition between wise and restrained old age and impetuous youth. The latter does not see or weigh the consequences of its acts, while the former is inclined to weigh them too much.

Humoradas

1. Ser fiel, siempre que quieres,[1] es tu lema;
pero tú ¿quieres siempre? He aquí el problema.

2. Todo en amor es triste,
mas, triste y todo, es lo mejor que existe.

3. Hay quien pasa la vida
en ese eterno juego
de hacer caer a la mujer y luego
rehabilitar a la mujer caída.

4. ¡Qué bien has aprendido en tu provecho
que ser mala es un cálculo mal hecho!

5. Con tal que yo lo crea,
¿qué importa que lo cierto no lo sea?

6. Para él la simetría es la belleza,
aunque corte a las cosas la cabeza.

7. Toda cosa es nacida
para tener un trágico destino
y girar y girar en remolino[2]
en torno del sepulcro: ésta es la vida.

8. ¡Quién de su pecho desterrar pudiera
la duda, nuestra eterna compañera![3]

9. Al mover tu abanico con gracejo
quitas el polvo al corazón más viejo.[4]

[1] Notice the untranslatable play on words, since *quieres* means either 'you are in love' or 'you wish.'

[2] *en remolino,* whirling

[3] How is *¡Quién . . . pudiera* to be translated? This little poem repeats something which Campoamor tells us in many other places—that doubt is the basis of his thought despite his yearnings for certitude.

[4] Although Campoamor thought he had invented a new form in these *Humoradas,* we can see that they are really epigrams. Their similarity to Spanish proverbs is also great.

Naturalism

ABOUT 1870, in France, a new concept of literature was set forth by Émile Zola. Based on realism, this new school added a certain scientific or pseudo-scientific aspect. It tried to make the novel even more faithful in its representation of life by precise documentation (that is, the author took from life masses of notes out of which he chose the material for his descriptions), and it attempted to apply to literature recent findings on the subject of heredity, which were interpreted to mean that everyone's life is predetermined by his ancestry. Naturalistic characters cannot decide their own course in life; their actions may seem voluntary but in reality they are merely the results of physical causes—heredity and, to a lesser degree, environment. Moreover, naturalism, in order to show more easily the results of heredity, deliberately chose abnormal characters, many times mentally unstable or even insane, and its situations were daring and violent, such as adultery and incest. Its emphasis was always on the seamy side of life.

Although naturalism influenced such authors as Galdós, its most vocal advocate in Spain was a woman, EMILIA PARDO BAZÁN (1851–1921). She set forth the theory of naturalism in a series of twenty articles collected under the title *La cuestión palpitante* (1883), and illustrated it in her best novel, *Los pazos de Ulloa* (1886), and its sequel, *La madre naturaleza* (1887). *Los pazos de Ulloa* tells the story of a degenerate Marqués living in a ramshackle palace of Galicia, who has as his mistress the daughter of the overseer of his estates. The latter readily consents to this arrangement as a means of acquiring money and power for himself. When the Marqués marries a cousin from Santiago de Compostela, the innocent bride, discovering the relations between her husband and his mistress, seeks consolation from an idealistic young priest, and the greedy overseer spreads the rumor that they are carrying on an affair. The book ends with the death of the wife. The sequel tells of the love affair between two children of the Marqués, one by his wife, the other by his mistress, who are horrified when they finally discover their relationship.

As one can gather from these summaries, Pardo Bazán has the daring situations of naturalism. She also has an abundance of accurate descriptive detail. But since she was always a good Catholic, she never could accept the belief in determinism, so essential to naturalism. Furthermore, her descriptions of vicious situations are always purely external, never giving the inner feeling or the psychological sensation of the situation. We are not surprised that Pardo Bazán gave up naturalism about the end of the century and later denounced it as a false system. During the twentieth century, her work takes on a tinge of Christian idealism quite opposed to the tone of her earlier production.

Pardo Bazán also handled the short story with a sureness and technical mastery which have been equalled by few Spanish writers.

Another outstanding proponent of naturalism in Spain was LEOPOLDO ALAS, generally known under the pseudonym of *Clarín.* A professor of law in the University of Oviedo, Clarín was a great liberal. He is better known as an essayist and critic of literature than as a novelist. In his essays he is greatly concerned with 'the Spanish problem,' the future and the improvement of his country. Hence in many ways Clarín reminds us of Larra. His greatest novel, *La regenta* (1884), is naturalistic in theme—adultery—and in detailed description and documentation, but Clarín, too, gave up naturalism about 1890 and, like Pardo Bazán, turned to a more spiritual concept of life.

Emilia Pardo Bazán

El disfraz

La profesora de piano pisó la antesala toda recelosa y encogida. Era su actitud habitual; pero aquel día la exageraba involuntariamente, porque se sentía en falta. Llegaba lo menos con veinte minutos de retraso,[1] y hubiese querido esconderse tras el repostero, que ostentaba los blasones de los Marqueses de la Ínsula, cuando el criado, patilludo y guapetón, la dijo, con la severidad de los servidores de casa grande hacia los asalariados humildes:

—La señorita Enriqueta ya aguarda hace un ratito . . . La señora Marquesa también . . .

No pudiendo meterse bajo tierra, se precipitó . . . Sus tacones torcidos[2] golpeaban la alfombra espesa, y al correr, se prendían en el desgarrón interior de la bajera, pasada[3] de tanto 5 uso. A pique estuvo de[4] caerse, y un espejo del salón que atravesaba para dirigirse al apartado gabinete donde debía de impacientarse su alumna, la envió el reflejo de un semblante ya 10 algo demacrado, y ahora más descompuesto por el terror de perder una plaza[5] que, con el empleíllo del marido, era el mayor recurso de la familia.

15 ¡Una lección de diez y ocho duros! Todos los agujeros se tapaban con ella.[6] Al panadero, al[7] de la tienda de

[1] *con veinte minutos de retraso,* twenty minutes late
[2] *torcidos,* worn on one side, crooked
[3] *la bajera, pasada,* her petticoat, worn out
[4] *a pique de,* at the point of
[5] *plaza,* here, position, job
[6] *Todos los agujeros se tapaban con ella,* freely, All their worst debts were covered by by it (the money from the lesson)
[7] *al,* understand, *al hombre*

la esquina, al administrador implacable que traía el recibo del piso, se les respondía invariablemente: «La semana que viene . . . Cuando cobremos la lección de la señorita de la Ínsula . . .» Y en la respuesta había cierto inocente orgullo, la satisfacción de enseñar a la hija única y mimada de unos señores tan encumbrados, que iban a Palacio[8] como a su casa propia, y daban comidas y fiestas a las cuales concurría lo mejor de lo mejor, grandes, generales, ministros . . . Y doña Consolación, la maestra, contaba y no acababa[9] de la gracia de Enriquetita, de la bondad de la señora Marquesa, que la[10] hablaba con tanta sencillez, que la distinguía tanto . . .

Todo era verdad—lo de la sencillez, lo de la distinción . . . —pero la profesora no por eso se sentía menos achicada—hasta el extremo de emocionarse—cuando la madre de su alumna, siempre vestida de terciopelo, siempre adornada con fulgurantes joyas, la dirigía la palabra, la hablaba de música . . . Porque la Marquesa de la Ínsula, que no sabía ni cuáles eran las notas del pentagrama,[11] disertaba a veces con verbosidad, repitiendo lo que oía decir a los entendidos en su platea.[12] Y doña Consolación, sin enterarse de lo que explicaba aquella voz tan suave, a menudo imperiosa en su dulzura, contestaba indistintamente:

—Verdad . . . Así es . . . No cabe duda . . . Tiene razón la señora . . .

¡Si por culpa de la tardanza perdiese la lección! ¡Si, al verla entrar, la Marquesa hiciese un gesto de contrariedad, de desagrado! El corazón fatigado de la profesora armaba un ruido de fuelle que la aturdía . . . Se detuvo para tomar aliento. Y, en el mismo instante, oyó que la llamaban con acento cordial, afectuoso. Era su discípula.

—¡Doña Consola! ¡Doña Consola!—repetía la niña, en el tono del que tiene que dar una noticia alegre—. Venga usted . . . ¡Hay novedades!

«Doña Consola» corrió, no sin grave peligro de enganche y caída. La Marquesa, llena de cortesía, se había levantado, de lo cual protestó la maestra, exclamando:

—¡Por Dios!

La chiquilla batía palmas.

—¡Mamá, mamá, díselo pronto! . . .

—Dame tiempo . . . —contestó risueña la madre—. Doña Consolación, figúrese usted que deseamos . . . Vamos a ver: ¿no tiene usted muchas ganas de oír *Lohengrin*?

—Yo . . .

La profesora se puso amoratada, que es el modo de ruborizarse de los cardíacos.

—Yo . . . *¡Lohengrin!* ¡Ya lo creo, señora! —prorrumpió de súbito, en involuntaria efusión de un alma que hubiese podido ser de artista si no fuese de madre de familia obligada a ganar el pan de tres chiquitines—. ¡Ya lo creo! Sólo una vez oí una ópera . . . ¡y hace tantos años ya! ¡Y *Lohengrin!* Se dice que lo cantan divinamente . . .

—¡Oh! ¡Ese Capinera! ¡Y la Stolli! ¡Si es un bordado![13] Bueno; pues se trata de que esta noche tenemos dos asientos . . .

El amoratado fué morado oscuro. ¿Estaría soñando? ¿La convidaban al palco? ¿Al palco, con la Marquesa?

—Son dos butacas que le han enviado a nuestro jefe—prosiguió la dama—, y yo no sé por dónde lo ha sabido este diablillo de Enriqueta, que además ha averiguado que el jefe no

[8] *Palacio,* the Royal Palace
[9] *y no acababa,* and couldn't say enough
[10] *la* for *le,* as not infrequently heard even in the speech of cultivated people
[11] *pentagrama,* musical scale
[12] *platea,* box (at the opera)
[13] *¡Si es un bordado!* Why, it's an artistic triumph!

quiere aprovechar esas localidades, ni para sí, ni para su hijo; ¡prefieren irse a Apolo![14] . . . Y ha sido su discípula de usted quien ha pensado en seguida . . .

—¡Mil gracias, Enriquetita! . . . ¡Mil gracias, señora! —balbuceó la maestra, ya recobrada de su primera emoción—. Agradezco tanta bondad, y disfrutaría mucho oyendo la ópera, que no conozco sino en papeles[15] . . . ; pero ni mi esposo ni yo tenemos ropa . . . , vamos . . . , como la que hay que tener para ir a las butacas del Real.

—¡No importa! —gritó Enriqueta, que no renunciaba a su benéfico antojo—. Mamá le da a usted un vestido bonito . . . ¿No lo dijiste? —añadió colgándose del cuello de su madre como un diablillo zalamero, habituado a mandar—. ¿No dijiste que aquel vestido que se te quedó antiguo, de seda verde? ¿Y el abrigo de paño, el de color café, que no lo usas? ¿Y ropa de papá, un frac ya antiguo, para el marido de doña Consola?

—Sí, todo eso es verdad—confirmó la Marquesa—, y si doña Consolación no tiene inconveniente . . .

La profesora no sabía lo que la pasaba. Ignoraba si era pena, si era gozo, lo que oprimía su corazón enfermo y mal regulado. Pero Enriquetita, tenaz, aferrada al capricho bondadoso y a la diversión de la mascarada, insistía.

—¡Doña Consola! ¡Doña Consolita! Mire usted que lo pasará divinamente. Verá: mandamos un recado a su señor esposo, y le traen en un coche. Usted ya no se va. Les darán de cenar aquí. Toinette les viste . . .

—¿También va Toinette a vestir al marido de doña Consolación?— preguntó la Marquesa, contagiada del buen humor de la chiquilla.

—No; quise decir que Toinette la viste a usted, y a su marido le visite Lino, el ayuda de cámara de papá. ¡Ande usted, diga que sí! . . . Luego les tomamos otro coche, ¿no dijiste que se lo tomabas, mamá?, y se van ustedes al teatro.

La Marquesa hacía señales de aprobación, y, entretanto, la maestra meditaba . . . ¡Desnudarse delante de aquella Toinette, la doncella francesa, remilgada y burlona, que vería la ropa interior desaseada, los bajos destrozados, el corsé roto, de pobre dril gris! ¡Mostrar los estigmas de la miseria sufrida heroicamente, la flojedad de las carnes, que olían al sudor enfriado de tantas caminatas hechas a pie, por ahorrarse los diez céntimos del tranvía! ¡Enseñar su faldilla de barros, con el desgarrón, que no había tenido tiempo de remendar! Una vergüenza, una humillación dolorosa la impulsaban a gritar: «No, no iré, no me vestirán de carnaval con la librea de lujo . . .» Pero los ojos preciosos, límpidos, de Enriqueta, expresaban tal buena voluntad, tal afectuoso empeño de proporcionar a su profesora, por una noche, los goces de los privilegiados, que doña Consolación tuvo miedo de negarse a aquella humorada o gentil travesura. «Pueden quedar descontentos . . . Puedo perder esta lección de ricos, los diez y ocho duros al mes, casi tanto como gana Pablo con su empleo . . .» Y, en voz alta, tartamudeó:

—Pues lo que quiera Enriquetita . . . Lo que quiera . . .

Dos horas después estaba vestida y peinada doña Consola. Sobre su ropa blanca, perfumada de *foin,*[16] crujía la seda musgo[17] del traje, antiguo para la elegante Marquesa, en realidad casi de última moda, primorosamente

[14] *Apolo,* for *el Teatro de Apolo,* a theatre which specialized in light one-act plays
[15] *en papeles,* in newspaper accounts
[16] *foin,* (French) hay (name of a perfume)
[17] *musgo,* moss, here, moss-colored

adornado con bordados verde pálido y rosas en ligera guirnalda; en la cabeza un lazo de lentejuela hacía resaltar el brillo del pelo castaño, rizado con arte. Las mangas de la almilla[18] de algodón habían estorbado,[19] porque la manga del traje terminaba en el codo; pero Toinette, con alfileres, lo arregló, y la maestra lucía guantes blancos, largos, que le hacían la mano chica. Enriqueta bailaba de contento. No hacía sino contemplar a su profesora y repetir:

—¡Si se ha vuelto tan guapa! ¡Si no parece la de los demás días!

Bajaban la escalera interior doña Consolación y su consorte, para meterse en el cochecillo, y apenas se atrevían a mirarse; tan raros se encontraban, él de rigurosa etiqueta, envarado;[20] ella emperifollada, sintiéndose, en efecto, bonita y rejuvenecida dos lustros[21] . . . Al arrancar el simón,[22] el marido murmuró, bajo y como si se recatase:

—¿Sabes que me gustas así?

Y ella—pensando en que al otro día iba a recobrar sus semiandrajos,[23] su traje negro, decente y raído, y que la vida continuaría con los ahogos económicos y físicos, las deudas y los ataques de sofocación al subir tramos de escaleras—, se echó en brazos de él y rompió en sollozos.

[18] *almilla,* undershirt
[19] *habían estorbado,* had been in the way
[20] *envarado,* sitting up straight
[21] *lustro,* a period of five years
[22] *simón,* a type of horse-drawn cab
[23] *semiandrajos,* half-rags

The Generation of 1898

THE literature of the first twenty-five or thirty years of the twentieth century is dominated in the main by a group of authors that we call the 'Generation of '98.' Some critics have claimed that these men do not form a true literary group or school; perhaps their relationship is not so much literary as ideological. The date attributed to this group refers to the Spanish-American War, and to the Spaniard that war was a national catastrophe. The young men who grew up and began to write under the influence of this disaster blamed it on the self-satisfied attitude of the past generation. They regarded the nineteenth century as a total failure in its attempts to reform governmental and social institutions. The desire for a complete break with the nineteenth century was common to all the new generation.

The young men of '98 felt that their first duty was to see Spain clearly, to lay aside the rose-colored glasses of optimism and see all the faults and shortcomings of their fatherland. Even in the description of landscape they avoided the smiling aspects of nature. In choice of characters and settings they also exposed the sores and wounds of the nation. With themselves they were no more indulgent. They pried into the recesses of their own minds and souls with the desire of finding out why they (and all the young people of their generation) were failures. They discovered within themselves an overwhelming lack of will to face the struggles of life. Thus their first principle was to discover the ills of Spain in order to attempt to heal them.

But when it came to positive suggestions for reforms and improvements, the Generation of '98 had no strikingly new solutions to offer. Its social program was largely a continuation of ideas of Larra, Galdós, and other less known nineteenth-century reformers. However, many new ideas were brought in from outside Spain, and the young authors felt enthusiasm for Nietzsche, Ibsen, and many other European thinkers. Spain itself produced philosophers of outstanding caliber and originality for the first time in over two hundred years.

All this with regard to the social, political, and philosophical side of the Generation of '98. From the strictly literary point of view we find two characteristics in most of its members. The emphasis on originality of style is infinitely greater than ever before. All the young authors wished to break with the rhetorical style of the nineteenth century with its long sentences and frequent improvisation. No common style was established, each author being completely independent, but careful workmanship and a nervous, concise manner of writing was the rule. A great interest in the materials of their art—in this case, words—and the variety of new effects possible through new combinations is seen in these writers, just as a similar interest in materials can be observed in the young painters of the time. In the second place, many of this group of authors show a new kind of realism, tortured by pain, which appears in both landscape and characters. Oftentimes the characters reflect in their mental disturbances the mentality of the new generation, introspective, analytical, and thoroughly dissatisfied with itself.

Novelists

PÍO BAROJA (1872–1956), a rough, virile Basque, naturally turned to action as the remedy for the ills of life. But he felt that the checks and restrictions of society had robbed him of the freedom to act. Consequently a deep hatred for all branches of society runs throughout his work. As if to compensate for his own frustration, he turned to writing of men of action, men in conflict with society and indifferent to its laws. A great many of his heroes are adventurers or vagabonds; but he also has a type of hero who, like himself, suffers from the inability to act. His narratives relate, in a deliberately rough style, devoid of all literary devices and sham, the rather haphazard adventures of his protagonists.[1]

RAMÓN DEL VALLE-INCLÁN (1869–1936) contrasts sharply with Baroja and with his whole generation in that he escapes from the problems of everyday life into a poetic, unreal world. Externally it resembles his native Galicia, but his imagination peoples it with primitive peasants filled with ancient superstitions and semi-pagan beliefs, and with despotic, cruel noblemen. Like Bécquer, Valle-Inclán never could distinguish what he imagined from what he really saw. He has an aristocratic distaste for the common stuff of life, and the artist's desire to remove himself from humdrum, bourgeois existence.

While seeking violent and weird emotions, Valle-Inclán falls into a decadent enjoyment of sensation for itself. Perhaps his attitude is best expressed by the word 'perverse,' for he often gives us exactly the contrary emotion to one which we normally expect. For instance, he portrays with

[1] Important novels: *Zalacaín, el aventurero; La busca; Camino de perfección; Paradox, rey*

approval a feudal nobleman who hates his sons and is in turn bitterly hated by them.

All this matter is written in an unusually lyric style, more like poetry than prose. It is no doubt mannered, but it possesses beautiful rhythms and is expressed in words often chosen not so much for their sense as for their power of suggestion.[2]

AZORÍN (real name, José Martínez Ruiz) (1874–) is really more of an essayist than a novelist. He gives a splendid example of the Generation of '98's scrutinizing attitude towards Spain and the problem of personal adjustment to the world. All of his attention centers on two things: the landscape or atmosphere of Spanish life, and himself. His novels are his own spiritual history. He depicts himself as a shy, over-refined young man, too developed intellectually and too analytical to have will for action. In painting atmosphere, Azorín fixes his attention on small, humble things and is fond of describing minutely everything in a landscape, a street, or a room—as, for example, all the utensils and tools in a farm kitchen. He feels that these minute details are suggestive of the feeling of the whole scene. Moreover, while many great and important things pass away with time, the small, humble, everyday objects continue to exist. Azorín likes to give us the sensation of the passage of time through this device of showing how small things continue while men and even civilizations pass away.[3]

Azorín, too, has a very personal style. He seldom uses any but the present tense and is fond of using subject pronouns and of repetition of words.[4]

Philosophers

MIGUEL DE UNAMUNO (1864–1936) was, like Baroja, a Basque and had similar qualities of roughness and vitality. But Unamuno was also a widely read, cultured professor of Greek and president of the University of Salamanca. From these opposing elements, a spiritual conflict developed within him between his vital instinct, leading to an intense desire for immortality, and his European culture, which led him to skepticism. This inner battle between intuition and logical thought was what Unamuno had in mind when he defined himself by saying: 'I am a man of contradiction and of strife.' His yearning for immortality, his terror at the thought

[2] Important novels: *Sonata de estío; Romance de lobos; Flor de santidad*

[3] Thus Azorín developed the ideas and techniques used so successfully by the French writer Proust some years later.

[4] Important novels: *La voluntad; Doña Inés*
Important collection of essays: *Castilla; Los pueblos*

of ceasing to be, turned him more and more towards intuitive faith. He concluded his greatest work with the words: 'And[5] if what is reserved for us [after this life] is nothingness, let us act so that this will be an injustice.'[6]

JOSÉ ORTEGA Y GASSET (1883–1955), as well as Unamuno, believes that the living man must be the center of all philosophical thought. But this author is a refined, cultured man with little sympathy for the masses and what he calls 'mass-ideas.' He believes that Spain's difficulties lie precisely in the lack of a select minority and that the nineteenth century as a whole is characterized by the triumph of the commonplace through a false application of democracy to non-political spheres such as art, education, and philosophy. He says man became less and less important throughout the nineteenth century and things (cf. the materialism of science, manufacturing, and business) took precedence over man. Ortega, therefore, hopes for a violent break with the nineteenth century and a shaking off of the bonds of materialism. He, like Unamuno, concludes that intuitive thought is more important than logic, as it places greater value on man's feeling towards things than on the things in themselves. Ortega y Gasset has been widely read in translation outside of Spain and is much admired in the English-speaking world.[7]

Dramatists

JACINTO BENAVENTE (1868–1954) began his career as a playwright with severely realistic pictures of Spanish life, showing a cold, cynical attitude towards the shortcomings of his characters. Benavente was born in Madrid, and in his early works he portrays the upper and middle classes of the capital. His tendency is to see the evil they do much more clearly than the good and to present it without moralization and with a frigid indifference to reform. In this early period he also deliberately tones down the dramatic intensity of his work.

Later in life he modifies all these characteristics. He often sets his plays in imaginary places, thus getting rid of the realism imposed by the Madrid atmosphere; he begins to moralize and to champion Goodness and Kindliness (which he finds only in women); and he often allows himself the most intense dramatic situations and violent action.

Benavente captured the stage from his great predecessor, Echegaray, and

[5] «Y si es la nada lo que nos está reservada, hagamos que sea una injusticia esto,» from *Del sentimiento trágico de la vida*. Compare this attitude with the Stoicism of Quevedo, Vol. I, pp. 233–4.

[6] Important works: *Del sentimiento trágico de la vida; La agonía del cristianismo; Ensayos* (many volumes)

[7] Important works: *España invertebrada; La rebelión de las masas; El tema de nuestro tiempo*

broke almost completely with Spanish tradition. He sought his models outside of Spain, in Shakespeare, Molière, Ibsen, and the contemporary French dramatists. The new direction he gave the drama was followed by all the younger group, including Martínez Sierra and Linares Rivas, and to some extent by the Quintero brothers.[8]

Pío Baroja

Ayer y hoy

Los requetés[1] *en Vera*[2]

Yo paso gran parte del año en Vera del Bidasoa, y estaba en casa cuando estallaron los acontecimientos revolucionarios que perturban a España. Hace ocho días supimos que había llegado al pueblo un camión cargado de comunistas y de gentes del Frente Popular de Irún,[3] que recorrieron las calles de la aldea, y a la mañana siguiente, después de vitorear a la República y dedicarse un poco a la pedantería de los puños en alto[4] y de «¡Salud, camaradas!», volvieron a Guipúzcoa[5] e hicieron saltar[6] el puente de Endarlaza. Dos días después entraban en Vera los requetés salidos de Pamplona.[7] Al salir de mi casa, por la mañana, me dijeron: «Ahí están.» Efectivamente, en mi barrio, que llaman de Alzate, delante de una casa de dos pisos, con un balcón con una muestra[8] donde se leía «Círculo de la Unión Republicana,» había un grupo de veinte a treinta hombres con traje amarillo «kaki,» boina roja y un fusil brillante, moderno. Me pareció una escena del tiempo de la guerra carlista y del cura Santa Cruz.[9] Un oficial, desde el balcón, arrancó el palo del asta de bandera e hizo saltar a hachazos el letrero y lo tiró al suelo. Después fué sacando libros y amontonándolos en la calle, donde los soldados les prendieron fuego. Entre los libros ha-

[8] Important plays of Benavente: *Los intereses creados; La comida de las fieras; La noche del sábado; La malquerida; Señora ama.* Of Martínez Sierra: *Canción de cuna; El reino de Dios.* Of Linares Rivas: *La garra; El abolengo.* Of Los Quintero: *Malvaloca; Doña Clarines*

[1] *requetés,* members of the private army of absolute monarchists, organized with the idea of overthrowing the Spanish republic. Their center of activity was Navarre and the Basque provinces. The distinctive element of their uniform was the red beret (*boina roja*).

[2] *Vera* is a small town on the Bidasoa River, not far from the French border, in the province of Navarre. In later life Baroja owned a house there.

[3] *Frente Popular,* an alliance of leftist political parties which controlled the government of the republic at the outbreak of the Spanish Civil War (July 1936). *Irún,* the city near the mouth of the Bidasoa River, the chief point of entrance into Spain from France at the western end of the Pyrenees.

[4] *puños en alto,* the raised fist; that is, the salute of the Popular Front.

[5] *Guipúzcoa,* the Basque province adjacent to Navarre, in which Irún and San Sebastián are located.

[6] *hicieron saltar,* they blew up

[7] *Pamplona,* the chief city and capital of Navarre

[8] *muestra,* here, sign

[9] *la guerra carlista;* there were two Carlist wars, 1834–40 and 1872–76. The supporters of Don Carlos (see p. 256) were absolutists, who fought against any liberalization in government or religion. The *requetés* were their ideological offspring. Baroja was very interested in the second Carlist war and wrote many novels set in that period. *El cura Santa Cruz,* a priest who became noted as the leader of a guerrilla band during the second Carlist war. He is a character in some of Baroja's works.

bía algunos míos que había regalado al pequeño casino. Allí quedaron carbonizados.

Estas tropas del requeté tenían cierto aspecto. En su mayoría eran hombres pequeños, casi todos de la Rivera de Navarra.[10] Había un muchacho alto y grueso, con una boina de borla amarilla, y uno viejo con gran aire de antiguo guerrillero. Después de destrozar la pequeña biblioteca del círculo, pusieron un letrero que decía: «Dios, patria, fueros[11] y Rey.» Estuve hablando con los requetés. Uno me preguntó qué habían hecho los comunistas al pasar por el pueblo. Yo les dije que nada. «¡Lástima que no los hayamos encontrado!» dijo uno. «¿Y ustedes—les pregunté—, están dispuestos a la guerra?» «No, pero no nos darán miedo las balas. Bien confesados y bien comulgados, para morir lo mismo da hoy que mañana»—me contestá uno pequeño. «¿No tendrá usted hijos?» preguntó una mujer. «Sí, tengo cinco, tan pequeños que caben en esta cartuchera.»

Vamos a Almandor

Al día siguiente se habló en Vera de que venían más tropas del requeté, que iban al límite de Navarra con Guipúzcoa al mando del coronel Beorlegui. Los dos médicos del pueblo fueron a las proximidades de Endarlaza para establecer una ambulancia de la Cruz Roja. El miércoles por la tarde uno de los agentes de policía de Vera me dijo:

—Hoy tiene usted an espectáculo interesantísimo. Va a llegar una columna de Pamplona al mando del coronel Ortiz de Zárate, que entrará por el vecino pueblo de Lesaca y marchará a forzar el camino de Oyarzún para acercarse a San Sebastián.

Esta es una de las marchas que hacía con frecuencia el cura Santa Cruz. Cuando me decían esto se encontraba conmigo un médico del pueblo, Dr. José Ochoteco y un policía. El Dr. Ochoteco había venido en un automóvil pequeño con una gran cruz roja en el parabrisa. Llevaba en la manga un brazal con la misma cruz. El policía dijo:

—Ochoteco podría llevarnos en su coche para ver el paso de la columna.

—Muy bien—contestó el médico—, vamos en seguida.

—Vamos—repliqué.

Subimos los tres al automóvil y nos encaminamos hacia Lesaca. A la entrada del puente sobre el Bidasoa, vimos a dos oficiales, uno de los cuales conocía al médico.

—No ha llegado aún la columna—le dijeron—, pero debe estar cerca.

Yo le dije al médico que me parecía que lo mejor sería volver.

—¿A usted le importa[12] —me preguntó el médico—que vayamos hasta Almandor para ver a mi mujer que está algo enferma?

—A mí, no.

Llegamos a Almandor; fuimos a casa del suegro del doctor y desde el balcón comenzamos a ver el avance de la columna medio militar, medio carlista.[13] Irían de 700 a 800 hombres en

[10] *La Rivera de Navarra,* the southern part of Navarre, along the Ebro River. In other works, Baroja shows disdain for the inhabitants of this region.

[11] *fueros,* local laws or exemptions from national law. The Basques and Navarrese clung tenaciously to their special exemptions, an important element in their traditionalistic point of view.

[12] *le importa . . . que,* here, does it make any difference to you if

[13] *medio militar, medio carlista,* half regular army, half *requetés*

varios camiones, requetés de boina roja, soldados de artillería con piezas ligeras y automóviles de oficiales y jefes. Los requetés gritaban y saludaban al estilo fascista; los soldados de artillería, con casco de acero y trajes obscuros, se mostraban serios y no hacían manifestaciones de entusiasmo. Pasó toda la columna y nosotros pensamos abandonar Almandor y salir para Vera. Nuestro médico tenía prisa y cuando encontramos los últimos camiones detenidos, empezamos a adelantarnos.[14] Era seguramente una imprudencia. Bajamos la cuesta hasta Mugaire, siempre adelantando a los camiones, entre mujeres y sacerdotes que nos aplaudían como si fuéramos de la comitiva.

Nos prenden

De pronto se comenzaron a oír grandes voces de ¡Alto! ¡Alto! Nosotros nos detuvimos y oímos la voz de uno que gritaba:

—A ver ese automóvil donde va Pío Baroja.

Cuatro o cinco hombres altos, de aspecto amenazador, nos hicieron bajar del coche y uno de ellos gritó:

—¡Pónganse en fila!

Entonces nos amenazaron con pistolas y nos registraron. Yo creí, a la verdad, que en aquel momento nos fusilaban. «Nos van a matar aquí—pensé con cierta indiferencia—. Yo gritaré «¡Viva la libertad!» Tras un momento nos registraron y al policía le arrancaron violentamente la placa, la pistola y todo lo que llevaba en el bolsillo. En aquel momento yo no tenía todo el miedo que lógicamente debía tener. Sentía un fondo de desprecio por esta escenografía repugnante. Setecientos hombres para asustar a tres personas inofensivas era demasiado. No sé si esperaban de nosotros algún acto de desesperación. Después de tenernos algún tiempo rígidos en la carretera, amenazados con pistolas, subimos al automovil con orden de seguir detrás de otro que nos señalaron. Este aparato, esta pedantería nietzschiana,[15] se me antojaba absurda . . .

Seguimos al automóvil que nos indicaron y llegamos a la entrada del pueblo de Santesteban. El pueblo tiene un camino que pasa por un puente para unirse a la carretera. En esa encrucijada se aglomeraban los requetés y el público. Entonces el hombre alto que me había amenazado con una pistola se acercó a nuestro coche y dijo, señalándome y mostrándome a los requetés:

—Este es el viejo miserable que ha insultado en sus libros a la religión y al tradicionalismo.

Yo nada contesté. «Hay que matarlo,» dijeron los requetés. Me chocó la mansedumbre del público, pues nadie hizo la menor objeción. Un fotógrafo pretendió hacer una fotografía, pero alguien dió un manotazo a la máquina, que cayó al suelo. Algunos de los requetés y de los soldados venían a mirarme la cara, como a una fiera. Después de media hora, un jefe dijo que teníamos que ir a Vera, y en ese momento un puño entró[16] violentamente y me rozó la cara. Aquí pensé que alguno iba a agarrarme del brazo, a sacarme violentamente y a dejarme tendido en la carretera.

Salimos de Santesteban y llegamos a Vera. No sé qué conciliábulos hubo

[14] *adelantarnos,* to advance, passing the trucks

[15] *pedanteria nietzschiana,* showing off like supermen

[16] *entró,* supply *en el coche*

allí, pero al cabo de una hora nos mandaron volver a Santesteban. «Allí nos matan,» pensé. A la entrada del pueblo nos rodearon cuatro guardias civiles y en medio de la gente, tocada con boinas rojas, fuimos a la cárcel que se encuentra en el sótano del Ayuntamiento.

Al entrar en ella dije a mis compañeros:

—Aquí creo que ya estamos en seguridad.

Horas después se presentó el oficial del estado mayor de la columna, hombre amable. Me dijo que podía salir de la cárcel e irme a dormir al hotel. Yo contesté:

—Me quedo aquí, no sólo por compañerismo, sino porque me encuentro más seguro; en un hotel podrían matarme con mucha más facilidad.

El oficial del estado mayor dijo que a los tres nos pusieran en libertad una hora después de salir la columna del pueblo, pero a poco se presentó un sargento de la guardia civil y nos dijo que en la comida que habían tenido los oficiales se decidió que era impropio y de mal efecto encarcelar a gente inocente. Así que el médico y yo podíamos marcharnos y que el policía se quedaría en la cárcel por no haber dejado pasar a Francia un automóvil de uno de los señores fascistas que iban de expedición.[17] Dejamos al pobre policía en la cárcel y marchamos a casa de un compañero del doctor Ochoteco, el médico Aguirre.

Escapada

Al llegar a casa de éste comencé a tener un gran pánico y a perder la serenidad. El sargento de la guardia civil que nos acompañaba nos dijo que le diéramos palabra de no salir de casa de Aguirre hasta las dos de la tarde del día siguiente. Nos tendimos Ochoteco y yo en la cama y estuvimos sin poder dormir. Teníamos la esperanza de que la columna abandonara pronto el pueblo. Efectivamente, a eso de las cinco o seis de la mañana empezamos a oír ruido de motores y gritos de ¡Viva España!, ¡Viva la religión! y ¡Viva el clero! Estaba yo relativamente tranquilo cuando a eso de las ocho o nueve de la mañana empezaron nuevamente a pasar camiones. Uno de éstos habíase volcado, quedando un muerto y varios heridos, y además la expedición había encontrado uno de los puentes en el camino de Leiza roto. De nuevo se llenó el pueblo de boinas rojas.

—Yo he tenido mucho miedo—me decía el médico—, pero ya se me va pasando. Dentro de unos días no me acuerdo de esto. Usted ha estado muy sereno.

—Sí; pero ahora me empieza el pánico a mí y es posible que ya no se me quite.

Hablamos con el Dr. Aguirre de cómo se podría salir de Santesteban, sin peligro, y pensamos que mejor sería hacerlo después de comer, porque en estos primeros días los requetés se dedicaban a comer y beber alegremente y probablemente después a dormir. El sargento de la guardia civil nos dió un salvoconducto para llegar a Vera. Después de comer. fuimos a la cárcel con ánimo de saludar al policía compañero de viaje pero no pudimos. Salimos a la carretera bajo un sol de fuego. En todos los pueblos del tránsito había jóvenes armados, gente petulante con fusiles

[17] *iban de expedición,* who were members of the expeditionary force

y escopetas modernos. En Sumbilla nos pararon un momento, después seguimos adelante hasta Vera, donde mi hermano, cuando le conté lo que me había pasado, me dijo que iría al pueblo para preguntar a los carabineros si me podían dar un salvoconducto para llegar a Francia, pero le dijeron que no. Yo me decidí a marchar a pie. A los dos kilómetros de andar, vi que subía un automóvil y lo detuve. El dueño era un español de apellido francés. En la carretera no había obstáculos, pero antes de llegar al punto avanzado apareció un carabinero. «Este me fastidia,» me dije. El carabinero pidió los papeles al propietario del automóvil y luego me dijo:

—¡Usted es Pío Baroja!

—Sí, señor.

—Usted ha sido preso. Así lo dice el «Diario le Navarra.»

—Es verdad, pero me soltaron.

—¿Y ahora a dónde va?

—Voy a uno de estos caseríos de España.

Entonces el carabinero se echó a reír:

—Ya veo que va usted a Francia; yo no se lo impediré, que cada cual se salve como pueda.

—Pues, muchas gracias.

En la frontera varias personas se interesaron por saber lo que me había pasado. Por la noche me llevaron hasta Hendaya,[18] a casa de unos amigos.

He ido después a la frontera de Vera, en el collado de Ibardin, para ver si no hay ya vigilancia y comunicarme con mi familia, pero allí siguen las boinas rojas y los hombres con arma al brazo montando la guardia.

En esta situación, un tanto mísera, no es fácil tener serenidad de juicio para contemplar los sucesos de manera clara y objetiva. Intentaré hacerlo en otro artículo de manera clara y personal. Parece que el escritor tiene algo de rumiante y que vive más de los recuerdos que en los hechos, porque ahora, en salvo, me tiembla la mano al escribir como si el recordar el peligro fuera para mí más desagradable que el afrontarlo y tenerlo delante.

Comentarios

Quiero insistir en que no estoy de acuerdo, en la teoría ni en la práctica, con las derechas ni con las izquierdas. Mi punto de vista es solamente personal e individual. Lo único que deseo infervientemente es que el estado de España se normalice y que pueda vivir el que trabaja. Varias cuestiones o problemas se plantean hoy a los españoles y a los extranjeros ante la revolución desencadenada en España. La obscuridad de estos problemas depende de muchas causas . . .

España es el país más vario de Europa en su naturaleza . . . pero esta variedad no es principalmente variedad en la riqueza, sino más bien en la pobreza. España es un mundo en pequeño. Un país así puede tener, evidentemente—y lo tiene—, mucho interés para el escritor y el psicólogo, pero un interés muy poco práctico. Actualmente, el interés así no se cotiza. De aquí que España sea un pueblo que vive en el aislamiento, como encerrado en una campana neumática, y que sólo sus productos culturales antiguos tengan valor en el mundo . . .

Como falta el conocimiento de los

[18] *Hendaya,* the French town (Hendaye) across the river from Irún

hechos y la filosofía sobre ellos, falta también un concepto claro y aproximado de lo que es la realidad del país. La información falla en muchos órdenes de la vida. La cultura también. En el ambiente no hay más que lugares comunes y dogmas, la mayoría venidos de fuera. Esto produce el feo contraste de un pueblo naturalmente original, dedicado a la vulgaridad y a la imitación. Un pueblo que pretende ser otra cosa de lo que es. Asi, sintiéndose nacionalista, defiende el internacionalismo, y encontrándose individualista, quiere implantar el comunismo. Las dos tendencias políticas que tienen raíces en el fondo psicológico del español son el tradicionalismo y el individualismo anarquista . . .

Otra cuestión que interesa a muchos es preguntarse: ¿Cómo ha surgido la violencia? No es fácil, ni casi posible, que unos tengan toda la culpa. Mucha gente ignoraba, porque no se hablaba de ello en los periódicos, pero muchos lo sabíamos, que casi todos los días había asesinatos políticos en la capital. Socialistas y fascistas se atacaban a traición, y dejaban a cada paso cadáveres en las calles . . . Después de la lucha de callejuela, individual, ha estallado la guerra civil, con caracteres 5 parecidos de violencia y de barbarie. Estas manifestaciones violentas y sanguinarias de los españoles se explican en el extranjero y en nuestro país por los eternos lugares comunes pues- 10 tos en circulación desde hace siglos. En uno de estos periódicos de Francia del Sur, con mucha solemnidad se decía hace días, como quien dice algo importante y nuevo: «España es afri- 15 cana.» La idea es muy vieja, y se ha atribuído a muchos. ¿A qué pueblo de Africa se parece España? ¿A Egipto, a Argelia, a Marruecos, a Túnez, al Transvaal? No se parece en nada a 20 aquellos países, ni en la historia, ni en la étnica. También se dice que tenemos la sangre de los árabes. ¿Qué sangre árabe van a tener los vascos, los navarros, los asturianos y los galle- 25 gos, en donde la violencia se da como en todas partes? Todas estas teorías valen poco, o no valen nada. Es explicar lo mal conocido por algo completamente desconocido . . .

Mi opinión

Alguno me preguntará: ¿Y su opi- 30 nión? Ciertamente, yo no me recato en darla. En estos momentos soy partidario de una dictadura militar que esté basada en la pura autoridad y que tenga fuerza para dominar los instintos 35 rencorosos y vengativos de la masa reaccionaria y de la masa socialista. Yo no puedo tener simpatía por esa turba tradicionalista, defensora de la religión, que es capaz de insultar y 40 probablemente de matar a un escritor porque no comparte sus ideas. Tampoco experimento la menor estimación por esa plebe socialista de Madrid, que lanzó hace meses la estúpida noticia de que las damas católicas daban caramelos envenenados a los chicos, lo que la autorizaba para incendiar, robar y maltratar. Tanto una masa como otra me parecen lo peor del país, lo más brutal, lo más despótico y lo más sanguinario. No creo que sea raro que un hombre como yo desee que aparezca el domador de esas bestias feroces, y que lo haga, no como el legendario Orfeo, con la lira en la mano, sino con el filo de la espada.

Ramón del Valle-Inclán

El miedo

Ese largo y angustioso escalofrío que parece mensajero de la muerte, el verdadero escalofrío del miedo, sólo lo he sentido una vez. Fué hace muchos años, en aquel hermoso tiempo de los mayorazgos,[1] cuando se hacía información de nobleza para ser militar. Yo acababa de obtener los cordones de Caballero Cadete.[2] Hubiera preferido entrar en la Guardia de la Real Persona,[3] pero mi madre se oponía, y siguiendo la tradición familiar fuí granadero en el Regimiento del Rey. No recuerdo con certeza los años que hace, pero entonces apenas me apuntaba el bozo y hoy ando cerca de ser un viejo caduco. Antes de entrar en el Regimiento, mi madre quiso echarme su bendición. La pobre señora vivía retirada en el fondo de una aldea, donde estaba nuestro pazo[4] solariego, y allá fuí sumiso y obediente. La misma tarde que llegué mandó en busca del Prior de Brandeso para que viniese a confesarme en la capilla del pazo. Mis hermanas María Isabel y María Fernanda, que eran unas niñas, bajaron a coger rosas al jardín, y mi madre llenó con ellas los floreros del altar. Después me llamó en voz baja para darme su devocionario y decirme que hiciese examen de conciencia:

—Vete a la tribuna,[5] hijo mío. Allí estarás mejor . . .

La tribuna señorial estaba al lado del Evangelio,[6] y comunicaba con la biblioteca. La capilla era húmeda, tenebrosa, resonante. Sobre el retablo campeaba el escudo concedido por ejecutorias de los Reyes Católicos al señor de Bradomín, Pedro Aguiar de Tor, llamado el Chivo y también el Viejo. Aquel caballero estaba enterrado a la derecha del altar: El sepulcro tenía la estatua orante[7] de un guerrero. La lámpara del presbiterio[8] alumbraba día y noche ante el retablo,[9] labrado como joyel de reyes: Los áureos racimos de la vid evangélica[10] parecían ofrecerse cargados de fruto. El santo tutelar era aquel piadoso Rey Mago que ofreció mirra al Niño Dios: Su túnica de seda bordada[11] de oro brillaba con el resplandor devoto de un milagro oriental. La luz de la lámpara, entre las cadenas[12] de plata, tenía tímido aleteo de pájaro prisionero como si se afanase por volar hacia el Santo. Mi madre quiso que fuesen sus manos las que dejasen aquella tarde a los pies del Rey Mago los floreros cargados de rosas, como ofrenda de su alma devota. Después, acompañada de mis hermanas, se arrodilló ante el altar: Yo desde la tribuna solamente oía el murmullo de su voz, que guiaba moribunda las avemarías, pero cuando a las niñas les tocaba

[1] *mayorazgo,* first born son of a noble family; the estate which this son inherited, and which could not be sold or donated to anyone else. The law permitting the sale of entailed estates was passed in 1837, hence, this story is set before this date.

[2] *cordones de Caballero Cadete,* the shoulder knot (insignia) of a gentleman cadet (in the military forces)

[3] *Guardia de la Real Persona,* the king's bodyguard

[4] *pazo,* a manor house. (A word used in Galicia, Valle-Inclán's native region.)

[5] *tribuna,* gallery

[6] *lado del Evangelio,* the left hand side of the altar area

[7] *orante,* praying, kneeling in prayer

[8] *presbiterio,* chancel, area before the altar

[9] *retablo,* altar screen, reredos

[10] *la vid evangélica,* the carved grape vine ornamenting the altar screen, symbolizing the wine of the communion.

[11] Images in Spanish churches are frequently dressed in real clothes of costly materials.

[12] *cadena,* chain. The lamp is supported by chains from the ceiling.

responder, oía todas las palabras rituales de la oración. La tarde agonizaba y los rezos resonaban en la silenciosa oscuridad de la capilla, hondos, tristes y augustos, como un eco de la Pasión. Yo me adormecía en la tribuna. Las niñas fueron a sentarse en las gradas del altar: Sus vestidos eran albos como el lino de los paños litúrgicos. Ya sólo distinguí una sombra que rezaba bajo la lámpara del presbiterio: Era mi madre que sostenía entre sus manos un libro abierto y leía con la cabeza inclinada. De tarde en tarde, el viento mecía la cortina de un alto ventanal: Yo entonces veía en el cielo, ya oscuro, la faz de la luna, pálida y sobrenatural como una diosa que tiene su altar en los bosques y en los lagos . . .

Mi madre cerró el libro dando un suspiro y de nuevo llamó a las niñas. Vi pasar sus sombras blancas a través del presbiterio y columbré que se arrodillaban a los lados de mi madre. La luz de la lámpara temblaba con un débil resplandor sobre las manos que volvían a sostener abierto el libro. En silencio la voz leía piadosa y lenta. Las niñas escuchaban, y adiviné sus cabelleras sueltas sobre la albura del ropaje y cayendo a los lados del rostro iguales, tristes, nazarenas. Habíame adormecido, y de pronto me sobresaltaron los gritos de mis hermanas. Miré y las vi en medio del presbiterio abrazadas a mi madre. Gritaban despavoridas. Mi madre las asió de la mano y huyeron las tres. Bajé presuroso. Iba a seguirlas, y quedé sobrecogido de terror. En el sepulcro del guerrero se entrechocaban los huesos del esqueleto. Los cabellos se erizaron en mi frente. La capilla había quedado en el mayor silencio, y oíase distintamente el hueco y medroso rodar de la calavera sobre su almohada de piedra. Tuve miedo, como no lo he tenido jámas, pero no quise que mi madre y mis hermanas me creyesen cobarde, y permanecí inmóvil en medio del presbiterio, con los ojos fijos en la puerta entreabierta. La luz de la lámpara oscilaba. En lo alto mecíase la cortina de un ventanal, y las nubes pasaban sobre la luna, y las estrellas se encendían y se apagaban como nuestras vidas. De pronto, allá lejos, resonó festivo ladrar de perros y música de cascabeles. Una voz grave y eclesiástica llamaba:

—¡Aquí, Carabel![13] ¡Aquí, Capitán! . . .

Era el Prior de Brandeso que llegaba para confesarme. Después oí la voz de mi madre trémula y asustada, y percibí distintamente la carrera retozona de los perros. La voz grave y eclesiástica se elevaba lentamente, como un canto gregoriano:

—Ahora veremos qué ha sido ello . . . Cosa del otro mundo no lo es, seguramente . . . ¡Aquí, Carabel! ¡Aquí, Capitán! . . .

Y el Prior de Brandeso, precedido de sus lebreles,[14] apareció en la puerta de la capilla:

—¿Qué sucede, señor Granadero del Rey?

Yo repuse con la voz ahogada:

—¡Señor Prior, he oído temblar el esqueleto dentro del sepulcro! . . .

El Prior atravesó lentamente la capilla: Era un hombre arrogante y erguido. En sus años juveniles también había sido Granadero del Rey: Llegó hasta mí, sin recoger el vuelo[15] de sus hábitos blancos, y afirmándome una mano en el hombro y mirándome la faz descolorida, pronunció gravemente:

—¡Que nunca pueda decir el Prior de Brandeso que ha visto temblar a un Granadero del Rey! . . .

No levantó la mano de mi hombro,

[13] *Carabel,* name of one of the dogs
[14] *lebrel,* greyhound
[15] *vuelo,* flight; here, fullness

y permanecimos inmóviles, contemplándonos sin hablar. En aquel silencio oímos rodar la calavera del guerrero. La mano del Prior no tembló. A nuestro lado los perros enderezaban las orejas con el cuello espeluznado.[16] De nuevo oímos rodar la calavera sobre su almohada de piedra. El Prior me sacudió:

—¡Señor Granadero del Rey, hay que saber si son trasgos[17] o brujas! . . .

Y se acercó al sepulcro y asió las dos anillas de bronce empotradas[18] en una de las losas,[19] aquella que tenía el epitafio. Me acerqué temblando. El Prior me miró sin desplegar los labios. Yo puse mi mano sobre la suya en una anilla y tiré. Lentamente alzamos la piedra. El hueco, negro y frío, quedó ante nosotros. Yo vi que la árida y amarillenta calavera aún se movía. El Prior alargó un brazo dentro del sepulcro para cogerla: Después, sin una palabra y sin un gesto, me la entregó. La recibí temblando. Yo estaba en medio del presbiterio y la luz de la lámpara caía sobre mis manos. Al fijar los ojos las sacudí con horror: Tenía entre ellas un nido de culebras que se desanillaron silbando, mientras la calavera rodaba con hueco y liviano son, todas las gradas del presbiterio. El Prior me miró con sus ojos de guerrero que fulguraban bajo la capucha como bajo la visera de un casco:

—Señor Granadero del Rey, no hay absolución . . . ¡Yo no absuelvo a los cobardes!

Y salió de la capilla arrastrando sus hábitos talares.[20] Las palabras del Prior de Brandeso resonaron mucho tiempo en mis oídos: Resuenan aún. ¡Tal vez por ellas he sabido más tarde sonreir a la muerte como a una mujer! . . .

Miguel de Unamuno

Mi religión

Me escribe un amigo desde Chile diciéndome que se ha encontrado allí con algunos que, refiriéndose a mis escritos, le han dicho: «Y bien, en resumidas cuentas, ¿cuál es la religión de este señor Unamuno?» Pregunta análoga se me ha dirigido aquí varias veces. Y voy a ver si consigo, no contestarla, cosa que no pretendo, sino plantear algo mejor el sentido de tal pregunta.

Tanto los individuos como los pueblos de espíritu perezoso—y cabe[1] pereza espiritual con muy fecundas actividades de orden económico y de otros órdenes análogos—propenden al dogmatismo, sépanlo[2] o no lo sepan, quiéranlo o no, proponiéndose o sin proponérselo. La pereza espiritual huye de la posición crítica o escéptica.

Escéptica, digo, pero tomando la voz escepticismo en su sentido etimológico y filosófico, porque escéptico no quiere decir el que duda, sino el que investiga o rebusca, por oposición al que afirma y cree haber hallado. Hay quien escudriña un problema y hay quien nos da una fórmula, acertada o no, como solución de él.

En el orden de la pura especulación filosófica, es una precipitación[3] el pedirle a uno soluciones dadas,

[16] *con el cuello espeluznado,* with the hair of their necks standing on end
[17] *trasgo,* goblin, sprite
[18] *empotrado,* embedded
[19] *losa,* flagstone
[20] *hábitos talares,* full length robes
[1] *cabe,* here, is compatible
[2] *sépanlo,* whether they know it
[3] *precipitación,* a getting ahead of oneself

siempre que haya hecho adelantar el planteamiento[4] de un problema. Cuando se lleva mal un largo cálculo, el borrar lo hecho y empezar de nuevo significa un no pequeño progreso. Cuando una casa amenaza ruina o se hace completamente inhabitable, lo que procede[5] es derribarla, y no hay que pedir que se edifique otra sobre ella. Cabe, sí, edificar la nueva con materiales de la vieja, pero es derribando antes ésta. Entretanto, puede la gente albergarse en una barraca si no tiene otra casa, o dormir a campo raso.

Y es preciso no perder de vista que para la práctica de nuestra vida rara vez tenemos que esperar a las soluciones científicas definitivas. Los hombres han vivido y viven sobre hipótesis y explicaciones muy deleznables y aun sin ellas. Para castigar al delincuente no se pusieron de acuerdo sobre si éste tenía o no libre albedrío, como para estornudar no reflexiona uno sobre el daño que puede hacerle el pequeño obstáculo en la garganta que le obliga al estornudo.

Los hombres que sostienen que de no creer[6] en el castigo eterno del infierno serían malos, creo, en honor de ellos, que se equivocan. Si dejaran de creer en una sanción de ultratumba, no por eso se harían peores, sino que entonces buscarían otra justificación ideal a su conducta. El que siendo bueno cree en un orden trascendente, no tanto[7] es bueno por creer en él cuanto que[7] cree en él por ser bueno. Proposición ésta que habrá de parecer oscura o enrevesada, estoy de ello cierto, a los preguntones de espíritu perezoso.

«Y bien, se me dirá: cuál es tu religión?» Y yo responderé: «Mi religión es buscar la verdad en la vida y la vida en la verdad, aun a sabiendas de que no he de encontrarla mientras viva; mi religión es luchar con Dios desde el romper del alba hasta el caer de la noche, como dicen que con El luchó Jacob.[8] No puedo transigir con aquello del Inconocible[9]—o Incognoscible, como escriben los pedantes—, ni con aquello otro de «de aquí no pasarás.» Rechazo el eterno *ignorabimus.*[10] Y en todo caso quiero trepar a lo inaccesible.»

«Sed perfectos como vuestro Padre que está en los cielos es perfecto,» nos dijo el Cristo, y semejante ideal de perfección es, sin duda, inasequible. Pero nos puso lo inasequible como meta y término de nuestros esfuerzos. Y ello ocurrió, dicen los teólogos, con la gracia. Y yo quiero pelear mi pelea, sin cuidarme de la victoria. ¿No hay ejércitos y aun pueblos que van a una derrota segura? ¿No elogiamos a los que se dejaron matar peleando antes que rendirse? Pues ésta es mi religión.

Esos, los que me dirigen esa pregunta, quieren que les dé un dogma, una solución en que pueda descansar el espíritu en su pereza. Y ni esto quieren, sino que buscan poder encasillarme y meterme en uno de los cuadriculados en que colocan a los espíritus, diciendo de mí: «Es luterano, es calvinista, es católico, es ateo, es racionalista, es místico,» o cualquier otro de estos motes, cuyo sentido claro desconocen, pero que les dispensa de pensar más. Y yo no quiero dejarme encasillar, porque yo, Miguel de Unamuno, como cualquier otro hombre

[4] *planteamiento,* formulation, stating
[5] *proceder,* here, to come first
[6] *de no creer,* if they don't believe
[7] *no tanto . . . cuanto que,* not so much . . . as. (This sentence contains one of Unamuno's typical paradoxes.)
[8] See Genesis 32. 24–28.
[9] In his youth Unamuno was attracted to Herbert Spencer's philosophy, which declared that God was the unknowable. Now he rejects this doctrine.
[10] *ignorabimus,* (Latin) we shall not know

que aspire a conciencia plena,[11] soy una especie única. «No hay enfermedades, sino enfermos,» suelen decir algunos médicos, y yo digo que no hay opiniones, sino opinantes.

En el orden religioso apenas hay cosa alguna que tenga racionalmente resuelta, y como no la tengo, no puedo comunicarla lógicamente, porque sólo es lógico y transmisible lo racional. Tengo, sí, con el afecto, con el corazón, con el sentimiento, una fuerte tendencia al cristianismo, sin atenerme a dogmas especiales de esta o de aquella confesión cristiana. Considero cristiano a todo el que invoca con respeto y amor el nombre de Cristo, y me repugnan los ortodoxos, sean católicos o protestantes—éstos suelen ser tan intransigentes como aquéllos—, que niegen cristianismo a quienes no interpretan el Evangelio como ellos. Cristiano protestante conozco que niega que los unitarios sean cristianos.

Confieso sinceramente que las supuestas pruebas racionales—la ontológica, la cosmológica, la ética, etc., etc.—de la existencia de Dios no me demuestran nada; que cuantas razones se quieren dar de que existe un Dios me parecen razones basadas en paralogismos[12] y peticiones de principio.[13] En esto estoy con Kant. Y siento, al tratar de esto, no poder hablar a los zapateros en términos de zapatería.

Nadie ha logrado convencerme racionalmente de la existencia de Dios, pero tampoco de su no existencia; los razonamientos de los ateos me parecen de una superficialidad y futileza mayores aún que los de sus contradictores. Y si creo en Dios, o, por lo menos, creo creer en El, es, ante todo, porque quiero que Dios exista, y después, porque se me revela, por vía cordial, en el Evangelio y a través de Cristo y de la Historia. Es cosa de corazón.

Lo cual quiere decir que no estoy convencido de ello como lo estoy de que dos y dos hacen cuatro.

Si se tratara de algo en que no me fuera la paz de la conciencia y el consuelo de haber nacido, no me cuidaría acaso del problema; pero como en él me va mi vida toda interior y el resorte de toda mi acción, no puedo aquietarme con decir: ni sé ni puedo saber. No sé, cierto es; tal vez no pueda saber nunca, pero «quiero» saber. Lo quiero, y basta.

Y me pasaré la vida luchando con el misterio y aun sin esperanza de penetrarlo, porque esa lucha es mi alimento y es mi consuelo. Sí, mi consuelo. Me he acostumbrado a sacar esperanza de la desesperación misma. Y no griten: ¡paradojas!, los mentecatos y los superficiales.

No concibo a un hombre culto sin esta preocupación, y espero muy poca cosa en el orden de la cultura—y cultura no es lo mismo que civilización—de aquellos que viven desinteresados del problema religioso en su aspecto metafísico y sólo lo estudian en su aspecto social o político. Espero muy poco para el enriquecimiento del tesoro espiritual del género humano de aquellos hombres o de aquellos pueblos que, por pereza mental, por superficialidad, por cientificismo, o por lo que sea, se apartan de las grandes y eternas inquietudes del corazón. No espero nada de los que dicen: «¡No se debe pensar en eso!»; espero menos aún de los que creen en un cielo y un infierno como aquel en que creíamos de niños, y espero todavía menos de los que afirman con la gravedad del necio: «Todo eso no son sino fábulas y mitos; al que se muere lo entierran, y se acabó.» Sólo espero

[11] *a conciencia plena,* very conscientiously
[12] *paralogismo,* false reasoning
[13] *petición de principio,* begging the question

de los que ignoran, pero no se resignan a ignorar; de los que luchan sin descanso por la verdad y ponen su vida en la lucha misma más que en la victoria.

Y lo más de mi labor ha sido siempre inquietar a mis prójimos, removerles el poso del corazón, angustiarlos, si puedo. Lo dije ya en mi *Vida de Don Quijote y Sancho,* que es mi más extensa confesión a este respecto. Que busquen ellos como yo busco, que luchen como lucho yo, y entre todos algún pelo[14] de secreto arrancaremos a Dios, y, por lo menos, esa lucha nos hará más hombres, hombres de más espíritu.

Para esta obra—obra religiosa—me ha sido menester, en pueblos como estos pueblos de lengua castellana, carcomidos de pereza y de superficialidad de espíritu, adormecidos en la rutina del dogmatismo católico o del dogmatismo librepensador o cientifista; me ha sido preciso aparecer unas veces impúdico e indecoroso; otras, duro y agresivo; no pocas, enrevesado y paradójico. En nuestra menguada literatura apenas se le oía a nadie gritar desde el fondo del corazón, descomponerse, clamar. El grito era casi desconocido. Los escritores temían ponerse en ridículo. Les pasaba y les pasa lo que a muchos que soportan en medio de la calle una afrenta por temor al ridículo de verse con el sombrero por el suelo y presos por un polizonte. Yo, no; cuando he sentido ganas de gritar, he gritado. Jamás me he detenido el decoro. Y ésta es una de las cosas que menos me perdonan estos mis compañeros de pluma,[15] tan comedidios, tan correctos, tan disciplinados hasta cuando predican la incorrección y la indisciplina. Los anarquistas literarios se cuidan, más que de otra cosa, de la estilística y de la sintaxis. Y cuando desentonan, lo hacen entonadamente; sus desacordes tiran a ser[16] armónicos.

Cuando he sentido un dolor he gritado, y he gritado en público. Los salmos que figuran en mi volumen de *Poesías* no son más que gritos del corazón, con los cuales he buscado hacer vibrar las cuerdas dolorosas de los corazones de los demás. Si no tienen esas cuerdas, o si las tienen tan rígidas que no vibran, mi grito no resonará en ellas y declararán que eso no es poesía, poniéndose a examinarlo acústicamente. También se puede estudiar acústicamente el grito que lanza un hombre cuando ve caer muerto de repente a su hijo, y el que no tenga ni corazón ni hijos de queda en eso.

Esos salmos de mis *Poesías,* con otras varias composiciones que allí hay, son mi religión, y mi religión cantada y no expuesta lógica y razonadamente. Y la canto, mejor o peor, con la voz y el oído que Dios me ha dado, porque no la puedo razonar. Y el que vea raciocinio y lógica, y método y exégesis, más que vida, en esos mis versos, porque no hay en ellos faunos, dríadas, . . . y otras garambainas más o menos modernistas, allá se quede con lo suyo, que no voy a tocarle el corazón con arcos de violín ni con martillo.

De lo que huyo, repito, como de la peste, es de que me clasifiquen, y quiero morirme oyendo preguntar de mí a los holgazanes de espíritu que se paren alguna vez a oírme: «Y este señor, ¿qué es?» Los liberales o progresistas tontos me tendrán por reaccionario y acaso por místico, sin saber, por supuesto, lo que esto quiere decir, y los conservadores y reaccionarios tontos me tendrán por una especie de anarquista espiritual, y unos y otros, por un pobre señor afanoso de singularizarse y de pasar por original y cuya

[14] *pelo,* here, bit, particle
[15] *compañeros de pluma,* fellow writers
[16] *tiran a ser,* tend to be

cabeza es una olla de grillos.[17] Pero nadie debe cuidarse de lo que piensen de él los tontos, sean progresistas o conservadores, liberales o reaccionarios.

Y como el hombre es terco y no suele querer enterarse, y acostumbra después que se le ha sermoneado cuatro horas a volver a las andadas, los preguntones, si leen esto, volverán a preguntarme: «Bueno: ¿pero qué soluciones traes?» Y yo, para concluir, les diré que si quieren soluciones acudan a la tienda de enfrente, porque en la mía no se vende semejante artículo. Mi empeño ha sido, es y será que los que me lean piensen y mediten en las cosas fundamentales, y no ha sido nunca el de darles pensamientos hechos. Yo he buscado siempre agitar, y, a lo sumo, sugerir más que instruir. Si yo vendo pan, no es pan, sino levadura o fermento.

Hay amigos, y buenos amigos, que me aconsejan me deje de esta labor y me recoja a hacer lo que llaman una obra objetiva, «algo que sea—dicen—definitivo, algo de construcción, algo duradero.» Quieren decir algo dogmático. Me declaro incapaz de ello y reclamo mi libertad, mi santa libertad, hasta la de contradecirme, si llega el caso. Yo no sé si algo de lo que he hecho o de lo que haga en lo sucesivo habrá de quedar por años o por siglos después que me muera; pero sé que si se da un golpe en el mar sin orillas, las ondas en derredor van sin cesar, aunque debilitándose. Agitar es algo. Si merced a esa agitación viene detrás otro que haga algo duradero, en ello durará mi obra.

Es obra de misericordia suprema despertar al dormido y sacudir al parado, y es obra de suprema piedad religiosa buscar la verdad en todo y descubrir dondequiera el dolo, la necedad y la inepcia.

Ya sabe, pues, mi buen amigo el chileno lo que tiene que contestar a quien le pregunte cuál es mi religión. Ahora bien: si es uno de esos mentecatos que creen que guardo ojeriza a un pueblo o una patria cuando le he cantado las verdades a alguno de sus hijos irreflexivos, lo mejor que puede hacer es no contestarles.

[17] *olla de grillos,* pandemonium

José Ortega y Gasset

Pepe Tudela vuelva a la Mesta[1]

No será indiferente a los amigos de Pepe Tudela notificarles que éste se va a hacer ganadero. Es Pepe Tudela un muchacho soriano,[2] que vino a Madrid para estudiar carrera, hizo luego oposiciones al Cuerpo de Archiveros,[3] y habiendo triunfado en ellas, se reintegró a la provincia maternal como jefe del archivo de Hacienda.[4] Durante sus años madrileños, Tudela ganó la amistad de nuestros hombres de letras y ciencias, cultivó a críticos e historiadores del arte y fué asiduo miembro de la tertulia que en «El Gato Negro» gobierna con mano hábil don José María Soltura.[5] Yo siempre había estimado su gesto sencillo y discreto, su culto delicado a las cosas excelentes y una como sanidad moral que emana de su persona. Por todo ello me ha complacido, después de algunos años, volverle a hallar este verano en una excursión que desde Soria hice a la altura de Numancia.[6]

El cadáver milenario de Numancia yace sobre un cabezo de empinadas laderas que impera a un magnífico valle castellano. El perímetro de la urbe ciñe exactamente el del cabezo, de suerte que el perfil de las murallas, peraltado[7] sobre el paisaje, debía irradiar sobre el ancho contorno una incesante gesticulación. Hoy de la ciudad ejemplar sólo queda una huella geométrica, la planta de sus calles y habitaciones. Sobre este esquema numantino vamos haciendo vía. Pepe Tudela, que es buen arqueólogo, me hace notar la existencia de dos Numancias superpuestas: la villa celtíbera que Escipión[8] arrasó, y la urbe romana construída sobre aquélla. Medio metro de escombros separa una de otra, lo que me obliga a preguntar frecuentemente a cuál Municipio pertenece la tierra que voy pisando, cuidadoso de acomodar mis emociones a la arqueología.

Porque es lo cierto que en lugares como Numancia no sabe uno qué sentir. Hay hombres envidiables, provistos de un espléndido patriotismo de convención que al llegar aquí se sienten inmediatamente legítimos herederos de las virtudes que ejercitaron los arevacos,[9] y son capaces de inclinar el torso sobre el bisel[10] del cerro, tender hacia el valle el puño e insultar a Escipión Emiliano. Son los mismos que ante los dibujos rupestres de Alta-

[1] *la Mesta,* the organization of sheep raisers; *vuelve a la Mesta,* goes back to the farm

[2] *soriano,* from Soria (see Bécquer, p. 373, n. 5, and A. Machado, p. 567.)

[3] *hizo . . . oposiciones al Cuerpo de Archiveros,* he took the competitive examinations for the Corps of Archivists

[4] *Hacienda,* Treasury

[5] *José María Soltura,* a friend of Ortega

[6] *Numancia,* the ancient city of the Celtiberians, which held out heroically against the Romans until the death of the last inhabitant. It is a symbol of Spanish heroism and love of country.

[7] *peraltado,* here, raised

[8] *Escipión,* Scipio Emilianus, the Roman general who destroyed the original city of Numancia

[9] *arevacos,* the name of the tribe of inhabitants of Numancia

[10] *bisel,* bevel, here, slope

mira[11] experimentan doméstico orgullo, por considerar a los cavernarios dibujantes como gente de la familia.

Por mi parte, no sé bien qué sentir sobre esta colina famosa. En rigor, lo único que me conmueve hondamente es la magnífica desnudez del panorama y la gracia con que el sol actual vierte su flúida exaltación sobre esta tierra limpia. En cambio, de los arevacos me separan, no sólo veintitrés siglos, sino cosas mucho más difíciles de salvar. Así, todos los discursos donde el nombre de Numancia, conjugado con los de Otumba y Lepanto,[12] ha servido para idiotizar a mis compatriotas; así también, los innumerables cuadros académicos en que la ciudad celtíbera, rendida al hambre, está representada por unos mozos desnudos, de rolliza carnalidad, que en correctas posturas de cuadro plástico yugulan a sus mujeres o perforan las propias entrañas. Ciertamente que la historia de Numancia es una página de las más pulcras y simpáticas que hay en la historia. Estos arevacos de cabellos rizados—*torti crines,* dice Tito Livio[13]— y vestidos con negras pieles, poseían una egregia porción de dignidad. A las infidencias de los capitanes romanos respondieron siempre con inspirada nobleza.

Roma atravesaba un período de corrupción. Intrigas de subsuelo decidían del nombramiento de los generales que, ineptos y venales, desmoralizaban las legiones y agostaban las provincias. Un puñado de celtíberos bastaba para poner en franca huída a todo un ejército de latinos. No hubo más remedio, a la postre, que enviar contra los numantinos a un hombre apto, honesto e inteligente, y entonces Roma tuvo que enviar a un «intelectual.» Porque esto era Escipión Emiliano, única figura respetable que había a la sazón en la alta vida de la República. Es frecuente que los militares mediocres pretendan excusar su falta de adiestramiento mental, diciendo que ellos son soldados, como si el ejercicio bélico eximiese a los hombres de ser cultivados y sagaces. Por esta razón conviene recordar que los grandes capitanes han sido siempre gente letrada, de fina espiritualidad y exuberante afición a las ideas y las artes. Escipión Emiliano fué no sólo un «intelectual,» sino, lo que es peor todavía, un «intelectual europeizante.» Verdad es que Europa no existía aún, pero lo mismo da. Lo que para nosotros es Europa fué para los romanos Grecia. Escipión fué el primer helenizante de Roma; su casa, la primera donde se habló el griego, y su círculo vivero donde germinaron todos los pensamientos de reforma que, al cabo, habían de triunfar en la historia romana, no obstante la hostilidad de los patriotas castizos. Hombres como él, obcecados en el estudio, son los que mayor bien han solido labrar a su patria, y no los que casquivanamente se entretienen dictaminando sobre el patriotismo de los demás.[14]

Pero, a seguir estas rutas ideales que desembocan en el pasado, prefiero escuchar lo que Pepe Tudela me cuenta de su vida presente.

—¡Vuelvo al campo!—me dice—. He arrendado una dehesa, y el mes que viene, para comenzar, echo cien ca-

[11] *dibujos rupestres de Altamira,* cave drawings of Altamira. Altamira is not far from Santander.

[12] *Otumba,* a plain in Mexico where Cortés won a decisive battle over the Aztecs; *Lepanto,* the famous naval victory over the Turks, in which Cervantes took part

[13] *Tito Livio,* Livy, the Roman historian, who speaks of the 'curly hair' of the Arevacos

[14] Ortega was a proponent of 'Europeanizing' Spain, that is, bringing her abreast of the best new ideas and social reform that prevailed in northern Europe. He finds a parallel in the Hellenizing trend exhibited by Scipio Emilianus. But Ortega's enemies claimed that he was un-Spanish and unpatriotic in seeking to change their old traditional ways.

bezas de ganado. Acaso no sospeche usted todo lo que esto significa para mí. Es haber hallado la calma moral y un centro de segura gravitación a mi existencia. Mis años de Madrid fueron de inquietud sin riberas, de íntimo desasosiego, de caos espiritual. Al tornar a esta gleba mía, a la pequeña ciudad campesina, inspeccionada perpetuamente por los cerros inmediatos, el caos se ha ido ordenando, la inquieta y contradictoria diversidad de ideas y deseos se ha simplificado, y una ilusión directriz—volver al campo—presenta rumbo firme a mi vida. Y es el caso que, otros paisanos míos, después de haber estudiado carreras en Madrid, hacen lo mismo que yo y se sienten animados de idéntica ilusión. Pertrechados con una preparación científica de que hasta ahora ha carecido el campesino, reharemos la ganadería y mejoraremos el campo.

Así habló Pepe Tudela mientras descendíamos de la colina arqueológica, camino de Soria. Yo comprendo que sus palabras despierten escasísimo interés en quien no se halle, como yo, habituado de tiempo atrás por la idea de que asistimos al final de una larga bicentenaria contienda entre la cuidad y el campo. ¿Es un hecho esporádico y sin trascendencia el retorno a la gleba nativa de esos jóvenes sorianos, o es un síntoma de la época? ¿Se inicia aquí y allá la succión de la campiña sobre la capital, o seguirá imperturbada la tiranía de las ciudades tentaculares?[15]

Hay quien piensa que la vida europea no puede continuar inspirada por las urbes, y que, so pena de sucumbir, habrá de renovarse ruralizándose. Por otra parte, no cabe negar que la propensión a la existencia urbana es característica de nuestro destino meridional. La historia de los pueblos clásicos comienza con una fundación de ciudad, con una fiesta municipal. Detrás de Rómulo y Remo nos parece vislumbrar los instrumentos de una charanga, y casi oímos un elocuente discurso de primera piedra.[16] ¿Qué había pasado antes? No acertamos a imaginarlo: el griego y el romano exigen, para ser reconocidos, un fondo arquitectónico. Se opondrá a esto que aun los hombres prehistóricos fueron inquilinos de casas, o al menos de cavernas. Pero una ciudad, al menos en el sentido europeo, no es una casa ni una aglomeración de ellas. En Atenas y en Roma las habitaciones son mero pretexto: el órgano esencial de la ciudad es la plaza, el ágora[17] o foro. Fundar una ciudad es crear una plazuela. Fuera, pues, erróneo atribuir su origen al mismo instinto y las mismas necesidades que llevaron a fabricar la morada, el hogar, la habitación. La ciudad clásica nace de un instinto opuesto al doméstico.

Se edifica la casa para estar en ella; se funda la ciudad para salir de la casa y reunirse con otros que también han salido de sus casas. Un sentimiento de insuficiencia dentro del círculo doméstico, un afán de romper éste, de hacer nuestra vida tangente a otras vidas, de convivencia, de trato, de sociabilidad ultradoméstica, engendrá la urbe antigua. Por eso, mientras el semita, que ignora propiamente la ciudad, pondera la virtud de la hospitalidad, esto es, el arte de recibir a otro en nuestra casa, la virtud esencial de la urbe es la *urbanitas,* la urbanidad; esto es, el arte de comportarnos fuera de casa en el trato que con otros tenemos sobre la vía pública. Para decirlo de una vez: el impulso creador de la

[15] *tentacular,* here, octopus-like
[16] *discurso de primera piedra,* address made at the laying of a cornerstone
[17] *ágora,* agora (the forum of the Greek cities)

ciudad grecolatina no fué el hogar, ni el mercado o zoco,[18] ni la defensa, ni el templo, fué simplemente un apetito genial de conversación. Aquellos locuaces mediterráneos necesitaban de la charla y la disputa. No es un azar que la palabra más prestigiosa en Grecia fuese la palabra «palabra,» el *logos,* el hablar. La ciencia suprema que descubrieron fué llamada «dialéctica,» que quiere decir conversación, y cuando una divinidad semítica conquista sus corazones, lo más alto que de ella saben decir es que era el *logos,* el verbo hecho carne.[19]

Sin embargo, la urbe antigua, con la única excepción de Roma en el medio y bajo imperio, no deja de ser campesina. No sólo se ve desde la plaza la campiña que asiste, como mentor, a la existencia urbana, sino que el ciudadano sigue siendo labrador. Sus ideas, sus sentimientos, conservan la raíz hincada en el terruño. Sobre todo en el romano persiste intacto hasta el siglo II, después de Cristo, el carácter agrícola, y su historia es predominantemente una historia agraria. Cuando el gesto labriego desaparece de las fisonomías senatoriales, se inicia la decadencia definitiva del gran Estado latino. Rotos los conductos de moral nutrimiento que unen a la ingente ciudad con la gleba circundante, Roma pierde su poder creador, se le anquilosa el alma,[20] y, la plebe desruralizada vive servilmente de pan y de circo. La destrucción del Imperio habría sido más rápida si los emperadores no hubieran abandonado la capital para vivir en perpetua emigración por las provincias, habitando aldeas o pequeñas ciudades, con frecuencia campamentos. El secreto de la perseverancia del mundo antiguo está en el título de *Peregrinus*[21] que adoptaron sus emperadores. Su vida trashumante les dotó de cierta sensibilidad vivaz para las nuevas necesidades del mundo, que se habría embotado en el aire confinado de Roma.

Cuando los germanos penetran en el foro—en aquella tertulia de diez siglos—, y lo destruyen, comienza una nueva civilización. La irrupción del bárbaro en la ciudad que destruye simboliza la restauración de los derechos del campo sobre la historia humana. Viento nuevo sopla en Europa; va a retoñar la historia de nuevas raíces rurales. El germano no es labrador, pero es también campesino; más aún, es selvático. Guerrero y cazador, prefiere el aislamiento. En vez de una ciudad, erige un castillo, un burgo[22] de ofensa y defensa, que es como la guarida a la fiera y la peña al aguilucho. En torno de la mansión aguileña se agrupan las cabañas de los agrícolas; es el tipo de la nueva población, hecha por el campo y para el campo. El puño del señor feudal va así organizando, estructurando las glebas medievales de que han surgido las naciones modernas.[23] Mas de la antigua civilización quedan restos magistrales: algunos municipios romanos siguen en pie con sus ágoras verbipotentes. Y es curioso perseguir la contienda, a lo largo de la Edad Media, entre el puño feudal y la lengua urbana, entre el castillo campal y la plazuela parlanchina. Son dos principios opuestos: el derecho germánico,

[18] *zoco,* market place in an Arabian or North African town. The word is Arabic.

[19] See John I. 1: 'In the beginning was the Word, and the Word was with God, and the Word was God.'

[20] *se le anquilosa el alma,* its soul becomes hardened

[21] *Peregrinus,* wanderer

[22] *burgo,* fort, castle (German *Burg*)

[23] Ortega praises the feudal system (in his *Tema de nuestro tiempo*) because its feudal lords gave rise in later times to the select minority of well-rounded leaders which is necessary for the direction of a nation. He deplores the fact that the feudal system was not well developed in Spain (See Vol. I, p. 9).

personalista y sentimental, contra el derecho romano, colectivista y conceptual.

Los monarcas, apoyándose en la gente de la plazuela—abogados, prestes, comerciantes—, dieron la batalla a los señores feudales, es decir, pusieron cerco a la inspiración rural de la vida humana. La suerte andaba muy dudosa cuando en el siglo XVII aparece el capitalismo, y con él el lujo, y con ambos la ciudad moderna. Werner Sombart ha demostrado[24] que los grandes hacinamientos de población, característicos de los últimos tres siglos, se han formado al compás de la riqueza suntuaria. Lo que ha juntado las enormes masas ciudadanas de nuestras urbes ha sido el lujo de unos cuantos, de los capitalistas. París, Londres, Berlín, Madrid, están habitadas por consumidores en torno a los cuales se agrupan todos los intermediarios del consumo.

La ciudad moderna no produce, consume. Y esto, que es verdad en el orden económico, ¿no lo es también en los demás? La vida que ha palpitado en nuestras ciudades—creencia, arte, moral—, ¿no es propiamente el resto del impulso campesino anterior a ellas? El hombre de la gran capital—¿quién lo duda?—es más pulido, más agudo e ingenioso que el campesino. Pero esas calidades son virtudes adscritas exclusivamente a la periferia de nuestra personalidad. Tal vez el vecino de la gran ciudad ha cultivado su yo social, que es sólo nuestra corteza psíquica, aquel haz[25] de nuestra persona que roza con la ajena, a costa del yo íntimo, fuente de nuestra propia vitalidad. Ved el arte y la política que hoy hacemos: ¿no les faltan entrañas, latido de vísceras ocultas bajo la grácil apariencia? En su intimidad, las almas urbanas viven hoy desmoralizadas, sin grandes entusiasmos ni prestigiosas disciplinas. Una existencia mecanizada va suplantando en nosotros el sentido orgánico de la vida. ¿No llegará un momento en que la población de consumidores se consuma a su vez? . . .

Entretanto, este amigo mío, soriano, Pepe Tudela, vuelve a educar su persona en la eterna y fecunda ley del campo. Con vaga desazón de envidia le entreveo que trashuma en los prados serranos, bajo la comba faz de lo azul, detrás de sus merinas, que avanzan dando corcovos por las viejas cañadas[26] de la mesta, guiadas por los moruecos[27] y los solemnes carneros adalides.[28]

[24] *Author's note:* En su interesantísimo libro *Lujo y capitalismo,* 1913. (Publicado en la *Biblioteca de la Revista de Occidente.*) *Editor's note:* Ortega was the founder and director of the *Revista de Occidente,* which, besides its magazine, published numerous translations, particularly of German scholarly books, as a part of the program of Europeanizing Spain.

[25] *haz,* surface

[26] *cañada,* here, sheep track

[27] *morueco,* ram

[28] *carnero adalid,* bellwether

Azorín

Las nubes

Calisto y Melibea se casaron—como sabrá el lector, si ha leído *La Celestina*[1]—a pocos días de ser descubiertas las rebozadas entrevistas que tenían en el jardín. Se enamoró Calisto de la que después había de ser su mujer un día que entró en la huerta de Melibea persiguiendo un halcón. Hace de esto[2] diez y ocho años. Veintitrés tenía entonces Calisto. Viven ahora marido y mujer en la casa solariega[3] de Melibea; una hija les nació que lleva, como su abuela, el nombre de Alisa. Desde la ancha solana[4] que está a la parte trasera de la casa se abarca[5] toda la huerta en que Melibea y Calisto pasaban sus dulces coloquios de amor. La casa es ancha y rica; labrada escalera de piedra arranca de lo hondo[6] del zaguán. Luego, arriba, hay salones vastos, apartadas y silenciosas camarillas, corredores penumbrosos, con una puertecilla de cuarterones en el fondo, que—como en *Las Meninas*,[7] de Velázquez—deja ver un pedazo de luminoso patio. Un tapiz[8] de verdes ramas y piñas gualdas[9] sobre fondo bermejo cubre el piso del salón principal: el salón, donde en cojines de seda, puestos en tierra, se sientan las damas. Acá y allá destacan silloncitos de cadera,[10] guarnecidos de cuero rojo, o sillas de tijera[11] con embutidos[12] mudéjares;[13] un contador[14] con cajonería[15] de pintada y estofada[16] talla,[17] guarda papeles y joyas; en el centro de la estancia, sobre la mesa de nogal, con las patas y las chambranas[18] talladas, con fiadores[19] de forjado hierro, reposa un lindo juego de ajedrez con embutidos de marfil, nácar y plata; en el alinde[20] de un ancho espejo refléjanse las figuras aguileñas, sobre fondo de oro, de una tabla[21] colgada en la pared frontera.

Todo es paz y silencio en la casa. Melibea anda pasito por cámaras y corredores. Lo observa todo; ocurre a todo. Los armarios están repletos de nítida y bien oliente ropa—aromada por gruesos membrillos[22]— . . .[23] Todo lo previene y a todo ocurre la diligente Melibea; en todo pone sus dulces ojos verdes. De tarde en tarde, en el silencio de la casa, se escucha el lánguido y melodioso son de un clavicordio: es

[1] The famous novel written at the end of the fifteenth century by Fernando de Rojas. Its hero and heroine, Calisto and Melibea, are passionate, ill-starred lovers. As we already know (Vol. I, p. 63), both die in the original version. During a rendezvous he falls from the high garden wall, and she commits suicide by leaping from the tower of the mansion. But Azorín has imagined a different outcome, and slyly makes the reader a party to his changes.

[2] *de esto,* from the present time

[3] manor house

[4] sun gallery

[5] to take in (here, visually)

[6] *lo hondo,* the back

[7] A famous picture in the Museo del Prado, Madrid, showing the princesses and their dwarf companions.

[8] Here, carpet

[9] yellow

[10] low armchair

[12] inlay work

[13] Moorish

[14] counting table, desk

[15] set of drawers

[16] ornamented

[17] carved wood

[18] frame

[19] catch, hook

[11] *silla de tijera,* X-shaped chair

[20] quicksilver (obsolete word)

[21] Here, picture

[22] quince

[23] A description of the rest of the house, rich in the details so dear to Azorín, has been omitted.

Alisa que tañe. Otras veces, por los viales de la huerta, se ve escabullirse calladamente la figura alta y esbelta de una moza: es Alisa que pasea entre los árboles.

La huerta es amena y frondosa. Crecen las adelfas a par de[24] los jazmineros; al pie de los cipreses inmutables ponen los rosales la ofrenda fugaz—como la vida—de sus rosas amarillas, blancas y bermejas. Tres colores llenan los ojos en el jardín: el azul intenso del cielo, el blanco de las paredes encaladas y el verde del boscaje. En el silencio se oye—al igual de un diamante sobre un cristal—el chiar de las golondrinas, que cruzan raudas sobre el añil del firmamento. De la taza de mármol de una fuente cae deshilachada, en una franja, el agua. En el aire se respira un penetrante aroma de jazmines, rosas y magnolias. «Ven por las paredes de mi huerto,» le dijo dulcemente Melibea a Calisto hace diez y ocho años.

Calisto está en el solejar, sentado junto a uno de los balcones. Tiene el codo puesto en el brazo del sillón, y la mejilla reclinada en la mano . . . Nada puede conturbarle ni entristecerle. Y, sin embargo, Calisto, puesta en la mano la mejilla, mira pasar a lo lejos, sobre el cielo azul, las nubes.

Las nubes nos dan una sensación de inestabilidad y de eternidad. Las nubes son—como el mar—siempre varias y siempre las mismas. Sentimos, mirándolas, cómo nuestro ser y todas las cosas corren hacia la nada,[25] en tanto que ellas—tan fugitivas—permanecen eternas. A estas nubes que ahora miramos, las miraron hace doscientos, quinientos, mil, tres mil años, otros hombres con las mismas pasiones y las mismas ansias que nosotros. Cuando queremos tener aprisionado el tiempo—en un momento de ventura—vemos que han pasado ya semanas, meses, años. Las nubes, sin embargo, que son siempre distintas, en todo momento, todos los días, van caminando por el cielo. Hay nubes redondas, henchidas, de un blanco brillante, que destacan en las mañanas de primavera sobre los cielos translúcidos. Las hay como cendales tenues, que se perfilan en un fondo lechoso. Las hay grises sobre una lejanía gris. Las hay de carmín y de oro en los ocasos inacabables, profundamente melancólicos, de las llanuras. Las hay como velloncitos iguales e innumerables, que dejan ver por entre algún claro un pedazo de cielo azul. Unas marchan lentas, pausadas; otras pasan rápidamente. Algunas, de color de ceniza, cuando cubren todo el firmamento, dejan caer sobre la tierra una luz opaca, tamizada, gris, que presta su encanto a los paisajes otoñales.

Siglos después de este día en que Calisto está con la mano en la mejilla, un gran poeta—Campoamor—habrá de dedicar a las nubes un canto en uno de sus poemas titulado *Colón.* «Las nubes—dice el poeta—nos ofrecen el espectáculo de la vida» . . . «Vivir . . . es *ver pasar.*» Sí; vivir es ver pasar: ver pasar, allá en lo alto, las nubes. Mejor diríamos: vivir es *ver volver.* Es ver volver todo en un retorno perdurable, eterno; ver volver todo—angustias, alegrías, esperanzas—como esas nubes que son siempre distintas y siempre las mismas, como esas nubes fugaces e inmutables.

Las nubes son la imagen del Tiempo. ¿Habrá sensación más trágica que aquélla de quien sienta el Tiempo, la de quien vea ya en el presente el pasado y en el pasado lo por venir?

En el jardín, lleno de silencio, se escucha el chiar de las rápidas golondrinas. El agua de la fuente cae deshi-

[24] *a par de,* along with

[25] nothingness

lachada por el tazón de mármol. Al pie de los cipreses se abren las rosas fugaces, blancas, amarillas, bermejas. Un denso aroma de jazmines y magnolias embalsama el aire. Sobre las paredes de nítida cal resalta el verde de la fronda; por encima del verde y del blanco se extiende el añil del cielo. Alisa se halla en el jardín, sentada, con un libro en la mano. Sus menudos pies asoman por debajo de la falda de fino contray;[26] están calzados con chapines de terciopelo negro, adornados con rapacejos[27] y clavetes[28] de bruñida[29] plata. Los ojos de Alisa son verdes, como los de su madre; el rostro, más bien alargado que redondo. ¿Quién podría contar la nitidez y sedosidad de sus manos? Pues de la dulzura de su habla, ¿cuántos loores no podríamos decir?

En el jardín todo es silencio y paz. En lo alto de la solana, recostado sobre la barandilla, Calisto contempla extático a su hija. De pronto, un halcón aparece revolando rápida y violentamente por entre los árboles. Tras él, persiguiéndole, todo agitado y descompuesto, surge un mancebo. Al llegar frente a Alisa, se detiene absorto, sonríe y comienza a hablarla.

Calisto lo ve desde el carasol y adivina sus palabras. Unas nubes redondas, blancas, pasan lentamente, sobre el cielo azul, en la lejanía.[30]

[26] a fine cloth
[27] border
[28] stud, nail
[29] burnished
[30] In precisely this same way, chasing his straying falcon, Calisto entered this same garden and saw Melibea for the first time. History is repeating itself. Calisto can guess the young man's words because the emotional situation is identical, and human emotion is the most unchanging element throughout the centuries of man's existence. So Calisto looks at the clouds and sees that they too are evanescent and fleeting, but withal ever returning and eternal.

Jacinto Benavente

El marido de su viuda

Comedia en un acto estrenada en 1908

PERSONAJES

CAROLINA — FLORENCIO
EUDOSIA — CASALONGA
PAQUITA — ZURITA
VALDIVIESO

En una capital de provincia.

ACTO ÚNICO

Decoración. Gabinete.

ESCENA PRIMERA

CAROLINA y ZURITA

ZURITA

(*Entrando.*) ¡Amiga mía!

CAROLINA

Amigo Zurita; muy amable en haber acudido tan pronto. Yo no sé cómo corresponder a sus atenciones.

ZURITA

Encantado siempre de servir a usted en algo, amiga mía.

CAROLINA

Hice que le buscaran a usted por todas partes. Usted perdone si le ha molestado, pero el caso era urgente. Me hallo en una situación dificilísima; todo el tacto es poco para no caer en uno de esos ridículos insostenibles . . . , si usted no me salva con sus consejos.

ZURITA

Cuente usted con ellos, cuente usted conmigo para todo. Pero, ¿usted en ridículo? No puedo creerlo.

CAROLINA

Sí, sí, amigo mío. Usted es el único de quien puedo aconsejarme.[1] Usted es una persona de buen gusto; sus artículos y crónicas de sociedad son el árbitro del buen tono; las decisiones de usted se respetan, se acatan por todo el mundo.

ZURITA

No siempre, no siempre . . . En otro tiempo, existía aquí una sociedad escogida; pero ahora no es lo mismo, usted lo sabe. Las fortunas improvisadas son tantas, y tantas las familias aristocráticas que han venido a menos . . . Nuestra sociedad ha cambiado mucho. Dominan los *parvenus*[2] . . . Y el dinero es insolente. Cree que se basta para improvisarlo todo: educación, buen gusto, maneras distinguidas . . . Y usted lo sabe, amiga mía, nada de eso se improvisa. La distinción es flor de estufa delicada . . . Y nos quedan tan pocas gardenias . . . como usted,

[1] *de quien puedo aconsejarme,* from whom I can get advice

[2] *parvenu* (French), newly enriched

amiga mía . . . En cambio, ¡tenemos cada cardo borriquero![3] No lo digo por las de Núñez.[4] ¿Cómo dirá usted que amenizan ahora sus miércoles? Con un gramófono, amiga mía, con un gramófono. Siempre es mejor que cuando cantaba la pequeña, recitaba la mediana y tocaban todas . . . Pero es horrible . . . Yo me sofoco por ellas, créalo usted.

CAROLINA

Ya sabe usted que yo no asisto a sus miércoles. Sólo los visito cuando sé que no están en casa.

ZURITA

Pero vamos al caso, estoy impaciente . . .

CAROLINA

El caso es, como usted sabe, que mañana es el día señalado para la inauguración de la estatua de mi marido . . . , de mi anterior marido . . .

ZURITA

Honor merecidísimo a la memoria de aquel grande hombre,[5] de aquel hombre ilustre, a quien tanto debe esta provincia, España entera. Para todos los que tuvimos el honor de llamarnos amigos suyos, debe ser motivo de satisfacción ver cómo se hace justicia a sus grandes merecimientos, aquí, donde por pasiones políticas, por envidias, se regatea siempre el mérito de los hombres más eminentes. Pero don Patricio Molinete no podía tener enemigos . . . El día de mañana nos consolará de muchas miserias locales.

CAROLINA

Sí, en efecto; debo estar orgullosa y agradecida. Pero comprenda usted lo delicado de mi situación . . . Casada en segundas nupcias, ya no llevo su nombre, pero tampoco puedo desentenderme de haberlo llevado, mucho menos cuando todo el mundo sabe que fuimos un matrimonio modelo . . . Yo habría salvado la situación ausentándome estos días, pretextando una indisposición . . . Pero, ¿cómo se habría interpretado? Como un desaire, acaso como una protesta . . .

ZURITA

Seguramente. Si por circunstancias de la vida, muy respetables, ya no lleva usted aquel nombre ilustre, no por eso puede usted dejar de compartir el honor de haberlo llevado dignamente. Para su actual marido no puede haber ofensa.

CAROLINA

No; ¡pobre Florencio! . . . Él fué el primero en indicarme que yo debía participar en todo . . . Mi pobre Florencio fué siempre el primer admirador de mi pobre Patricio . . . Sus ideas políticas eran las mismas, en todo pensaban lo mismo.

ZURITA

Así parece.

CAROLINA

Dígalo usted.[6] Mi pobre Patricio me quería tanto, que él, sin duda, hizo pensar a mi pobre Florencio en que algo había en mí para merecer el cariño de aquel gran corazón y aquella gran inteligencia . . . Del mismo modo, me bastó que Florencio fuera el amigo inseparable de Patricio para estimarle como le he estimado. Cierto que Florencio nunca brillará tanto por sus condiciones de carácter, pero no

[3] *cada cardo borriquero,* so many rough thistles

[4] *No lo digo por,* I'm not referring to (said ironically); *las de Núñez,* the Núñez women

[5] *grande hombre.* Apocopation of *grande* to *gran* does not usually occur before a noun beginning with a vowel sound.

[6] *Dígalo usted,* That's the truth (literally, you may say that)

es porque le falten grandes dotes de inteligencia . . . Pero no tiene ambición; conmigo, con su casita, con este hogar modelo, ve colmadas sus aspiraciones. Y yo estoy muy contenta; yo tampoco soy ambiciosa. Las temporadas que viví en Madrid con mi esposo, para mí fueron un tormento. Los ocho días que fué ministro de Hacienda, yo los pasé en una continua excitación nerviosa . . . Dos veces que estuvo a punto de tener un duelo por cuestiones políticas, creí volverme loca. Y si hubiera llegado a presidente del Consejo,[7] como le pronosticaba un periódico que él dirigía, entonces . . . me hubiera costado una enfermedad.

ZURITA

No es usted como la de Espinosa, nuestra senadora, ni como nuestra actual alcaldesa. Ya verá usted cómo ésas no descansan ni dejan descansar a nadie hasta que no vean a sus maridos en estatua.

CAROLINA

Pero ¿usted cree que ni Espinosa, ni el actual alcalde, tienen méritos para que les levanten estatuas?

ZURITA

Sí; en una plaza pública es difícil, pero en los altares en clase de mártires y esposos, es muy posible . . . Pero olvidamos lo que importa

CAROLINA

Pues bien, amigo Zurita: como ausentarme hubiera sido muy violento, según usted mismo reconoce, y al permanecer aquí debo asistir a la inauguración del monumento de mi pobre Patricio, a la velada en su honor, debo recibir a las Comisiones de Madrid, de la provincia, de todas partes. ¿Qué actitud debe ser la mía? Si parezco demasiado triste, nadie creerá en la sinceridad de mi sentimiento. Tampoco puedo mostrarme complacida; dirían que había olvidado demasiado pronto . . . Ya lo dicen . . .

ZURITA

¡Oh, no! Quedó usted viuda muy joven . . . La vida no podía haber terminado para usted.

CAROLINA

Sí, sí; ¡dígales usted eso a mis cuñadas! . . . En fin, considere usted que ni sé cómo debo vestirme en estos días . . . Un traje severo que parezca al luto . . . sería ridículo presentándome al lado de mi marido; un traje de más vestir, tampoco me parece indicado . . . Aconséjeme, amigo Zurita; aconséjeme usted . . . Usted, ¿qué se pondría?

ZURITA

Es difícil, es difícil acertar en el punto . . . Pero yo creo que un elegante vestido negro con alguna nota violeta. La inauguración de un monumento que perpetúa la gloria de un grande hombre, no es motivo para entristecerse. Su marido de usted ha entrado de lleno en la inmortalidad . . . y allí la espere a usted por muchos años.

CAROLINA

Mil gracias.[8]

ZURITA

De nada. Usted le ha llorado bastante . . . Usted ha respetado su memoria; si ha vuelto usted a casarse, ha sido con un caballero dignísimo, que era el mejor amigo de su esposo de usted. Usted no ha hecho lo que otras viudas que todos conocemos, la de Benítez sin ir más lejos, que sin pensar en casarse

[7] *presidente del Consejo,* prime minister

[8] She thanks him for wishing her many years of life.

ni ese es el camino,[9] lleva dos años en relaciones con el mayor enemigo que tenía su marido en la provincia.

CAROLINA

No compare usted.

ZURITA

En fin, amiga mía . . . , todo el mundo apreciará la situación de usted como es debido.[10]

CAROLINA

Mis cuñadas me tienen asustada. Aseguran que mi situación es ridícula y la de mi marido mucho más ridícula . . . Dicen que cómo tenemos valor a presentarnos ante la estatua de su hermano . . .

ZURITA

¡Señora! Sus cuñadas de usted exageran. Y a usted sólo puede importarle la opinión de su esposo.

CAROLINA

Por ese lado estoy tranquila . . . En este mundo el uno, y el otro desde el otro, sé que los dos han de apreciar la sinceridad de mis sentimientos. Pero los demás, los demás . . .

ZURITA

Los demás somos los buenos amigos de usted y de su segundo esposo, que lo fuimos también del primero y estaremos siempre con ustedes, o los enemigos, los indiferentes, que nada deben importarle a usted.

CAROLINA

Gracias, muchas gracias. Ya sé que es usted un buen amigo nuestro, que lo fué usted suyo.[11]

ZURITA

De los dos, de los tres; sí, señora, de los tres . . . Aquí tiene usted a su marido.

ESCENA II

DICHOS[12] Y DON FLORENCIO

ZURITA

¡Amigo don Florencio!

FLORENCIO

¡Queridísimo Zurita! . . . ¡Cuánto me alegro de verle! . . . Deseaba dar a usted las gracias por el precioso artículo que ha publicado usted a la memoria de nuestro inolvidable . . . Muy sentido, muy sentido . . . Era usted un buen amigo suyo . . . Muchas gracias, querido Zurita; muchas gracias. Carolina y yo le agradecemos mucho su precioso artículo. Nos hizo llorar. ¿No es verdad, Carolina?

CAROLINA

Sí, en efecto.

FLORENCIO

Estoy satisfecho, amigo Zurita. Por primera vez en la provincia se han unido los elementos más incompatibles para honrar como se debía al hijo preclaro de esta región desagradecida. ¿Ha visto usted el monumento? Muy artístico. La estatua es de gran parecido. Es él, es él . . ., y los motivos alegóricos, muy artísticos: tanto el desnudo de la Verdad como el del Comercio y de la Industria, son de una ejecución perfecta. No pueden estar más parecidos . . . Ya sabe usted las batallas que hemos reñido para imponer los desnudos. Los elementos reaccionarios no querían desnudos; el escultor se negaba a entregar la obra

[9] *ni ese es el camino,* nor anything of the sort

[10] *como es debido,* as one ought to, as is fitting and proper

[11] *lo fué usted suyo,* you were a good friend of his

[12] *Dichos,* the forementioned (the characters of the preceding scene)

si se suprimían los desnudos. Al fin conseguimos que triunfaran los sagrados fueros del Arte.

CAROLINA

Pues, mira, yo hubiera preferido que no hubiera desnudos. ¿Qué necesidad había de que nadie se molestara? Ya sé de algunos amigos que no asistirán a la inauguración por ese motivo.

FLORENCIO

Ridiculeces, preocupaciones que nos tienen en lamentable atraso . . . Pero tú no puedes pensar así; la que fué compañera de aquel espíritu tan liberal, tan amplio . . . Recuerdo el viaje que hicimos juntos por Italia. ¿No te acuerdas tú, Carolina? La admiración ante aquellos gloriosos monumentos del arte pagano y del Renacimiento . . . Aquel hombre era un gran artista sobre todo . . . ¡Ah! ¡Qué hombre! ¡Qué grande hombre! Antes que se me olvide, Carolina: para el extraordinario de su periódico, me ha pedido Gutiérrez todos los retratos que tú conserves, y yo quiero también que publiquen aquellos versos que te escribió al principio de vuestras relaciones . . . ¡Verá usted qué versos! Hubiera sido un gran poeta[13] . . . ¡Hubiera sido todo lo que hubiera querido! ¿Y sus cartas? ¿Usted no conoce alguna de sus cartas íntimas? Anda, Carolina, trae alguna de las cartas que te escribió cuando erais novios . . .

CAROLINA

Otro día . . . En estos momentos . . .

FLORENCIO

Es verdad . . . Para nosotros, en medio de la legítima satisfacción, son días muy tristes . . . , unidos por los mismos recuerdos . . . Yo estoy seguro que no podré contener mi emoción en el momento de descubrir[14] la estatua.

CAROLINA

¡Por Dios, Florencio! ¡No vayamos a dar un espectáculo! Sobreponte.

ZURITA

Sí; es preciso que se sobreponga usted.

FLORENCIO

Si[15] estoy sobrepuesto.

ZURITA

Si ustedes no mandan otra cosa . . .

CAROLINA

Muchas gracias, Zurita . . . No sabe usted cuánto le agradezco . . . Desde que sé cómo he de vestirme, ya no me parece tan difícil mi situación.

ZURITA

Lo creo. Las situaciones más difíciles para una señora, son aquellas en que no sabe qué ponerse.

CAROLINA

Hasta mañana.

ZURITA

Don Florencio . . .

FLORENCIO

Agradecidísimo por su sentido, sentido artículo. ¡Admirable! ¡Admirable! (*Sale Zurita.*)

Escena III

CAROLINA y DON FLORENCIO

FLORENCIO

Estás emocionada, ¿verdad? Hondamente emocionada. Como yo; no te esfuerces por ocultarlo.

[13] Supply, if he had wished
[14] *descubrir,* here, to unveil

[15] *Si* makes the statement more emphatic: But I *am* under control!

CAROLINA

Estoy . . . , qué sé yo, violenta;[16] esa es la palabra.

FLORENCIO

No te olvides de buscar esos retratos; sobre todo, aquel en que estamos los tres juntos en la segunda plataforma de la torre Eiffel: es un precioso recuerdo.

CAROLINA

Sí; ya lo buscaré. Pero, oye. Esas indiscreciones referentes a la vida privada, me parecen . . . , qué sé yo, en mi situación, en nuestra situación . . .

FLORENCIO

¡Ah, la mujer![17] ¡Qué espíritu tan poco amplio![18] Pero tú no debías ser como todas . . . La que fué compañera de aquel espíritu tan superior . . . Nada de cuanto se refiere a la vida de un grande hombre puede ser indiferente para la Historia, y los que fuimos testigos, y hasta cierto punto colaboradores, permítaseme la inmodestia, colaboradores en la obra de su vida, debemos toda la verdad a la Historia.

CAROLINA

Pues no te empeñes en que yo ande enseñando las cartas, y los versos menos.[19] Recuerda lo que dicen.

FLORENCIO

¡Bah! Ya recuerdo.

«Tengo clavado[20] un beso que me diste . . .»

Ya se sabe lo que son versos . . . Nadie toma al pie de la letra lo que se dice en los versos . . . Además, iba a ser tu marido . . . ¿Qué tenía de particular que . . . ?

CAROLINA

¡Florencio! ¿Qué vas a suponer? No insistas. Estoy temiendo que nos pongamos en ridículo.

FLORENCIO

¿Por qué hemos de ponernos en ridículo? Nadie más obligado que yo a prestar su concurso en estas circunstancias . . . Por lo mismo que soy tu marido, el marido de su viuda . . . De otro modo, se diría que yo pretendía eclipsarle, que me molestaba su recuerdo, y tú sabes que no; tú sabes cómo yo le admiraba, cómo le quería; y él a mí: verdad es que nadie sabía llevarle su genio como yo . . . , porque tenía su genio, bien lo sabes . . . , sus rarezas, rarezas de grande hombre, pero grandes rarezas . . . Estaba muy poseído de su valer,[21] como todos los grandes hombres; era muy terco, como todos los grandes caracteres . . . Cuando se empeñaba en una cosa, no había quien le apeara de su idea;[22] por respeto no me atrevo a decir de su burro . . . Sólo yo, a fuerza de habilidad, de paciencia . . . , bien lo sabes. ¡Cuántas veces no me habrás dicho!: ¡Ay, amigo Florencio! ¡No puedo más! Y yo te hacía reflexiones, y a él también, y cuando teníais algún disgusto, yo siempre al quite.[23]

CAROLINA

Florencio, no continúes en ese tono. Me disgusta oírte . . .

FLORENCIO

Está bien, mujer. Es que estos días, yo comprendo tu situación de espíritu;

[16] *violenta,* here, profoundly moved
[17] *la mujer,* you women
[18] *poco amplio,* narrow
[19] *menos,* even less
[20] *clavado,* fixed (in my memory)
[21] *poseído de su valer,* sure of his worth
[22] *quien le apeara de su idea,* anyone who could make him abandon his idea. (The usual phrase is *apearse de su burro,* to dismount from his ass, to give up his stupid notion.)
[23] *yo siempre al quite,* I always turned aside the danger. (An expression ordinarily applied to bullfighting, referring to the action of drawing the bull away from a bullfighter who is in danger.)

todo el mundo es a recordar[24] sus méritos, sus virtudes. Y yo quiero que tú recuerdes que aquel grande hombre tuvo también sus pequeñeces.

CAROLINA

¿Qué vas a decirme?

FLORENCIO

Que si me comparas con él . . .

CAROLINA

¡Florencio! Sabes que nunca he comparado. Las comparaciones son odiosas.

FLORENCIO

No, Carolina; si ya sé . . . ¿Verdad que no te pesa haber cambiado su nombre ilustre por el mío modestísimo? Aunque a ti te consta que si yo me hubiera propuesto brillar . . . , si yo hubiera tenido aspiraciones . . . Porque yo creo tener algún talento. ¿No lo crees tú?

CAROLINA

Sí, hombre, sí; pero no digas más tonterías.

FLORENCIO

Estás nerviosa . . . No se puede hablar contigo. ¡Uy, tus cuñadas! Esto sí que no. Di que no estoy en casa.

CAROLINA

No te preocupes. Nunca me preguntan por ti.

FLORENCIO

¡Cuánto me alegro! Te deseo una horita corta, y huyo.

CAROLINA

¡Pues también estoy de humor para oírlas! (*Sale don Florencio.*)

[24] *es a recordar,* is in the midst of recalling, is busy remembering

ESCENA IV

CAROLINA, EUDOSIA y PAQUITA

EUDOSIA

5 ¿No estorbamos?

CAROLINA

¡Qué pregunta! Adelante.

EUDOSIA

10 ¿Conque hoy estás en casa?

CAROLINA

Ya lo veis.

15

PAQUITA

Como siempre que venimos a verte da la casualidad de que has salido . . .

20

CAROLINA

Sí que es casualidad.[25]

EUDOSIA

La casualidad es encontrarte. (*Pausa.*)

25 A tu marido acabamos de ver en la calle.

CAROLINA

¿Estáis seguras?

30

PAQUITA

Muy bien acompañado por cierto.

CAROLINA

35 ¿Sí?

EUDOSIA

Paquita es quien le ha visto con la de Somolinos en la confitería de Sánchez.

40

CAROLINA

Es posible.

PAQUITA

45 ¿Y te quedas tan fresca? Con la fama que tienen la de Somolinos y la confitería de Sánchez.

[25] *Sí que es casualidad,* It is indeed chance

CAROLINA

De la confitería no sabía nada.

EUDOSIA

Que ninguna señora decente, o que quiera parecerlo, pone los pies en ella desde que Sánchez se casó con esa francesa.

CAROLINA

Tampoco sabía lo de la francesa.

EUDOSIA

Pues sí, se casó con ella. Decimos casado por no decir una palabrota[26] . . . Se casó, si eso puede llamarse casado, en Bayona, por lo civil, como se casa la gente en esa Francia de perdición . . .

CAROLINA

Cuánto lo siento, porque soy muy golosa, y bombones y *marrons glacés* como los de casa de Sánchez no los hay aquí ni en ninguna parte.

PAQUITA

Pues te aconsejamos que no se los compres; te criticará todo el mundo . . . Sólo la de Somolinos se atreve a entrar en casa de Sánchez y a tratarse con su mujer, que le ha dado la receta para pintarse el pelo. ¿No te has fijado cómo lo lleva ahora?

CAROLINA

No he reparado.

EUDOSIA

Ya no es color caoba como antes; ahora es un rubio bebé . . . Además, la francesa la arregla las manos dos veces por semana . . . ¿No te has fijado cómo lleva las uñas? No se habla de otra cosa. (*Pausa.*)

PAQUITA

¿Conque por fin ése se ha salido con la suya?

CAROLINA

¿Quién es ése?

EUDOSIA

Se me resiste[27] llamarle tu marido. ¡Pobre hermano nuestro!

CAROLINA

¡Ah! No sé a qué podéis referiros.

EUDOSIA

A que por fin ha colocado en el monumento de nuestro pobre hermano esas figuras desnudas.

PAQUITA

Y de tamaño natural.

CAROLINA

Pero Florencio no tiene la culpa . . . Eso es cosa del escultor, de la Comisión . . . ¿Y qué tiene de particular? En todos los monumentos hay figuras así; son figuras alegóricas.

EUDOSIA

Pase todavía que la estatua de la Verdad no esté vestida; siempre se ha dicho que la Verdad es así. Pero la Industria y el Comercio . . . , ¿no podían llevar una túnica? Sobre todo el Comercio creo que está indecente.

PAQUITA

Nosotras ya no iremos a la tribuna de preferencia;[28] es la que está de frente, y desde allí se ve todo.

EUDOSIA

¿Y tú insistes todavía en presentarte? ¿No ha habido nadie que te haya aconsejado mejor?

CAROLINA

Si he sido invitada, señal de que no parece inconveniente mi presencia.

[26] *palabrota,* an ugly word
[27] *Se me resiste,* I can hardly bring myself to
[28] *tribuna de preferencia,* the reserved grandstand

PAQUITA

La tuya, no . . . si estuvieras como debías estar; pero al lado de ese hombre . . . , el que fué su mejor amigo . . . A los tres años escasos.

CAROLINA

Largos.[29]

EUDOSIA

¡Te parecen largos! ¡Tres años! ¡Un día para los que le seguimos llorando!

PAQUITA

Para los que todavía llevamos su apellido, porque ninguno nos parece más digno.

EUDOSIA

Y por no dejar de llevarlo, hemos renunciado a partidos muy ventajosos.

CAROLINA

Pues habéis hecho mal, porque vuestro hermano ya sabéis que tenía gran empeño en veros casadas.

PAQUITA

Él creía que todos los hombres eran como él, dignos de una mujer como nosotras. ¡Pobre hermano! Si alguien le hubiera dicho que iban a olvidarle tan pronto . . . Si te ve desde el cielo, ¡qué disgusto el suyo!

CAROLINA

No creo que en el cielo nadie pueda tener disgustos; no valía la pena de estar en el cielo . . . Vosotras no queréis haceros cargo de mi situación. Una viuda joven, lo menos malo que puede hacer para evitar murmuraciones, es volver a casarse. Y yo era muy joven cuando quedé viuda.

EUDOSIA

Veintinueve años.

CAROLINA

Veintiséis.

EUDOSIA

Admitamos los veintiséis. Ya no eras una niña. Además, una mujer viuda nunca es joven.

CAROLINA

Ni una soltera es nunca vieja. Corriente. Lo que no veo es lo que puede haber de incorrecto en que yo presencie la inauguración de la estatua.

EUDOSIA

Comprende que en todos los discursos han de hablar de su muerte prematura, del sentimiento de todos por la pérdida de hombre tan ilustre. ¿Qué cara vas a poner al oírlo? ¿Quién va a creer que no estás más conforme que todos, viéndote tan compuesta y tan consolada al lado de ese hombre?

PAQUITA

Y cuando todos recuerden su talento . . . , ¿qué cara va a poner tu marido, que no tiene ninguno?

CAROLINA

Bien sabes que no era esa la opinión de vuestro hermano, que estimaba mucho a Florencio.

EUDOSIA

¡Le estimaba! ¡Pobre hermano mío! ¡Por tener todos los talentos, tenía también el de dejarse engañar!

CAROLINA

Esa suposición me ofende . . . ; nos ofende a todos.

EUDOSIA

¿Dónde has guardado eso, Paquita?

PAQUITA

Aquí lo traigo. (*Saca un libro.*)

[29] *Largos,* more than three, going on four

EUDOSIA

Entérate, entérate de ese libro que ha llegado hoy de Madrid y se vende en case de Valdivieso.

CAROLINA

¿Qué es esto? (*Leyendo la cubierta del libro.*) «Don Patricio Molinete y su obra. Biografía. Correspondencia. Intimidades.» Os agradezco . . .

PAQUITA

No, no agradezcas nada . . . Ya verás, ya verás lo que escribía nuestro pobre hermano en sus cartas dirigidas al autor de ese libro, íntimo amigo suyo.

CAROLINA

Recaredo Casalonga. ¡Ah, sí, un trapisondista que tuvimos que echarle de casa! . . . Y dices que trae unas cartas . . . Ya estoy alarmada, siendo cosa de ese desahogado de Casalonga.[30]

EUDOSIA

Lee, lee . . . Página doscientas catorce. ¿No es eso, Paquita?

PAQUITA

Empieza en la doscientas catorce; pero lo gordo[31] está en la doscientas quince.

CAROLINA

A ver, a ver . . . ¿Qué es esto? ¿Qué cartas son éstas? ¿Qué dice aquí? . . . Que yo . . . Pero esto no es verdad . . . ; esto no ha podido decirlo mi marido.

EUDOSIA

Cuando se atreven a publicarlo en letras de molde . . .

CAROLINA

Pero esto no puede ser. Este libro es una calumnia . . . Esto no es respetar la vida privada. ¡Lo más privado de la vida! Esto no puede quedar así.

EUDOSIA

Pues quedará, quedará; ya verás cómo queda.

PAQUITA

A estas horas se habrán agotado los ejemplares.

CAROLINA

¡Ah, ya lo veremos! . . . Se verá . . . ¡Florencio! ¡Florencio! Ven en seguida. ¡Florencio!

EUDOSIA

Si aún no habrá vuelto.

PAQUITA

Estaba tan entretenido.

CAROLINA

Si no ha salido de casa . . . ¡Sois unas chismosas!

EUDOSIA

¡Carolina! Esa palabra la habrás dicho sin reflexionarla.

PAQUITA

No creo haber oído bien. ¿Has dicho chismosas?

CAROLINA

Sí, sí; dejame en paz. No puedo sufriros. Vosotras tenéis la culpa de todo.

EUDOSIA y PAQUITA

¡Carolina!

CAROLINA

¡Florencio! ¡Florencio!

ESCENA V

DICHAS y FLORENCIO

FLORENCIO

¿Qué te ocurre, mujer? ¿Qué te ocurre?

[30] *ese desahogado de Casalonga,* that brazen-faced Casalonga

[31] *lo gordo,* the important part

¡Ah, están ustedes aquí! Tanto gusto . . .

EUDOSIA

Nosotras, sí; nosotras, que ahora mismo salimos para siempre de esta casa . . . , donde se nos insulta.

PAQUITA

Donde se nos llama chismosas.

EUDOSIA

Donde se nos dice que no pueden sufrirnos.

PAQUITA

Y cuando eso se dice . . . , ¡qué será lo que se piensa!

FLORENCIO

Pero Eudosia, Paquita, no comprendo . . . Por mi parte . . .

EUDOSIA

La que es hoy su señora se lo explicará a usted.

PAQUITA

¡Salir así de esta casa que fué de nuestro hermano!

EUDOSIA

¡Pobre hermano nuestro!

FLORENCIO

Pero Carolina . . .

CAROLINA

Déjalas, déjalas; son insoportables.

PAQUITA

¿Has oído, Eudosia¿ ¡Somos insoportables!

EUDOSIA

Ya lo he oído, Paquita. Creo que no nos queda más que oír en esta casa.

CAROLINA

Sí; insoportables como todas las viejas solteronas.

EUDOSIA

Aun nos quedaba más que oír . . . Vamos, Paquita.

PAQUITA

Vamos, Eudosia. (*Salen.*)

Escena VI

CAROLINA y FLORENCIO

FLORENCIO

¿Pero qué disgusto has tenido con tus cuñadas?

CAROLINA

Con ellas, no; por ellas: es lo mismo. Se complacen en llevar y traer noticias desagradables . . . Todo lo que puede molestar. ¿Tú te acuerdas de Casalonga?

FLORENCIO

¿Recaredo Casalonga? ¡No he de acordarme! Un tipo delicioso, gran filósofo de la vida, un humorista muy divertido . . .

CAROLINA

Sí, todo eso; pues ese filósofo, ese humorista ha tenido la humorada de publicar este libro.

FLORENCIO

A ver. «Don Patricio Molinete. Su vida y su obra. Biografía. Correspondencia. Intimidades.» ¡Hombre! ¡Qué idea! Sí que fueron muy amigos; pero no creo que el libro pueda ser muy interesante. Este pobre Casalonga, ¿qué novedad puede decirnos?

CAROLINA

A nosotros ninguna . . . Pero lee, lee.

FLORENCIO

¡Hombre! ¡Cartas de Patricio! ¿Dirigidas a quién?

CAROLINA

Al autor de este libro, según él asegura. Cartas muy íntimas, muy confidenciales. Lee, lee.

FLORENCIO

«Querido amigo: La vida es triste. ¿Quieres saber por qué estoy tan desilusionado? ¿Por qué no tengo fe ninguna en los destinos de nuestra desgraciada patria? . . . Quieres saber . . . » Esta carta está escrita cuando ya estaba enfermo. El pobre, con su padecimiento del hígado, lo veía todo negro . . . ¡Ah, los grandes hombres no debían estar sujetos a estas miserias! ¡La inteligencia esclava del hígado! . . . No somos nada. «Los destinos de nuestra desgraciada patria . . .»

CAROLINA

Bueno; eso no importa nada . . . Más abajo. Lee, lee.

FLORENCIO

«La vida es triste.»

CAROLINA

No vuelvas a empezar.

FLORENCIO

No, si es que lo vuelve a decir. Mira. «Yo no he amado más que una vez, y a una sola mujer, la mía . . .» Tú.

CAROLINA

Sigue, sigue.

FLORENCIO

«Yo no he creído más que en un amigo, mi único amigo, Florencio.» Yo.

CAROLINA

Tú, sí; tú. Sigue, sigue.

FLORENCIO

5 ¿A qué viene esto? ¡Ah! ¿Qué dice aquí? Que tú, que yo . . .

CAROLINA

Lee, lee.

10

FLORENCIO

«Pues bien: esa mujer, ese amigo, los dos grandes, los dos únicos, los dos sagrados afectos de mi vida, de mi 15 existencia . . . No me atrevo a decirlo. ¡Si no me atrevo a pensarlo! Se aman, se aman en silencio, acaso sin sospecharlo ellos mismos.»

20

CAROLINA

¿Qué te parece?

FLORENCIO

«Ellos mismos . . . Comprendo que 25 luchan por vencer su pasión culpable . . . Pero ¿lucharán siempre? En medio de todo, los compadezco . . . Pero ¿qué debo hacer? ¡Soy muy desgraciado!»

30

CAROLINA

¿Qué dices?

FLORENCIO

35 ¡Pero esto no puede ser! Él no puede haber escrito esto. Y si lo escribió no puede publicarse.

CAROLINA

40 Pues se ha publicado verdad o mentira, y ahí lo tienes. ¡Ah!, y eso no es nada; en las cartas siguientes sigue comunicando sus observaciones, y, la verdad, hay algunas . . . que sólo él podía 45 haber hecho . . .

FLORENCIO

De modo que tú crees, tú opinas que estas cartas son auténticas . . .

CAROLINA

Pueden serlo. Hay datos, detalles . . .

FLORENCIO

¡Y nosotros creíamos que él nada sospechaba!

CAROLINA

Poco a poco, Florencio . . . Él nada podía sospechar . . . Tú sabes mejor que nadie cómo supimos respetarle, a pesar de todo . . .

FLORENCIO

¡Pues ya ves de lo que nos ha servido!

CAROLINA

Él sólo pudo creer . . . la verdad . . . Que nos amábamos en silencio . . .

FLORENCIO

¡De bastante nos ha servido el silencio! ¡Para que él fuera a contárselo al botarate de Casalonga! Un trapisondista que ahora ha querido sacar partido de estas intimidades. No me negarás que ha sido una ligereza imperdonable; yo nunca hubiera sospechado esto de mi amigo. Si dudaba de mí, de nosotros, ¿por qué no nos dijo algo? Hubiéramos sido más prudentes, le hubiéramos tranquilizado . . . Pero esto de contarle al primero que se presenta . . . Comprende ahora mi situación, nuestra situación en estos momentos . . . Cuando todo el mundo consagra un recuerdo a su memoria, cuando yo me he afanado tanto por la realización de ese monumento, ¿qué dirá todo el mundo después de leer esto?

CAROLINA

Siempre te dije que el monumento nos daría más de un disgusto.

FLORENCIO

¿Con qué cara me presento[32] yo mañana ante el monumento?

5

CAROLINA

¡Van a salirse con la suya mis cuñadas! ¡Estamos en evidencia![33]

FLORENCIO

10 ¡Ah! . . . Pero esto no puede quedar así . . . Ahora mismo me dirijo a la Prensa, al Juzgado, al gobernador, a las librerías. Y en cuanto a Casalonga . . . ¡Ah! Yo daré con él, y, o rectifica

15 y declara que esas cartas son apócrifas de cabo a rabo[34] . . . , o le mato. Me batiré con él, pero muy seriamente.

CAROLINA

20 ¡Florencio! ¡No digas disparates! ¡Un duelo! ¡Exponer tu vida!

FLORENCIO

¿Pero no comprendes que esto no

25 puede consentirse? ¿Dónde iríamos a parar? ¿Es que no va a respetarse la vida privada de nadie?

CAROLINA

30 ¡Florencio! ¡Por Dios!

FLORENCIO

¡No me detengas!

35

CAROLINA

¡Florencio! Haz lo que quieras; pero un duelo, no.

FLORENCIO

40 ¡Ah! O rectifica y recoge la edición de este libelo, o de lo contrario . . .

CAROLINA

45 ¡Zurita!

[32] *¿Con qué cara me presento . . . ,* How can I possibly be present

[33] *Estamos en evidencia,* We are providing a spectacle

[34] *de cabo a rabo,* from beginning to end

FLORENCIO

Querido amigo . . . Llega usted a tiempo.

ESCENA VII

DICHOS y ZURITA

ZURITA

Don Florencio . . . Carolina . . . ¡No me digan ustedes nada!

FLORENCIO

¿Ha visto usted? . . . ¿Ha visto usted? . . . ¿En qué país vivimos?

CAROLINA

¿También usted ha leído . . . ?

ZURITA

Me enteré en el Casino; allí tenían el libro, lo comentaban . . .

FLORENCIO

¿En el Casino?

ZURITA

Tranquilícese usted . . . Todo el mundo dice que se trata de un *chantage,*[35] que esas cartas no pueden ser de don Patricio.

FLORENCIO

¡Ah! ¿Dicen eso?

ZURITA

Y si no fuera . . . , son asuntos de la vida privada que nadie tiene el derecho de lanzar a la publicidad.

FLORENCIO

Lo que yo digo, la vida privada, lo más respetable . . .

ZURITA

Me faltó tiempo[36] para dirigirme a la librería de Valdivieso, que es donde se vende el libro . . . Le encontré consternado, él no sabía nada; adquirió los ejemplares creyendo que se trataba de un asunto serio, de acutalidad[37] en estos momentos . . . Le faltó tiempo para retirar del escaparate los ejemplares y para dirigirse en busca del autor.

FLORENCIO

¿Del autor? Pero ¿está aquí el autor?

ZURITA

Sí; él mismo le ha vendido en firme[38] los ejemplares; llegó con ellos esta mañana.

FLORENCIO

¡Ah! ¿Conque está aquí ese pillete de Casalonga? ¿Y usted sabe dónde se encuentra? . . .

ZURITA

En el Hotel de Europa.

CAROLINA

¡Florencio! No vayas tú. ¡Deténgale usted! Quiere desafiarle.

ZURITA

¿Qué dice usted? No vale la pena. Usted está por encima de todo eso, y su señora de usted mucho más por encima.

FLORENCIO

Y la gente, amigo Zurita, ¿qué dirá la gente?

ZURITA

La gente lo ha tomado a risa.

FLORENCIO

¿A risa? Estamos en el ridículo más espantoso.

[35] *chantage* (French), blackmail
[36] *Me faltó tiempo,* I couldn't act fast enough; I rushed to . . .
[37] *de actualidad,* right up to date, the most recent novelty
[38] *en firme,* for cash settlement

ZURITA

No quiero decir eso . . . ; quiero decir . . .

FLORENCIO

No, amigo Zurita. Usted es un hombre de honor, usted sabe que yo necesito matar a ese hombre.

CAROLINA

Pero, ¿y si es él el que te mata a ti? No, Florencio; un duelo no. ¿Para qué están los Tribunales?

FLORENCIO

No, me batiré . . . , querido Zurita . . . Busque usted a otro amigo . . . Vayan ustedes en representación mía al Hotel de Europa. Vean ustedes a ese hombre, exíjanle ustedes una reparación inmediata . . . , una reparación completa, rotunda. O declara, bajo su firma, que esas cartas son una falsedad indigna, o de lo contrario . . .

CAROLINA

¡Florencio!

FLORENCIO

No reparen ustedes en las condiciones . . . , las más serias . . . , a pistola, con balas de verdad, avanzando[39] . . .

ZURITA

Pero don Florencio . . .

CAROLINA

No vaya usted, se lo ruego.

FLORENCIO

Es usted mi amigo . . . Vaya usted en el acto.[40]

CAROLINA

No, no irá usted.

ZURITA

5 Pero don Florencio . . . Una persona seria como usted . . .

FLORENCIO

Cuando a una persona seria se la pone 10 en ridículo, deja de ser seria. Considere usted mi situación mañana ante ese monumento. ¡Yo! Su mejor amigo . . . Ella, mi esposa, su viuda . . . Y la gente comentando esas cartas . . . 15 ¡Suponer que yo . . . , que ella! . . . Corra usted, corra usted . . . No vuelva usted sin esa reparación.

ZURITA

20 ¡Calle usted! Oigo la voz de Valdivieso.

FLORENCIO

25 ¿Eh? . . . Y la de Casalonga . . . ¡Pero tiene valor de presentarse en mi casa! . . .

ZURITA

30 Deje usted . . . ; cuando él viene, acaso se anticipe a rectificar . . . voy a ver . . . (*Sale.*)

CAROLINA

35 ¡Florencio! No veas a ese hombre, no le recibas . . .

FLORENCIO

Descuida, estoy en mi casa . . . No 40 me olvido de lo que me debo a mí mismo[41]. . . Veremos qué explicación da, veremos . . . Lo que sí te agradeceré es que nos dejes solos . . . Estos asuntos de honor no son para señoras.

[39] *con balas de verdad, avanzando,* with real bullets, moving forward (towards the opponent). (Some duels were arranged so that the contestants ran very little real danger. Florencio is willing to take any risk.)

[40] *en el acto,* right away

[41] It would be incorrect for a gentleman to do violence to a person enjoying the hospitality of his home. Florencio owes this gentlemanly conduct to himself.

CAROLINA

Está bien; pero me quedo cerca . . . No estoy tranquila. No tienes ningún arma, ¿verdad?

FLORENCIO

Mujer, ¿cuándo he llevado yo armas de ningua clase?

CAROLINA

Ten prudencia, ten calma, piensa en mí . . .

FLORENCIO

Estoy en mi casa, no tengas cuidado . . .

CAROLINA

Mira que como te oiga hoy muy acalorado no podría contenerme.

FLORENCIO

¿Qué haces, mujer?

CAROLINA

Me llevo estos cacharros, no te vaya a dar un pronto[42] y se los tires a la cabeza . . . Lo sentiría porque son recuerdo.

FLORENCIO

Anda, mujer.

CAROLINA

Mira que estoy muy nerviosa . . . Ten calma, por Dios; ten prudencia . . . (*Sale.*)

ESCENA VIII

FLORENCIO y ZURITA

ZURITA

¿Está usted más tranquilo?

FLORENCIO

Descuide usted . . . ¿Está ahí ese hombre?

ZURITA

Sí; le ha traído Valdivieso, que desea sincerarse con usted.

FLORENCIO

Bien . . . Pero el otro, ese Casalonga . . . , ¿qué pretende?

ZURITA

Hablar con usted también. Darle toda clase de explicaciones.

FLORENCIO

No hay más que una explicación posible.

ZURITA

Mire usted. Mi opinión es que le reciba usted. Por lo que he podido oírle, me parece un inconsciente.[43]

FLORENCIO

Diga usted un fresco.[44]

ZURITA

Eso es . . . No me atrevía a decirlo . . . Él no da ninguna importancia al asunto.

FLORENCIO

¡Claro! Para él, ninguna.

ZURITA

En fin . . . Yo creo que está dispuesto a todo: a rectificar, a desmentir, a retirar el libro de la circulación. Lo mejor es que hable usted con él . . . ¿Me responde usted de su serenidad? ¿Puedo decirles que pasen? . . .

FLORENCIO

Sí . . . , sí, que pasen.

ZURITA

El pobre Valdivieso está muy disgustado . . . ¡Le estima a usted tanto!

[42] *no te vaya a dar un pronto,* lest you have a fit of anger

[43] *inconsciente,* ignoramus, moron

[44] *fresco,* fresh guy

. . . Es usted una de las tres o cuatro personas que aquí compran libros. ¡Se alegrará tanto si usted le tranquiliza diciéndole que nunca le creyó usted capaz . . . !

FLORENCIO

No. ¡Pobre Valdivieso! Que pase, que pasen . . . (*Sale Zurita, y a poco entra con Valdivieso y Casalonga.*)

ESCENA IX

DICHOS, CASALONGA y VALDIVIESO

VALDIVIESO

¡Señor don Florencio! No sé cómo decirle a usted . . . Supongo que usted no dudará de mi buena fe en este asunto . . . Yo ignoraba . . . , yo no podía sospechar . . .

FLORENCIO

Con usted no va nada.[45] Pero este caballero . . .

CASALONGA

¡Calla, hombre, no me digas nada! Lo que menos podía yo sospechar es que iba a encontrarte aquí . . . y casado con la viuda. ¡Es gracioso!

FLORENCIO

¿Pero oye usted esto?

ZURITA

Ya le dije a usted que es un inconsciente.

FLORENCIO

¡Y yo le dije a usted que es un fresco, pero no creía que lo fuese tanto! ¡Señor mío . . . !

CASALONGA

¡Déjate de tonterías, no me vengas con esa cara! . . .

FLORENCIO

En primer lugar, no recuerdo que nos hayamos tuteado nunca.

CASALONGA

Sí, hombre; sí. Y si no nos tuteamos es lo mismo. Durante una temporada fuimos inseparables. ¡Y en tiempos muy difíciles para los dos! Pero, ¿qué importaba? Cuando el uno no tenía dinero se lo pedía al otro, y tan contentos.[46]

FLORENCIO

Sí, me acuerdo que el otro era siempre yo.

CASALONGA

¡Ja, ja, ja! Es posible, es posible . . . ¿Conque estás tan incomodado conmigo? ¡Qué tontería! No vale la pena.

FLORENCIO

¿Pero oyen ustedes?

VALDIVIESO

Crea usted que si yo hubiera sospechado . . . Le compré en firme los ejemplares, aprovechando la actualidad del monumento. Pero ¡si yo hubiera sabido . . . !

CASALONGA

Pues eso, aprovechando la actualidad. Yo ando muy mal, chico. Esta situación conservadora[47] tan prolongada, me tiene en las últimas[48] . . . Ya no sabe uno qué discurrir para sacar dinero.

FLORENCIO

¡Me gusta el descaro! ¿Y qué hace usted con un hombre así?

ZURITA

Eso digo yo. ¿Qué hace usted?

[45] *no va nada,* nothing is involved
[46] *y tan contentos,* and everything was O.K.
[47] *situación conservadora,* political situation with the conservative element in control
[48] *me tiene en las últimas,* has me flat broke

CASALONGA

Figúrate que hasta me puse a escribir cosas para el teatro . . . Como las de todo el mundo . . . , un poco mejores, por eso no gustaban . . . Figúrate que me casé con la última patrona que tuve. ¡De alguna manera tenía que pagarla! ¡Pero, chico, me armaba unos escándalos, que un día, después de tirarnos todos los trastos a la cabeza, acordamos separarnos amistosamente! ¡Después, no quieras saberlo![49]

FLORENCIO

No, si no quiero saber nada . . . , si . . .

CASALONGA

Una novela, una verdadera novela . . . Figúrate que hasta he andado por esos pueblos explicando las vistas de un cine . . . Ya conoces mi facilidad de palabra . . . En las cintas dramáticas tenía un éxito . . . Pero enfermé de la garganta . . . Ya no me quedaba que tocar ninguna tecla . . . Yo tengo muy buenas relaciones . . . Pero los amigos . . . ¡Ah, los amigos! En cuanto les pides algo ya no hay amigos . . . En esto me enteré de que aquí inaugurabas un monumento a la memoria de nuestro amigo Patricio. ¡Pobre Patricio! ¡Aquél sí era un amigo! ¡Allí había hombre siempre![50] Se me ocurrió escribir cuatro tonterías de recuerdos personales, publicar unas cuantas cartas que conservaba de él . . .

FLORENCIO

¡Feliz ocurrencia!

CASALONGA

¡El garbanzo,[51] el miserable garbanzo! Pensé que en ninguna parte podía venderse mejor que aquí, en su patria. Llegué esta mañana en tercera,[52] chico, en tercera . . . Me fuí a casa de este hombre, le coloqué dos mil ejemplares, que me pagó con un descuento horroroso . . . ¡Estos libreros!

VALDIVIESO

¡Oiga usted! Lo razonable cuando se compra en firme.

CASALONGA

Si no digo nada. La humanidad se divide en primos[53] y pillos . . .

VALDIVIESO

¿Pero oyen ustedes esto?

CASALONGA

Usted es de los pillos.

VALDIVIESO

¡Oiga usted! ¡Pues no hay duda que he hecho un bonito negocio! ¿Usted cree que yo voy a vender un ejemplar más de ese libelo, sabiendo que en él se ofende a mi particular y respetable amigo don Florencio y a su distinguida esposa?

FLORENCIO

¡Gracias, amigo Valdivieso; muchas gracias!

VALDIVIESO

Quemaré la edición, aunque ya ve usted la pérdida que me supone.

FLORENCIO

De eso no hay que hablar. Eso es cuenta mía.

CASALONGA

¿Lo ve usted? Florencio paga. Quéjese usted ahora. Pero mal hecho, chico; yo que tú no le daba un cuarto . . .

[49] *no quieras saberlo,* don't even ask about it
[50] *¡Allí había hombre siempre!* There was a man you could always count on!
[51] *¡El garbanzo!* My living! (See p. 462, n. 8.)
[52] *tercera,* third class coach
[53] *primo,* slang, sucker

VALDIVIESO

¡Oiga usted! Como usted ha cobrado a tocateja[54] . . .

CASALONGA

No le llame usted cobrar a eso . . . con ese descuento . . . El papel vale más.

FLORENCIO

Lo que vale más es su desahogo[55] de usted, señor mío . . .

CASALONGA

¡Ja, ja, ja! Si no me ofendo, si tienes razón. Pero, ¿qué quieres? Cuando ha tocado uno todas las teclas[56] . . . ¿Vas a matarme?

FLORENCIO

Por mi parte pondré los medios[57] . . . ¿Usted cree que esto puede quedar así? . . . Y si se niega usted a batirse lo llevaré a los Tribunales.

CASALONGA

Deja ese tono trágico. ¿Un duelo? ¿Entre nosotros? ¿Y por qué? Porque la mujer de un amigo . . . , que hoy es tu mujer, se la pegaba contigo.[58] ¡Si hubiera sido con otro!

FLORENCIO

¡Que no le consiento a usted esas suposiciones!

CASALONGA

Será el primer hombre que se ofende porque le dicen que ha tenido relaciones con su mujer . . . ¿No comprendes que eso es ridículo? ¿Cómo vas a batirte por eso?

ZURITA

En el fondo hay algo de verdad.

FLORENCIO

5 Patricio nunca pudo escribir esas cartas, y menos a usted.

CASALONGA

Di lo que quieras; las cartas son au-
10 ténticas . . . Ahora que Patricio hiciera una tontería en escribirlas . . . , ya es más discutible . . . Yo las publiqué por dar un poco de amenidad al libro; al público le gusta siempre la
15 nota intencionada[59] . . . Por lo demás, ¿qué interés tenía yo en molestarte, criatura?

FLORENCIO

20 ¡Y dale con la confianza![60]

ZURITA

¿Y qué hace usted con un hombre así?

25

FLORENCIO

Eso digo yo. ¿Qué hace usted?

CASALONGA

30

Ya sabes que yo siempre te he querido mucho . . . , porque tienes mucho talento.

FLORENCIO

35

¡Gracias!

CASALONGA

Mucho más talento que el pobre
40 Patricio . . . , que era una excelente persona, pero, entre nosotros que estamos en el secreto, un completo besugo.[61]

[54] *a tocateja,* hard cash
[55] *desahogo,* brazen conduct
[56] *Cuando . . . teclas,* When one has tried every recourse
[57] *pondré los medios,* I'll do what I can
[58] *se la pegaba contigo,* was sweet on you
[59] *nota intencionada,* insinuation
[60] *¡Y dale con la confianza!* Drop that intimate tone!
[61] *besugo,* a kind of fish (sea bream); slang, simpleton

FLORENCIO

¡Hombre, no tanto![62]

CASALONGA

De esas reputaciones que se hacen en este país. ¡Si él hubiera tenido tu talento, tu clarísimo talento!

FLORENCIO

¡Hay que dejarle hablar![63]

CASALONGA

Di[64] que tú has sido siempre muy modesto y te has quedado en la sombra para que él luciera y brillara. Pero, ¿quién no sabe que sus mejores discursos pudo pronunciarlos gracias a ti?

FLORENCIO

¡No me descubras![65]

CASALONGA

Sí, señores, sépanlo ustedes . . . Este hombre era el verdadero talento; él es quien merecía la estatua . . . Este amigo admirable, único . . .

FLORENCIO

¡Es que no hay modo de reñir con este hombre!

CASALONGA

Por lo demás, yo ahora mismo envío un comunicado diciendo que esas cartas son apócrifas . . . , lo que tú quieras . . . , como tú quieras . . . ¡No faltaba más! Eso no tiene ninguna importancia . . . Yo estoy por encima de esas miserias . . . Y a este sujeto no le des más que lo justo . . . A dos reales por ejemplar, lo que él me ha dado a mí.

VALDIVIESO

No le permito a usted que se entrometa en mis asuntos . . . Es usted un trapisondista.

CASALONGA

¿Ha dicho usted trapisondista? Le advierto a usted que con usted sí me bato. Usted no es mi amigo. Usted es un explotador de la inteligencia ajena.

VALDIVIESO

¡Conmigo se atreverá usted! ¡Con un padre de familia! Después de haberme estafado.

CASALONGA

¿Ha dicho usted estafado? Eso me lo dice usted aquí.

VALDIVIESO

En todas partes.

FLORENCIO

¡Señores, señores! ¡Está usted en mi casa, en casa de mi señora!

ZURITA

¡Pero Valdivieso! . . .

CASALONGA

(*A Florencio.*) Te nombro mi padrino, y a usted también, mi querido amigo . . . ¿Cómo se llama usted?

VALDIVIESO

¿Pero van ustedes a hacerle caso? ¿Ustedes creen que yo voy a batirme con el primer desahogado que se presente? . . . ¡Un padre de familia!

CASALONGA

¡No admito explicaciones! ¡Mis amigos se entenderán con los de usted! Que todo quede arreglado esta misma tarde.

VALDIVIESO

¿Y le oyen ustedes con esa calma? ¿Y serán ustedes capaces de hacerle caso? Es muy cómodo, cuando es usted el

[62] *¡Hombre, no tanto!* I wouldn't go *that* far!

[63] Said with mock resignation: I just can't stop him!

[64] *Di,* here, You can say

[65] *¡No me descubras!* Don't give away my secret!

que debía batirse, tomarme a mí por cabeza de turco[66] . . .

FLORENCIO

¡Amigo Valdivieso! No le tolero a usted apreciaciones sobre mi conducta . . . Después de todo . . . ¡si usted no hubiera tratado de lucrarse de mala manera con ese libro, sabiendo que en él se me ofendía gravemente! . . .

VALDIVIESO

Pero, ¿habla usted en serio?

FLORENCIO

Tan en serio.

CASALONGA

Sí, señor, que hablamos en serio. ¡Usted ha dado lugar a todo! Nadie compra sin enterarse. Pudo usted indicarme la indiscreción que yo había cometido . . . Por mi parte, si quieres batirte con él, te cedo mi puesto como primer ofendido . . . Yo tendré mucho gusto en apadrinarte con este querido amigo . . . ¿Cómo se llama usted?

ZURITA

Zurita.

CASALONGA

Mi querido amigo Zurita.

VALDIVIESO

Pero, ¿quieren ustedes volverme loco? ¡Por lo visto me han preparado ustedes una encerrona![67]

FLORENCIO

¡Amigo Valdivieso, que no le consiento a usted esas apreciaciones! En mi casa no se preparan encerronas.

ZURITA

¡Ah, y yo tampoco! Yo no le he traído a usted a ninguna encerrona.

[66] *cabeza de turco,* cat's-paw, scapegoat
[67] *encerrona,* trap

CASALONGA

Ha olvidado usted con quién habla.

VALDIVIESO

¡Vaya! Queden ustedes con Dios. Esto no puede sufrirse . . . Así se agradecen mis buenos oficios . . . Lo que haré es vender el libro . . . , y si no se vende, lo regalo . . . y que lo lea y lo comente todo el mundo . . . ¡No faltaba otra cosa!

FLORENCIO

Oiga usted, ¿qué está usted diciendo? ¡Pobre de usted[68] si vende un solo ejemplar!

ZURITA

Eso es; pobre de usted. A mí no me deja usted en evidencia.[69]

CASALONGA

Ni a mí tampoco.

VALDIVIESO

¡No escucho una palabra! Hagan ustedes lo que quieran . . . Yo haré lo que me pareczca. ¡No faltaba más . . . , no faltaba más! . . . (*Sale.*)

FLORENCIO

Deténgale usted.

CASALONGA

Descuida. Ahora mismo voy a su casa y recojo los ejemplares. Lo que pensabas pagarle por ellos me lo das a mí, que me hace más falta y soy tu amigo . . . Ese hombre no se ríe de mí . . . ¡Ah!, y esta noche comemos juntos; te espero en el hotel; no me faltes; mira que si no vienes me presento yo aquí y me convido a comer contigo.

FLORENCIO

¡No! ¿Qué diría mi mujer? ¡Contenta la tienes!

[68] *Pobre de usted,* Woe upon you
[69] *A mí . . . evidencia,* You're not going to leave me playing a ridiculous role

CASALONGA

¡Bah! Tu mujer ya me conoce y se divertiría mucho . . . Seguirá tan guapa, tan distinguida, tan inteligente . . . Y ahora será dichosa . . . ¡El pobre Patricio tenía tantas rarezas! . . . Y aquella figura . . . y le doblaba la edad . . . Hasta ahora, chico . . . ¡No sabes lo que me he alegrado de verte! ¡Un amigo como tú! ¡Venga un abrazo! Me conmuevo. Yo soy así . . . Hasta ahora . . . Si no vuelvo, es que he pegado a ese hombre y estoy en la cárcel. Ponme a los pies de tu señora[70] . . . Servidor de usted, amigo . . . ¡Ah! Zurita . . . ¡Qué cabeza ésta! Beso a usted la mano. (*Sale.*)

ESCENA X

FLORENCIO, ZURITA, *después* CAROLINA

FLORENCIO

¡Usted no habrá visto nada igual nunca! Yo tampoco . . . Y yo que le conocía de antiguo . . . Pero ha mejorado mucho en este tiempo . . .

ZURITA

¡Es de una frescura épica!

FLORENCIO

¿Pero qué hace usted con un hombre que toma las cosas de esa manera? No es cosa de matarle. (*Entra Carolina.*) ¡Ah! ¡Carolina! ¿Has oído, te has enterado? . . .

CAROLINA

Sí . . . , es gracioso en medio de todo.

FLORENCIO

Menos mal que Carolina está más conforme.

ZURITA

Habrá oído los piropos . . . ¡Ese hombre es irresistible!

FLORENCIO

Mira, en resumidas cuentas . . . nadie ha dado importancia al asunto . . . Sólo se habían vendido dos o tres ejemplares.

CAROLINA

Sí . . . , pero uno de ellos a mis cuñadas, que es como si se hubieran vendido cuarenta mil, porque se lo irán contando a todo el mundo.

FLORENCIO

Ya contaban antes lo mismo. No te apures.

CAROLINA

De todos modos, yo no me presento mañana en la inauguración, y tú tampoco debes asistir.

FLORENCIO

¡Pero mujer!

ZURITA

¡Ah, la inauguración! No he tenido tiempo de decírselo a ustedes.

CAROLINA

¿Qué?

ZURITA

Que se ha suspendido.

FLORENCIO

¿Como?

ZURITA

Sí; a última hora la Comisión se ha alarmado ante las protestas ocasionadas por los desnudos . . . Muchas señoras han visto las fotografías del monumento y se negaban a asistir. Han convencido al escultor, y por fin consiente en retirar la estatua de la Verdad y en poner una túnica a la Industria y un calzón de baño[71] al Comercio

[70] *Ponme . . . señora,* Give my best to your wife

[71] *calzón de baño,* swimming trunks

CAROLINA

¡Cuánto me alegro!

ZURITA

Todo esto llevará algunos días. Cuando pasen, la gente se habrá olvidado de todo.

ESCENA XI

DICHOS y CASALONGA, *que entra muy sofocado con los ejemplares, que deja caer de golpe, levantando una nube de polvo.*

CAROLINA

¡Ay!

CASALONGA

No se asuste usted . . . A los pies de usted . . . Aquí está toda la edición . . . Le he devuelto las mil pesetas que me había dado . . . , ni un céntimo más . . . Ya te lo dije. ¡No faltaba más! Ahora, tú verás . . . Yo nada te pido . . . Soy tu amigo . . . No me queda otra tecla que tocar . . . No te digo nada.

FLORENCIO

Cuenta con dos mil pesetas . . . ¡Pero cuidado con publicar la segunda edición!

CASALONGA

Descuida. Con ese dinero . . . tengo para ser persona decente . . . lo menos . . . lo menos dos meses . . . ¡Señora mía! ¿Usted no recuerda de mí? El mejor amigo de Florencio y el mejor amigo de Patricio; por lo tanto, el mejor amigo de usted.

CAROLINA

Sí, ya recuerdo.

CASALONGA

He cambiado mucho.

FLORENCIO

5 No lo creas. No has cambiado nada.

CASALONGA

Usted, en cambio . . . , está lo mismo . . . ¡Mucho mejor! En toda la opu-
10 lencia de su hermosura espléndida, realzada por la felicidad de un matrimonio venturoso . . . ¿No tienen ustedes hijos?

15 CAROLINA

No . . .

CASALONGA

Los tendrán ustedes.
20

FLORENCIO

¡Adulador!

CASALONGA
25
Quisiera marcharme esta misma noche . . . ¿Qué hago yo aquí?

FLORENCIO

30 No, ya lo has hecho todo. Dentro de un instante te mandaré eso al hotel.

CASALONGA

Si pudieras añadir un piquillo . . .
35 Para los gastos de viaje . . . Por no descabalarlas.[72]

FLORENCIO

40 Bueno, hombre; bueno.

CASALONGA

No molesto más. ¡Señora mía, siempre suyo! . . . Amigo Zurita . . . , amigo
45 Florencio . . . No quisiera morirme sin volver a verte.

[72] *por no descabalarlas,* so as not to break into them (the two thousand pesetas)

FLORENCIO

Pues yo sí, yo sí; puedes creerlo.

CASALONGA

Ya sé que no lo sientes. Eres un falso cínico.

FLORENCIO

Te llevo esa ventaja.

CASALONGA

¡Adiós, amigo; adiós! ¡Qué diferente nuestra suerte! Para ti todo . . . , amor, riquezas, satisfacciones . . . ¡No quiero que me veas llorar! (*Sale.*)

CAROLINA

¿De modo que te cuesta el dinero?

FLORENCIO

¿Qué quieres? Por ti, por evitarte un disgusto. Estabas tan nerviosa . . . Yo me hubiera batido, hubiera llevado las cosas al último extremo . . . Zurita lo sabe.

CAROLINA

¡Siempre dije que el monumento nos costaría caro! . . .

FLORENCIO

Ya lo ves. Dos mil pesetas ahora, veinticinco mil que di para el monumento . . . , el uniforme de jefe de Administración, que pensaba estrenar en la inauguración . . . , los obsequios a las Comisiones . . .

ZURITA

La gloria cuesta siempre más de lo que vale.

FLORENCIO

No puede uno ser célebre ni de segunda mano.

CAROLINA

¿Te pesa?

FLORENCIO

No, Carolina mía. La gloria de ser tu marido bien vale para mí los inconvenientes de ser el marido de su viuda.

Modern Poetry

WE have seen that during the last half of the nineteenth century poetry became more restricted, more local in interest, more regional in theme, and more prosaic in diction. At the end of the century, a great wave of regeneration, called *modernismo,* passed over Spanish poetry, not only in Spain but throughout all the Hispanic lands. The prophet of this new movement was Rubén Darío (1867–1916), undoubtedly one of the greatest poets ever to write in Spanish.

RUBÉN DARÍO was born in Nicaragua but, during a life of constant agitation, spent much time in Chile, the Argentine, Spain, and Paris. He was a man of childlike candor and often had difficulty in managing his practical affairs. While his debauches filled him with remorse, he felt that his true self—hidden within his 'inner kingdom'—remained unsullied by the world. With a poet's disdain for materialism, he made a precarious living with newspaper writing and diplomatic work.

Modernismo became generally accepted with the publication of *Prosas profanas* (1896). Here Darío shows himself a universal man, thoroughly alive to the currents of literary thought from all nations and all times, although particularly influenced by the French poets Hugo, Leconte de Lisle, and especially Verlaine. He incorporates these elements of most diverse origin into Spanish, thoroughly assimilating all of his borrowings and fusing them in new rhythms and new poetic diction. Despite his borrowings, Darío made *modernismo* a declaration of poetic independence, of the right of the poet to express the hidden recesses of his soul in whatever form and language he pleased. He made Spanish poetry once more universal in scope and brought it abreast of the innovations of other lands.

In another book of prime importance, *Cantos de vida y esperanza* (1905), our poet shows a more marked predilection for American themes. He calls upon the republics of Latin America to unite, asks of them a sympathy for the bleeding mother country, Spain, and extols the 'Latin race,' their great common source. Furthermore these later poems show fewer of the artifices of poetry and a greater profundity of emotion. They are not so much made as felt.[1]

[1] Principal works of Rubén Darío: *Azul; Prosas profanas; Cantos de vida y esperanza.*

The influence of Rubén Darío was as great in Spain as in Latin America. No poet of the twentieth century fails to show an indebtedness to the great master's art, but the three Spanish poets from whom we have chosen selections are perhaps the ones least directly influenced by Rubén Darío.

ANTONIO MACHADO (1875–1938), although born in Sevilla, spent the formative period of his life in Madrid and in the small Castilian city of Soria. He himself says: '*Cinco años en la tierra de Soria, hoy para mí sagrada — allí me casé; allí perdí a mi esposa a quien adoraba, — orientaron mis ojos y mi corazón hacia lo esencial castellano.*' And the essence of Castilla is to be found in his descriptions of the arid steppes alternately baked by the sun or frozen by the cold of winter. Antonio Machado is the greatest poet of the Generation of '98; he looks at the Castilian landscape and speaks of '*aquellas tierras tan tristes que tienen alma.*' His amount of production is small, and he had no imitators.[2]

About 1900 a second Spanish poet began to publish, JUAN RAMÓN JIMÉNEZ (1881–1958). An Andalusian, from the region near Huelva, Juan Ramón writes essentially subjective poetry, the internal music of the soul. Nothing very great or transcendental is discussed in his works, yet the poet's delicately shaded feelings are communicated to the reader. The method is impressionistic. By giving us little indications symbolical of his sensation, Juan Ramón creates in our minds his own feeling. His verse is always musical, and many times no other effect than music is desired. He is generally melancholic, yet at times the rhythms of Andalusian popular dance melodies give their color and vivacity to his verse. Juan Ramón was the recipient of a Nobel prize shortly before his death.[3]

Juan Ramón is the great master of the many competent poets who began to write in the 1920's. Most of them specialized in one element found in the more inclusive art of Juan Ramón. Thus FEDERICO GARCÍA LORCA (1898–1936) specialized in the popular and folklore elements. His poetry calls to mind the dances of his native Granada, especially those of the gypsies. Many times he assumes deliberately the naiveté of the nursery rhyme. His dramas, which represent a turning away from the realism of Benavente, emphasize fantasy, poetry, and a combining of music and ballet with the drama. This poet's tragic death during the Spanish Civil War did much to enhance his fame.[4]

[2] Principal work of Antonio Machado: *Campos de Castilla.*

[3] Principal works of Juan Ramón Jiménez: *Segunda antoljia poética; Diario de un poeta recién casado* (prose and verse); *Platero y yo* (prose)

[4] Principal works of Federico García Lorca: *Romancero gitano; Poema del cante jondo; Llanto por Ignacio Sánchez Mejías;* plays: *Bodas de sangre; Yerma*

Rubén Darío

Sonatina

La princesa está triste . . . ¿qué tendrá la princesa?
Los suspiros se escapan de su boca de fresa,
que ha perdido la risa, que ha perdido el color.
La princesa está pálida en su silla de oro,
está mudo el teclado de su clave sonoro; 5
y en un vaso olvidada se desmaya una flor.

El jardín[1] puebla el triunfo de los pavos reales.
Parlanchina, la dueña dice cosas banales,
y vestido de rojo piruetea el bufón.
La princesa no ríe, la princesa no siente; 10
la princesa persigue por el cielo de Oriente
la libélula[2] vaga de una vaga ilusión.

¿Piensa acaso en el príncipe de Golconda[3] o de China,
o en el que ha detenido su carroza argentina
para ver de sus ojos la dulzura de luz, 15
o en el rey de las islas de las rosas fragantes,
o en el que es soberano de los claros diamantes,
o en el dueño orgulloso de las perlas de Ormuz?[4]

¡Ay! la pobre princesa de la boca de rosa
quiere ser golondrina, quiere ser mariposa, 20
tener alas ligeras, bajo el cielo volar;
ir al sol por la escala[5] luminosa de un rayo,[6]
saludar a los lirios con los versos de Mayo,
o perderse en el viento sobre el trueno del mar.

Ya no quiere el palacio, ni la rueca de plata, 25
ni el balcón encantado, ni el bufón escarlata,
ni los cisnes unáimes[7] en el lago de azur.
Y están tristes las flores por la flor de la corte;
los jazmines de Oriente, los nelumbos del Norte,
de Occidente las dalias y las rosas del Sur. 30

[1] Object of *puebla* whose subject is *triunfo,* triumphal parade
[2] damsel-fly (a small, brightly colored dragon-fly)
[3] A city of India, whose princes possessed fabulous treasures of precious stones
[4] An Arabian town on an island in the Persian Gulf, still a center of pearl fishing
[5] stairway, ladder
[6] ray (of light)
[7] of one mind; here probably referring to the habit of swans of swimming all in one direction at the same time, often in single file. Some editions of this poem read *ecuánimes* here.

¡Pobrecita princesa de los ojos azules!
Está presa en sus oros, está presa en sus tules,
en la jaula de mármol del palacio real;
el palacio soberbio que vigilan los guardas,
que custodian cien negros con sus cien alabardas, 35
un lebrel que no duerme y un dragón colosal.

¡Oh, quién fuera[8] hipsipila[9] que dejó la crisálida![10]
(La princesa está triste. La princesa está pálida.)
¡Oh visión adorada de oro, rosa y marfil!
¡Quién volara a la tierra donde un príncipe existe 40
(La princesa está pálida. La princesa está triste.)
más brillante que el alba, más hermoso que Abril!

¡Calla, calla, princesa—dice el hada madrina[11]—
en caballo con alas hacia acá se encamina,
en el cinto la espada y en la mano el azor, 45
el feliz caballero que te adora sin verte,
y que llega de lejos, vencedor de la Muerte,
a encenderte los labios con su beso de amor![12]

(*Prosas profanas*)

Canción de otoño en primavera

Juventud, divino tesoro,
¡ya te vas para no volver!
Cuando quiero llorar, no lloro . . .
Y a veces lloro sin querer . . .

Plural[13] ha sido la celeste 5
historia de mi corazón.
Era[14] una dulce niña, en este
mundo de duelo y aflicción.

Miraba como el alba pura;
sonreía como una flor. 10
Era su cabellera oscura
hecha de noche y de dolor.

Yo era tímido como un niño.
Ella, naturalmente, fué,
para mi amor hecho de armiño,[15] 15
Herodías y Salomé[16] . . .

Juventud, divino tesoro,
¡ya te vas para no volver! . . .
Cuando quiero llorar, no lloro,
y a veces lloro sin querer . . . 20

La otra[17] fué más sensitiva
y más consoladora y más
halagadora y expresiva,
cual no pensé encontrar jamás,

Pues a su continua ternura 25
una pasión violenta unía.
En un peplo de gasa pura
una bacante[18] se envolvía . . .

[8] *quién fuera,* would I were
[9] butterfly
[10] chrysalis
[11] *el hada madrina,* the fairy godmother
[12] The princess is, of course, in love with love. The awakening of her heart is accompanied by a vague restlessness and unexplained melancholy.
[13] multifold
[14] Here begins the first of the many adventures of his heart.
[15] ermine (which, being pure white, symbolizes purity)
[16] Salome asked for the head of John the Baptist, instigated by her mother, Herodias, whom John had denounced as a sinful woman. Symbolically, these women represent killers of innocence.
[17] next
[18] bacchante, woman who indulges in excesses

En brazos tomó mi ensueño
y lo arrulló como a un bebé . . . 30
Y le mató, triste y pequeño,
falto de luz, falto de fe . . .

Juventud, divino tesoro,
¡te fuiste para no volver!
Cuando quiero llorar, no lloro, 35
y a veces lloro sin querer . . .

¡Y las demás! en tantos climas,
en tantas tierras, siempre son,
si no pretextos de mis rimas,
fantasmas de mi corazón. 40

En vano busqué a la princesa
que estaba triste de esperar.
La vida es dura. Amarga y pesa.[19]
¡Ya no hay princesa que cantar!

Mas a pesar del tiempo terco, 45
mi sed de amor no tiene fin;
con el cabello gris, me acerco
a los rosales del jardín . . .

Juventud, divino tesoro,
ya te vas para no volver . . . 50
Cuando quiero llorar, no lloro,
y a veces lloro sin querer . . .

¡Mas es mía el Alba de oro![20]

(*Cantos de vida y esperanza*)

Antonio Machado

Campos de Soria

I

Es la tierra de Soria árida y fría.
Por las colinas y las sierras calvas,
verdes pradillos, cerros cenicientos,
la primavera pasa
dejando entre las hierbas olorosas 5
sus diminutas margaritas blancas.

La tierra no revive, el campo sueña.
Al empezar abril está nevada
la espalda del Moncayo;[1]
el caminante lleva en su bufanda 10
envueltos cuello y boca, y los pastores
pasan cubiertos con sus luengas capas.

V

La nieve. En el mesón al campo
abierto[2]
se ve el hogar donde la leña humea
y la olla al hervir borbollonea. 15
El cierzo[3] corre por el campo yerto,[4]
alborotando en blancos torbellinos
la nieve silenciosa.
La nieve sobre el campo y los caminos,
cayendo está como sobre una fosa. 20
Un viejo acurrucado tiembla y tose
cerca del fuego; su mechón de lana
la vieja hila, y una niña cose
verde ribete a su estameña grana.[5]
Padres los viejos son de un arriero 25
que caminó sobre la blanca tierra,
y una noche perdió ruta y sendero,
y se enterró en las nieves de la sierra.
En torno al fuego hay un lugar vacío,
y en la frente del viejo, de hosco
ceño, 30
como un tachón[6] sombrío
—tal el golpe de un hacha sobre un
leño—.
La vieja mira al campo, cual si oyera

[19] Verbs, not adjectives

[20] Probably the Golden Dawn of Immortality

[1] *el Moncayo,* the same mountain mentioned by Bécquer, p. 373, n. 10.

[2] *al campo abierto,* amid the open fields; away from the city

[3] *cierzo,* north wind

[4] *yerto,* stiff; motionless; here, congealed

[5] *ribete,* border; *estameña grana,* scarlet serge

[6] *tachón,* cleft, furrow

pasos sobre la nieve. Nadie pasa.
Desierta la vecina carretera, 35
desierto el campo en torno de la casa.
La niña piensa que en los verdes prados
ha de correr con otras doncellitas
en los días azules y dorados,
cuando crecen las blancas margaritas. 40

VI

¡Soria fría, *Soria pura,*
cabeza de Extremadura,[7]
con su castillo guerrero
arruinado, sobre el Duero;
con sus murallas roídas[8] 45
y sus casas denegridas!

¡Muerta ciudad de señores
soldados o cazadores;
de portales con escudos
de cien linajes hidalgos, 50
y de famélicos galgos,
de galgos flacos y agudos,
que pululan
por las sórdidas callejas,
y a la media noche ululan, 55
cuando graznan las cornejas!

¡Soria fría! La campana
de la Audiencia[9] da la una.
Soria, ciudad castellana
¡tan bella! bajo la luna. 60

IX

¡Oh!, sí, conmigo vais, campos de Soria,
tardes tranquilas, montes de violeta,
alamedas del río, verde sueño
del suelo gris y de la parda tierra,
agria melancolía 65
de la ciudad decrépita,
me habéis llegado al alma,
¿o acaso estabais en el fondo de ella?
¡Gentes del alto llano numantino[10]
que a Dios guardáis como cristianas viejas, 70
que el sol de España os llene
de alegría, de luz y de riqueza!

Juan Ramón Jiménez

Convalecencia

Sólo tú me acompañas, sol amigo.
Como un perro de luz lames mi lecho blanco;
y yo pierdo mi mano por tu pelo de oro,
caída de cansancio.

¡Qué de cosas que fueron 5
se van . . . más lejos todavía!
Callo
y sonrío, igual que un niño,
dejándome lamer de ti, sol manso.

. . . De pronto, sol, te yergues,[1] 10
fiel guardián de mi fracaso,
y, en una algarabía ardiente y loca,

[7] *cabeza de Extremadura,* chief city of the frontier. Extremadura is now a province far from Soria, but in the Middle Ages this name was given to all the dangerous territory close to the Moors.

[8] *roído,* eaten away, crumbling

[9] *Audiencia,* courthouse

[10] *llano numantino,* Numancian plain. Numancia, the ancient Iberian city which heroically resisted Roman capture, was located only a few miles from Soria.

[1] *erguir,* to straighten up, rise

ladras a los fantasmas vanos
que, mudas sombras, me amenazan
desde el desierto del ocaso. 15

(*Estío*)

Anochecer de otoño

En la hora negra, fría y solitaria,
el muelle, que esta tarde
me pareció llevarme hasta el poniente de oro,
¡es tan pequeño, ¡ay!, tan de juguete!
Y yo, juguete oscuro y triste, voy soñando, niño grande 5
—en este nuevo juego, que, hace una hora,
creía realidad definitiva
de hombre que recuerda riendo sus juguetes
de niño, sus barquitos,—
juguete oscuro y triste, voy soñando 10
en unas cosas altas,
de las que son juguetes
el mar, la tierra, las estrellas . . .

(*Piedra y cielo*)

Ya están ahí las carretas

Ya están ahí las carretas . . .
—Lo han dicho el pinar y el viento,
lo ha dicho la luna de oro,
lo han dicho el humo y el eco . . .
Son las carretas que pasan 5
estas tardes, al sol puesto,
las carretas que se llevan
del monte los troncos muertos.
¡Cómo lloran las carretas,
camino de Pueblo Nuevo! 10
Los bueyes vienen soñando,
a la luz de los luceros,
en el establo caliente
que sabe a madre[2] y a heno.
Y detrás de las carretas, 15
caminan los carreteros,
con la aijada sobre el hombro
y los ojos en el cielo.
¡Cómo lloran las carretas,
camino de Pueblo Nuevo! 20
En la paz del campo, van
dejando los troncos muertos
un olor fresco y honrado
a corazón descubierto.
Y cae el ángelus desde 25

[2] *saber a,* to taste like; here, smell of; *madre,* here, home

la torre del pueblo viejo,
sobre los campos talados,[3]
que huelen a cementerio.
¡Cómo lloran las carretas,
camino de Pueblo Nuevo! 30

(*Pastorales*)

Federico García Lorca

Canción de jinete

Córdoba.
Lejana y sola.

Jaca negra, luna grande,
y aceitunas en mi alforja.
Aunque sepa[1] los caminos 5
yo nunca llegaré a Córdoba.

Por el llano, por el viento,
jaca negra, luna roja.
La muerte me está mirando
desde las torres de Córdoba. 10

¡Ay, qué camino tan largo!
¡Ay, mi jaca valerosa!
¡Ay, que la muerte me espera
antes de llegar a Córdoba!

Córdoba. 15
Lejana y sola.

Romance de la luna, luna

La luna vino a la fragua
con su polisón de nardos.[1]
El niño la mira, mira.[2]
El niño la está mirando.
En el aire conmovido 5
mueve la luna sus brazos
y enseña, lúbrica y pura,
sus senos de duro estaño.
—Huye[3] luna, luna, luna.
Si vinieran los gitanos, 10
harían con tu corazón
collares y anillos blancos.
—Niño, déjame que baile.
Cuando vengan los gitanos,
te encontrarán sobre el yunque 15
con los ojillos cerrados.
—Huye luna, luna, luna,
que ya siento sus caballos.
—Niño, déjame, no pises
mi blancor almidonado.[4] 20
El jinete se acercaba
tocando el tambor del llano.
Dentro de la fragua el niño
tiene los ojos cerrados.

Por el olivar venían, 25
bronce y sueño,[5] los gitanos.
Las cabezas levantadas
y los ojos entornados.

Cómo canta la zumaya,
¡ay, cómo canta en el árbol! 30
Por el cielo va la luna
con un niño de la mano.

Dentro de la fragua lloran,
dando gritos, los gitanos.
El aire la vela, vela. 35
El aire la está velando.

[3] where trees have been felled

[1] Subject, *yo*

[1] *polisón de nardos,* bustle of tuberoses. This metaphor suggests the roundness (bustle) and whiteness (the color of the tuberoses) which characterize the full moon.

[2] *mira, mira.* This poem is a sort of nursery rhyme, although a sophisticated one. As children repeat words to savor their sound, so the poet repeats *luna, luna* and *mira, mira.*

[3] The child is speaking.

[4] *no pises mi blancor almidonado,* don't step on my starchy white. A common children's game is to avoid stepping on the moonlit ground.

[5] *bronce y sueño,* these words suggest the bronzed skin and half closed eyes of the gypsies.

Vocabulary

The following abbreviations are used: *arch.*—archaic (indicating words no longer in common use), *adj.*—adjective, *adv.*—adverb, *fig.*—figurative, *n.*—noun, *plu.*—plural, *aug.*—augmentative, *dim.*—diminutive, *super.*—superlative.

This vocabulary does not contain all the words in the book. Omitted are all the common pronouns, conjunctions, prepositions, etc., as well as many of the commonest words (according to Buchanan's count) and a considerable number of words whose form and meaning are closely similar in Spanish and English. However, words that are not exact cognates and all less familiar cognates have been included. The meaning of adverbs ending in *-mente* must usually be sought under the corresponding adjective.

A

abad abbot, priest
abajar *arch.* to lower, bring down to earth
abajo down; downstairs; **por ——** below
abalanzarse to rush, leap; **—— a** (*or* **sobre**) to leap upon
abalorio bead work
abandonar to abandon, leave, give up
abandono abandonment, abandon; slovenliness, negligence; giving up, relinquishing
abanico fan
abarcar to take in, include
abastar to provide, provision
abatamiento depression, dejection
abatanar to pound, beat
abatido downcast, dejected
abatir to cast down; to strike down; to dismay; to humble
abeja bee
aberración aberration
abertura opening
abismar to sink
abismo abyss; *plu.* hell
ablander to soften, melt
abnegación abnegation, self-denial
abofetear to strike, slap
abogacía legal profession
abolengo lineage, family tree
abominar to abominate, hate
abonar to guarantee, recommend, speak for; to justify; **——se a** to subscribe to, take a season ticket for
abono favor, behalf; support
aborrecer to hate, abhor
aborrecible abominable, abhorrent
aborrecimiento abhorrence
aborto abortion; hideous offspring
abrasado hot, burning
abrasador burning
abrasar to burn
abrazador, -a embracer
abrazer to embrace
abrazo embrace
ábrego southwest wind
abreviadamente in brief, briefly
abreviar to shorten, abbreviate
abrigar to harbor, shelter, protect, cover up
abrigo shelter, protection; (over)coat; bed clothes
abrileño *adj.* April, of April
abrochar to fasten, button
abrojo thistle
abrumar to depress; to overwhelm; to pester
absolución absolution, forgiveness of sins
absolver (ue) to absolve; to excuse
absorbción absorption
absorber to absorb
absortar *arch.* to absorb
absorto wrapt, absorbed
abstenerse to abstain
abstinencia abstinence
abuela grandmother
abuelo grandfather; ancestor
abultar to enlarge
abundancia abundance
abundar to abound; *arch.* to adorn
abur so long; goodbye
aburrir to bore, tire
abusar de to abuse, impose on
abuso abuse
abyección abjection, abjectness
acá here
acabado finished, perfect
acabar to finish, end; **—— de** to have just; **no —— de** to be at a loss to; **se acabó** that's all, it's all over
acacia acacia tree
academia academy; university
académico *n.* academician; *adj.* academic; classical
acaecer to happen, occur
acalorado excited
acaloramiento ardor, excitement; moment of enthusiasm
acallar to quiet

acariciar to caress
acarrear to transport, bring
acartonado thick, dry
acaso *n.* chance; *adv.* perhaps; **por si ——** just in case
acatar to respect
acceder to accede, give in
accesible accessible
acceso access; attack (of sickness)
accidentado in a faint
accidente accident; attack (of sickness); swoon
acechar to lie in wait for, ambush
aceite oil
aceitoso greasy
aceituna olive; olives
acémila pack animal
acemilero mule driver
acento accent
acentuar to accentuate
aceña water mill
aceptar to accept
acequia irrigation ditch
acera sidewalk
acerado steely, of steel
acerbo bitter
acercar to bring near, approach; **——se** to draw near, approach
acero steel, *fig.* sword
acertado right
acertar (ie) to hit the mark, be right; to do right; to solve, guess; **—— a** to succeed in; to happen
aciago *n.* bitterness; *adj.* fatal, unfortunate, bitter
acíbar bitterness
acicalar to polish
acierto good sense; success
aclarar to explain, make clear, clear up, clarify; to cultivate
acobardar to make cowardly, frighten; **——se** to be terrified
acoger to receive, to take in; **——se** to take shelter
acogida reception; asylum; **dar —— a** to welcome, receive
acogimiento reception, welcome
acometer to attack; to accost; to undertake
acometimiento encounter
acomodado well-to-do, rich
acomodar to accommodate; to make comfortable; to furnish; to arrange
acomodo job, employment
acompañamiento company
acompañante companion
acompasadamente leisurely, slowly
acompasado rhythmical
acondicionado adapted
acongojar to grieve, afflict
aconsejar to advise
acontecer to happen
acontecimiento event
acoquinar to frighten, intimidate
acordado harmonized, harmonious; well-tuned
acordar (ue) to agree; to determine, decide on; to accord; to give; to tune; **——se de** to remember; **——sele (algo)** to remember (something)
acorde in harmony; well-tuned
acorralar to corral, round up
acorrer to succor, aid
acosar to harass
acostar (ue) to put to bed; **——se** to go to bed; to fall down
acostumbrar to accustom; to be accustomed
acotación citation
acotar to cite
acrecentar (ie) to increase
acreditar to authorize; to affirm; to give credence to; **——se** to prove (oneself), demonstrate
acreedor *n.* creditor; *adj.* deserving
activo active
acto act; **—— continuo** immediately afterwards
actual present, present-day
actualidad present state, up-to-date condition; timeliness; novelty
acuchillar to cut, slash; **——se** to fight with knives *or* swords
acudir to hasten, come; to help, rescue; to resort
acuerdo agreement; **de —— con** in accord with; along with
acullá there
acumular to gather, accumulate
acuñar to coin, make into coins
acurrucar to cuddle; **——se** to curl up, get comfortable
acusación accusation
acusador accusing
acusar to accuse; to complain of
acústicamente acoustically, from the point of view of sound
achacar to impute
achantado hidden
achaque attack; illness; **en —— de** on the pretext of
achicado humble
achicarse to humble oneself
adamar to win (as a bride *or* lover)
adarga shield
adarve top of wall
adecuado adequate, suitable
adefesio ridiculous person
adelantado *n.* governor of a border province (especially on the Moorish frontier); *adj.* advanced, ahead
adelantar to advance, go ahead; to progress; to further; **——se** to advance, go ahead; to be early
adelante forward; **calle ——** along the street
adelanto progress, improvement, advance
adelfa oleander
adeliñar *arch.* to go, direct oneself; **——se** to direct oneself, go
ademán manner, gesture, look
adentro *adv.* within; *n. plu.* insides; **en mis ——s** within me, inwardly
aderezar to set straight, set aright, fix
adestrar (ie) to guide, lead
adherirse a (ie) to join oneself to
adiestrado trained
adiestramiento training, skill
adinerado moneyed, rich
adivinar to guess, divine
adivinatorio prophetic
adminículo a necessary thing, necessity
administrar to administrate, direct, manage
admiración admiration; surprise, amazement

admirador admirer
admirar to admire; to astound, amaze; **——se de** to be astounded at
admitir to admit; to accept
adobado spiced (wine)
adobe mud brick
adolecer to suffer, grieve
adolescencia adolescence
adoptar to adopt
adorador adorer
adorar to adore
adormecerse to drowse, fall asleep
adornar to adorn
adornista painter
adquirir (ie) to acquire
adquisición acquisition
adrede on purpose
adscrito applying
aduana customhouse
aducir to adduce
adulación adulation, flattery
adular to flatter
adulator *adj.* flattering; *n.* flatterer
adúltero adulterous, corrupt
adusto austere, stern
advenedizo parvenu, adventurer, man of no position, upstart
adversario opponent
adverso adverse
advertencia warning; foresight
advertir (ie) to inform; to state; to note, notice, be aware, bear in mind
adyacente adjacent
aéreo airy, light
aeronauta aviator
afabilidad affability, pleasantness
afable pleasant, affable
afán anxiety, solicitude, tender care; longing, desire; worry
afanado anxious, eager, keenly interested
afanar to strive for; to win from; **——se** to toil, strive for; to worry
afanoso eager
afear to make ugly; to speak evil of
afección disease
afectación affectation, assumed appearance
afectado imaginary
afectar to affect; to assume
afecto affection, love
afectuoso affectionate
afeitar to shave
afeite cosmetic
afeminación effeminacy
aferrado clinging
afición affection, liking, fondness
aficionado *n.* fan (of sports); *adj.* **——** a fond of
aficionar to make fond, win
afilado sharp, pointed
afinar to polish; to tune; to make keen
afirmación affirmation
afirmar to state, affirm; to resolve; to be firmly established; **—— la mano** to strike a blow; to place one's hand firmly
afirmativa affirmative answer
afirmativo affirmative
aflictivo grievous, distressing
afligir to afflict, distress
aflojar to loosen; to diminish
afónico unharmonious
afortunado fortunate, lucky
afrancesado partisan of the French (in 18th and early 19th centuries)
afrenta affront, insult; *arch.* suffering
afrentar to insult; to attack; **——se** to be insulted
afrentoso insulting
afrontar to face
afuera outside; **¡——!** get out!
afufarse to run away
agachar to bend down, stoop
agalla gill
agarrado stingy, grasping, close-fisted
agarrar to clutch, seize, to get; **——se** to clutch
agasajar to entertain, regale, treat
agente agent
ágil agile
agilidad agility
agitación agitation
agitar to agitate, upset; to wave; to move (violently); **——se** to wave; to stir
aglomeración group, agglomeration
aglomerarse to congregate
agobiar to crush, overwhelm
agonía agony
agonizante dying, at death's door
agonizar to be in the throes of death; to die
agora *arch. for* **ahora**
agorero prophetic; addicted to augury
agostar to dry up, wither; to exhaust
agosto August; harvest
agotar to exhaust, dry up
agraciar to adorn; to favor
agradar to please
agradecer to be grateful (for), thank (for)
agradecimiento gratitude
agrado agreeableness
agrandar to enlarge; to lengthen
agrario agrarian
agravar to aggravate
agraviar to affront, insult
agravio insult, offense; harm, wrong
agraz: en —— unseasonably
agregar to add; to join
agreste wild
agrícola *n.* farmer; *adj.* agricultural
agridulce bitter-sweet
agrio bitter
agrónomo agricultural
agruparse to gather, form a group
aguacero shower, downpour
aguador water-seller
aguaducho water-seller's stand
aguamanos water for washing
aguantar to bear, endure
aguar to water, dilute; to spoil
aguardar to wait (for)
aguardiente a kind of cheap liquor; **—— de anís** liqueur of anise, anisette
agudeza sharpness; witticism
agudo acute, sharp; keen; clever; lean, thin
agüero augury
aguijar to spur
aguijón spur; goad
aguijonear to spur
águila eagle; *slang* shark
aguileño aquiline
aguilucho eaglet
aguja needle; spire

agujerado pierced with holes
agujero hole; hiding place
ah ah; ahoy; **—— del coche** hey, you in the coach
ahijado godson
ahinco eagerness; perseverance, persistence
ahito indigestion
ahogar to stifle, suffocate; to drown; to choke; *fig.* to tighten the screws, torture
ahogo suffocation; affliction
ahondar to delve, penetrate
ahorcar to hang
ahorita right now
ahorrar to save; to spare; **——se de** to avoid
ahorro saving
ahuecado loose
ahumado smoky
aijada goad
airado angry, wrathful
aire air; breeze
airoso airy, windy; graceful; brilliant
aislamiento isolation
ajar to crumple; to wither, fade, dry up; **——le a uno la vanidad** to wound one's vanity
ajedrez chess
ajenjo wormwood
ajeno that belonging to another person, another's; **—— de** foreign to; free from
ajetreado worn-out
ajetreo agitation, confusion; weariness
ajo garlic
ajuar trousseau; furnishings
ajuntar to gather, get
ajustar to adjust, fit; to hire; **—— una cuenta** to add up an account
al *arch.* another thing, anything else
ala wing; brim (of hat); **—— de mosca** *fig.* thin, colorless material
alabanza praise
alabar to praise
alabarda halbred
alabastro alabaster
alambicado very subtle, over-refined
alameda poplar grove, grove; public walk
álamo poplar tree
alarde display; parade
alargado long
alargar to lengthen, stretch out; to hold out, hand to; to protract, postpone
alarido howl, shriek
alarmante alarming
alazán sorrel
alba dawn
albahaca sweet basil
albañil mason
albarda saddle; packsaddle
albedrío will; free will
albergar to lodge
albergue shelter, dwelling
albo (snow) white
alborada dawn
alborear to dawn
alborotador agitator
alborotar to make noise, disturb; to stir up; **——se** to become excited
alboroto tumult, hubbub, disturbance
alborozo gaiety, joy
albricias reward (for good news); good news
albura *n.* pure white
alcabala a 10% sales tax
alcahueta procuress, go-between
alcaide jailer
alcalde mayor; warden; judge; **alcalde-corregidor** mayor
alcaldesa mayor's wife
álcali alkali
alcance extent; pursuit
alcanza *arch.* pursuit
alcanzar to overtake; to reach, arrive at; to get, attain; to succeed in; to ascertain; to comprehend; to obtain
alcarreño from la Alcarria, a region a few miles east of Guadalajara
alcázar castle
alcoba bedroom
alcotán lanner, bird of prey
alcuza flask
aldaba door-knocker; catch, hook
aldabilla *dim. of* **aldaba**
aldea village
aldeano, –a *n.* villager, peasant; *adj.* country, rustic
alderredor *same as* **alrededor**
alegar to allege
alejar to separate; to keep away; **——se** to move away
alemán German
alentado brave; dashing
alentar (ie) to breathe
aleteo fluttering
aleve treacherous
alevoso treacherous
alfamar blanket
alférez *arch.* lieutenant
alfiler pin
alfombra rug
alfombrado figured
alforja saddle bag (also worn over the shoulder as a knapsack)
alga seaweed, water plant
algarabía Arabic (language); din, clamor
algazara noise
algecireño from Algeciras
algo something; *arch.* wealth, wordly goods; **por ——** not for nothing
algodón cotton; cotton cloth
alguacil constable
alhaja jewel; fine furnishing
alhelí gilliflower
alianza alliance
alicantina deceit, swindle
aliciente incentive
aliento breath, breathing; courage; desire
aligerar to lighten
alijo contraband goods; bundle of smuggled goods
alimentación feeding
alimentar to feed; to sustain; **——se** to eat
alimento food
alinear to align; to line up
aliño spread, feast
alisar to smooth
aliviar to alleviate, relieve
alivio alleviation, relief, improvement
almacén store; warehouse
almacenista merchant
almagre red ochre
almanaque almanac; calendar of saints
almena battlement
almendra almond
almendro almond tree
almete helmet
almíbar syrup; sweet drink; preserves
almo venerable; revivifying
almohada pillow

almohaza currycomb
almorzar (ue) to lunch
almotacén office of market inspector
almuerzo lunch
alojamiento lodging, billeting
alojar to lodge, take lodgings
alongado away, at a distance
alpargatero maker of **alpargatas** (peasant's sandals); shoemaker
alquilar to rent
alquiler rent, hire
alquimia alchemy
alrededor *adv.* around; *n. plu.* surroundings; —— **de** around
altanería *plu.* lofty regions
altanero lofty; arrogant, haughty
altar altar
altarito *dim. of* **altar**
alteración irritation, strong emotion
alterar to anger, upset; to alter, change
altercar to dispute, bicker; —— **razones** to converse
alternar to alternate; to associate
alternativamente alternately; at regular intervals
alternativo alternate
alteza honor; height
Altísimo God, the Most High
altivez haughtiness, loftiness
altivo haughty, lofty
alto high; deep, profound; *n.* height; **lo** —— the upper part, the top; **dar de alta** to release (from hospital), to declare cured
¡alto! halt; **hacer** —— to halt
altura height; highland
alucinación hallucination
aludir to allude
alumbrar to light; to shed light; to enlighten
alusión allusion
alusivo allusive
alza: en —— on the rise (of the stock market)
alzada height
alzado raised; **cejas alzadas** arched eyebrows
alzar to raise; to gather up; to shrug
allá: más —— **de** beyond
allanarse to acquiesce; to resign oneself
allegar to procure
allende beyond; —— **de** beyond
ama housekeeper; mistress; hostess; nurse; —— **de llaves** housekeeper
amabilidad amiability, kindness
amable amiable, kind
amador lover
amagar to threaten
amancebado living with a concubine
amancebamiento concubinage
amancillar to stain
amanecer to dawn; to arrive *or* be at dawn; to awaken; **al** —— at dawn
amaneramiento mannerism
amansar to tame; to pacify, placate
amante lover
amargar to embitter
amargo bitter
amargura bitterness
amarillento yellowish
amarrar to moor; to tie
amartelado smitten
amasar to knead
amatar *arch.* to extinguish
amazona amazon; woman's riding costume
ámbar ambergris
ambicionar to desire, yearn for
ambiente atmosphere; —— **vital** life
ámbito compass, realm
ambos both
ambrosia ambrosia
ambulancia first-aid station; ambulance
amedrentado frightened
amenaza threat
amenazador *adj.* threatening
amenazante threatening
amenazar to menace, threaten
amenidad pleasantness
ameno pleasant, agreeable
americana (suit) coat, jacket
amigote *aug. of* **amigo** pal
amilanarse to be terrified; to be cowardly
amistad friendship
amistoso friendly
amo master
amodorrado in a stupor, stupefied
amonestación admonition
amonestar to admonish, warn, advise
amontillado fine Sherry wine
amontonar to pile up
amor love; *plu.* love affair; words of love; —— **propio** vanity
amoratado purple, purplish
amoroso amorous, loving
amoroso-pastoril on love and nature
amortecer to faint
amortecido in a swoon; at the point of death
amortiguar to deaden; ——**se** to die down
amostazar to irk, exasperate; ——**se** to become angry
amparar to shelter, protect
amparo shelter; protection
amplio broad, ample
ampo pure white
amueblado furnished
anafre small oven, stove
anal *plu.* annals
analizar to analyze
análogo analogous, in accord with, similar
anarquista *n.* anarchist; *adj.* anarchical
anatema anathema; prohibition
anatómico of anatomy
anca haunch, crupper; **a las** ——**s** on the back of one's horse
ancianía old age
ancianidad old age
anciano old; **ancianitas** old women's home
ancho wide; **a mis anchas** at my ease
andada track, trail; **volver a las** ——**s** to backslide, go back to one's old ways
andador fond of walking; fast-walking
andadura walk, pace
andaluz Andalusian
andamio stand
andanada broadside
andar *n.* step
andas stretcher, bier

andrajo rag; worn-out garment
andrajoso *n.* ragamuffin; *adj.* ragged
anegar to drown
anemia anemia
ángelus angelus
Angelus Domini prayer to the guardian angel
angosto narrow
angostura narrow place, pass
anguila eel
ángulo angle; corner
angustia anguish
angustiado anguished
angustiar to afflict, fill with anguish
angustioso filled with anxiety; difficult
anhelante longing, yearning, desiring
anhelar to yearn for; to pant (for breath)
anhelo yearning, desire
anheloso yearning, desiring, longing
anidar to nest
anilla ring
ánima soul
animación animation
animal animal; brute
animalote *aug. of* **animal**
animar to animate, incite, cheer, encourage; **——se** to take *or* show courage
ánimo mind, spirit; courage; intention
animoso courageous, spirited
aniquilar to annihilate, overcome, destroy
anís aniseed, anise
anoche last night
anochecer to grow dark; *n.* nightfall
anochecido after dark
anonadar to annihilate, exterminate; to stupefy
anónimo *adj.* anonymous; *n.* anonymous letter
anotación note
ansí *arch. for* **así**
ansia yearning; worry, anxiety, anguish
ansiar to long for, desire
ansiedad anxiety
ansioso anxious, eager
antaño last year; previously
ante before, in front of; **—— que** *arch. for* **antes que**
antecedente antecedent
antecesor predecessor
antecoger to drive before
antena yard-arm, spar
anteojo spyglass
anterior previous, foregoing, former
antes *adv.* before; rather
antesala waiting room
anticipado in advance
anticipar to take the lead; to anticipate
anticipo advance
anticristo Antichrist, devil
antigüedad antiquity, age
antiguo old, ancient
antiparras glasses
antipático disagreeable, unpleasant
antojadizo whimsical, capricious
antojársele a uno to occur to one, seem to one; to have a yearning for
antojo whim
anublar to cloud
anudar to knot
anular to annul
anunciar to announce
anuncio announcement; advertisement
anzuelo fish hook
añadidura: de —— *or* **por ——** in addition
añadir to add
añejo old
añil indigo blue
añoso aged, old
añudar to entwine
apacible peaceful
apadrinar to act as godfather; to aid, support
apagado wan
apagar to extinguish, put out (light); to pacify
apalear to beat
apandar to pilfer, steal
apañado clever; mended; clothed
aparato apparatus; equipment; pompous display
aparatoso showy
aparecer to appear
aparejado in pairs; together
aparejar to prepare
aparejo preparation, disposition; means; opportunity; *plu.* trappings; saddle
aparentar to pretend, feign
aparición apparition, vision
apariencia appearance; manifestation
apartado distant, remote; retired, solitary
apartamiento solitude; separation
apartar to withdraw, send away, draw away, draw aside, step aside; to remove, set aside, divert; **——se (de)** to step to one side, move away; to differ (from)
aparte aside; apart, separate
apasionado impassioned, passionate
apearse to dismount
apechugar con to put up with
apedrear to stone
apegado attached, devoted
apego fondness, attachment
apelación appeal; summons (to court)
apelar to appeal, have recourse (to), call (on)
apellidar to appeal to, call on
apellido surname
aperador overseer, foreman
apercibir to warn, advise; to get ready
apero implement, tool
apesadumbrar to grieve
apestar to stink
apestoso foul-smelling, sickening, offensive
apetecer to wish, hope for, desire
apetecible desirable, enticing
apetito appetite; desire
apiñar to crowd
apisonar to trample
aplacar to placate, quiet
aplaudir to applaud
aplauso applause; **en —— de** in favor of
aplicación application
aplicar to apply, devote; to impute; to judge
aplomo aplomb, self-possession
apocado meek, humble, pusillanimous
apocalíptico apocalyptical, of the Apocalypse (*or* Revelation)
apócrifo false, apocryphal
apoderarse de to take possession of
aporrear to club

aposentar to lodge
aposento room
apostar (ue) to bet; to post (a watchman); ——**se** to risk
apostólico apostolic
apostrofar to apostrophize, address
apóstrofe apostrophe, salutation
apostura bearing, disposition
apoyar to lean (on); to base one's assertions (on); to support
apoyo support, aid
apreciación judgment
apreciar to appreciate; to value, esteem; to become aware of
aprecio esteem; appreciation
apremiante pressing
apremio insistence
aprendiz apprentice
aprendizaje apprenticeship
apresurado swift, quick, hasty
apresurar to hasten; ——**se** to hasten; —— **el paso** to quicken one's steps
apretado tight, close
apretar (ie) to tighten; to press; to oppress, torture; —— **el paso** to hasten one's step; ——**se con** to press against
apretón pressure; —— **de manos** handshake
apretura difficulty; dunning
apriesa swiftly
aprieto strait, trouble
aprisa swiftly, quickly
aprisionar to imprison
aprobación approval; **estar a la** —— to be waiting for approval
aprobar (ue) to approve
aprovechado proficient; advantageous
aprovechamiento profit, advantage
aprovechar to take advantage of; to profit by; to be useful; ——**se de** to take advantage of
aproximar to bring near; ——**se a** to approach; ——**se de** to approach within
áptero wingless

apto capable, competent
apuesta bet, wager
apuesto graceful; elegant
apuntación note, jotting
apuntar to bet; to jot down; to point; to show up; to show faintly; to dawn; to start
apunte note; jotting; sketch, study (of painting)
apurar to drain, exhaust; to scrutinize; to harass; ——**se** to worry
apuro worry, trouble, difficulty
aquejar to grieve, afflict
aquese, -a *arch. for* **ese, esa**
aqueste, -a *arch. for* **este, esta**
aquesto *arch. for* **esto**
aquietar to calm, quiet
aquilón north wind
ara altar
arábigo Arabic
arado plow
arador plowboy
araña spider
arañar to scratch
arar to plow
arbitrio will; means, expedient; discretion, judgment
árbitro arbiter, judge
arboleda grove
arborescente arborescent, tree-like
arbusto bush
arca chest, money box, coffer, ark
arcabucear to shoot
arcabuzazo gun shot
arcángel archangel
arcano secret
arciprestazgo position of archpriest
arcipreste archpriest
arco arch; bow
archiduquesa archduchess
archipiélago archipelago
archipobre very poor
archivo archive, record
arder to burn
ardiente ardent, hot, burning
ardor heat; ardor; courage
ardoroso fiery, ardorous
arena sand
Argel Algiers
argentino silvery
argolla ring
argucia subtlety
argüir to argue; to show, reveal

argumento argument; summary
árido arid
arisco surly, fierce
arista chaff
Aristóteles Aristotle
aritmética arithmetic
arma arm, weapon
armada armada, fleet; expedition
armadura armor
armar to arm; to set up, establish, prepare; to begin; to wage
armario cupboard, wardrobe
armero arms' rack
armiño *n.* ermine; *adj.* of ermine
armonía harmony
armónico harmonious
armonioso harmonious
aroma perfume, scent, aroma
aromado perfumed
arpa harp
arqueología archaeology
arqueólogo archaeologist
arquero archer
arquitectónico architectural
arrabal suburb, quarter
arraigado deep-rooted
arraigar to root, take root; ——**se** to take root
arramblar to sweep over, sweep away
arrancar to tear from, tear out, tear away; to pull out; to start
arranque sudden start; outburst, burst
arras wedding gift; gift
arrasar to tear down, demolish
arrastrado *n.* rascal, good-for-nothing; *adj.* wretched
arrastrar to drag
arrayán myrtle
arre get up!
arrear to urge on, whip up (a horse)
arrebañadura last bit
arrebatado sudden, impetuous
arrebatar to snatch away; ——**se a** to act hastily in
arrebato transport, fit
arrebol dawn
arreciar to become stronger; ——**se** to gather one's strength

arredrar to terrify
arreglado moderate; at a moderate price
arreglar to arrange; to fix; **——se** to get along, make out, manage; to fix oneself up
arreglo arrangement; order, good management
arrellanar to settle comfortably, lean back
arremangado with sleeves rolled up
arremeter to attack; to launch forth
arremolinar to swirl; **——se** to churn about
arrendar (ie) to rent (out)
arrendatario renter
arreo dress, decoration; *plu.* trappings
arrepentimiento repentance
arrepentirse (ie) to repent
arriar to lower
arriate border (in gardens)
arriba up, above; upstairs; **por ——** above
arribar to arrive
arriero muleteer
arriesgar to risk
arrimado close; **—— a** leaning on
arrimar to approach, draw near, bring near; to stow; to put aside; **—— contra** to back (someone) up against; **——se** to approach; **——se a** to lean against, press against, support oneself on
arrimo shelter; prop
arroba weight of 25 pounds
arrobamiento ecstasy
arrodillado kneeling
arrodillamiento kneeling
arrodillarse to kneel
arrogancia bravery; arrogance
arrogante arrogant
arrojado bold
arrojar to cast, throw (away), send forth, hurl; to drive away; **——se** to dash, rush
arrojo impulsiveness, dash, boldness
arrollar to roll over, crush; to roll up
arroparse to bundle up
arropía taffy
arrostrar to face
arroyo brook; gutter
arroyuelo *dim. of* **arroyo**
arroz rice; rice dish
arruga wrinkle
arrugar to wrinkle, crumple
arruinar to ruin
arrullador *n.* luller, comforter; *adj.* lulling, soothing
arrullar to lull
arrullo cooing
arte art; sort, kind; trick; **con buen ——** cleverly; **por tal ——** in such a way; **de poco ——** of low degree; **por el —— de** of the style of, like
artero crafty, cunning
articular to join
artículo article
artífice craftsman
artificio craft; artifice, trick
arzobispal of the archbishop
arzobispo archbishop
arzón saddle-tree
as ace
asa handle
asador spit
asadura *plu.* insides, guts
asalariado employee, wage earner
asaltar to assault
asalto assault, attack
asar to roast
asaz sufficient(ly), quite
ascender (ie) to ascend; to reach, amount (to)
ascendiente ancestor; influence
ascensión climb, ascent
asceta hermit
ascético ascetic
asco nausea, repugnance; **poner ——** to cause nausea *or* repugnance; **tener ——** to be sickened, be repelled by
ascua glowing coal, ember; **estar en ——s** to be on pins and needles; **hecho ——** glowing
aseado neat
asechanza snare, stratagem
asediar to besiege
asegurar to assure, state
asemejar to make like, cause to resemble
asenderado persecuted
asentar (ie) to seat; to fix, establish, set; to settle, calm; to take service
asentimiento consent
asentir (ie) to assent
aseo neatness
asequible attainable
asesinar to murder, assassinate
asesinato murder, assassination
asesino assassin
asesorar to advise
asestar to aim; to shoot
asfixiante asphyxiating
así: —— . . . como in the same way . . . as; as much . . . as
asiduo assiduous
asiento seat, resting place; position; **hacer ——** to settle
asignación share; assignment
asignar to assign
asilo asylum
asimismo likewise
asir to seize; to cling (together)
asistencia aid, care; service, work as a servant
asistenta servant, cleaning woman
asistente assistant, helper
asistir to attend, be present (at); to take care of; to assist
asmático asthmatic, wheezy
asnal of a donkey, asinine
asno ass
asociar to associate; **——se a** to join in
asomar to appear; to show; to look out of; to look; **——se** to peek out, look out
asombrar to startle, astonish; to take by surprise
asombro astonishment
asombroso amazing
asomo sign, indication, trace, bit
asonante assonance
aspaviento fuss, emotional demonstration
aspereza roughness; asperity; *plu.* rough terrain
áspero rough, sharp
aspiración aspiration, desire, objective
aspirante *n.* aspirant, candidate; *adj.* aspiring
aspirar to aspire; to breathe breathe in, blow
asqueroso repugnant

asta shaft (of lance); (flag) pole; horn (of bull)
astil shaft (of lance)
astilla splinter; kindling
astillero rack
astro star; *fig.* destiny
astrología astrology
astucia astuteness, cunning
astur Asturian, from Asturias
asturiano Asturian
astuto astute, cunning
asunto subject; affair
asurar to burn
asustar to startle, frighten
atacar to attack
atadijo bundle
atajar to cut off
atapar *arch.* to cover
atar to tie, fasten, bind; **loco de ——** stark mad
atarazado mangled; torn; wounded
ataúd coffin
ataviado decked out
atavío gear, finery, adornment
atemorizar to frighten
atenacear to tear off the flesh with pincers
atenazar *same as* **atenacear**
atención attention; *plu.* affairs, obligations
atender (ie) to pay attention; to take care of; to expect; **——se a** to take account of, take into consideration
atenerse a to abide by, adhere to; to depend on
atentado attack
atento attentive, heedful
atenuación attenuation; moderation
atenuar to attenuate, diminish
ateo atheist
aterido numb, stiff (with cold), frozen
aterrador terrifying
aterrar (ie) to cast down; to terrify
atesorar to treasure up, hold
atestado crowded, full of
atestar (ie) to stuff, fill up
atestiguar to bear witness to, testify
ático classic; high-toned
atinado sensible
atinar to succeed in; to guess (correctly), divine; **—— con** to hit on
atizar to poke, stir; **—— friegas** to massage vigorously
atolondramiento recklessness, forwardness
átomo atom
atónito astonished
atontado stupefied
atormentador tormenter, torturer
atormentar to torment
atortolado intimidated
atosigar to poison
atracar to bring near, approach; to stuff
atractivo *n.* attraction
atraer to attract
atrancar to bar, bolt
atrapar to catch, get
atrasado behind the times; overdue
atraso backwardness; *plu.* arrears
atravesar (ie) to cross; to pierce; to go through; **——se** to change hands
atreverse to dare
atrevido bold, daring, insolent
atrevimiento daring
atribuir to attribute
atribular to grieve, afflict; **——se** to become despondent
atrocidad atrocity; unjust act
atronar (ue) to thunder, rumble
atropellar to crush; to trample; to push (through)
atropello outrage
atroz atrocious, frightful
atufar to anger
aturdido upset, befuddled, stunned
aturdimiento befuddlement, perturbation
aturdir to upset, confuse
aturrullar to bewilder, daze
atusar to smooth
audacia audacity
audaz audacious
audiencia audience, court (of law); **dar ——** to receive (official visitors)
auditorio audience
augurar to augur, betoken
augurio augury
augusto august
aullido howl
aumentar to augment
aumento increase; **ir en ——** to increase
aura breeze
áureo golden, gold colored
aurora dawn
ausencia absence
ausente absent
austeridad austerity, puritanical living
austero austere
austro south wind
auto act; document (of lawsuit)
autoridad authority
autorizar to authorize; to justify
auxiliar to aid; *n.* helper; *adj.* auxiliary
auxilio aid
avance advance
avanzar to advance
avariento avaricious, greedy
avasallar to subject, dominate
ave bird
avecinado settled
avecinarse to draw near
avellana hazelnut
avellanado withered, wrinkled
avellano hazelnut tree
avemaría Hail Mary
avenir to reconcile; **——se** to agree; to put up with
aventajado superior, great, superb; gifted, charming
aventajarse to excel; to have the advantage
aventura adventure; **por ——** peradventure, perchance
aventurar to risk, venture
aventurero *n.* adventurer; knight errant; *adj.* adventuresome
avergonzar (üe) to shame; **——se de** to be ashamed of
avería damage
averiguación inquiry
averiguado well-known
averiguar to find out
avestruz ostrich
avezado accustomed
aviado well provided for
ávido avid, eager
avinagrado sour

avío preparation; care; *plu.* utensils, things necessary; **al ——** let's get started
avisar to give notice, inform, advise; to take counsel
aviso notice, warning; information; advice; care, watchfulness
avivar to sharpen; to enliven, quicken; to inflame; **——se** to rally one's forces
ay oh!, ah!; **—— de mí** woe is me!
ayuda aid, help; **para —— de** to help toward; **—— de cámara** valet
ayudante aide, assistant
ayudar to help, aid
ayunar to fast; to do without
ayuno fast, fasting
ayuntamiento city council; city hall
azacán water-carrier; *fig.* one who works very hard, slave
azada adze
azafrán saffron
azahar orange blossom
azar hazard, chance; unfortunate moment *or* event
azaramiento bewilderment; alarm, anxiety; trouble
azaroso hazardous
azófar brass
azor falcon, hawk
azorado confused, nervous
azotar to whip, lash
azote whip, scourge; blow; *plu.* whipping
azotea flat roof
azúcar sugar
azucarillo stick of honeycombed sugar for sweetening drinks
azufre sulphur
azulejo tile
azumbre liquid measure, about two quarts
azur azure
azuzar to urge on

B

baba drivel, drooling, slobbering
babilonia disorder, confusion
bacalao codfish
bacanal drinking bout, bacchanal
bacía basin
bachiller bachelor (of arts, etc.); chatterbox
bachillerato undergraduate work
bailar to dance
bailarín dancer
baile dance
bajel vessel (*poetic word*)
bajeza baseness; disgrace
bajo *adj.* low; **por lo ——** in a low tone; **sala baja** downstairs room; *n. plu.* petticoat
bajón lessening; fall; backward step
bajura lowland
bala bullet
baladí ordinary, common
balar to bleat
balazo bullet wound
balbuciente stammering
balbucir to stammer
balcón balcony; window
baldado lame
balde: en —— in vain, fruitlessly; **de ——** free, gratis
baldonar to insult
baldosín tile
balido bleating
balsa pool
bálsamo balsam, ointment, salve
baluarte bulwark
ballena whale
ballesta crossbow
bambolearse to sway, wobble
banal banal
banca bank
banco bench
banda scarf; bandage; side; **por ——** on each side
bandeja tray
bandera flag, banner
bando proclamation
bandolera game bag
bandolero highwayman
banquero banker
banquillo *dim. of* **banco**
bañar to bathe
baraja pack of cards
barajar to shuffle (cards)
barandilla railing
baratija trifle
barato *n.* fee, tip; *adj.* cheap
baratura cheapness, low cost
barba beard; chin; **hacer la ——** to shave
barbado bearded
barbaridad barbarity; nonsense
bárbaro *n.* barbarian; *adj.* barbarous
barbero barber
barbudo bearded
barca small boat
barco ship, boat
bardal thicket of brambles
bargueño chest (of drawers)
barniz polish
barnizado glossy
barón baron
baroncita *dim. of* **barona** baroness
barquilla basket (of balloon)
barra bar; weight; **—— de nariz** bridge of nose; **sin daño de ——s** without injury or danger
Barrabás thief who was saved from crucifixion instead of Christ
barraca hut, cabin
barranco ravine
barredura sweeping
barrer to sweep
barrera barrier, wall; fortification
barricada barricade
barriga belly
barrio quarter (of town)
barrizal mire; mudhole
barro clay; mud
barrote heavy bar
barrunto conjecture
barullo commotion, confusion
bastante enough, sufficient; quite a lot
bastar to be enough, be sufficient
bastardo illegitimate
bastidor wing (of stage setting); framed needle work
bastón cane; staff
basura refuse; garbage
bata robe, dressing gown, negligée
batahola hubbub
batalla battle
batallar to battle, struggle
batallón battalion
batanear to bat
batiente leaf (of door)
batir to beat; to clap (hands); **—— se** to fight
batueco fool
baúl trunk
bautismo baptism
bautizo baptism

bayoneta bayonet
bazofia refuse, slops
beata woman who frequents the churches; hypocrite
bebé baby
bebedizo potion, philter
bebida drink
becerro calf
Belcebú Beelzebub, the devil
beldad beauty
bélico of war, warlike
bellaco rogue
belleza beauty
bellota acorn
bendición blessing, benediction
bendito blessed; **agua bendita** holy water
beneficencia charity; —— **domiciliaria** social service
beneficio benefit, blessing; profit
benéfico beneficent, generous
benemérito worthy, meritorious
benevolencia benevolence, kindness
benévolo benevolent
bengala staff, symbol of command
benigno benign
benino *poetic for* **benigno**
benjuí benzoin
beodo *n.* drunkard; *adj.* drunk
bergantín *n.* brigantine; *adj.* brigantine-rigged
bermejo reddish
bermellón vermilion
berrear to bellow
berrendo spotted
berrido bellow, shout
berruga *for* **verruga** wart
berza cabbage
bestia animal
bíblico Biblical
bicentario two hundred years old
bicicleta bicycle
bicho bug; creature
bieldo winnowing rake
bien *n.* good; happiness; *plu.* wealth, treasure, blessings; **con ——** safely; **hombre de ——** worthy man; **Sumo Bien** supreme good, God; *adv.* quite, very; indeed; **no ——** hardly, scarcely, as soon as
bienaventurado *n.* fortunate person; *adj.* fortunate, blessed
bienaventuranza blessedness, glory
bien-compuesto orderly
bienestar well-being
bienhacer charity, good deeds
bienhechor benefactor
bienquisto loved, well liked
bigardón loafer
bigotazo *aug. of* **bigote**
bigote mustache
bilioso bilious
billete ticket, banknote, bill; note
binar to cultivate for the second time
bisabuelo great-grandfather
bisoño tenderfoot
bizarría splendor; generosity
bizarro gallant; generous; splendid
bizcar to squint
bizco squinting; cross-eyed
bizcocho lady finger; sponge cake
blanca a copper coin, farthing
blanco *adj.* white; *n.* target, mark; **poner los ojos en ——** to show the whites of one's eyes
blancura whiteness
blandengue wishy-washy person
blando soft; gentle
blandura softness; blandishment; **tiempo de ——** weather too warm to keep fish
blanquear to be white, snow white
blanquecino whitish
blasfemar to blaspheme
blasfemia blasphemy
blasón coat of arms; device (of heraldry)
blasonar to boast
bobada silly notion, foolishness
bobalicón dunce, fool
bobo fool
boca mouth; **a —— de jarro** point-blank
bocado mouthful; bite; delicacy
bocanada puff
boceto sketch
bocona *n.* loudmouth
bochornoso humiliating
boda *or* **bodas** marriage
bodega cellar; wine cellar
bodegón wine cellar
bofetada blow, slap
bola ball
boleta card, ticket
boliche bowling
bolichera woman in charge of bowling
bolita *dim. of* **bola**
bolsa stock exchange; purse
bolsilla purse
bolsillo pocket; purse
bolsón large purse, pocketbook
bomba pump; fire-engine; bomb
bombonera candy box
bonachón good-natured; simple-minded
bonanza calm
bondad goodness, kindness
bondadoso kindly
bonete hat
bonitamente neatly
bonito pretty
bono coupon (for food)
borbollón: a ——es in gushes
bordado embroidery
bordadura embroidery
bordar to embroider
borde edge, border; **al —— de** at the edge of
bordón staff (of pilgrim)
borla tassel
borracho drunk
borrador rough draft
borrar to erase
borrasca squall
borrascoso squally, stormy
borrego (young) sheep, lamb
borrico, -a donkey
borrón blot, stain
boscaje grove
bosque woods, forest
bostezar to yawn
bota shoe, boot; wineskin; **—— de agua** overshoe
botarate blustering fellow
bote bound; bucking; jar
botecillo *dim. of* **bote**
botella bottle
botica drugstore
boticario apothecary, druggist
botín boot
botina *dim. of* **bota**
botón button
bóveda dome

bozo down, fine hair
bramar to bellow
bramido bellow, roar
brasero brazier, heater
bravío wild
bravo *n.* bully; *adj.* wild; fine
bravura bravery
braza fathom
brazal arm band
brazo arm; *arch.* sword arm
brea pitch
bregar to work hard, struggle
breva bargain, good deal
breve brief, short; small
brevedad brevity; speed
breviario breviary, prayer book
brial *arch.* silk skirt
bribonaza impostor; great cheat
brida bridle
brillante diamond
brillar to shine
brillo brilliance, lustre; renown
brincar to jump, jump up and down (for joy); to bounce
brinco jump; hopping
brindar to toast, drink a toast; to offer; to invite; **—— con** to treat with; to offer
brindis toast; dedication
brío spirit, dash; animation, life
brioso spirited; courageous
brisa breeze
brisca a card game; **—— cruzada** a card game
brizna sprig, blade; bit
brocado brocade
brocal curb (of well)
broche brooch
broma joke; **en ——** as a joke, jokingly; **andar con ——s** to fool around
bromista joking
bromuro bromide
bronce bronze
bronceado bronzed
broquel small shield
brotar to spring forth, come forth, bud
bruces: de —— face downward
bruja witch
brujo wizard
brújula compass
bruma mist
bruñir to polish, give luster to
brusco *n.* knee holly; *adj.* brusque
bruto *n.* animal, brute; *adj.* rough; sturdy
buba pustule
bucle curl
buche mouthful (of liquid); craw (of bird)
buenaventura fortune
buey ox
bufanda muffler
bufete desk
bufón court fool
bufonesco comical, clownish
buhardillón garret, attic
buho owl
buhonero peddler
buitre vulture
bula bull, indulgence
bulto bundle; form, bulk
bulla noise, bustle; **meter ——** to make a lot of noise
bullicio noise, stir, hubbub, bustle
bullicioso noisy; spirited, animated
bullir *or* **——se** to stir, move
buñolería cruller stand
buñolero selling crullers
buñuelo cruller
buque boat
burla joke, trick, mockery; **de ——s** jokingly
burlador trickster, libertine
burlar to mock, deceive; to evade; **——se** to joke, mock, make light of
burleta joke
burlón *n.* banterer, mocker; *adj.* mocking, bantering
burra ass, donkey
burro ass, donkey; **—— ciego** a card game; **—— con vista** a card game
busca search
buscón cheat
busilis crux, knotty point
busto bust
butaca armchair; orchestra seat (in theater)

C

ca *arch.* for
cabal perfect, precise(ly); **estar en sus ——es** to be in one's right mind
cabalgadura mount
cabalgar to ride (horseback); to mount
cabalgata cavalcade
caballeresco chivalrous; equestrian
caballería cavalry; cavalcade; chivalry; mount
caballeriza stable
caballero gentleman; knight; **—— en** mounted on
caballista horseman, expert on horses
caballo horse; queen (in cards)
caballote *aug. of* **caballo**
cabaña cabin
cabe next to
cabecera head of bed; pillow
cabellera hair; wig
cabello hair
caber to be contained in; to fit; to be possible; to be natural; to fall to one's lot; to belong; **no —— en sí** to be bursting; to be beside oneself
cabestro halter
cabeza head; **mala ——** uncontrolled person, 'bad actor'
cabezada blow with head
cabezo hilltop
cabezudo big-headed; stubborn
cabida acceptance; influence
cabildo (cathedral) chapter; town council; guild
cable cable
cabo end; envoy; **a —— de** at the end of; at the edge of; **al ——** finally; in short; **dar ——** to bring to an end
cabra goat
cabrerizo goatherd
cabrilla kid
cabrío of goats
cabrón goat
cacería hunting party
cacerola pan, casserole
cacicato position of political boss
cacique political boss
cacharro pot; vase
cachivache worthless utensil, junk

cacho strip, piece, slice
cadalso scaffold, gallows
cadáver corpse
cadavérico death-like
cadena chain
cadete youngster
caduco perishable; frail; old, worn-out
caer to fall; **dejar ——** to drop; to bring down; **ya caigo** I see, I catch on
cafetera coffee pot
caída fall
caja box; drum
cajón drawer, money drawer
cajoncito *dim. of* **cajón**
cal whitewash
calabaza pumpkin; **dar ——s** to refuse; **llevar ——s** to be refused
calabazada knock (with the head against something)
calabozo dungeon, prison cell
calamar squid, ink fish; **——es en su tinta** squid prepared in a sauce made of the black fluid they contain
calamidad calamity
calamitoso calamitous
calandria lark
calar to pierce, run through; to cock (a gun); to pull down (a hat)
calavera *n.* skull; wild fellow; *adj.* wanton, loose-living
calcular to calculate; to be scheming in
calculista calculating
cálculo calculation; scheming; plan
caldera caldron, kettle
calderilla small change
caldero kettle
caldo broth
calendario calendar
calentar (ie) to heat, warm; to animate; **—— la cabeza** to excite
calentura fever
calenturiento feverish
caletre mind
calidad nature; rank; quality
calificación qualification
calificar to qualify, classify; **—— de** to classify as
cáliz chalice, cup
calmante sedative
calmar to calm; **——se** to calm oneself
calomelano calomel (medicine)
calumnia slander
calumniador slanderer
calumniar to slander
caluroso hot
calva bald spot
calvo bald, hairless
calzado shoe; footwear
calzar to shoe; to wear (shoes); to put on (shoes *or* gloves)
calzas breeches
calzones breeches, trousers
callado silent
callar to be silent; to become silent; **tan callando** so silently
calle street
calleja narrow street
callejero street
callejón narrow street
callejuela narrow street
cama bed; **—— imperial** expensive coffin
cámara bedchamber
camarada comrade
camarero valet, steward
camareta *dim. of* **cámara**
camarilla bedchamber
camarín boudoir
camastro cot; poor bed
cambiar to change; to exchange
cambio change; exchange; **a —— de** in exchange for; **en ——** on the other hand
camilla stretcher; cot
caminante traveler
caminar to walk; to go; to travel
caminata traveling; hike, (long) walk
camino road, path; **—— real** highway; **de ——** in passing; in traveling costume; ready for traveling
camión truck
camisa shirt; chemise
camisola fancy shirt
camorra quarrel
campal in the country
campamento camp
campana bell
campanada stroke of a bell
campanario bell tower
campanilla *dim. of* **campana**
campanillazo ringing (of bell)
campanudo bell-like; pompous
campaña campaign; experience
campeador *arch.* surpassing in bravery, champion
campear to dominate; to excel
campeón champion
campesino, -a country man *or* woman; *adj.* rural, country
campestre country, rural
campiña countryside
campo country; field; **—— santo** cemetery
can dog
cana white hair
canalla rabble; cur, vile person
cananea (*Sancho's mistake for* **hacanea**) Canaanite
canario canary (bird)
cancela iron grating at entrance of patio
cancillería chancellery
cancionero book of poetry, anthology
candado padlock
candela light; candle
candelero candelabrum, candlestick
candente incandescent
cándido candid, pure; simple
candil lamp
candilón *aug. of* **candil**
candiotera wine cellar
candor candor
candoroso filled with candor, simple, unaffected
canela cinnamon
cangilón pitcher, jar
canícula midsummer heat, dog days
cano white-haired, gray-haired
canónico canonical; canon
canónigo canon, priest attached to a cathedral
cansado tired; tiresome
cansancio weariness; boredom
cansar to tire
cantábrico Cantabrian; **mar ——** Bay of Biscay
cantador singer
cantaleta serenade
cantar *n.* lay, song

cántaro jug, pitcher
cante hondo *see* **cante jondo**
cante jondo Gypsy music
cántico song, chant
cantidad quantity; sum
cantiga song, lay
canto singing; song; canto; chant
cantor *n.* singer; *adj.* singing
canuto tubular case
caña pointer; cane; wicker; pole; **jugar ——s** to joust
cañada ravine
cañizo wicker frame
cañón cannon; bristle; barrel (of gun)
cañonazo cannon shot
caoba mahogany
caos chaos
capa cape
capacete helmet
capacidad capacity; ability
capataz foreman
capaz capable
capelo (cardinal's) hat
capellán chaplain
capigorrón slovenly fellow
capilla chapel
capital *n. masc.* capital (funds); *n. fem.* capital city; large city
capitán captain
capitanear to captain
capítulo chapter
capote large cape
capricho caprice; whim; bizarre notion; **a ——** capriciously
caprichoso capricious
caprichudo capricious, given to whims, crotchety
capucha hood
capullo (rose)bud; cocoon
capuz cloak
carabinero border guard
caracol snail; curl (of hair); *plu.* the dickens!
caracolear to cavort
caracterizar to characterize
caramba the dickens!
caramelo (piece of) candy
carasol solarium, sun porch
carbón coal; charcoal
carbonizar to burn up
carbunclo precious stone; ruby
carcajada burst of laughter
cárcel prison, jail
carcomido worm-eaten, rotten
cardenal cardinal; bruise, welt
cardíaco cardiac, person suffering from heart disease
cardinal cardinal, most important
cardo thistle
carecer de to lack
carencia lack
carga burden, load; cargo
cargado loaded, laden, overcast; **estar —— de** to have one's fill of, be sick of
cargante boring
cargar to load; to carry; to charge; to run off with; **——se** to become peeved; **—— sobre** to be resting on
cargo charge; job, task; **hacer —— a** to blame, incriminate; **hacerse —— de** to take into consideration; **llevar (a) ——** to have in charge; **tener a ——** to be in charge
caricia caress
caridad charity
Cariñena a kind of wine
cariño affection
cariñoso affectionate
carirredondo round-faced
caritativo charitable
cariz aspect (of weather *or* sky); *fig.* appearance
carmelita Carmelite
carmín carmine
carminoso reddish
carnal blood (relation)
carnalidad physique
carnaval carnival, Mardi Gras
carnero sheep; mutton
carnicería butcher shop
carnicero butcher
carnívoro carnivorous
carnoso fleshy
caro dear
carrasca swamp oak
carrera run, dash; career; course; profession; way, road; **seguir** *or* **estudiar ——** to study for a profession
carreta wagon, cart
carretada cartload
carretera highway
carretero cart driver
carretilla wheelbarrow; **de ——** by heart, by rote
carricoche carriage; wagon
carrik reefer, jacket
carrillo cheek
carro cart; chariot; **—— fúnebre** hearse
carroza carriage
carruaje carriage
carta letter; playing card
cartel chart, placard; poster; **poner en ——es** to publicize
cartelón *aug. of* **cartel**
cartera card case, billfold
cartón cardboard
cartuchera cartridge box
cartucho roll (of coins); cartridge
casada married woman
casado married man
casamiento marriage
casar to marry (off); **——se con** to marry
cascabel bell (on harness)
cascada waterfall
cascar to crack, break; (*slang*) to die
casco *plu.* brains, mind
casería farmhouse
caserío farmhouse, farm buildings; group of houses
casero *n.* landlord; *adj.* domestic
caserón *aug. of* **casa**
caseta hut
casilla keeper's lodge
casino casino, club; dance hall
caso case; situation; condition; event; **hacer ——** to pay attention
casorio marriage
caspa dandruff
casquivano muddle-headed
casta race, breed
castaña bun (of hair)
castañeta castanet
castañetear to chatter
castaño *n.* chestnut tree; *adj.* chestnut-colored
castañuela castanet
casticismo the quality of being purely Spanish, without foreign influences or modern innovations
castigar to punish; to instruct, teach
castigo punishment
castillo castle
castizo pure, without foreign influence
casto chaste
casual casual; accidental

casualidad chance
casuco hut; den, dive
cataclismo upheaval
catalejo spy-glass
catalinaria violent speech, savage attack
catar to look at, see; to try out, have for the first time
catarata cataract
catarrazo bad cold
catástrofe catastrophe
catecismo catechism
catecúmeno catechumen, neophyte
cátedra professors' chair; lecture hall
catedral cathedral
catedrático professor
categoría class, category
categórico categorical, precise
catequizar to convert
caterva swarm
catre cot
cauce channel, watercourse, bed (of stream)
caudal *n.* wealth, funds, fortune; *adj.* having much water, great (of rivers)
caudaloso copious
causa cause; lawsuit, case
causador, -a causer
cautela caution; precaution; stratagem
cautivar to captivate, capture
cautivo, -a *n. and adj.* captive; *arch.* wretched
cavar to dig
caverna cave, cavern
cavernario of the cave
cavernoso hollow, deep
cavidad cavity, empty space
cavilación thought; worry
cavilar to ponder, think over carefully
cayado staff
caza hunt
cazador hunter
cazar to hunt
cazuelo pot
cebada barley
cebar to stuff
cebo bait
cebra zebra
ceder to give in to, yield
cedro cedar
cédula document; **—— con recargo** document with surcharge
céfiro zephyr
cegado blinded; deafened
cegar (ie) to blind; to become blind
ceguedad blindness
ceguera blindness
ceja eyebrow
celada helmet; **—— de encaje** helmet with neckpiece
celaje skyscape, cloud effect; bright cloud
celar to be jealous
celda cell
celebérrimo *super. of* **célebre**
celebrado famous
celebral *arch. adj.* brain
celebrar to celebrate; to honor, praise, applaud
célebre famous
celebridad fame
celemín peck; basket *or* measure containing a peck
celeste celestial, heavenly
celestial celestial
celillos *dim. of* **celos**
celo zeal; jealousy; *plu.* jealousy
celosía Venetian blind, shutter
celoso jealous; zealous
celtíbero *n.* Celtiberian; *adj.* of the Celtiberians
cementerio cemetery
cena supper
cenador outdoor dining room
cenagoso muddy
cenar to sup, have supper; **—— fuerte** to dine and wine well
cencerrada tin-pan serenade
cencerreo noise of cowbell
cencerro mule bell, cowbell
cendal gauze
ceniza ash, ashes
censura censure, blame
censurar to censure
centauro centaur
centella spark; lightning bolt; flash of light
centellear to sparkle
centén an old Spanish coin worth about twenty-five pesetas
centena three-figure number
centenar one hundred
centeno rye
céntimo one hundredth of a peseta
centinela sentinel
céntrico central
centro center; **fuera de mi ——** outside my orbit
ceñido tight-fitting; *fig.* bedecked
ceñidor belt
ceñir (i) to gird on; to encircle
ceño frown
ceñudo frowning; angry
cepa stump; strain, species
cepillo brush
cepo *plu.* stocks (for prisoners)
cera wax; candles
cerca *n.* hedge, fence; city wall
cercanía *plu.* nearby regions
cercano near
cercar to surround; to besiege
cercenar to cut through, cut off
cerco hedge; siege; ring
cerda bristle; coarse hair
cerdear to refuse to do something
cerdo pig, hog
cerebro brain, mind
ceremonioso ceremonious
cero zero
cerradura lock
cerrar (ie) to close; to seal
cerro hill
cerrojo bolt
certero sure
certeza certainty
certidumbre certitude
certificar to certify; to assure
certísimo *super. of* **cierto**
cerveza beer
cerviz neck
cesante unemployed person (especially a government employee out of work because his party is out of power)
cesantía period of unemployment
cesar to cease
césped sod
cesta basket; **—— de papeles** waste paper basket
cesto basket
cetrino yellowish, lemon-colored
cetro scepter
cicatrizar to heal
ciclista bicyclist
ciclón cyclone

ciego blind; **a ciegas** gropingly
cielo sky; heaven
ciencia science, knowledge
cieno mud
cientificismo scientism
científico scientific
cientifista scientific
cierto certain, true; **de ——** certainly, for sure; **por ——** indeed
ciervo stag
cierzo north wind
cifra figure; symbol; abbreviation
cifrado in résumé, summed up
cigarra locust, cicada fly
cigüeña stork
cilicio hair shirt
cima peak, top; **dar ——** to bring to a happy conclusion; **por —— de** above
cimbel decoy
cimbreante vibrating
cimera plumes (on helmet), crest
cimiento foundation
cincha cinch
cinchar to cinch up
cine movie
cínico cynic
cinismo cynicism
cinta ribbon; belt; film
cinto belt
cintura waist
cinturón belt
ciprés cypress
circo circus
circular to circulate
círculo circle; club
circundante surrounding
circundar to surround
cirio taper, candle
cirujano surgeon
cisne swan
cita rendezvous, appointment, meeting
citar to cite, mention, mention by name; to quote; to subpoena, call (to a meeting)
cítara zither
ciudadano *n.* citizen, townsman; *adj.* of the city
clamar to cry, exclaim
clamor noise
claridad clarity; brilliance, (strong) light, brightness
clarificar to clarify; to purify
claro *n.* opening; *adj.* clear, bright; light-colored; famous; **de —— en ——** from dusk to dawn
clásico classic; classicist, partisan of the classic point of view
clasificar to classify
claustro cloister
cláusula clause
clavar to nail, fix, fix firmly (to a spot), stick (to *or* into)
clave clavichord
clavicordio clavichord
clavija peg
clavo nail
clemencia clemency, mercy
clerical priestly
clérigo clergyman; theological student; student
clerigucho clergyman
cleriguicio clergy
clerizonte clergyman
clero clergy
cliente client; patron; patient
clima climate; region
club club; political gathering
coadjutor coadjutor, assistant
cobarde coward
cobardía cowardice
cobardón *aug. of* **cobarde**
cobertura cover
cobrador collector; bank messenger
cobranza collection
cobrar to collect; to acquire; to recover
cobrir *arch. for* **cubrir**
cobro shelter, safe place
cocer (ue) to boil, cook
cocido stew
cocina kitchen; cooking; **—— económica** stove
cocinera cook
coco bogeyman
coche carriage, coach, chariot
cochera carriage shed
cochero coachman
cochino *n.* pig; *adj.* vile, wretched
códice manuscript
codicia avarice, greed
codiciar to covet, desire
codicioso greedy; eager
código code of laws, law book
codo elbow
codorniz quail
cofre coffer
coger to catch, seize; to gather; to strike
cogida attack (of bull); **—— de coche** accident caused by a carriage
cogote back of the neck
cohecho bribery
cohete skyrocket; **—— tronador** explosive skyrocket
cojear to limp
cojín cushion
cojo lame
cola tail
colada wash
colar (ue) to flow (through)
colcha bedspread
colchón mattress, pad
colectivista community-centered
colegial student
colegio secondary school; private school
colegir (i) to deduce; to select
cólera wrath
colérico angry, wrathful, irascible
coleto jacket; **decir para su ——** to say to oneself
colgadura tapestry, hanging
colgajo hanging article, pendant
colgar (ue) to hang
colina hill
colmar to heap, fill to overflowing; to come to a climax; to overwhelm; to satisfy fully
colmena beehive
colocación position, job
colocar to place
colodrillo nape of neck
coloquio colloquy, conversation
color color; appearance; *plu.* blush
colorado red
colorar to color
coloso colossus
columbrar to make out
columna column, pillar
columpio swing; swaying motion
coluna *arch. for* **columna**
collada (mountain) pass
collado hill
collar collar; necklace
comarca region, district
comarcano neighboring
combate fight, duel, struggle

combatido battered
combatiente combatant, adversary
combatir to combat, fight
combo curved
comedido polite, courteous
comedimiento civility, politeness; polite expression
comedirse (i) to be kind enough, be obliging
comentar to comment on
comentariar to comment on
comentario commentary
comerciante merchant, storekeeper
comerciar en to deal in
comercio store; business
comestible *plu.* food, things to eat
cometa comet
cometer to commit; to attempt
cómico comical, ridiculous
comido fed
comienzo beginning
comisario agent; quartermaster
comisión commission, order; committee
comistrajo mess, hodgepodge
comitiva company; committee
cómoda commode, bureau
comodidad comfort; opportunity
cómodo comfortable; suitable; convenient
como que as if
como quiera que as
como quier que *arch.* although
compadecer to pity
compadecido de pitying, filled with compassion for
compadre crony
compaginar to bring into harmony; to unite
compañerismo companionship; spirit of solidarity
compañero, -a companion; pal
compañía company; **hacer ——** to keep company, do the same as
comparación comparison
comparsa group
compartir to share, divide
compás rhythm, time; compass; **a ——** in rhythm, rhythmically; **a —— de** in harmony with
compasión compassion, pity
compasivo compassionate
compatriota fellow citizen
compendio summary, compendium
compenetrarse to mingle
compensar to compensate
competencia competition
competente adequate
competir (i) to compete
complacencia complacency; pleasure
complacer to please; **——se en** to get pleasure by, enjoy oneself in
complejo complex
complemento complement
completo: por —— completely
complexión build, stature
complicado complicated
cómplice accomplice, one who shares guilt
componer to compose; to arrange, settle; to mend, fix; to prepare; to strengthen; **——se** to fix oneself up; to get one's hopes up; **—selas** to arrange things
comportarse to bear oneself
compostura modesty; composure, sedateness; structure
compra purchase; **ir a la ——** to go shopping
comprador buyer, shopper
comprimido restrained, held back
comprometer to compromise; to jeopardize; **——se** to be obligated
compromiso compromise; promise; engagement; predicament
compuesto well-arranged; composed; **interés ——** compound interest
compunción compunction
compungido afflicted
comulgar to receive communion
común common; **por lo ——** commonly
comunero member of party which upheld civic liberties against Charles V
comunicar to communicate; to instill in
comunidad community
conato attempt
concatenación concatenation, linking
concebir (i) to conceive
conceder to concede, grant
concejil public; **prado ——** common
concejo council, board of aldermen; **—— de guerra** court martial, military council
concepción conception
concepto concept; conceit, cleverly phrased thought
conceptual intellectual, rational
conceptuar to consider
concertar (ie) to arrange; to agree; to bring into harmony; **——se** to be joined; to harmonize; to make an agreement
conceto *arch. for* **concepto**
conciencia conscience; consciousness
concierto concert; plan; concord, agreement
conciliábulo consultation, deliberation
conciliar to reconcile; **—— el sueño** to get to sleep
concluir to conclude, finish; **——se** to come to an end
concordar (ue) to agree
concorde concordant, harmonious
concordia agreement, harmony
concurrencia group, gathering
concurrido crowded
concurrir to attend, frequent; to come together; to be in conjunction
concurso company, crowd; contest; aid, help
concha shell
conde count
condenación punishment; condemnation
condenar to condemn; to damn
condición condition, quality, nature, character; rank, state, station
condigno worthy
condolecerse to condole
condoler (ue) to commiserate
conducción transportation; leading

conducir to lead; to carry
conducta conduct
conducto conduit; **por —— de** through
condumio fare; food
conejo rabbit
confección confection, concoction
confeccionar to cook up, prepare
conferencia lecture; conference
conferir (ie) to confide
confesar (ie) to confess; to hear one's confession
confesión confession
confesionario confessional
confesor confessor
confianza confidence, intimacy, trust
confiar to trust; to entrust, confide
confidente, -a confident
confín end, limit
confirmación confirmation
confirmar to confirm
confite preserves
confitería candy shop
conflicto conflict
conformación conformation, shape, figure
conformar to conform; **——se con** to resign oneself to; to conform oneself with
conforme corresponding, accordant, in conformity; resigned; **—— con** in agreement with; in favor of
conformidad conformity; resignation
confortar to comfort
confundir to confound, abash; to mingle
confuso confused, puzzled; jumbled
congeniar to be congenial
congestionar to congest; **——se** to become flushed
congoja anguish; fainting spell
congojado afflicted, anguished
congojarse to be afflicted; to complain
congregar to gather, congregate
congrio conger eel
conjetura conjecture
conjeturar to conjecture
conjugar to join (with); to conjugate
conjunto whole, ensemble
conjurar to conjure, entreat, implore; to conspire
conjuro entreaty; incantation; charm
conmoción trembling; mental disturbance; shock
conmover (ue) to move, stir; **——se** to become excited; to be moved
conocer to know; to recognize
conocido acquaintance
conocimiento knowledge, consciousness, senses; understanding; acquaintance
conque to that
conquista conquest
conquistar to conquer, win
consabido aforementioned
consagrar to consecrate; to devote
consecuencia consequence
consecuente consistent
conseguir (i) to obtain, attain; to succeed in
conseja tale, yarn
consejar *arch. for* **aconsejar**
consejero adviser, counsellor
consejo council; advice, counsel; consultation; opinion; **—— de guerra** court martial
consentimiento consent
consentir (ie) to consent, permit
conservación preservation, upkeep
conservador conservative
conservar to keep
consideración consideration; thought, meditation; deduction; **tener —— con** to show consideration for
considerado esteemed, respected
considerar to consider; to think; to esteem; to notice
consignar to consign; to state in writing
consiguiente: por —— consequently
consistencia substance
consistir to consist; **—— en** to consist of
consolador consoling; *n.* consoler
consolar (ue) to console
consolatorio consoling
consonancia harmony
consorcio union
consorte spouse, husband, consort
constancia constancy, steadiness
constante constant
constar to be a fact, be evident; to consist; to be stated
consternación consternation
consternado overcome with consternation, horrified
consternarse to be consternated
constipado (head) cold
constituir to constitute, establish
constitutivo constitutional
consuelo consolation
consulta consultation
consumar to consummate
consumidor consumer
consumir to consume, burn out, use up
consumo consumption
consurrección revival, revivification
contabilidad bookkeeping
contado counted, limited in number, rare; **ser para ——** to be fit to be told
contador money cabinet
contadorcillo *dim. of* **contador**
contagiado de infected with
contagio contagion
contagioso contagious
contaminar to contaminate, infect
contar (ue) to count; to tell, relate; **—— con** to count on
contemplar to contemplate
contemplativo contemplative
contender (ie) to contend, dispute
contener (ie) to contain; to restrain; **——se** to restrain oneself
contenido contents
contentamiento contentment
contentar to content
contento *n.* happiness, joy, contentment; *adj.* happy
contienda quarrel, dispute
contiguo adjoining
continente *n.* mien, bearing; continent; *adj.* abstemious

continuación constant succession
continuo continuous; **de ——** constantly
contorno region; contour, outline, figure
contorsión contortion
contra: de —— on the contrary
contra: en —— mia against me
contrabando contraband, smuggled goods
contradanza quadrille
contradecir to contradict
contradicción contradiction; obstacle, difficulty
contradictorio contradictory
contraer to contract
contrahecho disfigured
contraminar to countermine; to get the better of
contrariedad vexation
contrariado vexed
contrariar to contradict; to thwart; to offend
contrario *n.* opponent, adversary; *arch.* adverse fortune, harm; *adj.* contrary, opposite; adverse; opposed; **al ——** on the other hand, on the contrary, quite the contrary
contraste contrast; officer *or* office of fair weights and measures
contratiempo mishap
contrato contract
contravenir to go against
contribución tax
contribuir to contribute
contrito contrite
conturbar to disturb
contusión bruise, contusion
convaleciente convalescent
convencer to convince
convención convention; **de ——** conventional
convenible fitting
conveniente fitting
convenio agreement
convenir to agree; to suit, be appropriate; **——se en** to agree on
convento monastery; convent
conversar to converse
conversión conversion, change
convertir (ie) to change, convert, turn
convexo convex
convidar to invite
convite invitation; party
convivencia living together, community life
convocar to call, convoke
convulso convulsed, convulsive
conyugal conjugal, of marriage
coordinar to coordinate
copa goblet, glass; treetop; *plu.* clubs (in cards)
copar to bet a sum equal to what there is in the bank (in gambling games)
copete forelock; vanity
copia copy
copiar to copy
copioso copious
copla stanza; verse; song
copo tuft
coqueta coquette
coquetear to flirt
coquetería coquetry, flirtation
coquito *dim. of* **coco**
coracha leather bag
coraje anger
coral coral
coraza breastplate, armor
corazón heart; courage
corazonada intuition, hunch
corbata necktie
corcel steed
corcovo caper
corchete policeman
corcho cork
cordel cord, string
cordelejo: dar —— to jest
cordelería shop where rope is made or sold
cordero lamb
cordial of the heart, cordial
cordillera mountain range
cordobés Cordovan, from Córdoba
cordón cord, ribbon, narrow sash
cordonera rope maker's wife
cordura good sense, sanity
corear to form a chorus; to chime in with
cornada blow, wound (with horn)
corneja raven, crow
cornisa cornice, ledge
coro chorus, choir; group; **de ——** by heart
corona crown; *fig.* the best
coronar to crown
coronel colonel
coronela wife of colonel
corporal corporal, bodily
corpulento thick, large
corral corral, barnyard, yard
corralera a type of folksong
corralón *aug. of* **corral**
corredor *n.* corridor; solicitor; *adj.* fast-running
corregir (i) to correct
correo mail; courier
correonazo blow with leather strap
correr to run; to spread; to be in course
correría excursion
correrse to become ashamed; to spread oneself
correspondencia reciprocation
corresponder to correspond; to pertain (to), belong (to); to love in return; **—— a** to pay back
correspondiente corresponding; fitting
corrida run; **—— de toros** bullfight
corridica *dim. of* **corrida**
corrido ashamed
corriente *n. and adj.* current; *adj.* running; agreed, admitted
corrillo group (of gossips)
corro group
corroído crumbled, weather-beaten
corromper to corrupt
corrompido corrupt, imperfect
corrupto decayed
corsario corsair, pirate
corsé corset
cortado confused, abashed; fashioned
cortar to cut, cut off
corte court, capital; *plu.* parliament
cortecilla little slice
cortedad shyness, timidity; diffidence
cortejo cortège, suite
cortés courteous, polite
cortesana *n.* courtesan
cortesanía courtesy
cortesano *adj.* courtly, courteous; citified, stylish; *n.* courtier
cortesía courtesy
corteza bark; covering

cortijo farm
cortina curtain
cortinaje curtain, hanging
corto short, brusque; small; **pecar de ——** to sin through omission
corveta caper, bound
corvo curved
corzo deer
cosa de que possible that
cosaria hang-out
coscorrón bump (on the head)
cosecha harvest
coselete corselet, breast plate
coser to sew
cosmético cosmetic
cosquillas tickling; teasing, joking; misgivings
costa cost; coast; **a toda ——** at all costs
costado side
costal sack
costanilla steep street
costar (ue) to cost
costear to pay for, stand the expense of
costilla rib
costoso costly
costumbre custom; **de ——** usual
costumbrista pertaining to local customs
costura sewing; seam
costurón scab
cotizarse to have a value
cotorra magpie; kind of parrot
coyuntura joint; opportune moment
coz kick
cráneo skull, cranium
craso greasy; crass
creador *n.* creator; *adj.* creative
crear to create
crecer to grow, grow up
creces: con —— abundantly
crecido lofty; full
crédito credit, credence
credo credo; moment
credulidad belief
creencia belief
crepúsculo dim light, twilight
cresta crest
cretense Cretan
cría offspring; colt
criado, -a servant; *arch. masc.* ward
criar to bring up, raise, rear; to cause to grow; **——se** to grow
criatura creature; child, baby
cribar to sieve
cribo sieve
crimen crime
crinado like a mane, long (of hair)
crisma pate, crown
crispar to make tense *or* rigid
cristal window pane; glass; crystal
cristalino crystalline, clear
cristianismo Christianity
criterio criterion, judgment
crítica criticism
criticar to criticize
crónica chronicle
crónico chronic
crucificar to crucify; to torment
crucifijo crucifix
crudo raw, uncooked; crude, rough
crujir to creak, squeak; to clash
cruz cross; burden, trial
cruzada crusade
cruzar to cross; to fold; to pierce; to traverse; **—— la cara a uno** to strike one in the face
cuadra stable; ward
cuadrado square; **elevado al ——** squared (*math.*)
cuadrante point of compass
cuadrar to suit
cuadriculado square (on graph paper)
cuadrilla band
cuadro square; picture; bed (of garden); **—— de costumbres** descriptive essay on everyday life
cuádruple quadruple
cuajado *n.* meat pie; *adj.* congealed, coagulated
cual *prep.* like
cualdidad quality
cuando when; *arch.* even if; **—— más** at the most
cuantioso large, vast, copious
cuanto: —— antes as soon as possible; **en ——** as soon as; **en —— a, —— a** as to, concerning
cuarentena about forty (of anything); forty days; quarantine
cuaresma Lent
cuartel barracks; quarter (of escutcheon); square; **—— general** general headquarters
cuarterón panel
cuartilla sheet (of paper)
cuarto room; apartment; a small coin (less than a cent); quarter; *plu.* money; **——s traseros** hind quarters
cuartucho wretched room *or* apartment
cuasi almost
cubierta cover; envelope
cubierto table silver
cubil lair (of beasts)
cuchara spoon
cucharón *aug. of* **cuchara**
cuchicheo whispering
cuchilla knife; sword
cuchillada blow (with knife *or* sword)
cuchillo knife; **—— de monte** hunting knife
cuchufleta jest
cudicia *arch. for* **codicia**
cuello neck; collar
cuenca valley, hollow
cuenta account, reckoning; bead; **a buena ——** on account; **caer en la ——** to realize; **darse —— de** to realize; **hacer ——** to make believe; take for granted; **más de la ——** more than proper; **tener ——** to keep account; **vamos a ——s** let's get down to brass tacks; **en resumidas ——s** in short, when all is said and done
cuento tale, short story; **sin ——** innumerable
cuerda string, cord, rope; match
cuerdo wise, sane, discreet
cuero skin; leather; **en ——s** naked; **en ——s vivos** stark naked
cuerpo body, form; person; **—— de guardia** guardhouse, headquarters; **en ——** in indoor clothing, without overcoat *or* cape; **no poder con su ——** to be scarcely able to move
cuervo crow

cuesta hill; a **——s** on one's back; burdened
cuestión question; argument
cueva cave; **—— de ladrones** nest of thieves
cuévano large deep basket
cuidado care, worry; delicate health; love affair, love; **de ——** serious; **perder ——** not to worry
cuidadoso careful
cuidar to care for, take care of; to think
cuita care, trouble
cuitado wretched, unfortunate; *n.* coward
culebra snake
culebrear to wind
culpa fault, blame
culpable guilty, blameworthy
culpado blamed, guilty
culpar to blame
culto *n.* cult; *adj.* cultured
cumbre mountain top, peak
cumplido fulfilled, passed; full, complete; large
cumplimiento compliment
cumplir to fulfill, carry out, do one's duty, pay up, attain; to be fitting, necessary *or* important; **—— (veinte) años** to reach the age of (twenty); **—— con** to carry out
cúmulo mass, lot, series
cuna cradle; source
cundir to spread; to grow
cuña wedge
cuñada sister-in-law
cuñado brother-in-law
cuño stamp; *fig.* sort
Cupido Cupid
cupiera *third person singular imperfect subjunctive of* **caber**
cupo *third person singular preterit of* **caber**
cura cure; convalescence; priest
curango priest
curar to care; to cure; **——se** to get well; to care; **—— de** to care about; to take care of
curia (law) court
curiosidad curiosity
curita *dim. of* **cura**
cursar to take a course in, study
curso course
curtido experienced
curva curve
cúspide point, peak
custodia custody; monstrance
custodiar to care for, look after

CH

chabacano rude, rough
chacota noisy mirth
cháchara chit-chat
chaleco vest
chambra house coat, dressing gown
champaña champagne
chamuscar to scorch, singe
chancear to joke; **——se** to joke
chanza joke; **ni de ——** not even in jest
chanzoneta joke
chapa sheet metal
chapear to veneer
chapín slipper
chaquet jacket
chaqueta jacket
chaquetón jacket
charada puzzle
charanga brass band
charco puddle
charla talk, chatting
charlar to chat; to chatter
charlatán humbug, fake
charretera epaulet
chasco: llevar un —— to be disappointed
chasqueado tricked, deceived
chato pug-nosed
chavala girl, 'kid'
chiar to squeak, chirp
chico *n* child; *adj* small, little
chicuelo *dim. of* **chico**
chillar to shriek, shout
chillería scolding
chillido shriek
chillón loud
chimenea fireplace
china pebble
chinche bedbug
chinesco Chinese
chiquillada childish deed
chiquillo *dim. of* **chico**
chirrido squeak, shrill sound
chisme *plu.* gossip
chismorrear to gossip, gabble
chismoso gossiper
chispa spark
chispeante sparking, giving off sparks
chistar to utter a word
chiste joke; **tener ——** to be a joke
chistera top hat
chitón silence!
chivo he-goat, buck
chocar to displease; to clash; to shock; to hit (against)
chochear to be doddering
chocho doddering; **—— por** doting on
chopo (*slang*) musket, gun
choque clash, shock
chorreante dripping
chorro stream, trickle
choza hut
chuleta chop
chulo, -a dandy *or* coquette of the lower classes
chupar to suck
chupón bloodsucker
churro fritter, kind of doughnut

D

dádiva gift
dado que provided that
daga dagger
dama lady; *plu.* checkers
damasco damask, fine figured silk cloth
dantesco of Dante, Dantesque
Danubio Danube
danzante dancer
danzar to dance
dañado harmful
dañar to harm, hurt
dañino harmful
daño harm
dañoso harmful, injurious
dar to give; to strike, hit; **——se** to be considered; **—— con** to find; to strike; to land (in); to slam (a window); **—— con su cuerpo** to land, fall; **—— de alta** to release (from hospital), to declare cured; **—— de comer** to feed; **—— de mano** to strike; **—— de pie** to kick; **—— en** to take to, hit upon, bring oneself to, come upon; **—— lugar** to give occasion; **—— lugar a** to

cause, permit; —— **por libre** to set free; —— **por hecho** to consider something a fact; ——**se por** to consider oneself (as); —— **sobre** to attack, fall upon; **lo mismo le da** it's all the same to him

dardo dart

datar to date

dátil date

dato information

deán dean

deber to owe; ought; *n.* duty

debido due

débil weak

debilidad weakness

debilitar to weaken

débito debt

decadencia decadence, decline

decantar to exaggerate; to praise

decena two-figure number

decencia decency; respectability

decente respectable

decidido resolved, determined

decidir to decide; to persuade; ——**se** to make up one's mind

décimo tenth

decisión determination

declaración explanation, elucidation; testimony

declarar to declare; ——**se** to make a declaration of love; **estar declarado** to be engaged

declinar to draw to an end

declive slope

decoración stage setting

decorar to memorize

decoro decorum

decoroso decorous, proper

decretar to decree

decreto decree

dechado mold, model

dedal thimble

dedicar to devote, dedicate

dedo finger

defecto fault, defect

defender (ie) to defend

defensa defense; safety

deferencia deference

deficiencia shortcoming, deficiency

definición definition; decision

definitivo definite, definitive

defraudar to defraud; to frustrate

defunto *popular for* **difunto**

degenerar to degenerate

degollar (üe) to behead

dehesa grazing land

deidad deity, divinity, divine nature

dejadez lassitude

dejar to leave; —— **de** to leave off, cease, leave aside, abstain from; to fail to

dél *arch. for* **de él**

delación accusation; scandalous information

delantal apron

delantero front, forward

delatar to proclaim

delectación pleasure, delight

deleitable delectable

deleitar to delight; ——**se** to enjoy

deleite delight

deleitoso delightful

deleznable slippery; frail; perishable

delgado slender, thin

delicadeza delicacy

delicado delicate

delicia delight

delicioso delightful

delincuente delinquent, guilty

delinquir to transgress, do wrong

delirante delirious

delirar to be delirious

delirio delirium, madness, passion

delito crime

della *arch. for* **de ella**

demacrado emaciated

demanda demand; petition; endeavor

demandadero a monastery servant

demandar to beg, ask (for)

demás: los —— others; —— **de** *arch.* besides

demasía excess; **en** —— excessively

demediar *arch.* to be half through; to be half enough

demencia madness

demente demented, crazy

demonio demon; **qué** —— what the dickens

demontre dickens

demostrar (ue) to represent, show

denegación negation, denial

denegrir to become black (by weathering)

dengoso finicky; affected

denostar (ue) to insult

denotar to denote

dentadura teeth

denuedo daring, bravery

denuesto insult

denunciar to denounce

deparar to provide; to present

departir to talk, converse

depender to depend

dependiente clerk

deplorar to deplore

deponer to put aside

deporte sport

depositar to deposit

depositaria depository, custodia

depositorio trustee, receiver

depósito storehouse, depository, depot; deposit, trust

depresión depression, hollow,

depurado purified, pure

de que *arch.* after

derecho *n.* right; law; fee; *adj.* straight; **al** —— properly; **a la derecha** to the right; **de derechas** rightist, conservative

derramar to pour; to shed; to strew, spread; ——**se** to fall (of water); to spill; to be diffused

derredor: en —— around

derrengado crippled

derretir (i) to melt

derribado low (of shoulders)

derribar to knock down, strike down, throw down; to take down; to conquer

derrochar to squander

derroche flood

derrota defeat, rout

derruir to demolish, tumble down

derrumbadero cliff

derrumbarse to fall

desaborido insipid; witless

desabrido disagreeable, rude

desabrimiento rudeness, harshness

desacato disrespect, incivility

desacierto error, blunder; lack of success

desacorde discord

desacreditar to discredit

desafiar to challenge; to rival, compete with
desafío challenge; duel
desaforado excessive, immense; given to excesses; very loud
desagradar to displease
desagradecido ungrateful
desagrado displeasure
desaguisado *n.* improper *or* unjust deed; *adj.* improper, senseless
desahogado *adj.* comfortable, easy; *n.* brazen-faced fellow
desahogar to unburden
desahogo relief, ease, comfort; outpouring
desahucio dispossession
desairado unpleasant, unbecoming, graceless
desairar to rebuff, scorn
desaire slight, rebuff
desalado hasty, impatient
desalentado breathless
desaliento discouragement
desalmado heartless
desalojar to dislodge
desalumbrado dazzled, flattered
desamar to hate
desamor lack of love
desamparado unprotected, helpless, abandoned
desamparar to abandon
desamparo helplessness
desandar to retrace
desangrar to bleed (to death)
desanillar to uncoil
desaparecer to disappear
desaparición disappearance
desapiadado pitiless
desarmar to disarm
desarrapado ragged
desarrollar to develop
desarrollo development
desaseado unkempt, rumpled
desasir to loosen, free, detach
desasosegado restless
desasosegar (ie) to upset; **——se** to become nervous
desasosiego restlessness, perturbation
desastrado disastrous, ill-fated, unfortunate, fatal
desastre disaster, misfortune
desastroso disastrous, unfortunate
desatar to untie, undo, loosen; **——se** to become frayed (of the nerves)
desatender (ie) to neglect
desatentado discourteous; injudicious
desatento heedless; rude, discourteous
desatinado senseless, stupid, unintelligent
desatinar to talk foolishly
desatino stupidity, foolishness
desavenencia disagreement
desavío aberration; upset
desazón uneasiness; upset (health)
desbancar to break the bank
desbarajuste disorder, confusion
desbaratado dishevelled, disorderly
desbaratar to destroy, break up
desbocado runaway (horse); broken-mouthed (jug)
descabalgar to dismount
descabellado crack-brained
descabezar: —— un sueño to nap
descalabrado wounded in the head
descalabradura wound in the head
descalabrar to break one's head, wound in the head
descalzar to take off (shoes or stockings)
descalzo barefoot
descansado restful, calm
descansar to rest; to ease
descanso rest, ease; (*military command*) at ease!
descarado barefaced, impudent
descargar to unload, unburden
descargo exoneration; excuse
descarnado bare; bony
descaro impudence, effrontery
descarriado straying, wandering
descender (ie) to descend; to get down
desclavado unnailed; disjointed
descolgar (ue) to hang down; to take down
descolorido discolored
descollar (ue) to stand out
descomedido discourteous
descomponer to distort; to disarrange, unsettle; **——se** to lose one's temper
descompuesto unprepared; slovenly, deranged; upset
descomunal extraordinary
desconcertado disarranged; garbled
desconcertar (ie) to disconcert
desconcierto disturbance, confusion
desconfiado doubtful, suspicious; lacking in self-confidence
desconfianza distrust; diffidence
desconfiar to mistrust, doubt
desconocido unknown
desconsiderado inconsiderate
desconsolado miserable, disconsolate
desconsolador disheartening, grief-inspiring
desconsuelo desolation, misery
descontar (ue) to discount; to keep out
descontentamiento discontent
descontentar to displease
descontento *n.* dissatisfaction; *adj.* displeased
descorazonado dejected; cowardly
descorazonar to discourage
descorrer to run back, draw aside
descortés discourteous
descortesía discourtesy
descoser to rip out
descuajar to dissolve
descubierta *n.* reconnoitering
descubierto unprotected
descubrir to discover, uncover, find; to reveal; **——se** to take off one's hat; to uncover oneself
descuento discount; discounting
descuidado careless; unaware, off-guard
descuidarse to neglect; to be at ease; **si me descuido** if I don't watch out
descuido carelessness
desdecir to deny; to be out of harmony with

desde luego immediately; of course
desdén disdain
desdeñar to disdain
desdeñoso disdainful
desdicha unhappiness, misfortune
desdichado unhappy, unfortunate, wretched, unlucky
desdoblar to unfold, open
desechar to reject, cast aside
desecho rubbish
desembarazado empty; unencumbered, free
desembarazar to clear; **——se** to free oneself from
desembarazo freedom; indifference, flippancy
desembarcadero landing place
desembaular to bring out, take out
desembocadura mouth (of river)
desembocar to debouch; to open; to enter; to end
desembozarse to unmuffle oneself
desemejado strange looking
desempedrado unpaved
desempeñar to perform, carry out; to redeem (from pawnshop)
desencadenar to unchain, unleash; **——se** to be unleashed
desencajado popping (of eyes)
desencuadernado unbound
desenfado ease, natural manner
desengañar to disillusion, undeceive; **——se** to become disillusioned
desengaño disillusionment, undeceiving; (bitter) truth
desenhebrado disjointed, disorganized
desenlace outcome
desenlazar to come to an end, have its outcome
desenojarse to calm oneself
desentender (ie) to ignore
desentonar to clash with, be out of harmony with
desentrañar to dig out
desenvainar to unsheathe
desenvoltísmo *super. of* desenvuelto
desenvoltura ease, facility, nonchalance
desenvolver (ue) to unwrap, undo; **——se** to develop
desenvuelto forward, free and easy; clever
deseoso desirous
desequilibrar to unbalance
desequilibrio lack of balance
desertor deserter
desesperación desperation, hopelessness
desesperado hopeless, desperate
desesperar to despair, be hopeless, desperate
desestimar to scorn, hold in low esteem
desfallecer to decline, diminish; to grow weak
desfallecimiento weakness, faintness
desfavorecer to disdain
desfigurar to disfigure
desfiladero narrow mountain pass
desgano lack of appetite
desgarrador rending, tearing
desgarrar to shred, tear
desgarrón rip, tear
desgastar to wear
desgracia misfortune
desgraciado unfortunate, miserable, luckless, unlucky
desgranar to fall to pieces
desgreñado disheveled
deshacer to undo; to muss up; to destroy; **——se** to be undone; to collapse; **——se en** to work hard at something, do a thing vehemently; to be overcome with
deshecho undone, consumed, destroyed
desherrar (ie) to unshoe (a horse)
deshilachar to shred
deshojado leafless; undone
deshojar to strip the leaves off of; to wither; **——se** to lose leaves; to fade *or* die
deshonesto indecent
deshonor dishonor
deshonrar to dishonor
deshora: a —— untimely; unexpectedly
desierto *n.* desert, wild region; *adj.* arid, desert
designar to designate; to show; to outline
designio design; qualification
desigual uneven, unequal; different
desigualdad inferiority
desinteresado disinterested, impartial
desistir to desist, refrain
deslenguado foul-mouthed
desligar to untie
deslizar to slip, slide; **——se** to slip
deslucir to tarnish
deslumbrar to dazzle
deslustrar to tarnish
desmandarse to get out of hand; to go so far as
desmañado clumsy, awkward
desmayar to fade, disappear; **——se** to faint, swoon
desmayo swooning, fainting, weakness; setting (of sun)
desmedido without measure, immense
desmedrar to deteriorate
desmelenado disheveled (hair)
desmentir (ie) to give the lie to, contradict; to deny
desmérito lack of merit, worthlessness
desmoralizar to demoralize
desnaturalizar to denationalize; to denaturalize
desnivel unevenness
desnudar to bare; to unsheathe (a sword); **——se** to undress
desnudez nakedness; simplicity
desnudo nude; bare, naked; unprovided for, empty-handed; **—— de** devoid of
desocupado unoccupied, idle, empty
desolado desolate
desollar (ue) to skin
desorden disorder
desordenado disorderly, haphazard
desorientar to confuse
despabilar to brighten by snuffing *or* trimming; to snuff out; to sharpen (one's eyes)
despacio slowly
despachar to dispatch, accomplish, finish; to attend to
despacho office

despavorido startled, terrified
despechado spiteful
despechar to spite, pique, anger
despecho spite; despair; **a —— de** in spite of
despedazar to break to bits, pulverize
despedida leave-taking, parting; dismissal
despedir (i) to discharge; to give off; to send (away); **——se** to take leave
despegar to part, open; to tear away; **——sele a uno** to dislike
despeinado uncombed, disheveled
despejado wide awake; bright; clear
despejar to clear; to unburden
despejo spriteliness, ease, smartness; wakefulness
despensa pantry
despeñadero cliff, precipice
despeñar to throw (from a precipice); **——se** to fall; to throw oneself
desperdiciar to waste; not to avail oneself of
desperdicio garbage, waste
despernado legless
despernarse (ie) to walk one's legs off
despertador arouser; stimulus
despertar (ie) to awaken
despiadado heartless
despintado unpainted
despintar to disfigure, disguise
desplegar (ie) to unfold, open
desplomarse to plunge, fall
desplumar to pluck; to strip *or* despoil of property; to clean out
despoblado *n.* uninhabited place; *adj.* unpopulated; bare
despojar to plunder, despoil, rob, take as booty
despojito left over bit; worthless portion
despojo plunder, spoils; *plu.* spoils; leavings; treasure
desposar to marry
despotismo despotism
despotricar to chatter
despreciable despicable
despreciar to despise
desprecio scorn
desprender to let fall; to loosen; **——se** to detach; to fall; to follow, be a consequence of; **——se de** to give up, give away
desprendido loosened; beginning to fall (of rain)
despreocupado unconcerned; unprejudiced
desprestigiar to lessen one's prestige, bring into disrepute
desprovisto devoid
despuntar to begin, start; to break (of the dawn)
des que *or* **desque** *arch.* after
desquiciamiento unhinging; overthrowing, destruction
desquitar to get even, make up for
desquite revenge, satisfaction
desruralizado removed from the country
destacar to cause to stand out; **——se** to stand out
destartalado sloppy, unkempt
deste *arch. for* **de este**
destello flash; spark
destemplado untuned, out of tune
desteñido faded, lusterless
desterrado exiled
desterrar (ie) to exile
destiempo: a —— untimely
destierro exile
destilar to distill; to run
destinar to destine
destino destiny, fate, lot; job
destornillado unbalanced; 'touched'
destreza dexterity, skill
destrozar to break, destroy; to tear; to ruin
destruir to destroy
desusado unusual
desvalido helpless, destitute
desván attic room; *plu.* attic, garret
desvanecer to cause to disappear, sweep away, dissolve; **——se** to fade away; to faint
desvariado extravagant, mad, delirious
desvariar to rave, be mad
desvarío mental disturbance, wandering, raving; strange idea
desvelado wakeful; sleepless
desvelarse to lie awake
desvelo vigilance; anxiety; pains
desventajoso unfavorable
desventura misfortune
desventurado unhappy; unlucky
desvergonzado shameless
desvergüenza shamelessness; shame
desviar to turn aside
desvío deviation; going astray; aversion, coldness
desvivirse to outdo oneself, make every effort
detallado detailed
detalle detail
detención delay, halt; **con ——** closely, carefully
detener to detain, hold back, restrain; to put off; **——se** to stop; to delay
detenidamente at length, carefully
deteriorado deteriorated
determinado definite; certain
determinante determining; **—— de** bringing about, conducive to
determinar to determine; to persuade; to ascertain; to decide; to define, outline
detestar to detest
detrimento detriment
deuda debt
deudo relative
deudor *n.* debtor; *adj.* owing, in debt
devanar to wind up; **—— los sesos** to rack one's brains
devaneo mental aberration, illusion, dream; giddiness, dissipation; vanity
devengar to draw, earn
devocionario prayer book
devolver (ue) to return
devorador devouring
devorante devouring
devorar to devour
devoto devout, religious; devoted; **——s míos** devoted to me
día day; **el mejor ——** some one of these days; **en el ——** at the present time

diablo devil
diablura mischief, prank, deviltry
diabólico diabolic
diáfono diaphanous
dialéctica dialectics; argument
diamante diamond
diantre demon
diario daily, every day
dibujante artist, one who sketches
dibujar to sketch, outline; to depict
diccionario dictionary
dictadura dictatorship
dictamen opinion
dictaminar to state (opinions)
dictar to dictate
dicha happiness; fortune; **por ——** by chance
dicho *n.* saying; *adj.* aforesaid
dichoso happy; blessed; (ironically) cursed
diente tooth
diestra right hand
diestro *n.* halter; fencing master; *adj.* right (hand); dexterous
dieta diet
diferir (ie) to differ
dificultarse to become difficult
dificultoso difficult
difundir to spread, diffuse; to infuse
difunto dead, deceased
difuso diffused, scattered
digerir (ie) to digest
dignarse to deign
dignidad dignity; high office
digno worthy
digresión digression
dije ornament, trinket
dilación delay
dilatado extensive, long
dilatar to dilate; to put off, delay
dilatorio delaying, postponing
dilema dilemma
diligencia errand; diligence, care, activity; precaution; stagecoach
diligente diligent, indefatigable
diluir to dilute
diluvio deluge, flood
dineral fortune
dinero money; obsolete silver coin
diocesano of the diocese
diosa goddess
diosecito little god
diputado deputy, congressman
dirección administration, management
directe directly
director, -a director, manager
directriz leading, directing
dirigir to direct; **——se (a una persona)** to address, direct oneself to, go toward
discernir (ie) to discern clearly
disciplina discipline, penance; *plu.* whip, scourge
discípulo pupil
discordancia discord
discorde discordant
discreción cleverness; discretion
discreto clever; discreet; intelligent
disculpa excuse, pardon; explanation
disculpable excusable
disculpar to excuse
discurrir to run; to discourse; to reflect; to think of
discurso speech, discourse; thought
discutible questionable
disertación dissertation, speech
disertar to discourse
disforme hideous
disfraz disguise
disfrazar to disguise
disfrutar to enjoy
disgustar to displease
disgusto displeasure; unpleasantness; quarrel
disimular to feign, pretend, dissemble, hide (one's feelings)
disimulo dissimulation
disipar to disperse, scatter, dissipate
dislate foolish idea
disminuir to diminish
disnea labored breathing
disonar (ue) to be dissonant, out of tune
disparado like a shot
disparar to shoot; to break out, begin suddenly
disparate crazy idea, stupidity, foolish notion
dispendioso expensive
dispensa dispensation
dispensar to pardon, excuse
dispersar to disperse, scatter
disperso dispersed
displicencia peevishness
displicente peevish, unpleasant
disponer to dispose; to prepare
disposición aptitude, bent; arrangement; appearance
dispuesto disposed; trained; ready
disputa dispute
disputar to dispute
distar to be distant
distensión stretching, distention
distinción distinction
distinguir to make out, distinguish; to show regard for
distinto distinct; different
distracción distraction, amusement
distraer to distract, amuse; **——se de** to be inattentive to
distraído absent-minded
disturbar to disturb
disturbio disturbance
diversidad diversity, difference
diverso different, diverse; several
divertido amusing
divertimiento amusement
divertir (ie) to divert, turn aside; **——se** to amuse oneself, have a good time
divinal divine
divinidad divinity, divine nature
divino divine, holy
divisar to make out, sight
divulgar to divulge, spread
do *arch.* where
doblar to double, bend, fold; to cross; to turn (a corner *or* a page); to toll (of bells); **——le la edad** to be twice as old as
doble double
doblegarse to bend
doblez fold
doblón doubloon
docena dozen
dócil gentle, docile; peaceful
docto learned

doctor learned man
doctrina doctrine; learning; **de gran ——** filled with learning
dogal hangman's noose
dolencia illness; pain, suffering
doler (ue) to ache, pain; to grieve; to take pity
doliente doleful, sorrowful; suffering
dolo deceit, fraud
dolor pain; grief
dolorido suffering; aching
domador trainer (of animals), master
domar to tame
domesticidad household
doméstico *adj.* family; domestic
domicilio domicile
dominador dominating
dominante predominant, dominant
dominar to dominate
dominguero *adj.* Sunday, related to Sunday
dominio domain; sway, rule
dompedro morning-glory
don gift
donación donation, gift
donaire witticism; wit; grace, charm
doncel youth; squire
doncella damsel, maiden: housemaid
dónde: ¿—— bueno? where are you off to?
donoso charming; witty
donosura charm
don-pedro *see* **dompedro**
doquier *arch. or poetic for* **dondequiera** everywhere, wherever
dorado golden; gilded
dorador gilder; dealer in art objects
dorar to gild, brighten
dormilón *adj.* sleepy
domir (ue) to sleep
dormitorio bedroom; dormitory
dosel canopy; curtain
dotar to endow
dote dowry; endowment
dríada dryad
dril drill (cloth)
dromedario dromedary
ducado ducat
duda doubt
dudar to doubt; to wonder
dudoso doubtful; indistinct
duelo duel; grief; group of mourners
dueña possessor; chaperon; lady-in-waiting; *arch.* woman
dueño owner, possessor; master; employer
dulcificar to sweeten
dulzón sugared; overly sweet
dulzor sweetness
dulzura sweetness, gentleness
duplicar to duplicate
duquesa duchess
duradero enduring
durar to last, endure; to remain
durazno variety of peach
dureza harshness; hardness; obstinacy
duro *n.* dollar (five-peseta piece, now worth about ten cents); *adj.* hard
dux doge

E

era well, all right, come on
ébano ebony
ebrio drunk, inebriated
écarté (*French*) card game for gambling
eclampsia convulsions
eclesiástico ecclesiastical
eclipsar to eclipse; to cause to disappear; to disappear
eco echo
economía thriftiness, saving, economy
económico financial; thrifty
ecuánime unruffled
ecustre equestrian
echar to throw; to pay (compliments); to put; to set out; to stretch out; to set aside; to dismiss; **—— de ver** to show; **—— menos** (cf. **echar de menos)** to miss; **—— por delante** to send ahead; **—— por otro lado** to turn aside; **—— un cigarro** to smoke a cigar; **—— un sermón** to lecture (*slang*); **—— un viaje** to take a trip; **——se** to lie down; to slip on (of a garment); **——se a** to begin; **——selas** to put on the air of; **——se a revolucionario** to plunge into revolutionary activity; **——se a la calle** to rush out; **echado adelante** daring, reckless
edad age; time; **—— media** Middle Ages
edén Eden, paradise
edicto edict
edificar to build
edificio building
educación rearing; breeding
educando pupil
educar to rear
efectivamente in fact
efectivo real
efecto effect; dramatic effect; result; **en ——** in fact
efectuar to carry out
efeto *arch. for* **efecto**
eficacia effectiveness; efficiency; strength, force
eficaz efficacious; efficient
efímero ephemeral
efluvio emanation
efusión effusion; expression
egipcio Egyptian
égloga eclogue, idyll
egoísmo selfishness, egotism
egoísta selfish
egolatría self-worship
egregio extraordinary
eje axle
ejecución execution
ejecutar to carry out, execute
ejecutivo executive
ejucatoria patent of nobility
ejemplar *adj.* exemplary; *n.* copy (of a book)
ejemplo example; fable; **por ——** for example
ejercer to exercise; to practice
ejercia rigging (of ship)
ejercicio exercise; task; military drill; employment
ejercitar to exercise; to train; **——se en** to exercise; to practice
ejército army
ejido commons; community
elección choice
eléctrico electric
elegancia elegance
elegante elegant, tasteful
elegantón *aug. of* **elegante**
elegir (i) to choose; to elect
Elena Helen
elevamiento absent-mindedness

elevar to raise; **——se** to rise
eliminar to eliminate
elocuencia eloquence
elogiar to praise
elogio praise, eulogy
emanar to emanate
emancipar to emancipate
embajada mission
embajador ambassador
embalsamar to perfume
embarazado embarrassed; encumbered
embarazar to embarrass; to hinder
embarazozo bothersome
embarcación ship
embarcarse to take ship, embark
embargar to check, hinder, hold back, suspend; to attach (legally)
embargo (legal) attachment
embebecer to enrapture
embeber to imbibe; **——se** to be enraptured
embelesado engrossed; enraptured
embelesar to enrapture
embestir (i) to attack
emblemático emblematic
embobado fascinated; astonished
embocarse to swallow in haste, wolf
emborracharse to get drunk
emboscarse to hide in the forest
embotar to blunt, dull
embozado *n.* masked person (with cape pulled over face); *adj.* muffled, disguised
embozar to wrap up, muffle up
embozo collar of cape pulled over the face; mask
embriagar to intoxicate
embriaguez intoxication
embridar to bridle
embrocación embrocation, application of a liquid medicine
embrollo tangle; deception; misunderstanding
embromar to make fun of
embuste trick, deceit
embustero *n.* deceiver; *adj.* deceitful
embutido inlay
embutir to stuff, cram; to set into, inlay
emigrar to emigrate
eminencia marvel; eminence
emisión emanation
emocionado moved, stirred
empacho shyness
empalmarse to join, unite
empañar to sully; to blur; to veil; to muffle
empapar to soak through
emparedar to wall up
empecatado incorrigible
empecer to harm
empecible harmful
empeñado en mixed up in, involved in
empeñar to insist; to pawn; to pledge; to swear (an oath); **——se** to insist; to persist; **la lucha está empeñada** the struggle has begun
empeño insistence; intense desire; care; influence, 'pull'; effort; pawning; **papeleta de ——** pawn ticket; **casa de ——** pawnshop
emperador emperor
emperatriz empress
emperifollado dressed elegantly, 'dolled up'
empero however
empezar (ie) to begin
empinado steep
empinar to raise; **—— el codo** 'to bend the elbow,' drink
empíreo celestial, empyreal
empleado employee, jobholder
emplear to employ, use
empleo job; use
emplomado leaded
empollar to hatch
empotrar to embed
emprender to undertake, engage in
empresa business; undertaking; affair
empujar to push, impel
empujón shove
empuñar to seize, grasp
emulación emulation, imitation
émulo emulator
enaguas petticoat
enajenación derangement
enajenarse de sí to make one beside himself
enamorada lover, mistress
enamorado *n.* lover; *adj.* enamored, lovesick
enamoramiento love-making
enamorar to inspire love in; to make love
enano dwarf
enarbolar to raise
enarcar to bend, arch
enardecerse to become heated, become angry
encajar to fit (into *or* on); to bring together, close; to pass off
encaje neck-piece (of helmet); lace
encalabrinar to make dizzy
encalar to whitewash
encaminar to direct; to destine; **——se a** to approach, go forward
encandilar to light up
encanijar to make sick
encantado charmed
encantador *n.* magician, enchanter; *adj.* enchanting
encantamento *arch. for* **encantamiento**
encantamiento enchantment
encantar to enchant
encanto charm, enchantment
encaprichado given to whims, headstong
encaramado mounted (on)
encaramar to exalt; **——se** to climb
encararse con to face
encarecer to enhance; to extol; to overrate; to exaggerate
encarecimiento exaggeration
encargado, -a agent, manager
encargado de in charge of
encargar to entrust, charge; to request, order; **——se de** to take charge of
encargo duty, commission
encariñado infatuated
encariñar to inspire affection
encarnado red
encarnar to incarnate, symbolize
encarnizado bloodthirsty
encarrilar to set on the path, set straight
encasillar to pigeonhole
encefálico encephalic, of the brain
encelarse to become jealous

encenagar to stir up, muddy
encender (ie) to kindle; to burn; **——se** to become angry
encendido flushed
encerado blackboard
encerrar (ie) to enclose, shut in, imprison
encierro enclosure; detention
encima on top; **por —— de** above, on a higher plane than; **venirle ——** to befall (someone)
encina evergreen oak
encinar oak grove
enclavado nailed
encoger to shrink; **—— los hombros, ——se de hombros** to shrug one's shoulders
encogido shy, timid
encogimiento shyness
encomendar (ie) to commend; to entrust
encomiador praiser, extoller
encomienda commission; decoration carrying with it the administration of and income from ecclesiastical estates
encomio praise, encomium
encontrado opposed, conflicting
encontrar (ue) to find, meet; **—— con (algo)** to come upon (something), find (something)
encorvado bent (down)
encrespar to curl; **——se** to ruffle
encrucijada crossroads
encuadernación binding
encuadernar to bind (books)
encubierto disguised
encubrir to cover, hide, shield
encuentro meeting, encounter; **salirle al —— a uno** to come out to meet one
encumbrado lofty
encumbrar to raise; **——se** to rise, soar
ende *or* **de ende** *arch.* of it, from it; from there; **por ——** on account of it, therefore
endecha dirge
enderezar to straighten; to go straightway; to direct; to prick up (the ears)
endiablado devilish, diabolical
endilgar to surprise; to send
endiosado deified; haughty
endulzar to sweeten
endurecer to harden
enemigo *n.* enemy; *adj.* inimical
enemistad enmity
enérgico energetic
energúmeno madman
enfadar to anger; to repel; to tire; **——se** to become angry
enfado anger; irritation, bore
enfadoso irking
enfermar to make sick; to become sick
enfermedad sickness
enfermero, -a nurse
enfermizo sickly
enflaquecer to weaken
enfrascar to bottle; **——se** to be wrapped up, absorbed
enfrenar to check, hold back
enfrente opposite, across the street
enfriar to cool; to become cold; **——se** to become cold
enfurruñado angry, peeved
enfurruñarse to get angry
engalanar to adorn
enganche (action of) hooking, tripping
engañador deceiving
engañar to deceive
engaño deceit, trick; deception
engañoso deceitful, treacherous
engarzar to set (jewels)
engendrar to engender, give life to
engolfar to engulf
engordar to grow fat
engreimiento self-satisfaction, conceit
engreír to encourage one's conceit; to elate
enhiesto upright
enhorabuena congratulations
enigmático enigmatic, unfathomable
enjaezar to harness; to saddle
enjalma pad
enjambre swarm
enjaretarse to insinuate oneself into
enjuagar to rinse
enjugar to dry
enjuto dry; lean
enlazar to bind, intertwine; **——de** to set round with
enloquecer to become mad; to madden
enlosado paved
enlutar to dress in mourning; to darken
enmendar (ie) to mend, amend
enmudecer to become silent, keep silent
enojar to anger; **——se** to become angry
enojo anger; annoyance; distress
enojoso burdensome, troublesome
enramada arbor; grove
enrarecido rarefied
enredadero climbing
enredado involved
enredar to tangle; to fool around; **——se** to entangle oneself, become involved in
enredo tangle; falsehood, deceit
enredoso involved, intricate
enrevesado tangled; mixed up
enriquecimiento enrichment
enronquecer to become hoarse
enroscar to coil
ensalada salad
ensalzar to exalt, raise up
ensanchar to enlarge; **——se** to broaden, widen; **—— el corazón** to cheer up
ensanche widening; freedom
ensangostarse to become narrow
ensañarse to vent one's fury
ensartar to string together
ensayar to try; to rehearse; **——se** *arch.* to try out one's powers, do one's first deeds, strike one's first blows
enseñanza teaching; **primera ——** elementary school; **segunda ——** secondary school
ensilar to ensilage, store away
ensillar to saddle
ensueño dream, illusion

entablar to start; to initiate
entapujarse *arch.* to cover oneself
ente being
entena yard-arm
entendederas understanding, brain
entendedor one who understands, wise man
entender (ie) to understand; to know (of); to believe; *arch.* to hear; **—— en** to give attention to, attend to; **——se (con)** to get along (with)
entendido well informed
entendimiento intellect, mind, intelligence
enterar to inform; **——se de** to find out about; to understand
enterito every bit
enternecer to move, soften; **——se** to be moved
enternecido moved, stirred
entero entire; firm, unshaken; (*math.*) whole number
enterrador grave-digger
enterrar (ie) to bury
entibiar to cool off
entonación tone; intonation
entonadamente in harmony
entonar to intone, chant, sing
entornar to half close
entrada entrance; foray
entrambos both
entraña entrail, vital organ; *plu.* heart; vitals; depths; bowels; **sin ——s** heartless
entrañable heartfelt; dear
entrar to enter; to bring in; **—— le a uno** to come over one
entreabierto half-opened
entrecano grayish
entrecejo brow
entrecuesto backbone
entrechocar to bump together; to rattle
entrega delivery; payment
entregar to hand over, give, give over; to pay; **——se** to devote oneself
entrellano level space
entremés farce
entresemana: días de —— week days
entretanto *adv.* meanwhile; *n.* interval
entre tanto que while
entretejer to intertwine; to string
entretela: de mis ——s of the cockles of my heart
entretener to converse with, keep one interested; to while away; to foster; **——se** to amuse oneself; to take time
entretenido amusing, interesting; amused
entretenimiento amusement, entertainment
entrever to glimpse, see vaguely
entrevista interview
entricado *arch.* intricate
entriega *arch. for* **entrega**
entristecer to sadden
entrometer to meddle
entrometido meddlesome
entronizar to enthrone
entumecido numb
enturbiar to disturb, stir up
entusiasmar to enthuse
entusiasmo enthusiasm
entusiasta enthusiastic
envainar to sheathe (a sword)
envejecer to grow old
envenenado poisoned
envergonzante modest, poor but proud
enverjado grating
enviado envoy, messenger
envidia envy
envidiable worthy of envy
envidiar to envy
envidioso envious
envilecer to vilify
enviudar to become a widow
envoltorio wrapping, package
envoltura wrapping, coating
envolver (ue) to wrap; to swaddle; to cover
epiceno: genero —— common gender
epicúreo epicure
epidemia epidemic
epifanía epiphany, appearance
epigrama epigram
epilepsia epilepsy
epílogo epilogue
epitalamio epithalamium, marriage song
época epoch
equilibrio balance
equis (the letter) X
equitación equitation, riding
equivocado mistaken
equivocar to mix up; **——se** to be mistaken
era field, plot (of vegetables); threshing floor
eregir (i) to build, erect
erguido lofty; tall and straight
erguir (ie, i) to erect; to hold high; to straighten up
erizado bristly
erizar to bristle; **——se** to stand on end (hair)
erizo hedgehog; porcupine
ermita hermitage
ermitaño hermit
errante wandering; stray
errar (ie) to err, to make a mistake in; to stray
erróneo wrong, erroneous
erudicíon erudition, learning
erudito learned
erupción eruption; breaking out, rash
esbeltez slenderness
esbelto slender, svelte
esbozar to sketch; to outline
escabechar to pickle
escabel footstool
escabrosidad rough region
escabroso rough; scandalous
escabullirse to slip away
escala ladder; stairway; scale
escalar to scale
escaldar to scald
escalera stairs, stairway
escalofrío chill, cold sweat; shiver
escalón step
escaloncito *dim. of* **escalón**
escalpelo scalpel, dissecting knife
escama scale
escanciadora pourer, woman who pours
escandalizar to scandalize
escándalo scandal
escandaloso scandalous
escaño bench
escapada escape
escapar to escape
escaparate display window
escape: a —— very fast; in a hurry
escapatoria escape; surreptitious trip
escapulario scapulary

escarbar to scratch, dig, pick (the teeth)

escarceo *plu.* prancing, capers

escarcha frost

escarlata scarlet

escarmiento warning; lesson

escarnecer to scorn

escarnio scorn, jeering, derision

escarpado precipitous, steep; craggy

escasear to be scarce

escasez scarcity; privation

escaso scanty

escatimar to hold back; to be stingy with

escena scene; stage

escenario stage; setting

escenografía staging; acting

escéptico skeptic

esclavina pilgrim's cloak (ornamented with shells which betoken a visit to the shrine of Santiago de Compostela, near the sea)

esclavitud slavery

esclavizar to enslave

esclavo, -a slave; humble servant

escoba broom

escobajo stalk

escoger to choose

escogido choice; **lo ——** choiceness

escolar *n.* student; *adj.* scholastic, of a school

escombrera dump

escombro ruin; *plu.* rubbish

esconder to hide

escondrijo hiding place; hoarding

escopeta shotgun, gun

escoria impurity, dross

escorpión scorpion

escribano notary

escribiente notary; scribe

escrito *n. plu.* writings

escritor writer, author

escritorio desk

escritura writing; **divina ——, sacra ——** Holy Scriptures

escrúpulo scruple

escrupuloso scrupulous; squeamish

escrutinio scrutiny

escuadra squadron; squad

escuadrón squadron

escuálido skinny, undernourished

escudar to shield

escuderil of a squire

escudero squire

escudilla trencher, wooden bowl

escudillar to dish out

escudo escutcheon, shield, coat of arms

escudriñar to scrutinize

esculpir to sculpture; to engrave

escupir to spit (forth)

escurecer *arch.* to make obscure; to surpass

escureza *arch.* darkness

escuridad *arch. for* **oscuridad**

escuro *arch. for* **oscuro**

escurridizo slippery

escurrirse to slip away; to slip

esencia essence

esfera sphere

esfinge sphinx

esforzarse (ue) to strive, make an effort

esfuerzo strength; effort; fortitude

esgrima fencing

esgrimidor fencer

eslabonado linked together

esmaltar to enamel; to adorn (with bright colors)

esmerado painstaking; delicate

esmeralda emerald

esmerarse to take care

esmero pains, special attention

espabilar to wake up, make wide awake

espacio space; region, place; room; occasion; time; **con ——** at leisure

espacioso spacious; slow

espada sword; *plu.* spades (in cards)

espadachín swordsman

espadín rapier

espalda shoulder; back

espantable frightful

espantajo scarecrow

espantar to frighten; to surprise, astound

espantoso fearful, frightful

españolismo the quality of being typically Spanish; love for typically Spanish things

esparcido gay, jovial

esparcir to scatter, spread, spread abroad, divulge

esparto esparto grass (used in rugs and seats of chairs)

espasmódico spasmodic

espatarrado spread-eagle

espatarrarse to stretch out one's legs

especie kind, species, sort

espectáculo spectacle

espectador spectator

espectro specter

especulación speculation; investment; business proposition

espejo mirror

espejuelos glasses

espera: sala de —— waiting room

esperpento absurdity; odd person

espeso thick; heavy

espesura thicket; thick woods; thickness; density; darkness

espía spy

espiga head of grain

espigado tall (for one's age)

espina thorn; quill; suspicion; **dar mala ——** to cause doubt, suspicion

espionaje spying

espíritu spirit; ghost

espiritual spiritual

esplendente splendid

esplendidez munificence; magnificence

espléndido splendid, magnificent

esplendor splendor; glow

espolear to spur

espolique groom

espontáneo spontaneous

esposa wife; *plu.* handcuffs

esposo husband

espuela spur

espuma foam

espumajo foam

esquela note

esqueleto skeleton

esquema plan, outline

esquila bell

esquina corner

esquividad isolation

esquivo elusive; isolated; harsh, cruel

estable *adj.* stable

establecer to establish

establecimiento establishment, business

establo stable

estaca stake

estación season; station

estada stay, being
estado state; rank (in society), station; a measure of length (about 2 yds.); —— **mayor** general staff
estafar to swindle
estallar to burst, burst out, explode
estampa print, picture; figure; printing; appearance
estampar to print, imprint
estampía: de —— in a rush; stormily
estancarse to cease flowing, stagnate
estancia stay, sojourn; room; dwelling place
estandarte standard, banner
estante shelf; bookcase
estaño tin
estar: —— por to have a notion to; to be in favor of; **—— de buenas** to be in a good mood
estatua statue
estatura stature, figure
estera grass rug, mat
estéril sterile, unproductive
esterilizar to make sterile
estética esthetics
estético esthetic
estigma mark, stigma
estilarse to be the style; to be common
estilística style; stylistics
estilo style; kind; **a —— de** in the manner of; **por el ——** of that kind, like that
estimación esteem; worth, value
estimar to esteem
estímulo stimulus, inducement, incitement
estío summer, dog-days
estipendio stipend, fee
estirado stiff
estirar to stretch
estirpe race; lineage, family
estocada sword thrust
estofado stew
estómago stomach
estopa tow; **——s de encenderse y apagarse** easily kindled and extinguished materials
estoque sword
estorbar to disturb; to impede
estorbo hindrance
estorcer (ue) *arch.* to turn aside
estoria *arch. for* **historia**
estornudar to sneeze
estornudo sneeze
estrado dais
estrafalario strange, extravagant
estrago loss, havoc, ravishing
estrechar to tighten; to bind more closely; to press; **——se** to become narrow
estrechez narrowness; constraint; straitened circumstances, straits
estrecho *n.* strait; *adj.* narrow; close, intimate; strict
estrella star; *fig.* fortune, fate
estrellado starry
estrellar to break to pieces; **——se** to burst; to break, be shattered; to bump
estremecer to tremble, shake
estremecimiento quivering, trembling
estrena beginning, first deed
estrenar to act a play for the first time; to inaugurate; to wear for the first time; **——se** to begin
estreno first night (of play); beginning
estrépito noise
estrepitoso noisy
estribar to rest (on); to lie (in)
estribo stirrup
estridente strident
estropear to ruin; to harm, hurt
estructurar to give structure to
estruendo loud noise; **de ——** sonorous
estruendoso noisy
estrujar to crush, press hard
estuche (jewel) box
estudio study; school; studio (of artist); painting
estudiosillo fairly studious
estufa hothouse
estupendo stupendous
éter ether
eternidad eternity
eterno eternal
ético ethical
étnica ethnology, racial makeup
etiqueta formal attire; **de ——** in formal dress
europeizante believing in a united Europe
europeo European
evacuar to take care of, perform
evangélico evangelical
evangelio scripture, gospel
evaporar to evaporate
evidencia evidence; **con ——** clearly
evitar to avoid
evocación evocation
evocador evocative
evocar to evoke, call, call up
evolución evolution; turn
exactitud exactitude, correctness
exacto assiduous
exageración exaggeration
exagerar to exaggerate; to increase
exaltación excitement; exaltation, uplifting
exaltar to exalt; **——se** to become excited
exánime in a faint, weak, lifeless
excelencia excellence; excellency; **por ——** extremely good *or* well
excelso noble, excellent
exceso excess
excitar to excite; to stimulate, urge
exclamar to exclaim
excomulgado *fig.* cursed
excomulgar to excommunicate
excomunión excommunication
excusa excuse
excusado es it's unnecessary
excusar to excuse; to avoid, turn aside; **——se** to spare oneself
exégesis exegesis, critical study
exentar to exempt
exequia *plu.* funeral services
exhalar to exhale
exhausto *adj.* exhausted
exigir to demand
eximir to exempt; **——se de** to free oneself from
existencia reality; existence
éxito success
exótico exotic
expedicionario member of an expedition

experiencia experience; experiment; **hacer —— de** to try out, experiment with
experimentar to experience, feel
experimento experiment
expiar to expiate
expirar to die
explanadita little level space
explanar to explain
explotable exploitable
exponente proposer, originator of a plan
exponer to expose; to expound, explain
expresivo expressive; amiable
exquisito exquisite, delicate
extasiado ecstatic, in ecstasy
extático ecstatic
extender (ie) to extend; to make out (a receipt)
extenso: por —— at length, extensively, in detail
extenuado extenuated
exterminador *n.* exterminator; *adj.* exterminating
exterminio extermination
extinguir to extinguish
extraer to extract, take away
extramuros outside (a walled city)
extranjero *n.* foreigner; foreign countries; *adj.* foreign
extrañar to surprise, amaze; **——se** to be surprised, amazed
extrañeza strangeness; surprise, wonder
extraño strange; foreign; *n.* stranger
extravagancia wild idea
extravagante eccentric
extraviado wandering, strayed
extravío wandering, aberration
extremado extreme, great
extremaunción extreme unction
extremo *n.* extreme, end; exaggeration; *adj.* extreme
extremoso exaggerated, vehement
extrínseco extrinsic, objective
exuberante exuberant, great
exvoto votive offering

F

fábrica building
fabricar to make, manufacture
fábula fable
fabulista writer of fables
fabuloso fabulous; fictitious
facción feature
facilidad facility; opportunity
factura bill
facultad faculty; subject (of curriculum)
facultar to empower
facha appearance, sight; frightful appearance
fachada façade
faena task
faetonte Phaethon; driver
faisán pheasant
faja sash, band
fajo bundle, sheaf
falange phalanx
falaz deceitful
falcón falcon
falda skirt; shirttail; slope (of mountain); **—— de montar** riding skirt; **—— espesa** thickly wooded slope
faldamenta tails (of coat)
faldear to skirt, traverse a slope
faldero lap; **perrillo ——** lap-dog
faldilla de barros petticoat
faldriquera pocket
falsar *arch.* to pierce
falsario fraud
falsía falsehood
falsificador falsifying, mendacious
falso false, counterfeit
falta lack; fault; flaw; **hacerle —— a uno** to need; **sin ——** without fail
faltar to be missing, be absent; to be lacking; to fail; **—— a** to offend against; **no faltaba más** that's the last straw
falto de lacking in; through lack of
faltón *adj.* defective, deficient
faltriquera pocket, bag
fallar to pass judgment, sentence; to fail; to be lacking
fallecer to die; to falter, fail; **—— de** to falter in
fallecimiento decease, death
fallo judgment, sentence
fama fame; reputation; rumor
famélico hungry, starving, ravenous
familiar *n.* dependent, domestic; bosom friend; *adj.* familiar; unceremonious; of the family
familión *aug. of* **familia**
fanal (large) lantern; lighthouse
fandango popular song and dance of Andalucía
fandanguero 'dizzy'
fanega land measure (about 1.59 acres); grain measure (about 1.60 bu.)
fanfarrón braggart
fanfarronada boasting, braggadocio
fantasear to day-dream, indulge in fantastic imaginings
fantasía fantasy, imagination; conceit
fantasma ghost, phantom, apparition
fantasmagoría illusion; melodrama
fantástico fantastic
fardel sack
farmacia pharmacy; medicine
farol lantern; light
fárrago farrago, jumble
farsante (*slang*) fake, stuffed-shirt
fascinación fascination
fascinar to fascinate
fascista fascist
fastidiar to bore, weary; to do harm to, give trouble
fastidio boredom, ennui
fastidioso annoying; boring
fatal fatal; unlucky
fatalidad unlucky chance; calamity, fatality
fatídico fateful
fatiga fatigue, toil, pain; hardship
fatigar to fatigue; to molest; **——se** to worry
fatigoso toilsome, debilitating
fauces jaws
fauna fauna
fauno faun
fausto happy
favorecedor favorer; flatterer

favorecer to favor
favorito favorite
faz face, surface
fe faith; **a** —— by my faith
fealdad ugliness
febril feverish
fecundidad fecundity, fertility
fecundo, fertile, fecund
fecha date
fehaciente trustworthy
felice *poetic for* **feliz**
felicidad happiness, felicity
feligrés parishioner
feliz happy
fementido false, perfidious
fenecer to die; to end
feo ugly; bad
féretro coffin
feria fair; market
fermento ferment; yeast
feroz fierce, ferocious, savage
férreo iron; unbending
ferrocarril railroad
ferruginoso containing iron
ferviente fervent
fervoroso fervent
festejar to entertain; to celebrate; to do honor to
festejo rejoicing
festín feast
festivo gay
fetidez evil smell, stench
fétido fetid
feudal feudal
feudalismo feudalism
fiar to trust; **——se de** *or* **en** to trust in
ficción fiction; imagining
ficticio fictitious
ficus (*Latin*) fig tree
fidelidad faithfulness
fiebre fever
fiel faithful
fiera wild animal, beast
fiereza fierceness
fiero fierce, wild, terrible, severe
fiesta party; festival; holiday; fun; *plu.* demonstrations of joy; **hacer —— a** to celebrate; **de ——** in a gay mood
figón low tavern
figura figure, build; face card; face; spectre
figurado imagined, imaginary
figurar to sketch, represent; to figure, take part in; to cut a figure, be of importance; **——sele a uno** to imagine
figurón *aug. of* **figura**
fijar to fix, establish; to fasten; to stop; **——se en** to notice, pay attention to
fijo fixed; **de ——** surely
fila rank, file
filete steak
filial filial
Filipinas Philippine Islands
filo edge, cutting edge
filomena nightingale
filósofo philosopher
filtrar to filter
filtro philter, love potion
fin end; object; objective; *plu.* conclusion; **en ——** in short, finally; **sin —— de** a great number of
financiero financial
finarse to die
finca farm; property; house
fincar *arch.* to remain; to rest on; to fix on
fineza delicacy; *plu.* courteous deeds *or* words
fingir to feign, pretend; to imagine
fino fine; refined, courteous; skillful; **labio ——** thin lip; **de lo ——** of the finest quality
finura fine manners, delicacy, politeness
firma signature; **estar a la ——** to be waiting for a signature
firmamento firmament, heavens
firmar to sign
firme firm, steadfast, constant; (*military command*) hold firm!
firmeza firmness; strength; steadfastness
fisco treasury
fisga banter
fisgonear to snoop
físico physical
fisiólogo physiologist
fisionomía physiognomy
fláccido flaccid, limp
flácido *see* **fláccido**
flaco thin; weak
flamante resplendent; brand-new
flamear to blaze
flamenco Flemish
flámula banner, flag
Flandes Flanders
flaquear to weaken, falter
flaqueza weakness, leanness
flato gas
flauta flute
flautista flute player
flecha arrow
flojedad flabbiness
flojo loose; slight
Flora Flora, goddess of flowers and gardens
florecer to flower; to flourish, thrive
florero (flower) vase
floresta forest
florete foil
florido flowery, in flower
flota fleet
flotante floating
flotar to float, drift
foco focus
fogón stove
fogoso fiery
follaje foliage
folletín newspaper serial novel
folleto pamphlet
fomentar to encourage
fonda inn
fondo bottom; depths, substance; background; backstage; **al ——** at the back
fontana spring; stream
forastero *n.* stranger; *adj.* foreign, strange
forcejear to struggle
forjar to forge
formación formation; ranks
forma form; manner
formal serious, solemn; well-mannered; grown-up, mature
formalidad good manners; seriousness
formalizar to execute, legalize; to carry out
fórmula formula; **de ——** prescribed
formular to formulate, form
foro law court, forum
forro cover
fortaleza strength; fortitude, fortress
fortificar to fortify
fortuna fortune, fate; **por ——** fortunately
forzado necessary
forzar (ue) to force; **—— la fuerza del tiempo** to force events
forzoso necessary

forzudo powerful
fosfórico phosphorescent
fósforo match
fotógrafo photographer
foso ditch
frac frock coat
fracaso failure; calamity; ruin
fragilidad fragility; frailty
fragoso broken; rocky
fragua forge
fraguar to forge; to make
fraile monk, friar
francachela huge meal, debauch
franciscano Franciscan
franco frank; generous; open, clear; free and easy; gratis
franela flannel
franja fringe
franquear to pass through *or* over
franqueza frankness
fraque frock coat
frasco flask
frase phrase; sentence
fraterno fraternal
fraude deceit
fray brother (of a monastic order)
frecuencia frequency; **con ——** frequently
frecuentar to frequent
fregar (ie) to scour, scrub
freír (i) to fry
frenesí frenzy
frenético frantic
freno brake; curb, restraint
frente forehead, brow; front; **a su ——** in front of him; **en** *or* **de —— de** in front of, opposite; **—— a** in front of, before; **—— por ——** opposite
fresa strawberry
fresca angry scolding; piece of one's mind
fresco *n.* cool air, fresh air; **tomar el ——** to enjoy the coolness, cool off; *adj.* cool; fresh
frescor coolness
frescura coolness; freshness; insolence
fresno ash tree
frialdad coldness
friega rubbing, massage
frisado fuzzy
frisar to border (on)
frito fried
frívolo frivolous
frondoso leafy
frontera frontier, limit
fronterizo frontier
frontero opposite
fructificar to flower; to bear fruit
fructuoso fruitful
fruncir to wrinkle; **—— las cejas** to frown
frutal *adj.* fruit
fruto product; fruit; **sin ——** fruitlessly, without result
fuego fire; **al ——** next to the fire
fuelle bellows
fuente fountain; source; spring; platter; tureen
fuera outside; get out!; **—— de sí** beside oneself
fuero privilege, legal exemption
fuerte *n.* fort, fortification
fuerza force, strength; **a —— de** by dint of, on account of; **a —— de derecho** by rights, rightly; **por ——** by force, necessarily; **sacar ——s de flaqueza** to make a great effort; to screw up one's courage; **ser ——** to be necessary
fuga flight; escape
fugarse to run away
fugaz fugitive(ly), fleeting
fugitivo fugitive
fulano so-and-so
fúlgido bright, shining
fulgor glow
fulgurante flashing, gleaming
fulgurar to shine brightly; to flash
fulminio giving off lightning flashes, flashing
fullero cheat
fumar to smoke
fumigar to fumigate
función function; party
funcionar to work
funcionario, -a functionary, official; bureaucrat
fundación foundation
fundado well-founded; serious
fundamento foundation, basis
fundar to found; to base; **——se en** to found one's belief on
fundir to fuse; to melt down
fúnebre funereal; **empresa de servicios ——s** undertaking establishment
funebridad undertaking; gloomy business
funeral funereal, tragic, death-like
funerario undertaker
funesto very unfortunate, fatal
furia fury
furibundo furious
furor fury, madness
furtivo furtive
fusil rifle; gun
fusilar to shoot
fusilería gunfire
fustán fustian (cotton cloth)
futileza futility
futuro future

G

gabán overcoat, outer coat
gabinete sitting room
gacela gazelle
gaceta gazette, the official newspaper
gacho bent down; **sombrero ——** hat with brim turned down
gaita bagpipe
gala adornment, finery; glory; accomplishment
galán *n.* lover, dandy, beau; *adj.* gallant; elegant
galano elegant; clever
galante gallant; flirtatious
galanteo courting
galantería gallant speech, compliment
galanura elegance
galardón gift; reward
galera galley
galería corridor, passageway
galgo greyhound
galopar to gallop
galopín *dim. of* **galopo**
galopo rascal
gallardete pennant, flag
gallardía elegance, handsomeness
gallardo gallant, dashing; graceful; charming
gallego Galician, from Galicia
gallina hen, chicken
gallineja *sing. or plu.* fried chicken intestines

gallo cock, rooster
gallofero tramp, vagabond, loafer
gamo deer
gana desire; appetite; **lo que me ha dado la ——** just as I pleased; **tener ——s** to desire
ganadería cattle raising
ganadero cattleman
ganado cattle; flock; goats; animal; (*slang*) rabble
ganancia gain, earnings; conquest
ganapán day laborer
ganar to gain, win; to reach
gancho hook; **punto de ——** crochet, crochet work
ganga bargain; (*slang*) cinch; marvel
ganso goose; stupid person
gañán farmhand
garabatear to scribble
garabato scrawl
garambaina ridiculous affectation
garantía guarantee
garbanzo chick-pea
garboso sprightly
garganta throat, gullet; narrow mountain valley
gárgara gargling
garguero throat
garito low dive
garra claw
garrafa carafe
garrote death penalty (by strangulation); club; walking stick
garza heron
gasa gauze
gaseosa soft drink, pop
gastado worn; *see also* gastar
gastar to spend; to waste; to indulge in
gasto expenditure; waste
gatera (large) hole
gato cat; (*slang*) stake, hoard
gaveta till, money drawer
gaviota sea gull
gazapón gambling den, dive
gaznate windpipe
gazpacho cold soup
gelatina gelatine, aspic
gemelo twin
gemido moan; moaning, suffering
gemir (i) to moan
genealogista genealogist
generación generation
género class, kind, type; goods
generoso generous; noble; brave
genial genial; full of genius; of one's native disposition
geniecillo *dim. of* **genio**
genio genius; disposition, temper; bad temper; **corto de ——** diffident, shy
gente people; *plu.* servants
gentezuela low people
gentil graceful; handsome; splendid, fine
gentileza nobility; courtesy
gentilhombre gentleman
gentuza low people
genuflexión kneeling, genuflexion
geranio-hiedra climbing geranium
germánico Germanic, German
germano German; Germanic tribesman
germen germ
germinar to germinate; to hatch
gesticulación gesticulation, expression
gesto expression (of face); face; attitude
gigante giant
giganteo of giants
gigantesco gigantic
gira excursion; outing; **—— campestre** picnic
girar to revolve, gyrate
girifalte hawk
giro gyration; turn
gitano gypsy
glacial icy
gladiador gladiator
gleba land, glebe
globo balloon
gloria glory; delight; **dar ——** to be a pleasure
gloriar to glorify
glorificar to glorify
glotón glutton
gobernador governor
gobernante governing
gobernar (ie) to govern; to control, manage
gobierno government; governing, managing, administration
goce joy, pleasure
godo Goth
golfo gulf
golondrina swallow
golosina sweetmeat, dainty
goloso gluttonous; fond of sweets
golpe blow; stroke; **en un ——** at one stroke; **de ——** suddenly; **—— de tos** fit of coughing; **—— de vista** insight, ability to size up a situation
golpear to beat (on), pound
golpeteo beating
goma rubber
gordo fat, big
gordura fatness
gorguera collar
gorjear to warble
gorra cap
gorrión sparrow
gorro cap
gota drop
gotear to fall (in drops), dribble
gótico Gothic
gozar to enjoy; **—— de** to enjoy
gozo joy
gozoso joyful, glad
grabado engraving, etching
grabar to engrave; to mark
gracejo grace; humor, witty talk; charm
gracia grace; attractive quality; witty saying; wit; stunt; **tiene ——** that's funny
grácil graceful, delicate
gracioso witty, funny, amusing; graceful; pretty; pleasant
grada step
gradación gradation
grado degree; will; pleasure; rank; **de buen ——** willingly
grana *n.* scarlet
granada pomegranate
granadero grenadier
granado pomegranate tree
grande *n.* grandee, nobleman of highest rank; **en ——** on a large scale
grandeza greatness, magnificence; nobility
grandiosidad grandeur
grandor bigness, size
granero granary
granizo hail
granjear to gain
granjería gain
grano seed; grain; grain (of weight)
granuja rascal

grasa grease
gratificar to recompense; to satisfy
grato pleasing
gratuito gratuitous, free; undeserved
grave heavy; grave
gravedad gravity
graveza *arch.* heaviness
gravitación gravitation
graznar to caw
graznido croak
Grecia Greece
gregoriano Gregorian
gremio guild, union
greña lock (of hair)
gresca revolt, riot
griego Greek
grieta crack, fissure
grillo *plu.* irons (for prisoners), shackles
grima horror, revulsion
gris gray
gritar to shout, call; to protest
grito scream, shout; **poner el —— en el cielo** to shout to high heaven
grosería bad manners, crudeness
grosero crude, rough, coarse, vile
grotesco grotesque
grueso heavy, stocky
gruñido grunt
gruñir to grumble
gruta cave, grotto
guadaña scythe
guantada blow (with glove), slap
guante glove
guapetón *aug. of* **guapo**
guapín *dim. of* **guapo**
guapo handsome, pretty
guarda guard; **guarda-agujas** switchman
guardado sheltered
guardar to keep; to save; to guard
guardarnés armor closet
guardesa guard's wife; switchman's wife
guardia guard; policeman; **cuerpo de ——** troop of guards; **—— civil** civil guard, national policeman, gendarme; national constabulary; **—— del orden** municipal police
guardián guardian; **padre ——** father superior
guardilla garret
guardillón garret
guarida den, lair
guarnamiento *arch.* adornment
guarnecer to adorn, embellish
guarnición trimming, ornament
guasón joker
guedeja lock
guerra war; **dar ——** to give trouble
guerrero *n.* warrior, soldier; *adj.* warlike
guerrilla band of irregular troops, guerrilla band
guerrillero partisan; member of a guerrilla band
guía *m.* guide; *f.* guidebook
guiar to guide
guija pebble
guijarro stone
guillar (*slang*): **me las guillo** I'll beat it
guinda cherry
guiñapo rag; ragged person
guiñar to wink; to close the eye to evil
guirnalda garland
guiropa stew
guisa way; manner
guisante pea
guisar to cook; **—— de comer** to cook
guiso dish
guitarra guitar
guitarrista guitar player
gula gluttony
gulusmear to nibble; to pry into
gusanera worm heap
gusano worm; **—— de luz** glowworm
gustar to please; to taste; **—— de** to like
gustazo *aug. of* **gusto**
gusto pleasure; taste; fancy, whim; **a ——** pleased, content; with pleasure

H

haba bean
habano of Havana
haber *n.* credit; property; *plu.* credit; property
hábil able, clever
habilidad ability
habilitado director; agent
habilitar to enable
habitación room; apartment
habitador dweller, inhabitant
habitar to live in, inhabit
hábito habit; robe; clothing
habituarse to become accustomed
habla speech
hablador talkative; slanderous
hablilla gossip
hacanea hackney, riding horse
hacendoso industrious
hacer to make; to do; to cause *with following inf.*; to hold (a market); **—— caso** to give attention to; **—— de** to act as; **—— por** to try; **—— que** to pretend; **—— ventaja** to be ahead of, surpass; **——se cargo de** to realize; **——se el tonto** to play the fool
hacerio *arch.* blame
hacienda estate; wealth, property, fortune; treasury
hacinamiento pile, accumulation
hacha torch; ax
hachazo blow with ax
hachero torch stand
hachón torch; **—— de viento** torch
hada fairy; Fate (mythological figure)
hadar to enchant, bewitch
hado fate
hala move along!, come on!; so there!
halagador flattering, cajoling
halagar to flatter; to please
halago flattery, insinuating way; caress
halagüeño flattering; endearing, alluring
halagüero flattering
halcón falcon
hambriento hungry; lean
hanega *same as* **fanega**
haraposo ragged
harina flour
harpa harp
hartar to satisfy, fill; **——se (de)** to get one's fill (of); to stuff oneself (with)
hartazgo satiety, fill (of food)

harto *adj.* sufficient, more than enough; satiated, satisfied; *adv.* quite, very; very well
hasta up to; until; even; as many as
hastiar to bore
hastío boredom
hatajo despicable flock
hato flock
haya beech tree
haz bundle; rank, file (of army); surface
hazaña deed
he behold, see; —— **aquí** here is
hebra thread; hair
hecha: de esta —— from this moment
hechicera witch, enchantress
hechicero *adj.* bewitching, charming
hechizar to bewitch, enchant
hechizo spell, charm
hecho fact; deed; *adj.* ready made
hechura make; form
hedor stench
helado frozen, cold
helar (ie) to freeze
helecho fern
helenizante lover of Greek culture
hembra female
hemisferio hemisphere
hemorragia hemorrhage
henchir (i) to stuff, fill
hendir (ie) to split open; to force one's way
heno hay
heredad field, land; fief
heredado having received an inheritance
heredamiento heritage
heredar to inherit
heredera heiress
heredero heir
hereditario hereditary
hereje heretic
herejía heresy; *fig.* blasphemy
herencia inheritance, legacy; heredity
herida wound
herir (ie) to wound; to strike
hermafrodita hermaphrodite
hermosear to beautify
héroe hero
heroico heroic
herradura horseshoe; **camino de** —— bridle path, lane
herramienta tool
herrería forge
herrero blacksmith
hervir (ie) to boil, seethe
hervor boiling; ardor, excitement
hez dreg
hidalgo nobleman (of low rank); gentleman; *adj.* noble
hidalgote *aug. of* **hidalgo**
hidalguía nobility
hiedra ivy
hiel gall, bitterness
hielo ice; cold
hierático hieratic, priest-like
hierba grass; weed; herb; —— **corrompida** weed; **mala** —— weed
hierro iron; bar
hígado liver
higiene hygiene
higuera fig tree
hilado thread; **huevo** —— a mixture of eggs and sugar made in the form of threads
hilandera spinner
hilar to spin
hilo string; thread; theme
himno hymn
hincar to fix; —— **de rodillas,** —— **la rodilla** to kneel; ——**se** to kneel down
hinchar to swell
hinojo: de ——**s** kneeling
hipérbole hyperbole, exaggeration
hiperbólico hyperbolical, exaggerated
hípico equestrian
hipo hiccup; urge; **darle el** —— **por** to have a yen for
hipocondría hypochondria
hipocresía hypocrisy
hipócrita *n.* hypocrite; *adj.* hypocritical
hipoteca mortgage; security
hisopo sprinkler for holy water
Hispania Hispania, the Iberian peninsula
hispano Hispanic
historia history; story
historiador historian
hito: de —— **en** —— fixedly
hocico *sing. or plu.* snout, nose (of animal)
hogar hearth, home
hoguera fire
hoja leaf; page; —— **de lata** sheet metal; tin
hojaldre kind of pastry
hojarasca dead leaves; rubbish
hojear to glance over (book, writing)
hola hello; here!
holgachón lenient, soft
holgado comfortable
holgar (ue) to enjoy, have a good time; to be pleased; —— **más** to prefer
holgazán lazy; idle
holgura ease; indulgence
hollar (ue) to tread, trample (on)
hombre man; one; —— **de bien** gentleman; man of worth
hombro shoulder
hombruno mannish, masculine
homeopático homeopathic
homicida murderer
homicidio murder
homilía homily, sermon
honda sling
hondo deep, profound
hondonada ravine
hondura depth
honestidad modesty; purity; honor
honesto respectable, decent
hongo mushroom; derby; **sombrero** —— derby
honra honor
honradez honesty
honrado honorable, honest; decent
honrar to honor
honroso honorable
hora hour; time; **a la** —— at once; **en buena** —— at a fortunate moment; very well
horca gallows
horcajada: a ——**s** astride
horda horde
horizonte horizon
hormiga ant
hornilla stove hole (in old coal range)
horno oven
horquilla hairpin
horrendo horrible
horrísono horrible sounding, deafening
horrorizar to horrify

hortaliza vegetable, vegetables, garden stuff
hortelano gardener
hospedaje lodging; billeting
hospicio refuge, asylum
hostia host, communion wafer; **hacer un pan como una** —— to make a splendid bargain
hotel hotel; private home
hoyuelo dimple
huebra *arch.* ornament
hueco hollow; little space
huella trace, track
huérfano orphan
huero sterile, empty; **salir huera una cosa** to turn out badly
huerta vegetable garden; garden
huerto orchard; garden
huesa tomb, grave
huesecillo *dim. of* **hueso**
hueso bone
huésped, -a guest; host *or* hostess
hueste host, army
huída flight
huir to flee
humanar to humanize, make human; **Dios humanado** God in man's form; the communion wafer
humanidad humanity; humane treatment
humanista humanist
humano human; humane, kindly
humareda cloud of smoke
humedad dampness
humedecer to moisten, water
húmedo damp
humildad humility, humbleness; **hacer** —— **a** to humble oneself to
humilde humble
humillación humbling; humiliation; loss of prestige
humillar to humiliate
humo smoke; *plu.* airs
humor humor, vein
humorada humorous idea
hundimiento sinking
hundir to sink; to plunge, fall
huracán hurricane
huraño shy, withdrawn
hurgón poker; brawl
hurón ferret
huronear to ferret out; to pry into, investigate
huronera den, hole
hurtar to steal
hurto theft
huso spindle

I

ida going, outward trip
ídem the same, ditto
ides *arch. for* **vais**
idílico idyllic
idiotizar to stupefy
idólatra idolater
idolatría idolatry
ídolo idol
idóneo appropriate
iglesia church; —— **mayor** cathedral
ignominia ignominy, shame
ignominioso ignominious
ignorar not to know, be ignorant of
igual *n. and adj.* equal; *adj.* same, similar; fitting; even
igualar to equal
igualdad equanimity
igualmente likewise; equally
ijada flank, side
ijar flank
ileso unharmed, unscathed
ilícito illicit
illuminar to light; to brighten; to enlighten
ilusión illusion, dream; hope
ilusorio illusory, fleeting
ilustración education
ilustrado enlightened; cultured
ilustrar to cultivate; to enlighten
ilustre illustrious
imagen image
imaginar to imagine; to invent; to scheme; to think
imaginativo thoughtful
imán magnet
imbécil imbecile
imbuído steeped
imitador imitator
imitar to imitate
impacientarse to grow impatient
impasible passive, unmoved
impávido fearless
impedir (i) to impede, prevent, stop
impenetrable impenetrable
impensado unexpected
imperar to rule over; to overlook
imperdonable unpardonable
imperial imperial; soldier of the emperor
imperio empire; domination, sway
imperioso imperious
impertinencia impertinence; impertinent words
imperturbado undisturbed
ímpetu impetus; rushing, headlong motion
impetuoso impetuous
impiedad impiety, lack of piety
impío impious; pitiless, heartless
implacable implacable, relentless
implorar to beseech, implore
imponente impressive
imponer to impose
importar to matter, be important; to be at stake
importunar to importune, bother
importunidad persistence, importunity, annoyance
importuno importunate, persistent, annoying
imposibilitado prevented
impostor impostor
impotencia impotence; weakness; inability
imprecación imprecation
impregnar to impregnate
imprescindible indispensable
impresionar to affect
imprevisión recklessness
imprevisor improvident
imprevisto unforeseen
imprimir to impress, print
ímprobo dishonorable; difficult, laborious
impropio unbecoming, unfitting
improviso unexpected; **de** —— unexpectedly
impudente shameless; thoughtless: impudent
impúdico immodest
impugnable inexpugnable, unconquerable
impulsar to impel
impulso impulse; **a** ——**s de** by force of
impune unpunished
impuro impure
inacabable unending
inaccesible inaccessible

inadvertencia unawareness, unpreparedness
inadvertido unwarned, unaware
inagotable inexhaustible
inanición inanition, weakness caused by hunger
inanimado inanimate
inasequible unattainable
inaudito unheard of
inaugurar to inaugurate
incansable tireless
incapaz incapable
incendiar to burn
incendio fire; flame
incensario incense burner
incentivo incentive; impulse
incesable unceasing
incesante incessant
incienso incense
incitar to incite
inclinación inclination; love
inclinado bent; resting; inclined
inclinar to bend down, bow; to win (over); ——se to take an inclination; ——se a to have an inclination for, be inclined
ínclito illustrious
incluso including
incógnito unknown, nameless
incoherente incoherent
incomodar to make uncomfortable; to disturb; ——se to become angry
incomodidad discomfort
incompatible incompatible
incomprensible incomprehensible
inconexo unconnected, incoherent
inconsciente unconscious
inconsecuencia inconsistency
inconsistente unsubstantial
inconsolable inconsolable
inconstante inconstant, fickle
inconveniencia undesirability; unsuitability
inconveniente *n.* objection; unpleasantness; disagreeable aspect; *adj.* objectionable
incorporarse to sit up; to stand up; to join
incorpórea bodyless
incorrección inaccuracy; breaking of the rules
increado uncreated
incredulidad incredulity
incrédulo incredulous
increíble unbelievable
increpar to rebuke, reproach
incruento bloodless
inculto uncultivated; uncultured
incumbencia task
incurrir to incur; to commit
indagación investigation
indagar to find out; to investigate
indecente indecent, low
indecible unspeakable
indeciso undecided
indecoroso unbecoming; bad-mannered
indefectible unfailing
indescriptible indescribable
indeterminado indeterminate, vague
indiano Spaniard who had spent some time in the American colonies and returned to Spain
indicar to point out, indicate
índice index
indicio indication, sign
indigencia poverty, indigence
indigestar to give indigestion
indignado indignant
indigno unworthy
indio Indian; American
indirecte indirectly
indiscreto indiscreet
indisculpable inexcusable
indispensable indispensable
indispuesto indisposed, ill
indistinto vague, indiscriminate
individuo individual; member
índole nature
indolente indolent
inducir to induce, persuade
indudable without doubt, certain
indulgencia indulgence
indulgente indulgent; compassionate
indulto pardon
indumentario pertaining to clothes
industria industry; trick
industriar to scheme
industrioso industrious; crafty
inédito unpublished
ineducado uncultured, unpolished
inefable ineffable, inexpressible
ineficaz ineffectual
ineluctable inescapable, irresistible
ineludible unavoidable
inepcia incompetency
ineptitud ineptitude
inercia inertia; laziness; immobility
inerme unarmed, defenseless
inesperado unexpected
inestabilidad instability
inexperto inexperienced
inexplicable unexplainable, inexplicable
inextinguible inextinguishable; ceaseless
infamante insulting, defaming
infamar to defame
infame infamous, base
infamia infamy, base thing
infancia infancy
infanta princess
infantazgo rank *or* estate of prince *or* princess
infante prince
infantería infantry
infantil childish, infantile
infantina little princess
infatigable indefatigable
infección infection; corruption
infecto tainted; stagnant
infeliz unhappy
inferir (ie) to infer
infestar to pollute
inficionar to infect, poison
infidelidad unfaithfulness, infidelity
infidencia broken pledge, treachery
infiel faithless, unfaithful
infierno hell
infiltrar to infiltrate, seep (into)
infinito infinity
inflamable inflammable; easily stirred
inflamado flaming
inflamar to kindle, inflame
inflar to inflate; to swell
influir to influence; to inspire
influjo influence
información information; (judicial) investigation
informante appraiser

informar to inform; to give evidence
informe report; *plu.* news, information
infortunio misfortune
infractor violator
infringir to infringe
infundado unfounded, untrue
infundio trickery, deceit
infundir to instill
ingeniero engineer
ingenio cleverness; genius; intelligence
ingenioso ingenious, clever; *arch.* insane, mad
ingénito innate
ingente huge
ingenuidad ingenuousness
ingenuo ingenuous
inglés English; (*slang*) money lender
ingratitud ingratitude
ingrato ungrateful
ingreso admission
inhabitable uninhabitable
inicial initial
iniciar to initiate, begin
iniciativa initiative
inicuo iniquitous
iniquidad iniquity, foul deed
injerto graft
injuria insult
injuriar to insult
injurioso insulting
injusto unjust; unworthy
inmaculado immaculate, spotless, pure
inmarchitable unwithering, evergreen
inmarchito unwithered
inmaterial incorporeal
inmediación *plu.* neighborhood
inmediato next, nearby
inmemorial immemorial
inminencia imminence
inmodestia lack of modesty
inmoralidad immorality
inmotivado unmotivated
inmóvil motionless
inmundicia filth; filthy hole
inmundo foul, filthy, unclean
inmutable immutable, unchangeable
innecesario unnecessary
innegable undeniable
inocente innocent
inopinado unexpected
inoportuno inopportune
inquebrantable irrevocable
inquietar to worry, disquiet, disturb; **——se** to worry
inquieto worried, disturbed; restless
inquietud worry; restlessness; problem
inquilino, -a renter, tenant; householder
inquirir (ie) to inquire
insano unhealthy
inseguro uncertain; insecure
insensatez senselessness
insensato senseless, foolhardy
insensible unfeeling
insidia ambush, snare
insigne famous, renowned
insignia insignia
insinuante insinuating
insistencia persistence
insistir to insist; **—— en** to emphasize; to harp on
insolente insolent
insolvencia lack of payment; insolvency
insomnio sleeplessness, insomnia
insoportable unbearable, insupportable
inspeccionado overlooked
inspiración inspiration
inspirar to inspire
instable unstable
instalar to install
instancia insistence, urging
instantáneo instantaneous
instante instant
instar to urge
instintivo instinctive
instinto instinct
instituído instructed, informed
instrucción education
instruir to instruct
instrumento instrument
insuficiencia lack of learning; lacking
insufrible unbearable, intolerable
ínsula *arch. for* **isla**
insulano islander
ínsulo *humorous for* **insulano**
insulsez insipidity
insultante abusive person
insultar to insult
insulto insult
integridad integrity; entirety
íntegro entire, complete
inteligencia intelligence; understanding
intendente: —— de ejército quartermaster general
intensidad intensity
intentar to try, attempt; to strive; to intend
intento intention, plan, purpose
interés interest; *plu.* money matters, financial interests
interesar to interest; to be important
interior interior, inner
interlocutor interlocutor, one who takes part in a conversation
intermediario middle man
intermedio intermediate
internarse en to penetrate, enter within
interpelación demand for an explanation
interpelar to appeal to, speak to
interpolar to interpolate; to assert
interponer to interpose
interpretar to interpret
intérprete interpreter
interrogar to interrogate, question
interrumpir to interrupt
intervalo interval
intervenir to intervene, take part; to play a part
intimar to become intimate
intimidad intimacy
intimo, -a intimate
intranquilo worried
intransitable impassable
intrépido intrepid
intricar *arch.* to make intricate
intriga plot, intrigue
intrincado involved, complicated
intríngulis (*slang*) hidden drive, mystery, 'trick'
introducir to usher in; to introduce; **——se (en)** to enter, penetrate; to extend
intruso intrusive
intuición intuition
inumerabilidad infinite number
inundación flood
inundar to inundate, flood
inútil useless
inutilizado disabled
invalidar to invalidate
inválido crippled, lame

invencible invincible, unconquerable
invención invention; trick, stratagem; cleverness; composition
inventar to invent
inventario inventory
inventivo inventive, clever
inverecundia shamelessness
inverosímil untrue; unbelievable
invertir (ie) to invest
invicto never conquered
invierno winter
inviolable inviolable, inviolate
invocación invocation
invocar to invoke, call upon
invulnerable invulnerable
ir to go; **me va la vida en ello** my life is at stake; **no va mucho en esto** this isn't very important
ira ire, wrath
iracundo wrathful
irascible irascible
irradiación radiation
irradiar to radiate
irrealizable unattainable
irreflexivo unthinking
irregularidad irregularity
irreverente irreverent
irrevocable irrevocable; unavoidable
irritado angered
irritarse to become angry
irrupción bursting into; invasion
isla island
islote *aug. of* **isla**
itálico Italian
ítem item; also; —— **más** also, furthermore
izquierdo left; **a la izquierda** to the left; **de izquierdas** leftist, radical

J

ja ha!
jabalí wild boar
jaca pony
jácara folk song (about deeds of violence)
jacarandaina ruffians
jacarandina ruffians
jacarear to sing; **jácaras** to have a noisy good time
jaco pony; nag
jactancia boasting
jactarse de to boast of
jadeante panting
jaez trappings (for horse); kind
jalear to urge on dancers by clapping
jaleo high time, excitement; type of peasant dance
jalma pack-saddle
jamelgo nag
jamón ham; —— **en dulce** boiled ham
jamugas side-saddle
jaque bully
jaqueca headache, migraine
jaquita *dim. of* **jaca**
jarana carousal
jardín garden
jarra jug, pitcher
jarrazo blow with jar
jarro pitcher, jug
jaspe jasper (an opaque colored variety of quartz)
jaula cage
jauría pack of hounds
jayán giant, burly fellow
jazmín jasmine
jazminero jasmine bed
jefe chief, head man, leader, boss; important person
jerarquía hierarchy, rank
Jeremías Jeremiah
jerez sherry
jerga serge, dark-colored cloth; jargon
jergón pallet, straw mattress
jeringado (*slang*) blasted, cursed
Jesú heavens!
jícara (chocolate) cup; (*slang*) nut, bean, head
jilguero linnet
jineta a style of horsemanship; **a la** —— in fancy style; **de** —— mounted
jinete rider, horseman
jipío blubbering, sobbing
jira *see* **gira**
jirón shred
jofaina wash basin
jornada act; journey, day's trip, expedition; circumstance
jornalero day laborer
Jove Jove, Jupiter
jovenzuelo *dim. of* **joven**
jovialidad gaiety
joya jewel
joyel piece of jewelry
joyero jeweler
ju whew!
jubileo jubilee, festival; indulgence
júbilo joy
jubón doublet
Judea Judea
judía green bean; bean
judío Jew; skin-flint
juego game; gambling; set; **dar** —— to mesh, gear in with
juez judge
jugador gambler; player
jugar (ue) to play; to gamble
juglar minstrel
jugo juice
juguete plaything, toy; **de** —— toylike
juicio judgment; good sense; **sano** —— right mind
juicioso sensible
jumento ass, donkey
junco rush, reed, cane
juntamente together; at the same time
juntar to join; to gather; **——se** to meet, come together
junto together; at the same time; *arch. plu.* both; all
jurado court (of law); judge
jurador blasphemous
juramento oath, pledge
jurar to swear
jurisdicción jurisdiction
justa joust
justador tilter, jouster
justicia justice; judge; police; court
justiciero giver of justice
justificar to justify
justo just, proper; precise(ly); **al mes** —— just a month after; **el Justo** the Just One, Jesus
juvenil youthful
juventud youth
juzgado court (of law)
juzgar to judge; to believe

K

kilo kilogram
kilómetro kilometer

L

laberinto labyrinth, maze
labia 'gift of gab'
labio lip
laboriosidad industry
laborioso industrious

labrado wrought; carved; built
labrador farmer, peasant
labradora farm girl; farmer's wife
labrandera seamstress, embroiderer
labranza farming
labrar to embroider
labriego *n.* farmer; *adj.* of a farmer
lacayo lackey
lacayuelo *dim. of* **lacayo**
lacerado miserable
laceria hardship; miserable portion
lacerio misery
lacónico laconical
laconismo laconism, brevity of speech
lacrimoso tearful, lachrymose
ladearse to move to one side
ladera side, slope
ladino sly; astute
lado side
ladrar to bark
ladrido bark, barking
ladrón, -a thief; **cueva de ——es** nest of thieves
lagar wine press
lago lake
lágrima tear
lagrimear to weep
lamentar to lament; **——se** to lament
lamento lament
lamer to lick; to lap
lámina engraving, print
lámpara lamp
lampiño beardless
lana wool
lance affair; difficult position; affair of honor; occasion; matter
lancero lancer
languidez languor
lánguido languid
lanteja *arch. for* **lenteja** lentil
lanzar to throw, cast; to give forth
lanzón short thick lance
largar to come out with; to let fly; to drive away; **——se** to get out; 'to light out'
largo long; **a lo —— de** along; through; **pasar de ——** to pass without stopping
larguillo *dim. of* **largo** longish
lástima pity; *plu.* lamentations; griefs
lastimado pitiful, poor
lastimar to pain, hurt, wound
lastimero pitiful, piteous
lastimoso pitiful
latania latania palm
latero (*slang*) annoying
latido beat; throbbing
latigazo blow with a whip
látigo whip
latino Roman, latin
latir to beat; to bark
laúd lute
laureado crowned
laurel laurel
lauréola mezereon (flowering shrub)
lauro laurel
lavabo washbowl and pitcher, wash stand
lavandera laundress
lazo knot; snare; bond; ribbon, ornament
lealmente loyally; truly
lealtad loyalty
lebrel greyhound
lector reader
lectura reading
lecho couch, bed
lechoso milky
lechuga lettuce, head of lettuce
lechuza barn owl
legajo bundle; sheaf; file (of papers)
legal *arch. for* **leal**
legalizar to legalize
legión legion, Roman regiment
legislador legislator, lawgiver
legítima inheritance
legítimo legitimate
lego *n.* lay brother; layman; *adj.* lay, secular; *fig.* uneducated, uninstructed
legua league
leído well-read
lejanía distance
lejano distant, far
lejos: a lo —— in the distance
lema motto
lencero linen seller
lengua tongue; language; **con media ——** stammering
lenguaje speech, language
lentejuela sequin
lentitud slowness
lento slow
leño firewood, wood
león lion
leona lioness
lercha wooden stringer
letal lethal
letanía litany, religious chant
letra letter; words; letter of credit
letrado educated, learned
letrero sign
levadura yeast, leaven
leve light; slight
levita Prince Albert coat
levitilla *dim. of* **levita**
ley law; rule; obligation; **a toda ——** under all circumstances; **de baja ——** of low standard; **de la mejor ——** of best quality, unsurpassable
leyenda legend
leyente reader
liar to bind, fasten
libar to suck
libelo slander, libel
liberal liberal; generous
libertar to free
libertinaje licentiousness
libra pound; **entran pocos en ——** are few and far between
libraco *aug. of* **libro**
librado: bien —— successful, lucky
librar to free; **——se** to deliver to, turn over to
librea livery
librecultista freethinker
librepensador *n.* freethinker; *adj.* skeptical
librería bookstore
libreta loaf of bread weighing a pound
licencia leave, furlough; permission
licenciado licentiate, bachelor of laws
licencioso wanton
lícito lawful; permissible
licor liquid; liquor
lid fight, battle
lidiar to fight, struggle
liebre hare
lienzo linen cloth; canvas
liga birdlime
ligadura binding
ligar to bind

ligereza swiftness; lightness; ease; thoughtlessness, lack of foresight
ligero light; swift, fast; slender; fine, delicate
lima lime
limar to file (down), make smooth
límite limit; boundary, border
limosna alms
limosnero *n.* almoner, almsgiver; *adj.* charitable
limpiar to clean, wipe off
límpido limpid
limpieza cleanliness; cleaning; clarity; emptiness
limpio clean; clear, straightforward; **poner en ——** to make a clear copy; to set aright; **sacar en ——** to see clearly
linaje lineage, family; kind
linajudo of noble descent
lince lynx
linde boundary
lindeza beauty; **a las mil ——s** very beautifully
lindo pretty, beautiful, handsome; fine; **de lo ——** in fine style
lino linen
lío bundle, roll; tangle, mixup
lira lyre
lirio lily
lisiado crippled
liso smooth
lisonja flattery; caress
lisonjear to flatter; to fondle
lisonjero flattering
listo ready; clever
listón ribbon, tape
lisura smoothness
litera litter
literato author, literary man
litografía lithograph
litúrgico liturgical, of the liturgy
liviandad licentiousness; frivolity
liviano frivolous; licentious; slight, light, faint
lívido livid, pale
loa praise; laudable reputation
loar to praise
lobo, -a wolf
lóbrego gloomy
local *n.* locale; office
localidad place; seat (in theater)
loco mad; extravagant
locuacidad loquacity
locuaz loquacious
locura madness; mad idea
lodo mud
logaritmo logarithm
lograr to attain, get; to succeed in
logro success; attainment
loma ridge
lomo back; loin
lona canvas
longaniza sausage
longura length
lontananza distance
loor praise, acclaim
loriga armor, cuirass
loro parrot
losa flagstone; stone slab; tombstone
lotería lottery; **caerle a uno la ——** to win the lottery
loza china
lozanía vigor; freshness; luxuriance
lozano strong, brisk
lúbrico lewd
lucero bright start; morning star
lucidez lucidity; brilliance
lucido brilliant
luciente bright
Lucifer Lucifer
lucimiento brilliance
lucir to shine; to show, show off
lucrarse to enrich oneself; to make a killing
lucha fight, struggle
luchador fighter
luchar to struggle, fight
luego immediately; afterwards; **desde ——** immediately; of course
luengo long
lueñe *arch.* distant
lugar place; village; occasion
lugareño, -a *n.* villager; *adj.* rustic
lúgubre lugubrious
lujo luxury
lujoso luxurious
lujuria lust
lujurioso lustful
lumbre fire; light; **echar ——** to burn (with fever)
lumbrera luminary
luminaria illumination
luminoso luminous, bright
lustre luster, brilliance
lustro period of five years
lustroso shiny, glossy, lustrous
luto mourning
luz light; intelligence; **de cortas luces** of little intelligence

LL

llaga sore; wound
llagar to wound
llama flame; light
llamado so-called
llamar to call; to knock; to ring
llamativo seductive
llanamente plainly
llano *n.* plain; *adj.* flat, level; clear, evident; plain, smooth
llanto weeping, tears
llanura plain
llave key
llavecita *dim. of* **llave**
llavín key
llegada arrival
llegar to arrive; **—— a** (*followed by infinitive*) to come to; to go as far as; **——se** to approach
llenar to fill; to fulfill; to cover
llevadero bearable
llevador *adj.* capable of bearing, long suffering
llevar to take, carry; to take away; to lead; to wear (clothes); **—— a mal** to take badly; **—— dos días, tres meses,** etc. to have been two days, three months, etc.
lloricón whining
lloro weeping, tears
llorón weeping
lloroso tearful, weeping
llovizna drizzle
lluvia rain

M

maceta flower-pot
macilento withered; pale; emaciated
macizo robust, husky
mácula stain
macho *n.* mule; *adj.* male

madeja skein; **coser madejillas** to tie up skeins
madera wood
madero beam
madrastra stepmother
madre mother; —— **política** mother-in-law
madreselva honeysuckle
madriguera rabbit warren
madrugada early morning
madrugador *n.* early riser; *adj.* early rising
madrugar to rise early; to arrive early
madurar to mature, ripen
madurez ripeness; maturity
maduro ripe; mature
maestra teacher; boss (*slang*)
maestrante member of an aristocratic riding club
maestre grand master (of religious order)
maestrescuela rector
maestría skill
maestro, -a master, teacher; expert
Magdalena Madeline; Mary Magdalen
magia magic
mágico magic
magín mind, imagination
magistral masterly
magnánimo magnanimous
magnético magnetic
magnificar to magnify
magnificencia magnificence; generosity
magnitud magnitude, immensity
mago, -a enchanter; **reyes magos** Magi, Wise Men
magullado mauled, bruised
Mahoma Mohammed
maitines matins (a church service)
majada fold
majadería silly speech *or* act
majestad majesty
majestuoso majestic
majo *n.* a dandy and bully of the lower classes in Andalucía; *adj.* elegant, dressed up
majuelo new vine
mal *n.* evil; ailment, sickness; misfortune; trouble
malacondicionado surly, disagreeable
malandante unfortunate
malaventurado unfortunate
maldad wickedness; *plu.* evil deeds
maldecir to curse
maldiciente *n.* slanderer; *adj.* slandering
maldición curse
maldito cursed
maleante villainous
maledicencia slander, calumny
maleta suitcase, bag
malévolo malevolent
maleza thicket
malhadado bewitched, cursed
malhechor evil-doer, criminal
malhumorado bad-humored
malicia malice, wickedness, perversity
malicioso malicious; sly; mischievous
maligno malign, evil
malmascado badly chewed
malograr to come to an untimely end
malquerencia ill-will
maltratado bruised
maltratar to abuse, mistreat; to wear out
maltrecho battered
malva mallow
malvado wicked
malla mail, armor
mamar to suckle
mamarracho grotesque figure, sight
mamotreto monstrosity
manada swarm; flock
manantial spring (of water); source
manar to well forth, spring forth
mancebo *n.* youth; *adj.* youthful
mancilla spot, blot
mancillar to stain
manco maimed; one-armed; one-handed
Mancha, La the southeast district of Castilla la Nueva
mancha stain, blot, spot
manchar to spot, stain
manchego from la Mancha
manchón *aug. of* **mancha**
mandado order
mandamiento commandment
mandar to send; to order; **como Dios manda** proper(ly), fitting(ly)
mandato command, order
mandil cloth (for wiping down horses)
mando command; power
manejar to manage; handle; to drive
manejo management
manera manner, means; **de** —— *arch.* in such a way; **a** —— **de** like
manga sleeve; ——**s de camisa** shirt sleeves
mangoneo meddling
manía mania, craze, whim
manicomio insane asylum
manifestación manifestation
manifestar (ie) to state; to show, manifest
manifiesto manifest
manjar dish, portion (of food)
mano hand; front foot (of animal); **tener buena** —— to be skillful; **tener mala** —— to be unskillful
manojo bundle, sheaf
manotada blow (with hand); **dar** ——**s** to paw the ground
manotazo blow (with hand)
mansedumbre gentleness, meekness
mansión dwelling place, mansion
manso gentle; quiet
manta blanket
manteca butter
mantel tablecloth
mantener to maintain, support, keep, sustain
mantenimiento maintenance; sustenance
mantilla light scarf worn on head
manto robe; mantle, cloak
mantón shawl
manuscrito manuscript
manzano apple tree
maña skill; cunning; trick; evil trait
mañana morning; tomorrow; **muy de** —— very early in the morning
mañoso clever
máquina machine; structure; fabric; apparatus
maquinal mechanical
maquinar to scheme
maravedí penny, small coin

maravilla marvel, wonder; **a las mil** ——**s** marvelously
maravillar to marvel; ——**se** to be surprised; ——**se de** to marvel at
maravilloso marvelous
marca brand
marcar to mark; to be noticed
marcial martial
marco frame; mark (about ½ pound)
marcha march; movement, progress; **en** —— en route **romper la** —— to set out
marchar to go away; to walk; to march
marchitar to wither
marchito withered
marea tide
mareante causing dizziness, heady
marear to make seasick; to make dizzy
marfil ivory
margen margin; shore
marido husband
marinero *n.* sailor, mariner; *adj.* seafaring
marina seascape, picture of the sea
marino of the sea
mariposa butterfly
mármol marble
marqués marquis
marquesa marchioness
marron glacé (*French*) candied chestnut
marroquí Moroccan
marrullero whining
Marte Mars
martillo hammer
mártir martyr
martirio martyrdom; suffering
martirizar to martyr; to torture
más: de —— unneeded, superfluous
masa mass; dough
mascarada masquerade; disguise
mástel *arch. for* **mástil** mast
mastín mastiff
mastranzo mint
mata underbrush
matadero slaughter-house
matador killer, assassin
matanza slaughtering, killing
matar to kill
materia matter; material
material material; **en lo** —— with respect to physical things; **lo** —— the flesh, the physical being
materialismo materialism; specific nature; material gain
materialista materialistic
materializarse to become materialistic
materialmente physically, in the flesh
maternal maternal; native
matinal morning
matiz shade (of color)
matizar to tint
matón ruffian, bully
matorral thicket
matraca nonsense, twaddle
matrimonio marriage; married couple
matrona matron
matutino morning
maulería trickery
mayonesa mayonnaise
mayor *n.* major; *adj.* greater, greatest; larger, largest; higher; important; chief; *plu.* betters; **persona** —— grown-up person
mayorazgo *n.* estate (inherited by eldest son); eldest son; *adj.* eldest
mayordomo steward
mayormente principally, especially
mazmorra dungeon
mazo hammer
mazorca ear of corn; bunch
mecachis the deuce!
mecánico mechanical
mecer to rock; to sway
mechón lock
media stocking
mediado: a ——**s de** toward the middle of
mediano medium; medium-sized; moderate; mediocre
mediante by means of, through, by virtue of
mediar to intervene
medicamento medicine
médico doctor
medida measure; **a** —— **que** as, in proportion as
medio *n.* means; middle; *adj.* half; **en** —— between
mediodía noon; south
mediquillo *dim. of* **médico**
medir (i) to measure; **vara de** —— yardstick
meditabundo pensive, meditative
meditar to meditate
medrar to get ahead, progress
medroso fearful; frightening
mejilla cheek
mejor: —— **que** —— better than ever; **estar** —— **con** to be on better terms with
mejora improvement
mejorar to better, improve
mejoría improvement
melancolía melancholy
melena mane; long hair
melifluo sweet, honeyed
melindroso prudish
melocotón peach
melodía melody, melodiousness
melón melon
melosidad honeyed tone
meloso honeyed
mella nick; impression
mellar to nick
membrado robust, husky
memorial proposition, brief (of proposal); **echar** ——**es** to make a proposition
mención mention
mencionar to mention
mendicante *n.* beggar; *adj.* mendicant, begging; of a beggar
mendicidad begging
mendigar to beg
mendigo, -a beggar; —— **de punto** beggar having a regular station
mendrugo crust
menear to move from side to side; to shake; to stir; to wiggle; to manage, direct; to move
meneo swaying motion
menester need; occupation; **haber** *or* **tener** —— to need; **ser** —— to be necessary
menesteroso needy
mengano what's-his-name
mengua lack, need; flaw, shortcoming, fault; shame
menguado reduced, slight; short; stupid; exhausted
menguar to lack; to diminish; **menguado de** lacking in

meníngeo pertaining to meningitis
menor younger; smaller, smallest, slightest; less; **—— edad** youthful age
menos: por lo —— at least; **venir a ——** to fall into bad circumstances
menospreciar to despise, scorn
mensaje message
mensajería message carrying
mensajero messenger
mensual monthly
mentar (ie) to mention
mente mind
mentecato *n.* fool; *adj.* foolish, crack-brained
mentido false
mentir (ie) to lie
mentira lie; error; **parece ——** it seems impossible
mentís: dar un —— a to give the lie to, accuse of lying
mentor mentor, counselor
menudear to become frequent, be frequent
menudo small, tiny; short; **a ——** often, frequently; **por ——** in detail
mequetrefe jackanapes
mercader merchant
mercado market
mercancía merchandise, goods
mercantil commercial
mercar to purchase
merced grace; favor; *arch.* thanks; **—— a** thanks to; **a —— de** under the influence of; a prey to; **hacer ——** to spare
mercenario mercenary
merecedor meritorious, deserving
merecer to merit, deserve
merecido due, deserts
merecimiento merit; rank; *plu.* deserts
merendero summer house (for picnics)
merendona *aug. of* **merienda**
meridiano noonday; southern
meridional southern
merienda snack; picnic; lunch
merina merino sheep
merino merino, kind of wool cloth
mérito merit
merluza hake
mermar to diminish
mero mere
merodeo marauding
mesa table, desk; branch, subdivision (of a government office)
mesar to tear (the hair)
Mesías Messiah
mesmo *arch. for* **mismo**
mesón inn
mesonero innkeeper
mestizo half-breed
mesura restraint
meta goal
metafísico *n.* metaphysician; *adj.* metaphysical
metal metal; timbre
metamorfosis metamorphosis, change
meter to put, put in, place; **——se a** to set oneself up as; **——se con** to meddle with, interfere with, pick a quarrel with
metimiento familiarity, intimate dealings
metrificar to compose poetry
metro meter
mezcla mixture; **de ——** mixed color, spotted
mezclar to mix, mingle
mezcolanza mixture
mezquino wretched; mean; puny
mezquita mosque
miaja bit
miasma miasma, infected air
microscópico microscopic
miel honey
miembro member; limb
mientes *arch.* mind; **parar ——** to fix one's attention on
mies grain; wheat
miga crumb; soft part of bread; **hacer ——s** to become *or* be friends
migaja crumb
milagro miracle
milagroso miraculous
milenario thousand year old; age-old
milicia troops, army; militia
militar *n.* soldier; officer (of armed forces); *adj.* military
milla mile
millar thousand; **a ——es** by thousands
mimar to indulge
mimbre willow
mimbrón *aug. of* **mimbre**
mimo indulgence; fondness
mina mine
minero spring (of water)
mínimo very small; smallest degree
ministro minister
minucioso minute, diminutive; thorough
minúsculo tiny, minute
minuta minutes; notes; copy
miopía near-sightedness
mira aim, object
mirada look, glance, gaze
mirado circumspect, strait-laced; **bien ——** well regarded; **mal ——** with evil intent
miramiento consideration; circumspection
mirar to look at; to pay attention to; *fig.* to consider, take into consideration, think; **—— a** to aim at
mirilla peephole
mirón onlooker
mirra myrrh
misa mass
miserable base; miserable, wretched, unfortunate
miserere Miserere (a religious chant)
miseria misery; baseness, meanness; poverty; filth; vermin; miserable amount
misericordia pity, compassion, mercy
misericordioso merciful
miseriuca wretched trait
mísero miserable; mean
misión mission
misionero missionary
misterio mystery
misticismo mysticism
místico mystic
mitad half; mid-point; **cara ——** 'better half'
mitigar to mitigate
mito myth
mixto mixed
mobiliario furniture, household goods, furnishings
mocedad youth
mocito *dim. of* **mozo**

moco mucus; drivel; **llorar a —— y baba** to cry violently
mocoso sniveling; (*slang*) small boy
moda style, mode
modal *plu.* manners
modelado modeling
modelo model
moderado moderate
moderar to moderate
modificar to modify
modo manner; good manners; sort; *plu.* means; **a —— de** a sort of, something like; **de —— que** so that; **de todos ——s** in any case
modorra stupor
modosito *dim. of* **modoso**
modoso modest; well-bred
modular to modulate
mofa mockery
mofarse to mock
mohín grimace; pouting expression
mohino peevish, pouting
moho mold; rust
mojama dried fish
mojar to soak, wet
molde form; **letras de ——** type, print
mole mass
moler (ue) to grind; to press; to beat
molestar to bother
molestia bother, trouble, annoyance
molicie softness
molienda grinding
molino mill; **—— de viento** windmill
mollar soft; simple
mollera head, pate
momentáneo momentary
momento: al —— immediately, instantly; **por ——s** at times
momia mummy
mona *n.* ape, monkey; **dormir la ——** to sleep off one's drunkenness
monacal monastic
monarca monarch
monasterio monastery
mondo clean; unembellished; trimmed
moneda coin; **monedita de veintiuno y cuartillo** a gold coin withdrawn from circulation in 1786, worth 21¼ **reales; casa de la ——** the Mint
monería cute action
monigote lay brother; poorly painted figure
monja nun
monje monk
mono *n.* ape; *adj.* cute
monomanía mania
monotonía monotony
monótono monotonous
monserga gibberish
monstruo monster; freak
montado a pelo on the ragged edge
montar to ride (horseback); to mount; to cock (a firearm); to set (precious stones)
montaraz wild; mountain
monte hill, mountain; forest, woods; card game; **vestido de ——** in hunting costume; **Monte de Piedad** government pawnshop and savings bank
montepío savings account (in the Monte de Piedad); savings
montero hunter
montiña mountain side
montón pile; lot
moño bun (of hair)
mora blackberry
morada dwelling place, house
morado purple
morador dweller
moral *m.* black mulberry tree; *f.* ethics; *adj.* mental; moral
moralista moralist
morar to dwell
morazo *aug. of* **moro**
morbidez smoothness
morcilla blood pudding; **—— de sesos** head pudding
mordelón biting
moder (ue) to bite
mordida bite
moreno dark; dark-skinned
morería Moorish camp; Moorish quarter (of city); Moorish people
moribundo dying
morilla *dim. of* **mora** Moorish woman
morisco *n.* a Mohammedan converted to Christianity; *adj.* Moorish; **a la morisca** Moorish fashion
moro *n.* Moor; *adj.* Moorish
morrión helmet (without attached parts), morion
morrocotudo dandy, swell
mortaja shroud
mortecino sickly; wan; deathly
mortificación mortification
mortificar to mortify
mosca fly; **—— de luz** firefly
moscón horsefly; annoying person
mostaza mustard
mosto grape juice; juice
mostrador counter
mostrar (ue) to show
mostrenco stupid
mota speck; burl, knot of thread
mote nickname; offensive title; motto, device
motejar to call offensive names; to mock
motivo motive, reason, cause
mover (ue) to move; to wage (war)
movible movable
moza lass, girl
mozo lad, youth; servant; **—— de caballo** groom, stable boy; **—— de cuerda** porter
mozuela *aug. of* **moza**
mucho: de —— much; **ni —— menos; ni con ——** nor far from it; **qué ——** what wonder
muchedumbre multitude
muda cosmetic
mudable fickle; undecided
mudanza change; move; fickleness; figure (of a dance); **estar de ——** to be in the process of moving
mudar to change; **——se** to be fickle
mudo dumb; silent
mueble *n.* piece of furniture; *plu.* furniture; furnishings; *adj.* movable; **capital ——** personal property
mueca grimace
muela tooth; molar
muelle *n.* spring; dock, pier; *adj* soft
muerto dead; *fig.* half dead, tired out
muestra sample; sign; face (of clock)

mugre filth
mugriento filthy
mujercita *dim. of* **mujer**
mujeriego womanish; **a mujeriegas** side-saddle
mujeril womanly
mujerona *aug. of* **mujer**
mula mule
mulato mulatto
mulero muleteer; servant in charge of mules
muleta crutch
mulo mule
multitud crowd, multitude
mullido soft
mundanal worldly
mundano worldly
mundo world; high society; **gran ——** high society
municipio city, municipality
munificencia generosity, munificence
muñeco doll; puppet
muralla wall, city wall
murciano from Murcia
murciélago bat
murmullo murmur
murmuración gossip; slander
murmurador gossiper
murmurar to murmur; to gossip, backbite, slander
muro wall
murria melancholy
mus a card game
musa muse
musculatura muscles
músculo muscle
musculoso muscular
musgo moss
música music; tune
músico *n.* musician; *adj.* musical
muslo thigh
mustio sad
musulmán Moslem
mutilar to mutilate
mutuo mutual

N

nabo turnip
nácar mother-of-pearl
nacer to be born
nacimiento birth
nadar to swim
nado swimming; **a ——** by swimming; **arrojarse a ——** to strike out swimming
naipe playing card
nalga buttock
napolitano of Naples, Neapolitan
naranja orange
naranjo orange tree
nariz nose; *plu.* nostrils
narrador narrator
narrar to narrate, tell
nata cream
natal native
nativo native
natura nature; kind
natural *n.* nature, character; *adj.* native
naturaleza nature
naturalidad naturalness
naufragio shipwreck
náufrago shipwrecked person
navaja razor; clasp knife; **—— de afeitar** razor
nave ship
navegar to sail, navigate
navidad Christmas
navío ship
nazareno Nazarene
neblí falcon
necedad foolishness, stupidity; *plu.* foolish words
necesidad need, necessity
necesitado needy
necio *n.* fool; *adj.* foolish, stupid
negar (ie) to deny; **——se a** to turn a deaf ear to; to refuse
negativa negative; denial; refusal
negociante businessman
negociar to handle
negocio business; affair; deal; matter
negro *n.* Negro; *adj.* black; wretched
nelumbo water lily
nemoroso wooded, bosky
nene baby; child
neófito neophyte, convert
nervioso nervous
neto genuine; pure
neumático airtight, pneumatic
neurosismo neurosis
nevado covered with snow
nevar (ie) to snow
nido nest
niebla mist, fog
nicho niche; grave
nieto grandson
nieve snow
nimiedad prolixity; excess
nimio prolix; enduring, constant
ninfa nymph
Nínive Nineveh
niñería childish thing
niñez childhood
nitidez neatness; whiteness
nítido clean; pure; bright; neat
nivel level
nobleza nobility; generosity
nocturno nocturnal
noche: de —— at night; night; in evening attire
nodriza nurse
nogal walnut tree; walnut wood
nómada nomad
nombramiento appointment, naming
nombrar to name; to appoint
nombre: mal —— depreciatory nickname
nómina appointment
nominativo nominative
non *arch.* no, not; odd (number)
normalizar to become normal
norte north; *fig.* guide; direction
nostalgia nostalgia; yearning
notable remarkable, extraordinary
notar to note
notario notary
noticia report; information; notice; *plu.* news
noticioso aware
notorio evident; notable
novato beginner
novedad novelty; change; innovation; surprise
novel *adj.* novice
novela novel
novelesco storylike, romantic
novelero beginner
novelista novelist
novena novena (series of religious devotions lasting nine days)
novia sweetheart; bride
noviazgo engaged couple; engagement
novio suitor; bridegroom
nube cloud; **poner por** (*or* **en) las ——s** to praise highly, extol

nublar to cloud
nubarrón heavy, dark cloud
núcleo nucleus
nudo knot
nuera daughter-in-law
nueso *arch. for* **nuestro**
nueva *n.* news
nuevo new; **de ——** again, anew
nuez walnut; Adam's apple
nulo null; nil
numantino *n.* inhabitant of Numancia; *adj.* of Numancia
numen god; inspiration
numérico numerical
nuncio messenger
nupcial nuptial
nupcias marriage
nutrimiento nutrition, nourishment
nutrir to nourish

O

obcecado blind; unyielding
obedecer to obey
obediencia obedience
obediente obedient
obelisco obelisk
obispado bishopric
obispo bishop
obligar to oblige; to cause; to place under obligation
obra work; deed
obrar to work; to act
obscurecer to darken
obscuridad darkness; vagueness
obscuro dark; gloomy; stupid (of people); **a obscuras** in the dark
obsequiar to treat; to entertain
obsequias *arch.* obsequies, funeral service
obsequio gift
observante strict
observatorio observatory; lookout
obsesión obsession
obstáculo obstacle
obstante: no —— nevertheless; in spite of
obstinado obstinate
obstinarse to persist; to insist
obstruir to obstruct
ocasión occasion; opportunity; situation; provocation; reason why
ocaso sunset; setting (of sun)
occidente west; occident
océano ocean
ocio idleness; leisure
ociosidad idleness
ocioso idle; useless, vain
octogenario octogenarian
ocultar to hide
ocultis: de —— on the sly
oculto hidden
ocupar to occupy
ocurrencia idea
ocurrir to happen; to occur; **—— a** to take care of; to think of
ochavo coin; *plu.* money
odalisca harem beauty
odiar to hate
odio hatred
odioso odious
ofender to offend; to attack; to insult, to do harm
ofensa offense
oficial officer (of army); official; tradesman
oficina office; (government) job
oficinista office worker; bureaucrat
oficio religious service; job; position; career; trade; political office
oficioso officious; accommodating
ofrecer to offer; **¿Qué se ofrece?** What do you wish?
ofrecimiento offer
ofrenda offer
ofuscar to darken; to confuse
oída hearing; **por ——s** by hearsay
oído ear
ojazo big *or* wide eye
ojeada glance
ojera circle under the eye
ojeriza ill will
ojeroso having rings under the eyes
ojival ogive, Gothic
ola wave
ole come on!; hurray!
oler (ue) to smell
olfatear to sense; to smell
olfativo olfactory
oliente smelling
olímpico Olympic
oliscar to sniff; to seek out; to ferret out
olivar olive grove
olivo olive tree
olmo elm
olor odor, perfume; fragrance; **agua de ——** toilet water; **—— de santo** odor of sanctity
olorcillo *dim. of* **olor**
oloroso fragrant
olvido forgetfulness; oblivion
olla pot; stew; *fig.* food, livelihood
omecillo hate
omitir to omit; to leave undone
omnipotencia omnipotence
omnipotente all-powerful
onda wave
ondulante undulating
ondular to undulate
ontológico ontological, based on the nature of being
onza ounce; a gold coin (worth about $8)
opaco opaque
opalino opalescent
opinante one who holds an opinion
opinión opinion; public opinion; reputation, honor
oponer to oppose
oportuno opportune
opresión pressure
oprimir to oppress; to weigh down; to constrict, choke
oprobio opprobrium; disgrace
óptica optics; **ilusión de ——** optical illusion
optimista optimistic
opuesto *n.* opponent; *adj.* opposite; opposed
opulancia opulence, wealth
opúsculo article, pamphlet
oquedad hollowness
ora now; **ora . . . ora . . .** now . . . now . . .
oración prayer; sentence
oráculo oracle
orador orator
orangután orangutan
orar to pray
oratoria oratory
oratorio oratory, place for prayer
orbe orb, earth
orden *m.* order; **guardia del ——** municipal police; **—— público** police; *f.* order, command; religious order; **recibir las órdenes** to be ordained
ordenación ordaining, ordination

ordenado well-ordered
ordenanza orderly; officers' handbook, manual of arms; **de ——** standard, of the regular issue
ordenar to order; to ordain
ordeñar to milk
ordinario ordinary; unrefined; **de ——** ordinarily
orear to refresh
oreja ear
orejera ear covering
orfandad orphan's estate
organista organist
órgano organ
orgía orgy
orgullo pride
orgulloso proud
oriente East, Orient; luster (of pearls)
origen origin
originar to originate
orilla border, edge; bank; shore
orín rust
oriundo de native to; coming from
ornar to ornament, decorate
orondo filled with vanity
osadía daring
osado bold, daring
osar to dare
oscilar to waver
oscuridad darkness; obscurity
oscuro dark; obscure; unimportant; **a oscuras** in the dark; ignorant
ostentar to show
otero (isolated) hill
otoñal autumnal
otoño autumn
otorgar to grant; **—— testamento** to make a will
otrosí *arch.* likewise
oveja sheep
overo peach-colored, sorrel

P

pabellón canopy
pábulo food; **dar ——** to encourage
pacer to pasture, graze
paciencia patience
paciente patient
pacto pact, agreement
padecer to suffer
padecimiento suffering
padrastro stepfather
padrenuestro Lord's Prayer
padrino godfather; second (of duelist)
padrón column *or* post with inscription
paga payment
pagador one who pays
pagamento payment
paganismo paganism
pagano pagan
pagar to pay; *arch.* to please; **——se de** to be pleased with
pagaré promissory note, I.O.U.
página page
pago: en —— de in payment for
paisaje landscape
paisano *n.* peasant; *adj.* from the same region
paja straw; **silla de ——** cane chair
pajarillo *dim. of* **pájaro**
pájaro bird; (*slang*) fellow, guy
paje page boy
pajecico *dim. of* **paje**
pala spade
palabra word; word of honor; **tomar la ——** to take the floor
palacio palace; mansion
paladar roof of mouth; palate
paladión safeguard; offering to Pallas
palafrén palfrey
palangana wash basin
palco box (in theater)
paletilla shoulder blade
palidecer to grow pale
pálido pale
palillo toothpick
paliza beating
palma palm; hand
palmada blow (with palm of hand), slap, pat; **dar ——s** to clap
palmar palm grove
palmatoria small candlestick
palmetazo slap, blow (with ruler)
palmito dwarf fan palm; (*slang*) (woman's) face *or* figure
palmo span (measure); palm; small amount
palo stick, club; blow (with stick)
paloma dove
palomar dovecot
palomica pigeon
palomino pigeon
palosanto lignum-vitae (a tropical wood)
palpar to feel
palpitación palpitation
palpitante palpitating
palpitar to palpitate, beat
pámpano vine leaf; vine shoot
panadero baker
panal honeycomb; stick of honeycombed sugar for sweetening drinks
pandero tambourine
pánico panic, terror
pantalón trousers, pants
pantano swamp
panteón pantheon, burial crypt
pantera panther
pantorrilla calf (of leg)
pantuflo slipper
pañizuelo handkerchief
paño woolen cloth; cloth; **—— de manos** hand towel; **—— de pared** tapestry
pañolito kerchief
pañuelo handkerchief
papa Pope; *plu.* nonsense
papel paper; role; note; promissory note; *plu.* wallpaper; **—— sellado** legal paper; **hacer un ——** to play a role
papelejo old piece of paper
papelera filing case
papeleta pawn ticket; ticket; paper; card
papelucho *aug. of* **papel** old paper
papilla pap, baby food
paquete package
par pair, couple; even (number); **a la —— con** equal to; **de —— en ——** wide (open); **—— de** next to
par *arch. for* **por**
parabrisa windshield
parada stop
paradero stopping place
paradoja paradox
paradójico paradoxical
parador inn; tenement house
paraíso paradise
paralítico paralytic
paramento adornment
parar to stop; to parry; **to** end; **——se** to stop
parche sticking plaster
Pardillo a kind of wine

pardo dark gray, brown
parecer to seem; to appear; **——se** to appear; **——se a** to resemble; *n.* opinion; **a mi ——** in my opinion
parecido *adj.* similar; *n.* resemblance, likeness; similarity
pared wall
paredilla *dim. of* **pared**
paredón *aug. of* **pared**
pareja pair, couple
parentesco relationship
pariente, -a relative
parihuela stretcher
parir to give birth to
parlanchín chattering, talkative
parlero talkative
parlotear to chatter
paroxismo paroxysm
párpado eyelid
parra grape arbor; vine
párrafo paragraph
parroquia parish church; parish
parte part; cause; place; party (of lawsuit); *plu.* talents, qualities; **de mi ——** on my behalf; **de —— de** on behalf of; **de —— en ——** from one side to the other; **en buena ——** with good intention; **dar ——** to inform; **en mala ——** with bad intention; **en todas ——s, por todas ——s** everywhere
participación sharing, share
participante participant, sharer
participar to share; to inform (of)
partícipe participant
particular special; peculiar; private
partida departure; group; match, game; *arch.* part
partidario partisan
partido game, match; band, party; marriageable person; decision
partir to depart, set out; to split, cut in two; to keep from; to take away; to divide, share
parto birth; confinement; offspring; **profesora en ——s** midwife
parva stack (of wheat ready for threshing)
pasada: de —— on passing
pasado *n.* past; *adj.* passed; last; previous
pasaje passage
pasajero passing, temporary
pasar to pass; to happen; to run through; to lead across; to get along; to swallow; to suffer; to bring; **—— a** to come to be, turn into; **—— de** to go beyond; to be more than; **——lo bien** to get along well; **——se** to bear; **——se al enemigo** to go over to the enemy; **——se sin** to get along without; **——se por** to pass over; **se me pasa** I forget
pasatiempo pastime
pascua festival; **buena ——** what a pleasure
paseante idler
pasear to walk; **——se** to walk, take a walk; to walk up and down; to ride; to travel
paseo walk; ride; **dar un ——** to take a walk; to take a trip; **mandarle a uno a ——** to give someone the gate; to brush him off
pasillo hall
pasión passion; emotion; suffering; illness
pasionado one who suffers
pasitamente softly
pasito softly
pasividad passiveness
pasmar to astonish, surprise; to chill; **——se** to be overcome; to faint; to be surprised
pasmo fainting spell; astonishment
pasmoso astounding
paso step; walk; pace; passage, way, course; difficulty; feat; **a ——** at a walk; **abrir ——** to open a way; **al —— de** in proportion to; **cortar el ——** to intercept, block; **—— contado** measured step; **de ——** in passing, incidentally; **—— tendido** long stride; **sala de ——** antechamber; **salir al ——** to intercept, come to meet.
pasta cookie
pastar to graze
pastel pastry; pie
pasto food; fodder; *fig.* meal; **a ——** with meals
pastor shepherd
pastora shepherdess
pastoril pastoral
pata foot (of animal); shank; **volverle patas arriba** to turn upside down; to defeat
patada kick
pataleo kicking, stamping
pataleta convulsion
patata potato
patatita *dim. of* **patata**
patatús fainting fit
pataza huge foot
patear to stamp one's foot; to kick
patente *n.* patent; mark; *adj.* obvious
paterno paternal
paternostre Lord's prayer
patíbulo scaffold, gallows
patiecillo *dim. of* **patio**
patilla sideburn, side whisker
patilludo with sideburns
patitieso stiff-legged; dumbfounded
pato duck
patria fatherland, country
patriarca patriarch
patrimonio patrimony
patrio native, of one's home
patriota *n.* patriot; *adj.* patriotic
patrón patron; patron saint
patrona landlady, woman who runs a boarding house
patrono patron
patulea disorderly band
pausado slow, deliberate
pavesa ember, coal; hot ash
pavimento pavement; stone floor
pavo turkey; **—— real** peacock
pavor fear, terror
payaso clown
paz peace
peal good-for-nothing
peana pedestal
pecado sin
pecador, -a sinner
pecaminoso sinful
pecar to sin
peculio purse
pecuniario pecuniary

pecho chest, bosom, breast; heart; tax; tribute; **tomar a ——** to take to heart; **hacer —— a** to stand up to
pedalear to pedal
pedante pedant
pedantería pedantry; stupidity
pedazo piece, fragment, bit; **—— de ángel** lovable person
pedernal flint
pedestal pedestal
pedestre pedestrian
pedigüeño demanding, grasping, begging
pedir (i) to ask for; to beg
pedrada stoning
pedregoso stony
pedrería jewelry
pedrusco rough stone
pegado stuck on, glued on
pegajoso sticky
pegar to stick; to beat; to press; to set (fire to); to infect, give (a disease); **——se** to be catching (of a disease); **—— gritos** to shout
pegujar small farm
peinar to comb; to dress one's hair
peine comb
pejuguar *see* **pegujar**
pelado plucked; hairless
pelar to pull out (hair); to peel
peldaño step
pelea fight, battle
pelear to fight
pelele nincompoop
peleón strong wine
pelgar ragamuffin; tramp
peligrar to be in peril
peligro danger
peligroso dangerous
pelmazo indigestible; hard to take
pelo hair; **venir al ——** to be very apropos
pelota ball; *jai alai*
pelotera quarrel, fight
pelucona *slang for* **onza**
peluquero hairdresser; barber
pella lump; (*slang*) nest-egg
pelleja hide
pellejo skin, hide
pellizco pinch; **dar ——s** to pinch; to nibble
pena penalty; pain; punishment; sorrow; suffering; **valer la ——** to be worth the trouble; **so —— de** under penalty of; **¡Qué pena!** What a pity!
penado grieved, grieving
penar to grieve
pendencia quarrel; struggle, combat
pender to hang
pendiente *n.* hill, slope; earring; *adj.* pending; hanging; **—— de** dependent on, living on
péndola clock
pendón banner, flag, pennant
penetrar to penetrate; to see; to see through
penitencia penitence; penance
penitente penitent, repentant
penoso painful, difficult
pensamiento thought; intention
pensativo pensive, thoughtful
pensil beautiful garden
pensión pension
penumbra shadow
penumbroso shadowy
penuria penury, poverty
peña rock, crag
peñasco crag
peón foot soldier; **—— de albañil** hod-carrier
peonza top
pepita seed
pepitoria stewed chicken
peplo tunic
pequeñez smallness; petty detail; pettiness
pequeñuelo *dim. of* **pequeño**
pera pear
percal percale
percatarse to observe
perceptible perceptible
percibir to perceive; to receive
percha clothes-hanger, hat tree
perchero hat tree, clothes rack
perder (ie) to lose; to ruin, bring to perdition
perdición perdition; **de ——** wicked
pérdida loss
perdidizo easily lost, subject to being lost
perdido *n.* debauchee, base fellow; *adj.* ruined, in wretched condition; **ratos ——s** spare moments
perdiz partridge
perdulario *n.* wastrel; *adj.* reckless
perdurable enduring, unending, everlasting
perecedero perishable
perecer to perish
peregrinación wandering, peregrination
peregrino *n.* pilgrim; *adj.* strange
perejil parsley
perenne perpetual
pereza indolence, laziness
perezoso lazy
perfidia perfidy, perfidious
pérfido perfidious
perfil profile
perfilar to outline
perforar to pierce
perfumar to perfume
perfume perfume
perfumear to give forth perfume
perfumera maker *or* seller of perfumes
pergamino parchment
pergenio disposition; appearance
pericial expert
perico parrot
periferia edge, periphery
perilla goatee
perímetro perimeter, boundary
período period; sentence
peripecia crisis, unforeseen event
perito skilled, expert
perjudicar to harm
perjuicio prejudice; harm
perjurar to swear, vow
perla pearl; **de ——s** wonderful, perfect
permanecer to remain
permanente permanent
perniquebrar (ie) to break a leg
perpetuador perpetuator
perpetuo perpetual
perplejo perplexed, perplexing
perra dog; **—— chica** five céntimo piece ($\frac{1}{20}$ of a peseta); **—— gorda** ten céntimo piece ($\frac{1}{10}$ of a peseta)
perrillo *dim. of* **perro**

perrita *dim of* **perra; —— de lana** poodle
perro *adj.* vile, base
persecución persecution; **en —— de** chasing
perseguir (i) to pursue; to persecute
perseverancia perseverance
perseverante persevering
perseverar to persevere, continue
persignarse to cross oneself
persistencia insistence, persistence
persistir to persist
personaje person, person of importance, personage; character
personalista centered in the individual
personarse to present oneself
perspectiva perspective; view
perspicacia perspicacity
perspicaz perspicacious
perspicuo perspicacious, clear-sighted
persuadir to persuade
pertenecer to belong
pertinacia persistence, stubbornness
pertinaz pertinacious, persistent, obstinate, opinionated
pertrechar to provide; to arm
perturbador *n.* disturber; *adj.* disturbing
perturbar to disturb
perverso perverse, wicked
pesadilla nightmare
pesado insistent; stupid; heavy
pesadumbre sorrow, trouble
pesar to weigh; to grieve, sadden; to feel sorry about
pesar *n.* sorrow, grief, woe; **a —— de** in spite of; **a —— mío** in spite of myself
pescado fish
pescador fisherman
pescuezo neck
peseta silver coin (1/5 of a **duro)**
pesia oath, curse
peso weight; burden; coin originally worth about a dollar; **tener en ——** to keep in abeyance
pespuntar to backstitch
pesquisa investigation
pesquisar to investigate, snoop
pestaña eyelash
peste plague
pestífero pestiferous
pestillo bolt; latch
petaca cigar case
petición petition; request
petitorio begging
petrificado petrified
petulancia petulance; conceit
petulante insolent
pez *m.* fish; *f.* pitch
piadoso pious; piteous, compassionate
picacho *aug. of* **pico**
picadero riding ring; slaughter-house
picajoso touchy, easily angered
picante ironical, stinging
picar to stick; to sting; to burn (of sun); to vex; to chop up fine; to pick; to spur; **—— en** to border on; to dabble in; **—— por** to go in for; **—— espuelas** to spur
pícaramente in a rascally fashion
picardía low trick
pícaro *n.* rascal, rogue; *adj.* roguish; sly
picaruelo *dim. of* **pícaro**
pico peak; point; corner; bit; talkativeness; mouth
picotear to chat, chatter
picotero chattering, talkative
pie foot; footing, basis; **al —— de la letra** literally
piedad pity; piety; act of mercy
piel fur; skin
pienso *n.* fodder
pierna leg; **hacer ——s** to prance; **dormir a —— suelta** to sleep soundly
pieza piece; way; game, quarry; coin; room; (artillery) piece; **—— de a dos** coin worth two silver **reales** (a fourth of a **duro**); **—— de a ocho** piece-of-eight, **duro**
pila baptismal font
pilar pillar
piloto pilot
piltrafa scrap (of food)
pillete rascal, crook
pillo rogue
pim zing; **—— pam** whizz bang
pimentón red pepper; paprika
pimienta black pepper
pimiento pepper
pinar pine grove
pincel brush
pindonguería trinket, cheap jewel
pingajo rag, tatter
pingo rag
pino pine
pinta edge
pintado excellent
pintar to paint, represent; to color, dye
pintiparado made to order, perfect
pintor painter
pintoresco picturesque
pintura painting, picture
piña pineapple; pine cone
piñón pine nut
piñonate candied pine nuts
pío *n.* chirping; *adj.* pious
piojoso lousy
pipa pipe; cask, hogshead
pique: a —— de at the point of
piquillo bit, small amount
piramidal pyramidal
pirámide pyramid
pirata *n. or adj.* pirate
piropo compliment
piruetear to pirouette
pisada footfall, step
pisar to tread
pisaverde foppish
piso floor; apartment
pisotear to trample underfoot
pista track
pistola pistol
pitañoso gummy
pitillera woman who sells cigarettes *or* works in a cigarette factory
pizarra blackboard
pizca bit, particle
placa badge, insignia
placentero pleasant, pleasing
placer to please; *n.* pleasure
plácido calm, placid
plagado plagued; filthy
plan plan
plancha sheet (of metal)
planchadora laundress
planchar to iron
planeta planet

plano *n.* plane; flat (of sword); **de ——** with the flat of sword; *adj.* flat
planta plant; sole (of foot); ground plan; *fig.* foot; **en ——** up and about
plantación planting
plantar to plant; to set up; to rebuff; **——se** to hurry
plantear to set up; to offer
plantel nursery
plañidero whining
plata silver
plataforma platform; level space
plateado silvery
platear to silver
platero silversmith
plática chat, talk
platicar to chat; to chatter
Platón Plato
platónico Platonic
playa beach, shore
plaza square; place; bull ring; employment, job
plazo time; period of time, term
plazuela small square
plebe populace, common people
plebeyo plebeian
plegar (ie) to fold
plegaria prayer
pleguería fold; roundabout phrase
pleito lawsuit; quarrel
pleno full, complete
pliego folded paper; envelope
pliegue fold; wave
plomo lead
pluguiera *imperfect subjunctive of* **placer**
pluma feather; pen
plumaje feathers, plumage
población population; town
poblado *n.* town; *adj.* populated; clothed (with vegetation)
poblar (ue) to people, populate; to fill
pobrete, -a *dim. of* **pobre**
probretería poor people
pobretón *aug. of* **pobre**
pobreza poverty
poco: a —— de after a short while of
podadera pruning hook
podenco hound
poder: no —— meños de not to be able to help; *n.* power; power of attorney
poderoso powerful
podredumbre rot, putrefaction
poético poetic
poetizar to poetize, make poetical
policía *m.* policeman; *f.* police force
polilla moths; mildew
política politics; policy
político *n.* politician; *adj.* political; **madre política** mother-in-law
polizonte 'cop'
polo pole (of the earth *or* sky)
poltrón indolent
polvo dust
pólvora gunpowder
polvoriento dusty
polvoroso dusty
pollino, -a ass's colt, young donkey
polla chicken; (*slang*) young woman, 'spring chicken'
pollo chicken; youth; dandy
pomito flask
pomo hilt, pommel
pompa pomp, ostentation
pomposo pompous
pómulo cheekbone
ponderación exaggeration; eulogy
ponderar to weigh, consider; to praise highly
poner to put; to arrange *or* furnish (a house); **—— blanco** to wash white; **—— la mesa** to set the table; **—— por obra** to set to work on; to carry out; **——se a** to begin; to take time to; **——se (el sol)** to set
poniente *n.* west; *adj.* setting
pontificio pontifical
ponzoña poison
ponzoñoso poisonous
popa poop, stern; **llevar el viento en ——** to sail before the wind, make good progress
popular popular, of the people
populoso populous; *fig.* thick-leaved
por *arch.* in order to; **—— que** (*followed by subjunctive*) so that; **—— si** in case
porcelana porcelain
porción portion
pordioseo begging
pordiosero beggar
porfía persistence; importunity; obstinacy; conflict; **a ——** in competition, each striving to outdo the other
porfiado stubborn
porfiar to insist; to persist
pormenor detail
poro pore
porquería dirty *or* disgusting thing
porrada blow; knocking
portada title page
portado dressed
portal entrance way, street door
portarse to bear oneself
porte bearing, carriage
portento marvel
portentoso astonishing, prodigious
portera janitress, janitor's wife
portería gatehouse; room of doorkeeper *or* janitor
portero doorman; janitor
pórtico entrance, portico
portón *aug. of* **puerta**
porvenir future
porvida oath, swearing
pos: en —— de after, behind, following
posada inn; rooming house; dwelling place, lodging
posar to rest; to lodge; **——se** to rest
posas buttocks, seat
poseedor possessor
poseer to possess
posesionarse de to take possession of
posible *adj.* possible; *n. plu.* means
positivista *adj.* positivistic, materialistic
poso sediment, dregs
posponer to put behind, put in second place
pospuesto put in second place, put behind
posta post
poste post, pillar
postema abscess; *fig.* nuisance, hindrance
posterior subsequent, following
posternado prostrate
posternar to prostrate
postigo postern gate, small door within a larger one

postizo false
postrar to prostrate
postre dessert; end
postrero last, rear
postrimería last days
postrimero last
postulante supplicant
póstumo posthumous
postura posture
potencia power; faculty (of mind *or* soul)
potentado magnate, potentate
potente powerful
potestad ruler
potinque concoction
potro steed; young horse, colt
poyo stone bench
pozo well
práctica practice, experience
practicable usable, workable
practicante doctor
práctico practical
pradecillo *dim. of* **prado**
pradera meadow
prado meadow
preámbulo preamble
preboste provost; **capitán ——** officer in charge of military police
precario precarious
precaución precaution
preceder to precede
precepto rule, precept
preciar to value, esteem; **——se** to pride oneself; **——se de** to boast of
precio price; worth
preciosidad darling; lovely thing
precioso cute, lovely, darling; dainty
precipicio precipice; gulf
precipitación haste
precipitado fast, hasty
precipitar to hurry, hasten, rush forward; to impel; **——se** to rush; to throw oneself
precisamente precisely; right now
preciso precise; necessary, urgent; **ser ——** to be necessary
preclaro illustrious, outstanding
precocidad precociousness
preconizar to praise
precoz precocious; early
predecir to predict
predestinación predestination
predicación preaching
predicador preacher
predicar to preach; to say
predicción prediction
predilección preference, predilection
predilecto favorite
predominio predominance
prefación preface
preferencia preference; **con ——** first
preferente of preference, choice
preferir (ie) to prefer; to take preference over
pregón announcement, proclamation
pregonar to cry out, proclaim
pregonero *n.* town crier; *adj.* loud; public
pregunta question
preguntón inquisitive; given to asking questions
prelado prelate, bishop, abbot
premiar to reward
premio reward; prize
premioso burdensome, difficult; slow
prenda object of value; treasure; good quality; token; garment; **juego de ——s** game of forfeits
prendarse de to become fond of, fall in love with
prender to arrest; to capture; to catch (fire); to set (fire to); *arch.* to take
prendido well groomed
prensa (printing) press; the press, newspapers
preñado pregnant
preocupación preoccupation; fixed notion
preocupar to preoccupy
preparativo preparation
presa prey; captive; prize, booty; dam; pond (formed by a dam); **tomar ——** to take, help oneself to
presagio prognostication, sign
presbiterio chancel, area around altar
presbítero priest
prescindir to dispense with, to ignore
prescrito prescribed
presencia presence
presenciar to witness
presentado as a present
presente *n.* present (time); gift; *adj.* present; **tener ——** to keep in mind
presentir (ie) to have a presentiment of
presidir to preside (over)
presión pressure
presita: tomar una —— to take something, help oneself
preso, -a *n.* prisoner; *adj.* captive, captured; seized, caught
prestamista money lender
préstamo loan
prestar to loan, lend; to contribute; **——se** to offer
preste priest
presteza haste, speed
prestigioso honored, prestigious
presto *adv.* quickly; *adj.* swift; **de ——** swiftly
presumido presumptuous, conceited
presumir to presume
presunción presumption, conceit; assumption
presura haste, swiftness
presuroso swift, fast, hurrying
pretencioso pretentious
pretender to try; to intend; to pay court to; to aspire to
pretendiente suitor
pretensión intention; suit, courting
pretérito past, preterite
pretextar to give as a pretext
pretexto pretext; **dar ——** to serve as a pretext
prevalecer to prevail
prevención warning; foresight; preparation
prevenir to warn, forewarn; to look after, attend to; to prepare, arrange; to forestall; to avoid; **——se** to prepare; to foresee
prever to foresee
previo *adj.* previous; *prep.* after
previsión foresight
prez glory, honor
priesa *same as* **prisa**
primaveral springlike
primero que before

primicia first fruit
primo, -a *n.* cousin; *adj.* first; **a prima noche** in the early evening
primogénito first born; heir
primogenitura birthright
primor delicacy; elegance
primoroso graceful; exquisite; dexterous
principal principal; first, foremost; most important; illustrious; main floor
príncipe prince
principio beginning; first step; principle; **al ——** at first
prior prior
prisa haste, hurry; **a ——** fast; **darse ——** to hurry; **de ——** in a hurry
prisión prison, jail; *plu.* shackles
privación privation
privado *n.* favorite; *adj.* private
privar to deprive
privativo private
privilegio privilege
pro advantage; **en —— de** in favor of
probanza proof
probar (ue) to prove; to try, test, try out, put to trial; to taste
proceder to proceed; *n.* act
proceso trial
procurador lawyer
procurar to try
prodigalidad prodigality
prodigio prodigy, marvel
producto product; income
proeza prowess; *plu.* deeds of bravery
profanación desecration
profano *n.* layman; *adj.* profane, worldly; uninitiated
proferir (ie) to utter; to proffer
profesar to profess
profeta prophet
profético prophetic
prófugo, -a fugitive
profundidad depth, profundity
profundizar to delve deep
profundo *n.* depths; *adj.* deep, profound
progresista progressive
prohibir to prohibit
prójimo neighbor (in Biblical sense); fellow man
prole offspring, children
prolijo prolix, tedious; constant; long
prólogo prologue
prolongar to prolong
promesa promise
prometer to promise
promover (ue) to stir up, set in motion; to move
pronosticar to predict, prognosticate
pronóstico prediction
prontitud speed
pronto ready, prepared; soon; quick; **de ——** suddenly; **por de ——** at first
pronunciar to pronounce, say; to enunciate
propaganda advertising
propagar to spread, propagate
propender to tend
propensión tendency
propenso inclined, disposed
propiamente properly speaking
propicio propitious; appropriate
propiedad quality, nature; *plu.* nature
propietario landowner; owner
propinar to give
propio own; characteristic; proper, appropriate; very; himself, etc; **lo ——** the same; **—— a, —— de** appropriate to
proponer to propose; to set forth
proporción proportion
proporcionado proportioned
proporcionar to provide, furnish, give
proposición proposal
propósito *n.* objective, intention, purpose, plan; subject; *adj.* appropriate, fitting; **a ——** on purpose; apropos; **a —— de** suited for
propuesto put in first place
prórroga postponement
prosa prose; prosaic thing
prosaico prosaic
prosapia lineage
proscenio front of stage
proseguir (i) to continue
prosperado prosperous
prosperar to prosper
proteger to protect
protervo perverse, evil
protestante Protestant
protoencantador arch-enchanter
protomiseria poverty itself
provecto mature
provecho profit, advantage
provechoso profitable, beneficial
proveer to dispose; to provide; to manage; **—— de** to confer (the rank of)
provenir de to come from, spring from
providencia providence
próvido provident, foreseeing
provincia province
provisión food
provisto provided
provocante provocative
provocar to provoke; to incite, tempt
próximo next; near; **—— a** about to
proyectil projectile
proyecto plan, project
prudencia prudence
prudente prudent
prueba proof; trial
prurito itch; intense desire
psicológico psychological
psíquico psychic
pubertad adolescence
publicar to make public, publish, declare
publicidad publicity; public knowledge
público public; well-known
puchero pot; stew
pueblo town, village; people; common people, lower class
puerco *n.* hog; *adj.* dirty
pueril puerile, childish
puerto (sea) port; mountain pass
pues *adv.* so; *conj.* since; for; then
puesto stand; post; place; *adj.* prepared
puesto caso que *arch.* although
puesto que *arch.* although, even though
pugilato struggle
pugnar to struggle; to fight
pujanza power, force, impetus
pujar to falter; to struggle

pulcritud pulchritude, beauty; neatness
pulcro beautiful; neat
pulga flea
pulgar thumb
pulido polished
pulido polished
pulir to polish
pulmón lung
pulmonía pneumonia
pulso pulse
pulular to swarm
pulla repartee, low wit; **echar ——s** to make smart remarks
pundonor honor; susceptibility (respecting honor)
pundonoroso punctilious; honorable
punir to punish
punta corner; end; point
puntada stitch
puntapié kick
puntear to strum
puntiagudo pointed
puntillas: de —— on tiptoe
punto point; bit; instant, moment, jiffy; dot; stitch (sewing); **al ——** instantly; **a —— fijo** precisely; **de todo ——** completely; **estar a ——** to be ready; to be just right; **poner ——** *or* **poner —— final** to bring to an end; **por ——s** frequently; **—— final** period
puntual punctual
punzante piercing
punzar to prick, pierce
puñada blow (with fist)
puñado handful
puñal dagger; **¡puñales!** darn it!
puñalada dagger thrust
puñetazo blow with fist
puño fist; cuff; hand; handle (of sword *or* cane); (physical) power
pupila pupil; eye
pupilaje boarding school
pupilero master of boarding school
pupilo boarder; ward
purgatorio purgatory
purificar to purify
puro *n.* cigar
púrpura purple; *n.* purple cloth
purpurino lavender, purplish
pusilánime pusillanimous
pusilanimidad pusillanimity, cowardice

Q

quebradero de cabeza puzzle
quebrantado in broken health, afflicted
quebrantar to break; to violate
quebranto weakness; affliction; broken health; rough road
quebrar (ie) to break; **—— la cabeza** to torment
quedar to remain; **—— mal** to be in a bad position, come out badly
quedo quiet, still
quehacer task
queja complaint; trouble
quejarse to complain
quejoso complaining
quejumbroso complaining, whining
quema: vino de —— new wine
quemadero burning place, stake
quemar to burn
querella complaint
querellar to complain; to bring charges
querencia affection
querer to want, wish; to will; to try; *n.* will
querido *n.* lover, beloved
quesito *dim. of* **queso**
queso cheese
quiá bah!
quicio door jamb
quietar to quiet
quietecito *dim. of* **quieto**
quietad quiet, repose
quilate carat; degree of excellence
quimera chimera; strange idea
quimérico chimerical, fantastic
quincena fortnight
quinta farm; estate; *plu.* draft
quinto fifth
quisquilloso touchy
quisto *arch. for* **querido**
quitar to take away, remove, take off; to get out of the way

R

rábano radish; *fig.* a bit; (*slang*) the dickens!
rabia anger, wrath
rabiar to be mad; to rage
rabioso mad, raging
rabo tail
racimo bunch
raciocinar to reason
raciocinio reasoning; argument
ración share, portion, helping; food
racional rational
racionalista rationalist; freethinker
radiante radiant
radical deep-seated; **—— numérico** root
radio radius
raído worn, threadbare
raigón big root
raíz root; **bienes raíces** real estate
ralo sparse
rama branch; roof
ramo branch; species; bouquet; administrative division
rana frog
rancio old
rapacidad rapacity, greed
rapagón lad
rapamiento shaving; trimming
rapar to shave; to crop the hair
rapaz rapacious, predatory; *n.* lad, youth
rapaza girl
rapiña plundering
rapiñar to plunder
raposa fox
rapto ecstasy, rapture
rareza rarity, strange trait, strangeness
raro curious, odd; rare
ras level; **ad —— de** on the level of; **ras ras** *the sound of tearing cloth or paper*
rascar to scratch
rasgado large (of eyes)
rasgar to tear; to scratch; to destroy
rasgo trait, feature; stroke; (splendid) deed; clever phrase
rasguear to strum
rasguñar to scratch
rasguño scratch

raso *n.* satin; *adj.* smooth; uninhibited; devoid; ignorant; **lo —— *or* campo ——** open country
rastras: a —— by dragging
rastro trail, track, trace
rata rat
ratero pickpocket
rato while; **dar mal —— a uno** to make things unpleasant for one; to make one suffer
ratón mouse
ratonar to gnaw
raudal flood
raudo swift
raya line; limit
rayar en to border on
rayo ray (of light); lightning flash
raza race
razón reason; right; word, speech, part of conversation; **dar ——** to give information; **en —— de** with respect to; **puesto en ——** reasonable; **ser ——** to be right; **tener ——** to be right
razonable reasonable; fairly good
razonadamente in reasoned form
razonamiento reasoning, argument; speech
razonar to talk; to reason (out); to rationalize
reacio obstinate, stubborn
real *n.* coin (of copper, ¼ of a **peseta;** of silver, ⅛ of a dollar or **duro**); camp; *adj.* real; royal; handsome, fine; **camino ——** highway
realizar to realize; to bring about; to make real
realzar to elevate; to re-establish; to increase
reanimado reanimated
rebajamiento lowering
rebajar to lower
rebanada slice (of bread)
rebañadura pickings
rebaño flock
rebasar to go past; to exceed
rebelde rebellious
rebeldía rebellion, revolt
rebelión rebellion
rebocillo *dim. of* **rebozo**
rebosar to overflow
rebotar to rebound; to exasperate
rebozado clandestine; muffled, disguised
rebozo shawl (worn over head); **sin ——** openly, frankly; **de ——** disguised
rebramar to roar
rebueno very good
rebullir to squirm
rebuscar to inquire thoroughly (into), make researches; to search carefully
rebutir to stuff
recado errand; message; **—— de escribir** writing set
recaer to fall
recalcado emphasized; **—— de facciones** with prominent features
recapacitar to meditate, think carefully; to recollect
recargo recurrence; increase (of fever)
recatado cautious; quiet
recatar to hide
recato modesty; prudence
recaudo care, precaution
recebir *arch. for* **recibir**
recelar to fear, distrust, suspect
recelo fear, misgiving
receloso timid, fearful
recentísimo very recent
receta recipe; formula
recibimiento reception; hall, entrance room
recibo receipt
recién *adj.* recent; *adv.* recently
recio strong, stout; heavy; hard; loud
recíproco reciprocal
recitar to recite
reclamación claim; demand
reclamar to claim, demand
reclamo lure; complaint; tale, yarn
reclinar to rest; to lean back
recluta recruit
recobrar to recover
recoger to pick up, gather, get; to take back; to pull in; to shelter; to recollect (the senses); **——se** to retire, withdraw; to take shelter
recogida arrest
recogido compact
recogimiento protection; withdrawal from the world, retirement; refuge, asylum
recomendar (ie) to recommend; to commend
recompensa recompense
recompensar to recompense
reconcentrar to bring together
reconciliar to reconcile
reconcomio suspicion
reconocer to recognize; to reconnoitre; to examine closely
reconocimiento gratitude; reconnaissance
recontar (ue) to recount
reconvenir to reproach
recordar (ue) to remember; to remind; to recall; *arch.* to wake up
recorrer to travel; to visit; to walk back and forth; to look over, glance through
recortadito cut very short
recortar to outline
recostar (ue) to lean, lean back, recline
recovero poultry dealer
recrear to delight, entertain
recreo recreation; expansion; indulgence
recrudecer to increase
rectificar to rectify
rectitud honesty, rectitude
recto straight; upright, honest
rector rector; priest
recuerdo memory, remembrance, recollection
recurrir to have recourse
recurso recourse; resort, resource
rechazar to reject, refuse
rechifla hissing, mockery, ridicule
red net
redacción editorial staff *or* office (of a newspaper)
rededor *plu.* surroundings, neighborhood; **en ——** around
redención redemption
redentor redeemer
redimir to redeem; to purchase redemption from
rédito return; *plu.* interest (on loan)
redoble roll (of drum)
redondamente roundly; flatly

redondo round; complete; **a la redonda** round about; **en ——** around
reducido small
reducir to reduce; to subjugate
redundante redundant, superfluous
redundar to redound
refajo sash
refectorio refectory, dining hall
referencia account
referir (ie, i) to tell, relate; **——se a** to refer to
refinado subtle; artful
refinamiento refinement
reflejar to reflect
reflejo reflection
reflexión reflection, thought
reflexionar to reflect
reforma improvement
reformar to reform; to amend; to rehabilitate; **—— conciencia** to salve one's conscience
reforzar (ue) to reinforce
refrán proverb; saying
refregar (ie) to rub, massage
refrenar to check
refrescar to refresh, cool
refresco refreshment; rest
refriega scuffle, struggle
refrigerio cool drink
refugiarse to take refuge
refugio refuge
refulgente refulgent
refundición reworking; amalgamation
refunfuñar to growl, grumble
refunfuño growling
regalado heartening; caressing; comfortable, well off
regalar to regale; to give (a present); to pet
regalo present; treat; easy life
regar (ie) to water, irrigate
regatear to bargain; to lower in worth
regazo lap
regidor alderman
regimiento regiment
regio regal
regir (i) to rule; to manage; to drive
registrar to search, examine
registro search; register; tone
regla rule; **en ——** in proper order
reglado moderate
reglamento regulation; **de ——** usual, expected
regocijado cheerful, merry
regocijar to make joyous
regocijo rejoicing, merrymaking
regresar to go back, return
regreso return
regulado regulated
regular regular; moderately good, ordinary; proper, right
rehabilitar to rehabilitate
rehacer to remake
rehusar to refuse
reinado reign
reinar to reign
reino kingdom
reintegrarse to rejoin, go back to
reja grating, window bars; plowshare
rejón short spear; thrust with spear
rejuvenecer to rejuvenate
relación relation, account; love affair; *plu.* love affair
relámpago lightning flash; flash, spark
relampaguer to flash (of lightning)
relatar to relate
relegar to relegate
relente dampness, dew
relevar (ie) to stand out; to exonerate
relieve relief; *plu.* remnants
religioso monk
relinchar to whinny
reliquia relic; trace, vestige
reluciente shining
relucir to shine
relumbrar to shine
relumbrón luster; tinsel
rematar to bring to an end, finish
remate end
remedar to imitate
remediar to help; to remedy
remedio remedy; help
remedo imitation
remembranza remembrance
remendado spotted; patched
remendar (ie) to mend
remendón: zapatero —— shoe repair man
remilgado affected, prudish
remilgarse to act terrified
remitir to remit, hand over; send; to lessen, become less intense; **——se** to send
remolino swirl, eddy; commotion
remontarse to rise; to climb
remorder (ue) to produce remorse
remordimiento remorse
remoto remote
remover (ue) to move, stir
remozar to rejuvenate
remusgo keen cold wind
renacer to be reborn
rencilla bad humor; dispute
renacimiento renaissance, rebirth
rencor spite, rancor
rencoroso spiteful
rendido worn out; submissive, abject, humble
rendija crack
rendir (i) to render; to pay; to humble; to surrender; to conquer, overcome; **——se** to surrender
renegado, -a renegade; Moor; *fig.* rough, harsh
renegar (ie) to disown
reniego oath, curse
renglón line
renovación renewal; replacement
renovar (ue) to renew
renta income
rentar to yield
rentista person having an income from investments
renuevo sprout, shoot
renunciar to renounce, give up
reñido con at odds with
reñir (i) to quarrel; to scold; to fight
reo criminal; **—— de muerte** man condemned to death
reojo: de —— from the corner of the eye
reparación reparation, amends; repairs
reparar to amend, correct; to redeem; to restore; **—— en** to notice, pay attention to
reparo repair; help
repartimiento distribution
repartir to divide; to spread, scatter; to distribute
repasar to iron, press; to review, look over

repelar to pull out the hair of
repelón hair pulling
repente: de —— suddenly
repentino sudden
repercutir to reverberate
repetir (i) to repeat, do again
repicar to ring
repiqueteo clicking
replegar (ie) to fold back; **——se** to bend back
repleto replete, full
replicar to answer; to talk back, answer impertinently
repliegue fold
reponer to replace; to reply
reportar to restrain
reposado calm
reposar to rest; **——se** to rest
reposo repose; calm
repostería pastry
repostero caterer; tapestry with coat of arms
reprender to scold
represa dam; stop
representación representation; imagination, supposition; appearance; acting (of play)
representar to represent; to depict, picture; to act (a play)
reprimenda reprimand
reprimir to repress
reprobación blame
reprobar (ue) to reproach
réprobo reprobate
reproducir to reproduce
repuesto recovered; re-established; retired, hidden
repugnar to dislike; to oppose
repulsa rebuff; refusal
reputar to repute; to consider
requebrar (ie) to pay compliments to; to court
requerir (ie) to require; to request
requiebro compliment
requilorio unnecessary trifle
requisito prerequisite, requisite
requisitoria (legal) requisition
res head of cattle; animal
resabio trace
resaltar to stand out
resbaladizo slippery
resbalar to slide, slip
resbalón slide
resbaloso slippery
rescatar to ransom
rescindir to cancel, annul
resentirse (ie, i) to become angry; to be offended; to be impaired
reserva caution; reserve
reservar to reserve
resfriado cold
resfriar to chill
resguardar to shelter
resguardo guard; customs guard; shelter; **a —— de** safe from
residir to reside
residuo residue; waste
resignación resignation; submission
resignar to resign
resistir to resist
resolución determination; **en ——** in short
resolver (ue) to solve; **——se** to make up one's mind
resollar (ue) to breathe heavily, take a breath
resonante echoing, resonant
resonar (ue) to resound, ring, rumble, make a noise
resoplido snort
resorte spring
respaldo back (of chair)
respecto: con —— a, —— de with respect to; **—— a** respecting, with respect to
respetar to respect
respeto respect
respetuoso respectful
respirar to breathe
respiro breath, breathing; respite
resplandecer to shine, be resplendent
resplandeciente shining
resplandor glow, radiance
responder to answer
respondonzuelo saucy
responsabilidad responsibility
responso response (religious chant)
respuesta reply
resquebrajo (*humorous mistake for* **requiebro**) compliment
restablecer to re-establish; **——se** to recuperate, recover
restablecimiento recovery
restañar to staunch
restar to remain; to subtract
restauración restoration
restaurar to restore
resto rest; remnant; relic, bones (of saint)
restregar (ie) to rub
resucitar to resuscitate
resuelto resolved, determined, resolute
resultado result
resultar to result, turn out
resumen résumé, summary, **en ——** in brief
resumido summed up; **en ——as cuentas** in brief
retaguardia rear guard
retahila string; series
retador challenger
retama furze, broom
retar to challenge
retardar to put off
retardo delay
retazo piece, remnant; wisp; patch
retener to retain, hold back
reticencia reticence
retintín tinkling; sarcastic tone
retirada retreat
retirar to take back, take away; to set back; to put away; set aside; to withdraw; **——se** to retire, leave
retiro retirement, seclusion; retreat
retocar to touch up
retoñar to sprout
retoño sprout, scion
retoque touch
retorcerse (ue) to writhe
retórica rhetoric, empty words
retórico rhetorician
retorno return; renewal
retozar to frisk
retozón frisking, frisky
retraerse to withdraw, retire
retraso delay
retratar to portray
retrato portrait
retrechería evasion
retroceder to draw back, move back
retruécano play on words, pun
rétulo *arch. for* **rótulo** sign, placard
reuma rheumatism
reumático rheumatic
reunión gathering; group

reunir to bring together, collect; **——se** to come together, meet
revelación revelation
revelar to reveal
reventar (ie) to burst; to burst out with; to break open; (*slang*) to die
reventazón bursting
reventón popping
reverberar to reflect
reverdecer to renew
reverencia reverence; bow
reverendo reverent; revered; reverend; **——ísimo** Right Reverend
revés backhand blow; **al ——** on the contrary, on the other hand; contrariwise, backwards, the other way around; **del ——** back to front; inside out
revestir (i) to invest with; to clothe
revisar to look over
revista review; **pasar ——** to pass in review
reviva hurray!
revoco plaster
revolar (ue) to flutter, hover
revolcar (ue) to knock down; **——se** to writhe
revolver (ue) to revolve, stir, churn; to dig around; to look over (books, papers); **——se** to be upset; to be nauseated; to writhe
revoltijo confusion, haphazard mixture
revuelta deviation, digression
revuelto mixed together
revulsivo revulsory (medicine)
rezago remnant
rezar to pray
rezo prayer; praying
rezumar to ooze
Rhin Rhine
riachuelo *dim. of* **río**
ribera bank; shore
ribeteadora seamstress
ricacho *aug. of* **rico**
rico-hombre *arch.* nobleman
ridículo *n.* ridicule; *adj.* ridiculous
riego irrigation
rielar to sparkle, glisten
rienda rein; **—— suelta** free rein
riesgo risk
rifar to wrangle
rígido rigid, stiff, unbending
rigor rigor, harshness; **en ——** *or* **en —— de verdad** in strict truth; **de ——** necessary, customary
rigoroso severe, rigorous, strict, harsh, unyielding
riguroso *see* **rigoroso**
rima rhyme
rimar to rhyme
rincón corner
rinconada corner
riña quarrel
riñon kidney; *plu.* small of back
riqueza wealth
risa laughter
risco crag
risotada laugh, chuckle
risueño smiling; cheerful
ritmo rhythm
rizar to ruffle; to curl
rizo curl
robador robber
robar to steal
roble oak
robo theft
robustez robustness, strength
robusto strong; stout
roca rock
roce contact
rociar to sprinkle
rocín nag; **—— de campo** traveling horse
rocinante nag
rocío dew
rodado dappled
rodar (ue) to roll; to pass; to tumble; to wander about; **echar a ——** to send rolling
rodear to surround; to turn around
rodela round shield
rodeo turn, twist; roundabout course, detour
rodilla knee; **de ——s** kneeling
rodillazo blow with knee
roer to gnaw
rogar (ue) to ask, beg; to pray, entreat
rojizo reddish
rolar to veer
rollizo roly-poly
romance ballad
romano Roman
romanticismo romanticism
romántico romanticist; romantic author
romantizar to romanticize
romero rosemary (plant); pilgrim
romper to break; to tear; to pierce; to open *or* begin (a statement)
roncar to snore
ronco hoarse
ronda avenue, boulevard; police patrol
rondar to prowl about; **—— la calle** to patrol the street; **——le la calle a una mujer** to flirt with a lady from the street
rondeña *n.* popular Andalusian folk song and dance, named for the city of Ronda; *adj.* from Ronda
rondón: de —— straightaway
roña imperfection
roñoso miserable, wretched; dirty
ropa clothes
ropaje dress, clothing
Roque: vive —— ye gods!
roquero: castillo —— castle built on a crag
rosa rose; **rosa-enredadera** climbing rose
rosada rosy
rosal rose bush
rosario rosary; prayers
rosquilla doughnut
rostro face
roto torn; broken; broken out; destroyed
rotundo round
rotura break; cut
rozar to rub (against), brush against, graze
rubí ruby
rubio blond
rubor blush; shame
ruborizarse to blush
rucio gray (horse *or* donkey)
rudo severe; gross; rough, uncultured
rueca distaff
rueda wheel
ruego plea, request; **a ——s de** at the request of
rufián ruffian
rufo *n.* ruffian; *adj.* redheaded
rugido roar
rugir to roar
ruido noise
ruidoso noisy
ruin base, vile
ruina ruin

ruindad baseness
ruinoso miserable; worthless
ruiseñor nightingale
rumbo course
rumboso *n.* swaggerer, show-off; *adj.* splendid, liberal
ruminante ruminant, animal that chews its cud
rumor noise
rumoroso murmuring
run run rumor, report
ruralizarse to return to the country
ruso Russian
rústico *n.* peasant; *adj.* rustic
ruta route
rutinario routine

S

sábana sheet
sabañón chilblain
saber to know; to taste; *n.* knowledge; **—— a gloria** to taste wonderful
sabidor wise, learned
sabiduría wisdom
sabiendas: a —— knowingly
sabio learned, wise
sable sabre; **reñir al ——** to fight with sabres
sabor taste, flavor, savor; **a mi ——** to my pleasure; **a —— de** in the light of
saborear to enjoy
sabroso savory, delicious
sacar to take out, bring out; to get; **—— en consecuencia** to come to the conclusion; **—— en limpio** to see clearly
sacerdocio priesthood
sacerdotal priestlike
sacerdote priest
sacerdotisa priestess
saciar to satiate, satisfy
saco sack
sacramento sacrament
sacre saker (a kind of hawk)
sacrificio sacrifice
sacrílego sacrilegious, unholy
sacristán sacristan
sacro holy
sacudida shock; shove
sacudimiento trembling
sacudir to shake; to brush off, shake off, free oneself from; to deliver (blows); to move (with vigor); to stir
saeta arrow
sagaz wise, sagacious
sagrado sacred
sahumerio incense; burning of incense
sainete a one-act play, realistic and humorous in nature
sal salt; grace; wit
sala room; living room
salado witty; vivacious; salted; pickled
salador one who pickles, pickler
salario salary; **a ——** on a fixed salary
salchicha sausage
saldar to pay up, liquidate
saleroso witty, clever
salicilato salicylate
salida departure; sally; outburst; exit, door opening upon; **—— del sol** sunrise
salir to leave, go *or* come out; to turn out, result
saliva saliva; **gastar ——** to talk
salmista psalmist
salmo psalm
salmorejo a sauce for rabbit
salón room, hall, salon, drawing room; social gathering
salpicar to splatter; to scatter
salpicón cold meat
salsa sauce
saltador jumping
salta-paredes wall climber; wild youth
saltar to jump, leap; **——le (a una) novio** to get a sweetheart; **——le a uno las lágrimas** to burst into tears
salteador highwayman
salto leap, bound, jump, start; **dar un ——** to jump; to make a hurried visit
salud health; salvation
saludable healthy; beneficial
saludar to greet; to salute
saludo greeting, salutation
salvado bran
salvaje savage, wild
salvar to save; to jump over, clear
salve hail!
salvo *adj.* safe, sure; **a —— de** safe from; **en ——** in safety; **sano y ——** safe and sound; *prep.* except
salvoconducto pass, safe conduct
sanar to cure; to get well
sanción sanction, punishment
sandez absurdity
sandio foolish, inane
saneado free from loans *or* mortgages; guaranteed
sangrar to bleed
sangre blood; **¡qué ——!** what a mean disposition!
sangriento bloody
sanguinaria bloodroot
sanguinario sanguinary, bloody
sanguinoso blood-colored; sanguinary
sanidad health, healthiness
sano healthy, well; wholesome; sane
santero sanctimonious
santidad holiness, sanctity
santiguarse to cross oneself
santo *n.* saint; saint's day; *adj.* holy, saintly; **viernes ——** Good Friday
santuario sanctuary, shrine
saña wrath, rage, madness
sapo toad
sarao soirée, party
sardina sardine
sardónico sardonic
sargento sergeant
sarmiento vine stalk
sarna itch; keen desire
sartal string
sartén frying pan
sastre, -a tailor
Satanás Satan
satisfacción satisfaction, explanation
satisfacer to satisfy; to explain
saturnal saturnalia
saúco alder, elder (tree)
savia sap
sayal robe; sackcloth
sayo jerkin, doublet, smock
sayón jailor; hangman
sayuelo little smock
sazón season; time, occasion
sazonado seasoned; delicious
sazonar to season
sebo tallow; grease
seboso greasy
secar to dry; to dry up
sección section, department

seco dry; **a secas** simply; —— **de carnes** lean
secreto *n.* secret; secrecy; *adj.* secret, hidden, recondite; **de** —— in secret
secundar to aid
seda silk
sedación calming
sedentario sedentary
sedicioso seditious, mutinous
sediento thirsty
sedosidad silkiness; softness
seducir to seduce; to entice, captivate
seductor *n.* seducer; *adj.* seductive
segar (ie) to reap; to cut
seguidamente successively; in an orderly way
seguidilla folk song and dance of Andalucía
seguido consecutive
seguridad sureness; security; certainty
seguro sure; safe; **de** —— certainly; **irse del** —— to leave the sure way; **sobre** —— on sure ground
selva forest
selvático rustic; of the forest
sellar to seal
sello seal
semana week; **entre** —— in the middle of the week
semblante countenance
sembrado sown field
sembradura sowing
semejante like, similar; such (a); *plu.* fellow men
semejanza likeness, similarity
semejar to resemble; to seem, appear
semiandrajo half rag; shabby clothes
semilla seed
seminario seminary, school
semita Semite, Semitic
semítico Semitic
sempiterno everlasting, eternal
senado senate
senadora senator's wife
senatorial of the senate *or* senator
sencillez simplicity
senda path
sendero path
sendo one apiece
senectud old age
seno hollow, cavity, recess; bosom, breast, chest; *plu.* bosom, chest
sensación sensation
sensibilidad sensitivity, sensitiveness; emotion; perception
sensible sensitive; perceptible, tangible
sensitivo sensitive
sensual sensual
sentar (ie) to seat; ——**se** to sit down
sentencia sentence, verdict; meaning; wise saying
sentenciado *n.* condemned criminal; *adj.* condemned
sentenciar to sentence
sentido *n.* sense; meaning; *adj.* deeply felt, moving
sentimiento sentiment, feeling; pain, grief, mourning
sentir (ie) to feel; to feel sorry, regret; to perceive; to hear; *n.* feeling
seña sign; scar; *plu.* address; description; **¿qué señas?** what does he look like?; **por más señas** to give more details
señá *popular for* **señora**
señal sign
señaladamente especially, signally
señalar to point out, show; to mark, brand; to fix, assign
señoría lordship, excellency
señorico *dim. of* **señor**
señorial noble, of the noble class
señoril of the master
señorío lordly estate; domain; upper class
séptimo seventh
sepulcral sepulchral
sepulcro sepulcher, tomb
sepultar to bury
sepultura grave, tomb
sequedad dryness, aridness; taciturnity
ser: ¿qué será de mí? what will become of me? *n.* being
seráfico angelic, seraphic
serafín seraph, angel
serena siren
serenar to calm
serenidad serenity, calm
sereno *n.* night watchman; *adj.* serene, calm; **al** —— in the open air
seriedad seriousness
sermón sermon
sermoncico *dim. of* **sermón**
sermonear to preach
serpear to bend, wind
serpentear to wind
serpiente serpent
serranilla mountain girl; poem about a mountain girl
serrano of the mountains
serreta nose piece (of bridle)
servicial helpful
servicio service; **estar de** —— to be on duty; —— **a domicilio** home delivery
servido pleased
servidor servant
servil servile, slavish
servilleta napkin
servir (i) to serve; to be of use; to do military service
sesera brain
seso brains, intelligence, mind, sense
severidad severity
severo severe
sibarítico sybaritical, epicurean, voluptuous
sibila sibyl, prophetess
sien temple, brow
sierra mountain range, mountains
siervo servant; serf
siesta nap after lunch, siesta; noonday heat
sigilo secrecy
siglo century; secular world
significado meaning
significante meaningful
signo sign, symbol
sílaba syllable
silbar to hiss; to whistle
silbante *adj.* whistling, hissing; *n.* scoffer
silbato whistle
silbido whistle; catcall
silbo whistle; whistling; whispering
silueta silhouette
silvestre wild
silla chair; saddle; —— **de caballo** saddle
silleta chair
sillón armchair
sima abyss
simbólico symbolical
simbolizar to symbolize

simetría symmetry
similar *n.* likeness; look-alike; *adj.* similar
simoníaco simoniacal; selfish
simpatía friendship, liking; charm
simpático pleasant, agreeable
simpatizar to be in harmony with
simpleza simpleness, foolishness
simplicidad foolish saying; stupidity
simplificar to simplify
simplilla naïve girl
simulacro imitation, representation
sinapismo poultice
sincerarse to justify oneself
sincero sincere; pure, uncontaminated
síncope fainting spell
sinfín great number, infinity
singular singular; strange, unusual, rare; —— **batalla** *arch.* single combat
singularizarse to set oneself apart
siniestro *n.* calamity; *adj.* sinister
sinnúmero multitude
sino *n.* fate
sinónimo synonymous
sinrazón unreasonable act; wrong
sintaxis syntax
sintetizar to synthesize, sum up
síntoma symptom
sinvergüenza shameless person
sinvergüenzonaza *double aug. of* **sinvergüenza**
siquiera even; if only, at least
Siracusa Syracuse
sirviente, -a servant
sisa filching
sisar to filch
sisona petty thief; maid who steals from the household money
sistema system
sitial chair, seat
so you—! (*used to reinforce an insult*); *arch.* under
soberano *n. and adj.* sovereign; *adj.* supreme; superb
soberbia pride, haughtiness, self-confidence
soberbio proud; noble; superb
sobón, -a over-indulgent
soboncita *dim. of* **sobona**
sobra excess; leaving, leftover; **de** —— unnecessary; only too well; thoroughly
sobrado too much, more than enough; splendid
sobrante excess, leftover, superfluous
sobrar to be left over; to be more than enough, be superfluous; to be abundant
sobre envelope; cover
sobrecogido overcome
sobredicho aforesaid
sobrehumano superhuman
sobremanera especially, extremely
sobremesa: de —— after dinner; table talk
sobrenatural supernatural
sobrenombre nickname; surname
sobreponerse to overcome, overpower; to control oneself
sobrepuesto one above the other
sobrepujar to surpass
sobresaltar to startle
sobresalto start; anxiety
sobreseer to suspend *or* drop (a lawsuit)
sobrevenir to come to pass, happen
sobrevivir to survive
sobriedad sobriety
sobrino nephew
socaliña trick
socarrón mischievous; joking; sly
socorrer to aid, help; to save
socorro help
soez dirty, vile
sofá sofa
sofisma fallacy
sofocación breathlessness
sofocado out of breath
sofocar to suffocate, stifle
soga rope
sojuzgar to subjugate
solana sun porch, solarium
solapa lapel
solapado sly
solar property, estate
solariego manorial, ancestral
solas: a —— alone
solaz solace; enjoyment
solazarse to amuse oneself
soldado soldier
soledad solitude; *plu.* lonely place
soledoso solitary, lonely
solejar sun gallery
solemnidad solemnity; solemn occasion
solene *arch. for* **solemne**
soler (ue) to be accustomed
solfear to sing; to drone out
solicitar to ask for, seek, solicit; to accost
solícito solicitous, anxious, diligent
solicitud solicitude; care; petition, request
soliloquio soliloquy
solitario solitary
solomillo filet mignon
solsticio solstice
soltar (ue) to loosen, let go of, set free; to come out (with); —— **el trapo** (*slang*) to start bawling
soltera unmarried woman
soltero *n.* bachelor; *adj.* unmarried
solterón *aug. of* **soltero** old bachelor
solterona *aug. of* **soltera** old maid, spinster
soltura ease, freedom
solventar to settle
sollozante sobbing
sollozar to sob
sollozo sob
sombra shade, shadow; ghost; **a la** —— in the shade *or* shadows
sombrío gloomy; shady, dark
somero superficial
someter to submit
somnolencia somnolence, stupor
son sound; tune; **en** —— **de** in the way of; as
sonable resonant, sonorous
sonámbulo sleepwalker
sonante resounding
sonar (ue) to sound, resound, ring; to rustle; —— **a** to sound like
sonatina sonatina
sonda probe
sondear to probe
soneto sonnet
sonido sound

sonoro sonorous, ringing
sonoroso sonorous, resounding
sonrisa smile
sonrojo shame
sonrosado rosy
sonsacar to pilfer
soñado imagined
soñador *n.* dreamer; *adj.* dreaming
soñar (ue) to dream
sopa soup; sop
sopista *n.* poor student; *adj.* student
soplar to blow; to breathe into; to inspire
soplo breath, puff; instant; bit; breeze
soponcio fainting spell
sopor stupor
soportar to bear, endure, tolerate
sorbo gulp
sordidez meanness
sórdido sordid
sordo deaf; dull (of sound)
sorprendente surprising
sorprender to surprise
sorpresa surprise
sortija (finger) ring
sortilegio sorcery
sosegado *adj.* calm
sosegar (ie) to calm, quiet; to repose; to be calm
sosiego *n.* calm
soslayo: de —— glancing
soso insipid; dull
sospecha suspicion
sospechar to suspect
sospechoso suspicious, doubtful
sospiro *arch. for* **suspiro**
sostén support
sostener to hold, hold up, support, sustain, keep up
sota jack (in cards)
sotabanco garret, attic
sotana cassock, priest's robe
sótono basement
sotita *dim. of* **sota**
soto grove
suave soft; gentle
suavidad gentleness; softness
suavizar to soften; to smooth
subida ascent
subido high
subir to rise; to go up, climb, mount; to raise, lift up; **—— de punto** to increase
súbito sudden; **de ——** suddenly
sublevar to cause to rebel
sublimado exalted
sublimar to elevate, exalt
sublime sublime
sublimidad loftiness
subsistir to exist; to last, subsist
substancioso substantial
subsuelo subsoil; **de ——** underhanded
subteniente second lieutenant
subterráneo *n.* basement; crypt; *adj.* subterranean
subyugar to subjugate
succión suction, drawing force
suceder to happen; **——se** to happen one after the other, succeed each other
sucesivo next; **lo ——** the future
suceso event, happening; *arch.* success
sucesor successor
sucio dirty; base
sucumbir to succumb
sudado sweaty; soiled
sudar to sweat
sudor sweat; labor
sudoroso sweaty
suegra mother-in-law
suegro father-in-law
sueldo salary
suelo floor; lower part; ground, earth; country, land
suelto *adj.* loose; free; stray; unfastened; *n.* change (money)
sueño sleep; dream
suerte luck, fate; sort; manner; **de esta ——** in this way; **de —— que** in such a way that, in such a condition that, so that
suficiencia aptitude, ability; **expresión de ——** profound expression
sufridero bearable
sufrido long-suffering
sufrimiento suffering; sufferance
sufrir to suffer; to bear
sugerir (ie) to suggest
sugestión suggestion
suicida *n.* suicide; *adj.* suicidal
suicidio suicide
Suiza Switzerland
sujeción subjection
sujetar to subjugate, conquer; to seize, hold
sujeto *n.* individual, person; *adj.* fixed, fastened; subject
sulfonal sulphonal
sulfúreo sulphurous
suma sum; **en ——** in short
sumar to add
sumergir to submerge
suministrar to provide, supply
sumir to sink; to plunge; **——se** to be sunk
sumiso submissive
sumo supreme, highest, greatest; **lo ——** the highest degree; at most
suntuario sumptuary, involved in luxury
superar to surpass
superficie surface
superfluidad superfluity, unnecessary things
superpuesto superimposed
superstición superstition
súpito sudden; impatient
suplantar to supplant
súplica supplication
suplicación entreaty
suplicante supplicating, begging
suplicar to supplicate, beg
suplicio suffering; punishment
suplir to supply; to supplement; to take part
suponer to suppose; *n.* supposition
suprasensible supersensible, beyond perception
suprimir to suppress
supuesto fictitious, assumed, supposed; **por ——** of course
surcar to furrow, plow
surco furrow
surgir to spring up, rise, arise; to appear suddenly
surtir to supply; **—— mal efecto** to have a bad effect
sus get up! go on! (to horse *or* dog)
suspender to suspend, discontinue; to hold back; to hold in suspense
suspensión distraction

suspenso astounded; distracted; in suspense; **—— de** hanging from
suspicacia distrust
suspirado longed for
suspirar to sigh
suspiretear to heave a sigh
suspiro sigh
sustancia substance, essence
sustancioso substantial; nutritious
sustentar to sustain, bear; to nourish; to maintain
sustento sustenance; support
sustituir to substitute
susto fright; **de ——** unexpectedly
sustraer to subtract; to remove
susurrar to whisper
susurro whisper, whispering; rustling
sutil subtle; slender, thin
sutileza subtlety; cunning
sutilizarse to be sublimated

T

tábano horsefly
taberna tavern
tabernero tavern keeper
tabernucha low tavern
tabique partition, wall
tabla plank, board; picture; **—— rasa** plank; **—— redonda** Round Table
tabladillo cot
tacañería miserliness
tacaño *n.* miser; *adj.* stingy, close-fisted
tacilla *dim. of* **taza**
taciturno taciturn
tacón heel
taconazo blow with heel; **dar ——s** to make a noise with one's heels
tacto touch; tact
tacha fault, bad point
tachar to find fault with; to accuse
tachuela tack
tafetán taffeta; scarf
tahur low gambler; **hecho un ——** gambling furiously
taimado sly, cunning
tajar to slice, cut through; to divide, share
tajo blow (with edge of sword), cut; gorge; chopping block
tal cual just as
talabarte sword belt
tálamo wedding bed, couch
talante will, desire; **de buen ——** good humoredly, willingly
talar to cut down; to destroy
talego bag, money sack
taleguillo *dim. of* **talego**
talente *arch. for* **talante** desire, wish, will
talento talent, cleverness
talla carving; figure, stature; hand (at cards); importance
tallar to carve; to deal (cards)
talle height; figure
taller workshop
tallo stalk, stem
tamaño *n.* size; *adj.* so great, so big
tambalearse to stagger
tambor drum; drummer
tamizado filtered, sifted
tangente tangent; in contact with, touching on
tantear to feel out, test
tanto *n.* bit; *adj.* so much, as much; *plu.* so many, as many; such and such; **en —— que, entre —— que** while; **por ——** therefore, consequently
tañer to play (a musical instrument); to ring (a bell)
tapa cover
tapar to cover; to hide; to stop up
tapete table scarf; carpet
tapia wall
tapial wall
tapiz tapestry
tapizar to cover, hang with tapestry
tarasca shrew, slattern, termagant
taravilla chatterbox
tardanza delay
tardar to be long, delay
tarde late; too late; **de —— en ——** rarely, once in a long while
tardo slow; tardy
tarea task
tarima low platform; rough bed
tarjeta card
tarjetazo petition by card
tarro jar
tartamudear to stammer
tasa measure, limit
tatarabuelo great-great-grandfather, ancestor
taza cup; basin (of fountain)
tazón *aug. of* **taza**
té tea
tea torch
teatral theatrical, dramatic
teatro theater; stage
tecla key (of piano)
teclado keyboard
techo roof; ceiling; attic
teja tile; **de ——s abajo** here below; **de ——s arriba** in heaven
tejado roof
tejer to weave
tejido web; fabric
tela cloth; **—— pintada de flores** flower print
telaraña spider web
telarañoso cobwebby
telón curtain
tema theme, subject; contention; obsession
temblar (ie) to tremble
temblor shaking, trembling
tembloroso trembling
temerario rash; daring
temeridad temerity, rashness
temible fearful
temido feared, dreaded
temor fear
temoroso fearful
tempestad storm
tempestuoso stormy
templado tempered; mild; tepid, lukewarm
templanza temperance
templar to temper; to moderate; to tune; to manipulate; **——se** to cool off
temple temper; disposition; harmony
templete little temple
templo temple
temporada season; period of time
temporal temporary; temporal
temprano *adj. and adv.* early
tenacidad tenacity
tenaz tenacious; stubborn; tight
tenaza (*or plu.*) pincers
tendal tent
tendencia tendency

tender (ie) to extend; to stretch, stretch out; **—— el vuelo** to fly; **—— los ojos, la vista** to cast one's gaze; **—— de** to hang with
tendero shopkeeper
tendido stretched; **paso ——** long stride
tenebroso dark, shadowy, gloomy
tenedor, -a holder; *m.* fork; **—— de libros** bookkeeper
tener to have; to hold; **——se** to hold on; to stop; **—— de** *arch. for* **—— que; —— en mucho** to esteem highly; **—— en poco** to scorn; **—— entendido** to understand, believe; **—— por** *or* **a** to consider as; **—— por bien** to agree to; **—— que ver con** to have to do with
tenería tannery
teniente lieutenant; **—— coronel** lieutenant colonel
tenor tenor; manner
tentación temptation
tentador *n.* tempter; *adj.* tempting
tentar (ie) to touch, feel; to tempt
tenue tenuous
teñir (i) to dye, tint, stain
teologal theological
teología theology
teólogo theologian
teoría theory
teórico theoretical
terapéutica remedy, cure
tercero, -a go-between, intermediary; third floor (not counting the lowest floor or floors)
terciado crosswise
terciar to lower (a lance); to mediate; to act as a go-between; **—— la capa** to fling the corner of the cape over the shoulder
tercio third; player; *arch.* regiment
terciopelo velvet
terco stubborn
término end, limit; term; **primer ——** foreground
ternejal bullying
ternera calf; veal
ternerita *dim. of* **ternera**
ternura tenderness
terrenal earthly, of the world
terreno *n.* terrain, territory, land; *adj.* earthly, worldly
terrero *n.* mark; *adj.* earthen
terrorífico terrifying
terruño region; earth
terso smooth
tertulia social gathering, circle; **estar de ——** to enjoy oneself
tesoro treasure; treasury
testador testator
testamentario executor
testamento will
testarudo stubborn
testigo witness; second (in duel)
testimonio testimony
tétrico gloomy
texto text
tez complexion
tibieza lukewarmness, tepidity
tibio tepid, cool
tiempo time; weather; proper moment; **a un ——** at the same time
tienda shop; tent
tiento examination (by feeling); staff; **a ——** groping; **con ——** cautiously, carefully
tierno tender; **ojos ——s** crossed eyes
tieso stiff
tiesto flower-pot
tifoidea typhoid fever
tigre tiger
tijera (*or plu.*) scissors
tijerazo action of scissors, cutting action
tila tea of linden flowers
tildar to stigmatize, brand
tilín ding dong; tinkling noise; ting-a-ling; **hacerle a uno ——** to please someone very much, be a great favorite with someone
timbre bell; timbre, tone
timidez timidity
tímido timid
timo: dar el —— to cheat
tin tin tinkling noise
tinaja hogshead
tiniebla shadow, darkness
tino judgment; tact
tinta ink; tint
tintero inkwell
tinto stained
tiña itch; desire
tío uncle; (*slang*) fellow, guy
tira ribbon
tirada aparte offprint
tiranía tyranny
tirano, -a *n.* tyrant; *adj.* tyrannical; evil
tirante *adj.* taut
tirantez tension
tirar to throw, throw away; to shoot; to draw; to deal (cards); **—— a** to tend towards; **—— de** to drag, pull on
tiritar to shiver
tiro shot
tirón jerk, pull
tiroteo shooting, gunfire, fusillade
tirria (*slang*) dislike, antagonism
tísico consumptive
tisú tissue, cloth
titánico gigantic, titanic
título title, heading; count; titled person
tiza chalk
tiznar to smudge, blacken with soot
tizne soot
toba tartar (of teeth)
toca headdress
tocado *n.* headdress; *adj.* wearing (on the head)
tocador dressing table; dressing room
tocante a respecting
tocar to touch; to play (an instrument); to ring (a bell); to fall to one's lot; to be one's turn; to affect; **—— a** *plus an infinitive* to sound the call for, be at the point of; to reach
tocino bacon
todo: del —— completely; *with neg.* at all; **de —— en ——** completely; definitely
tolerar to tolerate, permit
tolondrón concussion, bump
toma dose
tomate tomato
tomillo thyme
tonel cask
tono tone; **a este ——** in this style, of this sort; **darse ——** to give oneself airs
tontear to play the fool
tontería foolishness
tontillo *dim. of* **tonto** my silly dear
tonto foolish, silly; stupid
topacio topaz

topar to bump; to come upon, meet; —— **con** to encounter; **topóme Dios con** God made me come upon; ——**se** to come upon
tope butt; attack
toque touch
tórax chest, thorax
torbellino whirlwind
torcaz: paloma —— ring-dove
torcedor source of pain
torcer (ue) to twist; to turn aside; to warp; —— **el camino** to turn aside; —— **se** to turn about
tordo dapple gray
torero bull fighter
tormenta storm; tumult
tormento torment; suffering; torture
tornar to return; to turn; to change; —— **a** to do something again
tornasolado iridescent
tornátil well-turned
torneo tourney
torno *arch.* contour; **en** —— around; **en** —— **de** around
toro bull; *plu.* bull fight
torpe stupid, dull; disgraceful
torpeza stupidity; clumsiness
torre tower
torrente torrent, flood
torreón turret, tower
torrezno bacon
torso torso, upper part of the body
torta cake
tortícolis wry neck, stiffness of neck
tortilla cake, wafer
tórtola turtle-dove
tortolica *dim. of* **tórtola**
tortuoso winding, tortuous
tos cough
tosco rough, rude
toser to cough
tósigo poison
tostada (piece of) toast
tostado tanned
tostar (ue) to toast; to tan; to roast
tostón roasted chick-pea
total total; in short, when all is said and done
trabajado toilsome
trabajo work; hardship
trabajoso toilsome
trabar to bind; to seize, grasp; to form (friendship); *arch.* to blame; ——**se** to start
trabucar to mix up
trabuco blunderbuss
traductor translator
traer to bring; to have; —— **en boca** to bandy about
tráfago dealing, affair, business
tragar to swallow
trago swallow, draught
traguito *dim. of* **trago**
traición treachery; **a** —— treacherously
traidor *n.* traitor; *adj.* treacherous
trajeado clothed
traje suit; costume
trama woof (of cloth)
trámite step; channel
tramo flight (of stairs)
tramontar to set behind mountains (of the sun)
trampa trap; trick, deceit
tramposo *n.* cheat, swindler; *adj.* tricky, deceitful
trance peril; critical situation; **a todo** —— at any cost
tranco long stride
tranquilidad calm, peace
tranquilizar to calm
tranquilo tranquil, calm, quiet; easy
transacción compromise
transcribir to transcribe
transcurrir to pass
transcurso course
transeúnte transient, passer-by
transformar to transform
transfusión transfusion
transido exhausted
transigir to put up with; to compromise
tránsito passage; end, terminus; circulation
transitorio transitory, fleeting
translúcido translucent
transmisible transmittable
transmitir to transmit
transmutación change, transmutation
transparentado showing through
transparente transparent
transportar to transport, carry; ——**se** to be carried away, be in a transport
tranvía streetcar
trapera ragpicker
trapisonda subterfuge
trapisondista swindler, cheat
trapo rag, cloth
traqueteo shaking, jerking
tras behind, after; beyond; —— **de** behind
trascendencia great importance
trascendente transcendent; supernatural
trascordarse (ue) to forget
trascurrir to pass (of time)
trasegar (ie) to change bottles *or* casks (of wine)
trasero back
trasgo ghost
trashumante traveling; moving from one pasture to another (of sheep and cattle)
trashumar to take from one pasture to another
trasladar to transport; to transfer, move
traslado copy
traslúcido translucent
traslucir to show through
trasparencia transparency
traspasar to pass through, pierce; to set (of the sun)
trasplantar to transplant
trasponer to pass beyond; to traverse
traspontín mattress pad; (*slang*) buttocks
traste fret
trastienda apartment back of store; *fig.* intuition, foresight
trastornado upset; mad, unbalanced
trasto stuff; rubbish, trash; worthless fellow, good-for-nothing
trastornar to upset, agitate
trastorno upheaval, disorder
trasunto copy; likeness
tratable tractable
tratado treatise; chapter
tratamiento treatment
tratar to treat; to deal with; to discuss; —— **de** to try to; to discuss; —— **del género** to make purchases
trato manner, way of dealing with people, friendly intercourse; dealings; deal; treatment; pact

través: al —— through; a **—— de** across; through; **de ——** sideways
travesía short cut, alley
travesura prank
travieso cute; lively, mischievous
trayecto distance; stretch
traza appearance; plan, scheme
trazar to trace; to plan; to write
trazo outline; profile
trebejar to toy, play
trecho distance; **a ——s** here and there
tregua truce
tremebundo awesome, frightful
tremendo tremendous, immense
trémulo tremulous
tren train; pomp, ostentation
trencilla *dim. of* **trenza**
trenza braid
trenzar to braid
trepar to climb, scramble up
tresillo a card game
tribu tribe
tribulación tribulation, affliction, suffering
tribunal court
tribuno orator
tributo tribute; tax
trigo wheat
trigueño medium dark
trillo threshing tool
trinar to trill; to become furious
trincar to break; to catch; to drink; to slap on
trino warbling, trill
tripas tripe; stomach; intestines, guts
tripería tripe market
tristura *arch.* sadness
triunfal triumphal
triunfar to triumph
triunfo triumph; triumphal parade
trocar (ue) to exchange, change
trocha trail
troje storehouse, barn
trompa trumpet; trunk (of elephant)
trompada (*slang*) blow
trompeta trumpet
tronado quarrelsome
tronar (ue) to thunder
tronco tree trunk
troncho stalk
tronera loophole
trono throne
tropa troops, soldiers
tropel troop, band
tropezar (ie) to stumble; to slip; **—— con** to encounter
tropezón stumble; faux pas; stumbling block; **dar ——es** to stumble
tropiezo stumbling; slip
trotaconventos go-between
trote trot
trovador troubadour
Troya Troy
troyano Trojan
trozo fragment, piece
trueco exchange
trueno thunder; **—— gordo** debacle; great scandal
trueque change, exchange
truhán scoundrel, knave
trujo *arch. for* **trajo**
truncar to cut off, truncate
tuerto wrong; one-eyed man
tul tulle, gauze-like cloth
tullido maimed, crippled
tumba tomb
tumbado sprawled
tumbar to knock down
tumbo tumble; **dar ——s** to stagger
tumultuoso tumultuous
tunante rogue
tundir to clip
túnica robe
tuno rascal
tupido thick, dense
turba mob, crowd
turbación emotion; confusion, embarrassment; disturbance
turbado perturbed, disturbed
turbar to disturb, stir up; **——se** to become dizzy; to become alarmed; to become upset
turbio muddy; indistinct; **de —— en ——** from dawn to dusk
turbión squall, downpour
túrdiga strip (of hide)
turno turn; **entrar en ——** to take precedence
turrón nougat
turulato dumbfounded
tute a card game
tutear to use **tú,** speak familiarly
tutelar *adj.* patron, tutelary
tutor guardian

U

ubre udder
uced *arch. for* **usted**
ufano proud; haughty
úlcera ulcer
último: por —— finally
ultrajar to insult
ultraje outrage; indignation
ultramarinos groceries
ultratumba: de —— after death, in the afterlife
ulular to howl, ululate
umbral threshold
umbrío shady
umbroso shadowy, shady
unción extreme unction
unidad unit; unity
uniforme uniform
unir to unite, bring together, join
unísono unison; **al ——** in unison
unitario unitarian
uña finger nail; claw; **—— de vaca** hock of beef
urbanidad urbanity, courtly manners
urbano *adj.* city
urbe *n.* city
urgencia urgency
urgir to be urgent
urna urn
urraca magpie
usar to use; to be accustomed; to follow (a trade)
usía *arch.* you
uso use; custom; **a** *or* **al —— de** in the manner of, in the fashion of
usufructo usufruct
usura usury; interest
usurero usurer
usurpar to usurp
utensilio utensil
útil useful
utilidad utility; pragmatism

V

v. gr. *abbreviation for* **verbigratia** for example
vaca cow, beef
vacar to have a vacation
vaciar to empty
vacilación hesitance
vacilar to vacillate, hesitate; to sway

vacío *n.* space, void; *adj.* empty, void
vadera ford
vagabundo vagabond, good-for-nothing
vagancia vagrancy; **andar de ——** to live as a vagabond
vagar to wander
vago vague; wandering
vaguido dizzy spell
vahido dizzy spell, dizziness
vaho vapor, fume; breath
vaina sheath
vaivén coming and going; surge
vajilla set of dishes; plate (dishes of gold *or* silver)
val vale, valley
vale (*Latin*) farewell
valentía valor; arrogance, boasting
valer to be worth; to be the same as; to help; **——se de** to avail oneself of, make use of; *n.* worth
valeroso valiant
valía worth
valiente brave
valioso valuable
valona ruff
valor worth; valor
valladar wall
vallado hedge
valle valley, vale
vanagloria conceit
vanidad vanity
vano vain; useless; light, gentle; unreal, non-existent
vapor steam, vapor
vaporcillo small steamboat
vaporoso vaporous, airy, ethereal; filmlike
vapuleo beating
vápulo beating
vaquera shepherd girl
vaqueta sole leather; **cara de ——** a stern face
vara rod, staff, staff of authority; bridge (of nose); yard (measure)
varear to whip
variar to change, vary
vario various, several; varied
varita *dim. of* **vara**
varón *n.* man; *adj.* male
varonil manly, masculine
vasallo vassal
vasar shelf (especially for glasses)
vasco Basque
vasija vessel
vaso glass; vase
vástago offspring
vecindad neighborhood; neighborly relations
vecino, -a *n.* neighbor; townsman; *adj.* neighboring, near
vedar to prohibit
vee, vees *arch. for* **ve, ves**
vega fertile lowland
veinteno *arch.* twentieth
vehemencia vehemence
vejación vexation, irritation
vejancona oldish woman
vejar to vex
vejestorio shriveled old man
vejete *dim. of* **viejo**
vejez old age; age, years
vejiga bladder; ice-bag
vela candle; sail; wakefulness; **en ——** sleeplessly; **estar en ——** to stay up, stay awake
velada evening festival, celebration
velador small table; *adj.* wakeful
veladura veiled *or* hidden quality
velar to watch (over), keep a vigil; to veil, hide
velarte fine broadcloth
velero sailing ship
veleta weather-vane
velo veil
velocidad velocity, speed
veloz swift
velloncito little fleece
vellorí inferior broadcloth
velludo velvet
vena vein
venablo javelin
vencedor, -a *n.* conqueror; *adj.* surpassing, overcoming
vencer to conquer; to surpass; to win
vencido due (of interest *or* payment)
vencimiento conquering; expiration; due date
venda bandage; blindfold
vendar to bandage
vendedor seller; sales person
vender to sell; to betray
vendimiador grape harvester
Venecia Venice
veneciano Venetian
veneno poison
venenoso poisonous
venerable venerable, revered
venerando venerable
venerar to venerate
venganza vengeance
vengar to avenge
vengativo vengeful, desirous of revenge
venia permission
venial corrupt; venial
venida coming; visit
venidero future
venir: —— a (*followed by infinitive*) to end by (*followed by present participle*); **—— en** to agree to; **lo por ——** the future
venta inn; sale, (action of) selling; **en ——** on sale
ventaja advantage
ventajoso advantageous, profitable
ventanal large window
ventana-verjel window filled with flowers
ventanero fond of looking out the window
ventanón large window
ventilado airy
ventilar to air
ventura good fortune; happiness; **por ——** by chance; **sin ——** luckless, unfortunate
venturoso felicitous, fortunate, happy
ver to see; to examine; **—— de** to see about; to try to; **tener que ——** to have to do
veracidad veracity, truthfulness
veras truths; serious things; **de ——** seriously
veraz truthful
verbena verbena
verbigracia for example
verbipotente powerful through speech
verbo word; verb; the Lord
verbosidad verboseness, prolixity
verdad: de —— really and truly
verdadero true; real
verde green; youthful
verdín mold, mildew
verdinegro greenish black
verdiñal green-skinned
verdoso greenish
verdugo hangman, executioner
verdugón welt

verdura verdure; foliage; *plu.* vegetables
vergonzante shamefaced; proud
vergonzoso shameful; bashful
vergüenza shame; bashfulness
vericueto rough path; short cut
verídico true; truthful; real
verificar to fulfill, accomplish, carry out; **——se** to take place, happen
verja grating; gate
verjel flower garden
verosímil likely, credible
versado versed
verso line (of poetry); stanza; **—— heroico** heroic verse
vertedero dumping place
verter (ie) to shed; to pour
vertiente slope
vertiginoso dizzy, giddy
vértigo dizzy spell, lightheadedness
vestido dress; garb, costume
vestidura clothing
vestiglo horrid monster
vestimenta vestment
vestir (i) to dress; to put on; **de más ——** more dressy
vestuario wardrobe; dressing room
veterano veteran
veterinaria veterinary medicine
vetusto old
vez: a la ——, de una —— at the same time; **a su ——** in his turn; **en —— de** instead of; **hacer las veces de** to serve as; **una ——** once, once in a while; **tal ——** perhaps
vía road; way; **por —— de** by way of; **hacer ——** to walk, travel
viaducto viaduct
vial path
vianda food
víbora snake
vibrar to vibrate; to brandish
vicario vicar
vicio vice
vicioso vicious, corrupt
victima victim
víctor hurray (for)
victoria victory
vid grapevine
vida life; living; **ganarse la ——** to earn one's living; **en (tu) ——** never
vidriera window
vidrio glass; pane (of glass)
vidrioso of glass; fragile, delicate
viejecita little old woman
viento wind
vientre abdomen; belly
viga beam
vigilancia vigilance
vigilante vigilant
vigilar to guard, watch over; to keep a vigil
vigilia night of wakefulness; fast; *plu.* long studies
vigor vigor, strength
vihuela guitar
vil vile
vileza vileness
villa city, town
villanía villainy, base deed
villano peasant, serf, churl; *adj.* baseborn
villanchón *aug. of* **villano**
vinagre vinegar
vínculo bond, tie
viña vineyard
violar to violate
violentarse to go against one's own desires
violento violent
violeta violet
virar to tack (a ship), turn
virgen virgin
Virgilio Virgil
virreinato viceroyalty
virrey viceroy
virtud virtue; power
virtuoso virtuous
viruelas smallpox
virus virus, germ
visaje grimace, face
víscera vital organ, viscera
visera visor
visión sight; vision; **ver ——es** to build castles in the air
visita visit; visitor; **de ——** on a visit, visiting
viso glimmer
vislumbrar to make out, see dimly, glimpse
víspera eve; **en ——s de** on the eve of
vista sight, view, gaze; **de ——** on watch; **estar a la ——** to be obvious; **a —— de** in sight of
vistazo glance
visto: por lo —— apparently, obviously
vistoso brilliant, flashy, striking
vital *adj.* life, vital
vitalicio for life, lifelong
vitalidad vitality
vítor hurrah!
vitorear to cheer, shout
vituperar to vituperate
vituperio censure, blame
viuda widow
viudez widowhood; state of widow *or* widower
viudo widower
vivacidad vivacity, liveliness
vivaracho lively
vivaz keen, lively
víveres food, provisions
vivero nursery
vivez liveliness, keenness
viveza keenness, vividness
vivienda dwelling place
viviente living
vivificación vivification; enlivening
vivir to live; **vive Dios, viven los cielos** by heavens!; **viva** hurray (for)
vivo alive, living; spirited, lively; keen, intense; **al ——** vividly
vizcaíno Basque
vizconde viscount
voacé *arch. for* **usted**
vocablo word
vocación vocation, calling
vocear to shout
vocería clamor
vociferar to shout
volandas: en —— through the air; flying
volandero soaring
volar (ue) to fly, flutter
volatería flight
volcán volcano
volcánico volcanic
volcar (ue) to turn over
voltereta somersault; acrobatic feat; revolution
voluble voluble
volumen volume
volver (ue) to return; to turn; to carry back; **—— en sí** to come to one's senses; **——se** to turn around, turn back; **——sele** to become; **—— de comienzo** to begin over again; **—— a** *plus an infinitive* to do again

vomitar to vomit
voraz voracious
vos *arch. for* **os** *or* **vosotros**
votar to swear
voto vow; vote; opinion; curse, oath; —— **va** I swear
voz voice; cry, shout; word; rumor; **a media** —— in a low tone; **a voces** loudly; **dar voces** to shout; —— **entera** firm voice
vuelco turn; leap
vuelo flight; **de** —— flying, in great haste
vuelta return; turn; **a la** —— **de** around (a corner); **con** —— **a** at the corner of; **dar la** —— to turn back; to return; **dar la** —— **a** to walk around; **dar media** —— to turn around; **dar una** —— to take a walk; to return; to change; **dar** ——**s** to walk back and forth; **dar** ——**s a** to turn over, think over; **de** —— back
vueso, -a *arch. for* **vuestro, -a**
vulgar ordinary, common
vulgo common people
vulnerado wounded

Y

y *arch.* there
ya already, now, soon; oh, yes; **ya . . . ya** now . . . now, either . . . or
yacente lying
yacer to lie
ya que although; if
yedra ivy
yegua mare
yelmo helmet
yerba grass; herb
yermo desert place; wild region
yerno son-in-law
yerro error
yerto rigid, stiff; motionless
yodoformo iodoform (medicine)
yugo yoke
yugular to cut the throat
yunque anvil

Z

zafio coarse; ignorant
zafiro sapphire
zaga: no irle en —— **a uno, no quedarle en**—— **a uno** not to remain behind someone; to be as good as *or* equal to someone; **a** —— **de, en** —— **de** pursuing, following
zagal shepherd; youth
zagala shepherdess; maiden
zaguán entrance hall
zahareño wild, untamed
zalamería flattery
zalamero flattering; wheedling
zambullirse to dive
zampar to devour, gulp, 'wolf'
zancadilla tripping; **dar** ——**s** to trip
zancajo stride
zángano drone
zangoloteo shaking, rattling; hopping around
zanguango dunce
zapatería shoe shop
zapatero shoemaker
zarandear to shake
zarandeo 'whirl'; agitation
zarcillo earring
zarrapastroso ragged, slovenly
zarza bramble
zarzamora brambleberry
zinc zinc
zócalo base
zona zone; clime
zopenco dolt, blockhead
zorcico a folk song of the Basque country
zote dunce, fool
zozobra anxiety; foundering
zozobrar to sink (of ships); to ruin, destroy
zozobroso anxious, worried
zumaya barn owl
zumbar to buzz
zumo juice
zupia wine full of dregs
zurcido darning
zurrón sack, knapsack